Controversial Therapies for Developmental Disabilities

Fad, Fashion, and Science in Professional Practice

Controversial Therapies
for Developmental Disabilities

Fad, Fashion, and Science
in Professional Practice

John W. Jacobson
Sage Colleges Center for Applied Behavior Analysis

Richard M. Foxx
Penn State Harrisburg

James A. Mulick
The Ohio State University and Columbus Children's Hospital

2005

LAWRENCE ERLBAUM ASSOCIATES, PUBLISHERS
Mahwah, New Jersey   London

Lawrence Erlbaum Associates, Inc., Publishers
10 Industrial Avenue
Mahwah, New Jersey 07430

Cover design by Sean Trane Sciarrone

Library of Congress Cataloging-in-Publication Data

Controversial therapies for developmental disabilities : fad, fashion, and science
in professional practice / edited by John W. Jacobson, Richard M. Foxx, James
A. Mulick.
    p. cm.
Includes bibliographical references and index.
ISBN 0-8058-4191-1 (cloth : alk. paper)
ISBN 0-8058-4192-X (pbk. : alk. paper)
1. Developmental disabilities. 2. Developmentally disabled—Rehabilitation.
   3. Developmentally disabled—Care. 4. Developmentally disabled—
Services for. I. Jacobson, John W. II. Foxx, Richard M. III. Mulick, James A.
(James Anton), 1948–   .
RC570.2.C66 2004
616.85′8803—dc22   2004043443
                                                 CIP

Printed in the United States of America
10 9 8 7 6 5 4 3 2 1

John W. Jacobson, PhD passed away on May 8, 2004,
much too soon for his many friends and colleagues who
valued and admired his wisdom, tenacity, level headedness,
breadth of interests and knowledge, sharp wit, and prodigious
appetite for taking on professional challenges.

This book is dedicated to the people most dear to John, his wife
of 31 years, Pat, and his son and daughter who he loved and of
whom he so often spoke, Eric and Katie, and also to the values he
advanced as a scientist: intellectual honesty and critical analysis.

We are fortunate to know and collaborate with John,
and we trust that this book will serve as a fitting legacy
to a most distinguished career.

James A. Mulick
Richard M. Foxx

Contents

Preface

FAD, DUBIOUS, CONTROVERSIAL, PSEUDOSCIENTIFIC, AND POLITICALLY CORRECT TREATMENTS IN DEVELOPMENTAL DISABILITIES SERVICES

Since approximately 1978, one of the largest and most complex, and costly, human services systems in the United States, indeed, in the world, has evolved to serve individuals with mental retardation and developmental disabilities. In the United States, this system, including child, family, and adult services, consumes billions of service dollars annually, at a level greatly disproportionate to the number of people with developmental disabilities served relative to the number of others served through other programs. The breadth and depth of the clinical field, and related research activities, attest to an extensive and now longstanding public policy commitment to the betterment of people with developmental disabilities in the United States and many other nations. At the same time, this field has certain essential features that are common to other human services and that challenge the fidelity and effectiveness of care at the individual, practitioner, provider agency, and local, state, and national service system levels. These features include shifting philosophical positions that often drive regulatory action and change where and how, but not how well, people with developmental disabilities are served; and a broad reliance on the least trained and experienced personnel as the primary agents of service. These features are perhaps inherent both in the nature of the work to be done, which relies on human agentry as a service delivery process, and on the constraints on resources that are determined first by public policy, and second by the costs of providing services in a manner that conforms to market standards in the general community. Manual labor is involved in much of the work that needs to be done on behalf of people with developmental disabilities, and this work is done in real time. There are fewer opportunities for teaching service recipients self-care skills and fewer educated consumers of services, and there is often a degree of antagonism toward professionals who incorrectly estimate the service needs or independence of people with developmental disabilities. There are also persisting tensions among those who advocate for services based on how much costly professional support is really needed. This is because some regard disability as merely a "state of mind" that requires only attitude change on the part of those without disabilities and view the recommendation or offer of professional services as "evidence of discrimination." In contrast, others advocate for improved, validated, well-reviewed and critically evaluated services and supports for this vulnerable population.

Many allied health and human service disciplines do not emphasize scientific training in the preparation of practitioners and professionals. Unfortunately, over time many of these individuals rise to become influential managers in human services. As a result, the developmental disabilities field, like other human services fields, is pervaded by the delivery of services and design of supports that are less effective than they could be, and sometimes even damaging. Treatments often are provided based on unvalidated or even disproven models of human behavior or methods of intervention. Sometimes people with developmental disabilities may receive services that actually conflict and undermine effectiveness of care. These types of problems are not limited to adult human services. The education of people with developmental disabilities has been affected by the same forces. Expenditures for the education of children with special needs have continued to grow to the point where school districts budgets are stretched thin. Yet, many of these costs are for programs that are ineffective, poorly designed, and inappropriate and that actually retard student progress, or which are selected by practitioners (e.g., special educators, principals) based primarily on their endorsement or marketing by authorities or well-known professionals in education.

Workforce and employment dynamics are not the only factors that undermine the integrity of treatment or intervention. Parents of children with developmental disabilities, in particular parents of children with mental retardation or autism, are continually seeking, ever more assertively, to obtain more efficacious treatments and educational interventions than the ones they are being offered. The research literature documents both the inefficacy and efficacy of a wide variety of treatments and educational methods for children and youth with a variety of conditions. Research can be used as a fairly reliable guide to what actually works. However, effective treatments or interventions are not always among the choices that professionals inform or offer to parents. Sadly, parents tend to be hesitant to question credentialed professionals about the grounds for their recommendations, sometimes even hesitant to probe professional endorsement of what appear to be quite strange or illogical treatment options.

Local professionals, most of whom are not specialists in mental retardation or developmental disabilities, are most likely to recommend that parents use the types of services with which the professionals are most familiar. These are often not state-of-the-art, sometimes not even appropriate treatment or educational options, but merely the most common, and could be minimally effective or even damaging when used with some disability populations. Even specialists or local educational agencies may recommend methods that fall within their range of skills or that they provide, rather than referring children and families, or dependent adults and their families, to seek more appropriate and better validated alternatives.

Despite the fact that a large share of public health care funds is dedicated to services for people with developmental disabilities, generally a small proportion of these funds goes to pay for services delivered by clinical professionals who meet community standards of licensure or certification and who are disability specialists. One reason why is that fees for services are not lucrative or even, in many cases, competitive with reimbursement under managed care or sufficient to cover practitioner expenses. Specialists in some disabilities are exceedingly hard to find. In the not-for-profit service sector, which dominates adult developmental services, journeyman professionals typically lack funds to attend training in specialized topics, or to attend professional conferences, or to participate in extended training in empirically validated interventions. Often, as well, the ratio of professionals to the number of people with developmental disabilities they serve can be insufficient to permit them to effectively train and provide ongoing technical assistance to the staff who are often the actual direct therapists who carry out interventions. It is well-established that training is effective only when professional follow-up and technical assistance is available and provided. Thus, although there are numerous threats to the integrity of services, no one element of, or group of people in, the service system is responsible for the fragility of developmental disability services. Furthermore, shifting philosophical bases of care, which drive system reforms, have taken place at a rapid pace and have thereby perpetuated this fragile state.

Over the past 15 years, there has been a continuing movement from full participation of scientist–practitioners in all facets of developmental services to a greatly diminished role. This has occurred as a consequence of the organizing frameworks for the field shifting from dominance of clinical care to educational models of services. Unfortunately, education in the United States has no unified model and is itself in a perpetual state of disrepair and subsequent reform. Most licensed or certified educators lack many of the basic skills needed to be effective consumers of scientific research reports, or to faithfully communicate and translate demonstrated research findings into program and service innovations. Simply put, their training in the use and interpretation of research is often limited to a single collegiate graduate or undergraduate course and what they can pick up from public television and the Discovery Channel. Education in the United States is not a research-based profession (although there are a few sterling exceptions in some graduate training programs). As the field of developmental disabilities has turned increasingly to education as a touchstone for reform and improvement, supposed common sense, nevertheless uninformed by scientific research and evaluation studies, has become an ever greater component of that reform. As this "common" sense has pervaded the field, there has also been a growing susceptibility to repeating past mistakes at the level of service and policy, and to the adoption of fad treatments that have a patina of apparent effectiveness, but that may also have very negative side effects.

This book addresses the present status and perpetuation of fad treatments and elucidates the details of research in areas of controversy within the field. Fad, dubious, controversial, pseudo-scientific, and politically correct treatments are not readily designated as exclusively faddish or controversial; rather, a treatment may be both faddish and controversial, and politically correct as well, and still not be worth a tinker's damn.

Here, and in the chapters that follow, fad treatments are considered to have several characteristics. The most important characteristic is that they are introduced, rapidly increase in use, soon become pervasive, and then, following some extended period of pervasive use, rapidly decrease over time and are abandoned. Concurrently, fad treatments are often promoted or adopted based on testimonials from recognized, otherwise authoritative, or prominent professionals in a field, averring that they are highly effective in alleviating problems in everyday or advanced skill development that are common among people with developmental disabilities. Yet, no evidence is offered to back up these testimonials that is more than suggestive in nature or that is based on research or investigation that meets credible standards. Sometimes fads are further perpetuated by testimonials by prominent scientists, who really are trained and expert in other scientific fields (e.g., chemistry, physics), but not in the behavioral sciences, and who may be susceptible to the misunderstanding of well-established behavioral science findings regarding the nature, impact, and alleviation of developmental disabilities. Most often, fads are adopted and further disseminated by well-meaning professionals or paraprofessionals who do not have the skills, training, background, or inclination to investigate whether the methods they have been encouraged to adopt are well-grounded in valid research. Fad treatments sometimes decrease in use over time because researchers have investigated their effects and found them to be wanting, and conveyed this information to practitioners engaging in fad practices. Or fad treatments' demise may occur because they are succeeded by more novel (i.e., sometimes merely newer) fad treatments to address the same or kindred developmental and functional concerns. However, a final characteristic of fad treatments is that they are never completely abandoned; they persist in use by small groups of professionals and resurface through the activities of these professionals, or of advocates who are unaware of the history of similar therapies and their disuse, and believe the treatment they have rediscovered to be novel.

Treatments or therapies may be dubious or controversial because (a) their underlying theoretical (or at least stated) rationales are baseless, or require assumptions of their effectiveness; (b) there is little or no unambiguous evidence of their benefits; (c) the research underlying their use does not meet conventional standards of quality or specificity; or (d) there are much simpler and better verified explanations for apparent, superficial effects of their use. And, somewhat surprisingly, some therapies are both dubious and controversial because either their stated theoretical rationales have been effectively disproven or their stated benefits have been found, in evaluative and controlled research, to be evanescent or nil. Yet, some professionals who initially champion and promulgate such therapies broadly and assertively do not abandon their positions, but rather may harden them and may even attack the integrity of those who question whether the therapy works. The most sophisticated of advocates for dubious or controversial therapies will accurately note that scientific methods cannot formally disprove a premise that a therapy "works." However, these same methods can make it possible to discern that the assumptions underlying a therapy are unfounded and inconsistent with facts, and that under the circumstances when a therapy is purported to "work," in fact the observed effects are merely an appearance of benefit, far less notable and meaningful than claimed, or undetectable. Therapies are dubious when their rationales and purported effects are poorly substantiated; they are controversial when advocacy for their use persists despite evidence regarding the insubstantiality of rationale or impact. In some cases, dubious and controversial treatments are acknowledged by many professionals except for those trained in the discipline that most commonly uses those treatments; in such cases, professional training programs in colleges and universities are the culprits that perpetuate these practices.

Pseudoscientific practices of professionals and near-professionals are, simply stated, based on inadequate research designs that cannot actually document the effects claimed for a practice, or are based on a rationale that is stated in scientific terms, but is not itself founded on findings from relevant and basic scientific research. Pseudoscientific practices persist in circumstances where practitioners adhere to applying outmoded methods of clinical service that are disconfirmed by research conducted subsequent to their graduate training. These practitioners fail to consult the ever-expanding research base of their disciplines as a foundation for improving practices when they wholeheartedly and uncritically accept testimonial or anecdotal evidence of rationale from prominent authorities, or, in a small number of cases, when they knowingly pursue the perpetuation of practices that are lucrative but ineffective and groundless.

Finally, politically correct treatments are based on rationales that are somewhat scientific, nonscientific, pseudoscientific, or even antiscientific in nature. Such treatments are disseminated and adopted by professionals and managers because they resonate in their purported nature and effects with ideological perspectives, or because their use contributes to the realization of other, perhaps tangible, socially progressive goals or objectives of service delivery. There also is the element of financial and professional gain via obtaining large governmental grants and establishing a new field. The rationale for such treatments—which may not even consist of a therapy intended to ameliorate functional limitations, induce skills, or cure ills, but instead to possibly enhance, or appear to enhance, the social status of people with developmental disabilities—may be no more complex than "to do the right thing." However resonant with political reasoning, politically correct treatments seldom resonate in the same manner with either scientific findings within a discipline or with thoughtful and critical common sense. When they do, they can be both effective or beneficial, and politically correct. Reliance on socially progressive public policy rationales for a treatment ignores the fact that such policies are ever-changing, revised because they reflect a political consensus rather than substantiated fact, or may even be inconsistent with the attainment of greater independence and community engagement by some or many people with developmental disabilities. On the other hand, within the body politic of national organizations that pride themselves on their progressive policy postures, promotion and adherence to politically correct treatment selection can propel individual advocates to prominence, despite the fact that the treatments, or indeed, the particular policies they espouse, are without generality and of small benefit to the individuals for whom they advocate. Because the end goals are political and social acceptance, rather than the attainment of known or identifiable benefits to the people who are served, those who advocate for treatments, therapies, or methods that may (or factually may not) "contribute" to the social well-being of people with developmental disabilities may be among those most prone, and most motivated, to disregard or derogate findings from research that disconfirm their positions.

Any book that evaluates, across a number of disciplines, the various fads, treatments, and movements that have proved to be ineffective, dubious, harmful, or politically driven should acknowledge any biases on the part of the editors and chapter authors. We acknowledge here a shared bias toward science and empirically based treatments and decision making. Thus, our criterion for selecting authors was first and foremost that they had a history of critiquing faulty practices and spurious reasoning, especially in their own areas of expertise.

Using this criterion, we assembled a group of collaborators from a number of disciplines and theoretical perspectives who were bound to this project by a belief in science and seemed capable of sharing our outrage at what has been falsely done to individuals with developmental disabilities and their families. Once everyone was on board, the book became a labor of love fueled by a shared desire to protect some of our most vulnerable citizens and their families and loved ones from experiences that offer hope but deliver little or nothing.

Throughout this book, it may appear to some that many descriptions of effective, science-based alternatives to fads and dubious treatments seem to be behaviorally based. This is an accurate reading and is based on the simple fact that there is a very large body of peer-reviewed literature supporting the use of behavioral approaches with individuals with developmental disabilities and autism. However, non-behavioral approaches that have empirical or scientific support can be found throughout the book as well. Simply put, the issue is not behavioral versus non-behavioral approaches or models, but rather empirically supported versus empirically baseless treatments.

Another reason this book may appear to favor interventions that are behavioral is that we are behavior analysts. However, as mentioned earlier, we did not select our chapter authors according to some behavior-analytic litmus test, but rather on the basis of their ability to handle a selected topic. In virtually every case, the individuals selected were among those best suited by history and knowledge to write that chapter. Indeed, our collaborators break down into three general categories: (a) behavior analysts, (b) individuals who would not describe themselves as behavior analysts but who favor or are sympathetic to behavior-analytic approaches because of the strong science underlying them, and (c) those who appreciate or acknowledge the empirical base of behavior analysis but who would not identify with it professionally.

Some readers of this book also may conclude that in bringing together both research summaries and critiques of occasional or even prevalent practices in developmental services, we are indicting the field of developmental disabilities. Nothing could be further from the truth. Indeed, over the many years that each of us has been involved in various aspects of developmental services, we have found that the great majority of paraprofessionals and professionals are committed to the well-being of people with developmental disabilities. Professionals with different disciplinary backgrounds understandably differ in the factors they emphasize as indications of well-being or of progress in the field. But as in any circumstance, and they are common in human services, when social policy and clinical practice are interwoven, the integrity of both policy and research may be compromised. Policy formation is not the function of research, nor is the function of research to verify that politically correct or valued postures are correct in a larger or other sense. Policies can be contrafactual, in that their premises may not be factual, and often such policies have unintended impacts that are unforeseen. The formation and implementation of contrafactual policies cannot survive scrutiny of their outcomes when these are adequately researched, and scientific activity is a counterbalance to such policies, although science in itself does not constitute a sufficient basis for either social action or social policy. Our position is that when professionals waste public and private resources through the perpetuation of fad, dubious, controversial, ineffective, nonbeneficial, politically correct, and sometimes damaging or depriving treatments, or advocate for disuse of effective and valuable treatments they claim to be unacceptable on political grounds, they diminish themselves as trusted professionals, their professions, and the people they purport to serve. The very nature of professionalism requires responsibility on our part: responsibility to those we serve by displaying more self-reflection, more candor, more honesty, and the capacity to be more objective about our practices and their implications. The chapters in this book cover a wide range of treatments and interventions that have become common in educational and adult service settings for people with developmental disabilities, but we have not been able to include the full range of practices that may be, or have been found to be, dubious in nature. It is not reasonable to expect that professionals will be able to rely on high-quality scientific research as the foundation of every action taken and decision made in the course of providing services to vulnerable individuals. Nevertheless, in the chapters in this book, we can see recurrent patterns where the actual benefits of interventions or common practices have been found, through systematic scrutiny, to be greatly deficient in what they deliver. Yet some or many practitioners and professionals persist in each of these practices, or in reviving them. Their professions deserve better, and even more, so do the people they serve.

—*John W. Jacobson*
—*Richard M. Foxx*
—*James A. Mulick*

List of Contributors

EDITORS

John W. Jacobson, PhD, BCBA
Sage Colleges Center for Applied Behavior Analysis
Troy, NY

Richard M. Foxx, PhD, BCBA
Penn State Harrisburg
Harrisburg, PA

James A. Mulick, PhD
The Ohio State University and Columbus Children's Hospital
Columbus, OH

CONTRIBUTORS

Eric M. Butter, MA
The Ohio State University and Columbus Children's Hospital
Columbus, OH

Chris Cullen, PhD
Keele University
Staffordshire, UK

Judith E. Favell, PhD
Advo-Serv Programs
Mount Dora, FL

Stephen Greenspan, PhD
University of Colorado Health Sciences Center
Denver, CO

Cheryl Gunter, PhD
West Chester University
West Chester, PA

William L. Heward, EdD
The Ohio State University
Columbus, OH

Steve Holburn, PhD
New York State Institute for Basic Research
    in Developmental Disabilities
Staten Island, NY

Christine A. Hovanitz, PhD
University of Cincinnati
Cincinnati, OH

James M. Johnston, PhD
Auburn University
Auburn, AL

James M. Kauffman, EdD
University of Virginia
Charlottesville, VA

Shannon Kay, PhD
The May Institute
Chatham, MA

Mareile Koenig, PhD, CCC-SLP, BCBA
West Chester University
West Chester, PA

Martin A. Kozolff, PhD
University of North Carolina at Wilmington
Wilmington, NC

Kimberely A. Kroeger, MA
Xavier University
Cincinnati, OH

Bernard Metz, PsyD
Children's Hospital Behavioral Health
Columbus, OH

Devery R. Mock, PhD
University of Virginia
Charlottesville, VA and
University of Iowa
Iowa City, IA

Dennis Mozingo, PhD, BCBA
University of Rochester Medical Center
Rochester, NY

Daniel W. Mruzek, PhD
University of Rochester Medical Center
Rochester, NY

Oliver C. Mudford, PhD
TreeHouse Trust
London, UK

Crighton Newsom, PhD
Southwest Ohio Developmental Center
Batavia, OH

J. Grayson Osborne, PhD
Utah State University
Logan, UT

Constance E. Roland, MA
Penn State Harrisburg
Harrisburg, PA

Susan M. Silvestri, MA
The Ohio State University
Columbus, OH

Tristram Smith, PhD
University of Rochester Medical Center
Rochester, NY

Peter Sturmey, PhD
Department of Psychology Queens College
    and The Graduate Center
City University of New York
New York, NY

Edmond Tiryak, JD
Private Practice of Law
Philadelphia, PA

Susan Vig, PhD
Albert Einstein College of Medicine
New York, NY

Stuart Vyse, PhD
Connecticut College
New London, CT

Thomas Zane, PhD
The Sage Colleges Center for Applied Behavior Analysis
Troy, NY

Part I

General Issues

Where Do Fads Come From?

Stuart Vyse
Connecticut College

> But, above all, let it be considered that what is more wholesome than any particular belief is integrity of belief, and that to avoid looking into the support of any belief from fear that it may turn out rotten is quite as immoral as it is disadvantageous.
>
> —Charles Sanders Peirce (1992, p. 123)

WHAT'S IN A FAD?

Before anything can be said about how fad therapies emerge and why they are often adopted over more valuable approaches, we must understand what we are talking about. What is a fad therapy in the field of developmental disabilities and how does it stand in relation to other, non-fad therapies? When language is used to define social or functional categories, it is often because doing so benefits someone by codifying an inherent value system. The motivations behind the establishment of these categories may be honorable or dishonorable. For example, the application of the label "mental retardation," based on definitions involving intellectual and adaptive functioning, make it possible for a segment of the population to receive educational and social services that enhance their lives. At the same time, applying this label—as well as providing the services—may make these individuals more susceptible to stigmatization, prejudice, and discrimination (Danforth, 2002; Goode, 2002). Indeed, the current preference for the phrase "person with mental retardation" is aimed at diminishing the stigmatizing effect of the label. Furthermore, the concept of a "developmental disability" is even more effective in this regard because it more clearly refers to a specific aspect of the person—one ability among many—and is less likely to be taken as a global assessment of the individual.

Throughout this volume, the treatments that are its subject will be described using adjectives such as "fad," "alternative," "controversial," "pseudoscientific," and "unsubstantiated," among others. It must be acknowledged that these are—in some sense—terms of derision, and they reveal the value system of the authors who use them. I will return to the definition of a fad later, but what of the other terms? For example, if a therapy is "alternative" it can only be so in relation to some other standard or orthodox therapy (Wolpe, 1999). That which distinguishes orthodox from alternative or unorthodox therapies may or may not be the level of scientific support. A therapy is "controversial" in relation to some issue of controversy brought, presumably by those who are critical of its use. Thus, just as being honored has more to do with the honorers than the honored, being controversial has more to do with the behavior of a therapy's critics than with the therapy. Absent arguments against it, a therapy might be free of controversy, but being so says nothing of its value. The label "pseudoscientific" is a pejorative adjective that suggests the treatment in question appears to be—but is not—scientific. The therapy may employ a technical jargon that sounds authoritative, and it may include a theoretical support structure that makes reference to genuinely scientific content (e.g., neurotransmitters, the sensory system, the brain), all of which give it the look and feel of a scientifically based treatment. But if these trappings of science are not backed up by reliable evidence, the treatment is a sham that steals some of its appeal from the positive reputation genuine science has acquired over its history. Despite the abundant evidence to the contrary (e.g., Shermer, 1997, and—for that matter—a book like this one), we live in an age of science. Although many people reject scientific thinking in important aspects of their lives, appeals to the scientific basis of a belief, product, or treatment often lend credibility to it. So powerful is the allure of science as a method of argument that some have even attempted to use it to support beliefs that are clearly beyond its limits, such as the existence of an afterlife and the possibility that the dead can communicate with the living (Schwartz, Russek, Nelson, & Barentsen, 2001).

But the label "unsubstantiated" or similar terms, such as "non-evidenced-based treatments" or "treatments unsupported by evidence," are a more direct indication of the philosophy of this volume. If the chapters in this volume share a common bias, it is that developmental disabilities treatments should be backed up by evidence and that scientific evidence is to be valued over other forms. The only way to obtain this kind of evidence is through research conducted according to accepted standards of methodology in the behavioral, social, and medical sciences. This is an admittedly positivist stance, and there have been many recent postmodern arguments about whether objective truth can ever be obtained in the social sciences (Gergen, 2001). But these arguments do not hold much sway in this arena. People with developmental disabilities and those who work with and care about them do not always leap to scientific evidence—or *sound* scientific evidence—as the best way of evaluating treatments for developmental disabilities, but most agree in principle that this is the kind of evidence that should matter. Most believe that a treatment should be chosen not on the basis of whether it is enjoyable to administer, is consistent with the user's personal philosophy, or seems logical, but on the basis of whether or not it works. Unfortunately, there is less agreement about what constitutes proof of success. Although most of those concerned about people with developmental disabilities are seeking evidence for the treatments they are using, some have not embraced scientific evidence as the most valued kind, and others cannot separate out the good and bad information they encounter. The purpose of this book is to outline the standards for evaluating treatments and help differentiate treatments that have strong scientific support from those that have little or no support.

By using these labels to distinguish various treatments and therapies for developmental disabilities, we are establishing categories on the basis of the presence or absence of scientific support. This value system is also evident in the definition of a "fad" proposed by the editors of this book. A fad, for the purposes of this volume, is defined as "a procedure, method, or therapy that is adopted rapidly in the presence of little validating research, gains wide use or recognition, and then fades from use—usually in the face of disconfirming research, but often due to the adoption of a new fad" (J. W. Jacobson, personal communication, November 11, 2001). So a fad is a therapy that is not supported by scientific evidence and that has a fairly rapid rise and fall. The basic concern, however, is the question of evidence. There are other techniques—equally lacking in support—that nonetheless manage to maintain their popularity over relatively long periods of time. Though they are not fads, these more resilient therapies are also the appropriate concern of many of the chapters to follow. Understanding that these are relative terms, the short lifespan of a fad may sometimes be evidence of its lack of value, but conversely, the longer life of another therapy is not necessarily evidence of value. If popularity and longevity were correlated with usefulness, a book like this one might not be necessary. But for a variety of reasons, this is not so. In Darwinian terms, scientific support is not the only measure of a treatment's evolutionary fitness. Other factors may allow it to fill an ecological niche and survive repeated rounds of natural selection.

As we set up these categories of scientifically supported and unsupported—essentially, good and bad—treatments, it is useful to examine our motives. Science has a long history of theoretical and technological triumphs, but over the years, scientific arguments have often been used to further political or professional social agendas. The eugenics movement of the late 19th and early 20th centuries attempted to ground class and race discrimination in science (Gould, 1981). The system of classification known as the *Diagnostic and Statistical Manual of Mental Disorders* (*DSM*; American Psychiatric Association, 1994) was intended as a scientific aid to research, diagnosis, and treatment, but its publication by a professional organization, the American Psychiatric Association, serves to keep this profession at the top of the heap as the final arbiter of what represents a bonafide mental illness (Kutchins & Kirk, 1997). The link between this manual and health insurance reimbursement policies raises additional questions. One need only ask who benefits if the manual contains many mental disorders (the current total is 374) rather than just a few?

Yes, we believe in science. This is an ideological stand of sorts. But we believe in a science that promotes no particular product or profession. The most effective treatments described in these chapters have been and are being used by a variety of professionals and nonprofessionals. The use of scientific therapies is not restricted to certain individuals by professional standards, ethical guidelines, or licensing laws. In addition, there are few products being sold in connection with a scientific approach to developmental disabilities treatment, and the professional books, periodicals, and manuals that have been spawned provide little profit motive for their authors and publishers. Certainly individual careers have benefited from the adoption or promotion of scientific therapies, but nothing remotely similar to the relationship between the American Psychiatric Association and the health insurance and pharmaceutical industries exists in the field of developmental disabilities. The primary social motive is improving the lives of people with developmental disabilities, and truly effective treatments have the best chance of providing the skills needed for them to participate as fully and independently as possible in the community.

WHERE DO FADS COME FROM AND WHY ARE THERE SO MANY?

Why is this book necessary? In a world where scientifically validated, effective treatments exist for people with developmental disabilities, where do all the ineffective fad treatments come from? Why are they not naturally eliminated from the landscape and replaced by treatments that work? In the remainder of this chapter, I will outline the circumstances—essentially the market demands—that appear to encourage the development and promotion of fad therapies, and I will outline some of the reasons why consumers—parents and professionals—choose them over other options. The story is one of the gradual adoption of science as the final arbiter of value, and it mirrors, in many respects, the history of modern medicine. Thus, as an introduction to the circumstances facing the field of developmental disabilities treatment, I will first outline the history of medicine in America. Although the following section is about U.S. history, the arc of the plot—from nonscientific therapies to scientifically validated ones—takes a similar path in Europe and other areas that have endorsed western medical procedures. The specific events are different, but the endpoints are the same.

A BRIEF HISTORY OF AMERICAN MEDICINE

In the United States and other westernized nations, effective research-validated procedures are now the dominant approach to medical problems, but this is a relatively new development. Rigorous medical research of the kind we value today became a widespread phenomenon only at the beginning of the 20th century. Before then, medical practice both here and in Europe was characterized by a diverse array of practitioners and techniques. Today, in the field of developmental disabilities, scientifically validated techniques exist, but unlike contemporary medicine, these methods have yet to emerge as the single dominant approach to treatment. An examination of the history of western medicine provides a number of clues to the popularity of alternative, unsubstantiated treatments in developmental disabilities treatment.

American Medicine Before the Revolution

In the colonial period, medical services were provided by a variety of practitioners, the great majority of whom had no formal academic training. Barbers in England and the colonies were authorized to perform surgery, and training was passed on by the apprenticeship method. It was not until 1745 that surgeons separated from barbers to form their own guild (Duffy, 1993). Surgeons were not officially authorized to practice medicine, but in fact, they often served as general practitioners for the lower classes. Apothecaries also served the poor, providing drugs for the treatment of illness, and they were joined by a variety of other trades offering medical services, including folk healers, bloodletters, bonesetters, midwives, and herb doctors, among others.

In the American colonies, particularly in New England, a class of minister physicians emerged. While studying theology, many ministers who dissented from the prevailing church in England had also studied medicine as an alternative means of employment in the event they were dismissed from the church. As a result, a number of the ministers who arrived in the colonies also provided medical services. Cotton Mather was such a minister-physician, and he wrote a very eloquent medical essay on a measles epidemic of 1713, which claimed five members of his household (Duffy, 1976).

In the 17th century, those colonialists who had received formal training—such as the minister-physicians—were at the top of the medical hierarchy and were the practitioners most likely to treat the ailments of the wealthy. Often these physicians had studied at the great hospitals and universities in England and on the continent. The American Revolution interrupted contact with British institutions and slowed the adoption of new medical techniques, but by the time of the Revolution, one hospital and two medical schools were in operation in America. A number of medical societies had been formed, and several colonies had established medical licensure laws (Duffy, 1976). Nonetheless, the limited access to academic training meant that the majority of physicians acquired their skills by apprenticeship.

From the Revolution to 1900

Many of the forces that led to modern medicine of the 20th century were present in the period following the revolution. Throughout the 18th century, physicians had attained the highest status of all those providing medical services, but medicine rarely brought them wealth. Furthermore, their methods were not free of criticism. The most important American doctor of the late 18th and early 19th centuries was Benjamin Rush. Rush attended college in New Jersey and apprenticed with a physician in Philadelphia, but to improve his chances of success as a doctor, Rush traveled to Britain to study medicine. He attended the University of Edinburgh and studied with noted physicians in London and Paris. On his return to America, Rush was appointed professor of chemistry at the College of Philadelphia. During the 1770s, Rush was swept up in the political furor of the times, and he was eventually elected to the Second Continental Congress and became a signer of the Declaration of Independence (Duffy, 1993). Following the war, Rush returned to his medical practice and, until his death in 1813, he was one of the most influential forces in American medicine.

During the 18th century and into the19th century, physicians who used the traditional methods taught in the medical schools of Europe sought to distinguish themselves from the other forms of medical practice. They called themselves the "regulars" and referred to various purveyors of folk medicine and nonstandard treatments as the "irregulars." Despite being of higher status and having the attention of the wealthy sick of the colonies, the regulars did not achieve dominance until the beginning of the 20th century, and their eventual success was achieved only after adopting very different methods.

The problem with American medicine before the end of the 19th century is that it was not based on what we would now think of as scientific evidence. Techniques that were extremely harmful to the patient were not recognized as such, and as a result, for several centuries, the regulars of the medical profession—both in Europe and America—did more harm than good. This situation led Oliver Wendell Holmes to deliver this now famous assessment in a lecture given at Harvard Medical School: "I firmly believe that if the whole *materia medica* could be sunk to the bottom of the sea, it would be all the better for mankind and all the worse for the fishes" (cited in Wolpe, 1999, p. 222). Holmes' indictment was justified. The standard medical philosophy of the day was based on a theory first articulated by the ancient Greek physicians, Hippocrates and Galen. It asserted that illnesses were caused by an imbalance of four basic bodily humors: yellow bile, black bile, phlegm, and blood. Imbalances could be caused by an excess of one of the humors or by the putrefaction or fermentation of one of them. The standard treatment was something that became known as heroic medicine. Physicians sought to alter the balance of humors by bleeding, cupping, or purging the patient. Cupping was accomplished by heating a glass cup or jar and placing it on the patient's skin. As the air in the cup cooled, it created a vacuum that was thought to draw materials out of the body. Wet cupping involved cutting the skin under the cup so that blood was drawn out of the wound. Purging involved the administration of strong herbal formulas that created violent vomiting and diarrhea.

Bloodletting was perhaps the most popular of all heroic treatments, involving the draining of large amounts of blood from the patient's body. Benjamin Rush erroneously believed that the body contained 25 pounds of blood (in fact, it contains less than half that amount), and he recommended bleeding until four fifths of the fluid had been removed from the body. He used this technique throughout his career, and a paradoxical result of the Philadelphia yellow fever epidemic of 1793 was that Rush's popularity increased. The fever simply ran its course throughout the city, and Rush's methods of bleeding and purging patients undoubtedly increased the number of deaths. Nonetheless, perhaps due to his warm and enthusiastic personality, he drew many adherents to his techniques (Duffy, 1976).

Throughout the colonial period and well into the 19th century, heroic medicine was the standard approach of the most highly trained physicians. But the brutality of these methods fueled the development of other medical theories and techniques. In addition, the higher cost of treatment by physicians meant that people of the middle and lower classes continued to bring their ailments to a variety of irregular physicians.

During the 19th century, several strong, rival therapies rose up to challenge the regulars. One of these was Thomsonianism. Samuel Thomson was born into a poor New Hampshire family in 1769, and as an adult he developed an interest in botanicals. He had witnessed the death of his mother, which he blamed on the harsh medicines of her orthodox physician, and when his wife became ill and was subjected to bloodletting and purging, he rejected the physician in favor of a root and herb doctor. Based on these experiences, Thomson began to experiment with the use of botanicals to treat disease, and in 1822, he published a book describing his methods. During the next 20 years, Thomsoniansim grew in popularity, both because it was a more humane alternative to the prevailing wisdom and because of its connection with a number of social movements of the time. Samuel Thomson was a religious fundamentalist, and his approach to medicine was aimed in large measure at returning the practice of medicine to the common person—a message that was consistent with the democratic ideals of Andrew Jackson's presidency. During the Jacksonian period, restrictions on eligibility to vote were greatly reduced, and more states moved toward popular elections for president. The period from the mid-19th century through the early 20th century was one of great social reform movements, and Thomsonians fought the establishment of medical licensure laws and supported efforts against the use of alcohol, tobacco, coffee, and tea (Duffy, 1976).

Another popular but irregular treatment in the 19th century—which retains considerable popularity today—was homeopathy. Homeopathic medicine was developed by the German physician Samuel Christian Hahnemann, who had obtained a medical degree from the University of Erlangen. Homeopathy was based on two principles. First, *similia similibus curantur* or "like cures like." This principle suggested that to cure a disease, one must find an herb or substance that produces the same symptoms as the disease in a healthy person. Hahnemann developed this principle after taking doses of cinchona bark, which produced fever in him and, when given to a patient with malaria, cured the patient's fever. The second principle of homeopathy effectively nullified any possible therapeutic effect of its treatments. Hahnemann believed that his medicines were most effective when they were highly diluted—a process that turned all homeopathic medicines into functional placebos. Nonetheless, because they did no harm to the patient, homeopathic physicians undoubtedly enjoyed better results than regular physicians using heroic methods because the body's own restorative functions were given a chance to operate (Duffy, 1993).

Homeopathy arrived in the United States in 1825, brought by physicians who had studied in Europe. It quickly made inroads in the eastern part of the country and by 1935 the first homeopathic college in America was established in Allentown, Pennsylvania. The growing popularity of Thomsonianism and homeopathic medicine, as well as other competitors to the regulars, led to a number of defensive moves on the part of orthodox physicians—chief among these was the "consultation clause." The American Medical Association (AMA) was formed in 1847, but it is a testament to the strength of homeopathy that the first national medical organization in the United States was the American Institute of Homeopathy, which had been created 3 years earlier. By this time, the country had suffered epidemics of yellow fever and Asian cholera, and the benign interventions of the homeopathic physicians were far more effective than the standard methods of bleeding and purging. In southern states, which were more affected by these epidemics, homeopathy gained many converts. So when the AMA was formed in 1847, it adopted its first Code of Ethics. This document included a number of useful principles regarding the physician-patient relationship, but it also included a clause regarding consultation:

> But no one can be considered as a regular practitioner, or fit associate in consultation, whose practice is based on an exclusive dogma, to the rejection of accumulated experience of the profession, and of the aids actually furnished by anatomy, physiology, pathology, and organic chemistry. (Bell & Hays, 1847/1999, Chapter II, Article IV. 1)

The effect of the consultation clause was to forbid any regular physician from taking on a patient who was also being seen by a homeopath, and no physician could consult with a homeopath, even if the patient requested it (Duffy, 1993). The consultation clause effectively defined who was a physician, and it also helped to solidify the regular's control over municipal and state hospitals. During the Civil War, homeopaths were not allowed in the Army Medical Corps; however, it is noteworthy that homeopathy was sufficiently strong in New York that in 1882 the Medical Society of the State of New York deleted the consultation clause from its version of the ethics code (Warner, 1999), an action that led to the establishment of two competing state medical societies. In addition, the exclusion of homeopathic physicians from regular hospitals forced them to establish their own, many of which achieved reputations superior to those of the regulars. Finally, homeopaths fought back rhetorically by labeling orthodox medicine "allopathy," a term that angered the regulars (Warner, 1999).

A particular irony of this history is that science was lost in the battle for professional dominance. If anything, those physicians who were the most scientifically based, such as the advocates for experimental physiology, tended to be among the opposition to the AMA code of ethics, and those who most harshly criticized experimental therapeutics were among the code's defenders (Warner, 1999). But by the late 19th century, the war of competing dogmas was beginning to fade, and many of the influential physicians of the era stressed the importance of scientific evidence in support of medical therapies. In a move that helped to break down divisions within the profession, the University of Michigan, which had previously maintained separate departments of regular and homeopathic medicine, admitted a professor of homeopathy to the regular medicine department. Finally, by the beginning of the 20th century, scientific medicine began to emerge as the new orthodoxy. In the 1903 revision of its Code of Ethics, the AMA eliminated the consultation clause, and by 1910, Abraham Flexner, the president of the AMA, described allopathy and homeopathy alike as "medical sects," and urged that both must be abandoned in favor of "scientific medicine" (Warner, 1999, p. 65). Furthermore, during the early 20th century, gifts made by the Carnegie and Rockefeller foundations and other wealthy philanthropists helped build important new research institutes (Duffy, 1976). Although it represented a great step forward, the adoption of scientific methods by the field of medicine did not lead automatically to a morally sound and value-free profession. The late 19th and early 20th centuries was the era of social Darwinism, in which scientific arguments were used to further social agendas (Gould, 1981). Nonetheless, the rise of scientific medicine in the 20th century led to rapid technical advancement and rejection of medical dogma as the guide for medical practice.

The Origins of Fad Therapies

The history of medicine in America suggests a number of factors that can lead to the success of nonscientific therapies. Since 1900, science has become the dominant judge of value in many domains, but it does not mean that science-based therapies or beliefs are universally endorsed. Here are some of the conditions that appear to lead to the popularity of alternative, nonscientific therapies:

Incomplete Effectiveness of Available Therapies.   When a person is ill or when a child is diagnosed with a developmental disorder, the current circumstance stands in stark contrast to normal expectation. As a result, the sick person is highly motivated to return to health, and the parents of the developmentally disabled child have a similar strong desire to bridge the gap between the child they hoped would be theirs and the one they have. In the case of a medical condition, if the available therapy is effective enough to eliminate the disease entirely (e.g., smallpox, tuberculosis) or to make it no longer a significant threat (e.g., infections treated with modern antibiotics), then alternative therapies are not needed. However, there are many conditions for which science has yet to produce a uniformly successful treatment. This was true earlier in the HIV epidemic in the United States, before the introduction of protease inhibitors and the more effective polypharmacy therapies now available ("People with AIDS," 1991), and it is the current state of affairs in the field of developmental disabilities. For example, a study of applied behavior analysis (ABA), the most effective therapy for autism, produced the highest levels of success in only 47% of participants (Lovaas, 1987), and there is considerable debate about whether the effectiveness of ABA has been exaggerated (e.g., Herbert & Brandsma, 2002). Under these circumstances, an alternative therapy— for example, facilitated communication (FC)—can gain rapid acceptance. In the absence of a completely effective treatment, FC is attractive because it instantly erases the intellectual gap for all children. The physical deficit that is purported to hide the child's true abilities remains, but FC's promise—the exchange of a pervasive developmental disability for a mere physical one—is very appealing to many.

Best Available Treatment is Onerous or Distasteful for Parent or Client.   Heroic medicine was an easy foil for more mild forms of treatment such as Thomsonianism and homeopathy. Contemporary alternative cancer therapies undoubtedly gain popularity from the substantial discomfort produced by chemotherapy and radiation therapy (Okie, 2000). In the field of developmental disabilities, the best therapies are expensive, demanding to administer, and take years to complete—or are never fully completed. Thus, a gluten- and casein-free diet (Whitely, Rodgers, Savery, & Shattock, 1999) or holding therapy (Welch, 1988) may be appealing to some parents because it appears easier to administer or because the more effective treatment is thought to be "cold and manipulative" (Maurice, 1993, p. 63).

Alternative Treatment Supported by Ideology.   Many treatments in both medicine and developmental disabilities have survived because the proponents and consumers have adopted a theory about the disease or disorder in question. All the regular and irregular treatments of American medicine before 1900 were based on a theory of disease: the heroic/humorial system of the regulars, Thomson's botanical treatments, and Hahnemann's homeopathy. Often belief, based on the ideological appeal of a therapy, is sufficient to sustain the use of a treatment in the absence of any evidence that it is effective.

The attractiveness of ideology is greatest if it extends beyond the specific condition and makes contact with a more general personal philosophy or, alternatively, draws credibility from its apparent relationship to another, validated theory. The success of Thomsonianism was spurred by its association with Jacksonian democracy and a variety of 19th-century social reform movements. Similarly, a variety of modern alternative medical therapies derive much of their appeal from broad cultural trends that reject traditional organized medicine in favor of approaches emphasizing diet, exercise, vitamins, and holistic health (Cassileth, 1989; Vyse, 1997a). In the field of developmental disabilities, treatments based on holding (Welch, 1988) and dietary restrictions (Whitely et al., 1999) may benefit from their coherence with contemporary theories of parenting and nutrition, respectively. In addition, despite limited evidence of the effectiveness of gluten- and casein-free diets in the treatment of autism (Herbert, Sharp, & Gaudiano, 2002), these treatments gain a veneer of plausibility from their apparent similarity to dietary programs for validated metabolic disorders, such as phenylketonuria and diabetes. However, without sound evidence in support to these diets, they represent another case of pseudoscience.

Treatment Promoted by Proprietary Professional Group.   Quite often, a therapy originates with a professional group and goes on to be promoted by members of that group. Ineffective treatments can survive if they are based on an appealing ideology and are backed up by the authority of the profession. Furthermore, the promotion of a proprietary therapy strengthens the professional group. The regulars, who were most likely to be academically trained and who represented the orthodox medical approach from colonial times into the 19th century, had a proprietary interest in the methods of heroic medicine, and they sought to protect their professional turf with state licensing laws and the consultation clause of the AMA (Wolpe, 1999).

Even today there are examples of unsubstantiated alternative therapies that have emerged from specific professional groups. In medicine, therapeutic touch (TT; Mackey, 1995) is a practice developed by a Dolores Krieger, a professor of nursing, based on the premise that the body is surrounded by energy fields. Proponents argue that a variety of diseases and conditions can be treated by passing the hands a few inches above the body to smooth these energy fields. A recent review found that "the 'facts' of TT are that it has an unknown mechanism of action and its efficacy is questionable" (O'Mathuna, Pryjmachuck, Spencer, Stanwick, & Matthiesen, 2002, p. 171). TT is not exclusively practiced by nurses, but it remains closely associated with the nursing profession. In the field of developmental disabilities, sensory integration therapy (Ayres, 1994/1979) has its origins in occupational therapy and is most often promoted by members of that profession—despite the absence of support for this therapy in the research published to date (see Herbert et al., 2002, for a review).

It should be acknowledged that not all therapies primarily promoted by a single professional group are worthless. The use of drugs to treat physical, psychiatric, and developmental disorders has, until recently, been the exclusive privilege of physicians, and that privilege has been protected by state licensing laws and educational and accreditation standards. Without question, drug therapies are very effective in treating a wide variety of ailments; thus, promotion by a professional group alone is not proof of ineffectiveness. Nonetheless, any therapy, whether effective or ineffective, gains strength from the authority granted to the professionals who promote it. In some cases, when combined with the ideological appeal of the therapy, the force of professional authority is surprisingly influential in maintaining the popularity of unsubstantiated treatments.

These are some of the broad historical and cultural factors—the market trends—that contribute to the development of questionable therapies, but what about the individual consumer? When there are better options available, why do parents and professionals often choose unsubstantiated treatments over those with better support? Much of the answer is beyond the scope of this chapter and will be left to those that follow, but in the most general sense, the question is one of belief. How do parents and professionals acquire the beliefs they use to guide their decisions? In 1877, the American pragmatist philosopher Charles Sanders Peirce published an article titled "The Fixation of Belief" that has become a classic of the philosophy of science. In it, Peirce describes four ways people acquire beliefs and assesses the relative value of each method. Peirce's categories apply to beliefs of all kinds, and they provide a useful framework for understanding the adoption of fad therapies.

Authority.   Beliefs are acquired by the method of authority if we accept the word of another. Often we grant others the power to change our beliefs if they have higher social status or are assumed to have special knowledge. Religious beliefs are acquired by the method of authority, as are, in fact, most of our everyday beliefs. As a practical matter, it is impossible for any individual to test more than a few ideas empirically; thus, we must acquire much of our knowledge by the method of authority. For example, I believe the light on my desk glows because of the movement of electrons through its copper wires and tungsten element, but I have never observed this phenomenon directly—only its effects. Some authority instilled my belief in the action of electrons years ago. Although it is often necessary to take the word of others, authorities are frequently wrong. Unless we know the basis of a person's statements, we have little reason to trust in their authority.

The regulars of early American medicine were the authorities of their day, and it is a testament to the power of their position that their methods were dominant for centuries. In addition, early American homeopathic physicians undoubtedly gained some influence from the authority they commanded. Today, physicians and other health professionals are the primary medical authorities, and although most of them recommend procedures based on scientific evidence, much of the influence they enjoy is based on the authority granted them by contemporary society. In the field of developmental disabilities, where cures are hard to come by, parents are confronted with authorities from many helping professions advocating different—often contradictory—therapeutic approaches. To the extent they find these professionals persuasive solely because of their standing, parents fall into the trap of choosing therapies by the method of authority.

Tenacity.   Sometimes we hold onto a belief out of loyalty—merely because it is our own. According to Peirce, the tenacious man "goes through life, systematically keeping out of view all that might cause him to change his opinions" (1992, p. 116). At times we are all guilty of defending our beliefs in the face of strong contradictory evidence, but to do so will often lead us astray. It is a basic tenet of scientific thinking that theories must be jettisoned or modified in the face of clear conflicting data.

The regulars of early American medicine represent a striking example of tenacity. Somehow most were able to maintain belief in their methods in the face of what was often devastating effects. Of course, their judgment was undoubtedly affected by professional and financial incentives, as well. Recognizing the superior effectiveness of homeopathic and Thomsonian therapies would have led many physicians to sacrifice the status afforded by association with orthodox medicine. Nonetheless, as previously noted, some doctors, particularly in the southern states during the yellow fever and Asian cholera epidemics, were not blind to the devastating effects of heroic medicine and adopted the more benign methods of homeopathic medicine.

In the field of developmental disabilities, tenacity allows professionals and parents to remain committed to a therapy despite evidence that it is ineffective. If the ideology behind the therapy has a strong appeal, adherents will be reluctant to give it up. Today, despite ample evidence that facilitated communication is an ineffective, pseudoscientific technique (Herbert et al., 2002; Jacobson, Mulick, & Schwartz, 1995), several Web sites are devoted to promoting FC, and the technique remains popular with many parents. Of course, the promise (or dream) of FC—that one's child is merely physically disabled, not developmentally disabled—would be difficult to relinquish.

A Priori.   Beliefs are fixed by the a priori method if they make sense or feel right. This is a subjective measure of value, which is necessarily dependent on the accidents of one's prior experiences. Although the a priori method is widely used, it cannot be a path to objective truth. Honest people using this method of reasoning will come to very different conclusions, and unless one embraces fully the postmodernist view of science, this is an unacceptable situation. Nonetheless, many people make judgments and choose actions on the basis of this kind of subjective assessment. In the fields of medicine and developmental disabilities treatment, a priori reasoning is particularly evident when an appeal is made directly to the consumer, as in the case of Thomsonianism. Thomson's approach was to remove the intervening authority of the physician and return medicine to the people. By aligning his approach with dominant political and social themes of the day, he increased the likelihood that his theory would conform to the sensibilities of his audience.

Any approach that makes use of a plausible ideology—particularly one that draws on other broad, cultural themes—will make subjective sense to large numbers of people in search of a solution. For example, biological autism therapies, such as secretin (Horvath et al., 1998) and gluten- and casein-free diets (Whitely et al., 1999) gain an air of plausibility from the assumption that the etiology of autism is genetic or, in some sense, "biological." The underlying logic is that biological therapies are best for biological conditions. Dietary treatments may also benefit from popular contemporary beliefs about nutrition and food allergies. But it is dangerous to rely on our intuitive response to a treatment because the subjective appeal of an idea is no more reliable than the word of an authority.

The Scientific Method.   Peirce's answer to the problem of fixation of belief was the scientific method, but, of course, there is no one scientific method. There are several ways of conducting science, and researchers have long debated how behavioral science, in particular, should be done (Cohen, 1994; Johnston & Pennypacker, 1993; Sidman, 1960). Nonetheless, according to Peirce, when empirical methods are used with adequate controls they should lead to beliefs that have "external permanency" (1992, p. 120). Taking a strongly positivist stance, he asserted that there are "real things, whose characters are entirely independent of our ideas about them" (1992, p. 120), and if the appropriate tests are devised, we can find out what those real things are. In support of this view, he pointed to the many scientific advances that were evident to his readers in 1877.

The authors of this volume share Peirce's enthusiasm for the scientific method. Empirical evidence rigorously obtained is the best way to settle disputes about the value of a treatment. Of course, science is an iterative process that can lead in unexpected directions, particularly early in the process of discovery. For example, in researching the use of prism glasses as a treatment for children with autism, Kay and Vyse (chap. 16, this volume) found only two published studies in the available databases, both of which reported positive effects. Thus, their case study may be the only published report of a negative outcome with this rather improbable therapy. None-theless, given adequate time, science typically produces an unequivocal estimate of the value of any therapy.

IN SEARCH OF BARTHOLOW'S FUTURE

Peirce's list makes good sense. Most, if not all, the beliefs we hold have been ac-quired by one or more of his four methods. But, if as individuals, we are to live by his suggestions, we will have a difficult time. If we are to use the scientific method to form our beliefs, a lifetime of testing will provide us with only a fraction of what is needed to live our lives. Because the goal of testing every important idea is impossi-ble to achieve, we must rely on authorities to help us make our daily decisions, and parents of developmentally disabled children making decisions about their chil-dren's therapy have the same problem. They cannot all be scientists—indeed, there is no reason for them to be. There are plenty of behavioral scientists at work on these problems today. The person who wants to acquire sound beliefs about disabilities treatment need not conduct research him- or herself. Instead, the consumer must value scientific evidence, seek it out, and recognize it when he or she sees it.

And this is where the problem lies. We live in an age of science. The effects of sci-ence, in the form of technological innovations, are obvious throughout the western-ized world. In professional medicine, the scientific method is the dominant approach to settling issues of opinion. It does not always lead to uncontroversial truth (e.g., Taubes, 2002), but the profession has fully adopted the view that argu-ments must be based on scientific evidence. Fewer professionals in the field of de-velopmental disabilities have made a similar commitment to science, and so a book like this one is necessary. But the fundamental problem that faces us is one of cul-tural values. We may have adopted the fruits of science in the form of advances in technology and medicine, but not enough of us have adopted scientific thinking as the primary way of "fixing knowledge" (Vyse, 1997a, 1997b). To be certain, science does not have the answer to every question. Science will not tell you whom to marry, what is the most meaningful part of your life, or whether there is a god. But for mat-ters of testable fact, there is no better tool, and claims about treatments for people with developmental disabilities are easily testable. At least that is the belief of the authors of this volume. If we are to help people with developmental disabilities reach their fullest potential, we must teach the larger community the benefits of sci-entific evidence and thought (Vyse, 1997a).

In 1872, Roberts Bartholow, an early advocate for the scientific approach to medi-cine, wrote in a textbook of the day:

> Homeopathy and allopathy are dreams of a by-gone time. Modern science is indiffer-ent to Hippocrates and Hahnemann. The therapeutics of today rejects dogmas, and the therapeutics of the future will accept nothing that can not be demonstrated by the tests of science. (Bartholow, 1872, p. 636)

Bartholow's future may be here for medicine, but it has not yet arrived for the field of developmental disabilities treatment. More efforts like this volume will be needed before that time will come. But if the history of American medicine is an ex-ample, the effort will not be in vain. Bartholow's future is within our grasp.

ACKNOWLEDGMENT

The author would like to thank John H. Warner for his comments on an earlier draft of this chapter.

REFERENCES

American Psychiatric Association. (1994). *Diagnostic and statistical manual of mental disorders* (4th ed.). Washington, DC: Author.

Ayres, A. J. (1994/1979). *Sensory integration and the child*. Los Angeles, CA: Western Psychological Services.

Bartholow, R. (1872). Experimental therapeutics. Introductory address. *Cincinnati Lancet and Observer* (Medical College of Ohio), *15*, 635–636.

Bell, J., & Hays, I. (1999). Code of ethics. In R. B. Baker, A. L. Caplan, L. L. Emanuel, & S. R. Latham (Eds.), *The American medical ethics revolution: How the AMA's code of ethics has transformed physician's relationships to patients, professionals, and society* (pp. 324–334). Baltimore: Johns Hopkins University Press. (Original work published 1847)

Cassileth, B. R. (1989). The social implications of questionable cancer therapies. *Cancer, 63*(1), 1247–1250.

Cohen, J. (1994). The earth is round ($p < .05$). *American Psychologist, 49*, 997–1003.

Danforth, S. (2002). New words for new purposes: A challenge for the AAMR. *Mental Retardation, 40*(1), 51–55.

Duffy, J. (1976). *The healers: A history of American medicine*. Urbana, IL: University of Illinois Press.

Duffy, J. (1993). *From humors to medical science*. Urbana, IL: University of Illinois Press.

Gergen, K. J. (2001). Psychological science in a postmodern context. *American Psychology, 56*(10), 803–813.

Goode, D. (2002). Mental retardation is dead: Long live mental retardation. *Mental Retardation, 40*(1), 57–59.

Gould, S. J. (1981). *The mismeasure of man*. New York: Norton.

Herbert, J. D., & Brandsma, L. L. (2002). Applied behavior analysis for childhood autism: Does the emperor have clothes? *The Behavior Analyst Today, 3*(1), 45–50. Available from http://www.behavior-analyst-online.org/BAT/

Herbert, J. D., Sharp, I. R., & Gaudiano, B. A. (2002). Separating fact from fiction in the etiology and treatment of autism: A scientific review of the evidence. *The Scientific Review of Mental Health Practice, 1*, 25–45.

Horvath, K., Stefanatos, G., Sokoloski, K. N., Wachtel, R., Nabors, L., & Tildon, J. T. (1998). Improved social and language skills after secretin administration in patients with autistic spectrum disorders. *Journal of the Association for Academic Minority Physicians, 9*, 9–15.

Jacobson, J. W., Mulick, J. A., & Schwartz, A. A. (1995). A history of facilitated communication: Science, pseudoscience, and antiscience. *American Psychologist, 50*, 750–765.

Johnston, J. M., & Pennypacker, H. S. (1993). *Strategies and tactics of behavioral research* (2nd ed.). Hillsdale, NJ: Lawrence Erlbaum Associates.

Kutchins, H., & Kirk, S. A. (1997). *Making us crazy: DSM: the psychiatric bible and the creation of mental disorders*. New York: Free Press.

Lovaas, O. I. (1987). Behavioral treatment and normal educational and intellectual functioning in young autistic children. *Journal of Consulting and Clinical Psychology, 55*, 3–9.

Mackey, R. B. (1995). Discover the healing power of therapeutic touch. *American Journal of Nursing, 95*(4), 26–34.

Maurice, C. (1993). *Let me hear your voice: A family's triumph over autism*. New York: Knopf.

Okie, S. (2000, January 18). Maverick treatments find U.S. funding: Cancer therapy to be tested despite mainstream medical doubts. *The Washington Post*, p. A1.

O'Mathuna, D. P., Pryjmachuk, S., Spencer, W., Stanwick, M., & Matthiesen, S. (2002). A critical evaluation of the theory and practice of therapeutic touch. *Nursing Philosophy, 3*, 163–176.

Peirce, C. S. (1992). The fixation of belief. In N. Houser & C. Kloesel (Eds.), *The essential Peirce* (Vol. 1, pp. 109–123). Bloomington, IN: Indiana University Press. (Original work published in 1877)

People with AIDS are targets of phony cure schemes. (1991, December 29). *St. Louis Post-Dispatch*, p. 10C.

Schwartz, G. E. R., Russek, L. G. S., Nelson, L. A., & Barentsen, C. (2001). Accuracy and replicability of anomalous after-death communication across highly skilled mediums. *Journal of the Society for Psychical Research, 65.1*(862), 1–25.

Shermer, M. (1997). *Why people believe weird things: Pseudoscience, superstition, and other confusions of our time.* New York: Freeman.

Sidman, M. (1960). *Tactics of scientific research: Evaluating experimental data in psychology.* Boston: Authors Cooperative.

Taubes, G. (2002, July 7). What if it's all been a big fat lie? *The New York Times Magazine*, 22–27, 34, 45, 47.

Vyse, S. A. (1997a). *Believing in magic: The psychology of superstition.* New York: Oxford University Press.

Vyse, S. A. (1997b). Superstition in the age of science. *World Review, 2*(4), 13–15.

Warner, J. H. (1999). The 1880s rebellion against the AMA code of ethics: "Scientific democracy" and the dissolution of orthodoxy. In R. B. Baker, A. L. Caplan, L. L. Emanuel, & S. R. Latham (Eds.), *The American medical ethics revolution: How the AMA's code of ethics has transformed physicians' relationships to patients, professionals, and society* (pp. 52–69). Baltimore: Johns Hopkins University Press.

Welch, M. G. (1988). *Holding time: How to eliminate conflict, temper tantrums, and sibling rivalry and raise loving, successful children.* New York: Simon & Schuster.

Whitely, P., Rodgers, J., Savery, D., & Shattock, P. (1999). A gluten-free diet as an intervention for autism and associated spectrum disorders: Preliminary findings. *Autism, 3*, 45–65.

Wolpe, P. R. (1999). Alternative medicine and the AMA. In R. B. Baker, A. L. Caplan, L. L. Emanuel, & S. R. Latham (Eds.), *The American medical ethics revolution: How the AMA's code of ethics has transformed physicians' relationships to patients, professionals, and society* (pp. 218–239). Baltimore: Johns Hopkins University Press.

Sifting Sound Practice From Snake Oil

Judith E. Favell
AdvoServ Programs

Dubious interventions and pseudotreatments have long been in evidence in the human services arena. Though no area or enterprise has been immune to the phenomenon of unsubstantiated claims and controversial fads, the field of developmental disabilities appears particularly vulnerable to questionable ideas and movements. Although substantial and well-substantiated progress has been seen across the decades in dimensions such as the teaching of adaptive skills, treatment of behavior problems, and the overall quality of life of individuals with developmental disabilities, these well-grounded, positive developments have often been eclipsed by the steady appearance of "breakthroughs," "new models," "cures," and "revolutionary strategies" that typically promise results that are more rapid, more beneficial, and easier to achieve than any seen before (CBS News, 2003). Positive, indeed astounding, effects are said to be seen with this pill, that diet, exotic machines, techniques that release hidden capacities and expressions, or methods that place no stress or challenges on the individual. The promise and promotion of these new and better mousetraps is not only contrasted to the relatively poorer outcomes achieved by traditional approaches, but they often include a strident denunciation of all that has gone before. For example, when supports in developmental disabilities began to gravitate from institutions to the community, the potential benefits of such a movement were often framed principally in terms of the abusive, impoverished, and incarcerating circumstances from which individuals were being liberated (e.g., the publications of the Association for the Severely Handicapped). All institutional practices were bad, and the people who worked there were misguided at best. Thus, the new community movement not only promised a revolution in the way supports would be provided and positive outcomes achieved, but it did so, in part, by denigrating previous service models and arrangements. In a similar fashion, a parade of movements has promised new and improved ways of achieving beneficial outcomes that are less intrusive, costly, stressful, labor intensive, and risky than the methods that have preceded them.

While new and improved models and methods will continue to arise, and are fundamentally healthy, indeed essential, if the field of developmental disabilities is to remain vital and innovative, the issue lies in whether and how the veracity of claims made about these models and methods are assessed and substantiated.

THE RULES AND REWARDS OF SCIENCE

This book and chapter are predicated on the premise that science is virtually the only means by which the field of developmental disabilities can test the effects of any proposed "innovation," and either establish or disconfirm its value as a beneficial part of services and supports. The scientific method separates the wheat from the chaff through, for example, its quantitative, direct measurement of observable events to empirically verify effects, its use of analytic means to determine if an intervention functionally caused the effects obtained, and its insistence on replication to establish that the results are not confined to one individual, practitioner/researcher, or other unique and nonrepeatable set of circumstances. Through these and other elements of its rules and process, science can indeed sort the wheat from the chaff, separate substance from superstition, treatment from tricks, and sound practice from snake oil. Through the scientific process, an entire body of knowledge and technology has been accumulated and applied to the betterment of individuals with developmental disabilities. Through this process, the field developed functional means of teaching people to toilet properly, feed themselves, read, work, communicate, and fill their leisure time with enriching activities. Through this process, effective means of treating incapacitating behavior problems such as self-injury and aggression were discovered. Such problems were found to conform to lawful principles and to respond positively to comprehensive treatment that reduced their frequency and severity (National Institutes of Health, 1991). The gradual accumulation of empirically valid and reliable methods of education, training, and treatment in turn enabled the social revolution that emphasized the potential for growth in people with developmental disabilities, oriented supports to facilitate their development, and enabled their greater independence and enjoyment of life. Integrated living in the community among family and friends, remunerative work, life without barriers from excessive drugs, stigmatizing behavior problems or functional incapacity, all of these outcomes have been achieved through the process of scientific research, both basic and applied.

THE DISTRUST AND DISDAIN OF SCIENCE

Despite the essential contribution of science to the understanding and amelioration of barriers and problems associated with developmental disabilities, science has remained distrusted and disdained by large contingents within both the field of developmental disabilities as well as society at large (Danforth, 1997). A number of reasons underlie this reaction against the role and benefit of science. The process of science appears arduous and slow, requiring a seemingly inordinate period to conduct its investigations, arrive at its conclusions, and disseminate its results. The methods and analyses of science sometimes appear to defy logic and not conform to conventional wisdom and common sense. The scientific process appears arcane, complex, and confusing to the developmental disabilities community, the general public, and even to professionals who are not trained in the value, logic, or methods of science. Science as a tool for advancement of knowledge and for social change is not widely taught on even graduate levels in education, medicine, psychology, and other professional human service areas. When presented with new methods and movements, professionals highly trained in the content of their discipline, but not in the scientific methods by which to analyze the veracity of new developments, may resort to popular but faulty means of evaluating the legitimacy of these developments (Kauffman, 1999). One need not look far for numerous examples of practices sometimes adopted widely and at great expense by competent and well-intentioned professionals whose information had not been subjected to the rigors of scientific scrutiny and which was eventually found to be ill considered and incorrect.

Not only are science's means viewed as arduous and arcane, but its perceived preoccupation with its methodology sometimes appears to eclipse an interest in the meaningfulness of its results. Attention ranging from reports in the popular media to congressional investigations have highlighted examples of sometimes elaborate and costly research that have yielded "trivial" or "obvious" conclusions which have not appeared to result in meaningful outcomes for real people with real needs (Proxmire, 1975). Viewed in this light, science appears self-serving and self-stimulatory, detached from and unresponsive to the real issues confronting people with developmental disabilities.

Perhaps worst of all, the scientific process may not yield good news, but instead deliver an answer that is unexpected or unwanted. Science's hallmark as "value-neutral" risks results and outcomes that do not conform to prevailing beliefs, wisdom, or treatment and instructional philosophy. Thus, when employing the tools of science, one must be prepared to have a promising approach disconfirmed or a cherished hope dashed. This possibility is painful to families engaged in a desperate search for help, and sometimes to professionals whose positions, livelihood, and even identities are inextricably tied to a concept or approach.

Few scientists have aided this situation by directly explaining and interpreting the scientific approach to consumers, the public, or human service professionals. Oriented toward communicating with like-minded professionals, dissemination efforts are focused on scientific journals and professional meetings (Mike, Krauss, & Ross, 1998). Communicating beyond these channels and venues, for example, directly to consumers, may be valued but is too frequently short-shifted. Further, dissemination efforts rarely focus on the role, methods, and benefits of science, concentrating instead on the results achieved. Thus, consuming audiences do not gain an appreciation for the process of science, nor are they exposed to even the most basic means of discriminating between spurious claims and those based on solid empirical evidence. Whereas scientists publish in their journals and interact at professional conferences, families and professionals who are not part of the scientific circle are left vulnerable to faddish movements and fanciful promises.

THE CARE AND FEEDING OF FADS

Not only is science viewed as a slow, arcane, and insensitive enterprise conducted by a closed club of nerdy scientific types wearing pocket protectors, but the fads and fancies dangled in front of the developmental disabilities community often have compelling features that are easy to promote and popularize (Dwyer, 1993). If not harnessed to the wagon of science, the process of developing and disseminating a new idea or practice need not be labor intensive nor required to follow an ordained process, and thus can be quite rapid. An idea can be derived from a hunch, an observation, anecdote, or case study, organized into a theory or conceptual framework with associated terminology and principles, and disseminated directly to consumers and the public, for example, through the press, a book, the Internet, or speaking circuit. Families in desperate search of help, and the press in constant search of hype, always provide a receptive audience for novel ideas and approaches. In this rapid trajectory from concept to audience, critical scrutiny may begin to emerge only much later in the process, sometimes after the fad has been adopted widely and at great cost in terms of resources and emotional investment (Jacobson, Mulick, & Schwartz, 1995).

Not only is it possible to derive and disseminate a new approach with relative ease if one is not saddled with the need to rigorously substantiate its benefits, but phenomena in developmental disabilities lend themselves to faulty observations and conclusions. With behavior problems, for example, a great deal of variability occurs naturally, with rates and intensities that vary widely across time and situations. Aggression may be frequent and severe for days or weeks and then decline or even disappear for a period of time, only to return again, perhaps more intensely or in a new form. Such variability invites spurious and superstitious conclusions, especially when interventions are tried frequently and nonsystemically (Vyse, 1997). Was the improvement or deterioration in the problem due to the drug that was prescribed, the new treatment method employed, the diet tried, the moon phase that prevailed? Quixotic observations and accidental correlations invite incorrect attributions of cause and effect, which in turn spawn superstitious practices, not only in the arena of behavior problems but in all other domains of professional and paraprofessional activity as well.

With the uneven course of development in virtually all adaptive areas seen for many people with developmental disabilities, it is difficult to know what accounts for progress or regression in communication, sociability, work productivity, or self-care merely by everyday observation. As with behavior problems, the variability in the acquisition and performance of these and other skills lends itself to incorrect conclusions regarding the causes of the changes seen. Faced with this variability in the behavior, skills, and well-being of an individual, it is not surprising that families and professionals, in search of answers for these changes, seize on salient environmental events that appear correlated with improvement. This process, though understandable, can and has spawned practices and movements that are in fact nonfunctional or even harmful.

The genesis and promulgation of dubious and improbable treatments can also be attributed to other variables beyond the relative ease of their promotion and the inclination toward linking naturally occurring changes with interventions that may or may not have had a functional role in those changes. In some cases, the needs, dynamics, and reinforcers of the individuals promoting a method or movement must also be examined. The field of developmental disabilities, just as all other human endeavors, is populated with mere mortals, whose needs for positive regard, attention, and making a contribution, as well as their own advancement and income, cannot be ignored. The field has seen a full range of "gurus," from honest and earnest advocates of a particular approach, to what can only be called snake oil salesmen. Once again, however, the essential tool to separate snake oil salesmen from honest purveyors of substance is whether the "product" they are promoting is scientifically validated or not. The field may forgive individuals whose ideas are ultimately proven misguided or wrong; it should be far less charitable toward those who reject efforts to test the veracity of their ideas or continue claims despite evidence against them.

It is clear that a variety of factors, alone or in combination, may account for the development and promulgation of faddish methods and movements, including the ease with which they may be promoted in popular channels, the possibility of spurious conclusions based on faulty observations and analysis, and the varying needs and dynamics of some individuals promoting them. To this list of variables that promote change, whether superstitious or substantive, should be added the many philosophical or political currents that exert pressure on the field. Against the constant ebb and flow, waxing and waning in perspectives and practices, there are regular occurrences of salient events that produce large shifts in opinions and approaches. Although some of these events are positive, such as the highly publicized findings regarding the benefits of early intervention in autism (McEachin, Smith, & Lovaas, 1993), more often, shifts in policy and practice seem to derive from negative events (Johnston & Shook, 1987). Of these, the most painful and powerful are the tragedies that occur when an individual with a developmental disability is harmed in some way (Weiss, 1998).

An injury or worse, death, can catapult change, sometimes accelerating needed reform, and sometimes advancing policy or practice that is of dubious value and potential deleterious effects. The emotional and intellectual climate that surrounds situations in which a person has been harmed does not tend to foster thoughtful and well-planned approaches to problems, but instead reinforces proposals that promise instant relief and dramatic effects. One example of this phenomenon involves reactions to employing therapeutic restraint in light of press reports of injury and death associated with its use (Weiss, 1998). Thoughtful analysis of the risks and the benefits of using restraint as part of a comprehensive program for treating severe behavior disorders is quickly eclipsed by calls for its categorical prohibition (Favell, 1990). The debate on this topic continues in forms and forums ranging from news articles to proposed legislation. This context provides an opportunity for proponents on both sides to argue their positions, sometimes stepping beyond available evidence and knowledge. In this climate, solid data supporting the various positions are rarely entertained, and thus neither the proof behind the legitimate role for restraint or the viability of alternatives to restrain may be critically scrutinized. Under these circumstances, statements made in interviews and testimony remain unchallenged and are accepted as fact by the grateful public and hungry press who are looking for answers that are palatable more than treatments that are palliative.

All those dedicated to and engaged in the systematic, scientific process of developing truly effective treatments, including alternatives to the use of restraint, are ignored in this process. Their more moderate and measured positions, based on data, are lost in the cacophony of pontification and polemics. This example of the debate regarding whether and how restraint might be utilized for severe behavior problems is among many others in which serious and legitimate inquiry into issues affecting those with developmental disabilities sometimes ignites into highly charged emotional and political wars. In these circumstances, it is clear how the climate and contingencies foster extreme and unsubstantiated positions and may give rise to dubious and improbable approaches that promise relief, especially easy and painless relief, to difficult problems.

Applied Behavior Analysis: An Example of the Fruits of Science and the Foundation of Fads

In attempting to understand the inclination toward adopting fads and unfounded treatments, in part by denigrating preceding and alternative approaches, and the disinclination toward using the scientific method to sift out sound practice from snake oil, the case in point of applied behavior analysis combines and highlights the mysteries of each. Behavior analysis has played a vital role in revolutionizing treatment and training in developmental disabilities, virtually moving services from custodial care to community-based supports, freeing individuals from many behavioral and adaptive barriers that had kept them dependent and devalued. These advances are based on solid research that has yielded a universe of effective treatment and training strategies never before seen or even imagined (Konarski, Favell, & Favell, 1992). Despite these contributions to the understanding and amelioration of challenges facing individuals with developmental disabilities, applied behavior analysis has been and continues to be the subject of major criticism, evoking reactions from both the public and other professionals ranging from denial to denigration (Hobbs, Cornwell, & Chiesa, 2000; Lovett, 1996).

This lack of respect or acceptance is manifested, for example, by the fact that new fads or trends are often referenced or contrasted against behavior-analytic principles and methods. For example, "positive behavioral support" (PBS) is sometimes depicted as an alternative to rather than a derivative of behavior analysis, implying that the approach is wholly different from the behavior-analytic tradition and practices from which it in fact sprang. In contrasting the two, comparisons often evoke old and outmoded behavioral practices, which, although today viewed as primitive, were in fact the origin of effective treatment for behavior disorders, and have now evolved into the more sophisticated and comprehensive strategies that are utilized today, not just by those espousing PBS, but by all behavior analysts.

Similarly, the movement calling itself "person-centered planning," which focuses on the individual and builds a support plan based on strengths, preferences, and personal desires, is often contrasted as the values-based polar opposite of behavioral approaches to planning and support (Holburn, 2001). This characterization ignores the very foundation of behavior analysis, with its unequivocal focus on the individual, an emphasis on the uniqueness of the individual's preferences, reinforcers, strengths, and needs, and how plans must be built on those facts, not on overgeneralized assumptions about what is functional and good for the individual. Strength-based planning has provided a helpful orientation to design supports for individuals, but delivering it rests squarely on the well-researched behavioral principle of shaping (Osborne, 1999).

Despite the shared roots and striking commonalities of "new and improved" practices with behavior analysis, the latter still remains difficult to understand or adopt, perhaps because of the very reasons discussed earlier, relating to why science is eschewed and fads are embraced. The processes by which behavior analysis works are slow and methodical, difficult and expensive, empirical rather than values based, not at all as dramatic and fun as exotic machines and cheerful dolphins, and rarely result in claims of instant breakthroughs, miracles, or cures. The methods of behavior analysis do not necessarily conform to common sense and popular culture which, for example, still questions the role and right to positive reinforcement, and they continue to fly in the face of established constituencies such as public schools and the mental health establishment (Foxx, 1996). Indeed, it could be argued that behavior analysis would not have had a chance to prove itself at all if the psychiatric and medical community had not abrogated its interest in individuals with developmental disabilities and essentially "allowed" behavior analysts to address people and problems that it never could nor wanted to help. (The same could be said of the educational and psychological communities!) Thus, the antibehavioral view continues to sell books, draw participants to workshops, and, pertinent to this volume, serve as the source of many new trends and fads, the chief merits of which may rest principally on their perceived distance from, or presumed improvement on, behavioral theory and practice.

ESSENTIAL STEPS TOWARD SOUND PRACTICE

If the field of developmental disabilities is to maximize vital innovation by promoting worthwhile strategies that are of demonstrable benefit, and culling wild goose chases that are not, a variety of steps seem indicated.

First, it is important to recognize that new fads and movements are neither inherently good nor bad. It has been said that the way to have a good idea is to have lots of them, and for that reason, it becomes important not to suppress but instead encourage new models, methods, and movements. Within my career, most practices that ultimately benefited people with developmental disabilities began as a shimmering promise or a radical idea. Of these, the most salient example is applied behavior analysis.

In the interest of encouraging new ideas and strategies, it would appear helpful to concentrate less on the origin and nature of the methods proposed, emphasizing instead that the approach be systematically evaluated and analyzed (Jacobson et al., 1995). Ideas springing from virtually any philosophy or discipline should be amenable to a fair and full test as to their efficacy. If an idea appears dubious or improbable, perhaps because it derives from a profession other than one's own, it is not necessarily without merit, but instead may deserve an opportunity to demonstrate its effects.

The point is a simple one: New ideas, regardless of their origin and despite falling outside of the realm of familiar practice, may deserve empirical evaluation so long as it is agreed by the individual's family and supporting professionals that it is ethical and not likely to cause harm. In short, I suggest that the rhetoric and intransigence that often surrounds newly proposed methods and movements should be replaced by empirical analysis, to explore both their promise and pitfalls. Neither "side" should be allowed to derail this process. Those representing established practices, including applied behavior analysis, should remain responsive to exploring new ideas and lend their analytic and measurement tools to the process. Proponents of new approaches must also not be allowed to ignore or reject submitting their strategies to empirical tests. When proponents of movements eschew the need for research or denounce its findings (Biklen & Cardinal, 1997), consumers should certainly question their motives if not rebuff their methods.

The call for tolerance to new ideas, matched with their rigorous evaluation, raises a wealth of issues, ranging from the "how" of evaluation to the "who" of deciding what is beneficial. As indicated earlier, the optimal strategy for testing the efficacy of new methods and models rests clearly with scientific research. Empirical analysis of a proposed intervention is the surest means of answering questions about its true effectiveness. The advent of single-subject research designs, which eschewed the involvement of large groups of participants and focused instead on the analyses of effects within and across a small number of individuals, brought a new level of sensitivity and relevance to research in developmental disabilities (Johnston & Pennypacker, 1981). With these designs, it was possible to evaluate unique adjustments and effects with individuals and incorporate information gained into the conclusions drawn. Thus, the marriage of research and practice was firmly forged, enabling research to be conducted in the actual course of delivering services. This relationship is alive and well and can be expected to continue to yield the most convincing data and information on whether a new approach is bogus or beneficial.

Even in situations in which formally designed research is not achievable, empirical validation is still possible, indeed essential, to evaluate effects in an individual case. Regardless of whether the proposed approach rests on a robust record of research or has not yet been fully explored through experimental analyses, evaluation and verification in individual applications remains a requirement in most standards of best practice. Given the idiosyncratic response to treatment and the universe of variations that may be needed to adjust treatment to individual circumstances, measurement and evaluation are an essential part of any sound clinical or educational effort, as well as a valuable means of accumulating a body of information on newly proposed approaches.

Although not replacing more formal research analyses, evaluation in individual cases can begin to accrue a clinical track record about the merits and problems involved. Such a track record of individual cases cannot necessarily confirm that a proposed strategy yields positive results, but it can bring into focus, sometimes with astounding clarity, when an intervention is nonfunctional or even harmful. The promise of Secretin in autism was eventually laid to rest by well-controlled research, but prior to those more definitive answers, evaluations with individual children repeatedly yielded negligible or no effects (Unis et al., 2002). The error was not in the idea, but instead would have been in the wholesale use of Secretin without evaluation in individual cases.

Reliable and valid measurement of effects can be expected to address many of the issues that would otherwise be the subject of strong philosophical debate and heated emotional argument about both new and existing interventions. If, for example, a medication or a diet is proposed to address an individual's hyperactivity, such an intervention would be expected to result in a demonstrable increase in participation in organized activities and attention to task, as well as measurable decreases in vocal and motoric outbursts on social outings (e.g., Reichelt, Knivsberg, Lind, & Nodland, 1991). The effects, positive or negative, move the discussion from an emotional to an empirical level and may replace the polemics that might otherwise occur. Likewise, if two competing views exist about how best to address the aggression of a child in school, endless meetings can be replaced with direct measurement of the desired effects. With which method is the child's rate of aggression the lowest, with the fewest interruptions in instruction, with the most evidence of social interaction and engagement in activities? Questions asked in this way may not always yield clear and simple answers, but in focusing on actual outcomes and quarreling less about means, the dialogue becomes more rational and focused on individual well-being rather than on professional or ideological posturing.

Of course, measurement will not settle all disputes abut the efficacy and advisability of interventions. When arguments regarding the relative merits of an approach continue despite measurement of its effects, it sometimes appears that different proponents are focusing on different aspects of these effects. For example, though one view may highlight the lack of aggression seen following the introduction of a new medication, another perspective may note the decrement in all activity, including functional and social engagement. Similarly, while one contingent might celebrate the reduction of demand-induced self-injury, others might question the concomitant reduction in skill acquisition associated with the removal of instructional demands used to achieve those reductions. Such examples, repeated in countless variation over the years, punctuate the need to expand and refine the measures of efficacy applied in all evaluation efforts, both to the existing technology and to newly proposed approaches. Simple reductions in behavior problems are not sufficient to evaluate the efficacy of an intervention; the full array of outcomes and side effects must be examined. Have the reductions achieved improvement in the individual's life; what was compromised to obtain the effects? Likewise, qualitative and quantitative process measures such as practicality, cost, and social acceptability must be included in the comprehensive evaluation of a method. Interventions that realize positive effects, but involve prohibitive costs or require scarce professional talent and acumen, may be ruled out regardless of their effects.

Empirical validation of the effectiveness of proposed strategies, hopefully incorporating some level of scientific analysis and certainly encompassing a full array of measures of efficacy, is the foundation on which true innovation must be built (Konarski et al., 1992). However, the tools of science will not, by themselves, provide answers as to the "good" versus "harm" that a strategy may present to an individual.

Is living in one's own apartment "good"? Is it harmful to use restraint or another intrusive technique as part of a treatment program for a severe behavior problem? What is the right balance between accepting people as they are and challenging them to grow? As indicated, such questions must first be addressed by defining and measuring the desired and undesirable outcomes of alternative decisions. Direct measurement can answer, for example, whether an individual in an apartment is integrated into the fabric of a community life with activities and friends, or whether she is inactive and alone. Similarly, direct measurement can document both deleterious effects of restraint, such as time away from activities or actual occurrences of harm, and the benefits associated with its use, such as reductions in the use of drugs or decreases in injuries resulting from a problem behavior.

Though measurement can replace diatribe with data, the essential next step involves a decision regarding whether the processes and outcomes are good or harmful, beneficial or deleterious. These are value-based decisions which ultimately determine whether a strategy, method, or approach is in the best interests of an individual.

At the end of the day, someone or some process must decide if what is proposed and promised is right and appropriate for individuals who cannot decide for themselves. A variety of movements in developmental disabilities have attempted to move these decisions from those closest to the individual to arenas far removed from individuals and their families. Rather than tailoring decisions to individual circumstances, these movements have issued categorical pronouncements and advocated uniform solutions to issues, typically framed within their ideological parameters and beliefs. This or that strategy is not only the best for all, but then becomes the *only* means to employ. Such hubris usurps the rightful role and responsibility of the individual and their families. These are the people closest to the issues, and it is they who will experience the consequences of these decisions. They make mistakes in judgment and action, but their errors pale against those who act remotely, without information or investment in the well-being of the individuals they effect. Prescriptions and prohibitions made from afar are rarely relevant and appropriate for each individual covered within it.

Movements that espouse categorical and uniform "answers," applied sweepingly across all people, often frame their views explicitly or implicitly as "serving the greater good." The corollary seems to be an understanding that certain individuals may be harmfully affected in the interest of this greater good. Movements that are based on disavowing or disallowing certain treatment strategies or that espouse a single value-based model for all individuals are sacrificing the well-being of some individuals to the altar of their ideologies and concept of greater good (Smith, 1996). Such positions usurp the rights, roles, and responsibilities of individuals and their families. Movements can appropriately raise issues and offer alternatives, but only those closest to the individual can insure that sweeping prescriptions and proscriptions do not have deleterious consequences on the individual they love.

SUMMARY

Hopefully, new methods and movements will continue to appear frequently in the field of developmental disabilities. Such an infusion of new ideas is essentially healthy to the field and can be of great benefit to individuals with mental retardation, autism, and other developmental delays. The fundamental challenge is to differentiate which of these ideas are sound and actually help people, and which are without substance.

The scientific method is the only real means of sifting sound practice from snake oil, and yet its principles and processes have hardly been embraced. Science is viewed as an arcane process which is not responsive to, nor capable of, rendering meaningful solutions to real people with real problems, especially by the public and professionals not trained in its machinations and insulated from scientists whose top priority is not public dissemination of the role and rules of science.

The difficulty in accepting science as a source of information and vehicle for social change is contrasted by the ease with which fads and movements blossom and flourish, advanced by positions and promoters that offer solutions promising easy and painless approaches to a consuming public in desperate search of answers and to a media in constant search of hype, and fanned regularly by significant events that invite sweeping changes in public opinion, policy, and law (Department of Health and Human Services, 2001). The continued devaluation of scientific approaches and the proclivity toward promoting new methods and movements by sometimes denigrating approaches that have preceded them can be found in the recent targeting of applied behavior analysis.

Strategies for fostering worthwhile innovation while decisively controlling wild goose chases are not mysterious in either logic or practice. The developmental disabilities community must maintain a context that welcomes new ideas, including those arising from disparate disciplines and ideologies and falling outside of familiar practices. Rhetoric about the suitability and possible efficacy of new methods then must be replaced by empirical tests, which directly measure the full effects of the intervention, and in all cases possible, include an analysis of the functional role the intervention played in the measured outcome. This level of evaluation must be conducted both within and across individuals and be considered an essential part of all best practice. There are no substitutes, no short cuts to this fundamental process of empirical validation. If proponents refuse to submit their ideas to it, their motives as well as their methods must be questioned. If consumers and professionals are denied data, they should refuse to consider an approach until such proof is offered.

While the process of empirical validation remains the critical means by which efficacious approaches are adopted and fallacious ones abandoned, a final element in the process deserves special emphasis. The quantitative methods of science are inadequate, and the overreaching generalizations of ideologically driven movements are inappropriate, to make value-based decisions in individual cases. No idea, model, method, or movement should be allowed to ordain what is right or wrong for an individual. Data can inform, advocacy can exhort, but at the end of the day, decisions regarding the issues unique to an individual belong as close as possible to that individual. The challenge in the field of development disabilities is to continue to provide sound options, not those based on supposition, to those making such life-altering decisions for the people they love.

REFERENCES

Biklen, D., & Cardinal, D. N. (Eds.). (1997). *Contested words, contested science*. New York: Teachers College Press.

Danforth, S. (1997). On what basis hope? Modern progress and postmodern possibilities. *Mental Retardation, 35*, 93–106.

Dwyer, J. (1993). Fertile field for fads and fraud: Questionable nutritional therapies. *New York State Journal of Medicine, 93*(2), 105–108.

Faser, J. (2003, January 16). Breaking the silence. *60 Minutes II* [Television broadcast]. New York: CBS Broadcasting, Inc.

Favell, J. E. (1990). Issues in the use of nonaversive and aversive interventions. In S. L. Harris & J. S. Handleman (Eds.), *Aversive and nonaversive interventions: Controlling life-threatening behavior by the developmentally disabled* (pp. 36–56). New York: Springer.

Foxx, R. M. (1996). Translating the covenant: The behavior analyst as ambassador and translator. *The Behavior Analyst, 19*, 147–161.

Hobbs, S., Cornwell, D., & Chiesa, M. (2000). Telling tales about behavior analysis: Textbooks, scholarship and rumor. In J. C. Leslie & D. Blackman (Eds.), *Experimental and applied analysis of human behavior* (pp. 251–270). Reno, NV: Context.

Holburn, S. (2001). Compatibility of person-centered planning and applied behavior analysis. *Behavior Analyst, 24*, 271–281.

Jacobson, J. W., Mulick, J. A., & Schwartz, A. A. (1995). A history of facilitated communication: Science, pseudoscience, and antiscience science working group on facilitated communication. *American Psychologist, 50*, 750–765.

Johnston, J. M., & Pennypacker, H. S. (1981). *Strategies and tactics of human behavioral research*. Hillsdale, NJ: Lawrence Erlbaum Associates.

Johnston, J. M., & Shook, G. L. (1987). Developing behavior analysis at the state level. *Behavior Analyst, 10,* 199–233.

Kauffman, J. M. (1999). Commentary: Today's special education and its message for tomorrow. *Journal of Special Education, 32,* 244–254.

Konarksi, E. A., Favell, J. E., & Favell, J. E. (Eds.). (1992). *Manual for the assessment and treatment of the behavior disorders of people with mental retardation.* Morganton, NC: Western Carolina Center Foundation.

Lovett, H. (1996). *Learning to listen: Positive approaches and people with difficult behavior.* Baltimore: Brookes.

McEachin, J., Smith, T., & Lovaas, I. O. (1993). Long-term outcome for children with autism who received early intensive behavioral treatment. *American Journal of Mental Retardation, 97*(4), 359–372.

Mike, V., Krauss, A. N., & Ross, G. S. (1998). Responsibility for clinical innovation. *Evaluation & the Health Professions, 21,* 3–27.

National Institutes of Health. (1991). *Treatment of destructive behaviors in persons with developmental disabilities.* Washington, DC: NIH Consensus Development Conference, U.S. Department of Health and Human Services.

Osborne, J. G. (1999). Renaissance or killer mutation? A response to Holburn. *Behavior Analyst, 22,* 47–52.

Proxmire, W. (1975, March). *Golden fleece award to the National Science Foundation, National Aeronautics and Space Administration, and the Office of Naval Research for research on determinants of infrahuman and human aggression.* Retrieved January 31, 2003, from http://www.taxpayer.net/awards/goldenfleece/1975–1980.htm

Reichelt, K. L., Knivsberg, A.-M., Lind, G., & Nodland, M. (1991). Probable etiology and possible treatment of childhood autism. *Brain Dysfunction, 4,* 308–319.

Smith, T. (1996). Are other treatments effective? In C. Maurice, G. Green, & S. C. Luce (Eds.), *Behavioral intervention for young children with autism: A manual for parents and professionals* (pp. 45–59). Austin, TX: Pro-Ed.

Unis, A. S., Munson, J. A., Rogers, S. J., Goldson, E., Osterling, J., Gabriels, R., et al. (2002). A randomized, double-blind, placebo-controlled trial of porcine versus synthetic secretin for reducing symptoms of autism. *Journal of the American Academy of Child and Adolescent Psychiatry, 41,* 1315–1321.

U.S. Department of Health and Human Services. (2001). *Use of restraint and seclusion in residential treatment facilities providing inpatient psychiatric services to individuals under age 21* (CMS-2065-F). 66 FR 7148 (Int. final rule); 66 FR 28110 (IFR with clarification). Washington, DC: Author.

Vyse, S. (1997). *Believing in magic: The psychology of superstition.* Oxford, UK: Oxford University Press.

Weiss, E. M. (1998, October 13). A nationwide pattern of death. *The Hartford Courant.* Retrieved January 31, 2003, from http://courant.ctnow.com/projects/restraint/day3.stm

The Nature and Value of Empirically Validated Interventions

Crighton Newsom
Southwest Ohio Developmental Center

Christine A. Hovanitz
University of Cincinnati

All professions involved in developmental disabilities have ethical standards that include a principle requiring that the individual professional provide competent treatment. In some cases, "competent" remains undefined (e.g., American Physical Therapy Association, 2000; Council for Exceptional Children, 1997). In other cases, competence is linked to scientific knowledge in the field. For example, the American Psychological Association's Ethical Standards state, "Psychologists' work is based on established scientific and professional knowledge of the discipline" (American Psychological Association [APA], 2002, p. 5). Physicians are expected to "continue to study, apply, and advance scientific knowledge" (American Medical Association, 2001, p. 1). For various reasons, some of which we explore later, professional organizations typically avoid an explicit requirement that practitioners use *only* scientifically valid interventions. As a result, most of the professions involved in developmental disabilities tolerate clinicians who provide dubious therapies and managers who operate questionable residential, vocational, and community services.

In the absence of the universal acceptance of scientific criteria for identifying valid interventions, society has developed certain formal standards for judging the acceptability of treatments (Beutler, 1998). These come from the health service system and the legal system. *Cost-effectiveness criteria* predominate in health care accounting. Treatment acceptability is based largely on the number of people served and the cost of services. From this perspective, an optimal treatment is one that reaches the largest number of individuals and costs the least, regardless of patient outcome. The second and third standards are applied by courts in defining malpractice. According to the *standard of common practice*, an intervention is considered acceptable based on its frequency of use in the community. If many providers employ the technique, the method is considered appropriate. As with the cost-effectiveness criterion, the standard of common practice does not consider outcome; a treatment that proves ineffective or even harmful could be exempt from malpractice if it is popular. The third standard is the *doctrine of the respectable minority*. A treatment will not be considered malpractice if the treatment is based on an explicit theory and method of delivery and a "respectable" minority of professionals endorse the theory. Once again, objective success of the treatment is not part of the criterion; a harmful therapy could be considered acceptable under these conditions. Clearly, standards outside of professional fields are grossly inadequate to inform and permit choices regarding effective interventions.

How does the conscientious practitioner, human service manager, or consumer identify empirically validated interventions? Some professional organizations have undertaken the task of establishing criteria for defining such interventions, as we describe next. It is possible to summarize all sets of criteria in general terms by saying that empirically validated treatments are scientific treatments. Describing what makes an intervention "scientific" instead of "unscientific" requires a brief review of the essential elements of science.

ELEMENTS OF A SCIENTIFIC APPROACH

The heart of the scientific enterprise is the search for order in nature. *Order* refers to discoverable regularities in relationships between events, such as the relationship between energy, mass, and the speed of light, or between different reinforcement strategies and the percentages of correct responses on an academic task by children with developmental disabilities. The rules or statements that scientists make about such relationships may be expressed mathematically (e.g., $e = mc^2$) or, as is more often the case in the social sciences, verbally (e.g., "Higher probability behaviors reinforce lower probability behaviors when made contingent on them"). In either case, such statements must be objective, testable, and replicable.

A statement is *objective* when the key terms are stated so explicitly and unambiguously that a community of knowledgeable listeners can agree on the meaning of the statement. Anyone who knows what *probability*, *reinforce*, and *contingent* mean in behavioral science will immediately understand the general rule expressed in the previous sentence. Ambiguity is minimized by *operationalizing* the key terms in the statement, that is, defining them in terms of the measurement operations required to make the observations of interest. Measurements might entail counting how often or timing how long a behavior occurs. Continuing with the current example, an investigator might define "higher probability" by explaining that if we measure the duration of all of a child's behaviors in a situation in which there are no restrictions on behaviors, the one the child engages in for the greatest total duration is the highest probability behavior in that situation. The *reliability* of one observer's measurements can be checked by having an independent observer make the same measurements at the same time. Operational definitions make phenomena available for public evaluation, verification, and replication, which are impossible when events are described in terms of personal perception and intuition (Green, 1996).

As an example of the difficulties arising when personal perception and intuition are relied on heavily, consider the following statement from a text on sensory integration about a boy with poor motor coordination. We have italicized the important but undefined terms:

Speculating that the problem originated in Mario's ability to *process and integrate* tactile inputs within the central nervous system, we conclude that a treatment program designed to include enriched tactile experiences derived from participation in activities that Mario *enjoys and finds meaningful* will increase the likelihood that he will *take in, process, and integrate* tactile inputs as a basis for *planning* motor actions. While we cannot directly observe if this occurs, we can observe if Mario's motor behavior improves. (Fisher & Murray, 1991, p. 6, emphasis added)

This is not a scientific statement because the terms *finding meaningful, taking in, processing, integrating,* and *planning* can mean different things to different observers (and nothing at all to some observers). Without further specification, their use merely gives a patina of neurological respectability to casual, intuitive speculation.

Statements are *testable* to the extent that they can be verified or falsified by undertaking certain operations and manipulations (*conducting an experiment*) and measuring the effects of the manipulated variables on the phenomenon under study. Science is thus an active process that produces increasingly better descriptions of reality. Although scientists differ in the relative emphasis they place on inductive versus deductive strategies for doing research, all scientific research starts with a question implying some sort of hypothesis—a guess, a conjecture—about what might be related to something, for example, or which treatment works better than another, and then tests it out. It is the "testing it out" that crucially distinguishes science from other disciplines. A Nobel laureate once explained testability in elegantly simple terms:

We may collect and classify facts, we may marvel at curiosities and idly wonder what accounts for them, but the activity that is characteristically scientific begins with an explanatory conjecture which at once becomes the subject of an energetic critical analysis. It is an instance of a far more general stratagem that underlies every enlargement of general understanding and every new solution of the problem of finding our way about the world. The regulation and control of hypotheses is more usefully described as a *cybernetic* than a logical process: the adjustment and reformulation of hypotheses through an examination of their deductive consequences is simply another setting for the ubiquitous phenomenon of negative feedback. (Medawar, 1963/1996, p. 31)

Scientists apply a number of "rules of evidence" in testing their ideas. A primary concern is the simplification of the conditions under which observations are made. This entails eliminating some factors that are not currently being studied to prevent them from affecting the results. Equally important is the practice of changing only one factor at a time in order to be sure which factor is actually causing the effects observed. When relatively strong variables (those having easily observed effects) are studied, single-case designs can be used (Barlow & Hersen, 1984). The level of a behavior is measured when the variable of interest is absent, as a control condition (*baseline*), which is then compared to the level of the behavior when the variable is present (*treatment*). If repeated introductions and withdrawals of the variable produce corresponding changes in the behavior, we attribute causal status to the variable. When a variable is expected to have a relatively weak effect or we are interested in the average results across a number of participants, appropriate group designs and statistical analyses are undertaken. For example, in a *randomized control design*, participants are assigned randomly to one of at least two groups, a treatment group and a control group. After the treatment is applied to the members of the former group, statistical tests indicate whether the level of behavior measured in the treatment group is significantly different from that in the control group (Kazdin, 1980).

Returning to the example of the boy with coordination problems, the hypothesized relationships between neurological variables and motor behavior clearly fail the testability criterion, as there is no way to manipulate processing, integrating, and planning. In spite of admitting the speculative nature of the assessment of the child's problem and an inability to observe the hypothesized events inside his body, Fisher and Murray (1991) go on to prescribe a treatment that will purportedly change those events in such a way as to produce improved motor behavior. Such an approach will not provide evidence for the hypothetical causes of the problem and is not a guide to responsible treatment. Even if "activities that Mario enjoys and finds meaningful" were specified and their provision actually did improve motor behavior under conditions in which alternative explanations could be ruled out, the only scientifically valid statement possible would be, "Activities A, B, and C provided in accordance with schedule D resulted in improved motor behavior as indicated by changes in measured performances X, Y, and Z." Any additional attributions of taking in, processing, integrating, and planning would be superfluous, remaining just as speculative and potentially misleading as they were in the initial intuitive assessment.

Finally, statements about relationships between events are *replicable* if independent investigators can repeat the original operations and make the same observations. Statements about highly replicable findings may eventually acquire the status of well-established scientific *theories* or even *laws* if they successfully explain a range of phenomena and enable us to predict and influence them in those sciences where control is possible. Such statements never become infallible, however, and can be overturned in the light of compelling new evidence.

Science is the most self-critical and self-correcting kind of knowing there is. Its criteria of objectivity, testability, and replicability enable scientists to find convincing answers to the simple yet crucial question, "How do you know?" (Agnew & Pyke, 1969). A commitment to a scientific approach increases the breadth and quality of knowledge in a field, discriminates valid from invalid treatments, and enables interventions and services to become increasingly effective and beneficial (Barlow, Hayes, & Nelson, 1984; O'Donohue, 1997).

The foregoing core principles of science are evident in a variety of methodologies used in both basic and applied research and have long served the field of developmental disabilities very well. Numerous empirically validated treatments are available for a fairly wide variety of problems. Compilations of empirically validated interventions and service models appear regularly and enable the conscientious professional to keep up with developments in the field (e.g., Hanson, Wieseler, & Lakin, 2002; Iwata et al., 1997; Jacobson & Mulick, 1996; Konarski, Favell, & Favell, 1992; Paine, Bellamy, & Wilcox, 1984; Whitman, Scibak, & Reid, 1983).

Evaluating Scientific Evidence

In any field, when a number of treatments have been studied, it becomes possible to organize them according to some estimate of the quantity and quality of evidence supporting them. The first approach to organizing treatments is often simply to ask professionals in the field who know the research literature and have had considerable experience in using a number of treatments to rank them. The aggregated rankings are published under the auspices of the relevant professional association as "expert consensus guidelines" for the use of professionals and consumers in the field.

The American Association on Mental Retardation recently formed two expert groups to evaluate treatments for problem behaviors and psychiatric disorders, one group addressing psychosocial interventions and the other pharmacological interventions (Rush & Frances, 2000). Each judge rated several possible interventions for a variety of common behavior problems on a scale anchored at 9 ("extremely appropriate: this is your treatment of choice") and 1 ("extremely inappropriate: a treatment you would never use"). The results were averaged and categorized as *treatment of choice* (items rated 9 by at least half the judges) and *first-, second-, and third-line treatments*. For example, for a hypothetical person with severe/profound retardation and severe, persistent self-injurious or aggressive behavior, the psychosocial group ranked "managing the environment," "applied behavior analysis," and "client and/or family education" as first-line treatments of choice; "classical behavior therapy" as a second-line treatment; and "supportive counseling," "cognitive-behavioral therapy," and "psychotherapy" as third-line treatments. Specific behavior analysis procedures were ranked in similar fashion. The psychopharmacology experts provided ratings of drug classes and individual medications across a variety of psychiatric conditions and problem behaviors, as well as ratings of preferred ways of handling complications. Other questions, addressed by both groups, dealt with diagnosis, assessment procedures, and decisions about medication in initial treatment plans for different groups of clients. Expert consensus guidelines are obviously limited by several factors, including the range of interventions presented for rating, the number and types of problems and client groups addressed, and the sample of professionals serving as expert raters. Such guidelines do, however, provide some initial guidance that can be considered along with the particulars of a given case and they indicate which treatments have consensual validity among peers.

A more rigorous approach to guidelines development was used by the New York State Department of Health in creating its practice guidelines on assessment and intervention for young children with autism (New York State Department of Health, 1999). A panel of professionals, service providers, and parents screened the literature and reviewed the most relevant articles in depth to make recommendations regarding assessment and educational programming. Studies selected for in-depth review had to meet high standards for quality, including adequate information concerning the intervention methods, participants in the relevant age range, controlled experimental designs, and the evaluation of functional outcomes. The panel provided overall recommendations for early intervention programs, with an indication of the strength of the scientific evidence for each recommendation, as well as detailed summaries of the evidence on each of 18 types of interventions ranging from intensive behavioral and educational intervention programs to diet therapies.

In advocating the value of empirically validated treatments in developmental disabilities, it is instructive to look at some recent developments in medicine because this field often serves as the model of a well-established clinical discipline.

Although medicine is based on solid science, practicing physicians historically received relatively little training in scientific methods and research, typically far less than most graduate students in the physical and social sciences. Over the past two decades, medicine has undergone a dramatic shift from its traditional focus on pathophysiology (the physiology and biochemistry of diseases) to an emphasis on evidence-based practice in the way it delivers services and in the way it trains medical students. Cost-containment issues drive much of this emphasis. But another, more important rationale also exists: It is the belief that physicians who are up-to-date as a function of their ability to read the current literature critically are thereby able to distinguish stronger from weaker evidence and likely to make better treatment decisions. Similarly, physicians who understand the properties of diagnostic tests and are able to use a quantitative approach are likely to make more accurate diagnoses.

In the traditional approach to medical practice, it was assumed that unsystematic observations from clinical experience were a valid way of building and maintaining one's knowledge about prognosis, diagnostic tests, and treatment efficacy. Further, it was assumed that the study and understanding of basic mechanisms of disease and pathophysiologic principles were a sufficient guide for practice. According to this paradigm, clinicians had a number of options for understanding a patient's signs and symptoms. They could reflect on their own experience, consider the underlying biology, go to a textbook, or ask an expert colleague. The "Introduction" and "Discussion" sections of a journal article would be considered an adequate way of gaining the relevant information from it.

In the evidence-based approach, clinical experience and intuition are supplemented with observations recorded systematically in a standardized way to facilitate later retrieval and analysis. The study of basic mechanisms of disease is necessary but not sufficient as a guide to diagnosis and treatment, as the rationales indicated by pathophysiologic principles may sometimes be incorrect. Understanding how to define patients' problems clearly, conduct focused literature searches, and apply basic rules of evidence to the "Method" and "Results" sections of published papers are deemed essential to correctly interpreting the literature and to derive a sound treatment strategy. The main benefits of such an approach are that it gives physicians a way to deal directly with the uncertainties of clinical medicine and it enables them to cope with the growth of research and rapid technological innovation, as well as meet increasing demands for quality care (Evidence-Based Medicine Working Group, 1992).

The sheer size and importance of medicine in the United States confers many advantages, including not only a massive research establishment, but also an extensive network of support for the analysis and dissemination of research findings. One part of this network is concerned with identifying empirically validated interventions, and it includes the Agency for Healthcare Research and Quality (AHRQ) of the U.S. Department of Health and Human Services. The AHRQ supports 12 Evidence-Based Practice Centers affiliated with universities in North America, which specialize in producing evidence reports and technology assessments based on the world's medical literature. One recent project had the goal of describing systems for assessing the quality of individual scientific articles and rating the strength of a body of evidence pertaining to any particular issue (West et al., 2002). The investigators identified 19 recommended grading systems for rating the quality of published studies and 7 for rating the strength of evidence. In the latter systems, "strength of evidence" is usually defined in terms of three dimensions: quality, quantity, and consistency. *Quality* refers to the methodological rigor of the studies on a topic, and is defined as the extent to which their design, conduct, and analysis has minimized selection, measurement, and confounding biases. *Quantity* refers to the magnitude of treatment effect, the number of studies, and the overall sample size across all studies. *Consistency* is the extent to which similar findings are reported from both similar and different experimental designs. The foregoing dimensions were used in developing the criteria listed in Table 3.1, which shows one system for evaluating the strength of evidence on a topic (West et al., 2002, based on Greer, Mosser, Logan, & Halaas, 2000). An interesting aspect of the scheme shown in Table 3.1 is that unlike most other schemes, which evaluate reviews covering a large number of studies, it can be applied to as few as six "important" research papers on a given topic. This would seem to make it suitable for adaptation and use in other fields, such as those involved in developmental disabilities, where large numbers of experimental studies focusing on a particular treatment are the exception rather than the rule.

Turning to another discipline deeply involved in developmental disabilities, organized psychology has been slow to insist that the services it offers the public be empirically sound in spite of calls from influential psychologists over the years that it do just that (e.g., McFall, 1991; Rotter, 1971). This issue was given significant momentum by McFall's (1991) "Manifesto for a Science of Clinical Psychology," his presidential address to the Section for the Development of Clinical Psychology as an Experimental/Behavioral Science (subsequently renamed the Society for a Science of Clinical Psychology, a section of Division 12 [Clinical Psychology] of the APA). The cardinal principle of the manifesto was that "Scientific clinical psychology is the only legitimate and acceptable form of clinical psychology" (p. 2). There were two corollaries. The first was that psychological services should not be administered to the public (except under strict experimental control) until they have satisfied four criteria: (a) The exact nature of the service must be described clearly. (b)

TABLE 3.1

Scheme for Grading Strength of Evidence in Medical Research

Grade	Criteria
I	Evidence from studies of strong design; results are both clinically important and consistent, with minor exceptions at most; results are free from serious doubts about generalizability, bias, and flaws in research design. Studies with negative results have sufficiently large samples to have adequate statistical power.
II	Evidence from studies of strong design but there is some uncertainty due to inconsistencies or concern about generalizability, bias, research design flaws, or adequate sample size. Or, evidence consistent from studies using weaker designs.
III	Evidence from a limited number of studies of weaker design. Studies with strong design either have not been done or are inconclusive.
IV	Support solely from informed medical commentators based on clinical experience without substantiation from the published literature.

Note: From *Systems to Rate the Strength of Scientific Evidence* (p. 71), by S. West et al., 2002, Rockville, MD: Agency for Healthcare Research and Quality. Adapted from "A Practical System for Evidence Grading," by Greer et al., 2000, *Joint Commission Journal on Quality Improvement, 26,* p. 707. Copyright by Joint Commission on Accreditation of Healthcare Organizations. Reprinted with permission.

The claimed benefits must be stated explicitly. (c) These benefits must be validated scientifically. (d) Possible negative side effects that might outweigh benefits must be ruled out. The second corollary was that the primary and overriding objective of doctoral training programs in clinical psychology must be to produce the most competent clinical scientists possible.

In 1993, at the urging of its Society for a Science of Clinical Psychology, Division 12 adopted the report of a task force chaired by Diane Chambless that discussed the need to validate the treatments used by clinical psychologists. The Chambless report presented criteria for considering a treatment to be empirically supported and listed some of the interventions meeting those criteria. Two categories were created, "well-established treatments" and "probably efficacious treatments." The most recent criteria for each appear in Table 3.2 (Chambless et al., 1998). For a treatment to be considered *well-established*, it has to have been found significantly more efficacious than a comparison treatment or placebo in at least two group-design studies or a series of controlled single-subject studies, by at least two inde-

TABLE 3.2

Criteria for Empirically Supported Psychological Interventions

Well-Established Treatments

I. At least two good between-group design experiments demonstrating efficacy in one or more of the following ways:

  A. Superior (statistically significantly so) to pill or psychological placebo or to another treatment.

  B. Equivalent to an already established treatment in experiments with adequate sample sizes.

OR

II. A large series of single-case design experiments (N > 9) demonstrating efficacy. These experiments must have

  A. Used experimental designs and

  B. Compared the intervention to another treatment as in IA.

Further criteria for both I and II:

III. Experiments must be conducted with treatment manuals.

IV. Characteristics of the client samples must be clearly specified.

V. Effects must have been demonstrated by at least two different investigators or investigating teams.

Probably Efficacious Treatments

I. Two experiments showing the treatment is superior (statistically significantly so) to a waiting-list control group.

OR

II. One or more experiments meeting the Well-Established Treatment criteria IA or IB, III, and IV, but not V.

OR

III. A small series of single-case design experiments (N ≥ 3) otherwise meeting the Well-Established Treatment criteria.

Note: From "Update on empirically validated therapies, II," by D. L. Chambless et al., 1998, *The Clinical Psychologist*, 51, p. 4. Copyright 1998 by Division 12, American Psychological Association. Reprinted with permission.

pendent research teams following a written treatment manual. The key criterion is the inclusion of some kind of comparison condition, which may be another treatment (including medication), a placebo, or a wait-list or assessment-only group. For single-case experiments, emphasis is placed on the need to establish a stable baseline over an adequate period of time to rule out preexisting trends. Acceptable designs include the well-known ABAB design as well as multiple-baseline designs across behaviors, settings, or participants. A single-case intervention may be considered *probably efficacious* if shown beneficial for at least three participants by a single research group. To be considered *well-established*, at least three replications (with three or more participants each) by at least two independent research groups, along with an absence of conflicting results, are needed. As of 2001, 108 empirically supported treatments had been identified for adults and 37 for children (Chambless & Ollendick, 2001).

The value of identifying empirically supported treatments remains controversial in some quarters. One concern is with generalization from laboratory to clinic. Empirically supported therapies are developed under conditions that are far from typical. "Real-world" clients are less uniform demographically and more likely to have multiple diagnoses than participants in clinical trials. Likewise, therapists in most treatment settings will be less specialized and at a lower level of training than occurs in high quality intervention research. Thus, there is the belief that research on empirically supported therapies will simply not generalize to actual clinical conditions. However, research examining this issue has failed to find serious problems in generalization, although it has found that treatment effects in the community may not be as great as they are in controlled studies (Chambless & Ollendick, 2001).

Some psychotherapists have expressed the fear that sole reliance on empirically supported therapies could lead to a restrictive list of treatments reimbursed by third parties (Silverman, 1996). In addition, a limited pool of acceptable treatments raises the question that innovative techniques not yet subject to empirical evaluation could be vulnerable to malpractice suits (Kovacs, 1996). Arguably, such suits could be an appropriate action for society to take in some cases, but a way to reduce the likelihood of legal problems has been described by O'Donohue (1997), discussed in the next section.

Proponents of empirically supported therapies offer strong arguments in their favor. In the absence of scientific criteria, it is highly doubtful that therapists can make sound clinical judgments with any consistency. Practitioners possess the same tendencies toward bias and inaccurate perception as anyone else. Only to the extent that judgment is informed by the accumulated systematic, objective knowledge of the larger field does professional training improve quality of intervention. A second but related issue revolves around the consequences for the mental health field if we do not use scientific research as the basis for intervention. Some have argued that a failure to promote and disseminate scientific evidence of effectiveness will result in a de-emphasis or eventual elimination of psychological interventions by the health care delivery system (Barlow, 1996). This concern reflects an assumption that the public or funding agencies will increasingly use scientific information to judge the appropriateness of interventions. In this view, a failure to seek empirical support could, and probably would, eventually result in the discrediting of psychosocial treatments of all types.

BEHAVING SCIENTIFICALLY

What about the situation in which the practitioner encounters a problem for which no clear evidence exists favoring one course of action over another? Such situations arise frequently enough, but their existence does not justify a treatment approach based only on tradition ("doing what we learned in graduate school") or habit ("doing what we've always done"). A better option is "behaving scientifically" as a professional or a human services manager, that is, to take an explicitly experimental approach to all intervention efforts (O'Donohue, 1997). This approach has several components. First, one assumes fallibility, the recognition that one's current beliefs, despite all the attractions they hold, may still be wrong. At the same time, this acknowledgment does not imply that the practitioner should abandon either accumulated research findings or methods of scientific inquiry that are solid for mere speculation. O'Donohue listed several kinds of errors that can occur in treatment provision (here modified to include examples from developmental disabilities):

1. False descriptive statements: We may claim, for example, that an adolescent or adult client never thought of suicide in the previous week when in fact he thought of it four times.
2. False causal statements: We may believe that our client's aggression is attention-seeking when in fact it is escape-motivated.
3. False ontological statements: We can believe that things exist when in fact they do not. For example, we may believe that a child with severe mental retardation has well-developed but hidden language skills waiting to be discovered through facilitated communication when in fact she does not.
4. False relational claims: We may believe that procedure A usually results in a greater reduction in self-injurious behavior than procedure B when this is untrue.
5. False predictions: We may predict that an inclusive classroom placement will result in positive social benefits for a particular child, but it actually leads to teasing and isolation for this child.
6. False professional ethical claims: We can believe that it is ethically permissible to impose certain restrictions on a client without informed consent when it is actually wrong. Alternatively, we may give a client excessive latitude in making choices beyond his or her ability to evaluate carefully, some of which can result in serious harm to the client or others.

The second component of behaving scientifically is an awareness that all treatment and service offerings are based on knowledge claims which should be examined with respect to the quality of their sources. In some cases, professionals and managers may be committed to a problematic epistemology, accepting ideology, authoritative pronouncements, or anecdotal evidence as equivalent to established scientific knowledge. In other cases, there may be acknowledgment of science as the best source of knowledge but only a weak commitment to following its tenets in selecting, implementing, and evaluating treatments and services.

Next, professionals and managers must realize that errors in treatment and service delivery can cause serious harm. At the very least, ineffective treatments and services have opportunity costs; they displace the opportunity to participate in other, more effective treatments and services. More immediate harm can occur when decisions are dictated by the false beliefs mentioned in the preceding list. For example, using procedure A when procedure B is more effective needlessly prolongs the client's suffering (Van Houten et al., 1988). Providing treatments or services that are erroneously believed to benefit the client wastes everyone's resources. Such "epistemic mistakes" can destroy families stressed past the breaking point, lead to an adult client's inappropriate arrest and incarceration, or produce serious injury, illness, or death. The only certain way to minimize such outcomes is to conduct our professional behaviors in an explicitly self-critical, evaluative manner, that is to say, in a scientific manner. Thus, O'Donohue (1997) argues that the supreme duty in human services is an epistemic duty to respect truth, a duty that is no less important than the moral duty to respect human life.

It follows that a practitioner or manager who is motivated by something other than the truth when forming a belief, such as ideology or personal philosophy, will be intellectually irresponsible and negligent insofar as he or she considers only the evidence that supports a prematurely formed conclusion. O'Donohue (1997) gives the example of a therapist who practices facilitated communication in order to enjoy popularity with parents and colleagues, financial rewards, and avoidance of the more intensive, laborious effort required by a behavioral language training approach. The therapist refuses to read research evaluating facilitated communication and refuses to learn about behavior analysis procedures. By engaging in selective consumption of information, such a therapist is failing in his or her epistemic duties as a professional.

Finally, O'Donohue (1997) recommends that professional practice and services be informed by the following considerations:

1. Accept the general attitude that we may be wrong.
2. Find out if our beliefs are consistent with the scientific literature.
3. Seek criticism from peers, especially peers who have greater relevant scientific expertise. Ask our critics what their criticisms are and listen to them nondefensively.
4. Conduct clinical practice and manage human services in such a way as to gain frequent feedback about our decisions and actions through peer reviews, client satisfaction surveys, social validity interviews, program evaluations, long-term client follow-ups, and experimental research.
5. Give criticism to others, including those who are failing in their intellectual duties, and fulfill a duty to the public by criticizing unsound practices and services.

Early in the 21st century, the field of developmental disabilities finds itself faced with not only increasing demands for accountability from consumers, government agencies, and the general public, but also threats to the scientific tenets that have fueled progress in treatment development and program innovation. These threats include well-intended but ungrounded theories and treatments, such as sensory integration therapy (Smith, Mruzek, & Mozingo, chap. 20, this volume) and facilitated communication (Jacobson, Foxx, & Mulick, chap. 22; this volume). They also include the equally ungrounded epistemic relativism of postmodernist philosophies, currently fashionable in the humanities, education, and the larger disabilities community. Postmodernists tend to ignore the long tradition of questioning basic assumptions that have characterized the philosophy of science from the time of Francis Bacon through the present and like to describe their work as challenging the logic and authority of science. The argument is made that science is a hopeless quest because each culture and subculture constructs its own version of reality and there is no way to say that any one version is better than any other. It is asserted that elite groups in a culture invariably define and use scientific knowledge in ways intended to oppress marginal groups (e.g., Foucault, 1980). Standard postmodernist themes of malice on the part of professionals and their oppression of groups of people with disabilities are evident in most postmodernist papers on developmental disabilities (e.g., Danforth, 2000; Goodley & Rapley, 2001; Peter, 2000).

Perhaps the most charitable view of postmodernist writings is that they may have sensitized those few workers in the field not already aware of them to the disparities in power between people with and without developmental disabilities. Less charitably, a close reading indicates that while advocating greater sensitivity toward and "liberation" of people with disabilities, postmodernist writings actually display a surprising lack of knowledge or concern about them and trivialize their problems as mere "social constructs," all the while exhibiting contempt for the people actually liberating them from harmful practices and systems. To these and other threats to progress in the field, we suggest that the appropriate response of individuals committed to a scientific approach is to expose the hollow assertions of antiscientific thinking as they surface (e.g., Koertge, 2000; Sokal & Bricmont, 1999) and to continue offering the better alternatives of evidence-based knowledge and empirically validated interventions.

REFERENCES

Agnew, N. M., & Pyke, S. W. (1969). *The science game: An introduction to research in the behavioral sciences.* Englewood Cliffs, NJ: Prentice-Hall.

American Medical Association. (2001). *Principles of medical ethics* [On-line]. Available from http://www.ama-assn.org/ama/pub/category/2512.html

American Physical Therapy Association. (2000). *APTA code of ethics* [On-line]. Available from http://www.apta.org/PT_Practices/ethics_pt/code_ethics

American Psychological Association. (2002). *Ethical principles of psychologists and code of conduct.* Washington, DC: Author.

Barlow, D. H. (1996). Health care policy, psychotherapy research, and the future of psychotherapy. *American Psychologist, 51,* 1050–1058.

Barlow, D. H., Hayes, S. C., & Nelson, R. O. (1984). *The scientist-practitioner: Research and accountability in clinical and educational settings.* New York: Pergamon.

Barlow, D. H., & Hersen, M. (1984). *Single case experimental designs: Strategies for studying behavior change* (2nd ed.). Boston: Allyn & Bacon.

Beutler, L. E. (1998). Identifying empirically supported treatments: What if we didn't? *Journal of Consulting and Clinical Psychology, 66,* 113–120.

Chambless, D. L., Baker, M., Baucom, D. H., Beutler, L. E., Calhoun, K. S., Crits-Christoph, P., et al. (1998). Update on empirically validated therapies, II. *The Clinical Psychologist, 51,* 3–16.

Chambless, D. L., & Ollendick, T. H. (2001). Empirically supported psychological interventions: Controversies and evidence. In S. T. Fiske, D. L. Schachter, & C. Zahn-Waxler (Eds.), *Annual review of psychology, 52,* 685–716.

Council for Exceptional Children. (1997). *Code of ethics for educators of persons with exceptionalities* [On-line]. Available from http://www.cec.sped.org/ps/code.html

Danforth, S. (2000). What can the field of developmental disabilities learn from Michel Foucault? *Mental Retardation, 38*, 364–369.

Evidence-Based Medicine Working Group. (1992). Evidence-based medicine: A new approach to teaching the practice of medicine. *Journal of the American Medical Association, 268*, 2420–2425.

Fisher, A. G., & Murray, E. A. (1991). Introduction to sensory integration theory. In A. G. Fisher, E. A. Murray, & A. C. Bundy (Eds.), *Sensory integration: Theory and practice* (pp. 3–26). Philadelphia: Davis.

Foucault, M. (1980). *Power/knowledge: Selected interviews and other writings, 1972–1977*. New York: Pantheon.

Goodley, D., & Rapley, M. (2001). How do you understand "learning difficulties"? Towards a social theory of impairment. *Mental Retardation, 39*, 229–232.

Green, G. (1996). Evaluating claims about treatments for autism. In C. Maurice, G. Green, & S. C. Luce (Eds.), *Behavioral intervention for young children with autism* (pp. 15–28). Austin, TX: Pro-Ed.

Greer, N., Mosser, G., Logan, G., & Halaas, G. W. (2000). A practical system for evidence grading. *Joint Commission Journal on Quality Improvement, 26*, 700–712.

Hanson, R. H., Wieseler, N. A., & Lakin, C. K. (2002). *Crisis: Prevention and response in the community*. Washington, DC: American Association on Mental Retardation.

Iwata, B. A., Bailey, J. S., Neef, N. A., Wacker, D. P., Repp, A. C., & Shook, G. L. (Eds.). (1997). *Behavior analysis in developmental disabilities* (3rd ed.). Lawrence, KS: Society for the Experimental Analysis of Behavior.

Jacobson, J. W., & Mulick, J. A. (1996). *Manual of diagnosis and professional practice in mental retardation*. Washington, DC: American Psychological Association.

Kazdin, A. E. (1980). *Research design in clinical psychology*. New York: Harper & Row.

Kendall, P. C. (1998). Empirically supported psychological therapies. *Journal of Consulting and Clinical Psychology, 66*, 3–6.

Koertge, N. (Ed.). (2000). *A house built on sand: Exposing postmodernist myths about science*. Oxford, UK: Oxford University Press.

Konarski, E. A., Favell, J. E., & Favell, J. E. (1992). *Manual for the assessment and treatment of the behavior disorders of people with mental retardation*. Morganton, NC: Western Carolina Center Foundation.

Kovacs, A. L. (1996, Winter). "We have met the enemy and he is us!" *AAP Advocate*, pp. 6, 19, 20, 22.

McFall, R. M. (1991). Manifesto for a science of clinical psychology. *The Clinical Psychologist* [On-line]. *44*, 75–88. Available from http://pantheon.yale.edu/~tat22/manifest.htm

Medawar, P. (1996). Hypothesis and imagination. In P. Medawar, *The strange case of the spotted mice and other classic essays on science* (pp. 12–32). Oxford, UK: Oxford University Press. (Original work published 1963)

New York State Department of Health. (1999). *Clinical practice guideline: Report of the recommendations. Autism/pervasive developmental disorders, assessment and intervention for young children (age 0–3 years)* (Publication No. 4215) [On-line]. Albany, NY: Author. Available from http://www.health.state.ny.us/nysdoh/eip/autism/index.htm

O'Donohue, W. (1997, Spring). On behaving scientifically: Fallibilism, criticism, and epistemic duties. *Clinical Science Newsletter* [On-line], pp. 2–7. Available from http://pantheon.yale.edu/~tat22/cs_sp97.htm

Paine, S. C., Bellamy, G. T., & Wilcox, B. (1984). *Human services that work: From innovation to standard practice*. Baltimore: Brookes.

Peter, D. (2000). Dynamics of discourse: A case study illuminating power relations in mental retardation. *Mental Retardation, 38*, 354–362.

Rotter, J. B. (1971). On the evaluation of methods of intervening in other people's lives. *The Clinical Psychologist, 24*, 1–2.

Rush, A. J., & Frances, A. (Eds.). (2000). Expert consensus guideline series: Treatment of psychiatric and behavioral problems in mental retardation [Special issue]. *American Journal on Mental Retardation, 105,* 159–228.

Silverman, W. H. (1996). Cookbooks, manuals, and paint-by-numbers: Psychotherapy in the 90s. *Psychotherapy, 33,* 207–215.

Sokal, A., & Bricmont, J. (1999). *Fashionable nonsense: Postmodern intellectuals' abuse of science.* New York: St. Martin's Press.

Van Houten, R., Axelrod, A., Bailey, J. S., Favell, J. E., Foxx, R. M., Iwata, B. A., et al. (1988). The right to effective treatment. *Journal of Applied Behavior Analysis, 21,* 381–384.

Whitman, T. L., Scibak, J. W., & Reid, D. H. (1983). *Behavior modification with the severely and profoundly retarded: Research and application.* New York: Academic Press.

West, S., King, V., Carey, T. S., Lohr, K. N., McKoy, N., Sutton, S. F., et al. (2002). *Systems to rate the strength of scientific evidence* (AHRQ Publication No. 02E016) [On-line]. Rockville, MD: Agency for Healthcare Research and Quality. Available from http://www.ahrq.gov/clinic/evrptfiles.htm#strength

The Appeal of Unvalidated Treatments

Tristram Smith
University of Rochester Medical Center

Most developmental disabilities are now treatable but incurable. That is, current treatments can help individuals with developmental disabilities in important ways but seldom eradicate the disability. For example, two treatments with solid scientific support are applied behavior analysis (ABA) and psychotropic medication. With ABA interventions, many individuals with developmental disabilities learn skills they would not otherwise be able to master. These skills enable them to communicate, interact with others, take care of themselves, engage in leisure activities, and work at school or in a job. Still, the majority of individuals who receive ABA continue to have significant overall delays in these areas. Medications sometimes reduce behavior problems such as aggression, insistence on routines, and difficulty falling or staying asleep, but they seldom eliminate such problems. Beyond limited effectiveness, these treatments have other drawbacks. ABA is labor intensive, often involving many hours per week of intervention for years; medications are prone to unpleasant side effects and usually work only as long as the individual keeps taking them. Both ABA and medications require supervision by highly trained professionals.

It is not surprising, then, that virtually everyone who cares about individuals with developmental disabilities is eager for new and better treatments. This eagerness is beneficial, and even essential, because it spurs treatment research and implementation of interventions found to be effective. Unfortunately, though, such eagerness also fuels the development of dubious remedies that purport to be everything that scientifically validated treatments are not: cures, risk-free antidotes, nostrums that laypersons can administer readily, and so on. Consumers often give credence to these remedies because they perceive them as having scientific support, a strong theoretical basis, or both (Smith & Antolovich, 2000).

When scientifically validated treatments yield only modest improvements, unproven remedies described as having highly favorable outcomes, scientific backing, and theoretical justification may seem to be especially attractive alternatives. Nevertheless, such remedies usually turn out to be ineffective or worse, as documented in other chapters in this book. For this reason, it is a serious mistake to try each new treatment marketed for individuals with developmental disabilities. To avoid doing more harm than good, service providers and families need to make careful and informed judgments to discern whether a remedy is plausible and worth exploring or whether it is a pseudoscientific approach with a low probability of success.

Evaluating treatments is complicated by the huge variety of interventions offered. These include (but are not limited to) megavitamins, diets, medications, sensorimotor therapies, relationship therapies, computer software packages, and educational curricula. Still, particular claims about outcomes, supporting evidence, and theory are reliable "red flag" indicators that the treatment is pseudoscientific. Identifying such claims as distinct from claims made about scientifically validated treatments is a vital skill for service providers and families.

CLAIMS ABOUT TREATMENTS

Outcomes

Claims about scientifically validated treatments and pseudoscientific ones are summarized in Table 4.1. As indicated in the table, outcomes reported for validated interventions generally involve increasing skills in specific areas such as communication and self-care so that individuals with developmental disabilities function better in everyday settings. In contrast, pseudoscientific interventions often are said to "cure" the disability; alternatively, the claimed benefits may appear important but ill-defined.

Cure. Common synonyms for *cure* include *healing*, *miracle*, *breakthrough*, and *revolution*. Because any of these words implies that the treatment is all that service providers and families could possibly have hoped for, the temptation to try the treatment is strong. However, such claims are as implausible as they are enticing. History shows that progress in developmental disabilities occurs, but happens slowly. To illustrate, Table 4.2 displays the years in which some common developmental disabilities and their etiologies were identified. As shown, the etiologies of cerebral palsy and autism remain largely unknown even though these syndromes were identified many years ago; etiologies of other disabilities listed in Table 4.2 were discovered 25 to 94 years after the disabilities were first described. Cures do not yet exist for any of these disabilities.

Given this history, claims that the cause and cure of a disability have suddenly been discovered are almost certain to be false. Therefore, such claims should serve as a warning to avoid the treatment unless there is extremely compelling scientific evidence of effectiveness (as described in the next section). A number of recent examples confirm the wisdom of avoiding such treatments. Since 1990, new purported cures have included, among others, *facilitated communication* (trained facilitators guiding individuals with developmental disabilities to type messages on a keyboard), *auditory integration training* (playing music with certain sounds filtered out), and *gentle teaching* (using unconditional acceptance and soft touch to respond to individuals with developmental disabilities). Each of these interventions had a period of enormous popularity. However, all were found to be ineffective in controlled studies, and some of them, notably *facilitated communication*, created problems instead of eliminating them (Jacobson, Mulick, & Schwartz, 1995).

TABLE 4.1
Characteristics of Scientifically Validated Treatments and Pseudoscientific Interventions

Characteristics	Scientifically Validated Treatments	Pseudoscientific Interventions
Reported outcomes	Significant improvements in functioning in everyday situations	1. Cures 2. Important-sounding but vague benefits (e.g., increased focus) 3. Major gains that cannot be studied
Evidence	Controlled studies with objective measures of behaviors relevant to everyday functioning	1. Uncontrolled studies or studies with unvalidated measures 2. Sophisticated technology used in unvalidated ways 3. Opposition from the "establishment" 4. Criticisms of validated treatments 5. Subjective evidence — anecdotes — case histories — testimonials — surveys — popularity or longevity of treatment
Theory	Consistency with other knowledge	1. Hypothesis of core deficit in social relationships or sensorimotor function 2. Natural intervention

TABLE 4.2
Years That Selected Developmental Disabilities and Their Etiologies Were Identified

Disability	Syndrome Identified	Etiology Identified
Down syndrome	1866	1959
Cerebral palsy	1860s	—
Phenylketonuria	1934	1984
Autism	1943	—
Prader-Willi syndrome	1956	1981
Williams syndrome	1961	1993
Rett disorder	1963	1999

Note: Based on information presented in *Genetics and Mental Retardation Syndromes* (p. **??**), by E. Dykens, R. M. Hodapp, and B. M. Finucane, 2000, Baltimore: Brookes.

Important-Sounding but Vague Benefits. Examples of benefits that are described as important but are vague include "enhanced learning," "increased focus," "improved body awareness," "reduced tactile defensiveness," "greater well-being," and "better sense of self." Although these benefits are not as alluring as the promise of a cure, they are cited more often by families as reasons for trying unvalidated treatments (Smith & Antolovich, 2000), and they are extremely difficult to measure clearly in research studies.

One reason these benefits are attractive is that they are portrayed as "deeper" and more fundamental than specific improvements in everyday functioning. However, fundamental change, if it occurs, should translate readily into specific, directly observable progress. For example, enhanced learning and better focus should be reflected in more rapid skill acquisition. Likewise, improved body awareness and reduced tactile defensiveness should be associated with increased skill and interest in motor activities, as well as improvements in social interaction such as approaching others more readily. Greater well-being and improved sense of self should lead to more positive affect. Therefore, claims of vague benefits signal that a treatment approach may not have benefits at all. They also portend a lack of careful, scientific evaluations of the treatment by proponents of the approach; the benefits are so vague that tests of whether they occur will be difficult or impossible.

Sensory integration therapy provides an illustration. In this approach, practitioners aim to correct the sensory processing of individuals with developmental disabilities through exercises such as spinning their bodies, brushing their limbs, and squeezing their joints. Proponents contend that the treatment produces all of the benefits listed at the beginning of the preceding paragraph (Fisher, Murray, & Bundy, 1991). Although the intervention originated in major research institutions in the early 1970s and is now provided to roughly one fourth of all children with developmental disabilities in the United States (Shore, 1994), proponents of this treatment never conducted controlled studies on its effectiveness. Instead, they reported only uncontrolled studies on nebulous outcomes such as whether children's eyes stop moving when they finish spinning (Ayres & Tickle, 1980). Controlled studies by independent investigators consistently show that the intervention is ineffective in treating behaviors related to everyday functioning, such as aggression or ritualistic behavior (Shore, 1994).

A variation of the vague benefit claim is the contention that the benefits of treatment disappear whenever the treatment comes under scrutiny by outsiders. For example, proponents of facilitated communication asserted that the presence of an objective observer disrupted the therapeutic relationship so severely that treatment gains were lost (Biklen & Cardinal, 1997). However, to provide clinically meaningful help to individuals with developmental disabilities, benefits must not be so tenuous; rather, they must extend robustly across settings and people. Therefore, even if it is true that treatment gains occur but disappear under scrutiny, the treatment is not useful.

Evidence

In chapter 3 of this volume, Newsom and Hovanitz noted that the effectiveness of validated treatments such as ABA and medications has been confirmed in multiple scientifically rigorous studies. These studies have controls to ensure that individuals who received the treatment improved to a greater extent than they would have without the treatment. For instance, investigators may compare a group that received the treatment to a similar group that did not. In addition, they use objective measures to ensure that the improvements were real rather than due to wishful thinking or investigator expectation. For example, the research assistants who collect the data may not know the purpose of the study, and investigators may compare data obtained by different research assistants for the same participant to test whether the data are reliable. Further, the measures pertain to concrete behaviors that are clearly important to individuals with developmental disabilities and their caregivers, such as whether they started talking, learned to dress themselves, stopped hitting, or mastered a job skill. These safeguards make scientifically rigorous studies the most dependable method for obtaining evidence on the effectiveness of a treatment.

Uncontrolled Studies. Proponents of unvalidated treatments often make no distinction between rigorous and nonrigorous studies. For example, one of the most popular megavitamin therapies for autism and other developmental disabilities consists of giving vitamin B6 at doses that far exceed the recommended daily allowance set by the U.S. Food and Drug Administration (Smith & Antolovich, 2000). Proponents of this approach cite dozens of supporting studies, and they assert that this scientific support equals or exceeds that for any other intervention for individuals with developmental disabilities (Rimland, 1998). Most parents who decide to use this intervention for their children view it as scientifically based (Smith & Antolovich, 2000). However, every supporting study is uncontrolled, based on subjective measures, or both (Pfieffer, Norton, Nelson, & Shott, 1995), and the few available studies with experimental controls and objective measures indicate that B6 is ineffective (Findling et al., 1997). Thus, it is important to determine whether the studies cited in support of a treatment meet the same standards as those for scientifically validated treatments.

Technology. Pseudoscientific treatments often incorporate sophisticated medical or educational equipment, such as computerized software, specialized laboratory tests of urine or blood, and biofeedback on brain waves measured by electroencephalogram. Of course, all of these forms of technology have legitimate uses, but it is not the technology itself that makes them legitimate. Rather, their legitimacy comes from studies that support their use for specific purposes. For example, urine tests have scientific support for assessing some kidney disorders, but not for measuring neurotransmitter levels, gastrointestinal infections, or food allergies (Williams & Marshall, 1992). Similarly, electroencephalograms have scientific support when used to assess seizure disorders, but not when used to treat attention deficit disorder (Lohr, Meunier, Parker, & Kline, 2001). Consequently, it is necessary to establish whether the specific use of technology is reliable and whether controlled studies support its use for assessing or treating the particular problem to which it is applied.

Opposition From the "Establishment." Proponents of pseudoscientific treatments often contend either that they are unable to conduct rigorous studies or that such studies exist but are ignored because of opposition from the "establishment." They may compare themselves to great scientists such as Galileo and Darwin who faced hostility to their ideas during their lifetimes. Obviously, however, opposition can be either right or wrong. Therefore, the presence of opposition does not mean that a treatment is effective. For example, critics of facilitated communication compared this intervention to the Ouija board and, regrettably, turned out to be correct.

Numerous studies revealed that, presumably without awareness, the facilitator, not the individual with developmental disabilities, controlled the typing (Jacobson et al., 1995). On the other hand, for many years, writers have compared ABA programs to Nazi concentration camps, obedience schools for dogs, and Dr. Frankenstein's laboratory (Bettelheim, 1967). Although these accusations never had any basis in reality, they do *not* show that ABA is effective; they merely show that it has critics.

In view of these considerations, an emphasis on opposition from the establishment is an important red flag. To illustrate, proponents of B6 repeatedly complain of opposition from the establishment (Rimland, 1992). They charge that physicians are mercenary and do not study vitamins such as B6 because they cannot patent and profit from them. They also allege that physicians are power-hungry and refuse to endorse anything that people can buy over the counter instead of by prescription. Although such accusations may have a kernel of truth, they are grossly overstated and irrelevant to determining whether B6 is effective. At this writing, the database for research supported by the National Institutes for Health (www.crisp.gov) lists almost 1,000 ongoing, funded studies on nutritional supplements. Validated nutritional interventions for developmental disabilities include folic acid supplements for pregnant women to reduce the risk of spina bifida, various infant and child nutrition programs to promote healthy brain development, and dietary interventions to control phenylketonuria. More importantly, whether or not they are justified, accusations against physicians have no bearing on whether B6 is effective. Stated differently, they are a diversionary tactic and, as such, suggest that scientifically sound evidence for effectiveness is lacking.

Criticisms of Validated Treatments. Criticisms of validated treatments often come from proponents of pseudoscientific interventions. For example, writers may point out that gains made in ABA are specific to the treatment setting and do not generalize to everyday situations, or they may observe that medications can cause side effects. They may then use these criticisms to justify implementing their intervention instead of validated ones. These arguments are similar to the criticisms of the establishment in that they are overstated (i.e., researchers have improved generalization and reduced medication side effects) and, more importantly, irrelevant in determining whether other treatments are effective. Criticisms of one treatment or its practitioners do not constitute evidence for the effectiveness of another treatment. For this reason, such arguments should raise the suspicion that scientific support for the proponents' own treatment is absent.

Subjective Evidence. The only evidence for many unvalidated interventions consists of anecdotes, testimonials from parents, or case reports. Proponents of such interventions often assert that, because treatments for developmental disabilities are highly complex, the anecdotal impressions of caregivers and service providers offer a more appropriate source of information than do objective data. In the words of Bettelheim (1967), a study of children with developmental disabilities "cannot observe the rigors of a 'scientific' experiment since it must, in its course, pursue the vagaries of life which are nothing if not unpredictable" (p. 6).

However, complexity does not justify relying on subjective evidence; on the contrary, it may increase the need for controlled studies. For example, Bettelheim's therapy, which was supposed to provide unconditional love and acceptance, turned out to worsen children's behaviors. Investigators noted that controlled studies with precise measures were necessary to detect this problem for the very reasons that Bettelheim cited in support of subjective evidence: Because behaviors fluctuated over time, with numerous factors contributing to this fluctuation, controlled studies turned out to be the only way to isolate the effects of the treatment (Lovaas & Smith, 1994).

Diets provide another useful illustration. A popular intervention for individuals with developmental disabilities is to place them on diets that forbid certain foods, such as wheat and dairy products. Most parents who try such diets for their children report that the diets are effective (Smith & Antolovich, 2000). However, a variety of explanations for this report are possible: The diets may really work as intended, or the reported improvements may reflect parents' desire to see gains, rather than actual progress (i.e., expectations of benefit may lead to subjective ratings of benefit even though no improvement in behavior occurred). Alternatively, the diets may have medical effects other than those attributed to it. For example, a wheat- and dairy-free diet may lead to protein deficiency (Arnold, Hyman, & Mooney, 1998), which may cause behavior change. The diets may have nonmedical effects such as parents' spending more time with their child in order to implement the diet. As well, the diets may deprive children of their favorite foods and thus may be similar in their effects to depriving children of other favorite objects, such as television or computer games. This deprivation could motivate children to make behavior changes, such as increasing their requests or seeking other things to do.

It is not humanly possible to sort out these alternative possibilities based on subjective evidence. Only studies that systematically control for each alternative will lead to an answer. For example, investigators can prepare foods that appear identical but differ in that some contain wheat and dairy whereas others do not. They can give these foods without informing the recipient or family which is which, and then they can compare the effects of foods that contain wheat and dairy to the effects of foods without these substances. If a difference emerges, the difference is likely to be due to wheat and dairy content, as opposed to other factors.

Subjective evidence may appear in different forms. One common form is a survey, in which many consumers rate the effectiveness of a treatment. Because of the large number of reports, surveys may seem more convincing than individual anecdotes, testimonials, and case reports. However, a survey is simply a compilation of individual selective impressions. For this reason, it is prone to the same sort of problems as individual reports and cannot substitute for a controlled study. Indeed, many treatments have received favorable survey ratings, yet have not held up in controlled studies (Smith, 1996). The popularity or longevity of a treatment is another subjective form of evidence and does not necessarily mean that the treatment is effective. For example, Bettelheim (1987) asserted that, for many years, his psychoanalytic clinic for children with autism had 10 times as many applicants as openings. Notwithstanding its popularity, the treatment turned out to be harmful (Smith, 1996).

Theory

Proponents of validated treatments emphasize the consistency of the treatments with known principles about human behavior and physiology. For instance, ABA emphasizes the application of laboratory research on how humans and other organisms learn new behaviors (Cooper, Heron, & Heward, 1987). Writers continually propose ways to enhance ABA by incorporating recent laboratory findings (e.g., Wilkinson & McIlvane, 1997). Medications are based on known properties or neurotransmitters in the brain and usually have been tested with individuals who have other disorders before they are administered to individuals with developmental disabilities. In contrast, proponents of pseudoscientific treatments often say that their treatments overturn established knowledge. Explanations for the treatment usually emphasize either that it addresses the core problem or deficit in the developmental disability, or that the treatment is somehow more "natural" than other interventions.

Core Deficits. Proponents of pseudoscientific treatments often posit that individuals with developmental disabilities have a core deficit that, once corrected, will yield global improvements in functioning. Many treatments are based on the view that the core deficit is a lack of opportunity or ability to form reciprocal relationships. Examples of relationship therapies include psychoanalysis, gentle teaching, options, play therapies, and holding therapy. In many other treatments, the core deficit is considered to be a problem in processing or acting on sensory input. Sensorimotor therapies include sensory integration training, auditory integration training, patterning, and facilitated communication.

The idea that relationship or sensory problems underlie developmental disabilities and that a remediation would lead to general improvements in functioning has been popular for hundreds of years (Spitz, 1986) and still has intuitive appeal to many (Smith & Antolovich, 2000). One reason the idea is attractive is that it suggests a way to simplify treatment. If there is a core deficit, service providers can focus treatment on this deficit instead of having to address the array of problems that an individual with developmental disabilities might present in communication, social interaction, self-care, and so on.

However, treatments based on core deficits should provoke skepticism. Positing a core deficit and treatment for it is analogous to saying that one has found a cause and cure, which, as previously discussed, is highly unlikely. Also, proposing that changes in one behavior will by itself lead to changes in other behaviors goes against a large body of research on humans and other organisms in both clinical and laboratory settings (Detterman & Sternberg, 1995). Simply put, changes in one behavior may lead to changes in behaviors that serve the same function, but not to changes in the individual's entire behavioral repertoire. For example, teaching an individual to make verbal requests for an object may reduce tantrums that occur when the individual wants the object. However, this skill is very unlikely to lead to improved peer interaction or self-care unless these skills are also taught. Thus, unlike validated treatments, treatments based on core deficits are incompatible with other knowledge about human behavior. Therefore, as might be expected, controlled studies indicate an absence of therapeutic benefit associated with both relationship therapies (Smith, 1996) and sensorimotor treatments (Kavale & Forness, 1999).

Natural Therapies. Many pseudoscientific therapies are described as "natural." Nutritional supplements are said to fulfill a biological need (Rimland, 1998). Special diets are intended to eliminate food additives such as dyes and agricultural products such as wheat and dairy so that the individual eats like a "caveman" (Crook, 1987). Chelation therapy, in which an individual takes medications to remove heavy metals from the body, is used for purification (Defeat Autism Now, 2001). Vaccines are shunned to prevent exposure to microbes and preservatives (Wakefield & Montgomery, 2000). Antifungal medications are taken for alleged yeast infections attributed to a history of antibiotic use. (Shaw, 2002).

The idea of "naturalness" is attractive in a postindustrial, urban society. Also, as noted earlier, some nutritional and dietary interventions truly are beneficial for individuals with developmental disabilities. However, nature can also be dangerous. Too much water causes drowning; similarly, too many vitamins can cause toxic reactions. Many plant products are healthy, but others cause illness; therefore, nutritional supplements derived from plant products may or may not even be safe, much less effective. Organic, unprocessed foods may be preferable to packaged foods in some respects, but they are also more likely to spoil and cause food poisoning (Margen, 2001). Thus, "natural" does not mean that a treatment is safe and effective. In fact, there have been credible reports of negative effects for many natural therapies, including those cited here (Smith, 1996).

EVALUATING INTERVENTIONS

Based on the distinctions between scientifically validated and pseudoscientific treatments, the main considerations in evaluating a treatment are the kinds of outcomes ascribed to it, the level of scientific validation, and the plausibility of the theory on which the treatment is based. A treatment that is both validated and plausible for achieving improvements in everyday functioning is one that should be widely used. A treatment that is both unvalidated and implausible, with unrealistically favorable or vague outcomes, is one to avoid.

As an example of the latter, in 1998, news stories publicized an innovative medical treatment prescribing the pancreatic hormone secretin for children with autism or (less frequently) Down syndrome. However, the stories contained many red flags: Secretin was touted as a cure. The evidence for its use consisted of a subjective report on one individual with autism. Secretin was said to treat the etiology or core deficit in autism (conjectured to be gastrointestinal problems) and was described as natural (supplementing a hormone in the body). Although the promise of a natural cure is undeniably alluring, all the red flags indicated that the treatment was very likely to be pseudoscientific and ineffective, as studies soon revealed (Corbett et al., 2001).

Other interventions are harder to evaluate because they have scientific support but some implausible theoretical assumptions, or vice versa. As an example of the former, the natural language paradigm (Koegel & Koegel, 1995) includes the word *natural*, which raises a red flag about its theoretical basis. However, it is a validated teaching approach for achieving some goals, particularly promoting generalization and initiation of skills by children with autism (Koegel & Koegel, 1995). Another example is theory of mind training (instruction on how to recognize the thoughts and feelings of others; Hadwin, Baron-Cohen, Howlin, & Hill, 1997). This intervention raises a red flag because it is based on the hypothesis that problems in this area are the core deficit in autism; still, several controlled studies support the use of this instruction to enhance social skills as one part of a treatment program. Given that they have scientific support for achieving tangible benefits, the natural language paradigm and theory of mind training appear to have appropriate uses. Thus, they merit consideration by service providers and families despite their red flags. In general, scientific support is the single most important consideration in determining whether a treatment is likely to be effective.

An example of a plausible but unvalidated treatment is verbal behavior therapy. This approach is based on ABA theory but has not been rigorously evaluated. Moreover, its proponents assert that 0their treatment methods differ substantially from standard ABA approaches (Sundberg & Partington, 1998). Another example is floor time, in which adults playfully obstruct children's activities (Greenspan & Wieder, 1998). Although it has not been directly tested in controlled studies, this approach is similar to a validated instructional method called incidental teaching (Hart & Risley, 1982), which is often useful as one component of a treatment program. What makes these interventions plausible is that, like validated interventions, they are consistent with other knowledge about individuals with developmental disabilities and about people in general. Because they are plausible, it is possible that they are effective. However, because they are untested, they are more of a gamble than are validated treatments. Therefore, validated interventions may be the first ones to try, with plausible but unvalidated treatments as backups to be considered if validated treatments are unsuccessful.

Treatment Combinations

Service providers and families often combine pseudoscientific treatments with validated ones (Smith & Antolovich, 2000). They may recognize that the pseudoscientific treatments are unlikely to work, or they may not have considered this issue. They often believe that it "can't hurt" to check out other treatments, and these other treatments just might help. Thus, they may decide that they should try as many treatments as they can.

Some writers encourage combinations of treatments. For instance, proponents of megavitamin therapies sometimes state that these therapies are inappropriate as stand-alone treatments but are important adjuncts to behavioral intervention. Although a combination of treatments certainly may be more potent than either treatment by itself, each treatment needs to have tangible effects of its own. For example, if megavitamins accelerate progress in behavioral intervention, there must be a mechanism by which they do so (e.g., increasing the length of time that the individual spends on task). Investigators should be able to detect this mechanism by examining a megavitamin therapy in isolation. Therefore, claiming that a treatment has little impact alone, but is useful as a supplement to another intervention, is a warning sign that the treatment could be ineffective. Indeed, controlled studies of megavitamin therapies have shown no benefits (Kleijnen & Mattson, 1983).

Beyond being unhelpful, adding an ineffective treatment to an effective one may be detrimental. Although research is sparse, the available evidence indicates that such combinations can be less effective than relying on one validated treatment for individuals with developmental disabilities. For example, in a study of children with autism, Eikeseth, Smith, Jahr, and Eldevik (2002) compared ABA to an eclectic treatment comprised of both ABA and unvalidated educational interventions. Although the treatments were of equal intensity, the ABA group outperformed the eclectic group. Investigators have not yet studied why combining treatments would reduce effectiveness, but several possible explanations are apparent: Some treatments in the mix may be harmful. Even if merely ineffective, they likely divert time and resources away from interventions known to be effective. Moreover, treatments may interfere with each other; for example, ABA may emphasize helping individuals follow a structured routine while relationship therapies may discourage routine. In addition, service providers may become "jacks of all trades and master of none," implementing numerous interventions but not doing any of them well. Therefore, although it may seem as though there is nothing to lose and everything to gain by combining treatments, there is actually considerable risk. If one or more of the treatments are lacking in validation, the risks probably outweigh the potential benefits.

Experimenting

Regardless of the level of scientific support and plausibility of a treatment, service providers or families may decide to implement it by itself or in combination with other interventions. In this situation, the question is no longer whether to try the treatment but whether to continue it. Still, the primary consideration in answering this question is whether the treatment is validated and plausible.

Hyman and Levy (2000) offer the following recommendations for validating a treatment for a particular individual with developmental disabilities: First, make only one treatment change at a time so that other treatments are held constant. Second, identify specific target behaviors to be addressed by the treatment, and use objective measures to obtain a baseline of this behavior prior to treatment. Finally, monitor changes in the target behavior on an ongoing basis with objective measures obtained by raters who are blind to treatment (e.g., having a teacher who is unaware of changes in vitamin consumption rate). Because these procedures provide reliable evidence on whether or not the treatment is helping, they facilitate informed decisions on whether to continue the treatment.

CONCLUDING COMMENTS

It is discouraging that the appeal of so many treatments is deceptive and that it is generally best to stick with scientifically validated interventions, despite their many limitations for individuals with developmental disabilities. Nevertheless, there is a positive aspect to this situation. Distinctions have emerged between validated, effective treatments and unvalidated, ineffective ones. These distinctions are valuable not only for evaluating current treatments, as emphasized in this chapter; they also point the way toward identifying new, more effective interventions. Approaches such as proclaiming cures, relying on subjective evidence, and calling remedies "natural" have not been productive in the past and are unlikely to lead to progress in the future. In contrast, careful studies that build on existing knowledge have been successful and hold promise for continuing to improve outcomes for individuals with developmental disabilities.

REFERENCES

Arnold, G. L., Hyman, S. L., & Mooney, R. A. (1998). Amino acid profiles in autism. *American Journal of Human Genetics, 63*, A262.

Autism National Committee. (1998–1999). *Behaviorism and developmental approaches.* Plymouth, MA: Author.

Ayres, A. J., & Tickle, L. S. (1980). Hyper-responsivity to touch and vestiblar stimuli as a predictor of positive response to sensory integration procedures by autistic children. *The American Journal of Occupational Therapy, 34,* 375–381.

Bettelheim, B. (1967). *The empty fortress.* New York: Free Press.

Bettelheim, B. (1987). The therapeutic milieu. In J. K. Zeig (Ed.), *The evolution of psychotherapy* (pp. 222–235). New York: Brunner/Mazel.

Biklen, D., & Cardinal, D. N. (Eds.). (1997). *Contested words, contested science: Unraveling the facilitated communication controversy.* New York: Teachers College Press.

Cooper, J., Heron, T., & Heward, W. (1987). *Applied behavior analysis.* Columbus, OH: Merrill.

Corbett, B., Khan, K., Czapansky-Bielman, D., Brady, N., Dropik, P., Selinsky Goldman, D., et al. (2001). A double-blind, placebo-controlled crossover study investigating the effect of porcine secretin in children with autism. *Clinical Pediatrics, 40,* 327–331.

Crook, W. G. (1987). Nutrition, food allergies, and environmental toxins [letter]. *Journal of Learning Disabilities, 20,* 260–261.

Defeat Autism Now. (2001). *Mercury detoxification consensus group position paper.* San Diego, CA: Autism Research Institute.

Dykens, E., Hodapp, R. M., & Finucane, B. M. (2000). *Genetics and mental retardation syndromes: A new look at behavior and interventions.* Baltimore: Brookes.

Detterman, D. K., & Sternberg, R. J. (Eds.). (1995). *Transfer on trial: Intelligence, cognition, and instruction.* Norwood, NJ: Ablex.

Eikeseth, S., Smith, T., Jahr, E., & Eldevik, S. (2002). Intensive behavioral treatment at school for 4- to 7-year-old children with autism: A 1-year comparison controlled study. *Behavior Modification, 26,* 49–68.

Findling, R. L., Maxwell, K., Scotese-Wojtila, L., Huang, J., Yamashita, T., & Wiznitzer, M. (1997). High-dose pyramidine and magnesium administration in children with autistic disorder: An absence of salutary effects in a double-blind, placebo-controlled study. *Journal of Autism and Developmental Disorders, 27,* 467–478.

Fisher, A. G., Murray, E. A., & Bundy, A. C. (Eds.). (1991). *Sensory integration: Theory and practice.* Philadelphia: Davis.

Goldstein, S., & Reynolds, C. R. (Eds.). (1999). *Handbook of neurodevelopmental and genetic disorders in children.* New York: Guilford.

Greenspan, S., & Wieder, S. (1998). *The child with special needs -Enhancing emotional and intellectual growth.* Boston: Addison-Wesley.

Hadwin, J., Baron-Cohen, S., Howlin, P., & Hill, K. (1997). Does teaching theory of mind have an effect on the ability to develop conversation in children with autism? *Journal of Autism and Developmental Disorders, 27,* 519–537.

Hart, B., & Risley, T. R. (1982). *How to use incidental teaching for elaborating language.* Austin, TX: Pro-Ed.

Hyman, S. L., & Levy, S. E. (2000). Autism spectrum disorders: When traditional medicine is not enough. *Contemporary Pediatrics, 17*(10), 101–116.

Jacobson, J. W., Mulick, J. A., & Schwartz, A. A. (1995). A history of facilitated communication: Science, pseudoscience, and antiscience working group on facilitated communication. *American Psychologist, 50,* 750–765.

Kavale, K. A., & Forness, S. R. (1999). *Efficacy of special education and related services.* Washington, DC: American Association on Mental Retardation.

Kleijnen, J., & Mattson, P. D. (1983). Niacin and vitamin B6 in humans: A review of controlled trials in humans. *Biological Psychiatry, 26,* 931–941.

Koegel, R. L., & Koegel, L. K. (1995). *Teaching children with autism.* Baltimore: Brookes.

Lohr, J. M., Meunier, S. A., Parker, L. M., & Kline, J. R. (2001). Neurotherapy does not qualify as an empirically supported behavioral treatment for psychological disorders. *The Behavior Therapist, 24,* 97–104.

Lovaas, O. I., & Smith, T. (1994). Intensive and long-term treatments for clients with destructive behaviors. In T. Thompson & D. Gray (Eds.), *Treatment of destructive behavior in developmental disabilities* (Vol. 2, pp. 243–260). Newbury Park, CA: Sage.

Margen, S. (Ed.). (2001). *Wellness foods A to Z.* New York: Rebus.

Pfeiffer, S. I., Norton, J., Nelson, L., & Shott, S. (1995). Efficacy of vitamin B6 and magnesium in the treatment of autism: A methodological review and summary of outcomes. *Journal of Autism and Developmental Disorders, 25,* 481–493.

Rimland, B. (1992, June). The FDA's war against health. *Autism Research Review International, 6,* 4.

Rimland, B. (1998). "Efficacy of vitamin B6 and magnesium in the treatment of autism: A methodology review and summary of outcomes": Critique. *Journal of Autism and Developmental Disorders, 28,* 580–581.

Shaw, W. (2002). *Biological treatments for autism and PDD.* Overland Park, KS: Great Plains Laboratory.

Shore, B. A. (1994). Sensory-integrative therapy. *Self-injury Abstracts and Reviews, 3*(1), 1–7.

Smith, T. (1996). Are other treatments effective? In C. Maurice, G. Green, & S. Luce (Eds.), *Behavioral treatment of autistic children* (pp. 45–67). Austin, TX: Pro-Ed.

Smith, T., & Antolovich, M. (2000). Parental perceptions of supplemental interventions received by young children with autism in intensive behavior analytic treatment. *Behavioral Interventions, 15,* 83–97.

Spitz, H. (1986). *The raising of intelligence.* Hillsdale, NJ: Lawrence Erlbaum Associates.

Sundberg, M., & Partington, J. W. (1998). *Teaching language to children with autism or other developmental disabilities.* Pleasant Hill, CA: Behavior Analysts.

Wakefield, A. J., & Montgomery, S. M. (2000). Measles, mumps, rubella vaccine: Through a glass, darkly. *Adverse Drug Reactions and Toxicological Reviews, 19,* 265–283.

Wilkinson, K. M., & McIlvane, W. J. (1997). Contributions of stimulus control perspectives to psycholinguistic theories of vocabulary development and delay. In L. B. Adamson & M. A. Romski (Eds.), *Communication and language acquisition: Discoveries from atypical development* (pp. 25–48). Baltimore: Brookes.

Williams, K. M., & Marshall, T. (1992). Urinary protein patterns in autism as revealed by high resolution two-dimensional electrophoresis. *Biochemical Society Transactions, 20,* 189S.

Part II

Historical, Cultural, and Psychological Issues

Historical Approaches to Developmental Disabilities

John W. Jacobson
Sage Colleges Center for Applied Behavior Analysis

James A. Mulick
The Ohio State University and Columbus Children's Hospital

Richard M. Foxx
Penn State Harrisburg

The history of questionable treatments is as long as the history of educational and adult services for people with developmental disabilities (DDs), and indeed, may predate such services. Prescientific treatments, which almost by definition predate the 1900s, reflected the state of art in what gradually became the fields of medicine, education, and even later psychology, and culturally typical responses to people with disabilities in general. Histories of special education and adult services have placed a heavy emphasis on where people were served in different eras and how developmental disabilities and people with such conditions were viewed in those eras, and to a lesser extent can and do report about the manner in which they were taught or treated. In part, this is a ramification of the nature of surviving records, with preservation of philosophical and policy documents and the records of individuals who were prolific in their writing or became recognized as leaders in the development or organization of services, or in advocating for services, being superior to that of detailed and complete explications of methods of care, education, and treatment. As a result, today we know more about where people were served, and with what aims, than we do about how they were served, and the outcomes of those services.

Treatments before the 20th century were largely prescientific in nature in part because of the absence of systematic confirmatory studies. The methods attempted were submitted to empirical scrutiny very systematically by their progenitors, but their effects were neither independently assessed nor replicated. This does not imply that educators and physicians were not guided in their work by theories (because they *were* guided by theories and shrewd guesses about how things worked), or that they were unconcerned with the benefits of their work as applied to the growth and development of people with DD (see Seguin, 1879/1976). Rather, it reflects the fact that, generally, the history of early services is primarily one in which concerned educators and physicians provided services, and the role of the university or centers of higher education in relation to places where services were provided was limited (e.g., in the 1800s). There were few means financially, logistically, or academically, to launch and maintain systematic inquiries that could compare the benefits of variations in specific instructional or treatment practices. Nevertheless, early pioneers of theory-based intervention didn't really always know, sometimes couldn't know, whether their theories were true or consistent with related scientific facts, and there were in fact precious few facts to be had in their time. It is easier for us to recognize bogus and ineffective treatments today before they are even tried out because of many scientific, technological, and telecommunication and information science advances. As well, the capacity of services actually to serve people was typically outstripped by demand, and this factor also provided, as it often does today, an impetus to implement services with good intentions and little or no prior or concurrent confirmation of likely benefits. It was an age of trying things out to see if they worked.

As well, just as today, in the 1800s, mainstream, progressive, and conservative trends in society influenced the selection of methods and the goals of education and treatment. This meant that developments in other aspects of education (e.g., the education of people with hearing or vision impairments) or medical care (treatment of people with psychosis or depression) influenced strategies used with people with DD. Disorders were not as finely differentiated. As noted by Scheerenberger (1983), "new and popular techniques were attempted" including "hypnosis (and) application of the electrical induction coil for muscle stimulation" (p. 63), which at the time also saw favor among the public as recreational curiosities in the parlor. Phrenology, a simplistic formulation of neuropsychological factors, represented another popular preoccupation of the middle and upper classes, and had wide impact on treatment selection. Many early leaders in establishment of services, including Seguin (see Scheerenberger, 1983), also emphasized moral treatment (see Harpers, 1854, for a contemporaneous sense of this view), which entailed teaching of rules of social conduct, a "strong sense of values, obedience and participation, duty, and responsibility for work" (p. 79), a focus that has persisted to the present day. It is reflected in a focus on social skills development to support full inclusion, and has resurfaced assertively within regular education as "character education" (Muscott & O'Brien, 1999; Otten, 2000).

During the early 1800s, publicly and privately funded schools and residential settings for people with developmental disabilities, sometimes serving both purposes, were uncommon and notable for their very existence. One early institution was the American Asylum for the Deaf and Dumb, established in 1818 in Hartford, Connecticut, which provided services specifically for people with mental retardation and other significant handicaps. This was followed by a few other schools and asylums in Europe and North America in which instruction was emphasized (Brockett, 1858). Other communities relied on almshouses and prisons or work camps for people who could not support themselves, although it was not uncommon for communities to take less formal measures to deal with such people. These less formal measures included indentured servitude, assisting an undesirable person to leave town by loading him or her onto a cart to be dropped off at a goodly distance, and warning undesirables away, when they arrived in town, with the information that the town would not be responsible for the newcomer's misfortunes.

By 1900, public schools for children or youth with mental retardation and other developmental disabilities had been established in Boston, Cleveland, Chicago, New York City, Philadelphia, and Providence, RI (Scheerenberger, 1983, p. 129), but these cities only represented 11% of the U.S. general population. Nonetheless, despite the fact that special education began for the very few and has grown to a sizable segment of the educational sector, many continuities of purpose and strategy in special education are evident from the 1800s to the present than might be expected after the passage of more than 100 years.

For example, Seguin, who stressed "physiological" methods entailing training of the "senses and the brain" during the 1800s, sought to induce learning "involving perception, imitation, coordination, memory, and generalization" and used positive reinforcement and modeling, as well as punishment procedures in a systematic way (Scheerenberger, 1983, p. 79). Voisin favored orthophrenic treatment that "required that each case be reviewed on an individual basis and that treatment (medical and educational) should attempt to expand the youngster's intellectual sphere, repress or develop faculties, and foster the morals and standards essential to living in social harmony" (p. 81). Down believed that "intellectual training required a cultivation of the senses, basic self-care skills, elimination of defective speech, use and value of money, gardening, and vocational training .... Moral training was critical" (p. 81). J. B. Richards' "educational approach emphasized object-teaching, imitation, variety, repetition, constant review of sanitary conditions, and physical exercise" (p. 121). Whereas in the first special school established in Providence, RI, there was a "strong emphasis on sense training consistent with Sequin's training, basic academic subjects slightly modified, manual or industrial training, and nature study," ... "others would have added play" and "physical education" (p. 131). "(T)he team teacher, the resource person, and dual tracking—were all evident before the turn of the century" (p. 132).

PRESCIENTIFIC AND SCIENTIFIC ORIENTATIONS

What do the terms *prescientific* and *scientific* signify? Very broadly, science in the context of developmental disabilities entails systematically identifying cause and effect relationships among, for example, experiences or events, or social interactions, and changes in behavior (including both overt behavior and covert behavior such as attitudes or thinking), or making predictions about behavior, such as predictions of academic or social benefit from educational or therapeutic interventions. Mere description of phenomena or studies based on trial and error may contribute to the formation of a theory, or may clarify possible effects of interventions, but in and of themselves do not address the validity of a theory. In order to qualify as a scientific theory, a theory must make predictions about the results that stem from a particular action or intervention, it must be possible to test these predictions, and the theory must be modified based on findings from tests of the theory. Scientific inquiry relies on methods that identify cause and effect methods through "true experimental" research designs, in which there is random sampling of participants, random assignments of participants to an experimental group (who receive an intervention), and a control group (who do not receive that intervention or receive everyday intervention). In some research designs, such as time series designs or single-case research, there are no separate control groups; instead, participants serve as their own controls and participate at differing times in the experimental and control conditions. Replication, or the completion of identical, nearly identical, or directly related studies by the same and other researchers, is critical to the accumulation of evidence for a theory, or evidence of benefit. True experimental research is often seen as applicable in terms of addressing the alleviation of problem behavior or psychological dysfunction, but is also applicable to tests of the value of various instructional methods or efforts to build skills or knowledge.

For both practical and ethical reasons that are beyond the scope of this chapter, when studying either instructional or therapeutic interventions for children or adults with developmental disabilities, it is often not possible to select people randomly from the general population, although it is possible to randomly assign people to an experimental group or control group and to select samples of people who are representative of people with specific treatment needs or with particular characteristics, which is termed *purposive sampling*. When this is the case, and other procedural requirements are met, research is considered to be quasi-experimental in nature. The accumulation of results through replications of quasi-experimental studies can provide convincing evidence of cause and effect relationships. These other procedural requirements include unambiguously demonstrating that measures used in a study are reliable (give consistent results) and valid (measure what they are intended to measure). In order for the findings or results of a research study to be valid, they must be based on reliable measures.

Other forms of research, including causal-comparative studies (which compare intact groups of people who are not randomly selected or assigned), correlational studies (which identify a relationship between two measures or variables within a single group), descriptive case studies, one-shot designs (in which an intervention is used with a single group), and qualitative research, do not, and cannot, demonstrate cause and effect. Such studies may, however, provide information that can facilitate the design and development of more definitive and varied experimental or quasi-experimental studies.

Many past educational and therapeutic interventions used with people with developmental disabilities were founded on inadequate research; research which could not indicate cause and effect. Such practices were most often abandoned when they fell out of popular favor among educators or clinicians on the basis of philosophical considerations, the subjective appeal of other procedures, changes in training of educators or clinicians, or obvious indications of ineffectiveness detected by individual practitioners. Notably, in appraising the current empirical basis of educational practices, with implications as well for therapies in adult developmental disabilities services, Davies (1999) observes:

> It is often unclear whether ... (recent) developments in educational thinking and practice are better, or worse, than the regimes they replace. This is in part because educational activity is inadequately evaluated by means of carefully designed and executed controlled trials, quasi-experiments, surveys, before-and-after studies, high quality observational studies, ethnographic studies which look at outcomes as well as processes .... Moreover the research and evaluation studies that do exist are seldom searched for and read, critically appraised for quality, validity and relevance, and organised and graded for power of evidence. (p. 109)

SERVICES FROM 1900 TO MID-CENTURY

During the late 1800s, the focus of residential services for people with developmental disabilities had begun to shift from an emphasis on training, and in many cases, short periods of residence in special settings and return to the community, to a growing emphasis on long-term residence with more limited prospects of return (Scheerenberger, 1983; Smith, 1985; Trent, 1994). By the early 1900s, residential institutions or colonies had been established throughout the nation (Fernald, 1917). With persisting or increasing admissions, and diminished discharges, the numbers and occupancies of institutions for people with developmental disabilities grew at first gradually and then rapidly (Kuhlmann, 1940; Malzberg, 1940; President's Committee, 1977), peaking in the 1960s.

Although comprehensive formulations of the role of assessment and individualized intervention had been articulated early in the 1900s (Witmer, 1909), the extent to which this therapeutic orientation, or in fact any orientation, was pervasive or typical of services nationally is largely unknown. The period 1920–1939, however, has been noted by Scheerenberger (1983) as one in which the orientation of institutions shifted further from an educational or behavioral science model to a medical model, in which greater emphasis was placed on health care provision rather than more comprehensive services encompassing education, development, and health care needs maintenance that typified earlier, and later, years (see also Dybwad, 1941). In part, the increased emphasis on medicine doubtless reflected the growing impact of scientific medicine and surgical treatment on many of the secondary conditions that were associated with syndromes leading to cognitive and behavioral disabilities.

Developments in special education reflected growth in the availability of separate classes or separate schools, including classes located at institutions, and by 1940, special education was recognized legislatively in 16 states (Scheerenberger, 1983). By the mid-1900s, it had become evident that some practitioners were concerned about the preparation of psychological personnel and delivery of psychological services (Doll, 1940; Huesman, 1947), the utility of occupational therapy (Menzel, 1946) and educational methods (Buchan, 1943), the effectiveness of psychoactive medications and treatment of mental disorders among people with developmental disabilities (Cutler, Little, & Strauss, 1940; Pollock, 1945), and the effectiveness of institutional training (Shotwell, 1949) and counseling (Thorne, 1948). It was not so evident, however, that in either special education or institutional settings, the practices of educators or clinicians were founded on empirical findings from research.

During this period, a number of therapeutic interventions were attempted with varying success reported. Directive therapy was found to be beneficial, whereas nondirective and analytical nondirective counseling were not (Scheerenberger, 1983). During the 1940s and especially the 1950s, there was "rising interest in psychoactive medications," which came to be used "freely and often indiscriminately, especially in residential situations" (pp. 224–225). Medical therapies attempted during this period included glutamic acid treatment, which appeared to yield promising results initially that were not borne out by later research, and other therapies "that were tried, yielded mixed or poor results, and were soon abandoned, including electric shock (electrotherapy), lobotomy, and various vitamin therapies"

(p. 225; see also Angus, 1949; Goldstein, 1954; Quinn & Durling, 1950; Schutt, Gibson, & Beaudry, 1960; Stimson, 1959).

MID-1900S TO THE PRESENT

Considerably more information regarding fad, dubious, or pseudoscientific educational and adult developmental services practices is available for more recent times. Several factors contribute to this phenomenon. First, in the period since the 1950s, there has been an explosion in the number and subtopic areas of professional journals, making it possible for research or speculative articles to be more readily published. Second, the advent of computer technology has made it possible to establish and manage large scale research projects, with larger and more complex data sets, or to conduct studies that entail more complex analyses of numeric or text data more readily, and has generally eased some burdens of conducting research. Third, there has been continuing growth in the number of people enrolled in special education or adult developmental services, provided in an increasing number of places, and at least in adult services, involving an every growing number of provider organizations, increasing the likelihood that speculative methods or therapies will be attempted, and reported, somewhere. Fourth, basic advances in understanding biological processes and vastly more powerful instruments and research methods have generated theories of great generality and accuracy, which has made it easier for scientists to recognize errors, wishful thinking, and fraud in the treatments offered to the public.

Fifth, there has been a tremendous growth, since the 1960s, in funding, not only for special education and developmental disabilities services, but also for related research and for training of special educators and clinicians in colleges and universities—again increasing the likelihood that some academics will pursue highly speculative avenues of applied or action research. Sixth, some have noted an increasing pessimism regarding the utility of interventions in educational and developmental services settings when these result in growth and development, but not in cure (Sasso, 2001), increasing the subjective attractiveness of ideologically based practices (e.g., Danforth, 1997; Skrtic, Sailor, & Gee, 1996) and those which claim remarkable effects, despite insubstantial evidence (e.g., Biklen, 1993; Biklen & Cardinal, 1997). Finally, especially during the past 20 years, there has been a shifting philosophical perspective in educational research and development, somewhat less so in the behavioral sciences or adult developmental services, toward emphasis on qualitative forms of research, which may engender an impression of benefit from "innovative" interventions, or convince some practitioners that such benefits accrue to these interventions, despite the limitations of qualitative inquiry in this regard.

Since 1960, there have been a number of dubious or pseudoscientifically rationalized interventions that have been popularized and widely adopted as fads or on the grounds of either theory alone or in conformance with politically correct ideology. The most egregious examples include psychomotor patterning (Doman, Spitz, Zucman, Delacato, & Doman, 1960; Sparrow & Zigler, 1978), gentle teaching (Barrera & Teodoro, 1990; McGee, Menousek, & Hobbs, 1987), treatments based on sensory integration theory (Ayres, 1963; Hoehn & Baumeister, 1994) and auditory integration (Dawson & Watling, 2000), facilitated communication (Biklen, 1990;

Dillon, Fenlason, & Vogel, 1994; Jacobson, Mulick, & Schwartz, 1995), nonaversive intervention or positive behavioral support (Horner et al., 1990; Linscheid & Landau, 1993), and biological or alternative medical interventions (Autism Society of America, n.d.; Collet et al., 2001; Richman, Reese, & Daniels, 1999; Spitz, 1986).

Psychomotor Patterning

Psychomotor patterning is a classic example of an intervention that was pseudoscientific in nature and became a prevalent fad treatment in homes, schools, and community services. Patterning, as it was generally known, involved a series of exercises through which children (and some adults) with mild to more severe mental retardation or cerebral palsy engaged, or were passively guided through, movements of the head and limbs. It was claimed that these movements recapitulated the prenatal and postnatal movements of a young child (Committee on Children with Disabilities, 1999). Proponents maintained that these movements could improve the neurological organization (i.e., structure and functioning) of the central nervous system and enhance intellectual performance. Broadly stated, the underlying premise is that recapitulation of these movements will alter the structure of the brain, so as to resemble more closely the brain structure of a typical child. No convincing evidence of these effects has ever been presented, and convincing evidence has been presented that it produces no appreciable benefits (Cummins, 1992; MacKay, Gollogly, McDonald, 1986; Sparrow & Zigler, 1978). There are periodic resurgences of patterning and belief in its utility (Bridgman, Cushen, Cooper, & Williams, 1985), and in response to this, the American Academy of Pediatrics issued statements on patterning and its lack of benefits in 1968, 1982, and 1999. The periodic nature of these statements reflects the continuing need to inform practitioners in health care and educational and developmental services about the findings that this intervention is of little use, because many practitioners are unfamiliar with past fad treatments of questionable value.

Patterning evidences many classic attributes of fad interventions as well. It is based on interpretations of the impact of intervention on neurological organization, except that there is no research evidence of beneficial neurological changes resulting from patterning, and the hypothesized changes are not consistent with known aspects of nervous system organization (American Academy of Pediatrics, 1999; Novella, 1996). Thus, although the basis for the intervention could be claimed to be theoretical in nature, engendering the appearance of a scientific rationale, the theory is itself groundless. Patterning is very time-consuming, entailing hours of activities daily for intervals of months or even years, thus displacing or preventing participation in services or therapies with demonstrated ameliorative benefits (see Warren & Mosteller, 1993, for a discussion of ethical concerns), and decreasing the chances that parents will have contact with professionals aware of the related research. A second classic feature is that the underlying rationale for the theory is neurological (this is perhaps a lingering legacy of Seguin's invocation of, and strong emphasis on, physiological factors). A third classic feature is that proponents of the intervention persist in promoting its use despite convincing evidence that it is implausible and ineffective. Patterning was long promoted by the Institute for Applied Human Potential, which today as the Institutes for the Achievement of Human Potential still operates an Internet web page (at www.iahp.org), and which has offices or operations, and offers training for therapists in Brazil, France, Italy, Japan, Mexico, and Spain. Participants in training are limited to parents or immediate adult family members of children with brain injuries, who are unlikely to have knowledge of disconfirming research and so may be culled into adopting these interventions for their children.

Sensory Integration and Auditory Integration

Sensory integration (SI) is a theoretical orientation that has been dominant in the academic preparation and resulting therapeutic orientation of occupational therapists in the United States and some other nations. The progenitor of this orientation was Jean Ayres (1963), who published related studies extensively in professional journals from the mid-1960s to the late 1970s. Today it is quite common to see reviews of SI in professional journals that consider whether there is an empirical basis for those therapies (e.g., Forness, Kavale, Blum, & Lloyd, 1997; Lonigan, Elbert, & Johnson, 1998; Parker, 1990), and usually conclude that it comes up short. SI was one of the first "mainstream" interventions in schools and adult developmental services to be challenged on the basis of inadequate substantiating research to justify its use (see Arendt, Maclean, & Baumeister, 1988; Cohen, 1985; Ottenbacher & Short, 1985). Arendt et al. (1988) noted that despite endorsement by the American Occupational Therapy Association of SI therapy for children with learning disabilities or autism, this encouragement did not extend to including children or adults with mental retardation; however, a review of published studies by Arendt et al. suggested that this was nonetheless a prevalent practice. Contemporary interventions provided by occupational therapists include the use of SI therapy (Hoehn & Baumeister, 1994; Vargas & Camilli, 1999).

Like patterning, the method of SI therapy "involves full body movements that provide vestibular, proprioceptive, and tactile stimulation" with the goal of improving the "way the brain processes and organizes sensations" (Ayres, 1979, p. 184). Like patterning, in general terms, SI therapies utilize an ontogenetic rationale (i.e., the known sequence of neurological development of specific brain structures) for the design and characteristics of specific interventions. However, as noted by Arendt et al. (1988), the sequence of development does not necessarily indicate the importance of a particular structure to sensory motor functioning. Generally, commentators such as Cohen (1985) and Ottenbacher and Short (1985) challenged the adequacy of research on the effectiveness of SI therapy, but Arendt et al. and Hoehn and Baumeister also have challenged the integrity (e.g., basis) of the theory underpinning sensory integration therapy. All of these researchers have concluded that proof of the effectiveness of SI therapy is inadequate with respect to interventions for people with mental retardation, or other disabilities (see also Dawson & Watling, 2000; Griffer, 1999). Indeed, Hoehn and Baumeister (1994) concluded, "[T]he current fund of research findings may well be sufficient to declare SI [sensory integration] therapy not merely an unproven, but a demonstrably ineffective, primary or adjunctive remedial treatment for learning disabilities and other disorders" (p. 338).

Baumeister and colleagues are not alone in expressing concerns regarding the effectiveness or value of sensory integration interventions; a recent review by Vargas and Camilli (1999) of effectiveness studies found that the effects of interventions were much smaller in studies that were conducted more recently, and presumably were of higher quality, than in earlier studies. Even some occupational therapy practitioners have found the empirical basis for SI therapies wanting (Williamson, Anzalone, & Hanft, 2000). Direct tests of SI have also suggested that, in some cases, the use of these interventions may worsen behavior problems (Dura, Mulick, & Hammer, 1988; Mason & Iwata, 1990).

In recent years, classification of children as having SI disorder has been proposed (see ABC News, 2000; Washtenaw Intermediate School District, 2002) and is widely asserted in school planning documents for children in special education. Nevertheless, this condition remains unrecognized in medical, psychiatric, or psychological nomenclatures, perhaps because of the vague nature of the behavior said to be diagnostic or characteristic of it: "overly sensitive or under-reactive to touch, movement, sights, or sounds, easily distracted, social and/or emotional problems, activity level that is unusually high or unusually low, physical clumsiness or apparent carelessness, impulsive, lacking in self control, difficulty making transitions from one situation to another, inability to unwind or calm self, poor self concept, or delays in speech, language, or motor skills" (Washtenaw Intermediate School District, 2002, p. 1). These characteristics may occur, may even be severe enough to be considered pathological and disabling, singly or in subgroupings, but they go by other names in the scientific and epidemiological research literature. There is little empirical support for grouping them all together as they are under SI disorder, and none at all for characterizing them all as either "sensory," or as having anything to do with "integration," either *within* or *of* the nervous system.

At least some of the characteristics attributed to SI are so endemic among children or adults with developmental disabilities that it is difficult to imagine that there are many people with developmental disabilities who would not also be said to have an SI disorder. Correspondingly, a great many, if not most, children and adults in disability education or treatment programs are deemed to "need" SI.

Occupational therapists often use a screening instrument for young children, known as the Sensory Integration and Praxis Test (SIPT; training available from http://www.sensoryint.com/). Using the PsycINFO on-line database of journal articles, 23 articles were identified that used the SIPT from 1988 to the present, indicating it is probably a widely used instrument. However, although we were able to find studies involving the validity of the SIPT, we were not able to identify studies documenting the short-term or long-term stability of results from this screening test. Long-term stability of results is critical to its utility as a diagnostic tool because unless a test measures something that appears to be the same from one time to another, all other things being equal, it may just measure noise. Several researchers have noted that the factors consistent with various forms of dysfunction identified by the test may not be well-founded (Cummins, 1991; Hoehn & Baumeister, 1994), and one can reasonably ask whether it can validly identify children with "sensory integration problems," given that the description of SI disorder in use may be too vague to provide a standard (either gold or otherwise) for comparison of scores of children so identified. These problems of definition and measurement, however, fail to deter practitioners of SI from prescribing the treatment for many kinds of disorders, and in almost any setting, with almost any person they might encounter.

Auditory integration therapy (AIT) is a recent manifestation of a neurologically rationalized intervention, most often suggested for use with children or adults with autism. In general terms, this therapy attempts to reduce hypersensitive or hyper-acute hearing of children with autism and other conditions, which are said to cause or contribute to occurrence of problem behavior or autistic behavior, through expo-sure to recorded music played out loud volumes, from which the sound frequencies identified as being associated with hyperacuity have been removed. The method was developed by Berard, an otolaryngologist in France. These services are adver-tised widely on the Internet, where it is reported that AIT

has been successfully used to help individuals with attention deficit hyperactive disor-der (ADHD), autism, dyslexia, hyperactivity, learning disabilities (LD), language im-pairments, pervasive developmental disorders (PDD), central auditory processing disorder (CAPD), attention deficit disorder (ADD), and depression. In the large major-ity of Dr. Berard's cases, AIT significantly reduced some or many of the handicaps as-sociated with the disorders listed above. (The Counseling Center, 2002, http://www.auditoryintegration.net/)

A few studies have suggested that there are therapeutic benefits from the use of AIT (e.g., Brown, 1999; Edelson, et al., 1999; Rimland & Edelson, 1995; see Edelson & Rimland, 2001, for additional studies), although a large number of these are confer-ence papers and so have not been peer-reviewed—a process that usually increases the quality of research reporting because with peer review, publication is contin-gent on other researchers' agreement that the study was both original and method-ologically sound. On the other hand, many scientists and professionals have concluded based on their own research and that of others, variously, either that at the present time AIT makes no sense on the grounds of present knowledge of audi-tory functioning, is unproven and speculative as an intervention, or is ineffective (Berkell, Malgeri, & Streit, 1996; Dawson & Watling, 2000; Gillberg, Johansson, Steffenburg, & Berlin, 1997; Gresham, Beebe-Frankenberger, & MacMillan, 1999; Link, 1997; Mudford et al., 2000; Siegel & Zimnitzky, 1998; Tharpe, 1999).

Although AIT could be considered a speculative and experimental therapy to be provided only in the course of research and with informed consent and institutional oversight (Tharpe, 1999), it has nonetheless taken on some of the characteristics of a fad intervention, championed by the Society for Auditory Intervention Techniques, based in Oregon. The device used to perform AIT, the audiokinetron, has been banned from importation into the United States by the federal Food and Drug Ad-ministration due to inadequate evidence of medical (i.e., treatment) benefit, except for educational uses.

Facilitated Communication

Yet another fad treatment associated with a vaguely stated neurophysiological ra-tionale, in this case, "some kind of apraxia" (Biklen, 1990), is facilitated communica-tion (termed FC or FCT), which is both dubious and pseudoscientific in nature. FC consists of physically holding an arm or hand of a person with a developmental dis-ability (often someone with autism, but in practice, most likely a person with men-tal retardation) who usually does not speak, or speak very much, for the purpose of "supporting" him or her in using a communication device, usually some form of keyboard, letterboard, or adapted communication device. The extensive research on FC through the mid-1990s generally discredited the method, indicating, in many cases, that the content of the FC-derived communication was unknowingly either influenced or completely controlled by the person providing support, who is typically termed a *facilitator* (see review by Jacobson, Mulick, & Schwartz, 1995).

FC was introduced in Australia during the 1980s by Crossley (Crossley & McDonald, 1980; Crossly, 1994) and was imported and disseminated beginning with a qualitative research report published in a student-run journal, the *Harvard Educational Review* (Biklen, 1990), which was soon reiterated (Biklen, 1992) and expanded on (Biklen, 1993). Repetitive publication (a series of descriptive assertions rather than experimental research), all authored by the same person, may have made FC seem to be broadly supported. Studies disconfirming the validity or authenticity of typed communications used a variety of true experimental and quasi-experimental methods. Proponents of FC have persistently argued that the evidence was invalid because it challenged people to prove their communication was authentic through "confrontational naming" (a technical term for asking a person to state a word, or name a picture, presented to them). In actuality, many of these studies used methods other than this form of "confrontation." This argument is merely an empty appeal to negative emotion because controlled research is the only way to establish a causal relation.

In response to the experimental findings, some proponents of FC outrageously suggested that professionals, more specifically psychologists, were protecting their professional turf (e.g., manufacturing the negative findings) so that they could continue to exploit people with disabilities as a rationale for employment (e.g., Borthwick, n.d.; Borthwick & Crossley, 1993). Others suggested that people with autism were confused when engaged in FC because they were really reading the minds of their facilitators at the same time as they were attempting to type (Haskew & Donnellan, 1992). Although doubtless this would be confusing if true, it would require us to accept yet another unproven phenomenon as the explanation for the failure of FC to exhibit independent validity, hardly a rational option. Yet others have suggested cursory and nondefinitive means of detecting facilitator influence (Biklen, Saha, & Kliewer, 1997; Weiss & Wagner, 1997) or that the very means that would allow definitive documentation of authenticity somehow prevents it from being demonstrated (Cardinal & Biklen, 1997). Proponents of FC also note that some people have learned to communicate, by typing or through the emergence of speech, via FC, but these are so few in numbers as reported by these proponents (see reports at http://soeweb.syr.edu/thefci/) that the protestation of benefit is ironic if one considers that at one time FC was being used with tens of thousands of people, for sustained periods of time, in schools and community services throughout the United States. In this context, those few who were allegedly assisted in learning how to communicate independently actually demonstrates the low probability of benefit from FC.

By the mid-1990s, with the confluence of negative findings of the utility of FC from researchers and practitioners in many westernized nations, interest in validating communications through FC as research projects diminished for almost all but the proponents. Five studies with negative findings were published in 1995, six in 1996, one in 1997 (Kezuka, 1997), and two in 1998 (Kerrin, Murdock, Sharpton, & Jones, 1998; Konstantareas & Gravelle, 1998). In contrast, six studies presenting positive findings and using qualitative or mixed methods were published (Cardinal,

Hanson, & Wakeham, 1996; Olney, 1995; Schubert, 1997; Sheehan & Matuozzi, 1996; Weiss, Wagner, & Bauman, 1996), including a group therapy study using FC in which validity of these communications appears largely assumed (Eliasoph & Donnellan, 1995). Mostert (2001), who conducted a review of FC studies from 1995 to 2000, concluded that there was still little evidence of validity for facilitated communication.

However, as a fad treatment, the inception of FC is recent, and it has not yet run its course. An elective course in FC is taught in the graduate program in education at Syracuse University (2002), and related studies favoring FC are included in graduate courses for educators at locations such as Dominican College in New York, Southeast Missouri State University, the University of Maryland, and the University of Wisconsin. Personnel from federally funded university centers in developmental disabilities in Indiana, Maine, New Hampshire, and Vermont have provided or sponsored training in FC and generally continue to do so, and the New Hampshire Division of Developmental Services has issued guidelines supporting use of FC. However, courses offering an orientation to or encouraging use of FC as a educational strategy appear to have become outnumbered by course syllabi where it is featured as a fad, unproven strategy or intervention.

Gentle Teaching, Nonaversive Intervention, and Positive Behavioral Support

Gentle Teaching. Gentle teaching is a philosophy of treatment (Mudford, 1995) that purports to have achieved remarkable success with problem behaviors including extremely dangerous ones (McGee & Gonzalez, 1990; McGee, Menolascino, Hobbs, & Menousek, 1987). Although behavior-analytical components are present in gentle teaching, unconditional value giving and warm assistance and protection are central to the overall strategy of dyadic interaction enhancement or "bonding" between the client and caregiver (McGee & Gonzalez, 1990). It emerged in synchrony with the nonaversive movement in the mid-1980s (Newsom & Kroeger, chap. 24, this volume) and was promoted as the humane alternative to not only aversives, but behavior analysis. Key to its promulgation was its use of humanistic language to further contrast it with the sterile language of behavior analysis (Foxx, 1996).

The main practitioner of gentle teaching is McGee, who casts it in spiritual, political, and sometimes behavioral terms depending on the audience (Mudford, 1995). Like all fads, total belief in, and unconditional acceptance of, gentle teaching is required in order to apply it successfully (McGee & Gonzalez, 1990).

Claims of success with severe behavior problems include no treatment failures in over 600 cases (McGee et al., 1987). These extraordinary effects were obtained within a few days of morning and afternoon 2-hour sessions and without the benefit of peer review (Mudford, 1995). However, independent methodologically sound evaluations of gentle teaching have found that claims of its universal effectiveness were false (Jones & McCaughey, 1992; Mudford, 1995).

Interest in gentle teaching began to wane in the early 1990s and currently it enjoys minor cult status on the Internet (Cullen & Mudford, chap. 25, this volume). Some factors responsible for its failure to sustain interest include (a) its extraordinary claims of success that even among ardent nonaversive proponents were thought to be grandiose, (b) its noninclusion in the mainstream nonaversive movement and nonassociation with any major advocacy organization (Foxx, chaps. 18 & 28, this volume; Newsom & Kroeger, chap. 24, this volume) and (c) its diminished appeal caused by the emergence of positive behavior support and its emphasis of values and vision (Horner et al., 1990).

Nonaversive Intervention. The nonaversive movement began in the early 1980s. It was spawned by the civil rights movement and deinstitutionalization and fueled by special educators, the availability of alternative treatments for nonsevere problem behaviors, attention to the causes of problem behaviors, the inappropriate use or abusive use of aversive procedures, and reports that aversive procedures had limitations (Newsom & Kroeger, chap. 24, this volume). Other contributing factors included postmodernist philosophy and its rejection of science; deprofessionalization, which greatly increased the numbers of scientifically illiterate administrative and treatment personnel; and the movement of major professional and parent groups such as AAMR, TASH, ARC, and the Autism Society of America toward advocacy as their primary mission.

TASH, The Association for Persons with Severe Handicaps, began the movement in 1981 by passing a resolution that banned the use of aversives that could, among other things, inflict severe physical or emotional stress or death. In a 1987 report, TASH highlighted the similarities between aversive treatments used with the developmentally disabled and methods applied to political prisoners reported by Amnesty International (Guess, Helmstetter, Turnbull, & Knowlton, 1987; Mulick, 1990a, 1990b). Seeking to carve out the moral high ground, the report described behavior analysts as devaluing the people they sought to educate and treat (Guess et al., 1987). To further buttress the argument, various claims were made that nonaversive treatments were effective with all manner of severe and dangerous behaviors and that aversive procedures were ineffective (Donnellan & LaVigna, 1990; Meyer & Evans, 1989).

In an attempt to retain an individual's right to effective treatment, the Association for Behavior Analysis, ABA, issued a position paper (VanHouten et al., 1988). This effort was not welcomed by the nonaversive movement (Donnellan & LaVigna, 1990) and bitter acrimonious debates and positions were drawn by protreatment choice and nonaversive movement proponents.

When a 1989 National Institutes of Health consensus statement issued a cautious recommendation regarding the continued use of aversives in select situations (NIH, 1989), the movement responded to this agenda setback with sweeping condemnation of the report and exerted its political muscle to hold up publication of the consensus report for almost 2 years (Foxx, chap. 28, this volume). Positive effects of the nonaversive movement include accelerating progress towards changing treatment standards, championing functional assessment, focusing on antecedent control, and increasing focus on nonaversive procedures although most research has been primarily focused on the mild problems behaviors of children (Newsom & Kroeger, chap. 24, this volume).

Not laudable are the negative outcomes of the movement. These include extension of the definition of *aversive* to include positive reinforcement and the use of contingencies in general (Newsom & Kroeger, chap. 24, this volume); increased use of drugs and restraint in the community because of the absence of treatment success or contingencies (Foxx, chap. 18, this volume); the false promise that all behavior problems, especially severe ones, can be treated nonaversively (Foxx, chap. 18, this volume); promotion of an anti-inclusive ideology that individuals with developmental disabilities, in contrast to everyone else, should never experience unpleasant or annoying events (Tiryak, chap. 27, this volume); promotion of impractical, expensive support options that fail or cannot receive funding (Paisey, Whitney, Hislop, & Wainczak, 1991); and creation of bitter divisions within the educational and treatment community via faulty logic, coercive proselytizing, and antiscience adoption of postmodern philosophy (Mulick, 1990a, 1990b).

Positive Behavior Support. The political climate created by the nonaversive movement required that the U.S. government make every effort to demonstrate the effectiveness of nonaversive approaches (Foxx, chap. 18, this volume). To that end, a multimillion dollar grant titled "A Rehabilitation Research and Training Center on Community-Referenced Technologies for Nonaversive Behavior Management" was awarded in 1987 by the National Institute on Disability and Rehabilitation Research (NIDRR) to a multisite group of university-based researchers. Although the group did not demonstrate the universal effectiveness of nonaversive methods with what they term "challenging behavior," they did display an entrepreneurial talent by creating positive behavior support (PBS), a sophisticated packaging of science, values, vision, politically correct language, and nonaversive movement buzz words (Horner et al., 1990).

PBS is described as a framework for developing effective interventions and programs for individuals who exhibit challenging behavior and is characterized by three features: a person-centered value base, a recognition of the individuality of each person (which seems a bit oxymoronic), and working toward meaningful outcomes (Anderson & Freeman, 2000; Koegel, Koegel, & Dunlap, 1996). The typical PBS case study or PBS university newsletter often features uplifting titles such as "A Legacy of Love: Our Path to Freedom Through Positive Behavior Support" (Lucyshyn, Dunlap, & Albin, 2002) or "the ability to 'connect' can often be the miracle ingredient in behavioral changes" (Beach Center, 1997).

The creators of PBS did not adopt the extreme positions of nonaversive movement but did retain its basic agenda wrapped around an applied science of assessment. This strategy offered several advantages. First, PBS was widely embraced by governmental and educational agencies as the palatable and politically correct alternative to more fanatical approaches and groups. This acceptance resulted in continuous funding by NIDRR, the establishment of richly funded university centers of PBS, and widespread adoption within governmental and educational agencies that serve individuals with disabilities. Second, PBS was initially considered by both sides of the aversives debate as being somewhat balanced in its approach to the controversy. This resulted in PBS presentations being acceptable at TASH and ABA meetings. Although the PBS founders first published in TASH's journal, *JASH*, they eventually founded their own journal, the *Journal of Positive Behavior Interventions*, which offered its authors the benefits of not being associated with extremeness or subjected to the scientific rigor of the behavior-analytical journals. Third, because PBS emphasized analysis rather than treatment or education goals, it was widely accepted by educational agencies because it brought "credibility" rather than accountability. Fourth, because the PBS model was based on a social services support model rather than a behavior change model, PBS offered the fail-safe argument that any failure was the result of a lack of supports (i.e., money rather than personnel or system failure). Eventually, PBS was promoted as a new approach (Lucyshyn et al., 2002).

Despite claims to the contrary, PBS is not a natural development in the evolution of ABA (Lucyshn et al., 2002) nor a new science, technology, or professional field. Yet, the attempt to separate PBS from behavior analysis has resulted in a number of deleterious effects, including a de-emphasis on technology, a failure to build technical capacity in staff, a failure to teach complexities of antecedent technology, a reliance on psychiatric supports (i.e., medications and noncontingent restraint) for difficult cases, reductions in opportunities for effective habilitative services by failing to adequately consider the consequences of behavior, and a failure to provide empirically valid demonstrations of multi-element interventions in applied settings (Johnston, Jacobson, Foxx, et al., in preparation).

As a successful politically driven approach, PBS is without peer. Consider that it is actively promoted and endorsed by groups such as the Autism National Committee (1998) who are antibehavior analytic—which is the very scientific base that PBS claims. But this success comes at a cost because PBS has lost credibility among science-based and -oriented individuals (Foxx, 1998).

Alternative Biological and Medical Treatments

Unverified fad treatments offered to people with developmental disabilities generally involve diets, drugs and various compounds made from "natural" and unregulated botanical and nutritional extracts, and surgery. These have a long history, and represent the hunches and trial-and-error searches of both professionals and amateurs in search of cures for disabling conditions. In the United States, medical treatments that require a physician's prescription and designated medical devices are regulated by law. The U.S. Food and Drug Administration requires controlled clinical trials to be carried out for new drugs, biologics, and medical devices to establish safety and efficacy before they are approved for use by physicians with their patients. This process results in the approval of only a fraction of proposed medical interventions, even when they originally appeared to have great promise and to represent a hopeful advance. The proof is either established experimentally, or the intervention is not given FDA approval.

Similar rigorous standards of proof are not required for substances designated and sold as nutritional extracts, dietary or nutritional advice, or even for devices that are proffered as educational (unless the devices cause physical harm). Consumer protection in these areas is limited to protection from fraudulent claims of efficacy and injury, which is why labels and advertisements for such alternative treatments are vague with respect to direct effects. Many such products are endorsed by articles that are presented as informative but carefully provided in separate documents so as not to be considered a direct claim of efficacy for the product. Sometimes ineffective and unnecessary treatments and procedures are sold with disclaimers about their lack of demonstrated value explicitly stated or at least strongly implied in order to escape strict liability, but are located in a tiny footnote or are written in language that nonprofessionals and even careless professionals either overlook or misunderstand. It is always a good idea to read the fine print and to look up references, but how often do we do it?

Down syndrome is a chromosomal disorder that results in abnormal physical development, developmental learning delays, and can involve a variety of potentially serious medical problems (Cohen, 1999). Medical problems can include serious heart defects, skeletal defects, endocrine disorders, gastrointestinal disorders, and abnormal muscle tone, as well as cataracts, frequent otitis media (i.e., ear infections), and frequent respiratory infections. As such, it is a useful model for looking briefly at the interplay between beneficial and bogus medical care. Cardiac (Baciewicz, Melvin, Basilius, & Davis, 1989) and orthopedic surgery (Greene, 1998; Pueschel, 1998) can greatly improve health, function, and longevity when medically necessary. Hormonal treatments are often necessary for endocrine disorders such as hypothyroidism and diabetes that occur with increased frequency in Down syndrome. Many useful books are available to assist professionals and families with the complexities of caring for and fostering the best possible outcome for children with Down syndrome (Pueschel & Pueschel, 1992; Pueschel & Sustrova, 1997; Stray-Gundersen, 1995), and comprehensive guidelines for the appropriate medical care are available and periodically updated (Cohen, 1999b), but as might be expected there are also many pitfalls and false promises available. Like other developmental disabilities (not to mention chronic diseases and psychiatric syndromes), megavitamin and mineral supplement regimens have been offered to hopeful parents, but research has failed to verify their effectiveness (Cohen, 1999). Freeze-dried fetal animal cells have been administered to children with Down syndrome (Sica Cell Therapy), but have not been shown to have any benefit and may produce allergic reactions (Cohen 1999). Children with Down syndrome have small chins and sometimes large tongues. Controversial uses of cosmetic surgery to change the shape of the tongue in an effort to improve appearance and speech has been of dubious value and carries the risk associated with any irreversible surgery as well as the special risks of complication of the healing process in the moist environment of the mouth (Lynch, 1990; Siperstein, Wolraich, & Reed, 1994). Chiropractic manipulation can be dangerous to people with Down syndrome because of their reduced muscle tone and lax or stretchy ligaments and the increased frequency of spinal malformations that can, under some conditions, compress the spinal chord (Cohen, 1999).

There is an all too familiar pattern here. If a little bit of something can be helpful, perhaps a lot of that same something will help more. This is not necessarily true, of course. Vitamins, by definition, are necessary for health, but some are toxic at high doses and others are simply excreted if in excess of the needed amount. Surgery and drug treatments carry risks and should be evaluated for their potential benefit against the background of their cost and risk. Stressing cosmetic reasons is a poor justification for surgery unless some functional or medical benefit is likely and significant, and may seem unfair when viewed as a form of expressed prejudice against human variety. Active drugs should not be embraced unless their use is empirically supported or their experimental use is done with informed consent and strictly supervised. Above all, it should be remembered that medical treatments are only as powerful as they are well understood and knowledgeably used.

THE ALTERNATIVE OF NOT ADOPTING FADS

Kauffman (1996) has observed, with some irony, that it often seems that educators, and one suspects well-meaning developmental services personnel as well, are more likely to readily adopt fad or unproven interventions than well-validated interventions (see also, Detterman & Thompson, 1997). Some research (e.g., Blanton, 2000) suggests that practitioners may not rely as heavily on research findings in clinical decision making as they do on discussion with colleagues, personal experience, workshops, and how-to resources. It is possible that the same preferences are common among educators, and special educators, and that would account for some discrepancies in the nature of common practices and practices indicated to be of value through research. It is important to note that there are many educational and instructional practices that are well validated (Crandall, Jacobson, & Sloane, 1997; Forness et al., 1997; Lloyd, Forness, & Kavale, 1998; Symons & Warren, 1998).

For example, research has indicated that where a child is taught (i.e., more or less inclusive settings) is less important than how a child is taught. That is, the instructional methods are more important, especially for academic outcomes of growing concern to special educators (Forness et al., 1997; Hocutt, 1996; Lloyd et al., 1998), although inclusion and school reform are both considered to be paramount operational and programmatic issues in education, and their mirror images represent critical areas of activity in the further refinement of developmental services. Generally, when ideologically based practices have been submitted to organized and well-constructed research to identify consistent direct and indirect benefits to children and adults with disabilities, these purported benefits have been difficult to verify as real occurrences. This does not mean that simply because an intervention or practice is compatible with progressive social and political philosophy that it is necessarily ineffective, but it is possible that proponents who can rely on ideology as a primary justification for their recommendations are less likely to bother to determine whether there is evidence that real outcomes result when others change the way they provide services based on their recommendations.

In summary, today there are a number of factors, longstanding factors, that may make practitioners in educational or developmental services prone to acceptance of fad, dubious, or pseudoscientific interventions. These include:

1. A continued focus on the search for a magic bullet that can make a meaningful difference in raising intelligence, and pessimism regarding the value of conventional or well-founded interventions that are not curative (Spitz, 1986).
2. Diminished attention to, or at least continuing disinterest in the use of, behavioral science as a source of information in selecting interventions, and for that matter any manner of empirical validation, and reliance on agreement with one's peers or the suggestions of a persuasive authority figure as the basis for adopting or changing instruction or intervention practices (Carnine, 2000).
3. Increased focus on values as a basis for clinical decision-making without substantial consideration of the plausible effectiveness of the specific interventions that are values-driven, and even ignoring contraindications of effectiveness (Lucyshyn et al., 2002; Mulick & Kedesdy, 1988; Wolfensberger, 1983).
4. Continuing problems in differentiating between benign intent (which is likely shared by ideologues and scientist-practitioners alike) or statements of progressive philosophy, and indications that interventions are effective and beneficial, contributing, in fact, to higher quality of life for people with disabilities.

There continues to be confusion of reorganization of the way services are provided with heightening the effectiveness of intervention or its acceptability to people with disabilities, their families, or the public. Finally, and perhaps more critically, there is persisting emphasis within some federal educational agencies on acceptance and support for process over outcomes and related dubious practices with effects on special education and spillover in developmental services.

REFERENCES

ABC News. (2000, July 21). *20/20: Sensory overload: When children can't process stimuli* [Television broadcast]. Retrieved from http://abcnews.go.com/onair/2020/2020_000721_sensoryintegration_feature.html)

Anderson, C. M., & Freeman, K. A. (2000). Positive behavior support: Expanding the application of behavior analysis. *The Behavior Analyst, 23*, 85–94.

Angus, L. R. (1949). Prefrontal lobotomy as a method of therapy in a special school. *American Journal of Mental Deficiency, 53*, 470–476.

Arendt, R. E., Maclean, W. E., Jr., & Baumeister, A. A. (1988). Critique of sensory integration therapy and its applications in mental retardation. *American Journal on Mental Retardation, 92*, 401–411.

Autism National Committee. (1998). *An open letter to families considering intensive behavioral therapy for the child with autism*. Ardmore, PA: Author.

Autism Society of America. (n.d.). *Options to meet the challenges of autism*. Retrieved August 3, 2002, from wwww.autism-society.org/packages/options.pdf

Ayres, A. J. (1963). The development of perceptual-motor abilities: A theoretical basis for treatment of dysfunction. *American Journal of Occupational Therapy, 17*, 221–225.

Ayres, A. J. (1979). *Sensory integration and the child*. Los Angeles, CA: Western Psychological Services.

Baciewicz, F. A., Jr., Melvin, W. S., Basilius, D., & Davis, J. T. (1989). Congenital heart disease in Down's syndrome patients: A decade of surgical experience. *Thoracic & Cardiovascular Surgeon, 37*, 369–371.

Barrera, F. J., & Teodoro, G. M. (1990). Flash bonding or cold fusion? A case analysis of gentle teaching. In A. C. Repp & N. N. Singh (Eds.), *Perspectives on the use of nonaversive and aversive interventions for persons with developmental disabilities* (pp. 199–214). Sycamore, IL: Sycamore.

Beach Center on Families and Disability Newsletter. (1997, Winter). Lawrence, KS: Kansas University Affiliated Program.

Berkell, D. E., Malgeri, S., & Streit, M. K. (1996). Auditory integration training for individuals with autism. *Education & Training in Mental Retardation & Developmental Disabilities, 31*, 66–70.

Biklen, D. (1990). Communication unbound; autism and praxis. *Harvard Educational Review, 60*, 291–314.

Biklen, D. (1992). Autism orthodoxy versus free speech; A reply to Cummins and Prior. *Harvard Educational Review, 62*, 242–256.

Biklen, D. (1993). *Communication unbound*. New York: Teachers College Press.

Biklen, D., & Cardinal, D. (Eds.). (1997). *Contested words, contested science*. New York: Teachers College Press.

Biklen, D., Saha, S., & Kliewer, C. (1997). How teachers confirm the authorship of facilitated communication. In D. Biklen & D. Cardinal (Eds.), *Contested words, contested science* (pp. 54–78). New York: Teachers College Press.

Blanton, J. S. (2000). Why consultants don't apply psychological research. *Consulting Psychology Journal: Practice and Research, 52*, 235–247.

Borthwick, C. (n.d.). *Facilitated communication: An "inappropriate challenge to professional belief systems."* Retrieved July 6, 2002, from http://vhpax.vichealth.vic.gov.au/~borth/FC&PSYCH.htm

Borthwick, C. J., & Crossley, R. (1993). *The validation of facilitated communication.* Caulfield, Victoria, Australia: DEAL Centre.

Bridgman, G. D., Cushen, W., Cooper, D. M., & Williams, R. J. (1985). The evaluation of sensorimotor-patterning and the persistence of belief. *British Journal of Mental Subnormality, 31,* 67–79.

Brockett, L. P. (1858). Cretins and idiots. *Atlantic Monthly, 1*(4), 410–419. Retrieved May 11, 2003, from http://www.disabilitymuseum.org/lib/docs/1385.htm

Brown, M. M. (1999). Auditory integration training and autism: Two case studies. *British Journal of Occupational Therapy, 62,* 13–18.

Buchan, D. W. (1943). Educational methods applicable to adult mental defectives. *American Journal of Mental Deficiency, 48,* 87–95.

Cardinal, D. N., & Biklen, D. (1997). Suggested procedures for confirming authorship through research: An initial investigation. In D. Biklen & D. Cardinal (Eds.), *Contested words, contested science* (pp. 173–186). New York: Teachers College Press.

Cardinal, D. N., Hanson, D., & Wakeham, J. (1996). Investigation of authorship in facilitated communication. *Mental Retardation, 34,* 231–242.

Carnine, D. (2000). *Why education experts resist effective practices (And what it would take to make education more like medicine).* Retrieved July 27, 2002, from http://www.edexcellence.net/library/carnine.html

Cohen, H. J. (1985). School-aged children with motor disabilities. *Pediatrics, 76,* 648–649.

Cohen, W. I. (1999). Health care guidelines for individuals with Down syndrome: 1999 revision. *Down Syndrome Quarterly, 4,* 1–15.

Collet, J.-P., Vanasse, M., Marois, P., Amar, M., Goldberg, J., Lambert J., et al. (2001). Hyperbaric oxygen for children with cerebral palsy: A randomised multicentre trial. *The Lancet, 357,* 582–586.

Committee on Children with Disabilities, American Academy of Pediatrics. (1999). The treatment of neurologically impaired children using patterning. *Pediatrics, 104,* 1149–1151.

Crandall, J., Jacobson, J. W., & Sloane, H. (1997). What works in education. *Behavior and Society, 7,* 3–7.

Crossley, R. (1994). *Facilitated communication training.* New York: Teachers College Press.

Crossley, R., & McDonald, A. (1980). *Annie's coming out.* London: Penguin.

Cummins, R. A. (1991). Sensory integration and learning disabilities: Ayres' factor analysis reappraised. *Journal of Learning Disabilities, 24,* 160–168.

Cummins, R. A. (1992). Coma arousal and sensory stimulation: An evaluation of the Doman-Delacato approach. *Australian Psychologist, 27,* 71–77.

Cutler, M., Little, J. W., & Strauss, A. A. (1940). The effect of benzedrine on mentally deficient children. *American Journal of Mental Deficiency, 45,* 59–65.

Danforth, S. (1997). On what basis hope? Modern progress and postmodern possibilities. *Mental Retardation, 35,* 93–106.

Davies, P. (1999). What is evidence-based education? *British Journal of Educational Studies, 47,* 108–121.

Dawson, G., & Watling, R. (2000). Interventions to facilitate auditory, visual, and motor integration in autism: A review of the evidence. *Journal of Autism and Developmental Disorders, 30,* 415–421.

Detterman, D. K., & Thompson, L. A. (1997). What is so special about special education? *American Psychologist, 52,* 1082–1090.

Dillon, K. M., Fenlason, J. E., & Vogel, D. J. (1994). Belief in and use of a questionable technique, facilitated communication, for children with autism. *Psychological Reports, 75,* 459–464.

Doll, E. A. (1940). Psychological personnel. *American Journal of Mental Deficiency, 45,* 167–169.

Doman, R. J., Spitz, E. R., Zucman, E., Delacato, C. H., & Doman, G. (1960). Children with severe brain injuries: Neurological organization in terms of mobility. *Journal of the American Medical Association, 174,* 257–262.

Donnellan, A. M., & LaVigna, G. W. (1990). Myths about punishment. In A. C. Repp & N. N. Singh (Eds.), *Perspectives on the use of nonaversive and aversive interventions for persons with developmental disabilities* (pp. 33–57). Sycamore IL: Sycamore.

Dura, J. R., Mulick, J. A., & Hammer, D. (1988). Rapid clinical evaluation of sensory integrative therapy for self-injurious behavior. *Mental Retardation, 26,* 83–87.

Dybwad, G. (1941). The problem of institutional placement for high-grade mentally defective delinquents. *American Journal of Mental Deficiency, 45,* 391–400.

Edelson, S. M., Arin, D., Bauman, M., Lukas, S. E., Rudy, J. H., Sholar, M., et al. (1999). Auditory integration training: A double-blind study of behavioral and electrophysiological effects in people with autism. *Focus on Autism and Other Developmental Disabilities, 14,* 73–81.

Edelson, S. M., & Rimland, B. (2001). *The efficacy of Auditory Integration Training: Summaries and critiques of 28 reports* (January, 1993–May, 2001). Retrieved August 3, 2002, from http://www.up-to-date.com/saitwebsite/aitsummary.html

Eliasoph, E., & Donnellan, A. M. (1995). A group therapy program for individuals identified as autistic who are without speech and use facilitated communication. *International Journal of Group Psychotherapy, 45,* 549–560.

Fernald, W. E. (1917). The growth of provision for the feeble-minded in the United States. *Journal of Psycho-Asthenics, 17,* 34–59.

Forness, S. R., Kavale, K. A., Blum, I. M., & Lloyd, J. W. (1997). What works in special education and related services: Using meta-analysis to guide practice. *Teaching Exceptional Children, 29*(6), 4–9.

Foxx, R. M. (1996). Translating the covenant: The behavior analyst as ambassador and translator. *The Behavior Analyst, 19,* 147–161.

Foxx, R. M. (1998). *Self-injurious behavior: Perspectives on the past, prospects for the future.* Panel discussion presented at the annual convention of the Association for Behavior Analysis, Orlando, FL.

Gillberg, C., Johansson, M., Steffenburg, S., & Berlin, O. (1997). Auditory integration training in children with autism. *Autism, 1,* 97–100.

Goldstein, H. (1954). Treatment of mongolism and non-mongoloid mental retardation in children. *Archives of Pediatrics, 71,* 77–98.

Greene, W. B. (1998). Closed treatment of hip dislocation in Down syndrome. *Journal of Pediatric Orthopedics, 18,* 643–647.

Gresham, F. M., Beebe-Frankenberger, M. E., & MacMillan, D. L. (1999). A selective review of treatments for children with autism: Description and methodological considerations. *School Psychology Review, 28,* 559–575.

Griffer, M. R. (1999). Sensory integration effective for children with language-learning disorders? A critical review of the evidence. *Language, Speech, and Hearing Services in Schools, 30,* 393–400.

Guess, D., Helmstetter, E., Turnbull, H. R., III, & Knowlton, S. (1987). *Use of aversive procedures with persons who are disabled: An historical review and critical analysis* [Monograph]. Seattle, WA: The Association for Persons with Severe Handicaps.

Harpers New Monthly Magazine. (1854). *A chapter on idiots, 9*(49), 101–104. Retrieved May 11, 2003, from http://www.disabilitymuseum.org/lib/docs/1387.htm

Haskew, P., & Donnellan, M. (1992). *Emotional maturity and well-being: Psychological lessons of facilitated communication.* Madison, WI: DRI Press.

Hocutt, A. M. (1996). Effectiveness of special education: Is placement the critical factor? *The Future of Children, 6,* 77–102.

Hoehn, T. P., & Baumeister, A. A. (1994). A critique of the application of sensory integration therapy to children with learning disabilities. *Journal of Learning Disabilities, 27,* 338–350.

Horner, R. H., Dunlap, G., Koegel, R. L., Carr, E. G., Sailor, W., Anderson, J. A., et al. (1990). Toward a technology of "nonaversive" behavioral support. *Journal of the Association for Persons with Severe Handicaps, 15,* 125–132.

Huesman, M. (1947). Psychological services to the mentally handicapped in the Chicago public schools. *American Journal of Mental Deficiency, 51*, 632–636.

Jacobson, J. W., Mulick, J. A., & Schwartz, A. A. (1995). A history of facilitated communication: Science, pseudoscience, and antiscience science. Working group on facilitated communication. *American Psychologist, 50*, 750–765.

Johnston, J. M., Jacobson, J. W., Foxx, R. M., et al. (in preparation). *A critique of positive behavior support.*

Jones, R. S. P., & McCaughey, R. E. (1992). Gentle teaching and applied behavior analysis: A critical review. *Journal of Applied Behavior Analysis, 25*, 853–867.

Kauffman, J. M. (1996). Research to practice issues. *Behavioral Disorders, 22*, 55–60.

Kerrin, R. G., Murdock, J. Y., Sharpton, W. R., & Jones, N. (1998). Who's doing the pointing? Investigating facilitated communication in a classroom setting with students with autism. *Focus on Autism and Other Developmental Disabilities, 13*, 73–79.

Kezuka, E. (1997). The role of touch in facilitated communication. *Journal of Autism and Developmental Disorders, 27*, 571–593.

Koegel, L. K., Koegel, R. L., & Dunlap, G. (1996). *Positive behavior support: Including people with difficult behaviors in the community.* Baltimore: Brookes.

Konstantareas, M. M., & Gravelle, G. (1998). Facilitated communication. *Autism, 2*, 389–414.

Kuhlmann, F. (1940). One hundred years of special care and training. *American Journal of Mental Deficiency, 45*, 8–24.

Link, H. M. (1997). Auditory integration training (AIT): Sound therapy? Case studies of three boys with autism who received AIT. *British Journal of Learning Disabilities, 25*, 106–110.

Linscheid, T. R., & Landau, R. J. (1993). Going "all out" pharmacologically? A re-examination of Berkman and Meyer's "Alternative strategies and multiple outcomes in remediation of severe self-injury: Going 'all out' nonaversively." *Mental Retardation, 31*, 1–6.

Lloyd, J. W., Forness, S. R., & Kavale, K. A. (1998). Some methods are more effective. *Intervention in School and Clinic, 33*, 195–200.

Lonigan, C. J., Elbert, J. C., & Johnson, S. B. (1998). Empirically supported psychosocial interventions for children: An overview. *Journal of Clinical Child Psychology, 27*, 138–145.

Lucyshyn, J. M., Dunlap, G., & Albin, R. W. (2002). *Families and positive behavior support: Addressing problem behavior in family contexts.* Baltimore: Brookes.

Lynch, J. (1990, January). Tongue reduction surgery: Efficacy and relevance to the profession. *ASHA*, 59–61.

MacKay D. N., Gollogly, J., & McDonald, G. (1986). The Doman-Delacato methods, I: The principles of neurological organization. *British Journal of Mental Subnormality, 32*, 3–19.

Malzberg, B. (1940). Trends in the growth of population in the schools for mental defectives. *American Journal of Mental Deficiency, 45*, 119–126.

Mason, S. M., & Iwata, B. A. (1990). Artifactual effects of sensory-integrative therapy on self-injurious behavior. *Journal of Applied Behavior Analysis, 23*, 361–370.

McGee, J. J., & Gonzalez, J. (1990). Gentle teaching and the practice of human interdependence: A preliminary group study of 15 persons with severe behavioral disorders and their caregivers. In A. C. Repp & N. N. Singh (Eds.), *Perspectives on the use of nonaversive and aversive interventions for persons with developmental disabilities* (pp. 237–254). Sycamore, IL: Sycamore.

McGee, J. J., Menolascino, F. J., Hobbs, D. C., & Menousek, P. E. (1987). *Gentle teaching: A nonaversive approach to helping people with mental retardation.* New York: Human Sciences Press.

McGee, J. J., Menousek, E., & Hobbs, D. (1987). Gentle teaching: An alternative to punishment for people with challenging behaviors. In S. J. Taylor & D. Biklen (Eds.), *Community integration for people with severe disabilities* (pp. 147–183). New York: Teachers College Press.

Menzel, M. (1946). Methods and techniques used in occupational therapy treatment for the imbecile. *American Journal of Mental Deficiency, 51*, 286–295.

Meyer, L. H., & Evans, I. M. (1989). *Nonaversive intervention for behavior problems: A manual for home and community.* Baltimore: Brookes.

Mostert, M. P. (2001). Facilitated communication since 1995: A review of published studies. *Journal of Autism and Developmental Disorders, 31*, 287–313.

Mudford, O. C. (1995). Review of the gentle teaching data. *American Journal on Mental Retardation, 99*, 345–355.

Mudford, O. C., Cross, B. A., Breen, S., Cullen, C., Reeves, D., Gould, J., et al. (2000). Auditory integration training for children with autism: No behavioral benefits detected. *American Journal on Mental Retardation, 105*, 118–129.

Mulick, J. A. (1990a). The ideology and science of punishment in mental retardation. *American Journal on Mental Retardation, 95*, 142–156.

Mulick, J. A. (1990b). Ideology and punishment reconsidered. *American Journal on Mental Retardation, 95*, 173–181.

Mulick, J. A., & Kedesdy, J. H. (1988). Self-injurious behavior, its treatment, and normalization. *Mental Retardation, 26*, 223–229.

Muscott, H. S., & O'Brien, S. T. (1999). Teaching character education to students with behavioral and learning disabilities through mentoring relationships. *Education & Treatment of Children, 22*, 373–390.

National Institutes of Health. (1989). *Treatment of destructive behaviors in persons with developmental disabilities*. Washington, DC: NIH Consensus Development Conference, U.S. Department of Health and Human Services.

Novella, S. (1996). Psychomotor patterning. *The Connecticut Skeptic, 1*(4), 6. Available from www.quackwatch.com

Olney, M. (1995). Reading between the lines: A case study on facilitated communication. *Journal of the Association for Persons with Severe Handicaps, 20*, 57–65.

Otten, E. H. (2000, September). *Character education*. ERIC Digest (ED444932). Bloomington, IN: ERIC Clearinghouse for Social Studies/Social Science Education.

Ottenbacher, K., & Short, M. A. (1985). Sensory integrative dysfunction in children: A review of theory and treatment. *Advances in Developmental and Behavioral Pediatrics, 6*, 287–329.

Paisey, T. J. H., Whitney, R. B., Hislop, M., & Wainczak, S. (1991). Case study 5: George. In R. Romanczyk (Ed.), *Self-injurious behavior: Etiology and treatment* [Monograph]. Binghamton, NY: University at Binghamton.

Parker, R. M. (1990). Power, control, and validity in research. *Journal of Learning Disabilities, 23*, 613–620.

Pollock, H. M. (1945). Mental disease among mental defectives. *American Journal of Mental Deficiency, 49*, 477–480.

President's Committee on Mental Retardation. (1977). *MR 76—Mental retardation: Past and present*. Washington, DC: U.S. Government Printing Office (040-000-00385-1).

Pueschel, S. M. (1998). Should children with Down syndrome be screened for atlanto-axial instability? *Archives of Pediatric and Adolescent Medicine, 152*(2), 123–125.

Pueschel, S. M., & Pueschel, J. K. (1992). *Biomedical concerns in persons with Down syndrome*. Baltimore: Brookes.

Pueschel, S. M., & Sustrova, M. (Eds.). (1997). *Adolescents with Down syndrome: Toward a more fulfilling life*. Baltimore: Brookes.

Quinn, K. V., & Durling, D. (1950). Twelve months' study of glutamic acid therapy in different clinical types in an institution for the mentally deficient. *American Journal of Mental Deficiency, 54*, 321–332.

Richman, D. M., Reese, R. M., & Daniels, D. (1999). Use of evidence-based practice as a method for evaluating the effects of secretin on a child with autism. *Focus on Autism and Other Developmental Disabilities, 14*, 204–211.

Rimland, B., & Edelson, S. M. (1995). Brief report: A pilot study of auditory integration training in autism. *Journal of Autism and Developmental Disorders, 25*, 61–70.

Sasso, G. M. (2001). The retreat from inquiry and knowledge in special education. *The Journal of Special Education, 34*, 178–193.

Scheerenberger, R. C. (1983). *A history of mental retardation*. Baltimore: Brookes.

Schubert, A. (1997). "I want to talk like everyone": On the use of multiple means of communication. *Mental Retardation, 35*, 347–354.

Schutt, C. C., Gibson, D., & Beaudry, P. (1960). The efficacy of sedac therapy with maladjusted mentally retarded girls. *American Journal of Mental Deficiency, 64*, 978–983.

Seguin, E. (1976). Psycho-physiological training of an idiotic hand. In M. Rosen, G. R. Clark, & M. S. Kivitz (Eds.). *The history of mental retardation, collected papers* (Vol. 1, pp. 161–167). Baltimore: University Park Press. (Original work published 1879)

Sheehan, C. M., & Matuozzi, R. T. (1996). Investigation of the validity of facilitated communication through the disclosure of unknown information. *Mental Retardation, 34*, 94–107.

Shotwell, A. M. (1949). Effectiveness of institutional training of high-grade mentally defective girls. *American Journal of Mental Deficiency, 53*, 432–437.

Siegel, B., & Zimnitzky, B. (1998). Assessing 'alternative' therapies for communication disorders in children with autistic spectrum disorders: Facilitated communication and auditory integration training. *Journal of Speech-Language Pathology and Audiology, 22*, 61–70.

Siperstein, G. N., Wolraich, M. L., & Reed, D. (1994). Professional's prognoses for individuals with mental retardation: Search for consensus within interdisciplinary settings. *American Journal of Mental Retardation, 98*, 519–526.

Skrtic, T. M., Sailor, W., & Gee, K. (1996). Voice, collaboration, and inclusion: Democratic themes in educational and social reform initiatives. *Remedial and Special Education, 17*, 142–157.

Smith, J. D. (1985). *Minds made feeble: The myth and legacy of the Kallikaks.* Austin, TX: Pro-Ed.

Sparrow, S., & Zigler, E. (1978). Evaluation of a patterning treatment for retarded children. *Pediatrics, 62*, 137–150.

Spitz, H. H. (1986). *The raising of intelligence: A selected history of attempts to raise retarded intelligence.* Hillsdale, NJ: Lawrence Erlbaum Associates.

Stimson, C. W. (1959). The treatment of cerebral palsy in mentally retarded patients using high-frequency, low voltage, electric currents. *American Journal of Mental Deficiency, 64*, 72–80.

Stray-Gundersen, K. (1995). *Babies with Down syndrome* (2nd ed.). Bethesda, MD: Woodbine House.

Symons, F. J., & Warren, S. F. (1998). Straw men and strange logic: Issues and pseudo-issues in special education [Comment]. *American Psychologist, 53*, 1160–1161.

Syracuse University. (2002). *Graduate catalog* (School of Education, pp. 50–72). Syracuse, NY: Author.

Tharpe, A. M. (1999). Auditory integration training: The magical mystery cure. *Language, Speech, and Hearing Services in the Schools, 30*, 378–382.

The Counseling Center. (2002). *What is Berard auditory integration training?* Retrieved August 3, 2002, from http://www.auditoryintegration.net/

Thorne, F. C. (1948). Counseling and psychotherapy with mental defectives. *American Journal of Mental Deficiency, 52*, 263–271.

Trent, J. W. (1994). *Inventing the feeble mind: A history of mental retardation in the United States.* Berkeley, CA: University of California Press.

Van Houten, R., Axelrod, A., Bailey, J. S., Favell, J. E., Foxx, R. M., Iwata, B. A., et al. (1988). The right to effective treatment. *Journal of Applied Behavior Analysis, 21*, 381–384.

Vargas, S., & Camilli, G. (1999). A meta-analysis of research on sensory integration treatment. *American Journal of Occupational Therapy, 53*, 189–198.

Warren, K. S., & Mosteller, F. (Eds.). (1993). *Doing more good than harm: The evaluation of health care interventions.* New York: New York Academy of Sciences.

Washtenaw Intermediate School District, Project Perform. (2002). *Sensory integration: What are some signs of sensory integrative dysfunction?* Retrieved August 3, 2002, from http://wash.k12.mi.us/~perform/Sensory_Integration.htm#WHATISSI

Weiss, M. J. S., Wagner, S., & Bauman, M. (1996). A validated case study of facilitated communication. *Mental Retardation, 34*, 220–230.

Weiss, M. J. S., & Wagner, S. H. (1997). Emerging validations of facilitated communication: New findings about old assumptions. In D. Biklen & D. Cardinal (Eds.), *Contested words, contested science* (pp. 135–156). New York: Teachers College Press.

Williamson, G. G., Anzalone, M. E., & Hanft, B. H. (2000). Assessment of sensory processing, praxis, and motor performance. In Interdisciplinary Council on Development and Learning Disorders, *Clinical Practice Guidelines* (pp. 155–184). Bethesda, MD: American Occupational Therapy Association.

Witmer, L. (1909). The study and treatment of retardation: A field of applied psychology. *Psychological Bulletin, 6,* 121–126.

Wolfensberger, W. (1983). Social role valorization: A proposed new term for the principle of normalization. *Mental Retardation, 21,* 234–239.

Classification Versus Labeling

Susan Vig
Albert Einstein College of Medicine

There is general agreement within the field of developmental disabilities about the value of understanding the nature of different kinds of disabilities and of clearly identifying disabilities in order to provide beneficial intervention and services. There is less agreement about the classification and labeling processes undertaken to achieve these goals. Issues of classification and labeling are debated by families, clinicians, educators, and other professionals who serve people with disabilities. This chapter will discuss classification and labeling issues relevant to children.

CLASSIFICATION

Classification is a process that separates individuals into groups that share common characteristics. Zigler, Balla, and Hodapp (1986) have stated that classification systems provide rules for grouping individuals so that there is agreement across classifiers about class characteristics. If an individual is a member of a particular class or category, what is known about the class designation will give information about that individual. Classification is used to determine eligibility for services and entitlements; to make diagnoses; to plan, implement, and evaluate intervention services; and to conduct research. Classification approaches reflect the theoretical perspectives and beliefs of classifiers as well as the purposes for classification.

Classification to Determine Eligibility for Services

The Individuals with Disabilities Education Act (IDEA, PL 101-476) specifies the disabilities that entitle children to special education and related services (e.g., counseling, speech language therapy) at school. Kamphaus, Reynolds, and Imperato-McCammon (1999) characterize the classification approach exemplified by IDEA as "categorical." The child either has or does not have a particular disability (mental retardation, autism, speech or language impairment, serious emotional disturbance, specific learning disability, or other specified impairment). The purpose of this approach is to identify children who need special education services. The approach is not designed to explore the nature of children's developmental problems, or to provide comprehensive diagnostic insight.

Kamphaus et al. (1999) contrast this categorical approach with what they call a "dimensional" approach, which groups children according to constructs or dimensions (e.g., borderline personality disorder). The authors caution that a categorical approach may overlook children who have serious problems but do not meet full criteria for category membership. This might occur, for example, when a child with mental retardation has a coexisting mood disorder that does not qualify as "serious emotional disturbance," but causes irritability and outbursts of anger in the classroom. Cognitive needs may be addressed, but services may not be provided for the comorbid condition. Categorical classification may not identify children with mild impairments such as borderline intelligence, who would benefit from supports and services, but who fail to meet eligibility requirements.

Classification by Etiology

Classification by etiology involves grouping individuals with disabilities according to the causes of the disabilities. Durkin and Stein (1996) suggest that etiological classification is useful for planning primary prevention, understanding the nature of a disability, conducting epidemiological research, and providing information to families. The scientific study of mental retardation is often based on etiological classification.

Organic Versus Familial Retardation. Zigler et al. (1986) have proposed that individuals with mental retardation be divided into two groups: (a) those with organic defects and (b) a larger group with more mild impairment who do not have an organic etiology. The "organic" group often has IQs below 50, physical stigmata, siblings with normal intelligence, and a high prevalence of physical conditions such as epilepsy and cerebral palsy. All socioeconomic classes are represented in the families of these individuals. There is a demonstrable organic cause for their disability. The "familial" group has IQs between 50 and 71, a normal physical appearance, and at least one family member with lower intelligence or mental retardation. Families are generally of lower socioeconomic status. There is no demonstrable organic cause for their retardation.

In recent years, there has been a growing recognition of the complex, often interactive, influences that may cause mental retardation. The two-group etiological theory proposed by Zigler et al. (1986) does not adequately address this complexity. Durkin and Stein (1996) have criticized the theory for grouping many diverse causes of mental retardation into a single "organic" class. They have noted that, as knowledge of etiology increases, forms of mental retardation previously classified as "familial" may eventually be determined to be "organic." Human genome research has resulted in the identification of genetic causes for many previously unknown etiologies. Environmental and psychosocial risk factors (particularly risk factors associated with poverty) are another source of etiologic complexity. Ramey, Mulvihill, and Ramey (1996) have described the "new morbidity" (interaction of adverse biological, environmental, and behavioral influences on health and development). Baumeister and Woodley-Zanthos (1996) have noted that environmental context can affect the outcome of biological etiologies, and that environmental risk can have biological consequences. For example, maternal drug or alcohol use can have biological consequences for a child (e.g., premature birth, fetal alcohol syndrome) and can also compromise the childrearing environment.

Etiology has implications for prevention and intervention. Mental retardation due to some genetic causes can be prevented or ameliorated by medical or dietary intervention. For example, folic acid supplements can protect against neural tube defects; diet can prevent mental retardation in children with phenylketonuria; thyroid hormone averts adverse developmental consequences for children with congenital hypothyroidism (Baumeister & Woodley-Zanthos, 1996). Public health and education initiatives can increase awareness of environmental and psychosocial factors associated with developmental problems in children (e.g., exposure to lead, transmission of HIV and AIDS).

Syndromes. The usefulness of classifying by etiology is illustrated by the condition known as Down syndrome. This disability has a genetic cause and is generally identified at birth. Much is known about its prevalence, associated medical problems, the level of mental retardation to be expected by adulthood, and the kinds of interventions that may optimize development.

Hayes and Batshaw (1993) provide an extensive discussion of the medical problems associated with Down syndrome: obesity, vision and hearing impairments, cardiac problems that may require surgery, risk for dislocation of the knees and hips, and hypothyroidism. They suggest that physicians should provide frequent pediatric preventive health care visits, arrange genetic counseling, refer children to early intervention and special education programs, and provide support for parents by connecting them to information and support groups.

The developmental characteristics of children with Down syndrome have been studied extensively. Compared to other children, those with Down syndrome have been found to develop at a slower rate, reach a lower final level of attainment, exhibit less causality pleasure in exploring objects, and lose previously acquired skills (Spiker & Hopmann, 1997; Wishart, 1993). They have been found to have stronger expressive than receptive language (Carr, 1988) and to exhibit a smaller range of affect lability when separated from their caregivers (Cicchetti & Ganiban, 1990). Experts have suggested that intervention should inolve errorless learning, dramatic presentation of learning materials, and emphasis on review and skill maintenance (Spiker & Hopmann, 1997; Wishart, 1993).

Other syndromes also have been studied. The finding that children with fragile X syndrome did poorly on a test involving imitation of hand movements led investigators to suggest that these children might not do well with manual signs in early communication (Hodapp, Leckman, Dykens, Sparrow, Zelinsky, & Ort, 1992). Compulsive overeating and food-seeking behaviors associated with Prader-Willi syndrome imply a need for exercise, diet, weight management, and extra support when food is nearby (Fiedler & Hodapp, 1998).

Classification by Levels of Support

1992 AAMR Definition. The 1992 definition of mental retardation, published by the American Association on Mental Retardation (AAMR; Luckasson et al., 1992), eliminated previous levels of measured intelligence as a basis for classification of individuals with mental retardation. The definition instead specified that classification should be based on the intensities of supports needed by an individual in order to function in daily life. According to the 1992 definition, a diagnosis of mental retardation was to be based on subaverage intellectual functioning (an IQ standard score of approximately 70 to 75 or below) and limitations in two or more adaptive skill areas: communication, self-care, home living, social skills, community use, self-direction, health and safety, functional academics, leisure, and work.

By prioritizing the supports needed to optimize the daily functioning of people with mental retardation, the 1992 definition emphasized the environmental component of the interaction between person and environment (Jacobson & Mulick, 1996). With increased significance attributed to environmental influences, there was a decreased emphasis on the cognitive, affective, and behavioral functioning of individuals with mental retardation (Jacobson & Mulick, 1996).

The 1992 definition was criticized for replacing IQ severity levels (mild, moderate, severe, profound) with levels of support. Critics described potential difficulty operationalizing the definition (Turnbull, Turnbull, Warren, Eidelman, & Marchand, 2002); a lack of reliable or valid measures for determining support intensities (King, State, Shah, Davanzo, & Dykens, 1997; MacMillan, Gresham, & Siperstein, 1995); poor applicability of specified adaptive skill areas to children (Gresham, MacMillan, & Siperstein, 1995; Vig & Jedrysek, 1996); and the potential risk of confusing intensities of supports with previously specified degrees of intellectual disability (Borthwick-Duffy, 1993; Hodapp, 1995). Although early intervention efficacy research has shown that children with mild delays derive more benefit from intervention services than those with more severe impairments (Guralnick, 1991; Infant Health and Development Program, 1990), equating intensities of supports with severity of disability might mean that maximum resources are allocated to children with severe impairments whereas children with mild impairments, who could benefit most, receive little or no intervention.

2002 AAMR Definition. The 2002 AAMR definition of mental retardation (Luckasson et al., 2002) retains the idea of supports as a preferred direction for the field, but emphasizes that different classification systems can be used to address different purposes for classification. Classification may be based on intensities of supports, etiology, IQ ranges, levels of adaptive behavior, or other factors. The 2002 definition replaces the previous ten adaptive skill areas with three more general areas: conceptual, social, and practical.

Classification by Levels of Measured Intelligence

The 2002 AAMR definition of mental retardation permits classification by IQ-based severity levels: mild, moderate, severe, and profound. Because each level is associated with different characteristics and capabilities, classification based on measured intelligence can be useful for both research and practice.

Different degrees of mental retardation are associated with different developmental trajectories. Children functioning at different IQ levels progress at different rates, reach plateaus at different ages, and have different adult outcomes. Sattler (1988, p. 648) estimates adult mental ages of approximately 8:3 to 10:9 years for individuals with mild mental retardation, 5:7 to 8:2 years for moderate, 3:2 to 5:6 for severe, and below 3:2 years for profound mental retardation. Understanding what different levels of mental retardation mean for current and future functioning is helpful in planning intervention for children. The emphasis should be on adaptive skills, rather than academic achievement, for those with significant degrees of mental retardation. Knowledge of developmental trajectories can help parents advocate for developmental services and plan for future needs (vocational or residential programs, legal guardianship).

Different degrees of mental retardation have been associated with differential risk of maltreatment. There is a greater incidence of neglect experienced by individuals with mental retardation and IQs above 50 than those with IQs below 50 (Zigler et al., 1986). In a large study of institutionalized children and adolescents with mental retardation, those with mild impairments were found to be at greater risk of maltreatment (physical and emotional neglect, physical and sexual abuse) than those with severe impairments (Verdugo, Bermejo, & Fuertes, 1995). The investigators suggested that undesirable behavior was mistakenly attributed to the child's character for individuals with mild impairment, but correctly attributed to the disability for those with more severe impairment.

International Classification Systems

In an attempt to create greater international consistency, particularly for research, the World Health Organization has developed two classification systems: *Classification of Mental and Behavioral Disorders: Diagnostic Criteria for Research* (10th ed. [ICD-10]; World Health Organization, 1993) and the *International Classification of Functioning, Disability, and Health* (ICF; World Health Organization, 2001). The diagnostic criteria of ICD-10 are similar to those of the *Diagnostic and Statistical Manual of Mental Disorders* (4th ed. [DSM–IV]; American Psychiatric Association, 1994) and its text revision (DSM–IV–TR; American Psychiatric Association, 2000). The ICD-10 is used to identify mental retardation for health care data systems. The ICF system has a functional orientation. Disability is conceptualized in terms of interaction between person and environment rather than being a fixed trait. Neutral language is used to avoid potentially stigmatizing labels. In criticizing a draft of the ICF, Stein (2000) noted that trying to define disability in terms of interaction between person and environment would be very difficult to accomplish for different countries and different cultures.

IDENTIFICATION AND DIAGNOSIS

Classification emphasizes characteristics of groups and what group membership means for the individuals classified. Diagnosis focuses on characteristics of particular individuals. For individuals with disabilities, the process of clinical diagnosis results in one or more labels which best describe the disabilities.

Clinical diagnosis may be contrasted with the more general identification of children's developmental problems in educational settings. Although multidisciplinary teams may be involved in both processes, and sources of information may be similar, the goal in educational settings is to determine eligibility for services rather than to achieve diagnostic precision. General terms such as "preschool child with a disability" may be sufficient to establish eligibility. Clinical diagnosis uses more precise labels (autism, mental retardation, cerebral palsy, fragile X syndrome). Clinical diagnosis often seeks to determine etiology, and diagnostic labels reflect that emphasis.

Early Identification and Diagnosis

Legal mandates and funding for early intervention provide incentive to identify children's developmental problems before the age of 3 years. Participation in early intervention programs can prevent declines in cognitive development for children with mental retardation (Guralnick, 1991, 1998). Participation has been associated with less need for special education and fewer failing grades in subsequent schooling (Ramey & Ramey, 1992), and fewer maternally reported behavior problems (Infant Health and Development Program, 1990).

Early intervention has been associated with developmental gains for children with autism. Based on a review of eight well-established early intervention programs, representing diverse intervention strategies, Dawson and Osterling (1997) concluded that all of the programs produced measurable developmental gains and fostered positive school placements.

Some disabilities with distinctive physical characteristics, such as Down syndrome, can be diagnosed during infancy. Other diagnoses cannot be made until a child has failed to meet certain developmental milestones (motor milestones for cerebral palsy, cognitive milestones for mental retardation). Many children with autism are now being identified before the age of 3 years. Research showing that features of autism (e.g., deficits in pointing and showing) can be seen in home videotapes of first birthday celebrations (Mars, Mauk, & Dowrick, 1998; Osterling & Dawson, 1994) has helped practitioners recognize early symptomatology.

Parents as well as children can benefit from early intervention. Early intervention can reduce stress due to a child's disability and improve family interaction (Guralnick, 1998). Improved family interaction has been associated with better developmental outcomes for children (Hauser-Cram, Warfield, Shonkoff, & Krauss, 2001; Kelly, Moriset, Barnard, Hammond, & Booth, 1996).

Diagnostic Guidelines

In making formal diagnoses of children's developmental problems, clinicians generally use established diagnostic criteria. Formal diagnostic guidelines provide labels and/or codes to be used in characterizing children's problems. Although the guidelines present objective criteria for characterizing symptomatology, more subjective clinical judgment comes into play in deciding whether the symptoms do, or do not, meet the diagnostic criteria. Because some of the guidelines were not developed specifically for children, their application is not always an easy task.

The *DSM–IV* and *DSM–IV–TR* (American Psychiatric Association, 1994, 2000) are commonly used for clinical diagnosis. For diagnoses of mental retardation and autism, criteria are identical in the two editions.

With recent interest in early diagnosis, there has been a recognition that diagnostic criteria developed for adults or older children are not suitable for children under 3 years of age. In an effort to present more age-appropriate guidelines for this age group, the National Center of Clinical Infant Programs developed the *Diagnostic*

Classification of Mental Health and Developmental Disorders of Infancy and Early Childhood (Zero to Three, 1994). These guidelines emphasize issues relevant to infant mental health and parent-child interaction.

Checklists and observational systems are often used for clinical diagnosis of autism. The Checklist for Autism in Toddlers (CHAT; Baron-Cohen, Allen, & Gillberg, 1992) is used to identify autism in 18-month-old children. Practitioners observe a young child's eye contact, pointing, following an adult's pointing, and pretend play. The Childhood Autism Rating Scale (CARS; Schopler, Reicher, & Renner, 1988) presents 15 behaviors to be rated for severity. Other instruments used for young children include the Pre-Linguistic Autism Diagnostic Observation Schedule (PL-ADOS; DiLavore, Lord, & Rutter, 1995); the Autism Diagnostic Interview (ADI; LeCouteur, Rutter, Lord, Rios, Robertson, Holdgrafer, & McLennan, 1989); the Autism Diagnostic Interview-Revised (ADI-R; Rutter, Lord, & LeCouteur, 1995); and the Communication and Symbolic Behavior Scales (CSBS; Wetherby & Prizant, 1993). The ADOS and ADI require extensive training prior to use.

LABELING

Clinical diagnosis, which aims to clarify a child's developmental status, usually results in the use of diagnostic labels. Within this context, labels represent specific diagnoses. The more general process of identifying children's developmental problems to establish eligibility for services, undertaken in educational settings, may also involve labeling. Within the educational system, a label represents special education status (MacMillan, Jones, & Aloia, 1974).

The use of labels for individuals with disabilities has been criticized by those who find labels stigmatizing. There has been concern about labeling children who have mild mental retardation, belong to minority groups, and have low socioeconomic status. Use of the label *educable mentally retarded (EMR)* has been particularly controversial. Criticisms involve the ineffectiveness of EMR classes for labeled children; bias of IQ tests on which labels are based; and overidentification of minority children (MacMillan et al., 1974). The Larry P. v. Riles case (Larry P. v. Riles, 1979) resulted in an injunction in which California banned the use of standardized individual intelligence tests to evaluate African-American children for placement in EMR classes. A 1986 modification banned the use of the tests for any special education placement for these children (Larry P. v. Riles, 1986).

Reluctance to use the label "mental retardation" is suggested by increased use and substitution of the label "learning disability" in educational settings. In a study of school referral practices, few students with IQs at or below 75 were classified as having mental retardation (MacMillan, Gresham, Siperstein, & Bocian, 1996). Baroff (1999) has cited data from the U.S. Department of Education stating that the number of children served as "learning disabled" increased 202% from 1994 to 1997. Those designated as "mentally retarded" decreased 38%.

Discomfort with the term "mental retardation" has generated discussion about using different terminology and changing the name of the American Association on Mental Retardation. Alternative terminology has been suggested for both the disability and the organization: "general learning disorder" (Baroff, 1999); "intellectual disability" (Gelb, 2002); "cognitive-adaptive disabilities" (Walsh, 2002); "American Society of Intellectual Disabilities" (Schalock, 2002); "American Association on Intellectual Disabilities," "American Association on Developmental-Cognitive Disabilities," "American Association on Developmental Disabilities" (Warren, 2002). Turnbull et al. (2002) note that, although the term "mental retardation" may seem to be offensive to individuals with that disability and their families, the real problem occurs for derivatives of the label (e.g., informal use of the pejorative term "retard"). They state that the term "mental retardation" is understood by legislators, the press, and the general public, and that the Special Olympics has inspired positive associations to it.

Effects of Labeling on Children's Self-Concepts, Teacher Expectations, and Peer Attitudes

Do labels affect children's feelings of self-worth? Based on a comprehensive review of studies investigating the effects of the label "mental retardation," MacMillan et al. (1974) did not find evidence of a direct relationship between labeling and self-concept. Children in some studies already had poor self-esteem before being labeled. In other studies, children's self-esteem improved when they were placed in special education classes and worsened when they were delabeled and returned to regular education classes.

Critics of labeling have suggested that labels can negatively affect teachers' expectations for labeled children. It has been thought that labels create a self-fulfilling prophecy by causing teachers to form negative expectations, leading to differential treatment of labeled children in the classroom, and resulting in poor student achievement. There has not been strong empirical support for the idea of a self-fulfilling prophecy. In a study of regular first-grade classrooms, Brophy and Good (1970) found that teachers praised teacher-ranked low achievers less frequently and demanded less of them than higher achievers. Although this was thought to contribute to further declines in achievement, it could be argued that the teachers were simply being realistic about the children's abilities. Yoshida and Meyers (1975) investigated the effects of the label "educable mentally retarded (EMR)" on the expectations of regular and special education teachers who viewed a videotaped teaching interaction between a teacher and student (described as a sixth grader or labeled as mentally retarded) The EMR label did not result in lower teacher expectancies. Based on a meta-analysis of 47 studies of labeling and teacher expectations, Smith (1980) found full support for formation of expectations, partial support for the differential effects of labels on teacher behavior and student achievement, and little support for the effects of that process on student ability. Brophy (1983) reviewed research on the self-fulfilling prophecy and concluded that teachers revise their expectations as they gain new information about their students. Sattler (2001) similarly noted that teachers may form provisional expectations based on a label, but revise their expectations as they see how a child is actually performing.

Peer attitudes toward labeled children have also been investigated. In studies by Gottlieb (1974), fourth graders of higher and lower socioeconomic status viewed videotapes of 12-year-old boys, with and without a label of mental retardation, who were described as good or poor spellers. High ratings on a social distance scale were associated with high academic competence, but there was no effect for the label. In a study by Bak and Siperstein (1986), fourth and sixth graders viewed videotapes of two children reading. The videotaped children, with and without labels of mental retardation, were described as socially withdrawn or aggressive. In a social rating procedure, the label of mental retardation was found to have a protective effect for the videotaped child described as socially withdrawn. Using audiotaped vignettes accompanied by photographs, Siperstein, Budoff, and Bak (1980) found that fifth and sixth graders had more favorable attitudes toward children clinically labeled as "mentally retarded," even when described as academically deficient, than to those informally labeled as "retard."

Non-Labeling

Some of those who object to the potentially negative impact of labeling propose that labeled children would fare better if stigmatizing labels such as "mental retardation" were not applied to them. Studies of individuals with cognitive limitations who have never been labeled, or have received euphemistic labels, suggest that unlabeled individuals do not necessarily fare well.

At a time when special education programs were less available, Johnson (1950) studied the social position of unlabeled children, with IQs indicating mental retardation, who were in regular classrooms. As assessed through sociometric analysis, peers had negative attitudes toward unlabeled children with low IQs, which worsened with decreases in IQ. Zetlin and Murtagh (1990) studied post-school adjustment of 17- to 19-year-olds who had borderline intelligence but had been labeled as "learning disabled" and received services under that label. Many of the students had dropped out of high school, and 80% worked at unskilled jobs from which they were fired or laid off. The investigators concluded that avoidance of the label "borderline intelligence," due to its potentially stigmatizing effects, meant that the needs of individuals with more mild intellectual impairments were not addressed.

Children with disabilities who are not formally labeled are nevertheless at risk for informal derogatory labeling (Kamphaus et al., 1999). Reynolds, Lowe, and Saenz (1999) note that if noncategorical funding for services were to replace current eligibility determination approaches, informal labeling by teachers and parents would continue and most likely worsen the problems of exceptional children.

Permanence of Labels

One often-heard criticism of labeling is that once applied to a child, a label is likely to remain with the child far into the future or for life. For children with mental retardation, it is the nature of the disability (a chronic and lifelong condition), rather than the diagnostic label, which causes academic difficulties during school years and ongoing problems with social and vocational adjustment in adulthood.

The chronicity of mental retardation is suggested by longitudinal studies documenting IQ stability. Vig, Kaminer, and Jedrysek (1987) studied children with borderline intelligence or mild mental retardation, who were first tested as preschoolers and retested during early elementary school. Despite intervention, the majority of the children remained within the same IQ classification range in follow-up testing. Bernheimer and Keogh (1988) found that children initially tested at a mean age of 34 months, and retested at 52, 74, and 109 months, had IQs which changed little over time (means of 67, 74, 71, and 70, respectively). In a study by Carr (1988), children with Down syndrome were found to have developmental quotients of 80 at 6 months, 45 at 4 years, 37 at 11 years, and 42 at 21 years. Results of these investigations suggest that most children with early cognitive delays will continue to need special education services throughout their schooling. The goal should be to optimize development rather than "cure" the disability.

Professionals' Reluctance to Label

Studies of parent–professional communication reflect professionals' ambivalence about diagnostic labels. This may take the form of delaying referral or diagnosis (Goodman & Cecil, 1987; Quine & Pahl, 1986). Professionals may use euphemisms or vague language to cover their own uncertainty or their wish not to distress families. In a study of parent-professional communication during informing interviews following multidisciplinary evaluation of children with borderline intelligence or mild mental retardation, Svarstad and Lipton (1977) found that evaluating professionals discussed test results in less than half of the cases, and explained the concept of mental retardation in less than one third of the cases. Following the interviews, many parents expressed their belief that their children had normal intelligence. Abrams and Goodman (1998) analyzed audiotaped informing interviews following multidisciplinary evaluation of preschool children with mental retardation. Professionals avoided use of the label "mental retardation," instead describing the child as "slow" or speaking of the child's "problem."

Parents have expressed dissatisfaction with professionals' reluctance to label, and a preference for being told the truth about their child. In Quine and Pahl's (1986) study, parents said that they wanted early diagnosis and full information about their child's disability, including diagnostic labels. Parents participating in Abrams and Goodman's (1998) study expressed dissatisfaction with evasiveness during informing interviews. In a study of communication between pediatricians and parents of children with mental retardation, parents reported long periods of anxiety if the disability was not obvious, and indicated a preference for being informed early of their child's disability (Quine & Rutter, 1994).

In providing guidelines for communication between pediatricians and parents, experts caution that pediatricians should avoid vague terminology and translate degrees of mental retardation into expectations for the present and future (Doernberg, 1982; Kaminer & Cohen, 1988). If this is not done, parents may interpret children's behavior as stubbornness, rather than inability, which can increase risk of maltreatment.

Benefits of Labeling

Expectations. Understanding the disability represented by a diagnostic label helps parents and others formulate appropriate expectations for progress and behavior, and can protect a child from ridicule or maltreatment. This may be particularly important if a disability is not immediately obvious through physical appearance. A label of "mental retardation" can help parents and teachers understand why a child may progress slowly and reach a plateau in achievement despite special education and appropriate intervention services. A label of "autism" or "pervasive developmental disorder" can help others understand a child's difficulties with socialization, distress with imposed demands, atypical language, mannerisms, and stereotyped behaviors. Because the majority of children with autism also have mental retardation (Lord & Rutter, 1994; Myers, 1989; Volkmar, Burack, & Cohen, 1990), their rate of progress is apt to remain slow even when intervention improves other symptomatology. Including the label "mental retardation" as well as "autism" in a child's diagnosis can help others understand the child's rate of progress.

Intervention Planning and Implementation.   Provision of diagnostic labels enhances the process of planning and implementing intervention for children with disabilities. Although general terminology is sufficient to establish eligibility for services, the use of precise diagnostic labels results in better targeted services.

Support for Families.   The use of diagnostic labels can be helpful to families. Sattler (2001) notes that parents may experience a sense of relief when they realize that their child's problem is understood. Labels can lead parents to useful information, resources, advocacy organizations, and support groups. Many parents obtain information about their child's disability by accessing relevant literature or information available through the Internet. General or euphemistic terminology (e.g., "special needs") deprives parents of this opportunity. Use of specific diagnostic labels (e.g., cerebral palsy, autism, attention-deficit hyperactivity disorder, mental retardation) leads parents to the kind of appropriate information that will address their particular concerns. Targeted information in turn helps them develop realistic expectations, understand and manage their child's behavior, and serve as effective advocates for the child. Many national organizations (Autism Society of America, Down Syndrome Society, Association for Retarded Citizens) have local advocacy and support groups for parents. Because many developmental disabilities are lifelong, early contact with these organizations can support parents and help them know what to expect over time. The prerequisite is having a label for a child's developmental problem.

CONCLUSION

Although the classification and labeling of children with disabilities will probably continue to be controversial for some time to come, it is important for professionals and parents to base their opinions on empirical data rather than personal ideology. Classification approaches which help parents, professionals, and researchers gain greater understanding of developmental disabilities, and diagnostic labels which accurately address the characteristics and needs of individual children, can be beneficial to the field of developmental disabilities and to the children and families it serves.

REFERENCES

Abrams, E. Z., & Goodman, J. F. (1998). Diagnosing developmental problems in children: Parents and professionals negotiate bad news. *Journal of Pediatric Psychology, 23*, 87–98.

American Psychiatric Association. (1994). *Diagnostic and statistical manual of mental disorders* (4th ed.). Washington, DC: Author.

American Psychiatric Association. (2000). *Diagnostic and statistical manual of mental disorders* (4th ed.), Text revision. Washington, DC: Author.

Bak, J. J., & Siperstein, G. N. (1986). Protective effects of the label "mentally retarded" on children's attitudes toward mentally retarded peers. *American Journal of Mental Deficiency, 91*, 95–97.

Baroff, G. S. (1999). General learning disorder: A new designation for mental retardation. *Mental Retardation, 37*, 68–70.

Baroff, G. S. (2000). Eugenics, "Baby Doe," and Peter Singer: Toward a more perfect society. *Mental Retardation, 38*, 73–77.

Baron-Cohen, S., Allen, J., & Gillberg, C. (1992). Can autism be detected at 18 months? The needle, the haystack, and the CHAT. *British Journal of Psychiatry, 161*, 839–843.

Baumeister, A. A., & Woodley-Zanthos, P. (1996). Prevention: Biological factors. In J. W. Jacobson & J. A. Mulick (Eds.), *Manual of professional practice in mental retardation* (pp. 229–242). Washington, DC: American Psychological Association.

Bernheimer, L. P., & Keogh, B. K. (1988). Stability of cognitive performance in children with developmental delays. *American Journal on Mental Retardation, 92*, 539–542.

Borthwick-Duffy, S. (1993). Review of Mental Retardation: Definition, Classification, and Systems of Supports (9th ed.). *American Journal on Mental Retardation, 98*, 541–544.

Brophy, J. E. (1983). Research on the self-fulfilling prophecy and teacher expectations. *Journal of Educational Psychology, 75*, 631–661.

Brophy, J. E., & Good, T. L. (1970). Teachers' communication of differential expectations for children's classroom performance: Some behavioral data. *Journal of Educational Psychology, 61*, 365–374.

Carr, J. (1988). Six weeks to twenty-one years old: A longitudinal study of children with Down's syndrome and their families. *Journal of Child Psychology and Psychiatry, 29*, 407–431.

Cicchetti, D., & Ganiban, J. (1990). The organization and coherence of developmental processes in infants and children with Down syndrome. In R. M. Hodapp, J. A. Burack, & E. Zigler, E. (Eds.), *Issues in the developmental approach to mental retardation* (pp. 169–225). New York: Cambridge University Press.

Dawson, G., & Osterling, J. (1997). Early intervention in autism. In M. J. Guralnick (Ed.), *The effectiveness of early intervention* (pp. 307–326). Baltimore: Brookes.

DiLavore, P. C., Lord, C., & Rutter, M. (1995). The Pre-Linguistic Autism Diagnostic Observation Scale. *Journal of Autism and Developmental Disorders, 25*, 355–379.

Doernberg, N. (1982). Issues in communication between pediatricians and parents of young mentally retarded children. *Pediatric Annals, 11*, 438–444.

Durkin, M. S., & Stein, Z. A. (1996). Classification of mental retardation. In J. W. Jacobson & J. A. Mulick (Eds.), *Manual of diagnosis and professional practice in mental retardation* (pp. 67–73). Washington, DC: American Psychological Association.

Fiedler, D. J., & Hodapp, R. M. (1998). Importance of typologies for science and service in mental retardation. *Mental Retardation, 36*, 489–495.

Gelb, S. A. (2002). The dignity of humanity is not a scientific construct. *Mental Retardation, 40*, 55–56.

Goodman, J. F., & Cecil, H. S. (1987). Referral practices and attitudes of pediatricians toward young mentally retarded children. *Journal of Developmental and Behavioral Pediatrics, 8*, 97–105.

Gottlieb, J. (1974). Attitudes toward retarded children: Effects of labeling and academic performance. *American Journal of Mental Deficiency, 79*, 268–273.

Gresham, F. M., MacMillan, D. L., & Siperstein, G. (1995). Critical analysis of the 1992 AAMR definition: Implications for school psychology. *School Psychology Quarterly, 10*, 1–9.

Guralnick, M. J. (1991). The next decade of research on the effectiveness of early intervention. *Exceptional Children, 58*, 174–183.

Guralnick, M. J. (1998). Effectiveness of early intervention for vulnerable children: A developmental perspective. *American Journal on Mental Retardation, 102*, 319–345.

Hauser-Cram, P., Warfield, M. E., Shonkoff, J. P., & Krauss, M. W. (2001). Children with disabilities. *Monographs of the Society for Research in Child Development, 66*, (Serial No. 266). Ann Arbor, MI: Society for Research in Child Development.

Hayes, A., & Batshaw, M. L. (1993). Down syndrome. *Pediatric Clinics of North America, 40*, 523–535.

Hodapp, R. M. (1995). Definition in mental retardation: Effects on research, practice, and perceptions. *School Psychology Quarterly, 10,* 24–28.

Hodapp, R. M., Leckman, J. F., Dykens, E. M., Sparrow, S. S., Zelinsky, D. C., & Ort, S. I. (1992). K-ABC profiles in children with fragile X syndrome, Down syndrome, and non-specific mental retardation. *American Journal of Mental Deficiency, 97,* 39–46.

Individuals with Disabilities Education Act Amendments of 1997. Public Law No. 105-17, III, Stat 37, (1997).

Infant Health and Development Program. (1990). Enhancing the outcomes of low-birth-weight, premature infants. *Journal of the American Medical Association, 263,* 3035–3042.

Jacobson, J. W., & Mulick, J. A. (1996). Introduction. In J. W. Jacobson & J. A. Mulick (Eds.), *Manual of diagnosis and professional practice in mental retardation* (pp. 1–8). Washington, DC: American Psychological Association.

Johnson, G. O. (1950). Social position of mentally handicapped children in regular grades. *American Journal of Mental Deficiency, 55,* 60–89.

Kaminer, R. K., & Cohen, H. J. (1988). How do you say, "Your child is retarded?" *Contemporary Pediatrics, 5,* 36–49.

Kamphaus, R. W., Reynolds, C. R., & Imperato-McCammon, C. (1999). Roles of diagnosis and classification in school psychology. In C. R. Reynolds & T. B. Gutkin (Eds.), *The handbook of school psychology* (3rd ed., pp. 292–306). New York: Wiley.

Kelly, J. F., Moriset, C. E., Barnard, K. E., Hammond, M. R., & Booth, C. L. (1996). The influence of early mother-child interaction on preschool cognitive/linguistic outcomes in a high-social-risk group. *Infant Mental Health Journal, 17,* 310–321.

King, B. H., State, M. W., Shah, B., Davanzo, P., & Dykens, E. (1997). Mental retardation: A review of the past 10 years. Part I. *Journal of the American Academy of Child and Adolescent Psychiatry, 36,* 1656–1663.

Larry P. v. Riles, 495 Supp 926 (ND Cal 1979).

Larry P. v. Riles, 495 F Supp 926 (ND Cal 1979), att'd in part, rev'd in part, 793 F 2d 969 (9th Cir 1986).

LeCouteur, A., Rutter, M., Lord, C., Rios, P., Robertson, S., Holdgrafer, M., et al. (1989). Autism Diagnostic Interview: A standardized investigation-based instrument. *Journal of Autism and Developmental Disorders, 19,* 363–387.

Lord, C., & Rutter, M. (1994). Autism and pervasive developmental disorders. In M. Rutter, E. Taylor, & L. Hersov (Eds.), *Child and adolescent psychiatry* (pp. 569–593). Boston: Blackwell.

Luckasson, R., Borthwick-Duffy, S., Buntinx, W. H. E., Coulter, D. L., Craig, E. M., Reeve, A., et al. (2002). *Mental retardation: Definition, classification, and systems of supports* (10th ed.). Washington, DC: American Association on Mental Retardation.

Luckasson, R., Coulter, D. A., Polloway, E. A., Reiss, S., Schalock, R. L., Snell, M. E., et al. (1992). *Mental retardation: Definition, classification, and systems of supports* (9th ed.). Washington, DC: American Association on Mental Retardation.

MacMillan, D. L., Gresham, F. M., & Siperstein, G. N. (1995). Heightened concerns over the 1992 AAMR definition: Advocacy versus precision. *American Journal on Mental Retardation, 100,* 87–97.

MacMillan, D. L., Gresham, F. M., Siperstein, G. N., & Bocian, K. M. (1996). The labyrinth of IDEA: School decisions on referred students with subaverage general intelligence. *American Journal on Mental Retardation, 101,* 161–174.

MacMillan, D. L., Jones, R. L., & Aloia, G. F. (1974). The mentally retarded label: A theoretical analysis and review of research. *American Journal of Mental Deficiency, 79,* 241–261.

Mars, A. E., Mauk, J. E., & Dowrick, P. W. (1998). Symptoms of pervasive developmental disorders as observed in prediagnostic home videos of infants and toddlers. *Journal of Pediatrics, 132,* 500–504.

Myers, B. A. (1989). Misleading cues in the diagnosis of mental retardation and infantile autism in the preschool child. *Mental Retardation, 27,* 85–90.

Osterling, J., & Dawson, G. (1994). Early recognition of children with autism: A study of first birthday home videotapes. *Journal of Autism and Developmental Disorders, 24,* 247–257.

Quine, L., & Pahl, J. (1986). First diagnosis of severe mental handicap: Characteristics of unsatisfactory encounters between doctors and patients. *Social Science and Medicine, 22,* 52–62.

Quine, L., & Rutter, D. R. (1994). First diagnosis of severe mental and physical disability: A study of doctor-parent communication. *Journal of Child Psychology and Psychiatry, 35,* 1273–1287.

Ramey, C. T., Mulvihill, B. A., & Ramey, S. L. (1996). Prevention: Social and educational factors and early intervention. In J. W. Jacobson & J. A. Mulick (Eds.), *Manual of diagnosis and professional practice in mental retardation* (pp. 215–227). Washington, DC: American Psychological Association.

Ramey, C. T., & Ramey, S. L. (1992). Effective early intervention. *Mental Retardation, 6,* 337–345.

Reynolds, C. R., Lowe, P. A., & Saenz, A. L. (1999). The problem of bias in psychological assessment. In C. R. Reynolds & T. B. Gutkin (Eds.), *The handbook of school psychology* (3rd ed., pp. 549–595). New York: Wiley.

Rutter, M., Lord, C., & LeCouteur, A. (1995). *Autism Diagnostic Interview* (Rev. 3rd ed.). Available from C. Lord, Department of Psychiatry, University of Chicago.

Sattler, J. M. (1988). *Assessment of children* (3rd ed.). San Diego, CA: Author.

Sattler, J. M. (2001). *Assessment of children: Cognitive applications* (4th ed.). San Diego, CA: Author.

Schalock, R. L. (2002). What's in a name? *Mental Retardation, 40,* 59–61.

Schopler, E., Reicher, R. J., & Renner, B. R. (1988). *The Childhood Autism Rating Scale.* Los Angeles: Western Psychological Services.

Siperstein, G. N., Budoff, M., & Bak, J. J. (1980). Effects of the labels "mentally retarded" and "retarded" on the social acceptability of mentally retarded children. *American Journal of Mental Deficiency, 84,* 596–601.

Smith, M. L. (1980). Meta-analysis of research on teacher expectations. *Evaluation in Education, 4,* 53–55.

Spiker, D., & Hopmann, M. R. (1997). The effectiveness of early intervention for children with Down syndrome. In M. J. Guralnick (Ed.), *The effectiveness of early intervention* (pp. 271–305). Baltimore: Brookes.

Stein, R. E. K. (2000). Commentary: Can one size fit all? *Journal of Clinical Epidemiology, 53,* 111–112.

Svarstad, B. L., & Lipton, H. L. (1977). Informing parents about mental retardation: A study of professional communication and parent acceptance. *Social Science and Medicine, 11,* 645–651.

Turnbull, R., Turnbull, A., Warren, S., Eidelman, S., & Marchand, P. (2002). Shakespeare redux, or Romeo and Juliet revisited: Embedding a terminology and name change in a new agenda for the field of mental retardation. *Mental Retardation, 40,* 65–70.

Verdugo, M. A., Bermejo, B. G., & Fuertes, J. (1995). The maltreatment of intellectually handicapped children and adolescents. *Child Abuse and Neglect, 19,* 205–215.

Vig, S., & Jedrysek, E. (1996). Application of the 1992 AAMR definition: Issues for preschool children. *Mental Retardation, 34,* 244–253.

Vig, S., Kaminer, R. K., & Jedrysek, E. (1987). A later look at borderline and mildly retarded preschoolers. *Developmental and Behavioral Pediatrics, 8,* 12–17.

Volkmar, F. R., Burack, J. A., & Cohen, D. J. (1990). Deviance and developmental approaches in the study of autism. In R. M. Hodapp, J. A. Burack, & E. Zigler (Eds.), *Issues in the developmental approach to mental retardation* (pp. 246–271). New York: Cambridge University Press.

Walsh, K. K. (2002). Thoughts on changing the term mental retardation. *Mental Retardation, 40,* 70–75.

Warren, S. (2002). The name game. Part 2. *AAMR News and Notes, Spring, 2002, 3,* 8.

Wetherby, A. M., & Prizant, B. (1993). *Communication and Symbolic Behavior Scales.* Itasca, IL: Riverside.

Wishart, J. G. (1993). The development of learning difficulties in children with Down's syndrome. *Journal of Intellectual Disability Research, 37,* 389–403.

World Health Organization. (1993). *Classification of mental and behavioral disorders: Diagnostic criteria for research* (10th ed.). Geneva, Switzerland: Author.

World Health Organization. (2001). *International classification of functioning, disability, and health.* Geneva, Switzerland: Author.

Yoshida, R. K., & Meyers, C. E. (1995). Effects of labeling as educable mentally retarded on teachers' expectancies for change in a student's performance. *Journal of Educational Psychology, 67,* 521–527.

Zero to Three/National Center for Clinical Infant Programs. (1994). *Diagnostic classification of mental health and developmental disorders of infancy and early childhood.* Arlington, VA: Author.

Zetlin, A., & Murtaugh, M. (1990). Whatever happened to those with borderline IQs? *American Journal on Mental Retardation, 94,* 463–469.

Zigler, E., Balla, D., & Hodapp, R. M. (1986). On the definition and classification of mental retardation. *American Journal of Mental Deficiency, 89,* 215–230.

The Self-Esteem Fallacy*

Richard M. Foxx
Constance E. Roland
Penn State Harrisburg

Given the obsession with self-esteem among the general public, regular educators and therapists (Roland & Foxx, 2003), it should come as no surprise that it is ardently espoused as being of great importance for individuals with developmental disabilities. This is especially true of those advocating for educational inclusion (Jacobson, 2000) because assessment of one's inclusionary status is thought to determine one's self-esteem. Yet, a close examination of self-esteem reveals that it easily meets the definition of a fad, as there is little or no empirical evidence that it is of any real value to those having or lacking it (Roland & Foxx, 2003). Self-esteem also has been labeled as a myth and a major contributor to overindulgent childrearing practices (Damon, 1995).

We begin by looking at why the general public and the psychological/educational community view self-esteem as important. We next examine why its importance is highly questionable. The chapter concludes with a case from a due process hearing that illustrates how those touting inclusion in the education of individuals with developmental disabilities and autism have linked it to increases in the self-esteem of special and regular education students that make no educational sense.

A BRIEF HISTORY

The concept of self-esteem is grounded in the theories of self-concept. As such, self-esteem is a self-evaluation of competency ratios and opinions of significant others that results in either a positive or negative evaluation of one's worthiness. James first discussed self-esteem as part of his theory of self-concept (Marsh, Byrne, & Shavelson, 1992). His definition of *social self* (the importance of the evaluations of others) is closer to what we currently regard as self-esteem than what he described

*The authors greatly appreciate the critical comments of Edmond Tiryak on an earlier version of the chapter.

as self-esteem. Brown (1993) has argued that self-esteem is grounded in affective, rather than cognitive, processes and that feelings are most important to individuals. Thus, individuals do not just think positive or negative thoughts about themselves, they feel good or bad about themselves.

When individuals seek inclusion in a group or when their inclusionary status within a group is threatened, they are motivated to behave in ways that will maintain their inclusion or increase the potential for inclusion. This motivation could be positive, for example, attending and participating in math club and wearing a pocket protector in order to be accepted as a math whiz, or negative, for example, defacing a school building in order to be accepted as a gang member. In effect, in their effort to increase self-esteem, individuals can behave without serious thought as to positive or negative consequences of their actions.

Self-esteem is regarded as a key to understanding normal, abnormal, and optimal behavior (Bednar, Wells, & Peterson, 1989; Markus & Wurf, 1987; Wells & Marwell, 1976). Many parents and caregivers believe that if their children or charges do not feel good about themselves, that is, have high self-esteem, they will be at risk for any number of emotional and psychological problems. Higher levels of self-esteem are said to be associated with high ego functioning, personal adjustment, internal control, favorable therapy outcomes, positive adjustment to old age, and autonomy (Bednar et al., 1989). A lack of self-esteem is suggested to be related to negative outcomes, including some mental disorders such as depression and suicide (Marciano & Kazdin, 1994) and social problems such as substance abuse, teen pregnancies, school dropout rates, and delinquency (Mecca, Smelser, & Vasconcellos, 1989).

Many therapists have accepted the notion that if "we could only enhance their self-esteem, then everything would be so much better" (Mruk, 1995, p. 57). Parallel with the belief that low self-esteem causes emotional distress and dysfunctional behavior is the belief that high self-esteem is related to optimal mental health. "Its general importance to a full spectrum of effective human behaviors remains virtually uncontested" (Bednar et al., 1989, p. 1). Branden, one of the leading popularizers of self-esteem, stated that he could not think of a single psychological problem that was not traceable to low self-esteem (Branden, 1994). He also believed that as someone's self-esteem increased, there was an increased likelihood of that person treating others with respect, kindness, and generosity. Mecca et al. (1989) identified self-esteem as a causal factor in personal and social responsibility.

In 1986, The California Task Force on the Importance of Self-Esteem embarked on a major effort to prove scientifically that low self-esteem is a causal factor of the types of behavior that become social problems. "We all know this to be true, and it is not really necessary to create a special California task force on the subject to convince us. The real problem we must address … is how we can determine that it is scientifically true" (Smelser, 1989, p. 8). The task force's work included review of several thousands of studies and journal articles; yet, it was unable to find more than a weak correlation between behavior and self-esteem. "The news most consistently reported, however, is that associations between self-esteem and its expected consequences are mixed, insignificant, or absent" (p. 15). Despite the lack of scientific evidence supporting their contention, the task force continued to argue for programs designed to increase self-esteem.

THE NATIONAL PREOCCUPATION WITH SELF-ESTEEM

Some have raised concerns regarding "the national preoccupation" with self-esteem (e.g., Baumeister, Heatherton, & Tice, 1994; Dawes, 1994; Leary & Downs, 1995; Mruk, 1995; Pipher, 1997). Baumeister et al. (1994) perhaps said it best: "In our view, America is not suffering from low self-esteem. It suffers from a spreading epidemic of self-regulation failure" (p. 5).

There is a growing body of evidence that contradicts the overall popular belief that high self-esteem is the antidote to emotional and behavioral problems. Self-serving attributions, a strategy often employed to increase self-esteem, can create social difficulties when others realize that this tactic is in use (Forysth, Berger, & Mitchell, 1981). Baumeister, Heatherton, and Tice (1993), found that in situations where ego was threatened, high self-esteem individuals allowed self-enhancing illusions to affect decision processes and committed themselves to goals they were unable to meet. There is also an association between excessively high self-esteem and high dysfunctional and undesirable behaviors, as studies have found relationships between high self-esteem and childhood bullying (Olweus, 1994), rape (Scully, 1991), and violence in youth and adult gangs (Jankowski, 1991). A multi-disciplinary review of studies related to aggression, violence, and crime conducted by Baumeister, Smart, and Boden (1996), found "that violence appears to be most commonly a result of threatened egotism—that is highly favorable views of self that are disputed by some person or some circumstance" (p. 5). Baumeister et al. (1996) added that history is replete with atrocities committed against humanity by individuals who, because of their sense of superiority, believed they had the right to manipulate, dominate, and harm others.

The public "self-esteem fallacy" in the popular culture is a direct result of psychologists emphasizing its importance. Although it was noted in 1959 that individuals who seek psychological help are often suffering from feelings of unworthiness, inadequacy, and anxiety (Coopersmith, 1967), psychologists really became enamored with self-esteem in the 1970s. Pipher (1997) suggested that many therapists trained in the 1970s are made uneasy by issues of morality: "Speaking in terms of duty was called 'musterbation,' and the worst word in the English Language was 'should' " (p. 123). She continued by explaining that clients have been shaped and taught to expect their therapists to agree with them and be concerned only with how they feel. Baumeister et al. (1994) suggested that understanding self-esteem and one's identity became important when the baby boomers were in their adolescence and trying to "find" themselves.

Moskowitz (2001) finds that Americans reflexively turn to psychological cures involving, among other things, a consideration of self-esteem to be troubling because so many of these cures are vapid therapies that involve no rigorous psychological thinking.

By focusing on self-esteem instead of good character, therapists often end up feeding narcissism. When clients are concerned mostly with "massaging the self" (Pipher, 1997, p. 158), they neglect the work that is necessary to build a solid foundation for meaningful personal behavioral change. The American educational system has also been affected by this "fallacy" as evidenced in the subordinating of its standards to the "fostering of self-esteem independent of performance" (Herrnstein & Murray, 1994, p. 432).

As noted earlier, individuals who focus on maintaining or enhancing their self-esteem may not be objectively evaluating their responses. Sometimes the quest to feel good results in dysfunctional or dangerous behaviors (Baumeister, 1991; Mecca et al., 1989). Leary and Downs (1995) believe that if individuals do not "engage in an adequate conscious and rational assessment of the consequences of engaging in such behaviors" (p. 139), they may attempt to maintain self-esteem at a personal cost.

Dawes (1994) suggested that the most prevalent cultural and therapeutic belief is that childhood experiences are the major determinant of adult behavior, especially those that enhance or diminish self-esteem. This has led to the belief, despite virtually no empirical evidence, that self-esteem is a causal variable of behavior.

Pipher (1997) has found in her years as a therapist that many adults try to bolster their self-esteem with self-affirmation tapes and self-help books. These media are designed to convince the listeners or readers that they are good people and should feel good. Although these messages may benefit some people, they mask the need for concrete changes in one's goals and behaviors (Dawes, 1994). If one's work is meaningless or one's relationships are fragmented, approaches are needed that are specific in terms of the behaviors that can bring about change (e.g., Borkovec & Costello, 1993; Halford, Sanders, & Behrens, 1994).

Based on his sociometer theory, Leary (1999) has suggested that "some people ought to have low self-esteem" (p. 215). Those who behave in destructive and inappropriate ways that lead to exclusion experience low self-esteem because their sociometer has accurately detected that they are unwanted. McFarlin, Baumeister, and Blaskovich (1984) found that individuals scoring high on measures of self-esteem may engage in nonproductive persistence. They concluded that "high self-esteem can mean delusionally conceited as easily as low self-esteem can mean pathologically insecure" (p. 153). Some have suggested that one of the reasons parents are having difficulty raising self-sufficient children is that they have become overly concerned with the development of specific talents in order to raise their children's self-esteem. Parents are hurrying to take their children to coaches, tutors, and private teachers rather than spending time teaching them common sense and responsibility. In effect, children are being outsourced, rather than learning self-reliance. In his discussion of the childrearing literature of the past few decades, Damon (1995) noted that by focusing on self-esteem boosting rather than pride of achievement, parents have encouraged self-centeredness in their children and adolescents.

In terms of therapy and societal functioning, a system that demands accountability and responsibility from individuals seeking or providing services has little use for self-esteem (Roland & Foxx, 2003). A therapist's first responsibility is to provide services that have sound empirical evidence demonstrating their effectiveness. Dawes (1994) reported that many mental health professionals have abandoned the commitment made at psychology's inception, that is, "to establish a mental health profession that would be based on research findings, employing insofar as possible well-validated techniques and principles" (p. vii). Rather, many mental health professionals base their treatment protocols on an "intuitive understanding" that they have gained from experience, rather than on the large body of research that has developed over the last 40 years. After reviewing a large body of empirical investigations and summaries of investigations, Dawes concluded that those who practice from an intuitive basis are no more effective than minimally trained professionals who lack the credentials for licensure. Of major concern is the profound effect that mental health professionals, working without a scientific basis for their "expertise," have had on the cultural beliefs regarding "what constitutes a good life, what types of behavior are desirable, and—most important—how people 'should' feel about the world" (p. 9).

In discussing the implications of the sociometer hypothesis for clinical and counseling psychology, Leary (1999) suggested that low self-esteem may be an indication of the underlying nature of a problem: "a sense of relational devaluation or rejection" (p. 26). It is not, however, the cause of dysfunctional behavior or emotional distress. Therefore, instead of approaching therapy as an attempt to raise self-esteem, therapists should focus on helping the client to understand the circumstances surrounding their feelings of relational devaluation (Roland & Foxx, 2003). If rejection is a result of such behaviors as lack of social skills, aggressive behavior, or faulty cognitions, it is appropriate to develop a behavioral or cognitive-behavioral plan with measurable objectives that address these deficits. Leary noted that strategies designed to raise self-esteem by teaching behaviors to increase social acceptance (i.e., social skills, self-control) are valuable. On the other hand, strategies that rely on messages designed to convince individuals that they should feel good about themselves may discourage them from taking action to resolve real problems. When unfair rejection underlies feelings of low self-esteem, it is important for clients to understand that self-esteem is not a reflection of individual worth, but simply a measure of how others have treated or regard them. Leary contended that if individuals understand unwarranted rejection as a result of others' weaknesses and shortcomings, they can learn to avoid self-deprecation and form relationships in which they are valued.

The sociometer hypothesis (Leary & Downs, 1995; Leary, Tambor, Terdal, & Downs, 1995; Leary, 1999) proposed that high self-esteem is related to perceived inclusion. Furthermore, there were no criteria regarding the characteristics of the social group providing the exclusionary or inclusionary cues. Therefore, when individuals do not have competing motivations that prevent association with a particular group, they may allow their self-esteem needs to be met by destructive or criminal individuals and social groups. Dishion, Patterson, and Griesler (1994) reported that the strongest correlate of antisocial behavior in adolescents is association with deviant peers. Despite findings that antisocial children are disliked by peers (Coie & Kupersmidt, 1983; Dishion, 1990; Dodge, 1983) and are deficient in critical social, academic, and problem-solving skills (Dishion, Loeber, Stouthamer-Loeber, & Patterson, 1984; Freedman, Rosenthal, Donahoe, Schlundt, & McFall, 1978), antisocial adolescents report large peer networks (Dishion, Andrews, & Crosby, 1995). These studies demonstrate that antisocial adolescents are able to meet their needs for inclusion and may very well experience high self-esteem despite engaging in behaviors that display disrespect for themselves and others. Recognizing this, some school-based character building programs have attempted to point out that bad behavior should pose a threat to one's self-esteem because it is important to really feel good about yourself (Hunter, 2000).

In summary, the current public conception of self-esteem, its emphasis on "feeling good," and the potential benefits that feeling good has on the individual and on society have created behavior that can be destructive to the self and society. When individuals are encouraged to do whatever is necessary to feel good about themselves, rather than to tackle the hard work necessary to effect behavioral change and psychological growth, neither they nor society benefits. Glennon, author of *200 Ways to Raise a Girl's Self-Esteem* (1999), made this point clearly when he stated that he wondered if nurturing his daughter's self-esteem had a dark side because he had neglected to develop her wisdom and compassion. From the dark side, he saw three major problems emerging: entitlement, control, and intolerance (Glennon, 2002).

We have argued elsewhere that self-respect is more important to individual functioning than self-esteem (Roland & Foxx, 2003). The major distinction between the two concepts is that whereas competency ratios and others' opinions are central to self-esteem, autonomy is central to self-respect. In contrast to self-esteem, individuals with self-respect are not dependent on the opinions or presence of others and display increased accountability and responsibility because their feelings of worthiness come from their consideration of themselves and others and their attainment of their goals and aspirations (Roland and Foxx, 2003).

Self-esteem appears to be an important concern of advocates for educational inclusion. Jacobson (2000) reported that his survey of ERIC from 1990 to 2000 revealed 85 references to the key terms *inclusion and self-esteem* but only 45 to *mental retardation* and *self-esteem*. Yet, Daniel and King (1997) suggested that inclusive groupings are associated with greater instances of behavior problems, student gains in only one instructional area, and lowered levels of self-esteem. The following case supports their contention as well as a number of the points made in Kauffman and Hallahan (1995).

THE SELF-ESTEEM/INCLUSION ILLUSION: A CASE EXAMPLE

Several years ago one of the authors was asked by a school district to evaluate whether or not a 10-year-old boy's educational needs were being met. The school district had requested an Individual with Disabilities Education Act (IDEA) hearing before a special education officer because it contended that it could not provide FAPE (A free and appropriate public education) to the boy by keeping him in a regular classroom as his parents and their inclusion expert insisted. Rather, the district sought to place the boy in a resource setting for several hours per day. The author's evaluation included a review of voluminous records; the inclusion expert's reports over the years; interviews with the boy's teachers, aide, and parents, the school principal, the school district's special education director, and attorney; and direct observations of the boy in all of his school settings. After filing the report, the author would be serving as the school's expert witness at the hearing.

The boy was nonverbal, not toilet trained, aggressive, and took food from others in the cafeteria. In kindergarten through second grade, he was included in regular education classes with support from a one-to-one aide in the classroom and received one hour per day of pull-out services from a special education teacher. In Grades 3 and 4, he continued to be included in regular education classes and receive one-to-one support but his pull-out services were terminated.

By Grade 5, the school district requested the IDEA hearing because it contended that it could not provide FAPE to the boy in the regular classroom but could do so in a resource setting. The district noted that over the prior 2 years, it had been very difficult to either schedule an ARD (Areas of Disagreement) meeting with the parents, finish a meeting, or participate in a meeting that was not highly contentious. Perhaps not surprisingly, one item from a list of points of agreement between the school and parents was that the boy's diaper would be checked each hour and changed if appropriate.

The battle lines were clearly drawn. The school district, with the author serving as an expert, sought to meet the boy's educational needs via a plan that addressed his needs and level of functioning. The parents, local advocacy group and its attorneys, and an inclusion expert sought to maintain the status quo wherein the boy remained included throughout most of the school day. One of their bedrock issues, was that the boy's "self-esteem" as well as that of his regular education classmates would and had been positively affected by the inclusion experience.

To frame the issues, we shall discuss the reports and classroom observations of the inclusion expert, an independent autism specialist's report and the author.

Inclusion Expert's Reports

The expert's initial inclusion plan and observations were written when the boy was in third grade. It had been followed for 2 years and was a major part of the expert's testimony. A second report was written for the hearing. Both reports had all of the requisite inclusion concepts, buzzwords, and underlying ideology (see Kauffman & Hallahan, 1995).

Inclusion Plan

Inclusion Builds Self-Esteem and Acceptance. The expert indicated that inclusion in regular classroom activities would raise the boy's self-esteem by heightening his feelings of acceptance by classmates and the other students in the school. The regular education teacher was urged to take ownership of the boy in order to have him perceived as a legitimate member of the class. By taking ownership, the teacher would prevent the boy from being "velcroed to his aide and this, in turn, would enhance his positive perception of himself." The students would perceive the boy as a classmate and one of them rather than as a visitor or outsider.

Inclusion Must Be Maintained at All Costs to Prevent a Loss of Self-Esteem. The expert strongly felt that once the boy was accepted by the other students, they would have greater tolerance for the problem behaviors that he was known to display. Furthermore, it was important to his self-esteem that when he had a behavior episode that he remain in the classroom unless it became *"totally impossible to conduct classroom activities or for the other students to attend to their work"* (italics added).

The More Opportunities for Inclusion, the More Appropriate the Service Delivery and the Greater Opportunity to Raise Self-Esteem. The expert equated the appropriateness of service delivery with the extent and number of opportunities available to the boy to participate in the regular curriculum. For example, it was suggested that during spelling exercises, the boy have the opportunity to select the word others were to spell. Picking the word for his classmates was said to be a reward and a way of keeping him on task. Additionally, it would build his self-esteem.

Inclusion Is Learner Centered and Builds Self-Esteem. The report indicated that it was important to make the curriculum inclusive for all students and that doing so offered benefits in regards to self-esteem. Inclusive methods were reported to be much more learner centered than traditional methods. Being learner centered, these methods were uniquely designed to help the student have a positive experience in school. They also were regarded as more creative than traditional methods.

Classroom Observations

The inclusion expert's observations in the classroom revealed the boy's actions did not suggest that his self-esteem was being enhanced by his inclusion experience.

The boy was described as sometimes sitting with other students but not participating in their activities. He appeared distracted and inattentive when other children were asked to interact with him. He seemed bored since he acted tired, closed his eyes and wanted to rest frequently. On some occasions he became quite agitated such as when the lights were turned out or when he attempted to grab food in the cafeteria.

Autism Specialist Report

A year later, an autism specialist was asked to consult on the boy's case. The purpose of the consultation was to help the teaching staff develop strategies for the boy's problem behaviors. The consultant reviewed the boy's records, Individual Education Plan (IEP), and conducted observations at the boy's school on two occasions.

Several issues related to problem behavior were noted. The consultant reported that during lunch, the boy took food from another student's plate. The consultant also saw him grabbing food during a social game. The boy was observed smiling and pulling a staff member's hair and clothing. Other behaviors observed included falling asleep at his desk or on the floor. He observed some instances of stereotypy. Other behaviors reported but not observed included biting and kicking other students, and banging objects. One of the consultant's suggested interventions was to coach the boy's classmates to be ready to block his attempts to steal food or aggress.

The inclusion plan and regular classroom did not seem to be appropriate for meeting the boy's educational needs. The consultant reported surprise that the boy's IEP contained at least 50 objectives. After identifying priority objectives, the consultant wondered if the regular classroom was the best environment in which to achieve them. The academic objectives on the boy's IEP that were part of his inclusion plan were especially troublesome. Although the goal of the inclusion plan was for the boy to learn the content of the class, the consultant stated that the boy did not seem capable of processing the language and concepts that would permit this to occur.

The Author's Report

Later that year, one of the authors observed the boy, looked at his records, interviewed all of the relevant parties, and issued a report.

Observations

The boy's preferred activities were observed to be sleeping, flopping, pinching his knees, slapping a ball, hopping up and down, listening to music, and engaging in self-stimulation. He resisted most attempts to have him engage in any activity that was on his academic schedule. It was clear that he was not motivated to engage in activities that made no sense or had no purpose in his world.

During the regular education class math period, the students discussed measures of capacity and weight. The teacher led them in a discussion that included pints, quarts, gallons, ounces, converting ounces to pounds, liters, and metric measurement. The teacher had the children define capacity as the amount of liquid a container could hold. During this period, the boy's aide was attempting to stop him from hopping up and down, tapping his chair, and flopping in his chair and have him look at his desk in an attempt to match some numbers. The whole scene had a surreal aspect to it, which raised the question of just how much valuable educational time had been wasted in the past 5 years.

Conclusions

The author's report contained a number of sharply worded conclusions. One concerned the inclusion expert's assertion that the boy's self-esteem would be raised in a regular classroom. The author pointed out that the expert offered no way of measuring self-esteem or building it other than blind faith. Furthermore, being pulled from a regular class is no more embarrassing or stigmatizing than receiving help in the classroom (Jenkins & Heinen, 1989).

Next, the report addressed the boy's overall lack of progress since kindergarten. He still was not toilet trained although he was capable of mastering this skill (Foxx & Azrin, 1973). His lack of progress in basic independent living skills, communication skills, and social interaction skills was directly attributable to his receiving very little quality one-to-one instruction in a distraction-free environment (Foxx, 1982) such as an effective pull-out program (Kauffman, 1989; Maurice, Green, & Foxx, 2001). It was noted that little had changed from descriptions of the boy's behavioral excesses and deficits reported several years earlier.

The author recommended that the boy's pull-out program consist largely of individualized applied behavior analysis because it is the most effective educational intervention for students with autism/pervasive developmental disorder at the boy's level of functioning (see Matson, Benavidez, Compton, Paclawskyj, & Baglio, 1996). Typically, children in these studies have made substantial, functional gains in several core areas, such as everyday living and communication skills (Jacobson, Mulick, & Green, 1998). Hence, applied behavior analysis must be a major component of any educational intervention effort.

The inclusion plan received criticism. The boy's educational needs were not being met via inclusion and it was preventing him from progressing at a satisfactory rate or achieving goals that are educationally appropriate for him. It simply defied logic to contend that the majority of the boy's educational needs could be met in a general classroom. In this case, the desirability of regular classroom inclusion made no more sense than placing an ICU patient in a general hospital ward for ideological or economic reasons (Diamond, 1995). As Diamond (1995) so aptly put it, "It might ... provide a cheerier setting and support the illusion of normalcy, but that will mean little when the patient dies. I am afraid that extremists who regard the 'least restrictive environment' to be the only classroom in the neighbor school will condemn some of our most precious young people to a dead end, educationally and personally" (p. 252).

The boy's problem behaviors were not being addressed, especially those directed at other students. The boy did not have the right to jeopardize others by his aggressive acts of biting, hitting, pulling hair, or stealing food. These behaviors had the effect of further separating him from the students without disabilities and reducing the amount and quality of his social interactions (see Fuchs & Fuchs, 1994). They also could be construed as a violation of the other students' opportunity to learn in the most appropriate environment (Diamond, 1995).

The report concluded that the dispute between the school district and the boy's parents reflected the division in special education between process (placement with same-aged peers to enhance, among other things, self-esteem) versus outcome (the boy learning) and between social philosophy (inclusion at all costs) versus scholarly research (sound educational practices appropriately developed for an individual).

The due process hearing lasted several days and included testimony by the author, inclusion expert, regular and special education teachers, the school district's special education director, and the boy's parents. The hearing officer ultimately agreed with the school district and concluded that the school district could not continue to provide FAPE to the boy unless he received instruction in a resource setting for several hours per day. The hearing officer did not address whether or not the boy's self-esteem would be affected as a result of the decision.

REFERENCES

Baumeister, R. F. (1991). *Escaping the self.* New York: Basic Books.

Baumeister, R. F., Heatherton, T. F., & Tice, D. M. (1993). When ego threats lead to self-regulation failure: Negative consequences of high self-esteem. *Journal of Personality and Social Psychology, 64*(1), 141–156.

Baumeister, R. F., Heatherton, T. F., & Tice, D. M. (1994). *Losing control: How and why people fail at self-regulation.* San Diego, CA: Academic Press.

Baumeister, R. F., Smart, L., & Boden, J. M. (1996). Relation of threatened egotism to violence and aggression: The dark side of high self-esteem. *Psychological Review, 103*(1), 5–33.

Bednar, R., Wells, G., & Peterson, S. (1989). *Self-esteem: Paradoxes and innovations in clinical theory and practice.* Washington, DC: American Psychological Association.

Borkovec, T. D., & Costello, E. (1993). Efficacy of applied relaxation and cognitive-behavioral therapy in the treatment of generalized anxiety disorder. *Journal of Consulting and Clinical Psychology, 61*(4), 611–619.

Branden, N. (1994). *The six pillars of self-esteem.* New York: Bantam.

Brown, J. D. (1993). Self-esteem and self-evaluation: Feeling is believing. In J. Suls (Ed.), *Psychological perspectives on the self* (Vol. 4, pp. 27–58). Hillsdale, NJ: Lawrence Erlbaum Associates.

Coie, J. D., & Kupersmidt, J. B. (1983). A behavioral analysis of emerging social status in boys' groups. *Child Development, 54,* 1400–1416.

Coopersmith, S. (1967). *The antecedents of self-esteem.* San Francisco: Freeman.

Damon, W. A. (1995). *Greater expectations: Overcoming the culture of indulgence in America's homes and schools*. New York: Free Press.

Daniel, L. G., & King, D. A. (1997). Impact of inclusion education on academic achievement, student behavior and self-esteem, and parental attitudes. *Journal of Educational Research, 91*(2), 67–80.

Dawes, R. M. (1994). *House of cards: Psychology and psychotherapy built on myth*. New York: Free Press.

Diamond, S. C. (1995). Special education and the great god, inclusion. In J. M. Kauffman & D. P. Hallahan (Eds.), *The illusion of full inclusion: A comprehensive critique of a current special education bandwagon* (pp. 247–254). Austin, TX: Pro-Ed.

Dishion, T. J. (1990). The peer context of troublesome child and adolescent behavior. In P. E. Leone (Ed.), *Understanding troubled and troubling youth* (pp. 128–153). Newbury Park, CA: Sage.

Dishion, T. J., Andrews, D. W., & Crosby, L. (1995). Antisocial boys and their friends in early adolescence: Relationship characteristics, quality, and interactional process. *Child Development, 66,* 139–151.

Dishion, T. J., Loeber, R., Stouthamer-Loeber, M., & Patterson, G. R. (1984). Skill deficits and male adolescent delinquency. *Journal of Abnormal Child Psychology, 12*(1), 37–54.

Dishion, T. J., Patterson, G. R., & Griesler, P. C. (1994). Peer adaptations in the development of antisocial behavior: A confluence model. In L. R. Huesmann (Ed.), *Aggressive behavior: Current perspectives* (pp. 61–95). New York: Plenum.

Dodge, K. A. (1983). Behavioral antecedents of peer social status. *Child Development, 54,* 1386–1399.

Forysth, D. R., Berger, R. E., & Mitchell, T. (1981). The effects of self-serving vs. other-serving claims of responsibility on attraction and attribution in groups. *Social Psychology Quarterly, 44* (1), 59–64.

Foxx, R. M. (1982). *Increasing behaviors of persons with severe retardation and autism*. Champaign, IL: Research Press.

Foxx, R. M., & Azrin, N. H. (1973). *Toilet training individuals with developmental disabilities: A rapid program for day and nighttime independent toileting*. Champaign, IL: Research Press.

Freedman, B. J., Rosenthal, L., Donahoe, C. P., Jr., Schlundt, D. G., & McFall, R. M. (1978). A social-behavioral analysis of skill deficits in delinquent and nondelinquent adolescent boys. *Journal of Consulting and Clinical Psychology, 46*(6), 1448–1462.

Fuchs, D., & Fuchs, L. S. (1992). Limitations of a feel-good approach to consultation. *Journal of Educational and Psychological Consultation, 3*(2), 93–97.

Fuchs, D., & Fuchs, L. S. (1994). Inclusive schools movement and the radicalization of special education reform. *Exceptional Children, 60,* 294–309.

Fuchs, D., & Fuchs, L. S. (1995). Inclusive schools movement and the radicalization of special education reform. In J. M. Kauffman & D. P. Hallahan (Eds.), *The illusion of full inclusion: A comprehensive critique of a current special education bandwagon* (pp. 213–242). Austin, TX: Pro-Ed.

Glennon, W. (1999). *200 ways to raise a girl's self-esteem*. York Beach, ME: Conari Press.

Glennon, W. (2002). Her dad: When self-esteem runs amok. *Daughters* (newsletter, p. 1). July/August. Duluth, MN: Dads & Daughters.

Halford, W. K., Sanders, M. R., & Behrens, B. C. (1994). Self-regulation in behavioral couples' therapy. *Behavior Therapy, 25,* 431–452.

Herrnstein, R. J., & Murray, C. (1994). *The bell curve: Intelligence and class structure in American life*. New York: Free Press.

Hunter, J. D. (2000). *The death of character*. New York: Basic Books.

Jacobson, J. W. (2000). Self-esteem: A nod is as good as a wink to a dead horse. *Psychology in Mental Retardation and Developmental Disabilities, 26*(1), 1–6.

Jacobson, J. W., Mulick, J. A., & Green, G. (1998). Cost-benefit estimates for early intensive behavioral intervention for young children with autism: General model and single state case. *Behavioral Interventions, 13,* 201–226.

Jankowski, M. S. (1991). *Islands in the street*. Los Angeles: University of California Press.

Jenkins, J. R., & Heinen, A. (1989). Students' preferences for service delivery: Pull-out, in-class, or integrated models. *Exceptional Children, 55,* 515–523.

Kauffman, J. M. (1989). The regular education initiative as Reagan-Bush educational policy: A trickle-down theory of education of the hard-to teach. *The Journal of Special Education, 23,* 256–278.

Kauffman, J. M., & Hallahan, D. P. (Eds.). (1995). *The illusion of full inclusion: A comprehensive critique of a current special education bandwagon.* Austin, TX: Pro-Ed.

Leary, M. R. (1999). The social and psychological importance of self-esteem. In R. M. Kowalski & M. R. Leary (Eds.), *The social psychology of emotional and behavioral problems* (pp. 197–221). Washington, DC: APA Books.

Leary, M. R., & Downs, D. L. (1995). Interpersonal functions of the self-esteem motive: The self-esteem system as a sociometer. In M. H. Kernis (Ed.), *Efficacy, agency, and self-esteem* (pp. 123–144). New York: Plenum.

Leary, M. R., Tambor, E. S., Terdal, S. K., & Downs, D. L. (1995). Self-esteem as an interpersonal monitor: The sociometer hypothesis. *Journal of Personality and Social Psychology, 68*(3), 518–530.

Marciano, P. L., & Kazdin, A. E. (1994). Self-esteem, depression, hopelessness, and suicidal intent among psychiatrically disturbed inpatient children. *Journal of Clinical Child Psychology, 23,* 151–160.

Markus, H., & Wurf, E. (1987). The dynamic self-concept: A psychological perspective. *Annual Review of Psychology, 38,* 299–337.

Marsh, H. W., Byrne, B. M., & Shavelson, R. J. (1992). A multidimensional, hierarchical self-concept. In T. M. Brinthaupt & R. P. Lipka (Eds.), *The self: Definitional and methodological issues* (pp. 44–95). Albany, NY: State University of New York Press.

Matson, J. L., Benavidez, D. A., Compton, L. S., Paclwaskyj, T., & Baglio, C. (1996). Behavioral treatment of autistic persons: A review of research from 1980 to the present. *Research in Developmental Disabilities, 17,* 433–465.

Maurice, C., Green, G., & Foxx, R. M. (2001). *Making a difference: Behavioral intervention for autism.* Austin, TX: Pro-Ed.

McFarlin, D. B., Baumeister, R. F., & Blascovich, J. (1984). On knowing when to quit: Task failure, self-esteem, advice, and non-productive persistence. *Journal of Personality, 52,* 138–155.

Mecca, A. M., Smelser, N. J., & Vasconcellos, J. (Eds.). (1989). *The social importance of self-esteem.* Berkeley, CA: University of California Press.

Moskowitz, E. S. (2001). *In therapy we trust: America's obsession with self-fulfillment.* Baltimore: Johns Hopkins University Press.

Mruk, C. J. (1995). *Self-esteem: Research, theory, and practice.* New York: Springer.

Olweus, D. (1994). Bullying at school: Long-term outcomes for the victims and an effective school-based intervention program. In L. R. Huesmann (Ed.), *Aggressive behavior: Current perspectives* (pp. 97–130). New York: Plenum.

Pipher, M. (1997). *The shelter of each other.* New York: Ballantine.

Roland, C. E., & Foxx, R. M. (2003). Self-respect as a concept separate from self-esteem. *Philosophical Psychology, 16*(2), 247–287.

Scully, D. (1991). *Understanding sexual violence: A study of convicted rapists.* London: HarperCollins Academic.

Smelser, N. (1989). Self-esteem and social problems: An introduction. In A. M. Mecca, N. J. Smelser, & J. Vasconcellos (Eds.), *The social importance of self-esteem* (pp. 294–326). Berkeley, CA: University of California Press.

Wells, L. E., & Marwell, G. (1976). *Self-esteem: Its conceptualization and measurement.* Beverly Hills, CA: Sage.

8

The Delusion of Full Inclusion

Devery R. Mock
James M. Kauffman
University of Virginia

The place in which instruction occurs—not instruction itself—has become the central issue in special education (Crockett & Kauffman, 1999). "Place-based education" (Smith, 2002) has been described, although it is not explicitly part of the full inclusion movement (FIM) in special education. Place-based education is consistent with the FIM assumption that place either can make or does make instruction effective. Blackman (1992) stated about special education:

> 'Place' is the issue .... *There is nothing pervasively wrong with special education.* What is being questioned is not the interventions and knowledge that have been acquired through special education training and research. Rather, what is being challenged is the location where these supports are being provided to students with disabilities. (p. 29, italics in original)

The ideas that place is the paramount issue, that education should be based on one's location, and that changing the place of instruction is the key to improving it are likely among the most fatuous contemporary notions about teaching and learning. The idea that special education will become effective if we merely change its location may be laughable, but the idea has not been proposed as a joke. To be sure, the place of instruction constrains it, since all instruction cannot be offered with equal finesse and effectiveness in the same place and at the same time (Kauffman & Hallahan, 1997; Kauffman & Lloyd, 1995). However, the logic of this observation merely refutes the FIM.

Of greater concern is that we see the FIM as fitting Worrall's (1990) criteria for fraud or quackery: It is contrary to common sense, inconsistent with what we know about disabilities, and devoid of credible supporting evidence. Fads, pseudotreatments, slogans, and misleading statements have captured the public imagination and the attention of many professional educators today (Kauffman, 2002). One of the most popular pseudotreatments is changing the place in which teaching is proffered. Another is asserting that whatever is or can be offered in a "mainstream" setting (considered by proponents of the FIM as *the* place to be) is better than what is or

113

can be offered in a separate, special setting. That is, proponents of the FIM assume that the normalizing influence of the general education classroom is more important and powerful than specialized, therapeutic interventions, even in the face of evidence that separate, special environments produce better outcomes for some students (e.g., Carlberg & Kavale, 1980; Kavale & Forness, 2000; Stage & Quiroz, 1997). The FIM is consistent not only with Worrall's (1990) description of quackery but also with Shermer's (2001) description of pseudoscience. Shermer describes how pseudoscience claims an apparent scientific revolution, but the claim will not withstand careful scrutiny. Pseudoscience portrays science as too conservative, not open to radical new ideas. "But science is conservative. It cannot afford not to be. It makes rigid demands on its participants in order to weed out the bad ideas from the good" (p. 64).

The idea that place or location is prepotent over the details of instruction is a particularly noxious delusion when special education is under attack. The delusion is especially noxious because it distracts attention from important issues and holds out the false hope that the FIM will result in better instruction for students with disabilities while undercutting fiscal support for special education. Some have suggested in popular media that the cost of special education is too high, in part because of expensive placements (e.g., Cottle, 2001; Soifer, 2002). Much of the additional cost of special education is spent on space (separate classes), staff (special teachers), and intensified instruction (lower pupil-teacher ratios). The FIM thus seems to be cost saving, as more students with disabilities could be served in general education classes by regular teachers, thereby saving at least the costs of space and staff, if not instructional costs as well.

ATTACKS ON SPECIAL EDUCATION

Special education is receiving particularly intense scrutiny at the beginning of the 21st century. Legislators are preparing to correct the "problems" plaguing special education, which some say is a waste of money (Cottle, 2001; Fletcher, 2001). Critics contend that special education misidentifies students and provides them with services that are too expensive and of poor quality. Children in special education, they argue, are prevented from achieving their true potential because disabilities are poorly defined, instructional practices are fragmented, teachers have low expectations and poor training, and students are separated from the mainstream (Alexander, Gray, & Lyon, 1993; Lyon & Fletcher, 2001; Gartner & Lipsky, 1987; Lipsky & Gartner, 1996, 1997, 1998; McGill-Franzen, 1994; Slavin, 2001; Slavin & Madden, 2001a, 2001b). Ending separation from the mainstream is the central focus of the advocates of the FIM. Most critics of special education advocate full inclusion and the dissolution of special education as a separate, identifiable entity. Although special education surely needs significant improvement, it is the improvement of instruction itself—not the place in which it is offered—that is critical (Kauffman, 1999a, 2002; Zigmond, 1997).

The FIM has its historical and conceptual roots in Dunn (1968) and Deno (1970). The publication of Dunn's article was a watershed event in special education (MacMillan, Gresham, & Forness, 1996). Dunn suggested that special education of children with mild mental retardation was morally and educationally wrong because homogenous grouping damaged these children's self-esteem and caused their educational disadvantage. He urged educators to stop "segregating" students through special self-contained programs. Deno (1970) echoed Dunn's concerns and argued against categorizing students in special education. She suggested that special education should "work itself out of business" (p. 233) by giving general educators the techniques it had developed.

The sentiments of Dunn and Deno helped shape the regular education initiative (REI) of the 1980s. The REI was based on the assumption that all students are very much alike, eliminating the necessity of special education for at least many, if not most, students and returning responsibility for many or most students with disabilities to regular classroom teachers (Kavale & Forness, 2000). The FIM of the 1990s, however, carried integration a step further, advocating the complete elimination of special education as a separate entity (see Fuchs & Fuchs, 1994). Proponents of the FIM have called for "a fundamental change of the existing dual, failing, and costly special and general education systems ... toward the broader matter of educating students with disabilities in a unitary system that will prepare them to participate in society" (Lipsky & Gartner, 1997, p. 69). The FIM suggests that the current "dual system" of regular (or general) and special education is especially harmful to students with disabilities.

Opponents of the FIM maintain that the dissolution of special education would be especially harmful to students with disabilities (Kauffman & Hallahan, 1995). Many arguments against full inclusion focus on students whose disabilities are severe and hence particularly troublesome to general education teachers. However, Walker and Bullis (1991) noted that the characteristics of students with behavioral disorders "make delivery of specialized intervention services within regular classrooms highly problematic" (p. 84). Kauffman, Lloyd, Baker, and Riedel (1995) concurred.

Crockett and Kauffman (1998, 1999) described how parents of children with severe disabilities found general education to be unhelpful for their children. Regarding the mother of a child with autism they noted, "She observed that so much is counterintuitive in the treatment of autism that her son Daniel's general education teachers often hinder rather than help him learn to cope with his classroom environment" (Crockett & Kauffman, 1999, p. 180). For students with severe disabilities, even the most basic aspects of general education classrooms (e.g., interactions with peers, unpredictable reinforcement schedules, and environments filled with desks, chairs, books, and many other objects) serve as triggers for problematic behavior. Perhaps the greatest parental objection to full inclusion is that effective teaching of their child is delayed or denied by the placement (Crockett & Kauffman, 1999; Palmer, Fuller, Arora, & Nelson, 2001). Teachers simply cannot teach a general education class effectively and at the same time offer the intensive, focused, relentless instruction that many children with disabilities require if they are to make reasonable progress. Palmer et al. (2001) noted the pros and cons of full inclusion and reported a parent's observations on the matter:

I have two children with disabilities; this survey is about one. He is uncomfortable around other children and in close spaces. He expresses dislike of normal students. He is also disliked by them and they tell me about his behavior when I'm on campus. Mainstreaming to a large extent would not do anyone service in this case.

My other son has been fully and successfully mainstreamed for years. I know the downfalls, I know the up side. I consider mainstreaming as something that *must be de-*

cided on a case-by-case basis. Like any other fad, it is being evangelized as a cure-all. It isn't. It is terrific in some cases. In others, it is child abuse. (p. 482)

Although arguments such as these make evident the problems inherent in educating all students in the general classroom, they do not directly defend a continuum of alternative placements (CAP) for students with less obvious disabilities. The CAP is a wide range of alternative placements, including regular classroom placement, resource rooms, special classes, special day schools, and special residential schools (see Hallahan & Kauffman, 2003, pp. 13–17, for description). Learning disability (LD), for example, is not obvious to the casual observer (Forness, Sinclair, Jura, McCracken, & Cadigan, 2002). The majority of students with LDs now spend most of their instructional day in the regular classroom (U.S. Department of Education, 2000). These students constitute most of the "gray area" in the inclusion debate, the students whose disabilities can most readily be denied or passed off as minor differences that require little or nothing special or as normal variations that general education teachers can easily accommodate. These students are the pawns in the FIM game plan.

ATTACKS ON THE CONTINUUM
OF ALTERNATIVE PLACEMENTS (CAP)

Sarason (2001) discusses society's initial responses to the virus that causes AIDS. After he notes that science, sociology, psychology, and medicine at first responded ineffectively to both the virus and the illness, Sarason concludes that there are lessons to be learned from the AIDS story.

First, when a field is confronted with new and puzzling phenomena, the odds are very high that it will seek to understand them in ways that were productive in the past. Second, that understanding will, for varying lengths of time, turn out to be very oversimple. Third, the approach to the problem will markedly downplay the ways the phenomenon has cause and effect transactions with existing social attitudes, different interest groups .... There are correspondences that can be summed up in two statements: The problem is far more complicated than was initially thought. The more you know, the more you need to know. (pp. 58–59)

The FIM, rife with ignorance and irrelevant claims of cause and maltreatment, may parallel Sarason's example of the AIDS story. Attacks on the CAP make use of strategies and tactics that have been discussed elsewhere (e.g., Kauffman, 1999a, 2002; Sasso, 2001): nonsequiturs, oversimplifications, and willful ignorance.

Nonsequiturs

Special education has been based not merely on the applied sciences of medicine and education but also on the idea of social justice (Mock, Jakubecy, & Kauffman, 2002). In many instances, social advocates organized and worked to secure federal policies that provided both protection and opportunity for individuals with disabilities (Hallahan & Mock, 2003). This is a history that should engender pride; however, it is also a history often predicated more on conviction than observable truth. Kavale, Fuchs, and Scruggs (1994) warned that "without a properly rendered research base, policy analysis becomes policy advocacy because reason alone and the influence of values goes unchecked" (p. 76; see also Sasso, 2001). Advocates of the FIM argue for policies unchecked by empirical science. As Sasso (2001) observes, argument unaccompanied by reliable scientific evidence is simply propaganda.

Stainback, Stainback, East, and Sapon-Shevin (1994), have proposed that the goal of full inclusion is to "create a world in which all people are knowledgeable and supportive of all other people" (p. 487). In this way, their logic suggests, students learn that all persons are equally valued members of society and that inclusion of all persons is the most important of all goals. In yet more impassioned pleas, proponents of the FIM have likened current special education to racial segregation. These arguments are based on a misapplication of the landmark U.S. Supreme Court case, *Brown v. the Board of Education of Topeka* (see Kauffman, 2002; Kauffman & Lloyd, 1995). They evoke shameful memories of legalized racial segregation and define the issue of full inclusion as a matter of civil rights (Gallagher, 1998; Gartner & Lipsky, 1987; Stainback et al., 1994; Stainback, Stainback, & Stefanich, 1996). Additionally, advocates of full inclusion have intensified this emotional appeal, likening current special education to both apartheid (Lipsky & Gartner, 1987) and slavery (Stainback & Stainback, 1988). Through such nonsequiturs, advocates of full inclusion attempt to rally public opinion against special education practices born of concerns for social justice.

Legalized segregation was a far too monstrous and systematic policy to be likened to education in a resource or special class or special school for students with disabilities or to the CAP. Appealing to *Brown* as justification for the FIM trivializes the experiences of those who lived through or currently live with the repercussions of racial segregation. Racial segregation and special education are built on entirely different legal, moral, and educational premises (see Crockett & Kauffman, 1999; Kauffman, 2002; Kauffman & Lloyd, 1995).

However, even if argument from *Brown* were not a nonsequitur, it would not be convincing. In 1954, the Supreme Court (in *Brown*) ordered the desegregation of all public schools. Almost 50 years later, urban schools are more racially segregated than ever before (Sarason, 2001), and citizens in cities like Cincinnati, Ohio, are boycotting hotels, restaurants, and stores in protest of systemic racism (Pierre, 2002). The U.S. Supreme Court decision clearly did not end segregation at the societal or even the school level. Such evidence is clearly disturbing, especially to individuals who had hoped that a simple change in a law or policy would effect immediate social change.

In explaining the naiveté of social scientists who had expected immediate change to accompany the *Brown* ruling, Sarason (2001) wrote, "My own explanation of the unpreparedness of American social science was that it viewed segregation as basically a moral issue and when that moral issue received the appropriate legal-political resolution, implementation would not encounter, except perhaps initially, serious obstacles" (p. 19).

Social scientists distilled the practice of segregation into a single issue of morality. Clearly, they oversimplified a very complex issue. Likewise, when full inclusionists distill criticisms of special education into the single issue of segregation, they also oversimplify a very complex issue in addition to using an argument (segregation) that does not rest on the same premise as special education. They beg the field to solve current problems using tools of the past and tools not appropriate for the problems, and hence to choose social activism over logical thinking and scientific evaluation.

Oversimplifications

Full inclusionists propose redesigning schools to create environments in which all children are known individually and, consequently, have all of their needs met (Lipsky & Gartner, 1997). This utopian goal, apparently shared by some teachers and administrators but rejected by others, may be in some respects inviting, but it is based on oversimplified understandings of schools, students, and research (see Crockett & Kauffman, 1999; Hallahan & Kauffman, 2003; Palmer et al., 2001).

Middle schools and high schools are complex environments. They are often characterized as both balkanized and resistant to change (Sarason, 1990, 2001). It is therefore not surprising that the majority of articles about full inclusion focus on elementary schools. Conceptually, full inclusion becomes more difficult to envision in the upper grades. For instance, would all students be included in calculus? Would all students be included in Spanish-IV? How would placement decisions be made so as not to exclude any student?

The policy of full inclusion would affect all students with disabilities, more than half of whom receive educational services in middle or high school settings. McIntosh, Vaughn, Schumm, Haager, and Lee (1993) studied the instruction offered to students with LD in mainstreamed high school classes. They found that teachers provided few adaptations, and instruction was generally not differentiated to meet the needs of students with disabilities. Students with LD infrequently asked the teacher for help, seldom volunteered to answer questions, and interacted with both the teacher and peers at a low rate. At present, there is not sufficient empirical evidence to support the full inclusion of students with LD, much less students with other more severe disabilities, at the middle or high school level.

Lipsky and Gartner (1997) suggested that to successfully accomplish full inclusion, general educators should use instructional strategies that experienced and qualified teachers use for all children. These strategies included (a) cooperative learning, (b) curricular modifications, and (c) whole language instruction. Each of these recommended strategies will now be examined in the light of relevant empirical data.

In cooperative learning, teachers group students to work together on assigned tasks. These tasks may range from practicing teacher-taught skills to attempting to discover new, student-identified knowledge. Tateyama-Sniezek (1990) reviewed 12 studies in which cooperative learning was the independent variable and academic achievement the dependent variable, finding that the opportunity for students to study together did not guarantee gains in academic achievement. Over 10 years later, McMaster and Fuchs (2002) conducted another literature review of cooperative learning. They concluded that the use of empirically supported cooperative elements may be an important, but not a sufficient, determinant of cooperative learning's effectiveness, specifically for students with LD. A reasonable person would ask, "Why would we expect classmates to be better at helping LD students learn than professional teachers using an empirically validated curriculum?"

The curricular adaptations that full inclusionists advocate are reminiscent of medicines dispensed to cure all that ails a person, better known as quack remedies (see Worrall, 1990). That is, teachers are urged to dispense weak, palliative treatments in response to problems that are often quite severe. Proponents of full inclusion often fail to specify whether these adaptations (which may range from special seating arrangements to modified assignments) are in fact accommodations or modifications. Additionally, many descriptions are such that it is difficult to ascertain how the adaptation is implemented, let alone how it is to be effective. For example, Stainback et al. (1996) wrote:

> For many students an objective for a lesson may be to learn to write letters to friends. But for other students a more appropriate objective might include dictating a letter into a tape recorder .... Developing separate or different objectives for one or a few students can lead to their isolation or segregation within the classroom. (p. 14)

Given such an assumption, it is difficult to understand how the decision to adapt a curriculum is to be made. Despite this level of ambiguity, Stainback et al. (1996) assure readers that developing curricular accommodations is relatively easy. Research in both testing and instructional accommodations demonstrates that nothing could be further from the truth (Bielinski, Ysseldyke, Bolt, Friedebach, & Friedebach, 2001; Fuchs & Fuchs, 2001; Johnson, Kimball, & Brown, 2001; Pitoniak & Royer, 2001).

Fuchs, Fuchs, Hamlett, Phillips, and Karns (1995) found that the instructional adaptations that general educators make for students with LD are typically oriented to the group, not the individual, and are relatively minor in substance. Additionally, Fuchs et al. (1995) observe that most adaptations are made in a rather indiscriminate manner, thus questioning the very validity of both the adaptation and the instruction. In another study, McIntosh et al. (1993) reported that due to inappropriate adaptation of class work, as well as instruction aimed at the large group, most students with LD were not engaged in the learning process. Instructional adaptations do not appear to have the palliative effect that full inclusionists have described.

Stainback et al. (1996) also encouraged readers to implement constructivist practices such as whole language in full inclusion classrooms. The 1980s whole-language instructional approach was introduced by reformers who openly and explicitly rejected the value of quantitative evidence of effectiveness and held to the belief that learning to read is as simple as learning to speak (Dudley-Marling & Fine, 1997; Garan, 1994; Goodman, 1992, 1994). Using this philosophy, specific skill instruction was abandoned in favor of a focus on the reading process as a whole—reading as using language rather than reading as decoding written language. After the whole language philosophy had been implemented, the results of the 1992 and 1994 National Assessment of Educational Progress demonstrated that more than 40% of fourth graders instructed using a whole language approach were unable to read grade-appropriate texts (Adams, 1997). Researchers have since questioned the way in which whole language was so universally adopted in the absence of any credible evidence of its efficacy (Adams, 1995; Slavin, 2001). The lessons from this example are multiple. Whole language does not have sufficient evidence to warrant its use with students with or without disabilities. Additionally, wholesale changes in educational practice in the absence of empirical support have proven harmful to student progress.

Willful Ignorance

The research we have reviewed to this point illustrates that the FIM is based on false premises. However, other research and, in addition, misrepresentations of research by proponents of the FIM, also reveals that full inclusion will not withstand careful scrutiny.

Beginning with the REI, supporters of inclusionary practices have used efficacy studies to question the effectiveness of special education practices (Kavale & Forness, 2000). Research outcomes that demonstrated a lack of efficacy for resource room models served as an impetus for the FIM (Lyon, Fletcher, Shaywitz, Shaywitz, Torgesen, Wood, et al., 2001). For example, Lipsky and Gartner (1997) wrote:

> Outcomes for students who participate in the separate special education system are severely limited. This is true across a variety of metrics: dropout rates, graduation rates, postsecondary education and training, employment, and residential independence. The widespread failures that are documented in the special education system provide a strong basis for change. (p. 11)

Other studies (Rea, McLaughlin, & Walther-Thomas, 2002; Wallace, Anderson, Bartholomay, & Hupp, 2002) suggested that students in general education classrooms achieved better outcomes on some measures than did their peers in pull-out programs. Unfortunately, these studies and others like them violated at least one standard of rigorous empirical research: random assignment to treatment groups. Thus, the more able students with LD were served in general education classrooms while their more disabled peers were served in resource rooms. This difference in disability level accounts for some of the differences in the outcomes.

Additionally, advocates of full inclusion use efficacy studies to suggest that current special education practices cause students with disabilities to fall further behind their general education peers. Ysseldyke and Bielinski (2002) found this assertion untenable. In monitoring a group of students who remained classified as LD over a 5-year period, the researchers found that the rate of progress for this group remained relatively constant. When this group was modified to account for students placing in and out of the LD category, the mean achievement level dropped and the gap widened. Ysseldyke and Bielinski explained that students with higher achievement placed out of special education and were then replaced by newly identified students with lower achievement. This change in group membership resulted in lower mean achievement for those receiving special education. Ysseldyke and Bielinski concluded that special education group membership should not be a focus in examining achievement trends. Simmerman and Swanson (2001) found that when researchers failed to (a) control for teacher effects, (b) establish a criterion level of instructional performance, (c) use standardized measures, (d) use the same measures between pretest and posttest, (e) control for sample heterogeneity, and (f) use the correct unit of analysis, they reported inflated or unreliable treatment outcomes. Thus, the efficacy studies used to discredit special education practices are compromised by methodological shortcomings and do not warrant the dissolution of special education's continuum of alternative placements (CAP).

Proponents of full inclusion tend to disregard the nature of cause and effect transactions as they pertain to disability. Lipsky and Gartner (1996) wrote, "For students with disabilities, the critical challenge will be how we view and treat difference—as an abnormality or as an aspect of the human condition" (p. 788). The sentiment expressed in that statement is profound; yet, the reality conveyed is overly simplified. Perhaps the critical challenge for an individual will be, as Lipsky and Gartner asserted, to feel included and accepted, but perhaps the critical challenge will be to learn to read or to learn to feed oneself. Additionally, social acceptance of a disability does not cause the disability to vanish. Disability status is not merely a matter of semantics. Perhaps the critical question is whether we assume that all human conditions deserve the same treatment or, if not, treatment in the same location.

Critics of special education often distill disability into an absolute set of measurable constructs. Many researchers guilty of this oversimplification do not define themselves as full inclusionists; yet, they propose reforms that would, in all likelihood, result in full inclusion. Lyon and Fletcher (2001) explained the causes of the prevalence of LD in this way:

> We propose that the rise in the incidence of LD is largely the result of three factors. First, remediation is rarely effective after 2nd grade. Second, measurement practices today work against identifying LD children before 2nd grade. Third, federal policy and the sociology of public education itself allow ineffective policies to continue unchecked. (p. 2)

Lyon and Fletcher (2001) seem to imply that controlling these three variables will result in the disappearance of the disability. Is the cause and effect relationship really that direct? Oversimplified understandings of cause and effect engender oversimplified solutions to disability. These understandings move critics of special education, be they full inclusionists or individuals advocating inclusionary practices, to propose reforms aimed at erasing disability. Three such reforms proposed by Lyon and Fletcher focused on (a) the definition and identification of LD, (b) teacher preparation, and (c) prevention, early intervention, and remediation.

Like Gartner and Lipsky (1987), many researchers have questioned the validity of LD (Lyon & Fletcher, 2001; Lyon et al., 2001; Shaywitz , Escobar, Shaywitz, Fletcher, & Makuch, 1992; Siegel, 1989; Vellutino, Scanlon, & Lyon, 2000; Vellutino, Scanlon, & Tanzman, 1998). They argue that students with LD are not readily distinguishable from students with low achievement. Despite research showing that students with LD demonstrate achievement that is the "lowest of the low" (Kavale, Fuchs, & Scruggs, 1994), Lyon et al. (2001) proposed that effective intervention can occur without the identification of disability. Lyon (personal communication, March 20, 2002) suggested replacing the term *learning disability* with *learning difference*, as everyone demonstrates learning differences. Any label that applies to all rather than a subset of the population perpetuates the incorrect assumption that students with a disability (including LD) do not differ significantly from the general population (Fuchs & Fuchs, 1995; Kauffman, 2002).

Lyon and Fletcher (2001) maintained that highly intensive, systematic instruction can only be accomplished when the number of children with reading difficulties declines. Additionally, asserting that most early reading difficulties are similar regardless whether the student is served in special or compensatory education programs, Lyon et al. (2001) argued for the delivery of services in the regular classroom. Critics of special education have argued that teacher training in special education is inadequate and ineffective (Alexander et al., 1993; Lyon & Fletcher, 2001; Gartner & Lipsky, 1987; Lipsky & Gartner, 1997, 1998; McGill-Franzen, 1994; Slavin, 1997, 2001; Slavin & Madden, 2001a, 2001b). Assuming that this ineffectiveness results from lack of depth and intensity of training, it is difficult to imagine how a general educator could be more effective with even less deep and extensive training. This logic is even worse than that used when making decisions regarding class size. Sarason (2001) wrote, "The assumption is: A teacher who is inadequate or mediocre with a class of 25–30 students will become adequate with a class of 15–20 students" (p. 102). Likewise, individuals advocating inclusionary practices seem to suggest that returning all students to the regular classroom will improve teacher efficacy or that the efficacy of all teachers can be improved to the point at which all children will thrive in regular classrooms. This suggestion ignores both logic and evidence.

The National Reading Panel (2000) concluded that systematic phonics instruction produces significant benefits for students in kindergarten through sixth grade and for students with reading disabilities regardless of socioeconomic status. However, Mather, Bos, and Babur (2001) suggested that teachers are ill-prepared to offer such instruction. Surveying preservice and inservice teachers of grades kindergarten through third grade, Mather et al. found that only 16 % of preservice and 47% of inservice teachers were able to match the term *digraph* with its definition. Additionally, only 48% of preservice and 37% of inservice teachers knew that phonics was a reading method that teaches the application of sounds to letters. Once again, cause and effect has been drastically oversimplified. Returning students with disabilities to the regular classroom does not ensure that teachers will be equipped to effectively instruct them.

Special education has been criticized for its reliance on a "wait-to-fail" model (Lyon et al., 2001; Lyon & Fletcher, 2001). Thus, proponents of the FIM have advocated a shift from an emphasis on remediation to an emphasis on prevention, wherein regular classroom teachers use effective instructional programs that ensure that most students achieve success the first time they are taught (Slavin & Madden, 2001a). Special education researchers have agreed that primary prevention aimed at averting the manifestation of disabilities represents an important focus for research and funding (Andrews et al., 2000). It is generally agreed that prevention is a good thing, and evidence does suggest that primary prevention is sometimes possible (e.g., Kauffman, 1999b).

Unfortunately, the best prevention we can devise will not eliminate all failure or all disability. The cause and effect relationship is just not that simple. Primary prevention, when implemented effectively, reduces the manifestation of dysfunction. The most effective primary prevention programs are comprehensive, sustained across age levels, and based on empirically validated practices (Coie et al., 1993; Cowen, 1996; Zigler, Taussig, & Black, 1992). Even with such preventative interventions, some individuals manifest dysfunction and require additional intervention— secondary or tertiary prevention after a disorder or "failure" has occurred. When, as Lyon and Fletcher (2001) have suggested, primary prevention is the work of both special and regular education, and when special educators focus on early identification and the implementation of specialized interventions within the regular classroom (Lyon et al., 2001), where will the students who manifest disabilities resistant to primary prevention receive instruction? Additionally, who will instruct these students? And this point must not be lost: Effective prevention requires unequivocally that, at least in the beginning years of implementation, more students, not fewer, must be served (Kauffman, 1999b).

Long ago, Kauffman (1989) pointed out how proponents of the REI (now the FIM) ignored or misinterpreted research findings like those of Carlberg and Kavale (1980). Ignorance and misrepresentation of research continue. Perhaps additional statements about instructional research should give pause to those who promote the FIM:

> In reform-based lessons, low achievers face the challenge of becoming part of a community of learners in which students are to construct their own understanding of mathematical concepts through conversations with peers and the teachers. An underlying assumption is that students can exchange ideas and learn from each other (Baxter, Woodward, & Olson, 2001, p. 543) .... The assumption that all students will flourish with the challenging mathematics curricula and pedagogy that comprise reform needs to be questioned. (Baxter et al., 2001, p. 545)

CONCLUSION

Kavale et al. (1994) were correct in suggesting that the formulation of LD policy "is a fragile endeavor" complicated by ideology (p. 76). Advocates of full inclusion have adopted an ideology—a delusion, in our judgment—that being in the same place as others is a necessary, if not sufficient, condition for fair treatment of students with disabilities. This delusion includes at least one of the following assumptions, if not all of them: (a) If all students receive instruction in the same setting, they will receive the same opportunities to learn. (b) Fair treatment of students with disabilities can be achieved only when these students are in the same place as students without disabilities. (c) Students with disabilities should be treated like all other students (see Ysseldyke, Algozzine, & Thurlow, 2000, p. 67, for a statement of the last assumption).

Special education is by nature paradoxical, in that it is a way of achieving equal opportunities through treatment that is different (and therefore unequal). In attempting to provide students the same access and opportunity afforded to everyone, we treat students with disabilities differently and individually. It is impossible to offer such treatment to all students. In order to maximize equity, we offer special education to students with disabilities (see Crockett & Kauffman, 1999; Hockenbury, Kauffman, & Hallahan, 1999–2000). This reality may prove difficult for some to accept, as they see equal treatment as the key to equal opportunity. Students with disabilities benefit from specialized interventions (Foorman, Francis, Fletcher, Schatschneider, & Mehta, 1998; Forness, Kavale, Blum, & Lloyd; 1997; Fuchs, Fuchs, Mathes, & Martinez, 2002; Lloyd, Forness, & Kavale, 1998; Torgesen, Alexander, Wagner, Rashotte, Voeller, & Conway, 2001; Vaughn, Gersten, & Chard; 2000). Without different treatment, unfairness is assured.

Perhaps the FIM is popular because if offers what appears to be a road to quick and easy success. It is much quicker and easier to move bodies than to teach well. If the goal is to move students into mainstream classes, this can be accomplished quickly, with little effort or money, and with virtually certain and easily documented success. People start out in one place and are moved to another. All done! Right? Perhaps not. However, if the goal is to teach students exceedingly well, regardless of their characteristics, then success cannot be claimed as quickly. The task requires great effort and monetary costs, the outcomes are uncertain (especially for students with more severe disabilities of any nature), and success may be difficult to document. The ideology of full inclusion may, in our opinion, be fairly characterized as delusional because it meets Worrall's (1990) criteria for fraud: It is simply unreasonable based on what we know.

REFERENCES

Adams, M. J. (1995). *Beginning to read: Thinking and learning about print.* Cambridge, MA: MIT Press.

Adams, M. J. (1997). The great debate: Then and now. *Annals of Dyslexia, 47,* 265–276.

Alexander, D., Gray, D. B., & Lyon, G. R. (1993). Conclusions and future directions. In G. R. Lyon, D. B. Gray, J. E. Kavanaugh, & N. A. Krasnegor (Eds.), *Better understanding learning disabilities* (pp. 343–350). Baltimore: Brookes.

Andrews, J. E., Carnine, D. W., Coutinho, M. J., Edgar, E. B., Forness, S. R., Fuchs, L. S., et al. (2000). Bridging the special education divide. *Remedial and Special Education, 21,* 258–260, 267.

Baxter, J. A., Woodward, J., & Olson, D. (2001). Effects of reform-based mathematics instruction on low achievers in five third-grade classrooms. *Elementary School Journal, 101,* 529–547.

Bielinski, J., Ysseldyke, J. E., Bolt, S., Friedebach, M., & Friedebach, J. (2001). Prevalence of accommodations for students with disabilities participating in a statewide testing program. *Assessment for Effective Intervention, 26*(2), 21–28.

Blackman, H. P. (1992). Surmounting the disability of isolation. *The School Administrator, 49*(2), 28–29.

Carlberg, C., & Kavale, K. (1980). The efficacy of special versus regular class placement for exceptional children: A meta-analysis. *The Journal of Special Education, 29,* 155–162.

Coie, J. D., Watt, N. F., West, S. G., Hawkins, J. D., Asarnow, J. R., Markman, et al. (1993). The science of prevention: A conceptual framework and some directions for a national research program. *American Psychologist, 48,* 1013–1022.

Cottle, M. (2001, June 18). Jeffords kills special ed. reform school. *The New Republic,* 14–15.

Cowen, E. L. (1996). The ontogenesis of primary prevention: Lengthy strides and stubbed toes. *American Journal of Community Psychology, 24,* 235–249.

Crockett, J. B., & Kauffman, J. M. (1998). Taking inclusion back to its roots. *Educational Leadership, 56,* 74–77.

Crockett, J. B., & Kauffman, J. M. (1999). *The least restrictive environment: Its origins and interpretations in special education.* Mahwah, NJ: Lawrence Erlbaum Associates.

Deno, E. (1970). Special education as developmental capital. *Exceptional Children, 37,* 229–237.

Dudley-Marling, C., & Fine, E. (1997). Politics of whole language. *Reading and Writing Quarterly: Overcoming Learning Difficulties, 13,* 247–260.

Dunn, L. (1968). Special education for the mildly retarded—Is much of it justifiable. *Exceptional Children, 34,* 5–22.

Fletcher, M. A. (2001, October 5). Overhaul planned for special education. *The Washington Post,* p. A3.

Foorman, B. R., Francis, D. J., Fletcher, J. M., Schatschneider, C., & Mehta, P. (1998). The role of instruction in learning to read: Preventing reading failure in at-risk children. *Journal of Educational Psychology, 90*, 37–55.

Forness, S. R., Kavale, K. A., Blum, I. M., & Lloyd, J. W. (1997). What works in special education and related services: Using meta-analysis to guide practice. *Teaching Exceptional Children, 29*(6), 4–9.

Forness, S. R., Sinclair, E., Jura, M. B., McCracken, J. T., & Cadigan, J. (2002). *Learning disabilities and related disorders.* Los Angeles: Wallis Foundation.

Fuchs, D., & Fuchs, L. S. (1994). Inclusive schools movement and the radicalization of special education reform. *Exceptional Children, 60*, 294–309.

Fuchs, D., Fuchs, L. S., Mathes, P. G., & Martinez, E. (2002). *Social standing of students with learning disabilities in PALS and No-PALS Classrooms.* Manuscript submitted for publication.

Fuchs, L. S., & Fuchs, D. (1995). What's "special" about special education? *Phi Delta Kappan, 76*, 522–530.

Fuchs, L. S., & Fuchs, D. (2001). Helping teachers formulate sound test accommodation decisions for students with learning disabilities. *Learning Disabilities Research and Practice, 16*(3), 174–181.

Fuchs, L. S., Fuchs, D., Hamlett, C. L., Phillips, N. B., & Karns, K. (1995). General educators' specialized adaptations for students with learning disabilities. *Exceptional Children, 61*, 440–460.

Gallagher, D. J. (1998). The scientific knowledge base of special education: Do we know what we think we know? *Exceptional Children, 64*, 493–502.

Garan, E. (1994). Who's in control? Is there enough "empowerment" to go around? *Language Arts, 71*, 192–199.

Gartner, A., & Lipsky, D. K. (1987). Beyond special education: Toward a quality system for all students. *Harvard Educational Review, 57*, 367–390.

Goodman, K. S. (1992). I didn't found whole language. *The Reading Teacher, 46*, 188–199.

Goodman, K. S. (1994). Reading, writing, and written texts: A transactional sociopsycholinguistic view. In R. B. Ruddell, M. Rapp Ruddell, & H. Singer (Eds.), *Theoretical models and processes of reading* (4th ed., pp. 1093–1130). Newark, DE: International Reading Association.

Hallahan, D. P., & Kauffman, J. M. (2003). *Exceptional learners: Introduction to special education* (9th ed.). Boston: Allyn & Bacon.

Hallahan, D. P., & Mock, D. R. (2003). A brief history of the field of learning disabilities. In H. L. Swanson, K. Harris, & S. Graham (Eds.), *Handbook of learning disabilities.* New York: Guilford.

Hockenbury, J. C., Kauffman, J. M., & Hallahan, D. P. (1999–2000). What's right about special education. *Exceptionality, 8*(1), 3–11.

Johnson, E., Kimball, K., & Brown, S. O. (2001). American Sign Language as an accommodation during standards-based assessments. *Assessment for Effective Intervention, 26*(2), 39–47.

Kauffman, J. M. (1989). The regular education initiative as Reagan-Bush education policy: A trickle-down theory of education of the hard-to-teach. *Journal of Special Education, 23*, 256–278.

Kauffman, J. M. (1999a). Commentary: Today's special education and its messages for tomorrow. *The Journal of Special Education, 32*, 244–254.

Kauffman, J. M. (1999b). How we prevent the prevention of emotional and behavioral disorders. *Exceptional Children, 65*, 448–468.

Kauffman, J. M. (2002). *Educational deform: Bright people sometimes say stupid things about education.* Lanham, MD: Scarecrow Education.

Kauffman, J. M., & Hallahan, D. P. (Eds.). (1995). *The illusion of full inclusion: A comprehensive critique of a current special education bandwagon.* Austin, TX: Pro-Ed.

Kauffman, J. M., & Hallahan, D. P. (1997). A diversity of restrictive environments: Placement as a problem of social ecology. In J. W. Lloyd, E. J. Kameenui, & D. Chard (Eds.), *Issues in educating students with disabilities* (pp. 325–342). Hillsdale, NJ: Lawrence Erlbaum Associates.

Kauffman, J. M., & Lloyd, J. W. (1995). A sense of place: The importance of placement issues in contemporary special education. In J. M. Kauffman, J. W. Lloyd, D. P. Hallahan, & T. A.

Astuto (Eds.), *Issues in educational placement: Students with emotional and behavioral disorders* (pp. 3–19). Hillsdale, NJ: Lawrence Erlbaum Associates.

Kauffman, J. M., Lloyd, J. W., Baker, J., & Riedel, T. M. (1995). Inclusion of all students with emotional or behavioral disorders? Let's think again. *Phi Delta Kappan, 76,* 542–546.

Kavale, K. A., & Forness, S. R. (2000). What definitions of learning disability say and don't say: A critical analysis. *Journal of Learning Disabilities, 33,* 239–256.

Kavale, K. A., Fuchs, D., & Scruggs, T. (1994). Setting the record straight on learning disability and low achievement: Implications for policymaking. *Learning Disabilities Research and Practice, 9*(2), 70–77.

Lipsky, D. K., & Gartner, A. (1987).Capable of achievement and worthy of respect: Education for handicapped students as if they were full-fledged human beings. *Exceptional Children, 54,* 69–74.

Lipsky, D. K., & Gartner, A. (1996). Inclusion, school restructuring and the remaking of American society. *Harvard Educational Review, 66,* 762–796.

Lipsky, D. K., & Gartner, A. (1997). *Inclusion and school reform: Transforming America's classrooms.* Baltimore: Brookes.

Lipsky, D. K., & Gartner, A. (1998). Taking inclusion into the future. *Educational Leadership, 56,* 78–81.

Lloyd, J. W., Forness, S. R., & Kavale, K. A. (1998). Some methods are more effective than others. *Intervention in School and Clinic, 33,* 195–200.

Lyon, G. R., & Fletcher, J. M. (2001). Early warning systems. *Education Matters, 1,* 2–29.

Lyon, G. R., Fletcher, J. M., Shaywitz, S. A., Shaywitz, B. A., Torgesen, J. K., Wood, F. B., et al. (2001). Rethinking learning disabilities. In C. E. Finn, A. J. Rothrham, & C. R. Hokanson (Eds.), *Rethinking special education for a new century* (pp. 259–287). Washington DC: Thomas B. Fordham Foundation.

MacMillan, D. L., Gresham, F. M., & Forness, S. R. (1996). Full inclusion: An empirical perspective. *Behavioral Disorders, 21,* 145–159.

Mather, N., Bos, C., & Babur, N. (2001). Perceptions and knowledge of preservice and inservice teachers about early literacy instruction. *Journal of Learning Disabilities, 34,* 472–482.

McGill-Franzen, A. (1994). Compensatory and special education: Is there accountability for learning and belief in children's potential? In E. H. Hiebert & B. M. Taylor (Eds.), *Getting Reading Right From the Start* (pp. 13–35). Boston: Allyn & Bacon.

McIntosh, R., Vaughn, S., Schumm, J. S., Haager, D., & Lee, O. (1993). Observations of students with learning disabilities in general education classrooms. *Exceptional Children, 60,* 249–262.

McMaster, K. N., & Fuchs, D. (2002). Effects of cooperative learning on the academic achievement of students with learning disabilities: An update of Tateyama-Sniezek's review. *Learning Disabilities Research and Practice, 17,* 107–117.

Mock, D. R., Jakubecy, J. J., & Kauffman, J. M. (2002). Special education: History. In *Encyclopedia of education* (2nd ed., Vol. 6, pp. 2278–2284). New York: Macmillan.

National Reading Panel. (2000). *Teaching children to read: An evidence-based assessment of the scientific research literature on reading and its implications for reading instruction.* Washington, DC: National Institute of Child Health and Human Development.

Palmer, D. S., Fuller, K., Arora, T., & Nelson, M. (2001). Taking sides: Parent views on inclusion for their children with severe disabilities. *Exceptional Children, 67,* 467–484.

Pierre, R. E. (2002, April 2). Racial strife flares in Cincinnati over downtown business boycott. *The Washington Post,* p. A3.

Pitoniak, M. J., & Royer, J. M. (2001). Testing accommodations for examinees with disabilities: A review of psychometric, legal, and social policy issues. *Review of Educational Research, 71*(1), 53–104.

Rea, P. J., McLaughlin, V. L., & Walther-Thomas, C. (2002). Outcomes for students with learning disabilities in inclusive and pullout programs. *Exceptional Children, 68,* 203–222.

Sarason, S. B. (1990). *The predictable failure of school reform: Can we change course before it's too late?* San Francisco: Jossey-Bass.

Sarason, S. B. (2001). *American psychology and schools: A critique.* New York: Teachers College Press.

Sasso, G. M. (2001). The retreat from inquiry and knowledge in special education. *The Journal of Special Education, 34,* 178–193.

Shaywitz, S. E., Escobar, M. D., Shaywitz, B. A., Fletcher, J. M., & Makuch, R. (1992). Evidence that dyslexia may represent the lower tail of a normal distribution of reading ability. *The New England Journal of Medicine, 326,* 145–150.

Shermer, M. (2001). *The borderlands of science: Where sense meets nonsense.* New York: Oxford University Press.

Siegel, L. S. (1989). IQ is irrelevant to the definition of learning disabilities. *Journal of Learning Disabilities, 22,* 469–486.

Simmerman, S., & Swanson, H. L. (2001). Treatment outcomes for students with learning disabilities: How important are internal and external validity. *Journal of Learning Disabilities, 34,* 221–236.

Slavin, R. E. (1997). Including inclusion in school reform: Success for All and Roots and Wings. In D. K. Lipsky & A. Gartner (Eds.), *Inclusion and school reform: Transforming America's classrooms* (pp. 375–388). Baltimore: Brookes.

Slavin, R. E. (2001). Show me the evidence. *American School Board Journal, 188*(3), 26–29.

Slavin, R. E., & Madden, N. A. (2001a). *One million children: Success for All.* Thousand Oaks, CA: Corwin Press.

Slavin, R. E., & Madden, N. A. (2001b). Success for All: An overview. In R. Slavin & N. Madden (Eds.), *Success for All: Research and reform in elementary education* (pp. 3–16). Mahwah, NJ: Lawrence Erlbaum Associates.

Smith, G. A. (2002). Place-based education: Learning to be where we are. *Phi Delta Kappan, 83,* 584–594.

Soifer, D. (2002, June 23). Benefits, placements, funding and regulations are questionable at best. *Lexington Herald Leader,* p. F2.

Stage, S. A., & Quiroz, D. R. (1997). A meta-analysis of interventions to decrease disruptive classroom behavior in public education settings. *School Psychology Review, 26,* 333–368.

Stainback, S., & Stainback, W. (1988). Letter to the editor. *Journal of Learning Disabilities, 21,* 452–453.

Stainback, S., Stainback, W., East, K., & Sapon-Shevin, M. (1994). A commentary on inclusion and the development of a positive self-identity by people with disabilities. *Exceptional Children, 60,* 486–490.

Stainback, S., Stainback, W., & Stefanich, G. (1996). Learning together in inclusive classrooms: What about the curriculum. *Teaching Exceptional Children, 28*(3), 14–19.

Tateyama-Sniezek, K. M. (1990). Cooperative learning: Does it improve the academic achievement of students with handicaps. *Exceptional Children, 56,* 426–438.

Torgesen, J. K., Alexander, A. W., Wagner, R. K., Rashotte, C. A., Voeller, K. K. S., & Conway, T. (2001). Intensive remedial instruction for children with severe reading disabilities: Immediate and long-term outcomes from two instructional approaches. *Journal of Learning Disabilities, 34,* 33–58, 78.

U.S. Department of Education. (2000). *Twenty-second annual report to Congress on implementation of the Individuals with Disabilities Education Act.* Washington, DC: Author.

Vaughn, S., Gersten, R., & Chard, D. J. (2000). The underlying message in LD intervention research: Findings from research syntheses. *Exceptional Children, 67,* 99–114.

Vellutino, F. R., Scanlon, D. M., & Lyon, G. R. (2000). Differentiating between difficult-to-remediate and readily remediated poor readers: More evidence against the IQ-achievement discrepancy definition of reading disability. *Journal of Learning Disabilities, 33,* 223–238.

Vellutino, F. R., Scanlon, D. M., & Tanzman, M. S. (1998). The case for early intervention in diagnosing specific reading disability. *Journal of School Psychology, 36,* 367–397.

Walker, H. M., & Bullis, M. (1991). Behavior disorders and the social context of regular class integration: A conceptual dilemma? In J. W. Lloyd, N. N. Singh, & A. C. Repp (Eds.), *The regular education initiative: Alternative perspectives on concepts, issues, and models* (pp. 75–93). Sycamore, IL: Sycamore.

Wallace, T., Anderson, A. R., Bartholomay, T., & Hupp, S. (2002). An ecobehavioral examination of high school classrooms that include students with disabilities. *Exceptional Children, 68,* 345–359.

Worrall, R. S. (1990). Detecting health fraud in the field of learning disabilities. *Journal of Learning Disabilities, 23,* 207–212.

Ysseldyke, J. E., Algozzine, B., & Thurlow, M. L. (2000). *Critical issues in special education* (3rd ed.). Boston: Houghton Mifflin.

Ysseldyke, J. E., & Bielinski, J. (2002). Effect of different methods of reporting and reclassification on trends in test scores for students with disabilities. *Exceptional Children, 68,* 189–200.

Zigler, E., Taussig, C., & Black, K. (1992). Early childhood intervention: A promising preventative for juvenile delinquency. *American Psychologist, 47,* 997–1006.

Zigmond, N. (1997). Educating students with disabilities: The future of special education. In J. W. Lloyd, E. J. Kameenui, & D. Chard (Eds.), *Issues in educating students with disabilities* (pp. 377–390). Mahwah, NJ: Lawrence Erlbaum Associates.

Credulity and Gullibility Among Service Providers: An Attempt to Understand Why Snake Oil Sells

Stephen Greenspan
University of Colorado

INTRODUCTION

It is not surprising that people with cognitive limitations are often gullible or credulous, but it is important to understand that all human beings, even people with advanced degrees, are capable of being duped. Evidence can be found in the many works of fiction devoted to the topic, including Shakespeare's *Othello*, Collodi's *Pinocchio*, Melville's *The Confidence Man*, and Twain's *The Adventures of Tom Sawyer*. It can also be found in the large numbers of human service workers who jump on the bandwagon of the most ridiculous, unproven, and dubious of treatment fads. Can there be any other term to describe professionals who subscribe to such fad therapies than *gullible*?

Gullibility is a complexly determined, and little studied, phenomenon that has many causes. My colleagues and I (Greenspan, Loughlin, & Black, 2001) have proposed a heuristic model, loosely based on the work of Martin Ford (1992) for explaining gullibility in persons with disabilities. The same model can be used, I believe, to explain and study gullibility in service providers. The following sections are organized around some of the elements in the model. I omit a few elements (such as "communicative incompetence" and "physical incompetence") that are particularly relevant to understanding gullibility in persons with disabilities. In the last section, I attempt to integrate the various elements, by pointing out the interactive nature of the model and by making some practical recommendations for training and supervising human service workers. Before undertaking this analysis, I need to define two central terms.

Gullibility may be defined as a tendency toward being fooled or duped. All human beings can be fooled or duped in some situations, such as when one is betrayed by a spouse or close friend. The term *gullible* is usually used to refer to people who can be tricked repeatedly or in situations where there are obvious warning signs. Thus, the term suggests a personality trait, in that gullible people tend not to learn from experience, as in the example of human service professionals who advocate for a novel treatment fad after they have previously been burned by one or more earlier ones.

A related construct, and one which I believe is at the heart of much gullibility, is *credulity*. This term can be defined as a tendency to believe things that are unproven or unlikely to be true. Whereas gullibility involves some behavioral outcome, in that people demonstrate that they are tricked by doing something tangible (e.g., handing over a check), credulity is more a state of mind or belief. The two terms can be considered somewhat equivalent, however, and it may be that the phenomenon of interest in this book, namely the proliferation in the disability field of various fad treatments, is better covered by the credulity rubric.

SITUATIONAL FACTORS UNDERLYING GULLIBILITY TOWARDS FADS

To the extent that there has been research on gullibility, it has been conducted by social psychologists interested in group, rather than individual, manifestations. Examples are studies of "counselor gullibility" (Miller, 1986; the tendency of therapists to believe their clients' misrepresentations of reality), the "Barnum effect" (Layne, 1979; the tendency to believe statements about oneself made by reputed authorities), and the "compliance effect" (Milgram, 1974; the tendency to follow orders, even when told to do harm to others). The main lesson from these studies, and studies examining effective marketing tactics (Cialdini, 1984), is that some situational factors are more likely to result in gullible outcomes than others. Two situational factors that increase the likelihood that an individual will exhibit gullibility are social pressure and the existence of an ambiguous situation.

By social pressure, I am referring to the presence of two or more persons, particularly persons of status, who encourage belief in a phenomenon. A personal example involved my becoming caught up in betting on a shell game, when observing people on a street corner guessing correctly, and when encouraged by other onlookers to play the game. Both the observed winners and the encouragers were—I later found out—participants in the scam. (My falling for this scam was also facilitated by having been younger and more naïve at that time.)

Human beings tend to look to others for clues as to how to behave. Fads are described as "bandwagons" precisely because most of us are reluctant to be left behind when something worthwhile appears to be happening. Group pressure, in other words, can sometimes erase doubts, and the existence of such pressure, when combined with the charismatic personality and refined persuasion skills of many fad originators, can be difficult to resist.

The best known example of how social pressure works to erase doubts is, of course, the classic children's tale, *The Emperor's New Clothes* by Hans Christian Anderson. I saw an example of the same phenomenon in the human services when I attended a conference session early in the history of the facilitated communication (FC) craze. The session featured a demonstration of FC by Douglas Biklen, the chief American promoter of FC, and associates from Syracuse University (Biklen & Cardinal, 1997). As I remember it, there were three individuals being facilitated by persons (such as a sister, in one case) who were close to them. The demonstration had something of a quasi-religious quality, both in the nature of the miracles we appeared to be witnessing and the beatific state of grace that the facilitators appeared to be in. Witnesses were cowed either into belief or, in my case, silence (I remember wanting to shout "fake" but lacked the courage to do so).

Among the other situational factors that contribute to gullibility (all of which seem to be operating in the previous example) are (a) the degree of ambiguity or complexity in the problem or phenomenon being addressed (fads tend to flourish where more conventional approaches do not appear to be working very well, or where there are few clear-cut criteria for determining success or failure); (b) the desperate desire by family members and professionals for their relative or client to be "cured"; and (c) a lack of sophistication about research methods or the scientific literature pertaining to a particular disability. Because all three of these factors are often present in cases of autism, it is not surprising that autism is a disability category that has provided an extremely fertile field for fad therapies. The complexity of autism lies in the unusual mix of competence and incompetence that is often present, and its ambiguity lies in the difficulty in getting a clear handle on the nature of the disorder or the extent of a particular person's overall impairment. For this reason, family members and others often have unrealistic hopes for future attainment of normal functioning, and subjective and nonscientific evaluations of postintervention changes can be quite misleading.

A factor contributing to the susceptibility of service providers to fad therapies is the popularity in the human services of simplistic applications of behaviorist ideas. These applications tend to focus on specific behavioral deficits rather than underlying structural limitations and encourage excessive optimism about the extent to which previously intractable symptoms are "plastic" (i.e., can be improved dramatically through the skillful application of certain methods). Such an approach, which does not reflect current, more sophisticated, developments in behaviorist theory and practice, is grounded in a view of mental retardation as what Spitz (1986) termed a "learning disorder" (a paucity of behavioral schemas) as opposed to a "thinking disorder" (an inability to apply those schemas well in novel situations). A related problem is the tendency of some individuals claiming to be using behavioral methods to assume that etiology is relatively unimportant and to apply the same bag of techniques to a wide variety of conditions, even when the therapist may lack experience in, or deep understanding of, a particular condition.

The same objection may, conversely, be made about interventions that claim to be addressing underlying structural, personality, or cognitive processes, but which fail to address adequately the actual relevance of those processes or their susceptibility to intervention. In such an approach, commonsense notions about the importance of certain internal factors (e.g., high self-esteem, internal cognitive style, etc.) are applied uncritically and without empirical verification. Such an unsophisticated application of structuralist notions is comparable to the unsophisticated application of behaviorist notions, and contributes equally to the dissemination and acceptance of fad interventions.

AFFECTIVE FACTORS UNDERLYING GULLIBILITY TOWARD FADS

There is a human tendency to believe in miracles and the supernatural, as reflected in the fact that most people, even those with high IQs and advanced degrees, believe in God and a hereafter. There are realms of belief, in other words, that rely on affective processes and where rational thought processes are deliberately put on the shelf. That affective factors are operating in the fad realm can be found in the quasi-religious fervor of advocates for various fad treatments. People in the grips of such quasi-religious fervor dismiss questions about empirical evidence as beside the point, and even as insulting. The literature by FC adherents, for example, is re-plete with comments suggesting that those who require empirical proof are mis-guided and that the phenomenon will exist only if you truly believe in it, sort of like the "clap if you believe in fairies" (Tinkerbell resuscitation) scene in the musical ver-sion of *Peter Pan*.

The "true believer" nature of many disability treatment fads is tied to two related factors: (a) the desire to help and to "cure" those who appear to be beyond help and cure, and (b) the extent to which certain treatments are congruent with strong ideo-logical and political processes in the disability field. The first factor certainly explains the vulnerability of family members. For example, my late mother never stopped praying that my autistic brother would wake up "normal" one day and she became convinced after seeing the movie *David and Lisa* (Perry, 1998/1962) that he could be cured of his disability if she found him a wife. Interestingly, Israeli psychologist Reuven Feuerstein, whose name is associated with two other supposed (and now largely discredited) miracle cures—Feuerstein Instrumental Enrichment and facial surgery for children with Down syndrome—has recently been trumpeting to parents the amazing benefits that accrue from marrying off their adult children with disabili-ties (Ginsberg, 1998). Undoubtedly, such enthusiasm of professionals for various fad interventions also reflects a wish to bring about miracles, which may sometimes also be a reflection of a more general religiosity. This would appear to be the case with Feuerstein, perhaps the most active promoter of fad therapies in the mental retarda-tion field, and an ultra-Orthodox Jew who clearly believes that faith will bring about miracles, an explanation he has given for his own recovery from tuberculosis as a young man (H. Switzky, personal communication, April 12, 2001).

The second factor has to do with the extent to which some treatments come to be seen as more politically and ideologically correct than others. The best example of this is the extent to which the FC craze came to be used by adherents to the (equally fervent) full inclusion movement in special education and adult disability services to advance their agenda. The political and ideological link between FC and full in-clusion is also a personal one, in that many of the individuals (e.g., Douglas Biklen) and organizations (e.g., The Association for Persons with Severe Handicaps) in the forefront of the FC movement were already known for their outspoken advocacy for full inclusion. (In fact, Biklen discovered FC while on a trip to Australia to study ed-ucational inclusion practices in that country; see Biklen, 1993.) Undoubtedly, the appeal of FC to full inclusionists is that its many apparent success stories supported the argument that people with disabilities often have abilities that are underesti-mated by professionals. As pointed out by Wolfensberger (1994), however, it is a mistake to assume that the playing of normal social roles requires the demonstra-tion of normal abilities, especially when that demonstration is false.

As mentioned, advocates for fads often are true believers for whom the fad has some of the qualities of a religious article of faith. Twachtman-Cullen (1997) found this to be the case, for example, in her study of FC facilitators. Such a state of affairs helps to explain why skeptics are viewed as enemies and any call for controlled sci-entific validation is seen as a smoke screen. I experienced this myself when a promi-nent advocate whom I've known for years asked me if I believed in FC. When I hesitated, she said "Oh no, not you too," suggesting that she now saw me as having crossed over into the devil's camp. When fads become so much a part of a political and quasi-religious cause, it is hardly surprising that so many otherwise intelligent professionals refuse to use their critical faculties or, in some cases (perhaps reflecting a reluctance to alienate families), to share their concerns. Given that families rely on professionals for advice, the silence of professionals (whether due to gullibility or reticence) may serve to encourage families to adopt unproven or unwise fad interventions.

COGNITIVE FACTORS UNDERLYING GULLIBILITY TOWARD FADS

Gullibility can be viewed as a form of stupidity, so it is probably the case that cognitive factors play an important role in explaining gullibility toward treatment fads. It would be a mistake, however, to view gullibility merely as a manifestation of below average intelligence. Julian Rotter (1980), one of the few psychologists to study the phenomenon, saw gullibility as resulting from the intersection of low intelligence and high trust. Specifically, Rotter argued that while smart people are as likely as dull people to be very trusting, high intelligence comes in handy in situations where it would be foolish to be too trusting. Rotter used an experimental situation (a subject being urged to operate an electrical device that threw off sparks) where the dangers are physical and dramatic. In such a situation, trusting people who are otherwise bright are more likely to recognize the dangers and say "No thanks" than are trusting people who are otherwise not as bright. It remains to be seen, however, if above-average intelligence provides a similar protective function in situations (e.g., such as being exposed to a human service fad) that pose more subtle and complex challenges.

It is important to keep in mind, as several scholars have pointed out (Gardner, 1993; Greenspan & Driscoll, 1997; Guilford, 1967; Sternberg, 1988), that intelligence is a multidimensional construct. Specifically, one's IQ score, while a good predictor of academic (verbal and logico-mathematical) aptitude, does not directly tap practical, social, and other everyday aspects of intelligence. Limited social intelligence (understanding of people and social transactions) contributes to gullibility in that fad purveyors often emit clues about their own limitations or manipulative intentions, and someone with an ability to pick up and interpret those clues is, presumably, less likely to be manipulated. Limited practical intelligence (understanding of physical processes and phenomena) contributes to gullibility in that fad purveyors tend to provide pseudoscientific rationales for their fads (e.g., basing FC on the presumed motor apraxia of people with autism). A more sophisticated and knowledgeable professional is likely to be skeptical in the face of such pseudoscientific arguments, whereas naïve and poorly educated individuals are, presumably, more likely to find such arguments convincing.

Thus, even without considering affective, personality, or situational factors, it is very possible to imagine that an academically gifted person may have cognitive limitations that contribute to gullibility or credulity. This is aside from the issue of content expertise, or what Piaget termed "horizontal decalage," namely that people operate on different levels depending on how knowledgeable they are about a particular content area. An important survival skill is to be aware of one's limitations, and it is often the case that smart people, including scholars, tend to overestimate the breadth and depth of their knowledge. Furthermore, as Wason (1977) and others have shown, much of the time we rely on nonsystematic heuristic schemas and do not utilize our full logical powers to guide our actions or judgments in the everyday world.

Content expertise comes into play in understanding the credulity of many service providers toward dubious therapies when one understands that having a professional license, or an advanced degree, is no guarantee that one has the content expertise, or the research skills, to evaluate a given treatment fad. Some professions, or training institutes, do a poor job of preparing people to work in the disability field, and even those who are generally well-trained may lack training in a specific subarea, such as autism, physiology, genetics, experimental methodology, or other relevant subareas. We make allowances for untutored family members of individuals with disabilities when they jump on a fad bandwagon, precisely because we understand that they lack the theoretical or research skills, or the knowledge of the disability literature, to make informed judgments about such matters. But the fact is that some professionals know little more (and sometimes less) than family members about specific disabilities or treatments.

A partial explanation for the widespread appeal of fads in the disability field is that many of the disciplines active in treating individuals with disabilities can be considered "semi-professions" (Etzioni, 1969). A semiprofession is a field that lacks an underlying scientific base, or where that base is highly suspect, as in chiropractic, whose founder started with an interest in the now discredited theory of animal magnetism (Moore, 1993) and whose core diagnostic construct—subluxation of the spine—has never been shown to exist (Leach, 1994).

The typical practitioner in a semiprofession is unlikely to have meaningful training in ethics or research methodology, lacks knowledge of the research literature relevant to the populations served, and typically works within organizations rather than as a private practitioner. One reason why practitioners within semiprofessions have been so quick to adopt quack therapies is that it gives them a procedure that they can call their own (and seek insurance reimbursement for) and which advances attempts to give their disciplines independent and enhanced status. This partly explains why many nurses have adopted therapeutic touch (no-touch massage; Scheiber & Selby, 2000), why so many occupational therapists have adopted Snoezelen (Long & Haig, 1997), and why so many special educators and rehabilitation therapists have adopted FC.

CAN GULLIBILITY IN SERVICE PROVIDERS BE PREVENTED?

Faddism is hardly a new phenomenon, as can be found by perusing *Panati's Parade of Fads, Follies and Manias* (Panati, 1991). In the late 19th century, William Jones (1880), in his book, *Credulities Past and Present*, derided the human tendency to believe in nonsense. This tendency certainly extends to the helping professions, as pointed out by McCoy (2000) in his book *Quack* (a term that originated in the 1600s), which details the long history in the United States of questionable physical cures promoted by dishonest or self-deluded medical practitioners and accepted as valid by gullible practitioners and their patients. This trend is alive and well today, as pointed out in a slew of recent books with titles such as *Everyday Irrationality: How*

Pseudo-Scientists, Lunatics, and the Rest of Us Systematically Fail to Think Rationally (Dawes, 2001) and *Why People Believe Weird Things: Pseudoscience, Superstition and Other Confusions of Our Time* (Shermer, 1997).

For the most part, fad believers have been portrayed as people of limited intelligence or stability, but the popularity of human services fads requires one to consider the possibility that generally intelligent and emotionally stable people are often susceptible to holding questionable beliefs. Stanovitch (1999) has addressed this problem by making a distinction between "intelligence" as the possession of adequate cognitive problem-solving algorithms and "rationality" as the intentional application of those algorithms and thinking dispositions in addressing various real world goals and problems. Stanovitch (1994) addresses the phenomenon of smart people holding stupid beliefs by suggesting that they might have a form of learning disability which he terms "Dysrationalia," in which one's capacity to use reason is sidetracked by the intrusion of intuitively based cognitive styles. This argument is similar to my earlier statement that when affect and religious needs become activated, cognition often suffers. Stanovitch (1993) gives several examples of this phenomenon, as in the case of two Illinois teachers who mailed out 6,000 letters to parents protesting the requirement that they teach about the Holocaust, an event they were convinced had never occurred (presumably, they chose to send one letter for every 1,000 mythical murdered Jews).

Sternberg (2002) has extended the exploration of this phenomenon in a new edited book with the appropriate title *Why Smart People Can Be So Stupid*. In his concluding chapter, Hyman (2002) summarizes the various ways in which one can address this question. One approach, associated with Sternberg and his colleagues, is to view stupidity less as a function of low intelligence and more as a function of limited wisdom (a construct related to practical intelligence). Obviously, situational factors also enter into the equation, as heuristics that have worked in the past tend to be applied mindlessly in situations where there may be novel dangers or conditions that are not fully taken into account (an example used repeatedly in the book is Clinton's disastrous handling of the Lewinsky matter).

Hyman's chapter may be the only one in the Sternberg book that moves beyond domain modularity (e.g., having high academic intelligence but low practical intelligence) and which addresses the question of how one can be smart in a domain at Time 1 but stupid in the same domain at Time 2. This question has particular relevance for understanding how competent human services professionals can be so credulous and accepting of dubious fads.

For Hyman, the problem is not so much that gullible professionals are stupid, but rather that sometimes they can be too smart for their own good. For example, the popular conception that scientists are paragons of rationality is contradicted by the fact that outstanding scientists are often highly intuitive, contrarian, and affectively invested in the way they approach problems. Because such an approach has often worked for them in the past, they tend to rely on their intuitions even in situations where they might lead them astray. An example given by Hyman is Arthur Conan Doyle, a physician and writer who portrayed Sherlock Holmes as a monument to rationality but who devoted the latter part of his life to a book offering proof for the existence of fairies (relying on highly questionable photographic evidence), and who claimed that the magician and medium-debunker Harry Houdini was actually a secret medium who performed his amazing escapes by dematerializing himself.

Whereas Sherlock Holmes is typically portrayed, in contrast to Doyle himself, as an exemplar of the scientific method, it is interesting to note that Holmes rarely sought to empirically verify his intuitive deductions, and he lacked the most basic virtue of any good scientist, namely a willingness to acknowledge the possibility that his hypotheses might be incorrect. In a forthcoming book, Hyman discusses an even better example of this phenomenon, namely the case of Johann Carl Friedrich Zoellner, a professor at the University of Leipzig in Germany in the late 1800s and a great scientist who is considered the founder of the modern field of astrophysics. One evening, Zoellner, whose scientific breakthroughs owed much to his reliance on intuitively driven insights, attended a reception for a visiting American spiritualist. The spiritualist, Henry Slade, demonstrated various feats (e.g., making a rope tie and untie itself) and attributed these to his own paranormal abilities. Hyman, a cognitive psychologist and former magician who is able to duplicate all of Slade's feats, notes that Zoellner (who apparently never had seen a magic act before) became convinced that Slade must have been tapping into a non-material realm and later wrote a highly ridiculed book in which he set forth his case for the existence of this fourth dimension and for the reality of spiritualism.

In light of the cases provided by Stanovitch, Sternberg, Hyman, and others—which depict extremely intelligent people who are gullible toward the most incredible of notions—the answer to the question "Can gullibility in service providers be prevented?" is a resounding "No." As long as there are human beings—possessing affective or spiritual needs, limited in their experience, reliant on intuitive schemas, confronted by ambiguous phenomena, and manipulated by others—there will be dupes and gulls, even among the most educated and intelligent of people. The question we must address, therefore, is not whether we can prevent gullibility toward dubious fads but, rather, whether we can contain and minimize the consequences of this gullibility. The key to this containment process is, probably, to make avoidance of quackery a major agenda in the professionalization of the various disciplines and organizations that serve people with disabilities.

One of the differences between mature professions and semiprofessions is that the former have elaborate and very detailed ethics codes, which every practitioner is required to memorize and which are backed by active enforcement mechanisms, whereas the latter have very skimpy (often less than one page) and vague ethics codes with which many practitioners are unfamiliar and which are not backed by adequate enforcement mechanisms. Even mature disciplines may need to do more to limit fad use, as reflected in the case of the American Psychological Association (APA), which has stringent validation requirements for the use of psychological assessment measures, but which has avoided cracking down on the use by psychologists of arguably dubious therapy techniques, such as eye movement desensitization and reprocessing (Shapiro, 2000), which are routinely promoted in ads in APA journals. Still, practitioners in disciplines that strongly emphasize ethics training and enforcement are probably somewhat less vulnerable to fads, if only because they better understand the ethical issues, human costs, and potential career risks that are involved.

Complementing the development of discipline-specific ethics codes dealing with the general need to avoid fad use is the dissemination by various professional organizations and state regulatory bodies of occasional specific fad prohibitions. Critical to the stopping (or at least major derailing) of the FC craze was the almost universal denunciation of FC by various professional disciplines (these statements are listed in an appendix to Twachtman-Cullen, 1997). The demise of FC was also undoubtedly helped by the many lawsuits that were filed against FC practitioners and trainers by victims of that procedure, especially parents wrongly prosecuted for sexually abusing their children on the basis of accusations generated through FC. An example of how state regulatory bodies can be a force against faddism was the condemnation by the Colorado legislature of the teaching of therapeutic touch (a practice akin to laying on of hands by faith healers) in the University of Colorado School of Nursing. A discussion of that controversy can be found in Scheiber and Selby (2000).

Another way in which faddism can be contained though professionalization is by advancing the movement of various disciplines toward the status of true professions in which a grounding in, and familiarity with, scientific methods and literature is part of the training process. It is easy to forget that medicine was a prescientific discipline until fairly recently and that many horrific treatment fads (such as bleeding) were once quite prevalent. Specific medical disciplines, particularly neurology and psychiatry, have taken longer to become fully scientifically grounded, which might explain why lobotomy, a once-popular fad now universally condemned, was widely taught and used in prestigious teaching hospitals until a few decades ago (Valenstein, 1986).

Discussions of human service fads tend to emphasize their lack of evidence concerning treatment efficacy. But there is another dimension of fads that may be of equal importance as a "red flag": the superficiality and falseness of their theoretical rationales. Obviously, science advances in sometimes unexpected ways, and a blind and knee-jerk skepticism can sometimes cause legitimate advances to be resisted and delayed. But the dangers of unwarranted belief are much greater than the dangers of unwarranted skepticism, and a central tenet of the scientific method is to be skeptical of dramatic new claims until they are demonstrated, replicated, and, hopefully, explained. For the human services to be taken seriously, education about fads and how to spot them must become an important part of every practitioner's professional socialization. For individual practitioners and service agencies to be viewed as competent, it is essential that they be able to recognize worthless fads when they see them.

REFERENCES

Biklen, D. (1993). *Communication unbound: How facilitated communication is challenging traditional views of autism and ability/disability.* New York: Teachers College Press.

Biklen, D., & Cardinal, D. (Eds.). (1997). *Contested words, contested science: Unraveling the facilitated communication controversy.* New York: Teachers College Press.

Cialdini, R. (1984). *Influence: How and why people agree to things.* New York: Morrow.

Dawes, R. M. (2001). *Everyday irrationality: How pseudo-scientists, lunatics and the rest of us systematically fail to think rationally.* Boulder, CO: Westview.

Etzioni, A. (1969). *The semi-professions and their organization.* New York: Free Press.

Ford, M. E. (1992). *Motivating humans: Goals, emotions and personal agency beliefs.* Newbury Park, CA: Sage.

Gardner, H. (1993). *Multiple intelligences: The theory in practice.* New York: Basic Books.

Ginsberg, R. (1998, April). The transformer. *The Jewish Homemaker, 29*(3), 1–5. Available from www.ok.org

Greenspan, S., & Driscoll, J. (1997). The role of intelligence in a broad model of personal competence. In D. P. Flanagan, J. L. Genshaft, & P. L. Harrison (Eds.), *Contemporary intellectual assessment: Theories, tests and issues* (pp. 131–150). New York: Guilford.

Greenspan, S., Loughlin, G., & Black, R. S. (2001). Credulity and gullibility in people with developmental disorders: A framework for future research. In L. M. Glidden (Ed.), *International review of research in mental retardation* (Vol. 24, pp. 101–135). New York: Academic Press.

Guilford, J. P. (1967). *The nature of human intelligence.* New York: McGraw-Hill.

Hyman, R. (2002). Why and when are smart people stupid? In R. J. Sternberg (Ed.), *Why smart people can be so stupid* (pp. 1–23). New Haven, CT: Yale University Press.

Jones, W. (1880). *Credulities past and present: Including the sea and seamen, miners, amulets and talismans, rings, word and letter divination, numbers, trials, exorcising and blessing of animals, birds, eggs, and luck.* London: Chatto & Windus.

Layne, C. (1979). The Barnum effect: Rationality versus gullibility? *Journal of Consulting and Clinical Psychology, 47,* 219–221.

Leach, R. A. (1994). *The chiropractic theories: Principles and clinical applications* (3rd ed.). Baltimore: Williams & Wilkins.

Long, A., & Haig, L. (1997). How do clients benefit from Snoezelen? An exploratory study. *British Journal of Occupational Therapy, 55,* 103–106.

McCoy, B. (2000). *Quack: Tales of medical fraud from the museum of questionable medical devices.* Santa Monica, CA: Santa Monica Press.

Milgram, S. (1974). *Obedience to authority.* New York: Harper & Row.

Miller, M. J. (1986). Counselor gullibility. *Counselor Education and Supervision, 26,* 103–107.

Moore, J. S. (1993). *Chiropractic in America: The history of a medical alternative.* Baltimore: Johns Hopkins University Press.

Panati, C. (1991). *Panati's parade of fads, follies and manias: The origins of our most cherished obsessions.* New York: Harper Perennial.

Perry, F. (1998/1962). *David and Lisa* [Film]. New York: Fox Lorber Home Video.

Rotter, J. B. (1980). Interpersonal trust, trustworthiness and gullibility. *American Psychologist, 35,* 1–7.

Scheiber, B., & Selby, C. (Eds.). (2000). *Therapeutic touch.* New York: Prometheus.

Shapiro, F. (2000). *Eye movement desensitization and reprocessing* (2nd ed.). New York: Guilford Press.

Shermer, M. (1997). *Why people believe weird things: Pseudoscience, superstition, and other confusions of our time.* New York: Freeman.

Spitz, H. H. (1986). *The raising of intelligence: A selected history of attempts to raise retarded intelligence.* Hillsdale, NJ: Lawrence Erlbaum Associates.

Stanovitch, K. E. (1993). Dysrationalia: A new specific learning disability. *Journal of Learning Disabilities, 26,* 501–532.

Stanovitch, K. E. (1994). Reconceptualizing intelligence: Dysrationalia as an intuition pump. *Educational Researcher, 23,* 11–22.

Stanovitch, K. E. (1999). *Who is rational? Studies of individual differences in reasoning.* Mahwah, NJ: Lawrence Erlbaum Associates.

Sternberg, R. J. (1988). *The triarchic mind: A new theory of human intelligence.* New York: Viking.

Sternberg, R. J. (Ed.). (2002). *Why smart people can be so stupid.* New Haven, CT: Yale University Press.

Twachtman-Cullen, D. (1997). *A passion to believe: Autism and the facilitated communication phenomenon.* Boulder, CO: Westview.

Valenstein, E. (1986). *Great and desperate cures: Rise and fall of psychosurgery and other radical treatments.* New York: Basic Books.

Wason, P. C. (1977). Self-contradictions. In P. N. Johnson-Laird & P. C. Wason (Eds.), *Thinking: Readings in cognitive science* (pp. 114–128). Cambridge, UK: Cambridge University Press.

Wolfensberger, W. (1994). The "facilitated communication" craze as an instance of pathological science: The cold fusion of human services. In H. C. Shane (Ed.), *Facilitated communication: The clinical and social phenomenon* (pp. 57–121). San Diego, CA: Singular.

Developmental Disabilities and the Paranormal

John W. Jacobson
Sage Colleges Center for Applied Behavior Analysis

James A. Mulick
The Ohio State University and Columbus Children's Hospital

Belief in the paranormal is common in western societies, as well as in nations such as Russia (Gallup & Newport, 1990; Kruglyakov, 2002). More than 90% of Americans believe in one or more supernatural or paranormal phenomena (Gallup & Newport, 1990; Markovsky & Thye, 2001). Thus, it is culturally typical in this society to hold at least some beliefs in the supernatural or paranormal. In the United Kingdom, through a newspaper survey, 59% of respondents were believers in the paranormal, including 70% of women respondents and 48% of men (Blackmore, 1997). MacDonald (1995) also found that women were more likely to report telepathic experiences than were men.

Because there is little if any scientific support for the objective existence of paranormal phenomena, stipulation that paranormal phenomena are real, that they do exist, is a matter of pure faith. As a matter of faith, differentiating the paranormal from other aspects of faith in everyday life is valuable. Psychologists and sociologists have generally differentiated matters of religious faith, in terms of religiosity (engaging in prayer, attending religious services) and spirituality (belief in a divine entity), from spiritualism (belief in spirits, contacting the deceased through mediums and seances, psychic healing) and from faith in the paranormal or in psi.

While there are aspects of spiritualism that are consistent with some aspects of the paranormal, such as belief in an undetected and unmeasured field of energy within or about the human body, in general, psi is characterized by the claim that several or many special talents exist among humans, such as telepathy (knowledge of another's thoughts), clairvoyance (visualization of objects of events not within physical view), and psychokinesis (ability to move objects through exertion of will and without conventional physical intervention). Spiritualism implies a religious component to beliefs, which actually may or may not be consistent with principal teachings of avowed and conventional or traditional (e.g., Buddhist, Judeo-Christian, Muslim, and other) organized religious faiths, whereas paranormal beliefs may or may not be rationalized or characterized on the basis of individual religious faith. One may hold concurrent beliefs that are religious and spiritual, spiritualistic, and paranormal in nature, and, to the extent that there are logically or conceptually irreconcilable differences in the implications of these beliefs, there is a natural human tendency to discount or ignore such inconsistencies.

There is also a more mundane aspect of faith, and this form of faith is the mere belief or trust in some agency or source of information. People act on this form of faith in everyday tasks. People we trust inform us that taking a certain action will lead to a certain outcome, and we perform accordingly. An authority figure who has been trustworthy in the past gives us advice, and we follow it. A family member solves a problem that has stumped us or ameliorates a hurt that has been troubling us, and we place trust in that person to help us the next time an offer of help comes from that same individual in the future. A newspaper or television news agency provides information that turns out to be useful, and we expect useful information from the same source in the future. Such mundane forms of faith-generating experiences that we encounter lead us to rely on various resources to a greater or lesser extent. Because of the long period of human helplessness and dependency in childhood, it is a foregone conclusion that most people will develop trust and faith in many people and information resources long before critical evaluative faculties have a chance to emerge in their consciousness. In fact, as long as things proceed more or less comfortably, critical evaluation skills many never emerge, or if they do, may never be applied to certain potential sources of assistance and information. Trust, belief, and faith form intricate mutually reinforcing systems of guidelines, some in the form of laws and rules and some in unspoken patterns of compliance. Behavior may prove to be highly resistant to direct experiences of failure or inaccurate information, as long as other laws, rules, and a disposition to compliance based on previous learning continue to be useful and reinforcing.[1]

Matters of faith affect decision-making in a variety of human arenas, including politics and political action, benevolent involvements of individuals and groups (e.g., faith-based services), and presumably, decision making about such matters as the selection and use of health and behavioral services that may be secular, quasi-religious, or even paranormal in nature. This is a result of our ability to follow advice and rules that we are given, or that we construct for ourselves, on the basis of learning from our own experiences in dealing with other people and information.

FAITH IN CONVENTIONAL RELIGIONS AND DISABILITY

Many parents of children with autism or mental retardation find solace, hope, and comfort in religion. This is clearly evident in contemporary sources from the Internet. For example:

> The role of the parent becomes eternally essential for these children, who often suffer tremendous damage to their self-esteem. For them, it can be hard to remember that

---

[1]"If you give a man the correct information for seven years, he may believe the incorrect information on the first day of the eighth year when it is necessary, from your point of view, that he should do so. Your first job is to build the credibility and the authenticity of your propaganda, and persuade the enemy to trust you although you are his enemy." (Daugherty, 1958, p. 38)

they have a Heavenly Father who loves them and that their disabilities are a gift, not a punishment .... (Bittner, 2002, p. 1)

In despair we and others sought God to remove the Down syndrome from him. We will pray for this all our remaining days, or until God or one of His disciples brings forth Jacob's healing, or until Jacob tells us to stop. We also sought out, through the internet, other parents of Down syndrome (DS) to pray with us, but instead found a lot of Christians who believed God had put this on their children and that we needed to embrace DS as our friend. (Cardon Household, 2002, p. 1)

To Freddy being mentally retarded is not a disability. It may even be a BLESSING. I now see it as a gift from God and as the reason he is able to have such a positive effect on his environment and those who know him. (Slinn, 2002, p. 1)

We are so thankful to have found the Apert listserv online .... I only wish it had been there when Nick was born, but it is truly a God-sent blessing .... These kids are truly a gift ... as any special needs child. One smile from that little blonde curly-headed boy makes it all worthwhile. (Disorder Zone Archives, 2002, p. 1)

God created your child. God knew before you did that your child was Autistic. God still has a plan for your child's life. (Anonymous [a], 2002, p. 1)

It is also clear from religious sources on the Internet that they provide information that is generally contemporary in character for pastoral counselors who may be approached by families following the birth of a child with a developmental disability, with less conventional advice given at less conventional sites:

Leaders should not generally assume that mental disorders are a result of sin .... [T]he idea that a mental problem or suffering comes from God's anger or is due to an individual's becoming involved in sinful practices is far too narrow. While this can be the case, it usually is not .... [I]f the afflicted person knows of no unrepented sin, there is no need whatsoever to probe any further with the presupposition that there must be spiritual problems at the root of every mental disorder. It is destructive to suggest in such instances that family failures or some sin in the past created their loved one's mental illness or retardation. (Christensen, 2002)

Here are some "Do's and Don'ts" offered as a guide for those desiring to express their support and offers of help to families of children diagnosed with an autism spectrum disorder .... DON'T, if they are people with faith in God, tell them that their child would be cured if only they had enough faith. Not only is this an incredibly devastating, judgmental, and ignorant thing to say; it's wrong! Autism is neither a punishment for sin nor a test of God's power to heal. God made these children, too, and can perhaps do a greater work through their lives than through someone who appears to be "normal." ... DON'T tell them, either, that God has a special plan for this child or chose them to be parents of this special child, unless you know them very well. (Anonymous [b], 2002)

There are, of course, instances where unexpected substantial benefits of conventional medical or health interventions result in seemingly miraculous cures or divine intercession that are reported on the Internet. Because both intermediate- and long-term prognostications in medicine and health care, particularly with respect to child development, are often probabilistic in nature, there will always be some children for which adverse or pessimistic prognostications will be inaccurate. One such account, "Smell the Rain," which describes normal developmental attainments of a child born at very severe risk of disability, is ubiquitous on the Internet (e.g., Miller, 2002). Perhaps needless to say, medical science also recognizes the steady improvement of outcome in cases that were once thought to have been hopeless, but the improvement in these cases is highly correlated with advancements in science and medical technology. For example, it is now routine to expect very premature babies, born immature and very small with weights of less than 750 grams at birth, to have a fairly even chance of surviving without severe neurological sequale (Blaymore-Bier et al., 1994). In earlier decades, virtually all these very premature babies perished quickly.

Moreover, it should be recognized that there are instances when religious significance or aspects of religious experience imbue discussions of, and justifications for, unfounded or ineffective therapeutic procedures that already may have been thoroughly researched in a conventional manner (ReligiousTolerance.org, 2002; Sitzman, 2002). From time to time, concurrent religious belief and beliefs in the paranormal as phenomena related to developmental disability have been evident on Internet list services. In 1993, a series of messages were exchanged on the usenet group bit.listserv.autism, which contained such statements as "Believing that telepathy comes from God isn't new either. I think so—but you don't have to think anything at all about God to believe in telepathy. The link between autistic children and their parents … is extraordinary, we all know that. So I have no trouble believing in telepathic aspect of autism."

In 1996, a series of messages appeared in the usenet groups alt.paranormal and bit.listsev.tbi-support suggesting that traumatic brain injury "frees up" or releases paranormal powers. In 1998, a discussion on alt.folklore.ghost-stories involved traumatic brain injury and reported paranormal phenomena. In 1999, bit.listseve.autism autism discussions included the use of astrology (a spiritualistic practice) as a basis for predicting, prenatally, that a child will have autism or mental retardation. One skeptic in that exchange questioned how a method based on time of birth could make such a prediction. The question was essentially unanswered. It was, after all, a matter of faith.

FAITH IN THE PARANORMAL AND PSI IN SOCIETY AND AMONG INDIVIDUALS

Although there have been some research methods (e.g., use of ganzfeld apparatus, into which one inserts one's head and which is structured to present a featureless visual field with rounded surfaces all at equal distances from one's eyes) for which findings have accumulated over decades, methodological problems with earlier studies have limited the extent to which they provide support for the notion that psi exists (Milton & Wiseman, 2001). Milton and Wiseman also questioned the methodological soundness of many studies of paranormal abilities using a ganzfeld apparatus (which removes most or all visual perceptual cues), which have claimed to show substantial evidence of psi (see Bem & Honorton, 1994), arguing that these problems make it "impossible to interpret the results as evidence of extrasensory perception" (p. 434, abstract). Because the ganzfeld device presents the subject with a featureless visual experience (a form of visual sensory deprivation), it has been purported to facilitate emergence of paranormal perceptions.

Because beliefs in the paranormal are so prevalent, considerable research has examined the presence of factors that may be associated with such beliefs. Tobacyk, Miford, Springer, and Tobacyk (1988) found a modest positive relationship between the Barnum effect and extent of spiritualistic beliefs; they noted, the Barnum effect involves acceptance of "bogus" personality feedback consisting of trivial statements that could be descriptive of almost anyone. The types of statements made in daily newspaper horoscopes are characteristic of the feedback given to establish the Barnum effect in research. De Groot, Gwynn, and Spanos (1988) found that the susceptibility to hypnosis of women who were forewarned that they would be hypnotized was significantly correlated with scores on questionnaires about mystical experiences and paranormal beliefs. The susceptibility of women who were told afterward, or not at all, that susceptibility would be probed was not correlated with these questionnaire scores and neither was the susceptibility of men, regardless of whether or when they were told that susceptibility would be probed. As long as they tend to be credulous believers, people can have their tendency to follow instructions (e.g., be hypnotized) enhanced by just hearing that they will be hypnotized.

Others have studied the role of misperception, known as probability misjudgment or critical thinking, in belief in the paranormal (Blackmore & Troscianko, 1985; Musch & Ehrenberg, 2002; Royalty, 1995). The premise in this research is that believers in paranormal phenomena may "tend to wrongly attribute remarkable coincidences to paranormal causes rather than chance ..." (see also MacDonald, 1994). In other words, believers tend to underestimate the likelihood of (unexpected) events and misinterpret them as paranormal, selectively forget or make errors in recalling probabilities, and might feel that, under some circumstances, they can control what are essentially chance occurrences (Blackmore & Troscianko, 1985). The Blackmore and Trocianko, and Musch and Ehrenberg, studies found that believers were generally more likely to underestimate the likelihood of coincidental or chance events compared to nonbelievers, although Musch and Ehrenberg found that this difference was accounted for by cognitive ability; students with lower grades were more likely to believe and to have poorer reasoning skills about probabilistic events. In discussing the prevalence of belief in psi (paranormal or extrasensory phenomena), Bem & Honorton (1994) noted that "many laypersons treat all exotic psychological phenomena as epistemologically equivalent .... The blurring of this critical distinction is aided and abetted by the mass media, 'new age' books and mind-power courses, and 'psychic' entertainers who present both genuine hypnosis and fake "mind reading" in the course of a single performance" (p. 4).

However, other researchers (e.g., Roe, 1999) have found less support for a role of probability misjudgment in paranormal belief and have suggested that factors promoting belief may be more social in nature (e.g., culturally typical). Markovsky and Thye (2001) found that paranormal beliefs can be increased by passive social influence in small groups, especially when they are not presented as paranormal in nature, and that statements of belief increase when beliefs are stated by an individual with higher status (e.g., a respected professional or presenter at a conference). Complementary findings were reported by Blackmore (1997) from a newspaper survey, which, contrary to her other research, did not find that misjudgments of probability were associated with belief. Instead, she concluded that the "biggest difference" between those who believed and those who did not was the tendency of believers to claim that others had beliefs or experiences similar to their own. This finding illustrates the strong social component that is responsible for maintaining belief systems. Russell and Jones (1980) found that when subjects were confronted with disconfirming evidence about psi on follow-up, believers showed poorer recall of the evidence than did nonbelievers, suggesting that, like other beliefs, they may be resistant to change. Perhaps they had no one with whom to discuss the disconfirming evidence in their circle of friends, their friends having reinforced their beliefs in psi phenomena in the first place.

Grimmer and White (2001) investigated beliefs of college students in science, medicine, and the arts, with respect to "astrology and numerology, iridology and homeopathy, and biofeedback, telepathy in plants, and water divining," and found that arts students were least skeptical of these phenomena, and medical students were most skeptical. Messer and Griggs (1989) found that particular paranormal beliefs predicted lower grades for students in introductory psychology courses, which include considerable content on scientific methods and findings, even when the effects of Scholastic Aptitude Tests were taken into account. In another study, Banziger (1983) reported that among older learners (age 55 years and older), classroom instruction was effective in decreasing beliefs in the paranormal and these decreases endured up to 6 months.

Yet others have studied the relationship between religiosity and adversity (as measured by recent negative affect) on belief in the paranormal or supernatural. This relationship appears to be complex. For example, Beck and Miller (2001) found that research subjects who were religious were skeptical of paranormal phenomena but more accepting of supernatural phenomena than nonreligious subjects. Many religious systems embody considerable testamentary support for supernatural events and miracles as confirmation of their beliefs. Among religious subjects, negative affect over the past year was associated with decreased belief in the paranormal, whereas for nonreligious subjects, such affect was associated with increased belief in the supernatural and paranormal. In another study, MacDonald (1995) found that more frequent prayer was associated with more prevalent reports of telepathic experiences and greater financial dissatisfaction was associated with more prevalent reports of clairvoyance. In this study, however, life stress and crisis were not associated with reports of telepathic experiences.

The fact that people with some severe thought disorders or affective disorders will state that they communicate or speak with deceased persons or that their thoughts are affected or monitored by an outside force or conspiracy has led researchers to consider facets of personality or mental disorder that might be associated with paranormal beliefs. There appears to be little evidence of a relationship between paranormal belief and severe mental disorder or at least some personality characteristics. For example, Thalbourne (1998) found that extent of belief was no greater among people with major depression or schizophrenic disorders than among college students. Moreover, McBeath and Thalbourne (1993) found that skepticism regarding paranormal phenomena was unrelated to type A behavior. Tobacyk, Nagot, and Miller (1988) found that belief in superstition was related to lower measured personal efficacy (a sense that one can be effective in achieving goals) and lower interpersonal control (a sense that one determines one's own actions), but that other paranormal beliefs were not associated with locus of control. In summary, belief in psi or paranormal phenomena remains very difficult to predict on the individual level except as a general tendency to believe in things.

AUTISM AND THE PARANORMAL

Review of Internet and print sources discloses that although many therapies that are explained or posited on paranormal grounds are claimed to be relevant to the treatment of mental retardation, such therapies and claims of paranormal phenomena center on people, especially children, with autism spectrum disorders. Telepathy has been characterized as a "little understood but common ability in autistic individuals" (Georgiana Institute, 2002) or has been noted in specific instances to occur in children with autism (Auerbach, 1994; B. A. Bear Autism Foundation, 2002). This focus is most evident in discussions of savant syndromes and in rationalizations of apparent beneficial effects of facilitated communication.

Savant Syndrome

Miller (1999) recently reviewed much of the literature on savant syndrome. As identified originally by Down (1887), savant syndrome refers to the presence of remarkable, usually very specific skills among people with intellectual disability, and often both intellectual disability and autism (see also Treffert, 1988). These skills most commonly entail drawing, musical performance, or arithmetic feats (most frequently calendar calculating and deriving of prime numbers; Miller, 1999). Anecdotal reports are the primary source of published accounts of savantism, but Miller noted that whereas the skills appear to "consist of more than simple associate links or lists," it should be recognized that the vast majority of reported savants who have been tested have intellectual skills in the mild to "borderline" (a past classification) ranges of mental retardation, and others have been reported with very severe intellectual disability. Miller (1999) suggested that savant skills involve "elaborate pre-conceptual representational systems" (strategies for organizing information). Kehrer (1992) suggested that these capabilities entail automatic or automatized processes similar to those involved in perception of sensory (eidetic) stimuli.

However, O'Connor and Hermelin (1988) suggested that

> savant special abilities can neither be regarded as the sole consequence of practice and training, nor are such skills based only on an efficient rote memory. Instead, savants use strategies which are founded on the deduction and application of rules governing the material upon which their special ability operates. They also generate novel or new examples of such rule based structures just as we do in our use of language. (p. 395)

O'Connor and Hermelin (1988) suggested further that obsessive interest in very specific aspects of the environment (often seen to occur among people with autism spectrum disorders) may account for the development and continued manifestation of exceptional skills. People get better at what they practice, especially at what they practice to the exclusion of alternatives.

Although there has been, and continues to be, substantial research interest in savant syndrome, it remains very uncommon. In a prevalence study by Saloviita, Ruusila, and Ruusila (2000), it was found to occur at a rate of 1.4 per 1,000 people with mental retardation, with the most common special skills involving calendar calculation and exceptional memory skills. As people with mental retardation typically constitute fewer than 1% to 3% of the general population, savantism is indeed rare.

McMullen (1991) noted that several articles or book chapters on savant syndrome have uncritically reported or reiterated that some people with mental retardation or autism evidence psi or extrasensory perception, including telepathy (e.g., Rimland, 1978; Rimland & Fein, 1988; Treffert, 1988, 1989). Rimland and Hill (1984) also reported, based on anecdotal information, instances of savants with extrasensory perceptual talents. McMullen questioned the basis for these claimed talents, because the evidence offered in these sources consists of brief anecdotes, which in themselves reflect hearsay and uncritical acceptance of testimonials that psi talents do occur among savants, and have not been submitted to independent confirmation. More recently, Treffert and Wallace (2002) resummarized findings from research on savant talents, without referring to paranormal abilities in any way.

Facilitated Communication and Telepathic Conspiracy

The most extensive contemporary discussion of telepathy and autism is contained in a monograph on the topic of facilitated communication (FC) by Haskew and Donnellan (1992), which seems to be based entirely on anecdote, hearsay, and testimonial (to echo McMullin, 1991).

> Shortly after facilitation begins, and the initial concerns have been dealt with, facilitators often report that their communicators have an uncanny ability to know thoughts in their facilitators' minds. Exploration usually reveals that communicators have a well developed "sixth sense" that allows them both to understand what others think, feel, or know, and to transmit their own thoughts to other nonverbal acquaintances, and sometimes to their facilitators. (pp. 8–9)

> Reports that facilitated communicators are able to read their facilitators' and other people's minds surface whenever facilitation is attempted .... Among experienced facilitators its [telepathy's] occurrence is no longer controversial .... (p. 9)

> For many facilitators the ramifications of their communicators' spiritual lives prove profoundly moving, and sometimes frightening; and it ranks with the experience of telepathy as the most disturbing discovery of FC. (p. 11)

> Special education teachers in schools where FC is an established practice ... are accumulating ample evidence of nonverbal students acting in concert, often when they are not in the same classroom .... (p. 12)

> A special education teacher told us she found that having students conspire telepathically was the most troubling aspect of their mind reading abilities .... While caregivers often try to teach appropriate social cues, small talk and flirtation are difficult to describe and to teach. Paradoxically, a third stumbling block may lie in the ability to both hear what is being said and sense what is being thought. (p. 13)

> [I]n a world where telepathy may substitute for speech it is not always clear whose ideas are being facilitated. Sometimes a communicator simply defers to the thoughts

of a person with more perceived authority, like a facilitator, teacher or parent; but sometimes, we suspect, a communicator may become a "channel," typing an account of another nonverbal person's trauma. (p. 17)

[In referring to counseling]: Even when a good facilitating rapport has been established with a counselor, the "sixth sense" people without speech often possess can potentially interfere in the relationship. An example of telepathic communication over long distance when the first author received unsolicited support for his views on the treatment of traumatic stress from a person he has never met who lives over six hundred miles away! (p. 19)

Haskew and Donnellan's (1992) monograph was found to be cited prominently as recommended reading at the following websites found during an October 2002 search using Google: autism-resources.com, Autism Society of America, Autism Society of Southeastern Wisconsin Lending Library, maapservices.org, Minnesota Developmental Disabilities Council, Special Needs Project in Santa Barbara California, and State of Colorado Department of Human Services. Presumably, because this monograph is rife with claims of telepathy, recommendations that parents or families should read it constitute at least implicit endorsement of paranormal beliefs by these organizations and governmental or quasi-governmental agencies. On the other hand, James Randi (Correx Archive, 2002), a well-known debunker of spiritualistic phenomena, was unable to verify the authenticity of communication via FC, let alone telepathy as an element of the FC activity, in a case where he was asked to verify the accuracy of anecdotal evidence of telepathy involving a person with autism (see also chap. 22, this volume).

ENERGY-BASED OR PARANORMALLY RELATED THERAPIES AND DEVELOPMENTAL DISABILITIES

The marketing and sale of complementary and alternative therapies, some of which are founded on essentially paranormal premises, constitute a major industry. Eisenberg and colleagues (1998) conducted a comprehensive study of alternative therapies used in the United States between 1991 and 1997. They studied 16 alternative therapies; those that increased in use most during that period were energy healing, folk remedies, herbal medicine, homeopathy, massage, megavitamins, and self- help groups. Overall, the likelihood that people using health care would visit an alternative medicine practitioner increased from about 36% to about 42%. Expenditures for alternative health care were estimated by Eisenberg et al. at about $21.2 million during 1990–1997 and of this, $12.2 million was self-paid. Increases in use during this time period reflected increases in the proportion of the population seeking such services, rather than an increase in per patient visits (Eisenberg et al., 1998). Given that so many members of the general public both believe in some aspect of the paranormal and display a propensity for using alternative medical services, it would be remarkable if these services were not also sought at some time by a socially significant segment of parents for treatment of their family members with developmental disabilities.

Raso (1995) identified 31 practices in alternative medicine, including energy or vibrational methods, referring to them as a "'melting pot' of religion, occultism, folklore, parapsychology; pop psychology; pseudoscience, and medical guesswork. It overflows with theoretical rubbish"; and describes such methods as "mystical or super-naturalistic" (e.g., see Trieschmann, 2001, for distortions of findings in the physical sciences). Stevens (2001) noted that acceptance of many methods of complementary and alternative healing (e.g., homeopathy) involves magical thinking, which is not based on proof of cause and effect, but rather on perception and subsequent stipulation of assumed cause and effect, largely as a matter of innate perceptual biases that are neurologically based, serendipity, chance occurrence, or coincidences in which one perceives a pattern. Pseudoscience remains reported in the media as if it had substance. For example, Harrison (2001) reported in the *Telegraph* in the United Kingdom that scientists had discovered that the purring of cats is a "natural healing mechanism." Except, we suppose, when it isn't.

As one physician noted, parents and families who are dissatisfied with conventional treatments that cannot cure, but may alleviate, impacts of developmental disability may be prone to adopting use of complementary and alternative medicine (CAM) therapies:

> Outside the hospital environment, the cachet of respectability given CAM treatments by their identification as "complementary" medicine, can lead medical consumers to believe that they are legitimate medical practices. As a result, desperate consumers (once thought of, more compassionately, as "patients") can be lured into accepting CAM as first-rate medicine. In spite of the fact that scientists have pointed out the lack of proof for CAM treatments, the scientific illiteracy of the medicine-consuming public allows the marketing of disproven treatments as supplements to real care. Those who are ill have little practical choice but to "believe." (Green, 2002)

Even proponents of alternative therapies are aware of these vulnerabilities:

> The treatments of conventional medicine for autism are as speculative and trial-and-error based as the alternative therapies [an inaccurate and vague overgeneralization] …. The results of these comprehensive suites of therapies have not been sufficiently satisfying to prevent parents from seeking alternative therapies for the benefit of their children. If conventional medicine were completely successful in treatment of autism, no need would exist for alternative or innovative therapies. (Mehl-Madrona, 2002, comment added)

In addition, it is relevant to note that concerns about alternative health care practices transcend those stated by individual practitioners. The American Academy of Pediatrics (AAP; 2001) conclude that "many CAM approaches are based on inconsistent or implausible biomedical explanations and claims of effectiveness rest on anecdotal information and testimonials" (p. 601). AAP recommends to practitioners that "Families should be informed about placebo effects and the need for controlled studies. The pediatrician should explain that anecdotal and testimonial evidence is very weak. Families also should be advised to be vigilant for exaggerated claims of cure, especially if such claims are for treatments requiring intensive commitment of time, energy, and money on the part of the family" (p. 601).

Some energy-based and other paranormal-based therapies are marketed directly for people with developmental disabilities. For example, Internet sites aver that homeopathic therapies can be "definitely effective" for emotional disorders, including mental retardation (Shah & Shah, 2002; see also Ullman, 2002). It has also been reported that an "extremely important way that some naturopathic physicians can benefit the autistic patient is with constitutional homeopathy. Constitutional homeopathy (treating the entire person rather than the particular symptoms) can also result in significant behavior improvement and in some cases, there may be a complete cessation of the autistic behavior" (Lawton, 2002). There are no scientific studies, however, that demonstrate these effects, although there are discussions on the Internet of controlled research on the benefits of homeopathy (e.g., Lawton, 2002), which, in total, number much fewer than comparable studies published over the course of several years on behavioral treatment of autism alone, and are inconsequential compared to all studies in medicine and psychology focusing on autism (see also cautions suggested by the National Council on Health Care Fraud, 1994).

Energy therapies have been described as "therapy which invokes the cosmic energy from the cosmos and is transmitted to a person through the channel of an accomplished healer. This actuates overall healing of the person, apart from his/her specific short-term or chronic disease" (Devi, 2002). Claims by Devi include healing of mental retardation. One variant of energy therapy that has become notable in North America is thought field therapy (TFT) (Gaudiano & Herbert, 2000). Proponents of TFT aver "that it is imbalances in the bodies (sic) energy system which cause negative emotion" (Altaffer, 2002), and applicability to people with intellectual disabilities is suggested. "One of the wonderful benefits of TFT is that it is effective regardless of a person's verbal ability. There are tapping sequences for anxiety, depression, anger, and even physical pain .... With small children or people without language skills, it is only important that the person be experiencing the feeling when being treated" (Altaffer, 2002).

However, as Gaudiano and Herbert (2000) noted, "There are obvious problems with the theoretical basis for TFT, not the least of which is the complete lack of scientific evidence for the existence of 'thought fields'" (p. 30). Another energetic therapy indicated on the Internet as useful in treating autism, or in this case, cerebral palsy as well, is bi-aura therapy (Loch Ness, 2002). Like TFT, proponents of this therapy link physical health to energy blockages: "All illness and chronic pain is encoded in the energy matrix of the aura in the form of energy blockages or disturbances .... These blockages become locked in the auric field and obstruct the healing flow of energy" (Loch Ness, 2002).

Although it is not as readily recognized for its paranormal or spiritualistic component as other energy therapies, one such therapy that has been adopted by some practitioners providing otherwise recognized treatments is cranio-sacral manipulation. Cranio-sacral therapy is advocated for treatment of children with autism (Learningdiscoveries.org, 2002; Upledger, 2002), and also for those with cerebral palsy, developmental delay, degenerative neurological conditions, learning disabilities or hyperactivity, seizure disorders, or traumatic injury (Learningdiscoveries.org, 2002). One premise underpinning cranio-sacral manipulation is that "the body is kept alive by the presence of an energy field, which is known as the 'bio-electric field' in physiology, and the 'spirit' in religious traditions .... This fluctuating field of energy is not controlled by the body's nervous system, but is independent of it, and in an evolutionary sense, much older than it" (Dea, 2002). Another therapy, less well-known, vibro-acoustic therapy, purports to treat Rett syndrome and autism using the "energy of musical sound waves applied to the body" (Skille, 1989).

A Web site advocating use of magnetic field therapy (Alternatives for Healthy Living, 2002) states that mental retardation and epilepsy are among 42 health-related conditions that may be treated by wearing magnets. Sabadell (1998) reviewed research on therapies based on the use of magnets (as opposed to treatments now being researched using high intensity magnetic fields) in clothing, mattresses, or worn about the person. He noted that an underpinning assumption that "Earth's magnetic field has fallen fifty percent in the last centuries and five percent in the last hundred years. This falling has provoked an increase in common diseases. This is called Magnetic Field Deficiency Syndrome." In some manner, as yet unproven, it is claimed that deprivation of the influence of the "natural" magnetic field affects bioelectric cellular equilibrium (Sabadell, 1998). Evidence of benefit from magnetic therapy remains very limited and is consistent with effects that are minor compared to those claimed for this treatment (Livingston, 1998).

Thus, parents seeking alternative treatments that promise to achieve meaningful, if extremely vague, benefits for their children with developmental disabilities will find sources on the Internet and in popular culture that invite the adoption of energetic and paranormal therapies. But it is also possible that parents and their children with disabilities will encounter offerings of energy and paranormal-based therapies in the course of regular hospital care or chronic care services. Probably the most common of the energy-based therapies commonly offered, by nurses, in everyday healthcare settings, is therapeutic touch (TT). "In Toronto, where TT is practiced routinely in several hospitals, anyone seeking information about the technique can dial 65-TOUCH to reach the local TT network, which has 600 members in Ontario. At Denver's Presbyterian–St. Luke's Hospital, where nurses routinely practice TT, the staff has created a 'Department of Energy.' And at Bristol Hospital in Connecticut, a quarter of the caregivers have completed an in-house, 15-hour course in TT" (Jaroff, 1994).

One Web site on healing touch, a technique kindred to TT, notes that a therapist who was enrolled in the U.S. Navy "became a Certified Healing Touch Practitioner and Instructor October 1993. Before retiring, he taught 37 Healing Touch certification courses at five Naval Medical facilities (now seven) throughout the United States. He has taught over 200 certification courses in the Navy and civilian community" (Anderson, 2002). Starr, Landsman, Ochoteco, Carson-Groner, and Owens (2000) reported that TT is used in over 80 North American hospitals, taught in over 100 locations in 75 countries, and has been taught to more than 100,000 people, including 43,000 health care professionals. The explanation of the TT procedure provided by Starr et al. is that "the practitioner will scan the patient's energy field pattern using the hands as sensors .... The practitioner is able to assess the patient's energy by feeling various sensations given from the patient such as tingling, heat, cold, heaviness, and a drawing field .... The practitioner will then begin to focus intent on the specific direction of the patient's energy ...."

It is not uncommon to find TT included among continuing education requirements for nurses (e.g., Barton Community College, 2002), offered by colleges or accessible through sources like www.nurseCEU.com. Complementary therapies like TT are viewed by some academics in nursing as a usual or ordinary component of nursing practice (Snyder & Lindquist, 2001).

A typical representation of TT is provided by a Web site operated by St. Mary's Hospital, in Amsterdam, New York. That site reports: "The Center provides an energetic approach to healing in mind, body, and spirit through individual treatments and group programs .... All treatments and programs are supportive of the Mission of St. Mary's Hospital to care compassionately for those we serve with dedication to excellence and Christian ideals" (St. Mary's Hospital, 2002). The center offers healing touch, "administered with the intention for the person's highest good in mind, body, and spirit"; therapeutic touch, "a consciously directed process of energy transfer"; and Reiki, a "healing aid that balances and revitalizes the body, mind, and spirit" (St. Mary's Hospital, 2002). Conditions for which treatments are provided include "addictions, ... grief and loss, ... immune system disorders, ... multiple sclerosis, ... and panic attacks." In a September 2002 news segment on WXXA-23 television (Albany, NY), a staff member at this center stated that her intent while using such procedures could alter the endorphin level of a patient (Rowlands, 2002). Such claims are essentially claims for psychokinesis on a microphysiological level.

But, how effective is therapeutic touch? In their review of TT research, including federally funded studies (Selby & Scheiber, 1997), Starr et al. (2002) concluded, "Therapeutic touch has not been conclusively proven to be more effective than the placebo effect, but it has been proven to be effective" (see also Mucha, 2001). In contrast, most responsible health care researchers would conclude that a technique no more effective than a placebo is, in fact, ineffective. Elsewhere, others also have concluded that TT has not been found to be more effective than control conditions (e.g., placebo or "sham" TT) in research and hence "more rigorous research" is needed to support its utility as a nursing intervention (Peters, 1999, p. 59). Moreover, a critical recent study cast serious doubt on claims that TT practitioners can detect an energy field surrounding the human body (Rosa, Rosa, Sarner, & Barrett, 1998). In appraising TT, a review panel in Colorado concluded, "If an effect is observable, it can be measured. It is not adequate to state that TT involves mechanisms that exist beyond the five senses and which therefore cannot be proven by ordinary methods. Such comments are a disservice to science and the practice of healing and demonstrate a commitment to metaphysics and the mystical view of life" (Rosa, 1996). Given that disconfirming research on TT has been rejected by proponents of the therapy, Sarner (1998) posed the question of what research approach could produce findings that might discredit TT from their perspective.

The use of TT is not without its critics within the field of nursing, however, as indicated by Nardini (1996) in an article about TT at the University of Washington:

> Some are skeptical of the procedure, noting the lack of hard scientific evidence to prove how healing touch works.... "I've had nurses walk out of the room because they don't believe in healing touch, or that there even is an energy field," Olson said. Even some practitioners find its inner workings hard to explain. "It is a very creative process," said Mary Ellis, a healing touch practitioner at the Center for Creative Healing in Seattle. "It's like asking a painter how they paint." "A lot of therapists really don't know how it works," added Barbara Dahl, a certified healing touch practitioner and instructor in Seattle. "It's a lot of theory, and a little fact." Gary Olson, director of academic programs at the UW School of Nursing, said ... at times the UW has offered healing

touch classes as an elective. "The reason it is taught," he said, "is that we recognize that there are different therapies that work better in different situations."

Readers may wish to consider the vague nature of the rationale, "there are different therapies that work better in different situations," encouraging speculation leading to the unfounded conclusion that there are situations when TT results in more beneficial effects than conventional therapies, or for that matter, a sugar pill.

CONCLUSION

At the present time, there is no evidence that alternative therapies based on spiritualistic or paranormal premises are of any benefit in treatment for people with developmental disabilities. Yet, the high prevalence of beliefs in aspects of the paranormal in the general public and among parents of children with disabilities, as well as their commitment to the growth, development, and socialization of their children, make them vulnerable to adoption of dubious, energy-based and paranormal-based therapies for which shameless claims of effect made by well-meaning alternative therapists, charlatans, quacks, and fakirs alike are common.

Parents considering adoption of such therapies would be well-advised to consider sources that are more dispassionate in their appraisals. While some parents may find the sorts of content at comprehensive Web sites like csicop.org/si, pseudoscience.org, quackwatch.com, or skeptic.com/ss-skeptic.html to be unsuitable for their purposes, less daunting sites are available. Consider that a sizeable number of alternative therapies involving energy fields, and hence appealing to, or founded on paranormal beliefs, are reviewed on the Internet at Health. Yahoo.Com, including cranio-sacral therapy, applied kinesiology, magnetic field therapy, neurolinguistic therapy, sound therapies, and therapeutic touch. These reviews, which are very accessible to nonprofessionals, indicate there is little or no credible scientific evidence indicating that these therapies actually produce therapeutic or any benefits, except, perhaps to those providing them either emotionally or financially.

Parents also would be well-advised to be wary of charlatanism, of the practitioner who offers too much benefit and too little fact, or who is not able to back up claims with data and substantial research. Parents may also wish to be wary of discussions in popular tradebooks that may lead them, like other people, to make poor or less than fully informed decisions under pressure or under high stakes situations like making a commitment to use of a costly or time-consuming therapy (Gilovch, 1991; Stanovich, 2001). Parents also need to be aware that the use of alternative therapies may conflict with involvement in therapies that *do* have a sound basis, may postpone or discourage use of such therapies, or may consume scarce family financial resources that would be better spent on such therapies.

Pratkanis (2000) has extensively researched the use of propaganda techniques and has enumerated rhetorical (or written) strategies by which beliefs can be engendered or altered. These include the use of arguments that everyone else is in agreement, the use of generalities that are based on "intensely emotionally appealing" words, the use of vague rationales, oversimplification of issues, projecting negative qualities on others (e.g., skeptics of energy therapies), anti-intellectual content (e.g., identification of professionals as non-sympathetic or holding back or ignoring useful therapies), and encouraging the audience to identify with the propagandist (e.g., I'm a parent of a disabled child, I've committed my life to working with these children). Pratkanis also has noted that propaganda techniques include lying. Parents are well-advised to consider the degree to which strategic claims by purveyors of some alternative therapies are essentially the same as those of propagandists, who seek to manipulate hope and motives. In closing, perhaps parents should consider especially the observation by astronomer and popularizer of real science, Carl Sagan (1996), that "It is barely possible that a few ... paranormal claims might one day be verified by solid scientific data. But it would be foolish to accept any of them without adequate evidence" (p. 224).

REFERENCES

Altaffer, T. (2002). *Thought field therapy (TFT)*. Retrieved September 27, 2002, from Psychotherapy and Developmental Disabilities manuscript, http://home.att.net/~tom.altaffer/DEVTFT.HTM

Alternatives for Healthy Living. (2002). *Magnetic field therapy*. Retrieved October 19, 2002, from http://www.alt-med-ed.com/practices/magnetic.htm

American Academy of Pediatrics, Committee on Children with Disabilities. (2001). Counseling families who choose complementary and alternative medicine for their child with chronic illness or disability. *Pediatrics, 107*, 598–601.

Anderson, S. (2002). *Steve's healing touch practice*. Retrieved September 29, 2002, from http://stevehtouch.bizland.com/

Anonymous(a). (2002). *In his image: A word to Christian parents*. Retrieved September 29, 2002, from http://www.geocities.com/annamattautism/christianparents.html

Anonymous(b). (2002). *Help is only helpful when it actually helps: Do's and don'ts*. Retrieved September 29, 2002, from http://www.geocities.com/annamattautism/dosanddonts.html

Auerbach, L. (1994, August). *Psychic frontiers: New research in healing*, Retrieved September 28, 2002, from http://216.239.51.100/search?q=cache:MJT7sw6vp28C:www.mindreader.com/fate/articles/Fate0894.doc+autism+telepathy+foundation&hl=en&ie=UTF-8

B. A. Bear Autism Foundation. (2002). *Make a $20 donation*. Retrieved September 28, 2002, from http://b-a-bear.org/index2.html

Banziger, G. (1983). Normalizing the paranormal: Short-term and long-term change in belief in the paranormal among older learners during a short course. *Teaching of Psychology, 10*, 212–214.

Barton Community College. (2002). *Nursing continuing education*. Retrieved September 29, 2002, from http://www.barton.cc.ks.us/BCCC/coursedescriptions/nursingcontinuingeducation.htm

Beck, R., & Miller, J. P. (2001). Erosion of belief and disbelief: Effects of religiosity and negative affect on beliefs in the paranormal and supernatural. *Journal of Social Psychology, 141*, 277–287.

Bem, D. J., & Honorton, C. (1994). Does psi exist? Replicable evidence for an anomalous process of information transfer. *Psychological Bulletin, 115*, 4–18.

Bittner, T. L. (2002). *Your child's learning disability: A gift from god*. Retrieved September 29, 2002, from http://www.bellaonline.com/articles/art3793.asp

Blackmore, S. J. (1997). Probability misjudgment and belief in the paranormal: A newspaper survey. *British Journal of Psychology, 88*, 683–689.

Blackmore, S. J., & Troscianko, T. (1985). Belief in the paranormal: Probability judgements, illusory control, and the "chance baseline shift." *British Journal of Psychology, 76*, 459–468.

Blaymore-Bier, J., Pezzullo, J., Kim, E., Oh, W., Garcia-Coll, C., & Vohr, B. R. (1994). Outcome of extremely low-birth-weight infants: 1980–1990. *Acta Pediatrica, 83*, 1244–1248.

Cardon Household. (2002). *Down syndrome -preventing the mental retardation and improving the health.* Retrieved September 29, 2002, from http://home.austarnet.com.au/caradonhouse/down.htm

Christensen, J. J. (2002). *On dealing with mental illness and disabilities.* Retrieved September 29, 2002, from http://ldsmentalhealth.org/library/mi/milds/mildsauthor/angels/christiansen/leaders.htm

Correx Archive. (2002). *Facilitating communication: Giving voice to the speechless. Interview with James Randi.* Retrieved September 24, 2002, from http://www.abc.net.au/science/correx/archives/faccom.htm

Daugherty, W. E. (1958). *A psychological warfare casebook.* Baltimore: Johns Hopkins.

Dea, W. (2002). *What is craniosacral therapy?* Retrieved September 27, 2002, from http://www.headbonetailbone.com/article_clients-intro.html

de Groot, H. P., Gwynn, M. I., & Spanos, N. P. (1988). The effects of contextual information and gender on the prediction of hypnotic susceptibility. *Journal of Personality and Social Psychology, 54,* 1049–1053.

Devi, P. (2002). *Cosmic energy therapy.* Retrieved September 27, 2002, from http://www.geocities.com/prabhavatidevi/

Disorder Zone Archives. (2002). *Apert syndrome.* Retrieved September 29, 2002, from http://www.specialchild.com/archives/dz-020.html

Down, J. L. (1887). *On some of the mental afflictions of childhood and youth.* London: Churchill.

Eisenberg, D. M., Davis, R. B., Ettner, S. L., Appel, S., Wilkey, S., Van Rompay, M., et al. (1998). Trends in alternative medicine use in the United States, 1990–1997. *Journal of the American Medical Association, 280,* 1569–1575.

Gallup, G., & Newport, F. (1990). Belief in psychic and paranormal phenomena widespread among Americans. *Gallup Poll Monthly, 299,* 35–44.

Gaudiano, B. A., & Herbert, J. D. (2000). Can we really tap our problems away? A critical analysis of Thought Field Therapy. *Skeptical Inquirer, 24*(4), 29–33, 36.

Georgiana Institute. (2002). *A memo from Georgie.* Retrieved September 27, 2002, from http://www.georgianainstitute.org/text.htm

Gilovich, T. (1991). *How we know what isn't so: The fallibility of human reason in everyday life.* New York: Free Press.

Green, S. (2002). How did complementary medicine enter our hospitals. Retrieved October 14, 2002, from *Health facts and fears.com,* http://www.healthfactsandfears.org/

Grimmer, M. R., & White, K. D. (2001). Nonconventional beliefs among Australian science and nonscience students. *The Journal of Psychology, 126,* 521–528.

Harrison, D. (2001, March 18). *Feline purring shown to be effective vibrational energy healer.* Retrieved September 28, 2002, from http://www.telegraph.co.uk

Haskew, P., & Donnellan, A. M. (1992). *Emotional maturity and well-being: Psychological lessons of facilitated communication.* Danbury, CT: DRI Press.

Jaroff, L. (1994, November 12). A no-touch therapy: Critics attack a mystical hand-motion treatment spreading through nursing schools and hospitals. *Time magazine,* Retrieved September 29, 2002, from http://www.time.com/time/magazine/archive/1994/941121/941121.health.html

Kehrer, H. E. (1992). Savant capabilities of autistic persons. *Acta Paedopsychiatrica, 55,* 151–155.

Kruglyakov, E. (2002). Why is pseudoscience dangerous? *Skeptical Inquirer, 26*(4) 33–36.

Lawton, S. (2002). Autism. *Naturopathy online.* Retrieved October 14, 2002, from http://www.naturopathyonline.com/PatientRoles/autism.htm

Learningdiscoveries.org. (2002). *Craniosacral therapies.* Retrieved September 27, 2002, from http://home.iprimus.com.au/rboon/CranioSacralTherapy.htm

Livingston, J. D. (1998). Magnetic therapy: Plausible attraction? *Skeptical Inquirer, 22*(4), 25–30, 58. Retrieved September 26, 2002, from http://www.csicop.org/si/9807/magnet.html

Loch Ness Bi-Aura Practice. (2002). *How Bi-Aura therapy works.* Retrieved September 27, 2002, from http://212.67.202.143/~wonderful/bio/about.htm

MacDonald, W. L. (1994). The popularity of paranormal experiences in the United States. *Journal of American Culture, 17*, 35–42.

MacDonald, W. L. (1995). The effects of religiosity and structural strain on reported paranormal experiences. *Journal for the Scientific Study of Religion, 34*, 366–376.

Markovsky, B., & Thye, S. R. (2001). Social influence on paranormal beliefs. *Sociological Perspectives, 44*, 21–44.

McBeath, M. K., & Thalbourne, M. A. (1993). A technical note: The relationship between paranormal belief and some variables relevant to Type A behavior pattern. *Journal of Parapsychology, 57*, 411–415.

McMullen, T. (1991). The savant syndrome and extrasensory perception. *Psychological Reports, 69*, 1004–1006.

Mehl-Madrona, L. (2002). *Alternative and innovative therapies for development disorders.* Retrieved September 29, 2002, from www.eparent.com

Messer, W. S., & Griggs, R. A. (1989). Student belief and involvement in the paranormal and performance in introductory psychology. *Teaching of Psychology, 16*, 187–191.

Miller, L. K. (1999). The savant syndrome: Intellectual impairment and exceptional skill. *Psychological Bulletin, 125*, 31–36.

Miller, N. (2002). *Testimonials—true stories for god's glory: Smell the rain.* Retrieved September 29, 2002, from http://webspinners.futura.net/zumaltsp/smellrain.html

Milton, J., & Wiseman, R. (2001). Does Psi exist? Reply to *Storm and Ertel. Psychological Bulletin, 127*, 434–438.

Mucha, P. (2001, March 12). Tap therapy has its devotees and critics. *The Record,* Bergen County, NJ (Special from *The Philadelphia Inquirer Magazine*).

Musch, J., & Ehrenberg, K. (2002). Probability misjudgment, cognitive ability, and belief in the paranormal. *British Journal of Psychology, 93*, 169–177.

Nardini, J. (1996, August 7). Healing hands: Medical treatment focuses on soothing auras, energy layers. *The Daily at the University of Washington.* Retrieved September 20, 2002, from http://archives.thedaily.washington.edu/1996/080796/hands87.html

National Council on Health Care Fraud. (1994). *NCAHF position paper on homeopathy.* Retrieved October 14, 2002, from http://www.ncahf.org/pp/homeop.html

O'Connor, N., & Hermelin, B. (1988). Low intelligence and special abilities. *Journal of Child Psychology and Psychiatry, 29*, 391–396.

Peters, R. M. (1999). The effectiveness of Therapeutic Touch: A meta-analytic review. *Nursing Science Quarterly, 12*, 52–61.

Pratkanis, A. (2000). *Age of propaganda: The everyday use and abuse of persuasion.* (revised). New York: Freeman.

Raso, J. (1995). Mystical medical alternativism, *Skeptical Inquirer, 19*(5). Retrieved September 27, 2002, from http://www.csicop.org/si/9509/alternativism.html

ReligiousTolerance.org. (2002). *Hot! religious issues.* Retrieved September 27, 2002, from http://www.religioustolerance.org/conflict.htm

Rimland, B. (1978). Savant capabilities of autistic children and their cognitive implications. In G. Serban (Ed.), *Cognitive defects in the development of mental illness* (pp. 43–65). New York: Bruner/Mazel.

Rimland, B., & Fein, D. (1988). Special talents of autistic savants. In L. K. Obler & D. Fein (Eds.), *The exceptional brain* (pp. 472–492). New York: Guilford.

Rimland, B., & Hill, A. (1984). Idiot savants. In J. Wortis (Ed.), *Mental retardation and developmental disabilities* (Vol. 13, pp. 155–169). New York: Plenum.

Roe, C. A. (1999). Critical thinking and belief in the paranormal: A re-evaluation. *The British Journal of Psychology, 90*, 85–98.

Rosa, L. (1996). Therapeutic touch: Skeptics in hand to hand combat over the latest new age health fad. *Skeptic, 3*(1), 40–49.

Rosa, L., Rosa, E., Sarner, L., & Barrett, S. (1998). A close look at therapeutic touch. *Journal of the American Medical Association, 279*, 1005–1010.

Rowlands, C. (2002, September 17). *Therapeutic touch*. Television news segment on WXXA Fox 23 News, Albany, NY.

Royalty, J. (1995). The generalizability of critical thinking: Paranormal beliefs versus statistical reasoning. *The Journal of Genetic Psychology, 156*, 477–488.

Russell, D., & Jones, W. H., (1980). When superstition fails: Reactions to disconfirmation of paranormal beliefs. *Personality and Social Psychology, 6*, 83–88.

Sabadell, M. A. (1998). Biomagnetic pseudoscience and nonsense claims. *Skeptical Inquirer, 22*(4), 28. Retrieved September 27, 2002, from http://www.csicop.org/si/9807/magnet2.html

Sagan, C. (1996). *The demon-haunted world: Science as a candle in the dark*. New York: Ballantine.

St. Mary's Hospital, Amsterdam, NY. (2002). *Center for complementary therapies*. Retrieved September 20, 2002, from http://www.smha.org/department_descriptions.php

Saloviita, T., Ruusila, L., & Ruusila, U. (2000). Incidence of savant syndrome in Finland. *Perceptual & Motor Skills, 91*(1), 120–122.

Sarner, L. (1998). Therapeutic touch: Responses to objections to the JAMA paper. *Skeptic Magazine*. Retrieved September 25, 2002, from www.quackwatch.com

Selby, C., & Scheiber, B. (1997). Science or pseudoscience? Pentagon grant funds alternative health study. *Skeptical Inquirer*. Retrieved September 18, 2002, from http:// www.csicop.org/si9607/tt.html

Shah, R., & Shah, R. (2002). *Homeopathy for your child*. Retrieved September 28, 2002, from http:// www.indiaspace.com/homoeopathy/child.htm

Sitzman, Y. M. (2002). *The religious ramifications of facilitated communication*. Retrieved September 28, 2002, from http://www.goldenfc.com/articles/sitzman/rrofc.htm

Skille, O. (1989). VibroAcoustic therapy. *Music Therapy, 8*(1), 61–77.

Slinn, J. (2002). *Mental retardation: A father's view*. Retrieved September 29, 2002, from http:// www.parentsinc.org/newsletter/898/mentalr.html

Snyder, M., & Lindquist, R. (2001, May 31). Issues in complementary therapies: How we got to where we are. *Online Journal of Issues in Nursing, 6*(2), Manuscript 1. Retrieved September 29, 2002, from http://www.nursingworld.org/ojin/topic15/tpc15_1.htm

Stanovich, K. E. (2001). *How to think straight about psychology*. Boston: Allyn & Bacon.

Starr, J., Landsman, C., Ochoteco, T., Carson-Groner, J. L., & Owens, A. (2000). *The therapy of touch*. Retrieved September 18, 2002, from http://carbvon.hampshire.edu/~cjarvis/NS120/projects/TT/therap.htm

Stevens, P. (2001). Magical thinking in complementary and alternative medicine. *Skeptical Inquirer*. Retrieved September 26, 2002, from http://www.csicop.org/si/2001-11/alternative.html

Thalbourne, M. A. (1998). Technical note: The level of paranormal belief and experience among psychotics. *The Journal of Parapsychology, 62*, 79–81.

The Rosicrucian Fellowship. (2002). *Mental retardation*. Retrieved September 29, 2002, from http://www.rosicrucian.com/zineen/pamen029.htm

Tobacyk, J., Milford, G., Springer, T., & Tobacyk, Z. (1988). Paranormal beliefs and the Barnum effect. *Journal of Personality Assessment, 52*, 737–739.

Tobacyk, J. J., Nagot, E., & Miller, M. (1988). Paranormal beliefs and locus of control: A multidimensional examination. *Journal of Personality Assessment, 52*, 241–246.

Treffert, D. A. (1988). The idiot savant: A review of the syndrome. *American Journal of Psychiatry, 145*, 563–572.

Treffert, D. A. (1989). *Extraordinary people*. London: Bantam.

Treffert, D. A., & Wallace, G. L. (2002). Islands of genius. *Scientific American, 286*(6), 76–85.

Trieschmann, R. B. (2001). Spirituality and energy medicine. *Journal of Rehabilitation, 67*, 26–32.

Ullman, D. (2002). *Scientific evidence for homeopathic medicine*. Retrieved October 1, 2002, from http://www.healthy.net/asp/templates/article.asp?PageType=Article&ID=942

Upledger, J. E. (2002). *Autism – Observations, experiences and concepts*. Retrieved September 27, 2002, from http://altmedicine.about.com/gi/dynamic/offsite.htm?site= http%3A%2F%2Fwww.upledger.com%2FClinic%2Fautism.htm

Part III

Field-Specific Issues

Fads in General Education:
Fad, Fraud, and Folly

Martin A. Kozloff
University of North Carolina at Wilmington

The common view is that fads are ideas ("Bran is healthy"), materials (pet rocks), or activities (disco) that enter the social scene, acquire a certain cache as the "in" thing, gain momentum ("Everyone's doing it"), saturate the market or come to be seen as hard, silly, useless, or revolting (bran), and then disappear. The view assumes that the public is fickle but always desirous of something new, and gullible to a well-formed advertising pitch. ("It lowered my cholesterol".)

The common view does not adequately capture the history of innovations in education (ranging from questionable to destructive), such as additive-free diets, "gentle teaching," "sensory integration," "full inclusion," and "facilitated communication" for persons with autism and other developmental disabilities; whole language, invented spelling, learning styles, multiple intelligences, "brain-based teaching," constructivist math, portfolio assessment, self-esteem raising, "learning centers," "sustained silent reading," "developmentally appropriate practices," and "student-centered education" for more typical students.

For one thing, ordinary fads are cheap and harmless. A pastel blue leisure suit of the 1970s cost $39.95 and when passé (in about 2 months) could be given to the Salvation Army. In contrast, pernicious innovations in education waste time, learning opportunities, money, energy, hope, and the chances for beneficent outcomes. Instead of being taught to feed himself, walk, point to things he wants, operate a tape player or computer, look at the faces of his parents, and turn the pages of books, the fully included 16-year-old student with severe mental retardation sits strapped into a wheelchair in a high school history class. He learns nothing whatever; his teachers know the thing is a cruel hoax; but "inclusion specialists" are satisfied with "social progress" (increased tolerance and justice), and have higher self-esteem for a job well done.

Second, the list of wasteful and pernicious ideas (pedagogies), materials (curricula), and activities ("practices") in education is not limited to passing fads. Some destructive innovations exist for decades under the same name (*whole language*) and when finally assaulted by sufficient data and popular magazine articles revealing their damaging effects, merely change their name (*balanced literacy*).

ird, fads are isolated events in the culture. A pet rock inhabits an endtable only. ducation, a chronic, destructive innovation infects a larger circle. For example, onstructivism influences how education students are trained (they will discover how to teach); how learning is understood (knowledge can't be transmitted, it must be discovered anew by each learner); what the ends of education will be (appreciation—not necessarily mastery—of literature, celebration of—not necessarily knowing much about—different cultures); how schools will be governed and organized ("democratic communities of lifelong learners"); and how teachers and schools will be evaluated and certified (according to "rubrics" of airy psychological dispositions and educationally correct shibboleths; e.g., if a multiple choice question on a certification exam says "developmentally appropriate," that is the right answer).

Fourth, the history of education is characterized not only by faddish ideas and methods that don't work, but also by failure to institutionalize ideas and methods that do work (Finn & Ravitch, 1996; Ravitch, 2000). In other words, the good, the true, and the effective are often fads in education. For example, data on thousands of children in Project Follow Through (Adams & Engelmann, 1996; Gersten, Keating, & Becker, 1988; Meyer, 1984; Meyer, Gersten, & Gutkin, 1983) showed that direct instruction (DI) and applied behavior analysis (ABA) fostered the highest achievement in reading and math—in contrast to so-called progressive, child-centered, "developmentally appropriate" curricula. However, DI and ABA were attacked by proponents and sellers of the predominant, progressive, and largely ineffective curricula found wanting in Project Follow Through (Watkins, 1997), and until recently were tolerated and marginalized as, at best, useful only for disadvantaged children and children with special needs.

In summary, there are two sorts of pernicious innovations in education: (a) passing fads (e.g., state-level portfolio assessment of new teachers), and (b) chronic malignancy (e.g., whole language). Both are examples of folly and fraud. Folly is applied to innovations created and/or adopted by fools; that is, by persons and groups easily taken in by rhetorical devices (including their own), such as glittering generalities and evocative phrases ("authentic," "best practice"), and who don't know enough about research and verification to properly examine and discredit advertising claims.

Fraud is applied to innovations created and/or adopted by persons and groups operating in bad faith; that is, who

1. Claim to work in the interests of children, but in fact work in the interests of their own incomes, tenure, prestige, control, and self-importance.
2. Refuse to test the null hypothesis that their innovations do not work.
3. Refuse to conduct research according to the canons of verification; that is, to use comparison groups, longitudinal designs, reliability checks, and objective data that are examined by noninterested parties, but instead favor qualitative classroom research with uncontrolled field notes and informal interviews easily used to gather anecdotes to support (but not to test and possibly invalidate) self-serving assertions about effectiveness.
4. Denigrate research that challenges their claims (e.g., that the Report of the National Reading Panel is politically motivated) and continue to advocate, use, or require other persons (e.g., new teachers) to use methods that are at best of questionable effectiveness and safety.

It is tempting to believe that institutionalizing a scientific mode of thinking would reduce the rate and longevity of pernicious innovation in education. Many wise persons have argued this proposition (Ellis & Fouts, 1993; Carnine, 2000; Stone & Clements, 1998). The assumption seems to be that if only the field accepted the moral obligation to do no harm, and in service of this obligation field-tested innovations before they were disseminated—rejecting those that do not work—teachers and school children would no longer be ill-served by logically absurd "philosophies" and detrimental methods. The young Plato believed this. If his fellow citizens would only subject their beliefs to the rule of reason, they would know the true and the good, and would not choose falsehood and mischief. But Plato discovered that his fellow citizens did not much care to engage in behavior (reasoning) that jeopardized self-serving and class-serving beliefs. That is the case now. Purveyors of chronic malignancy in education simply reject the idea that human learning and the quality of teaching can be measured objectively, and that objective data have much to say of any importance. In this way, they make themselves invulnerable to criticism. Therefore, it seems that the more effective course is to focus upstream to discover where pernicious innovations come from and how they so easily spread and become institutionalized—so that they may be prevented.

THE SOCIAL ORIGINS AND INSTITUTIONALIZATION OF FAD, FOLLY, AND FRAUD

This section examines conditions (folly and fraud) that breed and nurture both acute and chronic infestations of pernicious nonsense in education and that also work to marginalize or destroy what is both true and beneficial. We focus on Romantic modernism; anomie and egoism; incentives for continual innovation; absence of contract, contact, and accountability; and education schools as the primordial soup of infection.

Romantic Modernism

Romantic modernism is a large thread in our culture that helps both to nurture and organize a critique of contemporary western society. Romantic modernism is a rejection of the modern world (technology, globalism) and its social institutions and value orientations, including capitalism (seen as aggressive, greedy, destructive), government (seen as authoritarian), the middle-class family (seen as patriarchal, stressing hard work and self-denial—no fun), organized religion (imposing an external morality), and schools (oppressive, biased toward western dead white patriarchal Europeans). Romantic modernism calls for a return to the alleged innocence, freedom, equality, naturalism, and community of older times (Grossen, 1998; Hirsch, 1996, 2001; Rice, 2002; Stone, 1996). Following are core propositions of Romantic modernism:

1. The individual is naturally good.
2. The individual is naturally a moral being who will choose the right.
3. The individual is naturally able to construct knowledge—create concepts, propositions, morals, and other generalizations.

4. The individual is naturally spontaneous and creative; health depends on un-
   stifled spontaneity.
5. Society is hierarchical, routinized, regimented; its knowledge systems contain
   pre-formed concepts, propositions, values, and other generalizations; its systems of roles, statuses, norms, and obligations (in schools, families, religions,
   and political associations) constitute pre-formed identities, moral codes, and
   life courses. In summary, society is naturally repressive; it inhibits the full development of the individual. It is crippling. It is the source of misery and of the
   perversion of natural goodness.

Romantic modernism is simplified Marxism without the effort to determine what
traditional societies really were and are like and whether contemporary society is as
crass, regimented, and stifling as claimed. Moreover, Romantic modernist propositions are the largest producer of pernicious innovation in education—namely,
so-called progressive, child-centered, holistic, developmentally appropriate education, with its "philosophical" wing of postmodernists and critical theorists—the
education "intelligentsia" (e.g., Henri Giroux, Michael Apple, Peter McLaren). In
other words, fads (such as portfolio assessment of new teachers) and chronic mischief (such as constructivism and whole language) are the spawn of Romantic modernism; their tenets are simple translations of Romantic modernist propositions
into education jargon.

Romantic Modernism Incarnate as Progressivism.   Following are some general
tenets of progressivism (easily found in publications such as Brooks & Brooks,
1993; Bredekamp & Copple, 1997; Davis, Maher, & Noddings, 1990; DeVries &
Zan, 1994; von Glasersfeld, 1984, 1995; and Zemelman, Daniels, & Hyde, 1998),
followed in the next section by their translation into the "philosophy" and practice of whole language.

1. *Instruction should be developmentally appropriate. We know what is and is not developmentally appropriate. Sitting at desks; responding quickly and reliably to teacher
questions and requests; teacher-directed lessons; instruction in reading, spelling, and
writing for young children; and instruction to mastery—these are not developmentally
appropriate.*
The phrase developmentally appropriate is a rhetorical device by which self-
styled "child-centered" educators and publishers try to convince gullible education students, teachers, and parents that what they sell ("inquiry learning," "discovery learning," "constructivism," "whole language") is good, and that direct
instruction, practice, and teaching elemental skills first are bad. There is no serious research whatever to support claims about what is developmentally appropriate. Instead, the validation is nothing more than repetition of this vapid
phrase—a chant. The pernicious side is that advocates of "developmentally appropriate practices" believe that preschool and early elementary age children
(even young children with known disabilities) should not be taught language
and reading in a systematic fashion because this would be unnatural. Consequently, advocates of "dap" either do not know (are so blinded by their beliefs
that they do not care) that disadvantaged students and students with disabilities

will be denied exactly the sort of instruction they need to catch up with advantaged peers. This is how "educational philosophy" means the same as "the higher immorality."

2. The teacher should be a facilitator rather than a transmitter of knowledge. Students must discover and construct knowledge on their own.

This claim rests on the fallacy of false binary opposition: Either teachers teach or students construct knowledge, but not both. It is a rhetorical device used by progressive educators to claim the moral and educational high ground. And it is consistent with the Romantic notion that bodies of knowledge impose categories on the individual and therefore suppress their natural ability to think and to be creative. However, the preponderance of scientific research supports the teacher actually teaching, that is, showing students how to solve problems, leading them through solutions, testing or checking to see if students have gotten it, correcting all errors, giving more examples, and providing more practice and opportunities for independent application in the future. Following is a quotation—riddled with logical fallacies, such as ad hominem, prejudicial language, and false binary opposition—that reveals the Romantic modernist opposition to teacher-directed instruction.

Following is a quotation from an influential book on "best practices." The quotation (as with much of the book itself) uses a false binary opposition (the left side is bad practice; the right side is best practice) that reveals the Romantic modernist opposition to (a caricature of) teacher directed instruction.

"Management by punishments and rewards → Order maintained by engagement and community

Teacher creates and enforces rules → Students help set and enforce rules

Students are silent/motionless/passive/controlled → Purposeful talk, movement, and autonomy

Rigid, unvarying schedule → Predictable but flexible time usage based on activities

Teacher presentation and transmission of material → Students actively experiencing concepts

Focus on memorization and recall → Focus on applying knowledge and problem solving

One-way assignments/lessons → Accommodations for multiple intelligences and learning styles

Forced constant silence → Noise and conversation alternates with quiet time

Distant, negative, fearful, punitive → Positive, respectful, encouraging, warm

Direct → Consultative." (Zemelman, Daniels, & Hyde, 1998, pp. 213–214)

3. Students do not need to be taught in a logical progression of tasks with precisely designed instructional communication. Most children learn well enough in 'messy,' natural environments.

This proposition rests on the Romantic opposition to technological progress, the idea that there can be bodies of knowledge external to the individual, and that there can be a set of uniformly effective ways to teach. The progressive educator feels stifled by the obligation to be technically proficient and to follow protocols created by other persons. However, these are not problems in medicine and other fields where professionals serve clients well precisely because professionals follow tested protocols. Note both the Romantic modernism and logical fallacies (of ad hominem and prejudicial language) embedded in the following critique of direct instruction.

Accompanying the call for the direct instruction of skills is a managerial, minimally democratic, predetermined, do-as-you're-told-because-it-will-be-good- for-you form of instruction. Outcomes are narrowly instrumental, focusing on test scores of skills, word identification, and delimited conceptions of reading comprehension. It is a scripted pedagogy for producing compliant, conformist, competitive students and adults. (Coles, 1998, para. 6)

4. *Homogeneous grouping based on students' current skills is bad. It lowers self-esteem and creates tracks. It is discrimination. Groups should be heterogeneous.*
This proposition, as with the others, trades on the alleged pro-egalitarianism and anti-authoritarianism of Romantic modernism. Grouping is essentially hierarchical; hierarchy is a perversion of natural equality. In fact, teachers learn very quickly that children in the same class are not equal, are not identical. Some students need more learning opportunities, assistance, individual attention, and practice than other students. Some students are ready for harder material than other students. Teaching to a heterogeneous group means that students get the same instruction despite their differences. Therefore, few students receive the kind of instruction from which they would most benefit. Ironically, the call for heterogeneous grouping means that students' initial differences really do become tracks because the neediest students fall even farther behind (Grossen, 1996). In special education, ideological antagonism to homogeneous grouping is found in the full inclusion movement—the result of which is that students with severe disabilities are placed in politically correct classrooms where they learn little that is useful.

5. *Teachers should not correct errors immediately and consistently. Error correction makes students dependent on the teacher and threatens self-esteem.*
This prescription flows from the Romantic and nativist notions that students construct knowledge and therefore should not be taught directly. The problem is that when teachers do not teach students what errors are and how to correct them, many students do not figure it out on their own. Therefore, errors are repeated and, in time, students have huge knowledge gaps that are impossible to fill without an enormous expenditure of time and effort (e.g., reteaching basic math skills to students who have no idea what is going on in algebra class; Anderson, Reder, & Simon, 1998). Predictably, these students end up both unskilled and with low self-esteem.

6. *Frequent practice is not an effective way to foster mastery and high self-expectations. Practice is boring and inhibits creativity. Drill and kill.*

This proposition rests on the Romantic deification of the individual. Practice and its product (uniform proficiency) are seen as regimentation and therefore an assault on individuality. In contrast, artists (martial, dance, music) and athletes know (and the preponderance of scientific research shows) that practice is the only sure route to mastery and the realization of some of the highest values, such as grace, endurance, and precision.

    7. Teachers should create their own curricula and lesson plans, rather than follow field-tested programs. Programs disempower teachers and hinder self-expression. This statement expresses the Romantic idea that to receive knowledge diminishes the individual and places him or her beneath the oppressive weight of external authority. However, as with other propositions in the Romantic dogma, this fosters sham, because teachers—with virtually no training in how to design instruction—are obliged to prepare not merely a few lessons but year-long curricula in reading, math, spelling, writing, science, and so on. The task is of course impossible and means that at best students receive ill-designed instruction. Moreover, it means that teachers are implicitly field-testing each lesson on their own students. It is doubtful that many families want their children to be part of such experiments.

    Instead of empowering teachers, this statement, in the end, leads to the disempowerment of teachers as they are denied the tools (field-tested programs) that would make them more effective. Doubtless an underlying reason why education professors and ed schools abhor effective field-tested programs in math, reading, spelling, writing, and other subjects is that these programs make education courses and education professors' endless innovations irrelevant to new and veteran teachers alike.

Progressivism Incarnate in Whole Language.   Following are quotations from prominent advocates of whole language. The quotations translate core Romantic modernist and progressivist propositions into educational jargon that serves whole language. However, every one of the propositions is contrary to the preponderance of scientific research on reading (National Reading Panel, 2000).

> Adults cannot actually teach children how to read or write, though they can demonstrate or model reading and writing to them. (Weaver, 1988, p. 86)

> All proficient readers have acquired an implicit knowledge of how to read, but this knowledge has been developed through the practice of reading, not through anything that is taught at school. (Smith, 1973, p. 184)

> When language (oral or written) is an integral part of functioning of a community and is used around and with neophytes, it is learned 'incidentally.' (Artwergen, Edelsky, & Flores, 1987, p. 145)

> Learning is continuous, spontaneous, and effortless, requiring no particular attention, conscious motivation, or specific reinforcement. (Smith, 1992, p. 432)

> … when parents and teachers plan children's environment and activities carefully so that literacy is an integral part of everything they do, then literacy learning becomes a

natural and meaningful part of children's everyday lives. When you create this kind of environment, there is no need to set aside time to teach formal lessons to children about reading and writing. Children will learn about written language because it is a part of their life. (Schickendanz, 1986, p. 125)

... 'sounding out' a word is cumbersome, time consuming, and unnecessary. By using context, we can identify words with only minimal attention to grapho-phonemic cues. (Weaver, 1980, p. 86)

Scientific Research at Odds With the Core Propositions of Folly (Romanticism and Progressivism).   Contrast the preceding propositions from the canons of Romanticism and progressivism (the source) and whole language (the incarnation) of fad and fraud, with the following propositions—which have the strongest and longest history of empirical support and on which rest effective field-tested curricula and instructional methods (Adams & Engelmann, 1996; Anderson, Reder, & Simon, 1998; Brophy & Good, 1986; Cotton, 1995; Ellis & Worthington, 1994; Kameenui & Simmons, 1990; Rosenshine, 1986, 1997; Rosenshine & Stevens, 1986; Walberg & Paik, 2000).

1. The teacher knows and can state *exactly* what he or she wants students to learn at all times; that is, the teacher can say exactly what students will be able to *do*.

"I am teaching the strategy for decoding words. By the end of the week, students will accurately and rapidly sound out *sit, sam, am, can, man, fit,* and *ran.*"

"I am teaching the concept *democracy.* By the end of the lesson, students will state the verbal definition of democracy, identify democratic and nondemocratic forms of political society, and develop examples and nonexamples of democracies."

"I am increasing fluency at math facts. By the end of the week, students will solve at least 10 one-digit adding and subtracting problems per minute with at least 90% accuracy."

When objectives are this clear, teachers are able to plan exactly how to teach and how to evaluate the effects of instruction.

2. The teacher systematically fosters the different sorts of changes that define mastery—acquisition (accuracy); fluency (accuracy and speed); assembling elements (e.g., knowledge of sound–symbol relationships and reading left to right) into larger compounds (sounding out words); generalization of knowledge to new examples; retention of skill over time; and independence from teacher supervision.

3. Instruction is a logically progressive sequence. It begins with elemental skills (e.g., counting, math facts) and moves to increasingly complex skills (adding, subtracting, solving word problems, using these skills in other places; e.g., adding the number of plates and cups in a cupboard at home). Students are always taught pre-skills needed for next lessons.

4. The curriculum focuses on a skill (e.g., the strategy for multiplying two-digit numbers) until it is mastered before the teacher moves to another kind of skill (e.g., decimals). Otherwise, students master nothing and basically have to start all over next year.

5. The teacher moves at a brisk pace to sustain attention and get more taught.

6. The teacher stays focused and keeps students focused on the task at hand. Lectures, demonstrations, and discussions do not wander off.

7. The teacher corrects all errors immediately. "That word is *snap*. What word? *snap*. Spell *snap*. s n a p. Read the sentence again."

8. The teacher immediately tests or checks whether students are getting what he or she is trying to teach. "Okay, your turn to read these words" or "Now, you solve this problem yourselves." If some students make errors, the teacher re-teaches the problem spot. This shows that the teacher understands that (a) the *only* solid measure of teaching effectiveness is students *using* what the teacher taught and (b) the teacher must check teaching effectiveness every time he or she teaches something new—the next letter–sound relationship (m says mmm), the next vocabulary word, the next rule, the next fact. This means that the teacher might be checking comprehension 30 or more times per lesson.

9. The teacher often asks questions of the whole group, and has the whole group respond together. "Who wrote the first draft of the *Declaration of Independence*?" The teacher also calls on individual students, asking the question first. "When was the *Declaration* signed? [Pause for think time] Johnny."

10. The teacher gives specific praise. "Excellent for reading that passage with no errors!" Not, "Good reading."

11. Homework is not used to teach the skill, for example, how to multiply, spell new words, or write a paper. (This should be done in school.) Homework is used to generalize or apply skills learned in school.

This section reveals a strong contrast between (a) the core beliefs of Romantic modernism and their translation into general so-called progressive, child-centered education, and then into chronic forms of pernicious pedagogy such as whole language, and (b) a set of empirical generalizations, instructional methods, and field-tested curricula derived from the preponderance of scientific research, which is largely rejected by progressivists, who at this time control education. The next section provides part of an answer to the question, How can a field so readily adopt and institutionalize ideas and methods (fad and fraud) that fly in the face of both common sense ("Teach kids the sounds made by the letters") and scientific research?

Anomie and Egoism

Medical doctors do not prescribe coffee enemas as a treatment for ovarian cancer, although some "New Age healers" have done so. No physician could logically deduce coffee enemas from the medical knowledge base on biology in general and cancer in particular. A physician suggesting such a treatment would be deemed mad. In other words, medical practice rests on a shared and strong knowledge base of empirically robust propositions. The knowledge base is part of the stock of common knowledge expected of qualified physicians. It helps to foster social cohesion among physicians (they see themselves as part of and sharing something larger) which in turn (a) lends moral authority to the knowledge base that is independent of the individual; (b) makes each physician morally responsible for acting in accordance with the knowledge base; and (c) makes each physician's actions (assessment, diagnosis, prescription, treatment) evaluatable in relation to the knowledge base and accountable to the field as a whole. In summary, physicians—as physicians—cannot think and act as they please (egoistically) and still consider themselves morally responsible, competent, and respectable. They cannot prescribe treatments that have no basis in research or that are known not to work, and avoid punishment. The same may be said of engineering, architecture, military operations, business decisions, farming, barbering, and other serious endeavors.

Not so in the field of education. Education does not have a knowledge base shared within and across teachers and education professors, schools, districts, states, and education schools—a knowledge base that rests on scientific research; that is, experimental, quantitative, longitudinal, replicated research whose findings are turned into conclusions and instructional implications only after they are examined in the light of the rules of right reasoning. Despite the preponderance of scientific research that yields clear and strong generalizations (listed previously), there is no agreement on such fundamental issues as (a) the desirability of logically precise communication and a logical progression of tasks; (b) error correction; (c) practice; (d) when teachers should be more directive and when students should guide their own endeavors; (e) when skills are best taught in isolation (e.g., word lists or math facts) and when they are best taught in context (in sentences, in problems); and (f) whether all tasks should be taught to near mastery before going on, or whether the same tasks should be revisited again and again until they are learned.

In other words, education is an *anomic culture*. Progressive ideas, methods, and curricula are not generated and legitimized by a solid and shared body of empirical propositions that say, If you do X, Y will happen. (Rather, they are generated and legitimized by beliefs in the dogma of Romanticism and progressivism.) Nor are progressive ideas, methods, and curricula rejected because they are logically absurd and harmful to children. (Rather, they are sustained by beliefs in the dogma of Romanticism and progressivism.)

For progressivists, few empirical research generalizations and rules for reasoning appear to be accepted as independent and as having an authority greater than what the education guru, ed professor, or ed school may think of them, and that therefore oblige intellectually honest persons to reject groundless beliefs and fanciful innovations. Indeed, Romantic modernism and its derivations, constructivism and postmodernism, attack the possibility that there can be any truths and rules for reasoning external to the individual. This is because independent truths and rules (given the egoism bred by the Romantic modernist thought world) are said to stifle the academic freedom and creativity of the individual.

Lacking institutionalized rules for reasoning (testing, falsifying) that say, "This is absurd. Go no further," and encouraged by Romantic beliefs that knowledge is relative and that individuals construct what is true for them, progressive education innovators operate in a state of *egoism*. They, as individuals and special "philosophy" groups, take themselves to be the final judges of what is true, effective, and good. Therefore, when critics ask for objective data and experimental research to test the claims of innovators, these requests are understood as attacks. Unfortunately, anomie and egoism help to sustain flawed curricula that damage the life chances of many children who depend on the honesty, humility, and rationality of educators. Note the interesting take on moral responsibility in these comments of a whole language advocate. "Saying that we are determined to teach every child to read does not mean that we will teach every child to read .... The best we can do ... is ... to ensure that, if not every child lives up to our hopes, there is a minimum of guilt and anguish on the part of teachers, students, and parents" (Smith, 1992, p. 441).

Incentives to Mischief Disguised as Child-Centered Innovation

Instruction in many subjects is or could be routine. Most children can be easily taught reading, math, spelling, writing, history, literature, and other subjects if instruction is well designed. This is true for students with and without disabilities. Moreover, knowledge of exactly how to teach these subjects could easily be put (and has been put) in a disseminable form, such as commercial curricula (e.g., *Reading Mastery* from SRA/McGraw-Hill, *Basic Skill Builders* from Sopris West, and *Skills for School Success* from Curriculum Associates). However, there is an incentive in education not to routinize and package effective instruction, although this would increase teachers' effectiveness and benefit their students. Instead, there is an incentive continually to revolutionize pedagogy and technique. This is because packaging effective curricula for easy distribution would mean that the field of education no longer has much business for education consultants, education professors, education researchers (on mundane subjects, such as reading and math, that have been pretty well covered by 100,000 articles), gurus, workshop promoters, and certifiers. Having little business, they would soon be out of business. This helps to explain why these self-interested parties in education work diligently to convince school systems, funding sources, government agencies, consumer groups, and families that there is still so much to learn; that teaching is an art, not a science; and that there are still so many problems to solve. Therefore, each next innovation (e.g., brain-based teaching) must be understood not as an example of increasing wisdom, but as creation of a new need and set of products.

Absence of Contract, Contact, and Accountability

In medicine, law, and business, clients contract with service providers; clients generally have direct contact with service providers, and clients can hold service providers accountable for failing to deliver contracted outcomes or for operating in violation of professional standards. This is not the case in education. Education innovators (e.g., professors, workshop promoters, publishers) do not have a contract with students, families, teachers, schools, or districts. They rarely interact in a direct way with the persons and organizations affected by their innovations. They receive no corrective consequences for "products" that were not properly field-tested or when they fail to deliver promised outcomes such as "Your students will be lifelong learners."

This distance between innovators and their subjects (not customers, clients, or partners) enables innovators to treat the whole process as a form of self-aggrandizing play. For example, education professors adopt a "new philosophy" (say, constructivism or postmodernism); they think of interesting ways it could be applied to schools (a discovery approach to teaching grammar); they have exciting conversations with like-minded colleagues; they get a grant (or at least get a school) that will enable them to implement their new idea; they take some kind of data that supports what they already believe; and they publish a series of articles and give papers at conferences, all validated by their peers' approval, that bring tenure and prestige. In time, the novelty wears off and they move on to another hot idea, leaving behind 10th graders who are still "struggling writers." In summary, there can be no compelling sense of moral responsibility where self-importance and arrogance are bred by egoism, where no adverse consequences follow fraud and folly, and where there is no external, professional code similar to the Hippocratic oath in medicine.

Primordial Soup of Fad, Folly, and Fraud

Too many schools of education are sources of pernicious innovations, the carriers of Romantic-progressivist doctrine. They induct new teachers and administrators into the Romantic-progressivist thought world and thereby ensure that another generation is prepared to receive and accept progressivist innovations (Hirsch, 1996; Ravitch, 2000). For example, a number of ed school teacher training curricula rest on and are misguided by empirically weak and logically flawed progressivist (constructivist, child-centered, developmentally appropriate) shibboleths concerning how children learn and therefore how children should and should not be taught. A small sample of these was listed in an earlier section (e.g., drill and kill, teachers should facilitate but not directly teach, students should construct knowledge). These are repeated in course after course, book after book, and exam after exam in education schools (Kramer, 1991).

At the same time, ed schools often do not adequately teach students the logic of scientific reasoning, specifically, how to define concepts and judge the adequacy of definitions and how to assess the logical validity of an education professor's or writer's argument and the credibility of his or her conclusions. Nor do ed schools commonly have students read original works (to see if, in fact, Piaget said what is claimed for him), original research articles, meta-analyses, and other literature reviews. The result is that most ed students do not have the skill to determine the validity of the progressivist propositions and curricula they are taught, but must rely on what their professors tell them to believe.

Moreover, a shared intellectual poverty that favors Romantic-progressivist doctrine is sustained because education professors typically read little that challenges what they already believe; they ignore research that invalidates their child-centered, constructivist thought world; and they mount disingenuous arguments against the preponderance of scientific research that challenges what they teach. For example, most do not as a matter of course and scholarly obligation read the Report of the National Reading Panel (one of many huge literature reviews), and do not have their students read this and other reviews. Or, they dismiss these reviews and teach their students to dismiss these reviews, with off-handed comments such as "All research is flawed" or "This document is biased." This self-imposed and self-defensive ignorance helps to ensure that what education professors believe and teach remains, to them, unchallenged. In addition, ed schools often sustain a Romantic-progressivist thought world by hiring persons who are educationally correct, that is, who believe the same doctrine as the committee that hires them and therefore won't upset existing relations of power or challenge anyone to think very hard.

There are two sorts of pernicious innovations in education: passing fads (e.g., multiple intelligence) and chronic malignancies (whole language). Both waste time, money, energy, teachers' efforts and goodwill, and children's opportunities to master skills. Both forms of pernicious innovation rest on the emotional appeal of an empirically empty Romantic modernist critique of contemporary social institutions and values (primary folly) translated into progressivist education shibboleths and jargon (derivative folly) that are used to generate and then to sustain allegedly novel (but rarely field-tested and almost always worthless) "practices" (fraud) that provide prestige, tenure, privilege, publication, easy money, and power to their promoters. Fads, folly, and fraud are perpetrated by too many faculty in education and will continue as long as they are allowed.

REFERENCES

Adams, G. L., & Engelmann, S. (1996). *Research on Direct Instruction: 25 years beyond DISTAR.* Seattle, WA: Educational Achievement Systems.

Anderson, J. R., Reder, L. M., & Simon, H. A. (1998). *Applications and misapplications of cognitive psychology to mathematics education.* Pittsburgh, PA: Department of Psychology. Carnegie Mellon University. Available from http://act.psy.cmu.edu/personal/ja/misapplied.html

Artwergen, B., Edelsky, C., & Flores, B. (1987). Whole language: What's new? *Reading Teacher, 41,* 144–154.

Bredekamp, S. B., & Copple, C. (1997). *Developmentally appropriate practice in early childhood programs.* Washington, DC: National Association for the Education of Young Children.

Brophy, J., & Good, T. (1986). Teacher behavior and student achievement. In M. Wittock (Ed.), *Third handbook of research on teaching* (pp. 328–375). Chicago: Rand McNally.

Brooks, J. G., & Brooks, M. G. (1993). *In search of understanding: The case for constructivist classrooms.* Alexandria, VA: Association for Supervision and Curriculum Development.

Carnine, D. (2000). *Why education experts resist effective practices (and what it would take to make education more like medicine).* Washington, DC: The Thomas B. Fordham Foundation. Available from http://www.edexcellence.net/library/carnine.html

Coles, G. (1998, December 2). No end to the reading wars. *Education Week.* Available from http://www.edweek.org/

Cotton, K. (1995). *Effective school practices: A research synthesis 1995 Update.* Available from http://www.nwrel.org/scpd/esp/esp95.html

Davis, R. B., Maher, C. A., & Noddings, N. (Eds.). (1990). *Constructivist views on the teaching and learning of mathematics* (pp. 125–146). Reston, VA: National Council of Teachers of Mathematics.

DeVries, R., & Zan, B. (1994). *Moral classrooms, moral children.* New York: Teachers College Press.

Ellis, A., & Fouts, J. (1993). *Research on educational innovations.* Princeton, NJ: Eye on Education.

Ellis, E. S., & Worthington, L. A. (1994). *Research synthesis on effective teaching principles and the design of Quality tools for educators.* Available from http://idea.uoregon.edu/~ncite/documents/technrep/tech05.pdf

Finn, C. E., & Ravitch, D. R. (1996). *Education reform 1995–1996. Part IV. Instruction. The tyranny of dogma.* Washington, DC: Thomas B. Fordham Foundation. Available from http://www.fordhamfoundation.org/library/epciv.html

Gersten, R., Keating, T., & Becker, W. C. (1988). Continued impact of the Direct Instruction model: Longitudinal studies of Follow Through students. *Education and Treatment of Children, 11,* 318–327.

Grossen, B. (1996). *How shall we group to achieve excellence with equity.* Eugene, OR: University of Oregon.

Grossen, B. (1998). *Child-directed teaching methods: A discriminatory practice of Western education.* University of Oregon. Available from http://darkwing.uoregon.edu/~bgrossen/cdp.htm

Hirsch, E. D., Jr. (1996). *The schools we need and why we don't have them.* New York: Doubleday.

Hirsch, E. D., Jr. (2001).The roots of the education wars. *Education Next,* Spring. Available from http://www.educationnext.org/unabridged/2001sp/hirsch.html

Kameenui, E. J., & Simmons, D. C. (1990). *Designing instructional strategies.* Columbus, OH: Merrill.

Kramer, R. (1991). *Ed school follies: The miseducation of America's teachers.* New York: Free Press.

Meyer, L. (1984). Long-term academic effects of the Direct Instruction Project Follow Through. *Elementary School Journal, 84,* 380–394.

Meyer, L., Gersten, R., & Gutkin, J. (1983). Direct instruction: A Project Follow Through success story in an inner-city school. *Elementary School Journal, 84,* 241–252.

National Reading Panel. (2000).*Teaching children to read.* Washington, DC: National Institute of Child Health and Development, U.S. Department of Health and Human Services.

Ravitch, D. R. (2000). *Left back: A century of failed school reforms.* New York: Simon & Schuster.

Rice, J. R. (2002). The therapeutic school. *Society, 32*(2), 19–27.

Rosenshine, B. (1986). Synthesis of research on explicit teaching. *Educational Leadership, 43,* 60–69.

Rosenshine, B. (1997). *Advances in research on instruction.* Available from http://epaa.asu.edu/barak/barak.html

Rosenshine, B., & Stevens, R. (1986). Teaching functions. In M. C. Wittrock (Ed.), *Handbook of research on teaching* (3rd ed., pp. 376–391). New York: Macmillan.

Schickendanz, J. A. (1986). *More than the ABC's: The early stages of reading and writing.* Washington, DC: National Association for the Education of Young Children.

Smith, F. (1973). *Psychology and reading.* New York: Holt, Rinehart & Winston.

Smith, F. (1992). Learning to read: The never-ending debate. *Phi Delta Kappan, 74,* 432–441.

Stone, J. E. (1996). Developmentalism: An obscure but pervasive restriction on educational improvement. Available from Education Policy Archives, http://www.olam.ed.asu.edu/epaa/v4n8.html

Stone, J. E., & Clements, A. (1998). Research and innovation: Let the buyer beware. In R. R. Spillane & P. Regnier (Eds.), *The superintendent of the future* (pp. 59–97). Gaithersburg, MD: Aspen.

von Glasersfeld, E. (1984). An introduction to radical constructivism. In P. Watzlawick (Ed.), *The invented reality* (pp. 17–40). New York: Norton.

von Glasersfeld, E. (1995). A constructivist approach to teaching mathematics. In L. P. Stefe & J. Gale (Eds.), *Constructivism in education* (pp. 3–16). Hillsdale, NJ: Lawrence Erlbaum Associates.

Walberg, H. H. J., & Paik, S. (2000). *Effective education practices* (Educational practices series. International Academy of Education. International Bureau of Education). Available from http://www.ibe.unesco.org/International/Publications/EducationalPractices/EducationalPracticesSeriesPdf/prac06e.pdf

Watkins, C. (1997). *Project Follow Through: A case study of contingencies influencing instructional practices of the educational establishment.* Cambridge, MA: Cambridge Center for Behavioral Studies.

Weaver, C. (1980). *Psycholinguistics and reading.* Cambridge, MA: Winthrop.

Weaver, C. (1988). *Reading process and practice.* Exeter, NH: Heinemann.

Zemelman, S., Daniels, H., & Hyde, A. (1998). *Best practice: New standards for teaching and learning in America's schools.* Portsmouth, NH: Heinemann.

Fads in Special Education: An Overview

Thomas Zane
The Sage Colleges Center for Applied Behavior Analysis

There is an old joke often heard in the field of special education:

Question: What are two things wrong with special education?

Answer: It's not special and it's not education.

Detterman and Thompson (1997) made the same point in their critique of the field. Although they said there is nothing special about the instruction and strategies in use for students with disabilities, it could be argued that the treatment fads found in special education are, in fact, "special" in that they are often quite unique and "stand out" from other more traditional strategies. As an example, consider craniosacral therapy, in which a therapist physically manipulates the skull to supposedly reduce the symptoms of autism and other learning disabilities. Such a strategy appears quite unique, albeit groundless and utterly ineffective.

Fads—treatments that are used which have no empirically derived, experimentally based research to show effectiveness—have historically existed in special education and continue to this day. Chaddock (1998) termed them the "reform du jour" (p. B1), a pattern of teachers trying new techniques on a regular basis, without first assessing the effectiveness of the technique or even considering if there are empirical studies that support effectiveness.

Fads in special education probably happen for several reasons. One relates to the importance of helping students with disabilities. Worrall (1990) suggested that because of the need to help students with learning and behavioral problems, there is pressure to try any technique or strategy for which there is even minimal proof or logic to suggest effectiveness. A good example of this is educational computer software designed to teach reading, writing, mathematics, and other skills. If such software were effective, then teachers could supply students with computers and there would then be a reasonable expectation that the students would learn. However, research (e.g., Zane & Frazer, 1992) has shown that there is little proof that such software actually does what the developers claim it can do. Therefore, as teachers, parents, and administrators seek "cures" and innovative practices that will maximize the learning of their students with disabilities (Chaddock, 1998), they may be more likely to attempt strategies with unknown or unproven effectiveness. Because of pressure (and desire) to help their students, professionals err by accepting and not questioning too demandingly different methods that could be useful (Detterman & Thompson, 1997). Others more skeptical (e.g., Vaugh, Klinger, & Hughes, 2000), posit that teachers continue to use methods known to not work because the teachers are familiar with such treatments and find it easy for them to implement them. That is, professionals might select a fad treatment to use because of faith that it will work, or in response to testimonials that aver the effectiveness of the treatment (Katsiyannis & Maag, 2001).

Another explanation focuses on issues surrounding the quality of research in special education. Chaddock (1998) noted that some professional journals in education do not have a peer-review requirement prior to publication of articles. This could lead to published articles that have an appearance of having passed a rigorous scientific analysis, but are replete with internal and external validity problems that are not communicated to readers. Parents and teachers who read such articles then believe there is empirical proof supporting the report of effectiveness. Acceptance of such proof relates to another potential explanation as to why fads occur in special education: a belief that the practitioners of special education are all honest, hard-working, and have only the best intentions for the students with disabilities. That is, all who practice special education are benevolent and would never be fraudulent (Worrall, 1990). In reality, there is no reason to believe that fraud will occur less in the education field than in other areas of society, or that researchers in special education will be less subject to the same interpretational excesses of their findings that, in part, are addressed by peer review.

From an even more disturbing perspective, the acceptance of postmodern thought may account for the continuation of fad treatments as well. Postmodern thinking takes the position that there is no universal body of knowledge about the physical and mental worlds; there is no "standard" knowledge or truths waiting to be discovered (Koertge, 1998; Sasso, 2001). Instead, postmodernists believe that most knowledge is "relative," in that what is known is influenced by social class and politics. Science, and the rules of science, are characterized as having been developed by men in power (demonstrably, a questionable position on science, because few scientists have any political or even social power) and thus these rules and methods are invalid. Another common premise is that there are multiple ways of knowing about something and these different perspectives are at least equal to, if not better than, empiricism and experimentation. For example, in his defense of the whole language approach to reading, Goodman (1992) wrote, "[T]he experimental researchers have demonstrated ... that their truth, their sources of evidence, are not those of teachers" (p. 356). Clearly, anyone who adheres to the position of postmodern thought has a lower criterion for accepting as valid, treatments for which there is little empirical evidence. For example, case studies and personal stories about the effectiveness of a method may constitute sufficient proof according to the postmodern, antiscientific perspective and may be considered evidence with a high degree of social validity. Belief in a method's effectiveness may substitute for research findings (Gage, 1989; Stahl, 1990).

A final hypothesis as to why fad treatments in special education occur is that people in the field—professionals, parents, and consumers—are uneducated, gullible, and may be duped. For example, when reading public documents, such as newspapers that contain a brief news article discussing how some fringe therapy helped a particular person or small group of subjects, many people latch onto that as evidence of a useful treatment, even though an article may contain no reference to research or scientific investigation (Kamhi, 1999). Indeed, several surveys (see Budiansky, 1986; Pepper, 1987; Young, 1988) show that even educated people are willing to try unproven treatments and are not as skeptical as they should be.

Adopting a fad treatment for use with students with disabilities has serious consequences. Using treatments for which there is no empirical evidence for effectiveness means that students may not progress as well as might be expected if other methods were to be used. Detterman and Thompson (1997) claim that measures of IQ and academic achievement of students served by special education services have not significantly changed over the past several years. Supporting this claim is Hettleman (2002) who cites statistics for children receiving special education services in Maryland. Students scoring in the "satisfactory" or better range on the state performance tests in reading represented only 9.6% of those in third grade. Percentages actually declined over the next two grades, at 5.6% in fifth grade and 1% in eighth grade. In addition, the gap in the scores between students in regular and special education widened over these years. Hettleman stressed that the issue today is finding high quality treatment for children receiving special education services. The lack of effective treatment is not a phenomenon particular to the United States. In England, for example, it is estimated that only 40% of the pupils leave school with adequate reading skills (MacLeod, 1997).

Sometimes fad treatments receive positive public (i.e., legislative or state or federal education department) recognition, which then provides an air of legitimacy to the treatment, which furthers its use. For example, the Senate of the state of Florida passed a resolution to make April 2002 "Craniosacral Therapy Awareness Month," recognizing the alleged importance and significance of this therapy that supposedly improves functioning of children with a variety of disabilities, including autism (Upledger Institute, 2002).

The existence of fad treatments in special education does damage in another way as well. The adoption of fads wastes money that could be spent on other instructional programs proven effective or that could be used to empirically evaluate treatments (Kean, 1993). In 1968, per pupil spending for special education was approximately $1,200 (Chambers, Parrish, & Harr, 2002). That figure has risen significantly over the past 30 years, with statistics from the 1999–2000 school year showing per pupil spending of $12,474. The federal government spent about $50 billion on special education services in the 1999–2000 school year. It is imperative that the money be well spent, that is, that this funding supports effective strategies leading to improved academic and skill performance. Unfortunately, the data do not support such a conclusion (e.g., Detterman & Thompson, 1997; Johnson & Kafer, 2001).

Some of the fad treatments that currently are being used with students in special education programs are described in the following sections of this chapter.

COGNITIVE SKILLS AND ACADEMICS

Numerous interventions exist to promote cognitive skills, but which lack the scientific credibility necessary for professionals to take seriously. Consider, for example, the use of nutritional supplements for persons with Down syndrome. For over the past 50 years, various so-called professionals have offered vitamin "cocktails" that supposedly improve the cognitive abilities and appearance of children with this syndrome (e.g., Haboud, 1955; Harrell, 1981). However, professional organizations have stated that there is no scientific proof that a mixture of different vitamins, nutrients, or chemicals is causally related to specific or general improvements in persons with Down syndrome (American College of Medical Genetics, 1996; National Down Syndrome Society, 1997).

Reading difficulties account for involvement of a large percentage of students in special education programs. The U.S. Department of Education (2000) reported that more than half of students labeled with a learning disability have serious reading deficiencies. The "Irlen lenses" were designed to solve these problems. The Irlen syndrome (n.d.) was first identified by Helen Irlen, a school psychologist in California (Irlen Institute, 2003, para. 2). Also known as scotopic sensitivity syndrome, some reading disabilities are hypothesized to be a result of a visual perception problem. Although the optical system is normal, an individual with this problem "sees" the printed page differently. Irlen describes some of the differences as "washouts," "rivers," and "seesaws." Each produces a visual array of the words on a printed page quite different from what normally skilled readers might see. Individuals with this scotopic sensitivity can be negatively impacted not only in their reading, but in attention span, motivation, handwriting, and self-esteem. Irlen (2002) even notes that about 50% of all persons diagnosed with autism may have this perceptual disorder. To determine the existence of the scotopic sensitivity syndrome, Irlen (1983) developed the Scotopic Sensitivity Symptom Checklist and the Irlen Differential Perceptual Schedule. For persons with the Irlen syndrome, the treatment involves the use of colored overlays placed on the reading material, or wearing of glasses that have colored (tinted) lenses. The colors supposedly reduce or eliminate the perceptual problems.

When reviewing the literature published on this method of treating reading problems, one discovers conflicting findings. Although Robinson and Conway (1990, 1994) found that subjects improved their attitude to school, academic skills, and reading rate after using colored lenses, reading accuracy was not improved. On the other hand, much of the published literature touting the success of this method is in the form of self-report data and case studies (Fletcher & Martinez, 1994), and is not submitted to a peer-review process (Spafford, Grosser, Donatelle, Squillace, & Dana, 1995). There is weak evidence supporting the validity of this approach. O'Connor, Sofo, Kendall, and Olsen (1990) showed an increase in comprehension after using colored filters to supposedly eliminate perceptual problems. Moreover, there is a lack of evidence from controlled studies that the colored overlays or lenses are causally related to actual improvements in reading ability (Fletcher & Martinez, 1994; Martin, Lovegrove, McNicol, & Mackenzie 1993). Indeed, there is skepticism that scotopic sensitivity syndrome even exists (Weiss, 1990). Due to the lack of comprehensive research data consistently showing a causal relationship between the use of colored overlays or lenses and improved reading accuracy and comprehension, one must view the Irlen approach with skepticism.

THE BASIS OF READING RECOVERY

Reading Recovery (Clay, 1985) is a method of teaching reading used in over 10,000 elementary schools in the United States, serving about 150,000 student in first grade yearly; over one million students have received Reading Recovery services since 1984 (Hoff, 2002). The method is believed by many to be one of the most effective remedial reading interventions currently available (e.g., Johnston & Allington, 1991).

The philosophy of Reading Recovery is, simply, that children will learn to read by being actually immersed in reading (Pinnell, 1991), placing the cart directly in front of the horse, because learning to say the sounds coded by letters in words is necessary before immersion in reading is practically possible. Clay (1985) emphasizes that the children need to learn the same reading strategies used by good readers. To that end, the basic Reading Recovery procedure involves one-to-one tutoring outside of the child's classroom. Teachers conducting Reading Recovery are required to be certified teachers receiving formal training in Reading Recovery methods for an academic year (Wasik & Slavin, 1993). They receive this training while working with their students. Students in the Reading Recovery program are tutored for 30 minutes daily, for up to 60 lessons. The target criterion for these children is to reach the reading ability of the "middle" or "average" readers in their respective classrooms (Wasik & Slavin, 1993).

There are numerous research reports supporting the contention that Reading Recovery results in helping students who are the poorest readers in the first grade reach grade level at the end of a program of up to 20 weeks (Hoff, 2002). For example, Clay (1985) reported that almost all of the children receiving Reading Recovery caught up with their peers and retained those gains for 3 years. Over the 18 years in which Reading Recovery has been used in the United States, advocates claim that 81% of all students who participated in the program reached their respective grade level in reading (Reading Recovery, 2002, Section 4). DeFord, Lyons, and Pinnell (1991) reported the success of Reading Recovery and considered it as one of the best reading methodologies available to Chapter I programs. Similarly, Pinnell (1989) reported positive results of Reading Recovery with first-grade children.

However, before accepting the hypothesis that Reading Recovery is causally related to reading improvement, one must consider alternative explanations for the apparent success. Clay is the developer of Reading Recovery and thus her conclusions must be regarded with caution as potentially biased. In some of the Reading Recovery research, only data on the children who were successfully "discontinued" from Reading Recovery were presented, and the data for the students who failed to successfully complete the Reading Recovery program were not. For example, in the Saginaw Public Schools (1992) study, of the 55 students who began the Reading Recovery program, 20 failed to finish it, perhaps literally voting with their feet. Other studies (e.g., Ramaswami, 1994) show similar attrition, in that a good portion of the sample not only failed to improve, but their failure was not accounted for in the final data presented in the research (Elbaum, Vaughn, Hughes, & Moody, 2000; Pinnell, Short, Lyons, & Young, 1986; Wasik & Slavin, 1993). If all children who began Reading Recovery are included, then the percentage of students reaching their grade level in reading ability decreases from 81% to about 60% (Reading Recovery, 2002, Section 4).

Further, independent researchers have found other conflicting results. For example, several investigators (e.g., Glynn, Crooks, Bethune, Ballard, & Smith, 1989; Pinnell, Lyons, DeFord, Bryk, & Seltzer, 1994; Wasik & Slavin, 1993) reported that the students who successfully graduated from Reading Recovery lost the gains made, from over a few months to as much as 3 years after completing the program. The initial increased likelihood of being promoted to the next grade following graduation from Reading Recovery was nonexistent by the third grade. Additionally, Wasik and Slavin reported that 27% of the original group of students who started in Reading Recovery failed to graduate from the program, even after the minimum 60 tutoring sessions. Others (e.g., Pinnell, 1988) reported about 30% of the students originally starting Reading Recovery dropped out without success. Thus, Reading Recovery boosted the reading performance of 73% of the original cohort.

Other uncontrolled variables in some studies prevent the confident assumption that Reading Recovery was responsible for gains in student reading ability, even at these reduced levels. For example, although Pinnell et al. (1994) reported that students in the Reading Recovery program showed considerable gains when compared to other tutoring methods, the teachers in this method were trained in the Reading Recovery method, whereas the teachers implementing the other tutoring methods were substitute teachers and the extent of their training in their respective tutoring methods was not fully explained. In the Pinnell et al. (1994) study, teachers in the Reading Recovery condition were trained for at least 2 years, whereas teachers in a comparison group were given 2 weeks of training. Thus, students in Reading Recovery could have done well not because of Reading Recovery, but because of better trained teachers (Rasinski, 1995a, 1995b). Elbaum et al. (2000) hypothesized that the critical variable is the instructional competence of the teacher, not the particular program or the teacher–student ratio (also see Acalin, 1995; Evans, 1996). Another uncontrolled variable that could account for the results of Reading Recovery is that the evaluation instruments and dependent measures used to assess student progress were developed by Clay, and the specific information assessed is explicitly taught in the Reading Recovery program (Wasik & Slavin, 1993). Thus, "children who were tutored in Reading Recovery were also more familiar with the assessment than were the children in the control groups" (p. 187). In addition, the official policy of Reading Recovery is to not serve students who had already been retained in first grade (Wasik & Slavin, 1993).

Other concerns permeate the debate about the efficacy of Reading Recovery. The method apparently does not raise school achievement scores (e.g., Hiebert, 1994; Pinnell & Lyons, 1995). Reading Recovery does not seem to reduce the need for special education or other remedial services (e.g., Pollock, 1994; Shanahan & Barr, 1995). And, there exists a considerable body of research findings suggesting that Reading Recovery is no better or worse than other methods. For example, meta-analyses (e.g., Battelle, 1995; Elbaum et al., 2000), in which findings from many different studies are combined statistically, provide data showing that Reading Recovery is no better than other individual tutoring strategies. Fincher (1991) found other methods superior to Reading Recovery. Grossen (2002) reported on research-based reading strategies that appear to be more effective than

Reading Recovery. In fact, there is such concern about the effectiveness of Reading Recovery that a group of educational researchers have formally gone on record as concluding that the effectiveness of Reading Recovery is questionable and it should not be considered a scientifically based treatment for reading problems (Baker et al., 2002, para. 1).

In summary, the causal relationship between Reading Recovery and reading gains remains tenuous at best. There are too many confounding variables involved in the research to make a confident prediction of causality.

THE BASIS OF WHOLE LANGUAGE

Whole language generally refers to a nontraditional, non-phonics-based approach to the teaching of reading and language arts. Some view whole language as not only a method incorporating theories of language, including the transactional view of reading and writing, and the social and personal views of learning, but as a curriculum (Goodman, 1992). Whole language practitioners are more closely aligned with the Piagetian constructionist and Vygotskian views of learning and perceive behavioral learning theory as "unscientific and inadequate for explaining human learning" (Goodman, 1992, p. 358). Whole language is "learner-centered" (Goodman, 1989), in that the student is the focus, not the content of the instruction. There is a curricular and methodological connection of both oral and written language on which whole language teachers focus (Bergeron, 1990). Children can learn to read and write simultaneously (Stahl, McKenna, & Pagnucco, 1994). It is assumed that children will naturally discover the rules of language use as they are immersed in using language (Eldredge & Baird, 1996). Specific instruction on how to write properly is ignored. During whole language instruction, students are active participants, bringing all different knowledges together (e.g., personal, experiential). According to Goodman (1992), whole language incorporates functional language, "authentic" speech, learner "ownership" of the process and product, and the use of prior and cultural experiences of the learner. Students are allowed (with some guidance by the teacher) to select their reading materials (thereby presumably increasing interest and motivation), and teachers refrain from giving standard worksheets or answers to problems. It is important for students to think through situations and come up with their own solutions and ideas. Additionally, the atmosphere in a whole language classroom is one of safety, free of abuse of any kind (Goodman, 1989, 1992). Teachers build a classroom community that provides a positive environment, encouraging learning and respect of all members (Goodman, 1989).

The teacher is partially an authority figure, but also viewed as a learner along with the students. The children and teacher discuss and agree on goals to achieve. Teachers build lessons around the experiences and histories of the children, in order to maximize the relevancy and motivation of the studies. The students are "in control" (Goodman, 1989, p. 114) of what they learn. What is being learned must be relevant and mean something to the students.

The popularity of the whole language movement is evidenced in many ways. Goodman (1992) reported that there are about 500 teacher support groups across the country. Teachers are reported to be using it even though their particular districts or school systems have policies promoting other reading methodologies (Goodman, 1992). The shift to whole language use of "tradebooks" (i.e., non-basal workbooks) has resulted in an increase in the sale of children's books (Goodman, 1992).

Whether there is empirical research to support the use of whole language procedures is difficult to answer. Even proponents of this approach acknowledge that such a research base is lacking (Stahl et al., 1994; Yatvin, 1993). However, to critically evaluate the research on the effectiveness of the whole language approach in improving reading and writing, there must first be a clear and precise definition of what exactly whole language instruction is. Instead, what seems clear is that there is not one precise definition or description of whole language instruction; there is little consistency across the professional literature about what exactly it is. Bergeron (1990) conducted a review of 64 papers published in professional journals on whole language. Each paper was read three times and checklists were completed analyzing each article along a number of dimensions (e.g., definition of whole language, instructional techniques used in whole language). An independent reader was employed to determine the reliability of agreement of completing the analysis. Interrater reliability was above 88%. There was disagreement across the authors about how whole language should be defined. About 34% of the authors thought whole language to be an approach toward instruction, about 23% a philosophy of instruction, 14% a belief, and 6% a "method." Furthermore, Bergeron found wide discrepancies across the published studies with respect to the instructional strategies that make up a whole language approach. A total of 21 different techniques were mentioned across the 64 studies, such as use of literature, invented spelling, independent reading, reading aloud, and use of student journals. Only the use of literature and "writing process" was mentioned in more than 50% of the published studies. Other features thought to be a critical part of the whole language experience—whole-to-part instruction, journal writing, charts, choral reading, and big books—were found in no more than a third of the published studies.

Nevertheless, there are published research reports on the effectiveness of whole language approaches. Many of these compared a whole language strategy to a more traditional basal reader program. In a meta-analysis conducted by Stahl and Miller (1989), 46 studies were identified that compared whole language instruction with the more traditional reading instructional methods (such as basals). Although they found that children in kindergarten classrooms responded better to whole language instruction, in terms of their "conceptual base for reading," Stahl and Miller concluded that whole language instruction was no better than traditional instruction.

Stahl et al. (1994) updated their 1989 literature review to evaluate more current research on the effect of whole language instruction. On reviewing the literature, they found 102 citations related to "research" on whole language; of these, only 14 had quantifiable data on which to report. It is interesting that despite the apparent widespread use of whole language, there is little measurable research analyzing its effectiveness. Furthermore, Stahl et al. found that the focus of recent research had shifted from measuring the effectiveness on improving reading achievement or comprehension, to a focus on changing the attitude, or motivation, of children toward reading. That is, whole language researchers seem to be concentrating more on getting children interested in reading, instead of making them better readers. O'Flahaven et al. (1992) reported that teachers they surveyed thought that increasing motivation to read was more important than pursuing research in terms of how to best improve reading comprehension. Putting aside for the moment whether there is an empirically supported causal relationship between attitude and behavior, there is little empirical evidence to suggest that such attitudes are in fact changed. Stahl et al. (1994) reviewed 17 studies investigating this particular question and found only two studies supporting a whole language approach actually improving attitudes more than traditional reading instruction. One study favored traditional instruction and the remaining 14 studies found no difference between the two methods. McKenna, Stratton, Grindler, and Jenkins (1995) found similar results when comparing whole language versus traditional basal instruction in over 900 children in Grades 1 to 5. Not only did the whole language approach produce no more positive attitudes about reading than the traditional approach, but attitude measures in the students who received whole language instruction declined over the grades. That is, whole language did not produce more positive attitudes in the subjects at the time of the study, and the subjects' attitudes about reading actually declined over later grades.

When analyzing the effectiveness of whole language instruction on various measures of reading ability, there are mixed results. Stahl et al. (1994) reported an insignificant effect size favoring whole language when reviewing studies focusing on reading comprehension. However, the authors cautioned that there were too few studies done to confidently make the assumption that the whole language approach was actually responsible for positive changes in comprehension. Most studies show no difference in effectiveness between whole language and traditional reading instruction.

Perhaps one reason for little empirical research on the effect of whole language on skill and comprehension development is that the whole language proponents claim that "teachers are regaining their confidence in their own professional judgment in evaluating themselves and their pupils" (Goodman, 1992, p. 355). That is, teachers can study what they believe to be important and use evaluative criteria they choose in order to determine how effective they are with their students. Furthermore, in attacking the evidence against whole language, proponents of this approach disparage so-called scientific research and findings as not objective, but biased in terms of the particular researcher's political views (Smith, 1988). If this is the perspective of whole language proponents, then postmodern thought seems to have taken over the whole language training movement.

Another attack on the findings showing other methods are as good as or better than the whole language approach comes from some supporters claiming that the critics are part of a political campaign to discredit whole language, as if there are no empirical findings on which to base criticism. Stahl (1990) referred to this as the "politicization of educational discourse" (p. 143). For example, Goodman (1992) referred to "far-right" or "right-wing" critics five times in two pages of his defense of the whole language approach. McKenna et al. (1995) fully discussed the political nature of whole language proponents. Edelsky (1990), an obvious supporter of whole language, admitted that the whole language perspective includes a political one, including "distribution of power" in schools and society.

Autism

The number of children diagnosed with autism spectrum disorder (including pervasive developmental disorder, Asperger syndrome, and autism) has been increasing alarmingly across the country (e.g., Department of Developmental
Services, 1999; Fombonne, 2003). Autism is now one of the most common pediatric
neurological conditions affecting young children (Greenwood, 2000). It is the
third most common pediatric developmental disorder, following mental retardation and cerebral palsy. Unfortunately, as the number of children with these conditions rises, so too, it seems, does the number of treatments used in the autism field
that have no empirical evidence for effectiveness. The New York State Department
of Health (1999) published *Clinical Practice Guidelines*, reviewing several treatments currently in vogue for this condition. Treatments ranged from educational
(applied behavior analysis, developmental education), to physical (sensory integration), and medical (sensory diet, secretin). The guidelines also delineated specific criteria for acceptable research findings of effectiveness. The reader is
referred to these guidelines for an excellent discussion of the role research should
play in determining which treatments parents and caregivers should pursue, and
a review of the research, if any, supporting each of the methods. Greenspan's approach, sensory integration, diet therapy, and secretin were all found to lack in
any organized, well-developed research base that could support the contention
that those methods are effective.

One treatment currently popular to treat autism is craniosacral therapy (CST;
sometimes also called cranial manipulative therapy, neural organizational technique, or craniopathy). According to Upledger (n.d.), CST is a "gentle" (note the
positive, comforting word usage) strategy that focuses on changing, through
physical manipulation, the "craniosacral" system of the body, consisting of the
cerebrospinal fluid that envelops the brain and is contained in the spinal cord. The
hypothesis of CST therapists is that there are disruptions in the flow or movement
of the cerebrospinal fluid and that by massaging different parts of the head and
body (described as tapping the skull with fingertips; Jarvis, 2001), they can change
the flow, remove restrictions of the flow, and thus improve the physical and mental health of the patient.

CST apparently can "do it all." A list of maladies that can be improved by CST
includes:

- autism
- learning disabilities, dyslexia
- attention deficit hyperactive disorder (ADHD), emotional difficulties
- infantile disorders, colic, bedwetting
- post-traumatic stress disorders
- orthopedic problems
- traumatic brain and spinal cord injuries, and
- color blindness. (Ferreri & Wainwright, 1985; Upledger, n.d.)

CST is said to affect all of these problems and body areas because of the extent to
which the spine and brain affect all parts of the body. Ferreri (2002), the developer of
neural organizational therapy (NOT), actually explains the logic of manipulating

the body to produce changes in the cerebral spinal fluid by referring to the old song, "the head bone is connected to the foot bone."

There is little basis for being confident that CST can be the cause of improvement in any of these conditions. First, one must be skeptical about the procedure. As Carroll (2002) points out, the flow or "rhythm" of the cerebrospinal fluid is somehow detected only by the therapist's hands; no instrument or other measurement device is used or can be used. As well, the client must "have faith" that the treatment will work, or it will not (Woodruff, 2002).

The most conclusive evidence against the efficacy of CST was collected by Green, Martin, Bassett, and Kazanjian (1999), who conducted a comprehensive review of this therapy. They found 34 studies related to this technique and critiqued them in terms of the quality of the research design and significance of outcomes. Green et al. reported that 11 studies focused on the motion of cerebral spinal fluid and whether or not detection of the spinal fluid is possible. These studies confirmed that it was, using precise measuring instruments (such as magnetic resonance imaging), not by therapist's hands. However, these studies did not support the hypothesis that changes in cerebrospinal fluid are related to changes in health. Green et al. reported on another 9 studies that focused on whether or not the adult skull can actually be physically manipulated. Indeed, the cranium is not fused solid and small movement among the cranial bones is possible, but none of these studies proved that these types of movements can be done through manual manipulation as suggested by CST. Lastly, Green et al. found 12 studies in which the researchers attempted to directly assess the effectiveness of CST. However, there were significant problems found with each of these studies, including poor interobserver reliability and the use of weak designs, such as case studies, that do not allow a confident assumption of a functional relationship (i.e., cause and effect). Indeed, any method related to chiropractic therapy is considered to be lacking a strong research base regarding effectiveness and should be judged as potentially harmful to children with autism (Gleberzon & Rosenberg-Gleberzon, 2001).

COMMUNICATION AND LANGUAGE

The phrase "augmentative and alternative communication intervention" (e.g., Light, 1999) describes the variety of procedures that are used in attempts to enhance functional communication by persons exhibiting language and communication delays. These procedures include sign language, computers and other electronic speaking devices, facilitated communication (FC), and picture communication boards. Although these methods are used throughout the special education population, there are few methods that have an empirical base of research to suggest effectiveness (Bedrosian, 1999; Beukelman, 1985; Calculator, 1991; Light, 1999).

FC is a good example of an augmentative communication fad that has little empirical evidence to support its effectiveness. Biklen (1990, 1993) popularized this communication approach in the United States. Once researchers began conducting carefully controlled studies to assess the effectiveness and validity of the technique, it quickly became apparent that positive results seemed to be due to either the facilitator influencing the communication or other uncontrolled factors (for reviews and findings, see Jacobson, Foxx, & Mulick, chap. 22, this volume; Jacobson, Mulick, & Schwartz, 1995; Wheeler, Jacobson, Paglieri, & Schwartz, 1993).

Auditory integration therapy (AIT) is another practice used but for which there is little empirical support. The American Speech and Language Hearing Association (1994) estimated that there were more than 200 audiologists, psychologists, social workers, teachers, and other professionals who were incorporating AIT into their practice at that time, and it is possible that the numbers of practitioners using AIT has grown. The theory of AIT is that some people who have attention and behavior problems, learning disabilities, aggression, depression, and autism hear sounds differently (Berard, 1993; Stehli, 1991), with some sounds heard "normally," whereas others are distorted. This distortion then leads to probable confusion and behavioral anomalies. Treatment consists of two or more 30-minute sessions daily, for about 2 weeks, in which the person with the disorder listens to music that has been digitally modified to eliminate sound frequencies to which that person shows particular sensitivity (Ziring, Brazdziunas, Cooley, & Kastner, 1998). The research that has been conducted on the efficacy of AIT has not supported the promise of such an approach. Gravel (1994) pointed out that there is, in fact, no difference in hearing sensitivities between children with and without autism. Much of the published research involves parent report data, which should be considered subjective, unreliable, and invalid (Tharpe, 1999). Although findings from a study by Rimland and Edelson (1995) showed a potential benefit of AIT, there were problems with the design of this study, including the absence of a control group, potential subject bias, and questionable functional impact of any improvement. Bettison (1996) used a better design and found no evidence that AIT differentially improved performance of some children with behavioral and learning difficulties. Other researchers used placebo treatment along with AIT and showed that AIT is no more effective than listening to regular music or even no music at all (Yencer, 1998; Zollweg, Vance, & Palm, 1997).

MINIMIZING FADS IN THE FUTURE

There is some hope that the adoption of fad treatments may be on the wane. The journals *Educational Researcher* (Vol. 26, No. 5, 1997) and *Exceptional Children* (Vol. 63, No. 4, 1997) have devoted issues to the topic of using practices with empirical support. In addition, Prometheus Books has begun publication of *The Scientific Review of Mental Health Practice*, a peer-reviewed journal devoted to the critical examination of unorthodox or fad treatments in the area of mental health. Vaugh et al. (2000) argued that there is an increased tendency for some professionals to demand research evidence to support the effectiveness of methods prior to adoption and implementation. Individual scholars (e.g., Stanovich, 1994) have begun to speak out about the need for teacher preparation programs to include coursework and competencies in the importance and characteristics of the scientific method. Further, the federal government, as part of the "Reading First" (2002, para. 2) education initiative, is funding "scientifically based" reading programs.

In the final analysis, the last line of defense against the use of fad treatments in special education consists of the special education teachers, teacher trainers, psychologists, therapists, and other professionals who are committed to helping those with mental and learning disabilities. It is these people who, through their professionalism, need to be trained in the scientific method, how to use educational strategies that have some empirical basis, and how to be critical readers of research (Sasso, 2001). They need to use their training and knowledge to critically evaluate new treatments and apply rigorous criteria before adopting them in use with their charges. As reported by Jarvis (2001), "By granting us a license to practice, the public trusts us to apply knowledge to treatment of their … problems. This implies that we must critically examine new ideas, decide if there is rational evidence for them, reject the bunk, and apply the knowledge that sifts through" (p. 1).

REFERENCES

Acalin, T. A. (1995). *A comparison of Reading Recovery to Project READ.* Unpublished doctoral dissertation, California State University, Fullerton, CA.

American College of Medical Genetics. (1996). *Statement on nutritional supplements and piracetam for children with Down Syndrome.* Retrieved November 21, 2002 from http://www.acmg.net/Pages/ACMG_Activities/policy_statements_pages/current/Down_Syndrome_Statement_on_Nutritional_Supplements_&_Piracetam_for_Children_with.asp

American Speech-Language and Hearing Association. (1994, November). *Auditory integration training, 36*(11), 55–58.

Baker, S., Berninger, V. W., Bruck, M., Chapman, J., Eden, G., Elbaum, B., et al. (2002). *Evidence-based research on reading recovery.* Retrieved October 16, 2003 from http://www.educationnews.org/Reading Recoveryisnotsuccessful.htm

Battelle Memorial Institute. (1995). *Longitudinal study of Reading Recovery: 1990–91 through 1993–94.* Columbus, OH: Ohio Department of Education.

Bedrosian, J. (1999). Efficacy research issues in AAC: Interactive storybook reading. *Augmentative and Alternative Communication, 15,* 45–55.

Berard, G. (1993). *Hearing equals behavior.* New Canaan, CT: Keats Publishing, Inc.

Bergeron, B. S. (1990). What does the term whole language really mean: Constructing a definition from the literature. *Journal of Reading Behavior, 22,* 301–329.

Bettison, S. (1996). Long-term effects of auditory training on children with autism. *Journal of Autism and Developmental Disorders, 26,* 361–367.

Beukelman, D. (1985). The weakest link is better than the strongest memory. *Augmentative and Alternative Communication, 1,* 55–57.

Biklen, D. (1990). Communication unbounded: Autism and praxis. *Harvard Educational Review, 60,* 291–315.

Biklen, D. (1993). *Communication unbounded: How facilitated communication is challenging traditional views of autism and ability/disability.* New York: Teachers College Press.

Budiansky, S. (1986, December). New snake oil, oil pitch. *U.S. News and World Report,* 68–70.

Calculator, S. (1991). Evaluating the efficacy of AAC intervention for children with severe disabilities. In J. Brodin & E. Bjorck Akesson (Eds.), *Methodological issues in research in augmentative and alternative communication* (pp. 22–35). Vallingby, Sweden: The Swedish Handicap Institute.

Carroll, R. T. (2002). Craniosacral therapy. *The skeptic's dictionary.* Available from http://skepdic.com/craniosacral.html

Chaddock, G. R. (1998). Resisting education's fads. *Christian Science Monitor, 90*(190), p. B1.

Chambers, J. G., Parrish, T., & Harr, J. J. (2002). *What we are spending on special education services in the United States, 1999–2002?* [Advance Report #1, Special Education Expenditure Project (SEEP)], Washington, DC: U.S. Department of Education.

Clay, M. M. (1985). *The early diction of reading difficulties.* Portsmouth, NH: Heinemann.

Deford, D. E., Lyons, C. A., & Pinnell, G. S. (Eds.). (1991). *Bridges to literacy: Learning from Reading Recovery.* Portsmouth, NH: Heinemann.

Department of Developmental Services. (1999). *Changes in population of persons with autism and pervasive developmental disorders in California's Developmental Services System: 1987 through 1998* (Report to the Legislature, March 1). Sacramento, CA: Author.

Detterman, D. K., & Thompson, L. E. (1997). What is so special about special education? *American Psychologist, 52,* 1082–1090.

Edelsky, C. (1990, November). Whose agenda is this anyway: A response to McKenna, Robinson, and Miller. *Educational Researcher,* 7–11.

Elbaum, B., Vaughn, S., Hughes, M. T., & Moody, S. W. (2000). How effective are one-to-one tutoring programs in reading for elementary students at risk for reading failure? A meta-analysis of the intervention research. *Journal of Educational Psychology, 92,* 605–619.

Eldredge, J. L., & Baird, J. E. (1996). Phonemic awareness training works better than whole language instruction for teaching first graders how to write. *Reading Research and Instruction, 35*(Spring), 193–208.

Evans, T. L. P. (1996). *I can read deze books: A qualitative comparison of the Reading Recovery program and a small-group reading intervention.* Unpublished doctoral dissertation, Auburn University, Auburn, AL.

Ferreri, C. A. (2002). *Neural organization technique.* Retrieved October 14, 2002, from http://www.positivehealth.com/permit/Articles/Kinesiology/ferr50.htm

Ferreri, C. A., & Wainwright, R. B. (1985). *Breakthrough for dyslexia and learning disabilities.* Pompano Beach, FL: Exposition Press.

Fincher, G. E. (1991). *Reading Recovery and Chapter I: A three-year comparative study.* Canton, OH: Canton City Schools.

Fletcher, J., & Martinez, G. (1994). An eye-movement analysis of the effects of scotopic sensitivity correction on parsing and comprehension. *Journal of Learning Disabilities, 27*(1), 67–70.

Fombonne, E. (2003). The prevalence of autism. *JAMA: Journal of the American Medical Association, 289,* 87–89.

Gage, N. L. (1989). The paradigm wars and their aftermath: A "historial" sketch of research on teaching since 1989. *Educational Researcher, 18*(7), 4–10.

Gleberzon, B., & Rosenberg-Gleberzon, A. L. (2001). On autism: Its prevalence, diagnosis, causes, and treatment. *Topics in Clinical Chiropractic, 8*(4), 42–58.

Glynn, T., Crooks, T., Bethune, N., Ballard, K., & Smith, J. (1989). *Reading Recovery in context.* Wellington, New Zealand: New Zealand Department of Education.

Goodman, K. S. (1992). Why whole language is today's agenda in education. *Language Arts, 69,* 354–363.

Goodman, Y. M. (1989). Roots of the whole-language movement. *The Elementary School Journal, 90*(2), 113–127.

Gravel, J. S. (1994). Auditory integrative training: Placing the burden of proof. *American Journal of Speech and Language Pathology, 3,* 25–29.

Green, C., Martin, C. W., Bassett, K., & Kazanjian, A. (1999). *A systematic review and critical appraisal of the scientific evidence on craniosacral therapy.* Vancouver, BC: British Columbia Office of Health Technology Assessment, The University of British Columbia.

Greenwood, J. C. (2000). *Autism: Present challenges, future needs – why the increased rates?* Hearing before the Committee on Government Reform, House of Representatives, 106th Congress. April 6, 2000. Serial No. 106–180:8–10.

Grossen, B. (2002). *Reading Recovery: An evaluation of benefits and costs.* Retrieved November 10, 2002, from http://darkwing.uoregon.edu/~bgrossen/rr.htm

Haboud, H. (1955). New therapeutic possibilities in mongolism, suggestions for specific treatments. *Arzeneimittel Forschung, 9,* 211–228.

Harrell, R. F. (1981). Can nutritional supplements help mentally retarded children? An exploratory study. *Proceedings of the National Academy of Sciences, 78,* 574–578.

Heibert, E. (1994). Reading Recovery in the United States: What difference does it make to an age cohort? *Educational Researcher, 23*(9), 15–25.

Hettleman, K. R. (2002, April 17). Still fighting the last war. *Education Week.* Retrieved November 15, 2002 from http://www.edweek.org/ew/newstory.cfm?slug=31hettleman.h21

Hoff, D. J. (2002, June 5). Researchers urge officials to reject Reading Recovery. *Education Week.* Retrieved November 12, 2002, from http://www.edweek.org/ew/ew_printstory.cfm?slug=39read.h21

Irlen Syndrome/Scotopic Sensitivity. What Is Irlen Syndrome? (n.d.). Retrieved November 10, 2002, from http://www.irlen.com/index_sss.html

Irlen, H. (2002). *Autism and the Irlen method.* Retrieved October 16, 2003 from http://www.irlen.com/autism_main.html

Irlen, H. (1983). *Scotopic sensitivity syndrome: Screening manual.* Long Beach, CA: Perceptual Development.

Irlen Institute. (2003). *Professional profile: Helen L. Irlen.* Retrieved October 16, 2003, from http://www.irlen.com/profile.htm

Jacobson, J. W., Mulick, J. A., & Schwartz, A. A. (1995). A history of facilitated communication: Science, pseudoscience, and antiscience. *American Psychologist, 50,* 750–765.

Jarvis, W. T. (2001). *Some notes on cranial manipulative therapy.* Retrieved October 15, 2002, from http://www.ncahf.org/articles/c-d/cranial.html

Johnson, K. A., & Kafer, K. (2001). Why more money will not solve America's education crisis. *Heritage Foundation Backgrounder,* June (No. 1448). Retrieved November 21, 2002, from http://www.heritage.org/Research/Education/BG1448.cfm

Johnston, P., & Allington, R. (1991). Remediation. In R. Barr, M. Kamil, P. Mosenthal, & P. D. Pearson (Eds.), *Handbook of reading research* (Vol. 2, pp. 984–1012). New York: Longman.

Kamhi, A. G. (1999). To use or not to use: Factors that influence the selection of new treatment approaches. *Language, Speech and Hearing Services in Schools, 30,* 92–98.

Katsiyannis, A., & Maag, J. W. (2001). Educational methodologies: Legal and practical considerations. *Preventing School Failure, 46*(1), 31–36.

Kean, P. (1993). Reading, writing and ripoffs. *Washington Monthly, 25*(7/8), 13.

Koertge, N. (1998). Scrutinizing science studies. In N. Koertge (Ed.), *A house built on sand: Exposing postmodernist myths about science.* New York: Oxford University Press.

Light, J. C. (1999). Do augmentative and alternative communication interventions really make a difference? The challenges of efficacy research. *Augmentative and Alternative Communication, 15*(1), 13–26.

MacLeod, A. (1997). Education fads get a royal rap. *Christian Science Monitor, 89*(140), 1.

Martin, F., Lovegrove, W., McNicol, D., & Mackenzie, B. (1993). Irlen lenses in the treatment of specific reading disability: An evaluation of outcomes and processes. *Australian Journal of Psychology, 45*(3), 141–150.

McKenna, M. C., Stratton, B. D., Grindler, M. C., & Jenkins, S. J. (1995). Differential effects of whole language and traditional instruction on reading attitudes. *Journal of Reading Behavior, 27*(1), 19–43.

National Down Syndrome Society. (1997). *Position statement on vitamin related therapies.* Retrieved October 2, 2002, from http://www.ndss.org/content.cfm?fuseaction=SearchLink&article=45

New York State Department of Health. (1999). *Critical Practice Guidelines.* Retrieved October 22, 2002, from http://www.health.state.ny.us/nysdoh/search/index.htm

O'Connor, P. D., Sofo, F., Kendall, L., & Olsen, G. (1990). Reading disabilities and the effects of colored filters. *Journal of Learning Disabilities, 23,* 597–603, 620.

O'Flahaven, J., Gambrell, L. B., Guthrie, J., Stahl, S. A., Baumann, J. F., & Albermann, D. A. (1992). Poll results guide activities of research center. *Reading Today, 10*(6), 12.

Pepper, C. (1987, Fall). Quackery: The need for federal, state, and local response. *The Skeptical Inquirer,* 70–74.

Pinnell, G. S. (1988). *Success of children at risk in a program that combines writing and reading.* Washington, DC: U.S. Department of Education, Office of Educational Research and Improvement. (ERIC Document Reproduction Service No. ED292061)

Pinnell, G. S. (1989). Reading Recovery: Helping at-risk children learn to read. *The Elementary School Journal, 90*(2), 161–183.

Pinnell, G. S. (1991). Teachers and children learning. In D. E. DeFord, C. A. Lyons, & G. S. Pinnell (Eds.), *Bridges to literacy: Learning from Reading Recovery* (pp. 171–187). Portsmouth, NH: Heinemann.

Pinnell, G. S., & Lyons, C. (1995). *Response to Hiebert: What difference does Reading Recovery make?* Unpublished manuscript.

Pinnell, G. S., Lyons, C. A., DeFord, D. E., Bryk, A. S., & Seltzer, M. (1994). Comparing instructional models for the literacy education of high-risk first graders. *Reading Research Quarterly, 29*(1), 8–39.

Pinnell, G. S., Short, A. G., Lyons, C. A., & Young, P. (1986). *The Reading Recovery project in Columbus, Ohio: Year 1—1985–1986.* Columbus, OH: Ohio State University.

Pollock, J. S. (1994). *Final evaluation report: Reading Recovery program 1995–1996.* Columbus, OH: Department of Program Evaluation.

Ramaswami, S. (1994). *The differential impact of Reading Recovery on achievement of first graders in the Newark School District.* Newark, NJ: Newark Board of Education, Office of Planning, Evaluation and Testing. (ERIC Document Reproduction Service No. ED374180)

Rasinski, T. (1995a). On the effects of Reading Recovery: A response to Pinnell, Lyons, DeFord, Bryk, and Seltzer. *Reading Research Quarterly, 30*(2), 264–270.

Rasinski, T. (1995b). Reply to Pinnell, DeFord, Lyons, and Bryk. *Reading Research Quarterly, 30*(2), 276–277.

Reading First. (2002). Retrieved October 16, 2003, from http://www.ed.gov/programs/readingfirst/index.html

Reading Recovery Council of North America. (2002). *Advocacy.* Retrieved November 10, 2002, from http://www.readingrecovery.org/sections/home/advocacy.asp

Rimland, B., & Edelson, S. M. (1995). Pilot study of auditing integration training on autism. *Journal of Autism and Developmental Disorders, 25*, 61–70.

Robinson, G. L., & Conway, R. N. (1990). The effects of Irlen colored lenses on students' specific reading skills and their perception of ability: A 12-month validity study. *Journal of Learning Disabilities, 23*, 589–596.

Robinson, G. L., & Conway, R. N. (1994). Irlen filters and reading strategies: Effect of coloured filters on reading achievement, specific reading strategies, and perception of ability. *Perceptual & Motor Skills, 79*(1), 467–483.

Saginaw Public Schools, Department of Evaluation Services. (1992). *Compensatory education produce evaluation: Reading Recovery Program 1991–1992.* Saginaw, MI: Author. (ERIC Document Reproduction Service No. ED350587)

Sasso, G. M. (2001). The retreat from inquiry and knowledge in special education. *The Journal of Special Education, 34*(4), 178–193.

Shanahan, T., & Barr, R. (1995). Reading Recovery: An independent evaluation of the effects of an early instructional intervention for at-risk learners. *Reading Research Quarterly, 30*, 958–996.

Smith, F. (1988). *Understanding reading* (4th ed.). Hillsdale, NJ: Lawrence Erlbaum Associates.

Spafford, C. S., Grosser, G. S., Donatelle, J. R., Squillace, S. R., & Dana, J. P. (1995). *Journal of Learning Disabilities, 28*(4), 240–252.

Stahl, S. A. (1990). Riding the pendulum: A rejoinder to Schickendanz and McGee and Lomax. *Review of Educational Research, 60*(1), 141–151.

Stahl, S. A., McKenna, M. C., & Pagnucco, J. (1994). The effects of whole language instruction: An update and a reappraisal. *Educational Psychologist, 29*(4), 175–185.

Stahl, S. A., & Miller, P. D. (1989). Whole language and language experience approaches for beginning reading: A quantitative research synthesis. *Review of Educational Research, 59*(1), 87–116.

Stanovich, K. E. (1994). Romance and reality. *The Reading Teacher, 47*(4), 280–291.

Stehli, A. (1991). *The sound of a miracle.* New York: Doubleday.

Tharpe, A. M. (1999). Clinical forum: Auditory integration training: The magical mystery cure. *Language, Speech & Hearing Services in Schools, 30*(4), 378–384.

Upledger Institute, Inc. (n.d.). *Cranio Sacral Therapy Awareness Month recognized by resolution in Florida Senate.* Retrieved November 2, 2002, from http://www.upledger.com/news/senate.htm

U.S. Department of Education. (2000). *Twenty-second annual report to Congress on the implementation of the IDEA.* Washington, DC: U.S. Government Printing Office.

Vaugh, S., Klinger, J., & Hughes, M. (2000). Sustainability of research-based practices. *Exceptional Children, 66*(2), 163–171.

Wasik, B. A., & Slavin, R. E. (1993). Preventing early reading failure with one-to-one tutoring: A review of five programs. *Reading Research Quarterly, 28*, 179–200.

Weiss, R. (1990, September 29). Dyslexics read better with blues. *Science News, 138*, 196.

Wheeler, D., Jacobson, J., Paglieri, I. L., & Schwartz, A. (1993). An experimental assessment of facilitated communication. *Mental Retardation, 31*, 49–60.

Woodruff, D. L. (2002). *Craniosacral therapy: A brief description*. Retrieved November 16, 2002, from http://www.vicpain.com/therapy.htm#CRANIO

Worrall, R. S. (1990). Detecting health fraud in the field of learning disabilities. *Journal of Learning Disabilities, 23*(4), 207–212.

Yatvin, J. (1993). Letter to the editor: Need for experimental research on whole language. *Reading Teacher, 46*, 636.

Yencer, K. A. (1998). The effects of auditory integration training for children with central auditory processing disorders. *American Journal of Audiology, 7*(2), 32–44.

Young, F. E. (1988, March). Allies in the war against health fraud. *The FDA Consumer*, 6–7.

Zane, T., & Frazer, C. G. (1992). The extent to which software developers validate their claims. *Journal of Research on Computing in Education, 24*(3), 410–419.

Ziring, P., Brazdziunas, D., Cooley, W. C., & Kastner, T. A. (1998). Auditory integration training and facilitated communication for autism. *Pediatrics, 102*, 431–433.

Zollweg, W., Vance, V., & Palm, D. (1997). The efficacy of auditory integration training: A double blind study. *American Journal of Audiology, 6*(3), 39–47.

The Neutralization of Special Education

William L. Heward
Susan M. Silvestri
The Ohio State University

Neutralize—To counteract, nullify, or destroy the force, influence, effect, etc., of; render ineffective.

By most accounts, special education has made good progress in the past 30 years. Not that long ago, access to an appropriate educational opportunity was the primary issue for many children with disabilities, particularly those whose disabilities were severe. Today, all children with disabilities receive special education and related services. Some children benefit from a special education that includes curricular elements and instructional technologies that were unavailable just a few years ago, and increasing numbers of students with disabilities are included in general education classrooms. Whereas special education can rightfully be proud of its accomplishments, the educational outcomes for many students with disabilities are disappointing. As a group, students with disabilities fare poorly on virtually every measure of academic achievement and social adaptation. Of special concern are the post-school adjustment outcomes for young adults with disabilities (Blackorby & Wagner, 1996; Frank & Sitlington, 2000).

We believe that these poor outcomes for students with disabilities reflect not so much the field's lack of knowledge about how to teach these students, as they are testament to education's collective failure to systematically implement available knowledge. We believe that implementation of research-based teaching practices is hampered in part by widely held beliefs about the nature of teaching and learning that support incompatible and weak instructional practices. As a result, many children with disabilities are receiving a special education that is not nearly as effective as it could be. In essence, the potential effectiveness of the special education received by many of the more than six million children who participate in special education today is neutralized by the presence of weak approaches that are selected on the basis of ideology instead of research results.

In this chapter, we (a) provide a definition of special education consistent with the discipline's historical development and mandated purpose in federal legislation; (b) make some assumptions about the status and role of research in special education; (c) describe several widely held beliefs about teaching and learning that impede implementation of special education's knowledge base and, as a result, neutralize the field's effectiveness; (d) offer some reasons why these ideologies and the weak practices they engender are so prevalent in education today; and (e) suggest four attitudes of professional practice that individual special educators might adopt in an effort to counter the neutralizing effects of illogical and unfounded beliefs about teaching and learning.

A DEFINITION OF SPECIAL EDUCATION

Although its historical roots can be traced back several hundred years (Safford & Safford, 1996), special education is a relatively young discipline. Special education is an integral part of society's response to the needs and civil rights of individuals with disabilities. It is a multidisciplinary field whose practices are influenced by developments in education, but also by events and currents in the cultural, social, economic, technological, medical, and legislative arenas. A thorough understanding of special education requires acknowledgment and appreciation of these many contributing influences. For example, special education can be seen as a legislatively governed activity concerned primarily with issues such as due process, informed consent, and the extent to which a school district's individualized education programs (IEPs) include all components required by federal and state laws. Some aspects of special education can also be understood as an outgrowth of litigation related to the civil rights movement. Such a view might give the impression that special education's primary goals are ending segregated placements in school, work, and community settings, ensuring equal access to educational supports and services, and improving society's attitudes about people with disabilities.

Although legal and sociopolitical perspectives have helped shape what special education is and how it is practiced, neither view reveals the fundamental purpose of special education, which is to provide instructionally based interventions designed to prevent (early intervention instruction), eliminate (remedial instruction), and overcome (compensatory instruction) the obstacles that might keep an individual with disabilities from learning and from full and active participation in school and society. In the federal Individuals with Disabilities Education Act (IDEA, PL 105-17), special education is defined simply as "specially designed instruction." A definition of special education consistent with the letter and spirit of IDEA and with consensus literature is provided by Heward (2003a): "Special education is individually planned, specialized, intensive, and goal-directed instruction. When practiced most effectively and ethically, special education is also characterized by the use of research-based teaching methods, the application of which is guided by direct and frequent measures of student performance" (p. 38).

SPECIAL EDUCATION'S RESEARCH BASE

Contrary to the conclusions of some critics (e.g., Gallagher, 1998; Poplin, 1988b; Skrtic, Sailor, & Gee, 1996), research has produced a significant and reliable knowledge base about effective teaching practices for students with disabilities (Greenwood, 2001; Lloyd, Weintraub, & Safer, 1997). Scientific research has yielded a substantial body of knowledge consisting of strategic approaches (e.g., functional assessment; Horner & Carr, 1997; Iwata, Dorsey, Slifer, Bauman, & Richman, 1994) and tactical procedures (e.g., constant time delay; Kratzer, Spooner, Test, & Koorland, 1993). Today's special educator can turn to a research base that includes many instructional strategies that did not exist when the Education of All Handicapped Children Act was signed into law in 1975, such as the following:

1. Embedding opportunities for language learning into preschool activity schedules (e.g., Horn, Lieber, Li, Sandall, & Schwartz, 2000; Robinson Spohn, Timko, & Sainato, 1999).
2. Low-tech methods such as response cards and guided notes to increase students' active engagement and achievement during group instruction (e.g., Heward, 1994; Lazarus, 1991).
3. Peer-mediated instruction/classwide peer tutoring systems (e.g., Fuchs et al., 2001; Maheady, Harper, & Mallete, 2001).
4. Methods for facilitating generalization and maintenance, such as the general case strategy (e.g., Sprague & Horner, 1984) or recruiting reinforcement (e.g., Alber & Heward, 2000).
5. Learning strategies instruction (e.g., Ellis, Deshler, Lenz, Schumaker, & Clark, 1991).

The research base is far from complete and no element of it is flawless. There is much that we still do not know about how to most effectively teach students with disabilities. Many questions remain to be answered, and the pursuit of those answers will lead to additional questions. While a significant gap exists between what is relatively well understood and what is poorly understood or not understood at all, the more distressing gap may be the one between what research has discovered about effective instruction and actual educational practice in many classrooms. For example, research has discovered a great deal about topics such as features of early reading instruction that reduce the probability of later reading problems (e.g., Coyne, Kame'enui, & Simmons, 2001; National Reading Panel, 2000); how to enhance the success of students with learning problems in content area classes (Deshler et al., 1999); and components that secondary special education programs should include to increase students' success in post-school environments (e.g., Patton, Cronin, & Jairrels, 1997). Numerous studies, however, report that the education received by many students with disabilities does not reflect that knowledge (e.g., Kauffman, 1996; Moody, Vaughn, Hughes, & Fischer, 2000; Wagner, Blackorby, Cameto, & Newman, 1994).

Much has been written about the importance of closing the research-to-practice gap and how that might be accomplished (Carnine, 1997; Gersten, 2001; Vaughn, Klingner, & Hughes, 2000). We believe the immense task of bringing the findings and implications of research closer to classroom practice must go beyond the expected difficulties (e.g., ramping up smaller scale interventions typical of controlled studies to the scale needed for application across many classrooms or schools) to somehow deal with the resistance and problems caused by widely held ideological beliefs that are inconsistent and incompatible with use of research-based instructional practices.

EXAMPLES OF ILLOGICAL BELIEFS ABOUT EDUCATION
THAT IMPEDE THE USE OF RESEARCH-BASED PRACTICES

In *Why People Believe Weird Things*, Michael Shermer (1997) wrote about demystifying claims of the supernatural and the paranormal by applying the methods of science and the attitude of skepticism. Shermer's "weird things" include alien abductions, ESP, and Holocaust denial. He qualifies things as weird if they are widely believed but have no sound scientific evidence to support them.

Education is a breeding ground and safe haven for weird and illogical beliefs. Heward (2003b) described 10 widely held but unfounded (i.e., weird) beliefs about teaching and learning that have the dual effects of supporting weak (and sometimes harmful) instructional practices and limiting the use of research-based instructional tools. We discuss five of those beliefs in this section.

Structured Curricula Impede True Learning
(or, Children Must Construct Their Own Meanings)

Some educators believe that there is no corpus of knowledge and skills that all children should learn. Stainback and Stainback (1992), for example, describe standard curriculum content as unnecessary, irrelevant, and boring to students and teachers alike. Instead of learning specific knowledge and skills described by a preset curriculum, they believe students should determine what and how much they will learn. "From a holistic, constructivist perspective, all children simply engage in a process of learning as much as they can in a particular subject area; how much and exactly what they learn will depend upon their backgrounds, interests, and abilities" (p. 72).

Similarly, Poplin (1988b) believes that a structured curriculum or lesson plan limits freedom and begets passivity. "Students' minds are allowed very little freedom when specific psychological processes, academic skills, and cognitive strategies are structured for them .... The more structured the curriculum, the more passive become our students" (p. 395).

Advocates of this notion contend that requiring teachers to follow a structured curriculum forces them to be a "sage on the stage," who forces students to learn knowledge and skills that may have no meaningful context for them. Instead of coercing students to learn knowledge that others have decided is important, teachers should facilitate students' exploration of learning by acting as a "guide on the side," who encourages children to construct their own meanings from materials and activities. "[T]he task of schools is to help students develop new meanings in response to new experience rather than to learn the meanings others have created" (Poplin, 1988a, p. 401).

Presumably, teachers need only encourage children to ask questions they may have about fun math problems and interesting stories. In the process of constructing their own meanings from these activities, the students will become skilled calculators and fluent readers. This sounds wonderful! But the fact that we have yet to see any evidence of this extraordinary claim should surprise no one. For it is facility with words and numbers that gives students the tools they need to solve problems and find answers to questions they may ask, not the other way around (Johnson & Layng, 1994; Simmons, Kame'enui, Coyne, & Chard, 2002).

Although children can benefit from constructivistic activities, they are more likely to do so if they possess relevant background knowledge and tool skills with which to explore and effectively manipulate relevant variables. Waiting for a child to miraculously construct the meaning and effective use of the principle of least common denominator—especially when a competent teacher could intervene with purpose and teach that knowledge directly and efficiently—is at best a waste of the child's precious time, and at worst just plain crazy (Finn & Ravitch, 1996).

The related beliefs that standard curricula are an impediment to learning and that students will construct their own meaningful truths are not only illogical and weird (i.e., unfounded), they are diametrically opposed to the standards-based testing movement (a.k.a. "the accountability fad," according to Kohn, 2002) and incompatible with the legal mandate in IDEA that students with disabilities participate in the general education curriculum and state- and district-wide assessments (Thurlow & Johnson, 2000; Thurlow & Thompson, 1999). These ideologies also stand in stark contrast to the role of the special educator as an expert designer, implementer, and evaluator of specialized instruction for the express purpose of achieving specified IEP goals and objectives.

Targeting Specific Skills for Instruction Precludes Authentic Learning

Because the whole of any complex skill (e.g., reading) is thought to be more than the sum of its component parts (e.g., decoding skills), some educators believe that component skills should never be isolated for instruction. Supporters of this belief contend that the only meaningful way to learn anything is in the context of the whole activity. For example, referring to the teaching of writing, Stainback and Stainback (1992) recommend that there should be "little focus on practicing skills such as punctuation, capitalization, or noun–verb identification in isolated ways—these are learned in the context of writing activities" (p. 70).

Poplin (1988b) contends that attempts to remediate specific skill deficits—an approach she calls special education's "reductionistic fallacy"—is responsible for the difficulties many students with disabilities have in generalizing and maintaining what they have learned. "For behaviorists, there are skills (often long lists of mechanical skills, Brigance assessments, DISTAR programs) that are necessary in order to read, though often they are divorced during assessment and instruction from the act of reading text itself" (p. 397).

Whether a particular skill targeted for instruction is divorced from meaningful context outside of the lessons in which it is acquired and practiced, or an important prerequisite for or a component of more complex behavior, cannot be determined by the form or topography of the targeted skill. The ultimate meaning of any skill can only be determined by assessing the effects of a student's acquiring and subsequently using the skill on his overall repertoire. For example, teaching *limestone* and *crystal* as sight words to a student with mental retardation may, at first glance, appear to be a splinter skill without context or meaning. However, being able to read those words may have tremendous relevance if the student has a rock collection (Browder, 2000).

Measurement Is Unnecessary (It May Even Be Harmful to Student Learning)

Direct, objective, and frequent measurement of student performance is one of the hallmarks of special education (Greenwood & Maheady, 1997). Curriculum-based assessment (CBA) is one form of direct and frequent measurement that enables teachers to make data-based instructional decisions (Deno, 1985). Extensive research shows increased academic achievement by students with disabilities when their teachers use CBA (e.g., Fuchs, Deno, & Mirken, 1984; Jones & Krouse, 1988; Steeker & Fuchs, 2000).

Nevertheless, measuring objectively defined aspects of student performance has been attacked vigorously in recent years. In two articles published in *Exceptional Children*, one of special education's flagship journals, Heshusius asserts

- "Because of the required quantification and measurement, teaching and learning often do not operate at the levels of what is meaningful to the child and what is worth doing" (1982, p. 7).
- "[Measurement tactics are] superimposed on but are unrelated to the human phenomena they claim to assess" (1992, p. 315).
- "Authentic learning does not occur in a stable, steadily progressing manner; rather, its visible outcomes are variable" (p. 325).
- "[Students are] *put through* [italics added] CBA/DI measurement and control procedures .... Measurement-driven ways of thinking about education thwarts authentic learning" (p. 325).

These excerpts suggest that (a) you may be able to pinpoint and measure a bit of behavior, but doing so will not tell you anything important; (b) if you measure student behavior, the behavior is no longer authentic; (c) if it is authentic learning, you cannot measure it; and (d) measurement may be damaging or harmful to students.

In criticizing standardized achievement tests, McNeil (as cited in Kohn, 1999) claimed, "[M]easurable outcomes may be the least significant results of learning" (p. 75). This statement is so absurd that, in the words of Wolfgang Pauli (as cited in Kame'enui, 1994), it is "not even wrong" (p. 149). Outcomes that are not measurable are not observable. If students are only "taught" unobservable skills, how will we or they know if they have learned anything?

Of course, defining, measuring, and charting some aspect of a student's performance does not make that behavior meaningful. But neither does measurement render the aspect measured meaningless. And claiming that measurement obviates the importance of what is measured is just weird.

Claims that measuring student behavior is a waste of time, an insult to students, and an impediment to their learning may provide comfort and relief to some teachers. Obtaining student performance data is hard work, and once obtained, the data often suggest that additional work is needed to modify instructional materials and restructure lesson plans. Moreover, measuring what one has taught requires a decision about what to teach (Bushell & Baer, 1994). As discussed previously, some educators today are reluctant to specify curricular objectives and learning outcomes for their students.

Eclecticism Is the Best Approach

Because no single theory or model of teaching and learning is complete and error-free, it is sometimes thought that incorporating components from a number of different models will cover the gaps or deficiencies found in any single model. At a superficial level, the logic underlying eclecticism may appear sound. However, the problems inherent in an unfettered eclecticism far outweigh its logical appeal (Heward, 2003b):

1. Eclecticism rests in part on a misplaced egalitarian view that every approach has something to offer. But not all theories and models are equally trustworthy and valuable, and the more models represented in the eclectic mix, the more likely that ineffective and possibly even harmful components will be included (Maurice, 1993, 2003).
2. Practitioners may not choose the most important and effective parts of each model, and might select weaker, perhaps ineffective components instead.
3. Some components of a model may be ineffective when implemented in isolation, without other elements of the model.
4. Elements from different models may be incompatible with one another. For example, children in a phonics-based program should practice reading with decodable text composed of previously learned letter–sound relationships and a limited number of sight words that have been systematically taught (Grossen, 2003). Using the less decodable and often predictable text typical of some whole language models limits beginning readers' opportunities to practice phonological skills with actual reading and encourages the use of prediction and context to comprehend a passage. Although prediction is a useful skill, children who must rely on the predictability of text will not become successful readers (Chard & Kame'enui, 2000).
5. An eclectic mix might prevent any model from being implemented continuously or intensely enough to obtain significant effects. A little bit of everything and a lot of nothing often reduces eclecticism to a recipe for failure (Kauffman, 1997).
6. Teachers may not learn to implement any of the models with the fidelity and precision necessary for best results. The eclectic practitioner is often an apprentice of many models but master of none.

Our skepticism of eclecticism does *not* mean we believe there is but one effective teaching method. Indeed, one defining characteristic of a good special educator is skill in the selection and proper use of a variety of instructional methods (Fuchs & Fuchs, 2003; Lovitt, 1996). Our wariness of eclecticism is based on (a) a commitment that students should only be taught with instructional tools that have empirical support for their effectiveness, (b) a research-derived knowledge that not all models are equally effective, and (c) the fact that some approaches have a harmful effect on student learning.

Creativity Is the Key to Teacher Effectiveness

There is widespread belief in education that creativity is a key to effective teaching. "You're so creative!" is considered high praise by many teachers. (And in fairness, who wouldn't like to be told the same?) There is, of course, an important role for creativity in teaching. Teachers have turned many ineffective lessons into effective lessons by adapting instructional materials, developing prosthetic devices, or changing the mode, form, timing, or other dimension of a response prompt. But the kind of creativity engendered by the invocation to "Be creative!" has little to do with systematically evaluating a student's interaction with carefully planned materials and lesson plans to detect flaws so that the teacher can then eliminate those flaws in some creative manner (Heward & Dardig, 2001).

Teachers are told time and time again that their profession is an art, not a science, and that not only is it permissible to teach in different ways from time to time, but that such change is good for students. Adding variety to instructional activities and materials in an attempt to make lessons more interesting and fun is one way in which teachers frequently try to be creative. Whereas creativity is highly valued in the arts, in many other professions it is considered counterproductive, if not harmful. Patients do not want doctors to perform surgery creatively, passengers do not want pilots to fly planes creatively, and investors do not want accountants to do math creatively. To do so would risk the lives and livelihoods of consumers and would constitute unnecessary risk taking with outcomes that are too important. For these same reasons, creativity for the sake of trying something different is counterproductive in education. Creative, inconsistent teaching methods are actually the opposite of evidence-based teaching methods.

Teacher creativity will always have an important place in the classroom, but the need and direction for that creativity should be guided and subsequently evaluated by students' achievements, not the whims of teachers.

THE CONSEQUENCES OF ILLOGICAL AND UNFOUNDED BELIEFS: LIMITING TEACHER EFFECTIVENESS AND NEUTRALIZING A PROFESSION

Direct Consequences for Students: Active Harm by Sins of Commission

Instructional practices cause direct harm when they require students to learn knowledge or skills that are incorrect or incompatible with adaptive knowledge. Such practices (sins of commission) can legitimately be considered instructional malpractice. For example, the belief that raising students' self-esteem is a teacher's first priority, may be responsible, in part, for two kinds of instructional malpractice in the classroom: using instructional materials that allow students to be "right for the wrong reason" and failing to correct students' mistakes (Heward & Dardig, 2001). From the primary grades through high school, teachers assign instructional materials that students can complete with 100% accuracy but without having to use the skill or knowledge the materials were intended to teach. Examples include the following: a "reading comprehension" activity that does not require students to even read the passage, let alone think about who did what to whom, because the correct answers to the comprehension questions are obvious by looking at the accompanying picture; a life-skills vocabulary worksheet that can be completed without reading the definitions—the student simply counts the number of letters in each term and matches that number with the number of spaces next to each definition; a language arts activity in which students "make" compound words by drawing lines to connect component words—but the student need not read any of the words and think about which ones go together, because *base* and *ball* are in blue boxes, and *bath* and *tub* are in green boxes.

Students' answers on such poorly designed materials are under the faulty stimulus control of irrelevant features (e.g., picture, number of letters in each word, color, and shape). As a result, the materials provide no meaningful practice with the knowledge or skills they were intended to teach (Vargas, 1984). Instructional materials that allow students to be "right for the wrong reason" do them no favors. Although students may initially feel good about getting the right answers so quickly and effortlessly, long-term effects on achievement and self-esteem are likely to be negative when students encounter everyday situations where they cannot apply the skill.

Misplaced emphasis on self-esteem (Foxx & Roland, chap. 7, this volume) may be responsible for hesitation by some teachers to correct student errors. Some teachers believe informing students that their work contains mistakes may harm their fragile self-esteem, which in turn will negatively affect achievement. But it is allowing students to repeat their mistakes that harms achievement and, ultimately, self-esteem as well. In addition, failing to correct students' mistakes wastes valuable instructional time because of the re-teaching that eventually must occur, perhaps as adult learners.

Indirect Consequences for Students: Benign Neglect by Sins of Omission

The most common student-related consequence of weak educational practices is the most insidious: Nothing happens. The students do not learn. However, students' lack of progress is likely to go unnoticed when specific curricular outcomes have not been identified and there is no commitment to direct and frequent measures of student performance.

Conventional wisdom holds that an extra measure of patience is required to be a good teacher of children with disabilities. This unfounded notion does a great disservice to students with special needs and to the educators who teach them. Although patience is a positive and valued trait, the idea that teachers must be patient with special education students often translates into a slower pace of instruction, lowered expectations for performance, fewer opportunities to respond, and fewer in-class and homework assignments.

Another widely held but unfounded belief about teaching special education students goes something like this: Students with disabilities can learn, but they learn more slowly than typical students; therefore, instruction should occur at a slower pace and they should be given extra time. In fact, research has found that slowing down the pace of instruction makes outcomes worse, not better for students with learning problems. For example, Carnine (1976) conducted an experiment in which instruction was presented to four first-grade remedial reading students at two paces: slow (intertrial interval of 5 seconds) and fast (intertrial interval of 1 second or less).

Fast-paced instruction resulted in more learning trials presented by the teacher, more responses per lesson by the students, better accuracy of student responses, and better on-task behavior. Systematic replications of Carnine's study with students of various ages and disabilities have yielded similar results (e.g., Carnine & Fink, 1978; Darch & Gersten, 1985; Ernsbarger et al., 2001; Koegel, Dunlap, & Dyer, 1980).

The combined result of active harm and benign neglect caused by teaching practices that find support from illogical and weird beliefs neutralizes the potential effectiveness and benefits of special education.

Consequences for Teachers and the Profession: Ineffectiveness, Stagnation, and Lack of Respect

The strange and illogical juxtaposition of some misguided and unfounded ideologies makes it difficult for individual teachers to know just what to do. For example, on the one hand, teachers are told that building students' self-esteem is of paramount importance; on the other hand, they are told they should not praise or reward students for their achievements (Kohn, 1993; Ryan & Deci, 1996). Another example of mixed messages: On the one hand, teachers are told that all children are the same, that there is no such thing as regular children and special children; then, they are told that every child learns differently, in his or her own unique way. So, which is it? Either all children are the same, or none are the same. It cannot be both.

Widespread belief in weird things in education also has outcomes for the field itself. By its failure to endorse evidence-based practices, education remains an immature profession "characterized by expertise based on the subjective judgments of the individual professional, trust based on personal contact rather than quantification, and autonomy allowed by expertise and trust, which staves off standardized procedures based on research findings that use control groups" (Carnine, 2000, p. 9). In contrast, mature professions, such as medicine, are distinguished by "a shift from judgments of individual experts to judgments constrained by quantified data that can be inspected by a broad audience, less emphasis on personal trust and more on objectivity, and a greater role for standardized measures and procedures informed by scientific investigations that use control groups" (Carnine, 2000, p. 9).

Our point here is not that special education should adopt a "medical model," but rather that mature professions recognize, by their standards of practice, that subjective judgment alone is not a sufficient foundation for professional activity. Immature professions risk not only stagnation and ineffectiveness, but disrespect as well. In order for education to make gains comparable to the technologies developed in medicine, engineering, and computer science, education must accept the responsibility of scientifically evaluating claims of effectiveness and systematically implementing only those curricula and instructional tools which have stood the test of scientific verification and replication.

WHY DO WEIRD BELIEFS AND ILLOGICAL PRACTICES FLOURISH IN SPECIAL EDUCATION?

Man prefers to believe what he prefers to be true.

—Francis Bacon

With the proviso that this analysis is speculative and very incomplete (e.g., we have not discussed financial issues and various response cost contingencies that may favor the adoption of ineffective practices), we suggest several factors that may contribute to the prevalence of weird beliefs and illogical practices in contemporary special education.

Changing the World Instead of the Student

Deconstruction of Disability. Special education was founded on the presumption that the learning and/or behavioral problems of some students make the general education curriculum and instructional methods inappropriate or ineffective (Reynolds & Birch, 1977). However, if disability is viewed as a social construction, there is much less urgency, if indeed there is any urgency at all, for early identification or prevention efforts, or for instructional interventions designed to change the repertoires of individual students (Kaufman, 1999). The student (any student) is okay as is; we need to alter our (society's) acceptance of, and sensitivity to, any differences in ability we perceive (Elkind, 1998; Smith, 1999).

From Amelioration to Accommodation: The Changing Conception of Special Education's Purpose. During the 1970s and 1980s, the overwhelming majority of special educators viewed the primary purpose of their field to be intervening with the intention of ameliorating the effects of disability (or the conditions which make a disability more likely). The past 15 to 20 years have witnessed a gradual, but we believe clearly evident, increase in the number of special educators who consider the field's primary purpose to be accommodating the special needs presented by an individual with disabilities. Increasingly, practitioners perceive special education as a system of curriculum modifications, testing accommodations, social supports, and related services all selected and designed to enable physical access to, and social acceptance in, integrated classrooms. Emphasis in professional training has shifted from developing and mastering knowledge of instructional tools to acquiring team-building skills, methods for collaborating with other educators, and working to change the attitudes of regular classroom teachers and nondisabled peers so that students with disabilities will be accepted and feel welcome in the regular classroom.

Kimball (2002) provides an excellent discussion of amelioration and accommodation as goals and guiding philosophies for special education, and he illustrates the differences (which are sometimes subtle) of how these two differing purposes would likely impact the use of a picture-based communication system with a child with autism (Bondy & Frost, 1994). A picture-based system implemented from the perspective of accommodating the child would be designed to meet the child's current repertoire, and no changes in the child's communicative responses would be expected or lamented if they did not occur. A picture-based system designed as an ameliorative intervention would also be designed to be compatible with the child's present skills, but various response prompts and differential consequences would be subsequently used "to firmly urge him along. Visual support would be faded to the greatest extent possible and, via judiciously applied consequences, skills would be built that were functional" (Kimball, 2002, p. 73).

Of course, amelioration and accommodation are not antithetical to one another; it is possible that both goals could be pursued in different environments or with respect to different components of a given individual's repertoire. Amelioration, however, best describes the intensive, goal-directed dimensions of special education as the field developed historically and as it is codified in IDEA. Special educators whose work is guided by a philosophy of ameliorating the effects of disabilities via preventive, remedial, and compensatory interventions are more likely to directly measure the effects of those efforts and therefore are less likely to subscribe to ideologies and non-research-based practices.

Profundity, Promises, and Pseudoscience

Rhetoric by Passionate Advocates.   Advocates who believe in ideologically based practices sometimes offer the very depth of their beliefs as the basis for the correctness and importance of implementing belief-based practices. Use of belief as a rationale for practice is common among advocates for whole language. For example, Nickel and Crowley (1999) encouraged whole language teachers to "stand together because our beliefs are *strong*" (p. 11, italics in original). Moreover, a recent issue of the Whole Language Umbrella's journal *Talking Points* was subtitled "Beliefs into Practice" (Crenshaw & King, 2000). It is remarkable—and weird and worrisome— that a profession responsible for the livelihood of its consumers would base its practices on their beliefs, particularly when evidence contrary to these beliefs is plentiful (National Reading Panel, 2000).

Advocates for ideologically based practices also use persuasive writing to convey the rightness of their beliefs. Heward (2003b) made the following comparison:

> Consider the language typically used by constructivist authors to describe the teaching practices and outcomes they prefer: *authentic, cooperative, creative, whole child, whole language, integrative, open-system, self-organizing*. These terms are used to paint a romantic and wholly positive picture of the teaching and learning process: Intrinsically motivated children exploring a world of unlimited learning opportunities, unfettered by expectations and pressures to respond in the 'correct way.' Their teachers, unburdened from the bureaucratic onus of having to monitor and quantify students' progress toward narrow, pre-determined learning objectives, are free to creatively follow their students' lead.

> By contrast, the following words appear frequently in the same authors' descriptions of systematic and explicit instructional practices: *mechanistic, top-down, narrow, simplistic, fragmented, competitive, closed-system, reductionistic, rote, linear, rigid, compliance, pre-determined, prediction, control*. These words are skillfully used to create a very different image of what goes on in the classroom: Uninterested children being cajoled, coerced, and/or bribed with unnecessary and harmful rewards to pursue isolated knowledge and skills that the children will practice and use only until their harried, script-bound teacher can measure and record them on a chart.

> Based on such portraits, what prospective teacher wouldn't choose the first classroom over the second? (p. 198)

Other rhetorical devices deployed by some advocates for ideologically driven practices include appeals to emotion and pleas to assess what might be considered the morally right or wrong thing to do. In *Regular Lives*, a film about the inclusion of a young boy with special needs, the narrator states that inclusion should be the norm for all students with disabilities, regardless of whether or not it works. "Even if it didn't work it would still be the thing to do, because it's right" (Goodwin, Wurzburg, & Biklen, 1987).

Relying on what is morally right or wrong avoids the issue of evidence. If evidence does not support a claim, it should not influence classroom practice. If a practice is right, it must have a beneficial outcome for the student, and if that outcome is observable, there is the potential for evidence to support the claim. The point is not that arguments about what is morally right and wrong are irrelevant; the point is that claims cannot be judged right or wrong without evidence.

Profundity and Promises. A profound explanation may seem more intriguing and important than a simpler one. And when the subject matter we seek to understand is complex, a complex and profound explanation seems necessary. Complex theories may also be more comforting because they seem to offer more apparent explanations for why learning does or does not occur (perhaps minimizing the responsibility of educators) and more options (that is, freedom) for action (or inaction) on our part.

Profundity is well represented in contemporary special education literature by postmodernism and deconstructivism (e.g., Brantlinger, 1997; Danforth & Rhodes, 1997; Elkind, 1998; Lather, 1992; Skrtic et al., 1996; Smith, 1999). These epistemologies have produced interesting and complex theories about how children learn (e.g., "spirals of knowledge" [Poplin, 1988a]; and "multiple intelligences" [Gardner, 1993]). In turn, these and other theories have spawned numerous prescriptions for classroom practice that promise grand outcomes.

Retreat from Objective Science

Antiscience. Unlike most professions in which practitioners' tools are thoroughly field-tested to ensure they are effective and reliable before they are implemented on a widespread basis, education has a long history of adopting new curricula and teaching methods with little or no evidence of effectiveness (Grossen, 1998; Spear-Swerling & Sternberg, 2001). Sadly, ideology, dogma, folklore, fashion, fad, and convenience have had greater influence on theory and practice in education than have the results of scientific research (Carnine, 1992; Gersten, 2001; Vaughn & Damann, 2001).

Some educators contend that science is an antiquated and mechanistic approach to knowledge generation based on a misguided empiricism of arbitrary variables that no longer fits the more sophisticated, postmodern understanding of teaching and learning (e.g., Gallagher, 1998; Heshusius, 1982, 1986; Poplin, 1988a; Skrtic et al., 1996). Supporters of this view believe that quantitative methods that rely on logical positivism should be replaced with the qualitative methodologies of deconstruction and discourse (e.g., Danforth & Rhodes, 1997; Elkind, 1998; Lather, 1992). Their position: There is no longer any need to conduct those artificial, manipulative, and irrelevant experiments; it is better to gather multiple perspectives on the phenomena of interest and to use those "voices" as the context for speculating about relationships among variables.

Pseudoscience.   The value and influence of carefully conducted science is also undermined by pseudoscience. With pseudoscience, one does not need real data to give the appearance and credibility of scientific support to favored treatments, therapies, or viewpoints. One simply makes up the data or reports only on a highly successful, and perhaps uniquely successful, student as evidence. Not only is invented knowledge much easier to acquire than discovered knowledge, it can be made to show exactly what the pseudoscientist wants it to show (cf., Green & Perry, 1999; Maurice, 1993). Coker (2001) provided the following indicators of pseudoscience, paraphrased here:

1. Indifference to the facts.
2. Sloppy research.
3. Aimed at proving a predetermined hypothesis.
4. Relies on subjective validation.
5. Avoids testing claims.
6. Often contradicts itself.
7. Deliberately creates mystery where none exits by omitting information.
8. Argues with rhetoric, propaganda, and misrepresentation rather than valid evidence .
9. Argues from alleged exceptions, errors, anomalies, strange events, and suspect claims.
10. Appeals to false authority (or authority w/out evidence), emotion, sentiment, or distrust of established fact.
11. Pseudoscientists invent their own vocabulary.
12. Relies heavily on anachronistic thinking—the wisdom of the ancients, the older the idea, the better.

Preparation and Changing Working Conditions of Special Educators

Education is particularly susceptible to weird things because of its philosophical roots. Critical theory and constructivism are the most popular philosophies in schools of education. They are based on the idea that truth is a social construct, and that each of us constructs our own knowledge and our own reality. With no agreed-on reality or truth, empirical validation is difficult or impossible. The constructivist philosophy is opposed to positivism, which requires scientific research and whose goal is the discovery of reliable relationships that facilitate pragmatic prediction and control.

During the past 10 to 15 years, we have witnessed the merger of previously free-standing special education departments and programs with teacher training programs in elementary and secondary education. Such mergers can yield distinct advantages, for example, faculty members collaborating on research, co-teaching arrangements, infusion of special education content into general education courses and vice versa, better appreciation by general and special education students of the challenges and responsibilities faced by one another, and the possibility of students obtaining dual certification or licensure in special and general education (Stayton & McCollum, 2002). Significant disadvantages have been noted as well; for example, combined certification programs typically mean preservice special education majors take fewer special education courses, and general education faculty often outnumber special education faculty, which can result in important decisions concerning such issues as departmental curriculum, resources, faculty hires, and promotion and tenure being determined by and split across the two programs as a function of differing philosophies. Although a discussion of the relative pros and cons of combined versus separate teacher training faculties and programs is far beyond the scope of this chapter, we will comment on a not uncommon experience of preservice special education majors in programs that require or involve a significant number of curriculum and methods courses taught by faculty in the general education program.

In preservice teacher education, the integration of general education philosophy with special education training creates a "precarious perch between things that are unknowable in any absolute sense and the unavoidable responsibility imposed on us for what we choose to do about them" (Gerber, 2001, p. 19). A preservice special education student learns in her special ed methods classes that direct and frequent measurement of children's performance is one of the hallmarks of a good teacher, that explicit and systematic phonics instruction is a critical component of early reading instruction, and that by using contingent teacher praise and other forms of positive reinforcement she can her help her students achieve success. During the same week (or day), professors in her general education methods classes explain that it is completely unnecessary to measure students' performance, that phonics is an outdated drill-and-kill approach sure to turn off children to reading for comprehension and pleasure, and that teachers who use extrinsic rewards risk harming children's intrinsic motivation for learning. Then, instead of receiving information about alternative methods for actually teaching academic tool skills or curriculum content to children, the preservice student is told that the most important way she can develop as an educator is to construct her own theory of teaching and learning from the ground up (Kozloff, chap. 11, this volume).

Increased exposure to postmodern perspectives and constructivist ideology that dominate general education programs and classes results in confusion for many preservice teachers. On graduation, many newly hired special educators will likely be working in an inclusive setting in which constructivist theories and practices are the norm.

Given the widespread support of these beliefs in general education, the inclusive schools movement means many students with significant disabilities are being exposed to the weak instructional practices encouraged by these notions. Acknowledging this possibility is not an indictment of either general education or inclusion, as such. It is well documented that placement in a special education setting is no guarantee that a student will receive an appropriate and effective education. Indeed, studies of curriculum and instruction in many special education classrooms have found that, other than limiting class size, there is often little that goes on in many special education classrooms that can rightfully be called "special" (e.g., Moody et al., 2000; Vaughn, Moody, & Schumm, 1998; Ysseldyke, Thurlow, Mecklenburg, & Graden, 1984). Nevertheless, the reality is that significant numbers of students with disabilities are spending large portions of the school day in classrooms with unstructured curricula, few requirements for academic productivity, and low expectations for achievement (Baker & Zigmond, 1990; Kauffman & Hallahan, 1994; Klingner, Vaughn, Hughes, Schumm, & Elbaum, 1998).

COMBATING WEIRD THINGS IN EDUCATION

Educating students with disabilities can be a daunting challenge. Four realities increase the difficulty level of this challenge and limit the potential effectiveness of even the best planned and expertly executed interventions. First, many students present numerous skill deficits or maladaptive behaviors, each of which could (but not necessarily should) be the focus of a teaching program. Second, the resources and time (including the student's time) available for designing and implementing instructional interventions are always limited. Third, in spite of the positive and optimistic description of the research base in special education, knowledge of how to teach is incomplete. Fourth, the teacher seldom, if ever, can control or even know all of the factors that are influencing a student's behavior.

Combined, these four factors produce a sobering bottom line: The difficulty and scope of the job is almost always greater than the resources, expertise, tools, and access available for doing the job. Adding to this challenge is the fact that special education is always a race against the clock. "[F]or children who are behind to catch up, they simply must be taught more in less time. If the teacher doesn't attempt to teach more in less time ... the gap in general knowledge between a normal and handicapped student becomes even greater" (Kame'enui & Simmons, 1990, p. 11).

Therefore, special education must be intensive and urgent; it must be designed and delivered with optimal effectiveness as one of its goals.

Four Attitudes of Professional Practice

> *Our beliefs may predispose us to misinterpret the facts, when ideally the facts should serve as the evidence upon which we base beliefs.*
>
> —A. M. MacRobert and T. Schultz
> (cited in Schick & Vaughn, 2002, p. 64)

Because special education can be no better than the quality of instruction students receive, it is important that teachers select and properly use instructional tools whose effectiveness has been established through scientific research. To reliably do so, teachers need to minimize the extent to which their work is neutralized by weird beliefs and ideologically based methods. The four "attitudes of special education practice" that follow may help teachers do that.

Strive for an Optimistic Realism.   The first step toward professional competence is an objective understanding of the nature and scope of the job's responsibilities. Special education is serious business. The learning and adjustment problems faced by students with disabilities are real, and they require intensive and systematic intervention.

> Be wary of the conception of disabilities as merely socially constructed phenomena; that all children who are identified as disabled would achieve success and behave well if others simply viewed them more positively .... Children with disabilities have skill deficits and difficulties in acquiring and generalizing new knowledge and skills—real disabilities that won't be "deconstructed" away. Don't let the needs of exceptional children get lost in such postmodern ideologies. (Heward, 2003a, p. 608)

Maintain a Focused Pragmatism. Special education is about making changes in the lives of students with disabilities. Special educators should focus their expertise and efforts on those aspects of a student's life that they can effectively control. Bloom (1980) called those things that both make a difference in student learning and can be affected by teaching practices, *alterable variables*. Examples of just a few of the many alterable variables at work during classroom instruction include the amount of time allocated for instruction, the sequence of activities within the overall lesson, the pacing of instruction, the frequency and form with which students actively respond during instruction, and the manner in which errors are corrected.

Although it is fashionable and may seem more exciting and important to learn about and debate the "big" policy issues of education, such as school reform, the merger of special and general education, and the merits of full inclusion and integrated curriculum, knowledge of any of these topics is no substitute for having skills and knowledge of sound instruction.

Depend on a Responsible Empiricism. Special educators owe it to their students, themselves, and to their profession to check out the trustworthiness of curricula and instructional methods. "If you are really interested in the truth, then you *must* use the scientific processes of logical inquiry … to arrive at it. Special educators are held accountable for what they say and do in a way that journalists, novelists, and postmodern critics are not. And that is how it should be" (Sasso, 2001, p. 187, italics in original).

Maintain a Healthy Skepticism. Be skeptical of extraordinary claims. Claims that sound too good to be true usually are just that. Teachers should critically examine the evidence themselves. Teachers can and should be as skeptical as researchers. A skeptical teacher treats education as a science.

Extraordinary claims require extraordinary evidence (Sagan, 1996; Shermer, 1997). What constitutes extraordinary evidence? In the strictest sense, and the sense that should be employed when evaluating claims of educational effectiveness, evidence is the outcome of the application of the scientific method to test the effectiveness of a claim, a theory, or a practice. The more rigorously the test is conducted, the more often the test is replicated, the more extensively the test is corroborated, the more extraordinary is the evidence. Evidence becomes extraordinary when it is extraordinarily well tested.

What doesn't constitute extraordinary evidence? Shermer (1997) listed several indicators: bold statements, anecdotes, and appeals to emotion that divert attention from evidence. When extraordinary claims are supported by extraordinary evidence, such smokescreens are not necessary. The use of scientific language, such as claims of reorganization of sensory processing in sensory integration therapy, does not add weight to evidence. Scientific language alone does not make a science. "Dressing up a belief system in the trappings of science by using scientistic language and jargon … means nothing without evidence, experimental testing, and corroboration" (p. 49). In addition, extraordinary evidence requires replication. A single study, anecdote, or theoretical article, no matter how impressive the findings or how complicated the writing, is not a basis for practice.

Claims that are based only on belief, authority, theory, or faith are claims with no basis for widespread classroom implementation. The difference between weird and valid educational practice is science, and the difference between science and dogma is evidence. Any claim in education may be extraordinary; the weight a claim carries, however, should be based on the quality and extent of its supporting evidence, not on its appeal. Sometimes an extraordinary claim becomes a weird thing when it is backed by an opinion instead of evidence. An extraordinary claim with extraordinary supporting evidence is a basis for best practice; an extraordinary claim based on anything but proportionally strong evidence is a weird thing.

REFERENCES

Alber, S. R., & Heward, W. L. (2000). Teaching students to recruit positive attention: A review and recommendations. *Journal of Behavioral Education, 10*, 177–204.

Baker, J. M., & Zigmond, N. (1990). Are regular education classes equipped to accommodate students with learning disabilities? *Exceptional Children, 56*, 516–526.

Blackorby, J., & Wagner, M. (1996). Longitudinal postschool outcomes of youth with disabilities: Findings from the National Longitudinal Transition Study. *Exceptional Children, 62*, 399–413.

Bloom, B. S. (1980). The new direction in educational research: Alterable variables. *Phi Delta Kappan, 61*, 382–385.

Bondy, A., & Frost, L. (1994). PECS: The picture exchange communication system. *Focus on Autistic Behavior, 9*, 1–9.

Brantlinger, E. (1997). Using ideology: Cases of nonrecognition of the politics of research and practice in special education. *Review of Educational Research, 67*, 425–459.

Browder, D. M. (2000). *Comments made as guest faculty for OSU teleconference seminar: Contemporary issues in special education.* Columbus, OH: The Ohio State University.

Bushell, D., Jr., & Baer, D. M. (1994). Measurably superior instruction means close, continual contact with the relevant outcome data: Revolutionary! In R. Gardner, III, et al. (Eds.), *Behavior analysis in education: Focus on measurably superior instruction* (pp. 3–10). Monterey, CA: Brooks/Cole.

Carnine, D. (1976). Effects of two teacher presentation rates on off-task behavior, answering correctly, and participation. *Journal of Applied Behavior Analysis, 9*, 199–206.

Carnine, D. (1992). The missing link in improving schools: Reforming educational leaders. *Direct Instruction News, 11*(3), 25–35.

Carnine, D. (1997). Bridging the research to practice gap. *Exceptional Children, 63*, 513–521.

Carnine, D. (2000, April). Why education experts resist effective practices. *Report of the Thomas B. Fordham Foundation.* Washington, DC: Thomas B. Fordham Foundation.

Carnine, D., & Fink, W. T. (1978). Increasing the rate of presentation and use of signals in elementary classroom teachers. *Journal of Applied Behavior Analysis, 11*, 35–46.

Chard, D. J., & Kame'enui, E. J. (2000). Struggling first-grade readers: The frequency and progress of their reading. *The Journal of Special Education, 34*, 28–38.

Coker, R. (2001). *Distinguishing science from pseudoscience.* Retrieved December 9, 2002, from http://www.quackwatch.org/01QuackeryRelatedTopics/pseudo.html

Coyne, M. D., Kame'enui, E. J., & Simmons, D. C. (2001). Prevention and intervention in beginning reading: Two complex systems. *Learning Disabilities Research and Practice, 16*, 62–73.

Crenshaw, S. R., & King, D. F. (2000, April/May). From the editors. *Talking Points*, p. 1.

Danforth, S., & Rhodes, W. C. (1997). On what basis hope? Modern progress and postmodern possibilities. *Remedial and Special Education, 18*, 357–366.

Darch, C., & Gersten, R. (1985). The effects of teacher presentation rate and praise on LD students' oral reading performance. *British Journal of Psychology, 55*, 295–303.

Deno, S. L. (1985). Curriculum-based measurement: The emerging alternative. *Exceptional Children, 52*, 219–232.

Deshler, D. D., Schumaker, J. B., Lenz, B. K., Bulgren, J. A., Hock, M. F., Knight, J., et al. (1999). Ensuring content-area learning by secondary students with learning disabilities. *Learning Disabilities Research and Practice, 16*, 96–108.

Elkind, D. (1998). Behavior disorders: A postmodern perspective. *Behavioral Disorders, 23,* 153–159.

Ellis, E. S., Deshler, D. D., Lenz, B. K., Schumaker, J. B., & Clark, F. L. (1991). An instructional model for teaching learning strategies. *Focus on Exceptional Children, 24*(1), 1–14.

Ernsbarger, S. C., Tincani, M. J., Harrison, T. J., Frazier-Trotman, S., Simmons-Reed, E., & Heward, W. L. (2001). *Slow teacher/fast teacher: Effects on participation rate, accuracy, and off-task behavior by pre-K students during small-group language lessons.* Paper presented at the 27th Annual Convention of the Association for Behavior Analysis, New Orleans, LA.

Finn, C. E., & Ravitch, D. (1996). *Education reform 1995–1996.* Washington, DC: The Thomas B. Fordham Foundation. Available from http://www.fordhamfoundation.org/library/epctoc.html

Frank, A. R., & Sitlington, P. L. (2000). Young adults with mental disabilities—Does transition planning make a difference? *Education and Training in Mental Retardation and Developmental Disabilities, 35,* 119–134.

Fuchs, D., & Fuchs, L. S. (2003). Inclusion versus full inclusion. In W. L. Heward (Ed.), *Exceptional children: An introduction to special education* (7th ed., pp. 80–81). Upper Saddle River, NJ: Merrill/Prentice Hall.

Fuchs, D., Fuchs, L. S., Thompson, A., Svenson, E., Yen, L., Al Otaiba, S., et al. (2001). Peer-assisted learning strategies in reading: Extension for kindergarten, first grade, and high school. *Remedial and Special Education, 22,* 15–21.

Fuchs, L. S., Deno, S. L., & Mirkin, P. K. (1984). The effects of frequent curriculum-based measurement and evaluation on pedagogy, student achievement, and student awareness of learning. *American Educational Research Journal, 21,* 449–460.

Gallagher, D. J. (1998). The scientific knowledge base of special education: Do we know what we think we know? *Exceptional Children, 64,* 493–502.

Gardner, H. (1993). *Multiple intelligences: The theory in practice.* New York: Basic Books.

Gerber, M. (2001). The essential social science of behavior disorders. *Behavioral Disorders, 7,* 12–20.

Gersten, R. (2001). Sorting out the roles of research in the improvement of practice. *Learning Disabilities Research and Practice, 16,* 45–50.

Goodwin, T., & Wurzburg, G. (Producers and Directors), & Biklen, D. (Executive Producer), (1987). *Regular Lives.* [Video Cassette]. Syracuse, NY: Syracuse University Department of Special Education and Rehabilitation.

Green, G., & Perry, L. (1999). Science, psuedoscience and antiscience: What's this got to do with my kid? *Science in Autism Treatment, 1*(1), 5–7.

Greenwood, C. R. (2001). Science and students with learning and behavioral problems. *Behavioral Disorders, 27,* 37–52.

Greenwood, C. R., & Maheady, L. (1997). Measurable change in student performance: Forgotten standard in teacher preparation? *Teacher Education and Special Education, 20,* 265–275.

Grossen, B. (1998). What is wrong with American education? In W. M. Evers (Ed.), *What's gone wrong in America's classrooms?* (pp. 23–47). Stanford, CA: Hoover Institution Press.

Grossen, B. (2003). Six principles for early reading instruction. In W. L. Heward (Ed.), *Exceptional children: An introduction to special education* (7th ed., pp. 248–250). Upper Saddle River, NJ: Merrill /Prentice Hall.

Heshusius, L. (1982). At the heart of the advocacy dilemma: A mechanistic worldview. *Exceptional Children, 49,* 6–11.

Heshusius, L. (1986). Paradigm shifts and special education: A response to Ulman and Rosenberg. *Exceptional Children, 52,* 461–465.

Heshusius, L. (1992). Curriculum-based assessment and direct instruction: Critical reflections on fundamental assumptions. *Exceptional Children, 58,* 315–328.

Heward, W. L. (1994). Three "low-tech" strategies for increasing the frequency of active student response during group instruction. In R. Gardner III, et al. (Eds.), *Behavior analysis in education: Focus on measurably superior instruction* (pp. 283–320). Monterey, CA: Brooks/Cole.

Heward, W. L. (2003a). *Exceptional children: An introduction to special education* (7th ed.). Upper Saddle River, NJ: Merrill/Prentice Hall.

Heward, W. L. (2003b). Ten faulty notions about teaching and learning that hinder the effectiveness of special education. *The Journal of Special Education, 36*(4), 186–205.

Heward, W. L., & Cooper, J. O. (1992). Radical behaviorism: A productive and needed philosophy for education. *Journal of Behavioral Education, 2,* 345–365.

Heward, W. L., & Dardig, J. C. (2001, Spring). What matters most in special education. *Education Connection,* 41–44.

Horn, E., Lieber, J., Li, S., Sandall, S., & Schwartz, I. (2000). Supporting young children's IEP goals in inclusive settings through embedded learning opportunities. *Topics in Early Childhood Special Education, 20,* 208–223.

Horner, R. H., & Carr, E. G. (1997). Behavioral support for students with severe disabilities: Functional assessment and comprehensive intervention. *The Journal of Special Education, 31,* 84–104.

Iwata, B. A., Dorsey, M., Slifer, K., Bauman, K., & Richman, G. (1994). Toward a functional analysis of self-injury. *Journal of Applied Behavior Analysis, 27,* 197–209.

Johnson, K. R., & Layng, T. V. J. (1994). The Morningside Model of generative instruction. In R. Gardner, III, et al. (Eds.), *Behavior analysis in education: Focus on measurably superior instruction* (pp. 173–197). Monterey, CA: Brooks/Cole.

Jones, E. D., & Krouse, J. P. (1988). The effectiveness of data-based instruction by study teachers in classrooms for pupils with mild learning handicaps. *Teacher Education and Special Education, 11,* 9–19.

Kame'enui, E. J. (1994). Measurably superior practices in measurably inferior times: Reflections on Twain and Pauli. In R. Gardner III, et al. (Eds.), *Behavior analysis in education: Focus on measurably superior instruction* (pp. 149–159). Monterey, CA: Brooks/Cole.

Kame'enui, E. J., & Simmons, D. C. (1990). *Designing instructional strategies: The prevention of academic learning problems.* Columbus, OH: Merrill.

Kauffman, J. M. (1996). Research to practice issues. *Behavioral Disorders, 22*(1), 55–60.

Kauffman, J. M. (1997). *Characteristics of emotional and behavioral disorders of children and youth* (6th ed.). Upper Saddle River, NJ: Merrill/Prentice Hall.

Kauffman, J. M. (1999). How we prevent the prevention of emotional and behavioral disorders. *Exceptional Children, 65,* 448–468.

Kauffman, J. M., & Hallahan, D. K. (1994). *The illusion of full inclusion: A comprehensive critique of a current special education bandwagon.* Austin, TX: Pro-Ed.

Kimball, J. W. (2002). Behavior-analytic instruction for children with autism: Philosophy matters. *Focus on Autism and Other Developmental Disabilities, 17*(2), 66–75.

Klingner, J. K., Vaughn, S., Hughes, M. T., Schumm, J. S., & Elbaum, B. (1998). Outcomes for students with and without learning disabilities in inclusive classrooms. *Learning Disabilities Research and Practice, 13,* 153–161.

Koegel, R. L., Dunlap, G., & Dyer, K. (1980). Intertrial interval duration and learning in autistic children. *Journal of Applied Behavior Analysis, 13,* 91–99.

Kohn, A. (1993). *Punished by rewards.* Boston: Houghton Mifflin.

Kohn, A. (1999). *The schools our children deserve.* New York, NY: Houghton Mifflin.

Kohn, A. (2001, September 26). Beware of the standards, not just the tests. *Education Week.* Retrieved December 9, 2002, from http://www.alfiekohn.org/teaching/edweek/botsnjtt.htm

Kohn, A. (2002, April 15). *The schools our young children deserve: Understanding the harms of direct instruction and standardized testing in early childhood.* Lecture given at National-Louis University, Evanston, IL.

Kozloff, M. A. (2001). *Insubstantial pageants: An analysis of ed school documents.* Retrieved October 15, 2002, from http://people.uncw.edu/kozloffm/pageants.htm

Kratzer, D. A., Spooner, F., Test, D. W., & Koorland, M. A. (1993). Extending the application of constant time delay: Teaching a requesting skill to students with severe multiple disabilities. *Education and Treatment of Children, 16,* 235–253.

Lather, P. (1992). Critical frames in education research: Feminist and post-structural perspectives. *Theory Into Practice, 33,* 86–99.

Lazarus, B. D. (1991). Guided notes, review, and achievement of secondary students with learning disabilities in mainstream content courses. *Education and Treatment of Children, 14,* 112–127.

Lloyd, J. W., Weintraub, F. J., & Safer, N. D. (1997). A bridge between research and practice: Building consensus. *Exceptional Children, 63*, 535–538.

Lovitt, T. C. (1996). What special educators need to know. In W. L. Heward (Ed.), *Exceptional children: An introduction to special education* (5th ed., pp. 84–86). Upper Saddle River, NJ: Merrill/Prentice Hall.

Maheady, L., Harper, G. F., & Mallete, B. (2001). Peer-mediated instruction and interventions and students with mild disabilities. *Remedial and Special Education, 22*, 4–14.

Maurice, C. (1993). *Let me hear your voice: A family's triumph over autism.* New York: Fawcett Columbine.

Maurice, C. (2003). The autism wars. In W. L. Heward (Ed.), *Exceptional children: An introduction to special education* (7th ed., pp. 490–492). Upper Saddle River, NJ: Merrill/Prentice Hall.

McNeil, L. (2001, September 26). Beware of the standards, not just the tests. *Education Week, 26.* Retrieved June 10, 2002, from http://www.edweek.org/ew/ew_printsotry.cfm?slug=04kuhn.h21

Moody, S. W., Vaughn, S., Hughes, M. T., & Fischer, M. (2000). Reading instruction in the resource room: Set up for failure. *Exceptional Children, 66*, 305–316.

National Reading Panel. (2000). *Teaching children to read: An evidence-based assessment of the scientific research literature on reading and its implications for reading instruction: Reports of the subgroups.* Available from http://www.nichd.nih.gov/publications/nrp/smallbook.htm

Nickel, M. A., & Crowley, P. (1999, October/November). California's literacy agenda. *Talking Points, 9*–11.

Patton, J. R., Cronin, M. E., & Jairrels, V. (1997). Curricular implications of transition: Life-skills instruction as an integral part of transition education. *Remedial and Special Education, 18*, 294–306.

Poplin, M. S. (1988a). Holistic/constructivist principles of the teaching/learning process: Implications for the field of learning disabilities. *Journal of Learning Disabilities, 21*, 401–416.

Poplin, M. S. (1988b). The reductionistic fallacy in learning disabilities: Replicating the past by reducing the present. *Journal of Learning Disabilities, 21*, 389–400.

Reynolds, M. C., & Birch, J. W. (1977). *Teaching exceptional children in all America's schools.* Reston, VA: The Council for Exceptional Children.

Robinson Spohn, J. R., Timko, T. C., & Sainato, D. M. (1999). Increasing the social interactions of preschool children with disabilities during mealtimes: The effects of an interactive placemat game. *Education and Treatment of Children, 22*, 1–18.

Ryan, R. M., & Deci, E. L. (1996). When paradigms clash: Comments on Cameron and Pierce's claim that rewards do not undermine intrinsic motivation. *Review of Educational Research, 66*, 33–38.

Safford, P. L., & Safford, E. J. (1996). *A history of childhood disability.* New York: Teachers College Press.

Sagan, C. (1996). *The demon-haunted world: Science as a candle in the dark.* New York: Ballantine.

Sasso, G. (2001). The retreat from inquiry and knowledge in special education. *The Journal of Special Education, 34*, 178–193.

Schick, T., & Vaughn, L. (2002). *How to think about weird things.* Boston: McGraw-Hill.

Shermer, M. (1997). *Why people believe weird things.* New York: Freeman.

Simmons, D. C., Kame'enui, E. J., Coyne, M. D., & Chard, D. J. (2002). Effective strategies for teaching beginning reading. In E. J. Kame'enui, D. W. Carnine, R. C. Dixon, D. C. Simmons, & M. D. Coyne (Eds.). *Effective teaching strategies that accommodate diverse learners* (2nd ed., pp. 53–92). Upper Saddle River, NJ: Merrill/Prentice Hall.

Skrtic, T. M., Sailor, W., & Gee, K. (1996). Voice, collaboration, and inclusion: Democratic themes in educational and social reform initiatives. *Remedial and Special Education, 17*, 143–157.

Smith, P. (1999). Drawing new maps: A radical cartography of developmental disabilities. *Review of Educational Research, 69*, 117–144.

Spear-Swerling, L., & Sternberg, R. J. (2001). What science offers teachers of reading. *Learning Disabilities Research and Practice, 16*, 51–57.

Sprague, J. R., & Horner, R. H. (1984). The effects of single instance, multiple instance, and general case training on generalized vending machine use by moderately and severely handicapped students. *Journal of Applied Behavior Analysis, 17*, 273–278.

Stainback, S., & Stainback, W. (Eds.). (1992). *Curriculum considerations in inclusive classrooms: Facilitating learning for all students.* Baltimore: Brookes.

Stayton, V. D., & McCollum, J. (2002). Unifying general and special education: What does the research tell us? *Teacher Education and Special Education, 25*, 211–218.

Steeker, P. M., & Fuchs, L. S. (2000). Effecting superior achievement using curriculum-based measurement: The importance of individual progress monitoring. *Learning Disabilities Research and Practice, 15*, 128–134.

Thurlow, M. L., & Johnson, D. R. (2000). High stakes testing of students with disabilities. *Journal of Teacher Education, 51*(4), 305–314.

Thurlow, M. L., & Thompson, S. J. (1999). District and state standards and assessment: Building an inclusive accountability system. *Journal of Education Leadership, 12*, 3–10.

Vargas, J. S. (1984). What are your exercises teaching? An analysis of stimulus control in instructional materials. In W. L. Heward, T. E. Heron, D. S. Hill, & J. Trap-Porter (Eds.), *Focus on behavior analysis in education* (pp. 126–141). Columbus, OH: Merrill.

Vaughn, S., & Damann, J. D. (2001). Science and sanity in special education. *Behavioral Disorders, 27*, 21–29.

Vaughn, S., Klingner, J., Hughes, M. (2000). Sustainability of research-based practices. *Exceptional Children, 66*, 163–171.

Vaughn, S., Moody, S. W., & Schumm, J. S. (1998). Broken promises: Reading instruction in the resource room. *Exceptional Children, 64*, 211–225.

Wagner, M., Blackorby, J., Cameto, R., & Newman, L. (1994). *What makes a difference? Influences on postschool outcomes of youth with disabilities.* Menlo Park, CA: SRI International.

Ysseldyke, J. E., Thurlow, M. L., Mecklenburg, C., & Graden, J. (1984). Opportunity to learn for regular and special education students during reading instruction. *Remedial and Special Education, 5*, 29–37.

Fads in Speech–Language Pathology

Mareile Koenig
Cheryl Gunter
West Chester University

Like all professionals serving individuals with developmental disabilities, speech–language pathologists (SLPs) are called on by consumers, insurance providers, and policymakers to justify their clinical practice through evidence-based outcome data. Yet Tharpe (1998) has noted that "the field of communicative disorders sorely lacks systematic documentation of clinical outcomes" and that "much of our current practice is based on opinions, theories, and personal experiences" (p. 178). Similar impressions were offered by Enderby and Emerson (1995). We examine these claims by describing speech–language pathology's (SLP) scope of practice; fads, controversial treatments, and related practices within SLP; the content of treatment efficacy information in journals published by the American Speech-Language and Hearing Association (ASHA); and factors contributing to fads and controversial treatments. We conclude with our recommendations for future directions in the field of SLP.

SCOPE OF PRACTICE

Speech–language therapy is not a single technique, and its practice is not rooted in a single theoretical framework. Rather, it includes a wide range of intervention targets and procedures. Specifically, it "includes prevention, diagnosis, habilitation, and rehabilitation of communication, swallowing and other upper aerodigestive disorders; elective modification of communication behaviors; and enhancement of communication" (ASHA, 2001, p. 1). While all of these practices apply potentially to the work of SLPs in the delivery of services to people with developmental disabilities (DD), the largest proportion of services to this population involves evaluation and treatment of speech and language disorders. "Speech disorders" include impairments of articulation, sequencing, and/or the rule-based production of speech sounds (e.g., Bauman-Waengler, 2000, pp. 1–10), whereas "language disorders" include impairments of form (grammar), content (semantics), and/or social-communication (pragmatics) in comprehension and/or production and across oral, written and other communication modalities (e.g., Paul, 2001, p. 3).

In most instances, SLP services are delivered to students with DD in school settings, where SLPs collaborate with other professionals as part of a treatment team. Moreover, SLPs are not the only professionals who target communication outcomes within the scope of their practice. Teachers, occupational therapists, reading specialists, and behavior analysts do so as well, either directly or indirectly (e.g., Mauer, 1999; Sundberg & Partington, 1998). Therefore, cross-disciplinary collaboration is essential.

The most integrated form of collaboration is the transdisciplinary model, which involves a degree of "role sharing" and "role release" by all participants (Nelson, 1998). In this context, an SLP may guide an occupational therapist in carrying out selected language intervention procedures. Similarly, an SLP may be taught to deliver selected sensory integrative therapy (SIT) procedures, or SLPs and occupational therapists may work together in providing a combination of services to individual clients. However collaboration is structured in a particular setting, it brings specialists from different professions into close contact with each other's clinical models, methodologies, and sadly, their fads and misconceptions.

Postgraduate education and a "commitment to lifelong learning" play a major role in the practice of SLP. However, the specific content and direction of continuing education will vary across clinicians. Many states offer continuing education seminars to public school practitioners on topics determined by complex formal needs assessments. Private schools with programs that are designed around particular therapeutic models may offer seminars focusing on these models. For example, if the setting places a primary emphasis on behavioral interventions, SLPs who work in these settings may attend workshops to increase their knowledge of behavioral interventions (e.g., verbal behavior, functional assessment) Similarly, if a setting emphasizes the sensory integration model (Ayres, 1972) or the "floor time" model (e.g., Greenspan & Wieder, 1998), SLPs are likely to expand their knowledge base in these areas. Agency philosophy can be a major determinant of continuing education, with little critical evaluation in many cases. Given this diversity in postgraduate experience and education, it would be inappropriate to suggest that all SLPs use the same intervention strategies, even if they are providing services to similar populations (e.g., individuals with DD). In our discussion of fads and controversial practices, we do not intend to imply that all SLPs utilize any or all of the procedures described.

FADS AND CONTROVERSIAL PRACTICES

Fads

In the field of developmental disabilities, there is a history of interventions known as "fads" (Jacobson, Mulick, & Schwartz, 1995). These treatments are adopted rapidly in the presence of little validating research. They gain widespread use or recognition, and then fade, often in the face of disconfirming research or due to the adoption of a new fad.

Facilitated Communication.   Facilitated communication (FC) is a method for providing "support" to persons with severe communication problems as they express messages (Biklen, 1990). Support is defined on many levels, including physical contact from the facilitator to the communicator while the communicator points to letters with the presumed intent to spell words that form a message. FC was developed by an educator (Biklen, 1990). Later, it was presented to SLPs at an ASHA convention (Biklen, 1992a) and in the *American Journal of Speech-Language Pathology* (Biklen, 1992b). Subsequently, and despite published concerns regarding its theoretical and empirical basis (e.g., Calculator, 1992a, 1992b; McLean, 1992), it was used by some SLPs for treating individuals with DD. However, when empirical evidence began to indicate that facilitators unwittingly authored messages that were falsely attributed to communicators, ASHA, AAMR, and APA published position statements indicating that the validity and reliability of FC remain scientifically unproven (ASHA, 1994; see also Jacobson, Foxx, & Mulick, chap. 22, this volume).

Whole Language.   The whole language (WL) movement may also be viewed on the spectrum of fads. The term was introduced by Goodman (1976) and it resembles the "language experience" approach to reading instruction described by Lee and Allen (1963). More recently, the phrase "balanced reading instruction" has been used by professionals who combine potentially promising features of WL with a skills-based approach to language instruction (Moats, 2000; National Association for the Education of Young Children [NAEYC], 1996).

A clear definition of WL is elusive because articles and books by WL proponents tend to avoid operational definitions. For example, Farris and Kaczmarski (cited in Chaney, 1990) stated, "There is no simple explanation of whole language .... The framework tends to be quite abstract" (p. 244). Others (e.g., Schory, 1990) have described WL as "an instructional philosophy that recognizes the importance of all areas of language in the acquisition of literacy" (p. 206). WL proposes that language (whether oral or written) is normally acquired in the context of meaningful communication, and that instruction that breaks language into discrete skills (e.g., sound segmentation, letter–sound correspondence, sound blending) is inconsistent with the WL approach. Meaning and purpose are the recommended goals of WL instruction, whereas explicit attention to features of the code is considered unnecessary (Goodman, 1986; Smith, 1977). Errors are viewed as "miscues." Explicit differential reinforcement for accurate decoding and explicit error correction are discouraged and even shunned (Paul, 2001). Instead, learners are presumed (not shown how) to notice conventional forms spontaneously when they realize that miscues contradict other contextual information within a reading experience.

Numerous scientifically unsupported premises are associated with the WL philosophy. For example, it is assumed that children and adults use the same strategies to read; learning to read is just like learning to talk (for which there is as yet no complete account); and that phoneme awareness, phonics, spelling, punctuation, and other skills of written language can be learned "naturally." A detailed description of these assumptions together with a summary of the disconfirming scientific evidence has been well documented previously (e.g., Chaney, 1990; Kozloff, 2002; Moats, 2000). In sum, the WL approach lacks supportive evidence for many of its crucial components.

Controversial Treatments

In the practice of SLP, treatments have been described which, unlike fads, continue to abound despite questionable theoretical frameworks, inconsistent or absent empirical support, limited evidence for lasting functional communication, and other considerations. These practices have been classified as "controversial" (Creaghead, 1999).

Sensory Integration Therapy (SIT).   This therapy is based on the unproven assumption that sensory integrative dysfunction contributes to delays in academic and communication development and that a "sensory diet" may attenuate or reverse a neurological disorder which would otherwise interfere with learning (e.g., Ayres, 1978, 1979). Because many children who qualify for SIT services also present with communication disorders, collaboration between SIT therapists and SLPs has become a widespread practice (Mauer, 1999). However, in separate reviews of the SIT literature, Griffer (1999) and Maurer (1999) concluded that, to date, there is insufficient evidence to support the use of SIT as a speech–language intervention strategy. (For a detailed analysis of the SIT literature, see Smith, Mruzek, & Mozingo, chap. 20, this volume.) Guidelines for conducting controlled empirical evaluations of potentially promising features of SIT can be found in Griffer, 1999; Maurer, 1999; and Smith, et al., this volume.

Fast ForWord.   Treatments designed to reduce temporal processing deficits have also been classified as controversial (Creaghead, 1999; Friel-Patti, Loeb, & Gillam, 2001; Gillam, 1999; Veale, 1999). Auditory temporal processing refers to an individual's perception of sounds (phones, phonemes, words) in time. Based on an extensive line of research, temporal processing deficits are considered by some researchers to underlie oral language deficits and subsequent reading problems demonstrated by children with specific language learning impairments (Veale, 1999). Based on this theory, Paula Tallal and colleagues at Scientific Learning Corporation developed a computer-based treatment protocol known as *Fast ForWord* (FFW). The aim of FFW is to help children with language impairments learn "specific auditory or phonological skills that have been related to the acquisition of speech and language" (Veale, 1999, p. 353).

Currently, FFW consists of seven computer games, all of which present auditory stimuli together with interesting visual displays. Three games target discrimination and memory for phonemes or syllables, and four games target vocabulary, syntax, and morphology. Each game requires a learner to make responses based on judgments about sounds, sound sequences, words, or sentences. Initially, auditory stimuli are presented with acoustic modifications to support successful responding. As a learner's response accuracy increases, the degree of acoustic modification decreases until the learner is responding to natural, unmodified speech. Response opportunities are presented within an intensive, discrete trial format for 100 minutes per day, 5 days a week, up to 6 weeks in a row until criterion performance levels are reached. (For a detailed description of these games and procedures, see Friel-Patti, DesBarres, & Thibodeux, 2001.)

To date, thousands of children have participated in FFW intervention, and efficacy research has been conducted with results that appear positive on the surface. These results, together with dramatic testimonials by professionals and consumers, are celebrated on the Scientific Learning Corporation's Web site (http://www.scilearn.com/edu/main=nclb/link=slc). A testimonial by Dr. Burns (an SLP who participated in the field trial of FFW) states that "This is the only training program I've seen in 30 years of practice that is based in science" and that "until now, most methods have been largely based on anecdotes and the individual inventions and dedication of speech therapists" (Scientific Learning Corporation, cited in Gillam, 1999, p. 363).

Despite dramatic testimonials, however, a closer examination of FFW's theoretical framework and efficacy data has raised questions within the professional community (Friel-Patti, DesBarres, et al., 2001; Gillam, 1999). Regarding FFW's theoretical framework, Gillam pointed to a body of evidence suggesting that "higher level phonological representation problems, not temporal processing deficits per se, may be fundamental to language and reading difficulties in school-age children ..." (p. 364). Further, many aspects of language do not require the perception of fine-grained temporal detail because redundancies in the communication signal would enable them to fill in the missing pieces (Leonard, 1998).

Concerns regarding the efficacy research have also been expressed. Based on two major studies published in peer-reviewed journals (Merzenich et al., 1996; Tallal et al., 1996), Scientific Learning Corporation claims that FFW yields 1½ to 3 years of language gain over a 6-week period. One concern noted by Gillam (1999) is that the major efficacy studies have been conducted by the developers of FFW. Other concerns pertain to the research methodology. The Merzenich et al. (1996) study included school-aged participants with receptive and expressive language delays, reading difficulties, and normal range nonverbal intellectual abilities. The intensive treatment protocol offered three components delivered over a 4-week period, including (a) two of the prototype FFW computer games, (b) eight speech and language activities structured by trained clinicians in a one-on-one context, and (c) daily homework assignments. Comparison of pre- and posttreatment measures indicated significant improvements in responses to the computer games, performance on a measure of temporal sequencing, formal measures of memory for commands, and formal measures of grammatical comprehension. Performance on speech and language activities was not reported. These results suggest that intensive treatment involving the previously mentioned elements leads to significant improvement on tests of auditory perception, memory, and language comprehension. However, the current FFW protocol does not include all of the treatment elements that were used in this study.

A second study (Merzenich et al., 1996; Tallal et al., 1996) involved 22 school-aged participants with language learning impairments. The participants were divided into two groups matched for nonverbal intelligence and receptive language. Children in both groups spent equal amounts of time attending laboratory sessions, playing computer games, receiving direct one-on-one intervention delivered by a clinician, and completing homework assignments. However, the children in one group listened to modified speech as they played the computer games, whereas children in the second group "received equivalent language training with natural speech materials" and they "played video games rather than these adaptive auditory-speech training games." (Merzenich et al., 1996, cited in Gillam, 1999, p. 366). Pre- and posttreatment measures were used to assess temporal processing, speech discrimination, and grammatical comprehension. Results indicated significant improvement by children in both groups on all measures. However, improvements for the participants treated with exposure to modified speech stimuli were greater than those of the participants who heard only natural speech. Although these results suggest the positive influence of FFW, it is important to remember that none of the participants received FFW alone. There is no way to determine from this study whether the same results would have been obtained if any of the other treatment components had been deleted from the intervention protocols for each group.

A third source of support offered by the developers of FFW is an unpublished study involving 500 children who received FFW training from 58 certified clinicians (Tallal et al., 1997). The children varied in age, degree of language learning impairment, and diagnosis (e.g., specific language impairment, autism, central auditory processing disorder, attention deficit disorder, dyslexia, and others). The length of treatment varied across children, as did the instruments used to measure pre- and posttest performances. Considering these sources of variability, it is difficult to interpret the data. Therefore, this study is not widely accepted as validation of FFW's success (Gillam, 1999).

Interestingly, neither of the first two FFW studies reported the participants' spontaneous language use pre- and postintervention, so it is not possible to determine whether improvements on structured and formal language tasks extended to the participants' general communication performance. However, some smaller scale studies conducted by independent researchers have examined this issue. Friel-Patti, DesBarres, and Thibodeau (2001) described five case studies of school-aged children with language learning difficulties who received FFW. Both standard test performance and conversational language performance were included in the pre- and postintervention assessment protocols. A comparison of these measures indicated modest improvements on the standardized tests but not on measures of conversational speech. Similarly, Loeb, Stoke, and Fey (2001) tracked the pre- and postintervention performances of three school-aged children who completed the FFW program. Their assessment protocol included formal language measures and measures of conversational language. Whereas modest increases were observed on formal language measures, very few changes were observed in the children's spontaneous conversational speech.

In a complex study by Gillam, Crofford, Gale, and Hoffman (2001), the effects of FFW were compared with the effects of a bundle of computer-based intervention programs published by the Laureate Learning Systems (LLS). None of the LLS programs included modified speech. Four school-age children served as participants. Based on random assignment, two of the children received FFW and two received LLS. Both forms of treatment were administered by the children's parents. The effects of each intervention were measured by pre–post performance on a standardized language test and by repeated measures of spontaneous conversational language within a multiple-probe single-subject design. All children made clinically significant gains on the standardized language measure. Three children (two receiving LLS and one receiving FFW) made clinically significant gains on mean length of utterance (a measure of conversational speech), but only one child, who received LLS, made fewer grammatical errors after treatment.

In sum, FFW has been delivered to thousands of children at great cost as measured in time and money. Although the initial efficacy studies offer important information, they fall short of confirming the efficacy of the FFW program. A number of smaller scale studies conducted by independent investigators confirmed the finding of improvements on some but not all important language measures. Clearly, further research is needed to resolve the controversy surrounding this intervention. In the words of Gillam, Loeb, and Friel-Patti (2001), "[G]iven the expansive claims that have been made about FFW, attempts to persuade school administrators to provide FFW training during the school day at considerable public expense, and the unprecedented media attention on FFW, a large-scale randomized clinical trial" (p. 269) is needed to assess this intervention.

Whole Language in Oral Language Instruction. We now turn to a third controversial treatment, which is the application of whole language to oral language instruction (WL–O). This application was proposed in 1990 by Norris and Damico as an alternative to what the authors characterized as "behaviorism and its fragmentation methodology." WL-O is described in reference to five "erroneous assumptions" and four intervention guidelines. According to Norris and Damico, it is erroneous to assume that

> 1) "targeting superficial forms of the language (sounds, words, grammatical forms, pragmatic rules) is the goal of language intervention …; 2) that teaching parts of language will provide learners with the tools for functional communication …; 3) language must be systematically targeted and taught in accord with a developmental sequence or a specific functional use …, 4) the role of the SLP is to enhance language development through modeling, shaping, and reinforcing correct responses; and that 5) outward forces, such as secondary reinforcers motivate learning and maintain a child's attention to a task …" (pp. 214–215)

As an alternative to the acceptance of these "erroneous assumptions," Norris and Damico (1990) advise SLPs to design language intervention by honoring four recommendations (pp. 215–219): 1) "Create an environment where there are opportunities for language to develop along the general to specific, familiar to unfamiliar continuums …;" 2) use theme-based activities (e.g., story book and authentic children's literature) to create repeatable contexts in which learners are motivated to hear and use language in the creation of meaning; 3) include collaborative activities which expose learners to the multiple functions of language; and 4) use scaffolding techniques to support the needs of learners. Scaffolding techniques include providing "assistance in communicating the message," initiating discussions that actively engage children; adjusting the complexity of language input to fit a learner's comprehension level, and attending to the content and form of a message. The latter is supported through the use of summarizing statements, close statements, requests for conversational repair, and prompts for elaboration.

Overall, the WL–O approach applies what is known about normal language development and recommends that SLPs use similar scaffolding strategies for assisting learners with speech–language impairments to communicate more effectively. Although Norris and Damico (1990) did not specify a target population, it appears that their recommendations are intended to apply to the entire range of learners, including individuals with specific language impairments, cognitive impairments, autism spectrum disorders, or developmental apraxia of speech.

This intervention is controversial for a number of reasons. We focus on two basic points: First, language is not always learned as a whole. There is evidence that "components of language are in some ways modular in development and, although they interact, they are not entirely integrated at all points in time" (Paul, 2001, p. 74; see also Bishop, 1997). For example, it is not uncommon for learners to demonstrate age-appropriate vocabulary, syntax, and pragmatics while presenting with speech production errors that are inconsistent with age-expectations. Similarly, many learners demonstrate age-appropriate semantic and speech production skills while grammatical performance ranks below age-expectations. In other words, even if language were acquired as an integrated whole by typical learners, this is not always the case for learners who present with DD. A recent review (conducted by a team of professionals, including SLPs) of treatment efficacy studies has recommended that interventions for learners with autism must be studied and evaluated with detailed attention to the individual profiles of learners (National Research Council, 2001). Given the wide range of variability within this population, "one size fits all" interventions are not defensible, regardless of the theoretical orientations from which they arise. We know of no studies that have tested the effectiveness of a whole language approach with learners who display a wide range of DD.

Second, we question the four "erroneous assumptions" described by Norris and Damico, particularly with respect to language instruction for children with pervasive developmental disorders such as autism spectrum disorders. A vast body of treatment efficacy data exists which validates the use of various behavioral interventions in language instruction for learners with DD (e.g., Goldstein, 2002; Matson et al., 1996; National Research Council, 2001), particularly learners with autism who (during early stages of development) often do not demonstrate the most fundamental feature of joint attention that is central to effective participation in transactional processes associated with normal language development such as whole language instruction. Finally, the very fact that many children who present with language impairments do so despite a history of participation in typical nurturing environments suggests that a different form of intervention is needed.

Although empirical evidence contradicts the basic assumption that language is always acquired (and should always be taught) as an integrated whole, other features of the WL–O model are consistent with commonly held clinical principles. One such principle is that intervention should enhance a learner's communicative success in the natural contexts of his life (Baer, Wolf, & Risley, 1968; Paul, 2001). Clearly, repeated opportunity to express meanings in natural contexts is a strategy consistent with this principle. However, discrete skills instruction followed by programmed generalization across contexts can also lead to this goal. Research indicates that while skills learned in the natural environment are more likely to be generalized spontaneously, some learners nevertheless require a more highly structured setting to establish individual skills, followed by planned generalization training (Fey, 1986; Paul, 2001).

In sum, WL–O includes features that are consistent with commonly held clinical principles, but it is based on assumptions that do not apply to all learners. We know of no data that support the use of WL–O with learners who present with a wide range of disabilities. For these reasons, WL–O must be considered for use only with caution.

Controversial Practices

Some SLP practices involve biases of a more general nature, often built into textbooks used in university-level training programs (e.g., Nelson, 1998; Owens, 1999; Paul, 2001). These biases seem to reflect an acknowledgment that major theories of language development generally include some supportable assumptions but that no single theory has been confirmed in its entirety. For example, Paul (2001) stated that "until definite research allows us to achieve consensus, each clinician must make an independent decision about them .... I believe that the descriptive-developmental model serves us best" (p. 19). However, she notes that other theories should not be excluded, because of the strengths that they bring to the clinical process.

Nelson (1998) states, "the best way to characterize a practice that blends the most desirable aspects of multiple theories is [to be] eclectic" (p. 90), citing Thatcher's (1980) definition of "eclectic" as "proceeding by the method of selection; choosing what seems best from others; not original nor following any one model or leader, but choosing at will from the doctrines, works, etc. of others" (p. 91). Moreover, Nelson is careful to distinguish "eclectic" from "disorganized and random practices" (p. 91), and we agree that an eclectic approach has merit when and if the decision to choose a strategy is tied to objective and systematic considerations. However, in the absence of these considerations, "what seems best" is left up to the interpretation of a clinician and poses risk for the kind of trial-and-error decision making consistent with disorganized and random practices. Science, after all, is the method by which people can actually show that one thing is better than another, truer than another, or differs in desirable ways from another practice. Why just urge professionals to select what "seems" best?

In his approach to the treatment of language disorders, Owens (1999) recommends a "functional framework." This framework includes interventions that provide many opportunities for learners to use and generalize language as a communicative tool within meaningful contexts (partners, settings, activities). He contrasts his framework to the "traditional model," which he describes as a "highly structured, behavioral one emphasizing the teaching of specific behaviors within a stimulus-response-reinforcement paradigm" (p. 6). Although this functional model includes many worthy features, it also welcomes the WL philosophy, and it appears to disregard some empirically validated methods.

We have no data to indicate how often fads, controversial treatments, or controversial practices may be used or experienced by SLPs. However, recent articles in ASHA journals have examined bases of clinical decision making (e.g., Apel, 1999, 2001; Creaghead, 1999; Duchan, et al., 2001; Kamhi, 1999), and ASHA's recent emphasis on evidence-based practices (discussed later) suggests that there are good reasons to reflect on this topic.

TREATMENT EFFICACY RESEARCH IN ASHA JOURNALS

Access to treatment efficacy data may be one means of attenuating the risk of fads and controversial treatments. Like other professionals, SLPs consult the universe of peer-reviewed professional literature pertaining to the particular issues and populations they serve (e.g., Jackson & Hale, 1990; Kuster, 2002). ASHA contributes four such journals, including the *American Journal of Audiology* (AJA), *American Journal of Speech-Language Pathology* (AJSLP), *Journal of Speech Language and Hearing Research* (JSLHR), and *Language, Speech, and Hearing Services in the Schools* (LSHSS).

As an index of the extent to which speech–language treatment efficacy research relevant to the DD population is offered by ASHA, we conducted a content analysis of the three journals that are likely to address this issue, including AJSLP, JSLHR, and LSHSS. Our content analysis covered a 5-year period from 1998 to 2002, including a total of 734 articles and reports.

In JSLHR, we analyzed all 407 articles/reports categorized under "Speech" and "Language" in the table of contents. In LSHSS, we examined all 157 articles/reports listed under "Article," "Report," "Clinical Forum," and "Clinical Exchange"; and in AJSLP, we examined all 170 articles/reports under "Clinical Focus," "Clinical Consult," "Tutorial," "Second Opinion," "Special Forum," "World View," and "Viewpoint."

Each article/report was coded with respect to the type of information it contained (R = research; P = pedagogical) and the topic it addressed (E = a speech–language treatment efficacy issue relevant to individuals with DD; O = some other topic). The second author independently coded a randomly selected 5% (20) of the articles/reports in JSLHR, 5% (8) of the articles/reports in LSHSS, and 9% (15) of the articles/reports in AJSLP. Intercoder agreements were calculated as 100%, 90%, and 93% respectively. The total number of items associated with each code was then identified, and the proportions of efficacy research, efficacy pedagogy, and other items were determined for each journal in reference to the total number of articles/reports reviewed over the 5-year period.

Figure 14.1 summarizes the data resulting from our analysis. As indicated, the proportion of research reports pertaining to treatment efficacy ranged from 5% in JSLHR to 12% in AJSLP; and the proportion of pedagogical articles pertaining to treatment efficacy ranged from 1% in JSLHR to 15% in LSHSS. The overwhelming proportion of articles and reports in the three journals pertained to other topics, ranging from 78% in LSHSS to 93% in JSLHR.

Overall, these results suggest that only a small proportion of articles and reports in ASHA journals pertain to the efficacy of treatments used for teaching speech and language to learners with DD. Because articles and reports were not coded for treatment efficacy relating to other disabilities (e.g., aphasia, apraxia, dysphagia, voice disorders), it is not possible to determine whether the amount of efficacy information pertaining to individuals with DD is proportionate to the wide range of issues included within the SLP scope of practice. Additionally, we would again emphasize that SLPs, like other professionals, routinely search a much wider database when seeking any type of information, including information about the efficacy of speech–language interventions used in treating individuals with DD. Nevertheless, these data suggest that articles published in ASHA journals contribute relatively little toward clarifying the efficacy of treatments for learners with DD.

FACTORS CONTRIBUTING TO FADS IN SLP

The use of fad treatments in SLP can be linked with a number of factors, including the failure of SLP to adopt an explicit scientist–practitioner model, the absence of a conventional clinical code, and social influences.

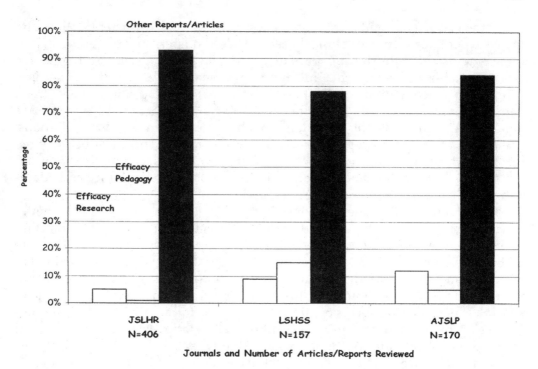

FIG. 14.1. The mean proportion of articles and reports addressing speech and language treatment efficacy for learners with DD in three ASHA journals from 1998 to 2002, inclusive.

Failure of SLP to Adopt an Explicit Scientist–Practitioner Model

Individuals pursuing a career in SLP commence with the completion of the mandates for the Certificate of Clinical Competence (CCC) from ASHA, which represent the influence of the clinical practitioner model. This model, which has been the basis for professional education across varied disciplines, stresses the development of the broad scope of clinical skills that will result in what the ASHA Code of Ethics (2003) conceptualizes as "competent" clinical service provision. We do not wish in any way to minimize the importance of intact technical clinical skills for SLPs. The continuous enhancement of these skills is essential to maintain acceptable levels of service for clients, ensure continued professional development for clinicians, and advance fundamental precepts of the discipline.

In addition to the clinical practitioner model, SLP has experienced the pervasive influence of the intuitive experience model. Kamhi (1999) alluded to this model in his description of the development of clinical expertise (Kamhi, 1994), when he noted that "Most clinicians described their approach as 'eclectic,' and often said that they used their particular approach 'because it worked.' I wanted clinicians to have a better justification of why they used a particular therapy approach" (p. 93). However, he subsequently noted that, while he wanted clinicians to have a view of therapy consistent with their philosophy or supported by empirical evidence, he "came to see that it was actually a very appropriate way to justify the use of a particular treatment approach" (p. 93). Consistent with the intuitive experience model, or clinical practice based on personal preferences, pronouncements of authoritative persons, personal experiences, and intuitive hunches, Kamhi characterized clinicians as "pragmatists" who, unlike scientists, have little problem with theoretical inconsistencies, and who embrace new treatment approaches that best lead to the most substantial functional outcomes. We do not wish to minimize the importance of clinical experience and the nebulous, but no less important, concept of clinical intuition for SLPs. The continuous refinement of the framework of clinical practice that stems from accommodation to and assimilation of new clinical experiences is essential for the flexibility and adaptability that client-centered practices demand.

However, even with these considerations, we assert that SLP would be better served with the explicit adoption of the scientist–practitioner model (SPM) for clinical practice. The SPM (Barlow, 1984) reflects several basic principles, including the application of critical reflection to clinical practice, the use of proven evaluation and intervention methods, the continuous evaluation of client performance and improvement, and practice informed from the scholarship in the discipline. These principles dictate such aspects of clinical practice as formulation of clinical questions, selection of evaluation and intervention frameworks, and interpretation and integration of client data. We do not wish to imply that the standards for professional education in SLP fail to embrace these concepts—they do. However, even a superficial review of the ASHA clinical certification standards reveals a predominant focus on specific clinical skills in discrete clinical areas, not the unified framework of the SPM in which the attitude of scholarship is woven into the fabric of clinical practice.

Hayes, Barlow, and Nelson-Gray (1999) characterize the SPM as one in which research and practice are not separate domains but are, instead, integrated. Practice is guided by science, and the practitioner is competent to conduct scientific research in practice and about practice. Competence is enhanced by both the completion of academic courses in research and the continued involvement in clinical research endeavors.

Evidence suggests that ASHA is moving in the direction of the SPM. Some perceptive, vocal proponents of explicit science-based practice have found appropriate venues to express their positions (e.g., Apel, 1999). Some proponents of the scientific approach to clinical practice have perpetuated this framework with those whom they mentor. On a broader scale, a recent revision of the ASHA clinical certification standards (to be implemented in 2005) has elevated research to a more central role. For instance, Standard III-F in the revised standards mandates "knowledge of processes used in research and the integration of research principles into evidence-based clinical practice," which indicates that "the applicant must demonstrate ... comprehension of the principles of basic and applied research and research design ... (and) should know how to access sources of research information and have experience relating research to clinical practice" (p. 13). Although this is a more explicit statement of the value of research than that contained in the present standards, it falls short of mandated engagement in clinical research.

In addition to revised certification standards, ASHA has shifted the focus of continued professional education to the theme of evidence-based practice and created evidence-based practice criteria (Wambaugh & Bain, 2002). Again, although this is more consistent with the principles of the SPM than an intuitive model, the concept of evidence-based practice still focuses on clinical outcomes, not on the broader concept of a scientific attitude as the basis for each dimension of the service provision continuum.

Several existing conditions contraindicate widespread acceptance of ASHA's movement towards the SPM. For example, some academic institutions with curricula in SLP provide opportunities for student participation in research, but most do not mandate undergraduate or graduate theses for completion of degrees. Further, the discipline of SLP continues to accept an artificial administrative schism between the "scientists" and the "practitioners," as seen in the ASHA Convention format of "research" presentations versus "professional" presentations and in the ASHA Executive Board structure, with separate Vice-Presidents for areas that could easily be integrated into the SPM.

In addition to these considerations, we have a particular concern about an emerging issue, that is, the perceived shortage of SLPs with earned doctorates. In fact, ASHA has devoted much attention to the recruitment and retention of doctoral students. Scott and Wilcox (2002) related the need for doctoral students to the needs for replacements of professors retiring from academic positions. However, they also noted that "our undergraduate and graduate coursework is weighted heavily toward clinical careers rather than academic ones, and the pressure to expand this focus increases as the scope of professional practice grows. This stands in stark contrast to many disciplines, where the curriculum builds more directly from undergraduate to graduate predoctoral and postdoctoral levels" (p. 5).

The schism between clinicians and researchers is further exacerbated in what appear to be sincere attempts to minimize the divide. Special themes of publications, for instance, that assert that clinicians and researchers should collaborate and that researchers should be more sensitive to clinicians' needs contradict the idea that one should be simultaneously both in such an intertwined fashion that these perspectives cannot be distinguished.

Absence of an Official Clinical Code

The discipline of SLP has no "official" system for the codification and differential diagnosis of communication disorders. Short of a document such as the *Diagnostic and Statistical Manual of Mental Disorders* (DSM; American Psychiatric Association, 1994), SLPs must depend on the *ASHA Desk Reference*, Volumes 1–4, which include, among other policies, Position Statements that delineate definitions and descriptions of conditions. The expectation of ASHA is that SLPs will view the *Desk Reference* as authoritative and that they will employ a consistent framework for the provision of clinical services. In a philosophical sense, SLPs may very well consider the professional association pronouncements the authoritative standards for clinical practice. However, on a practical level, inconsistent conceptualization of various clinical constructs abounds, facilitated by personal preferences and work site standards. The imposition of a mandated, unified code would, to some extent, resolve discrepancies in definitions and common application of terms. However, previous attempts by ASHA to codify communication disorders in a manner similar to the *DSM* never met with widespread adoption within the discipline. Because of that, SLPs encounter specific challenges. One challenge is the interchangeable use of clinical terminology. For example, the term *communication disorder* is accepted as the generic umbrella term for a vast array of conditions. Even so, a number of other terms (e.g., *delay, deviance, problem, impairment, handicap, syndrome*) capture the concept of "disorder" (Carrow-Woolfolk & Lynch, 1981). Often used in an interchangeable fashion, these terms, as defined on an individual basis, have distinct implications. The interchangeable use of terms with actual subtle distinctions can shift the focus of evaluation and intervention into inappropriate directions. In addition, terms abound, and are often inappropriately interchanged, for the actual problems themselves.

Related to the terminological problems just described are problems arising from the use of terms that are open to personal rather than shared interpretation. For example, sometimes clinicians adopt terms that are in the public vernacular as an act of camaraderie with a client, even if the use of such terms is technically incorrect (e.g., referring to speech production errors as "a problem with letters."). Those clinicians run the risk of violating ethical mandates to provide accurate information to the public. Sometimes SLPs adopt terms that other professionals present to them as possible labels for conditions, even if the use of such terms is inconsistent with the practice of SLP (e.g., using the term *speech* to mean 'language'). Those clinicians do those professionals a disservice in automatic acceptance of that term without qualification. The adoption of the search for shared, accurate terminology before clinical service provision can proceed would reduce much potential for confusion in both clients and professionals (Enderby & Emerson, 1986).

Finally, we would be remiss if we did not note our conclusion that the word *fad* is best used in retrospect. Given that a fad reflects a process that appears, becomes popular, receives accolades, then fades—without a substantial scientific validation—we are reluctant to use even the term *fad* without a clear operational definition of the construct. However, we have noted in SLP that *fad* is used in diverse forms, for example, when one is unfamiliar with or unimpressed with a procedure, when one holds views that contradict the provisions of a procedure, or even in derision. At present, SLP has no consensus as to what quantity and quality of evidence constitutes sufficient "proof" of the validity of a procedure, or, in concrete terms, when unsubstantiated or disputed crosses the line into "fad." With the ethical demands for the foremost consideration of the welfare of the client, we must protect clients from procedures with potentially harmful effects. At the same time, however, we must protect the process, often sustained over substantial periods of time, of scientific inquiry and not prematurely dismiss an avenue of potential benefit for clients.

Social Phenomena

We have identified four social trends that are linked with treatment fads. The first is a continued trust in folklore and folk remedies by some consumers. For example, we have heard colorful explanations of the causes of stuttering, ranging from a child's being scared by a snake or being tickled on the soles of the feet to being left outside in a rainstorm. Similarly, we have heard diverse assortments of presumed cures for conditions, such as those for deafness. Here, the folklore includes the ideas that pouring urine in the ears, jumping up and down, ingesting opium, dipping snuff, receiving electric shocks, and even bloodletting would immediately restore hearing. As the British Stammering Association (2003) noted, some people will experiment with claims of cure, many of which are very expensive; and people who have found the cure for a condition passionately believe they have something to offer to others. We do not doubt the sincere motives of people who wish to find the best, most effective route to a cure for a condition, and we are well aware of the appeal of unique "inside information" to those who experience a disability. However, the incessant acceptance of information not based in any theory of a condition, and not subjected to rigorous examination, is another factor that contributes to the perpetuation of fads.

Advertisement is another type of social influence on the development of trends. The exponential surge in advertisements for products and treatments has enhanced public awareness of some approaches but, at the same time, raised unrealistic hopes of some people with communication disorders. Some ads are extreme. For instance, one ad titled "Former Opera Singer Perfects Cure for Stuttering," states that for $259.00, with private, speech therapy sessions by phone, people who stutter can correct the stuttering in the privacy of their home (Stutter News, 2003). A demo tape entices people to review this product, and secondhand testimonials attest to the treatment's potent impact on their lives.

Some ads are particularly problematic for both clinicians and clients, when their claims include an apparent authoritative component. An example of this involves *Fast ForWord*. The Web site for this product contains a section summarizing the empirical results of studies conducted by respected researchers, including data that document improvements after participation in the protocol. At the same time, however, the serious attempt to show the validity of the protocol is undercut by "sound bite" quotes from professional endorsers and emotional testimonials from students and their parents. We wonder, in the end, which forms of evidence potential consumers consider authoritative in the decision of whether to consider this procedure.

A third social trend linked with fads involves the media's presentation of "sound bites" and encapsulated "headline" summaries of potential discoveries. One of the most extensive media campaigns affecting the field of SLP centered on the cochlear implant device. This device, manufactured by the 3M Corporation, aimed to enhance the hearing of people with profound hearing loss. Once the U.S. Food and Drug Administration announced its approval, the 3M Corporation stood poised to publicize its creation. While the intent was to promote public awareness of a device that could, in some cases, dramatically enhance life quality, we cannot discount the business considerations involved in the public relations efforts. Over a 6-month period, Public Communications, Inc. (n.d.) placed over 1,500 stories in the media and reached over 400 million audience members worldwide, while the 3M Corporation itself received over 5,000 requests from prospective consumers and health care individuals. We cannot be certain whether this response resulted from the device or the publicity that surrounded the device. However, the extensive coverage by the news media enhanced both the perceived credibility of the company and the demand for the product.

The fourth social influence linked with fads is the "never give up" attitude adopted by some consumers and SLPs. SLPs are bound by professional ethics to never assure clients of cures for communication disorders. Whereas statements of reasonable expectations for improvement can be provided, promises of outcome are not permitted, nor is continuation of treatment that has not proven efficacious for a client. Thus, while striving for maximum improvement in communication, SLPs recognize that a point can arise in treatment that marks the onset of diminished returns. Consumers and SLPs alike may find this point difficult to accept.

CONCLUSIONS AND RECOMMENDATIONS

Learners with developmental disabilities have a right to treatments with proven documentation of effectiveness. Moreover, speech–language treatment is provided at a substantial cost of time and public funding. For both of these reasons, it is important to examine treatment efficacy issues. Our examination has indicated that fads (e.g., facilitated communication, whole language), controversial treatments (e.g., sensory-integrative treatment, FastForWord, whole language applied to oral language instruction), and controversial practices (e.g., nonsystematic eclecticism) abound in the field of SLP as it is practiced in delivery of services to learners with developmental disabilities.

We are particularly concerned about the failure of SLP to adopt an explicit scientist–practitioner model. Clearly, ASHA and university training programs in SLP advocate science-based treatment. This advocacy is woven into ASHA's Code of Ethics and is reflected in the recent emphasis on evidence-based practices. However, in practice, SLPs have traditionally assumed separate roles either as researchers who study basic processes or as therapists who engage in clinical practice. We believe that this division has led some clinicians to overlook the scientific dimensions of clinical work. Clearly, sound clinical practices stem from multiple sources (Prizant & Rubin, 1999). However, "an understanding and application of science must be a vital part of clinical practice in order to ensure that treatment methods are theoretically sound and empirically based with measurable, cost-effective outcomes" (Blischak & Cheek, 2001, p. 11).

In the interest of fine-tuning and integrating a strong science-based approach in basic and applied areas of SLP, we offer the following recommendations, some of which may be relevant to other practitioner disciplines that must grapple with new rigors presented by evidence-based practice:

1. Adopt the science practitioner model. Reconceptualize clinical practice as a form of research, and collapse the distinction between researchers and clinicians.
2. Establish a standard clinical code for SLP.
3. Institute opportunities and requirements that students engage in scientific methods within "disorders" courses at the university level (e.g., Blischak & Cheek, 2001), and increase emphasis on science-based clinical practices.
4. Broaden the definition of "scholarly activity" to include basic, applied, integrative, and pedagogical forms.
5. Recognize both qualitative and quantitative forms of research (Brinton & Fujiki, 2003; Damico & Simmons-Mackie, 2003).
6. Inasmuch as a particular applied setting will shape the kind of scholarly contribution that a clinician can make, it is important to encourage smaller-scale efforts as well as larger controlled research studies.

These types of changes in preparation and practice would lessen the vulnerability of SLP professionals, and other professionals, to the application of fad treatments and promote science-based clinical practices to individuals with a full spectrum of impairments including developmental disabilities.

REFERENCES

American Psychiatric Association. (1994). *Diagnostic and statistical manual of mental disorders* (4th ed.). Washington, DC: Author.

American Speech-Language and Hearing Association. (1994). *Technical report on facilitated communication.* Rockville, MD: Author.

American Speech-Language and Hearing Association. (2001). *Scope of practice in speech-language pathology.* Rockville, MD: Author.

American Speech-Language and Hearing Association (2002). Knowledge and skills acquisition form for certification in speech-language pathology. Rockville, MD: Author.

American Speech-Language and Hearing Association. (2003). *Code of ethics.* ASHA Supplement.

American Speech-Language and Hearing Association. (in press). *Code of ethics* (revised). ASHA Supplement, 23.

Apel, K. (1999). Checks and balances: Keeping the science in our profession. *Language, Speech, and Hearing Services in Schools, 30,* 98–107.

Apel, K. (2001). Developing evidence-based practices and research collaborations in school settings. *Language, Speech, and Hearing Services in the Schools, 32,* 196–197.

Audiologic practices: What is popular versus what is supported by evidence. *American Journal of Audiology, 4*(1), 26–34.

Ayres, A. J. (1972). *Sensory integration and learning disorders.* Los Angeles: Western Psychological Services.

Ayres, A. J. (1978). Learning disabilities and the vestibular system. *Journal of Learning Disabilities, 11,* 30–41.

Ayres, A. J. (1979). *Sensory integration and the child.* Los Angeles: Western Psychological Services.

Baer, D., Wolf, M., & Risley, T. (1968). Current dimensions of applied behavior analysis. *Journal of Applied Behavior Analysis, 1,* 91–97.

Barlow, D. H. (1984). *The scientist practitioner: Research and accountability in educational settings.* New York: Pergamon.

Bauman-Waengler, J. (2000). *Articulatory and phonological impairments: A clinical focus.* Boston: Allyn & Bacon.

Biklen, D. (1990). Communication unbound: Autism and praxis. *Harvard Educational Review, 60,* 291–315.

Biklen, D. (1992a). *Facilitated communication with people with autism and other developmental disabilities.* Mini-seminar, ASHA Convention, San Antonio, TX.

Biklen, D. (1992b, January). Typing to talk: Facilitated communication. *American Journal of Speech-Language Pathology,* 15–17.

Bishop, D. (1997). *Uncommon understanding: Development and disorders of language comprehension in children.* East Sussex, UK: Psychology Press Limited.

Blischack, D. M., & Cheek, M. (2001, February). A lot of work keeping everything controlled: A class research project. *American Journal of Speech-Language Pathology, 10,* 1.

Brinton, B., & Fujiki, M. (2003). Blending quantitative and qualitative methods in language research and intervention. *American Journal of Speech-Language Pathology, 12*(2), 155–164.

British Stammering Association. (2003). *Stuttering cure.* Retrieved April 10, 2003, from http://www.stammering.org

Calculator, S. (1992a, January). Facilitated Communication: Calculator responds. *American Journal of Speech-Language Pathology,* 23–24.

Calculator, S. (1992b, January). Perhaps the emperor has clothes after all: A response to Biklen. *American Journal of Speech-Language Pathology,* 18–20.

Carrow-Woolfolk, E., & Lynch, J. I. (1981). *Language disorders in children: An integrative approach.* Boston: Allyn & Bacon.

Chaney, C. (1990). Evaluating the whole language approach to language arts: The pros and cons. *Language, Speech, and Hearing Services in Schools, 21,* 244–249.

Creaghead, N. A. (1999). Evaluating language intervention approaches: Contrasting perspectives. *Language, Speech, and Hearing Services in the Schools, 30,* 335–338.

Damico, J., & Simmons-Mackie. (2003). Qualitative research and speech-language pathology: A tutorial for the clinical realm. *American Journal of Speech-Language Pathology, 12*(2), 131–143.

Duchan, J. F., Calculator, S., Sonnenmeier, R., Diehl, S., & Cumley, G. D. (2001). A framework for managing controversial practices. *Language, Speech, and Hearing Services in the Schools, 32,* 133–141.

Enderby, P., & Emerson, J. (1986). *Does Speech and Language Therapy Work?* San Diego, CA: Singular.

Fast ForWord. (2003). Retrieved April 10, 2003, from http://www.scientificlearning.com

Fey, M. E. (1986). *Language intervention with young children.* San Diego, CA: College Hill Press.

Friel-Patti, S., DesBarres, K., & Thibodeau, L. (2001). Case studies of children using Fast ForWord. *American Journal of Speech-Language Pathology, 10,* 203–315.

Friel-Patti, S., Loeb, D. F., & Gillam, R. B. (2001). Looking ahead: An introduction to five exploratory studies of Fast ForWord. *American Journal of Speech-Language Pathology, 10,* 195–202.

Gillam, R. B. (1999). Computer-assisted language intervention using Fast ForWord: Theoretical and empirical considerations for clinical decision-making. *Language, Speech, and Hearing Services in Schools, 30,* 363–370.

Gillam, R. B., Crofford, J., Gale, M. A., & Hoffman, L. M. (2001). Language change following computer-assisted language instruction with Fast ForWord of Laureate Learning Systems Software. *American Journal of Speech-Language Pathology, 10*(3), 231–247.

Gillam, R. B., Loeb, D. F., & Friel-Patti, S. (2001). Looking back: A summary of five exploratory studies of Fast ForWord. *American Journal of Speech-Language Pathology, 10,* 269–273.

Goldstein, H. (2002). Communication intervention for children with autism: A review of treatment efficacy. *Journal of Autism and Developmental Disorders, 32,* 373–396.

Goodman, K. (1976). Reading: A Psycholinguistic Guessing Game. *Journal of the Reading Specialist, 6,* 126–135.

Goodman, K. (1986). *What's whole in whole language.* Portsmouth, NH: Heinemann.

Greenspan, S., & Wieder, S. (1998). *The child with special needs.* Reading, MA: Melroyd Lawrence.

Griffer, M. (1999). Is sensory integration effective for children with language-learning disorders? A critical review of the evidence. *Language, Speech, and Hearing Services in the Schools, 30,* 393–400.

Hayes, S. C., Barlow, D. H., & Nelson-Gray, R. O. (1999). *The scientist practitioner: Research and accountability in the age of managed care.* Boston: Allyn & Bacon.

Jackson, P. D., & Hale, S. T. (1990). *Journals in Communication Sciences and Disorders.* Rockville, MD: American Speech-Language and Hearing Association.

Jacobson, J. W., Mulick, J. A., & Schwartz, A. A. (1995). A history of facilitated communication: Science, pseudoscience, and antiscience. *American Psychologist, 50,* 750–765.

Kamhi, A. G. (1994). Toward a theory of clinical expertise in speech-language pathology. *Language, Speech, and Hearing Services in Schools, 25,* 115–118.

Kamhi, A. G. (1999). To use or not to use: Factors that influence the selection of new treatment approaches. *Language, Speech, and Hearing Services in Schools, 30,* 92–98.

Kozloff, M. (2002). Rhetoric and revolution: Kenneth Goodman's "Psycholinguistic guessing game." *Direct Instruction News, 2*(2), 34–41.

Kuster, J. M. (2002). Web-based information resources for evidence-based practice in speech-language pathology. *Perspectives on Language Learning and Education, 9*(1), 6–14.

Lee, D., & Allen, R. (1963). *Learning to read through experience.* New York: Appleton-Century-Crofts.

Leonard, L. (1998). *Children with specific language impairment.* Cambridge, MA: MIT Press.

Loeb, D. F., Stoke, C., & Fey, M. E. (2001). Language changes associated with Fast ForWord-Language: Evidence from case studies. *American Journal of Speech-Language Pathology, 10,* 216–230.

Matson, J. L., Benavidez, D. A., & Compton, L. S. (1996). Behavioral treatment of autistic persons: A review of research from 1980 to the present. *Research in Developmental Disabilities, 17,* 433–165.

Mauer, D. M. (1999). Issues and applications of sensory integration theory and treatment with children with language disorders. *Language, Speech, and Hearing Services in the Schools, 30,* 383–393.

McLean, J. (1992, January). Facilitated communication: Some thoughts on Biklen's and Calculator's interaction. *American Journal of Speech-Language Pathology,* 25–27.

Merzenich, M. M., Jenkins, W. M., Johnston, P., Schreiner, C., Miller, S. L., & Tallal, P. (1996). Temporal processing of deficits of language-learning impaired children ameliorated by training. *Science, 271,* 77–81.

Moats, L. C. (2000). *The illusion of "balanced" reading instruction.* Retrieved April 20, 2003, from http://www.edexcellence.net/library/wholelang/moats.html#foreword

National Association for the Education of Young Children. (1996). *Early years are learning years: Phonics and Whole language learning: a balanced approach to beginning reading.* Washington, DC: Author.

National Research Council. (2001). *Educating children with autism.* Committee on Educational Interventions for Children with Autism. Division of Behavioral and Social Sciences and Education. Washington, DC: National Academy Press.

Nelson, N. W. (1998). *Childhood language disorders in context: Infancy through adolescence* (2nd ed.). Boston: Allyn & Bacon.

Norris, J., & Damico, J. (1990). Whole language in theory and practice: Implications for language intervention. *Language, Speech, and Hearing Services in the Schools, 21,* 212–220.

Owens, R. O. (1999). *Language disorders: A functional approach to assessment and intervention.* Boston: Allyn & Bacon.

Paul, R. (2001). *Language disorders from infancy through adolescence: Assessment and intervention.* Philadelphia: Mosby.

Prizant, B. M., & Rubin, E. (1999). Contemporary issues in interventions for autism spectrum disorders: A commentary. *Journal of the Association for Persons with Severe Handicaps, 24,* 199–208.

Public Communications, Inc. (n.d.). *Marketing hearing implant for the deaf.* Chicago, IL: Author. Retrieved May 15, 2003, from www.pcipr.com/clients/casehistories/hcfp_0005.htm

Schory, M. E. (1990). Whole language and the speech-language pathologist. *Language, Speech, and Hearing Services in the Schools, 21,* 206–212.

Scientific Learning Corporation. (1998). *Fast ForWord* [Computer software]. Berkeley, CA: Author.

Scott, C., & Wilcox, K. (2002, November 19). The Ph.D. in CSD. *The ASHA Leader, 7*(21), 4–5, 16.

Smith, F. (1977). Making sense of reading—and of reading instruction. *Harvard Educational Review, 47,* 386–395.

Stutter News. (2003). *Former opera singer perfects cure for stuttering.* Retrieved April 10, 2003, from http://www.stutter.net/stutter_news.htm

Sundberg, M. L., & Partington, J. W. (1998). *Teaching language to children with autism or other developmental disabilities.* Danville, CA: Behavior Analysts, Inc.

Tallal, P., Merzenich, M., Burns, M., Gelfond, S., Young, M., & Shipley, J., et al. (1997, November). *Temporal training for language-impaired children: National clinical trial results.* Paper presented to the Annual Convention of the American Speech-Language and Hearing Association, Boston, MA.

Tallal, P., Miller, S. I., Bedi, G., Byma, G., Wang, X., Nagarajan, S. S., et al. (1996). *Language comprehension in language-learning impaired children: National clinical trial results.* Paper presented to the Annual Convention of the American Speech-Language and Hearing Association, Boston, MA.

Tharpe, A. M. (1998). Treatment fads versus evidence-based practice. In F. H. Bess (Ed.), *Children with hearing impairment: Contemporary trends* (pp. 179–188). Nashville, TN: Vanderbilt Bill Wilkerson Press.

Thatcher, V. S. (Ed.). (1980). *The New Webster encyclopedic dictionary of the English language.* Chicago: Consolidated.

Veale, T. K. (1999). Targeting temporal processing deficits through Fast ForWord: Language therapy with a new twist. *Language, Speech, and Hearing Services in the Schools, 30,* 353–362.

Wambaugh, J., & Bain, B. (2002, November 19). Make research methods an integral part of your clinical practice. *The ASHA Leader, 7*(21), 1, 10.

Part IV

Disorder- and Symptom-Specific Issues

15

Autism: A Late-20th-Century Fad Magnet

Bernard Metz
Children's Hospital Behavioral Health, Columbus, OH

James A. Mulick
Eric M. Butter
The Ohio State University and Columbus Children's Hospital

In April 2003, the California Department of Developmental Services reported its autism incidence figures during the period from 1987 to 2002, which suggested that the number of Californians diagnosed as having autism increased by approximately 637% (California Department of Developmental Services, 2003). Researchers currently estimate the incidence of autism spectrum disorders across the United States to be as high as 10 to 20 children per 10,000 rather than the historically reported incidence of 4 to 5 per 10,000 (Wing & Potter, 2002). However, it is unclear if this is a true increase in prevalence rather than the result of other factors, such as changes in diagnostic criteria and professional diagnostic practices. The apparent high prevalence of autism, the lifelong implications of the disorder, its severe impact on the functioning of the child and family, and the limited options for effective intervention have led many families to an often desperate quest for any treatment that might be effective.

Few other medical or neurodevelopmental conditions have been as fraught with controversial, fad, and unsupported treatments as the pervasive developmental disorders. We recently spent an hour performing an Internet search, using the Google search engine and the terms *autism* and *treatment*, and were able to identify over 65 distinct interventions advocated or proposed as efficacious for autism spectrum disorders. This includes interventions such as ADAM technology, which advocates unlocking autism through telepathy, injection of sheep stem cells, and use of fish oil and thyme, among others. It is unlikely to surprise the reader to learn that the vast majority of these treatments are being promoted on a commercial basis. It is also likely to be of little surprise that most of these proposed treatments have not been supported when subjected to the rigors of scientific study. Most have not been studied in any serious sense at all, however, mainly because serious researchers have failed to recognize the treatments' supporting rationales to be consistent with other accepted facts about autism, or sometimes even with physical causality. To date, only interventions based on the principles of applied behavior analysis have been shown to produce comprehensive, lasting results (Jacobson, 2000). This approach is tailored to the individual, builds on the child's strengths, and uses reinforcement to teach skills through many learning opportunities in many settings (Green, Brennan, & Fein, 2002).

In this chapter, we consider some of the most pervasive current fads and controversial, unsupported, and disproved treatments proposed as effective interventions for autism, especially in young children. We begin by attempting to clarify and establish some common definitions, terminology, and frameworks for evaluating the efficacy of proposed treatments.

THE NATURE OF FADS

Nobody creates a fad. It just happens. People love going along with the idea of a beautiful pig. It's like a conspiracy.

—Jim Henson

The tenth edition of the *Merriam-Webster Collegiate Dictionary* (1998) defines a fad as a practice or interest followed for a time with exaggerated zeal. Aquirre, Quarantelli, and Mendoza (1988) specified defining characteristics of fads; that is, they are homogenous, novel, and odd. They also described attributes of fad development: sudden, rapid spread, quick acceptance, and short lifespan. Bikhchandani, Hirschleifer, & Welch (1998) used social learning theory to explain fads as a form of herd behavior; imitative behavior based on incomplete information. Marsden (2003) succinctly noted that "contagion research shows that for an idea to be infectious, that is, to spread by contact, it should not only be '*beddable and spreadable*' (attractive and communicable), but should also '*resolve ambiguity or uncertainty*' " (para. 2).

According to Kozloff (chap. 11, this volume), a fad can be an activity, an idea, or material. Ordinary fads are frequently relatively inexpensive and harmless. They are typically isolated events in culture. Kozloff has taken great pains to differentiate between ordinary passing fads, which are generally benign, and what he calls pernicious innovations in education, which can be costly and destructive. Kozloff posits two types of pernicious innovations in education: passing fads and chronic malignancies. He attributes both to folly (lack of knowledge), fraud (promoted in bad faith), or both. We might add ideology as a third source for pernicious innovation in education or any other professional field. Stone (1996), for example, persuasively illustrated the damage caused by the push for instructional methodologies predicated on the doctrine of developmentalism at the expense of experimentally validated approaches.

Are fads necessarily bad? There can be positive elements to fads, for example, when consumer-driven interests lead to the development and appropriate implementation of scientifically validated interventions (Jacobson, 2000). But, in the area of autism treatment, fads tend to be harmful, fruitlessly expending limited time and monetary resources, falsely raising hopes and expectations, and distracting and detracting from efficacious efforts. Fads in relation to any illness or significant social problem may always be more harmful than not, because serious problems require serious efforts to find the truth about them as opposed to adopting a proposed solution because it is currently popular or personally appealing.

Why are parents of young children with autism prone to adoption of unproven fad treatments? We would like to suggest a number of possible reasons. The first set of reasons has to do with the nature of the disorder. Autism is lifelong and severe, impacting all facets of child and family functioning. Comorbidities, such as dangerous and socially inappropriate behavioral excesses and deficits, tend to be both pervasive and aversive to parents. Elements of the essential nature of autistic disorder, for example, poor joint attention and limited display of social affect, disrupt the basic nature of the parent–child relationship. The prognosis is poor. Immediate and early intervention is critical to improvement, but is sometimes hard to get. These factors can lead to desperation under time pressure to find interventions that may be helpful. Parents may buy into approaches that sound plausible and that offer hope, often trying shotgun approaches. Avoidance of guilt may also play a role in this behavior. After all, "What if I later find out that I could have done something?"

A second set of factors likely to contribute to parent susceptibility to unproven fad interventions may be rooted in the lack of knowledge that most parents are likely to have about autism and evidence-based intervention. Most parents are new to the diagnosis, because even at the reported increased rates, autism is still uncommon. Relatively few new parents have been trained in the principles of scientific inquiry, because scientific training is also uncommon and there is widely recognized scientific illiteracy in the general population (Gore, 2003). There is much information to be learned quickly. Although many parents strive to educate themselves about the disorder and potential interventions, it is unclear that this educational process occurs in a systematic, comprehensive fashion. It is likely that most parents rely on secondary and tertiary sources, which are summative, and do not learn about the principles used by authors to derive the conclusions that they promote. Parents may feel practices are valid even if they have not been subjected to scientific verification and peer review (Jacobson, 2000). They are bombarded with information from a variety of sources, including professionals, the Internet, and "word of mouth," and may be poorly equipped to evaluate it.

A third set of reasons underlying the proneness of parents to fad treatments is likely to be rooted in the nature of the systems with which parents must interact. While parents are new to the diagnosis and know little about it, there are also relatively few professionals who are well-educated about autism. Professionals may provide different, even conflicting information. Systems with which parents have to interact may have different, even competing, interests, perspectives, and considerations (e.g., school vs. health care professionals). Competition among expensive professionals and commercial products and proffered private services can be intense and insistent.

Competing interests and lack of knowledge may also account for the tendency of many professionals to be vulnerable to unproven fad treatments. Some practitioners may gravitate to interventions consistent with theoretical or philosophical frameworks to which they subscribe. In some cases, professionals may have insufficient awareness of the process of science, because their professional training may be only tangentially scientific. A significant subset of professionals may prefer to rely on clinical experience and judgment in contrast to scientific findings.

After all, daily successes and failures are a rich and prepotent source of direction that may shape a strong sense of conviction. Professionals may also be subject to pressures by stakeholders to come up with answers or to validate stakeholder assertions. Benelli (2003), for example, documented the role of the Italian media in promoting the Di Bella method, which purported to effectively treat all types of cancerous tumors, with no side effects—citing 10,000 successful cases in 20 years. This treatment required substantial patient out-of-pocket expense. The publicity in the press resulted in a public outcry supporting Professor Di Benelli, a physiologist, demanding reimbursement by the national health authority, and protesting against the health authorities, who were said to be "guilty" of insisting on "useless" validation studies of this therapeutic approach. Given these pressures, many may rely on practices advocated by other referent professionals, popular in the field, or pushed by stakeholders. In a number of instances, monetary gains or gains in status may also make professionals prone to unproven fad treatments.

THE NATURE OF EVIDENCE-BASED INTERVENTION

> One thing which emerges strongly from any case-by-case study of intellectuals is their scant regard for veracity. Anxious as they are to promote the redeeming, transcending Truth, the establishment of which they see as their mission on behalf of humanity, they have not much patience with the mundane, everyday truths represented by objective facts which get in the way of their arguments. These awkward, minor truths get brushed aside, doctored, reversed or are even deliberately suppressed.
>
> —Johnson, 1988

The push to identify and implement evidence-based intervention has become a priority in many disciplines. The Department of Social Policy and Social Work of the University of Oxford has recently introduced a Master of Science course of study in Evidence Based Social Work (University of Oxford, 2003). As noted in their brochure, "While social problems continue to increase, the resources to combat them are limited by fiscal and political pressures. The practical imperative of ensuring effective use of finite resources, together with an ethical imperative to demonstrate that intervention is doing more good than harm, require that practice be based on sound evidence."

Kasari (2002) has proposed a number of elements critical to well-designed treatment studies. These include use of appropriate treatment and comparison groups, clearly elaborated and detailed methodologies making use of treatment manuals, use of fidelity checks to ensure accurate procedural implementation, use of accepted and methodologically sound randomization or matching procedures, adequate statistical power, detailed description of sample characteristics, and proper use of reliable, valid, and appropriate measures. Kasari recommends use of large multi-site trials, multiple data points, and carefully examining components of individual treatment packages. We would add that appropriate use of single-subject experimental methods are also accepted as valid means of assessing change due to intervention.

In reviewing the evidence presented in support of various purported interventions for autism, we found a number of general problems. Many treatments presented *no* supportive studies. Evidence was often anecdotal or inconclusive.

Studies that were presented often had significant design flaws, such as poor or no controls, inappropriate measures, or inadequate sample sizes. Many studies made use of the same subjects in multiple studies. Studies often overgeneralized or overextended findings, making inferences or reaching conclusions unsupported by their own findings. Many of these studies were correlational, without any supporting theoretical framework and with inadequate controls for nonspecific effects. Every beginning science student is taught the truism, "correlation is not causation," but sometimes correlation is presented rather forcefully as though it is!

Of particular concern, many who promoted interventions made claims for efficacy supported by appeals to logic, used scientific-sounding rationalizations, and confused fact with hypothesis. Many used blatant marketing techniques, such as appeal to authority, unsupported assertions, or use of similar and attractive models, rather than any evidence at all, to attempt to attract prospective consumers.

We strongly believe that evidence-based interventions are those most likely to result in better outcomes, as demonstrated by scientific research. Treatments that repeatedly result in significant demonstrable benefit when properly implemented by numerous practitioners with many patients or clients should be retained and promoted. All others should be characterized as unproven, at best, and not advocated until such time as they can meet the rigorous standards of proof for effectiveness.

THE NATURE OF CONTROVERSY

According to Silver (1995), interventions are controversial if they are presented as efficacious in the absence of confirming studies, when pilot studies supporting them have not been replicated, when treatments go farther than the data that do support them, or, when treatment is used in an isolated fashion when multimodal approaches are actually needed. To these features, we would add the reverse of the latter criterion: Interventions are controversial if they are packaged with so many potentially active elements, or are so multimodal, that the effects of some of them are obscured or even counteracted. McWilliams (1999) has elaborated five criteria for controversial treatments. These include claims that the practice produces a cure, requirement of practitioner specialization, questionable research, high intensity requirement, and legal action. It appears that McWilliams views controversy as having primarily pejorative connotations. If this is indeed the case, then we can only agree with one of these criteria, questionable research. The other four may legitimately accompany any empirically supported intervention. We would be more sanguine about McWilliams' criteria if the term *controversial* was not value-laden. Thus, we prefer the definition proposed by Schwartz (1999), that an intervention becomes controversial when different users and beneficiaries assess its social validity differently (Schwartz & Baer, 1991; Wolf, 1978). Schwartz continues that the purpose of social validity is to assess the acceptability and sustainability of an intervention by asking the consumers to provide a description of how they perceive it. Social validity assessments are not meant to evaluate the effectiveness of an intervention, but to supplement evaluative information to attempt to figure out what the intervention means to consumers.

Is controversy necessarily bad? To the contrary, it has been argued that controversy is essential to progress in medicine (Donnan & Davis, 2003), by promoting the scientific scrutiny necessary to verify effective advances and produce guidelines for evidence-based practice. For example, the controversy (Eikeseth, 2001; Gresham & MacMillan, 1998) raised by Lovaas' (1987) assertions about the effectiveness of clinic-based programs based on principles of applied behavior analysis in treating autism in young children has led to replication and extension studies that have increased our understanding of effective intervention and identified some of the research questions that remain to be answered (Schreibman, 2000). The legal proceedings initiated by parents seeking more effective autism intervention in the schools have been instrumental in sensitizing educational and health systems to the need to provide more effective treatment for young children with autism (Jacobson, 2000).

Areas of Agreement in Autism Treatment

In reviewing unproven fad treatments, it is important to identify best practices about which a consensus exists. In reviewing documents recommending best practices for effective intervention for young children with autism, similar themes emerge.

Kabot, Masi, and Segal (2003) identified six guidelines for effective intervention for young children with autism. Intervention should be started at the earliest possible age. It must be intensive. Parent training and support is critical. Social and communication domains should be the foci of intervention. Treatment should be systematic, built on individualized goals and objectives tailored to the child. An emphasis on generalization is critical to effective intervention. The American Academy of Child and Adolescent Psychiatry (1999) has developed guidelines that emphasize the joint roles of health and educational systems in establishing appropriate educational goals, targeting and prioritizing symptoms and comorbid conditions for intervention, intervening in multiple domains of functioning (behavioral, adaptive, academic, and social-communicative), and monitoring the efficacy and side effects of any medications that are prescribed.

The National Research Council (2001) has elaborated characteristics of effective interventions in educational programs for young children with autism spectrum disorders. These include early entry into intervention, intensive instructional programming (defined as equivalent to a full school day, 5 or more days a week, 25 hours per week, year round, 12 months per year), use of planned teaching in frequent brief instructional bursts, one-to-one or small group instruction to facilitate attainment of individualized goals, use of specialized techniques such as discrete trial training and incidental teaching, systematic and individualized instruction, and emphases on development of spontaneous social communication, adaptive skills, appropriate behaviors, play skills, and cognitive and academic skills. The importance of monitoring progress, generalization of skills, use of skills in generalized settings, and of opportunities to interact with typically developing peers are also emphasized.

In the following sections of this chapter, we briefly examine exemplars of biomedical, mechanical, and psychosocial fad interventions that have been proposed for autism treatment. Some of them should never have been tried.

BIOMEDICAL FAD INTERVENTIONS

Volkmar (2001), one of the most respected medical researchers actively working in autism, has stated that there is general agreement that autism spectrum disorders develop as the result of some insult to, or abnormality in, the nervous system of the developing child, that multiple developmental processes are involved, and that there is both direct and indirect evidence that implicates several neurochemical systems. Hyman and Levy (2000) have noted that, despite the tentative and preliminary nature of this evidence, a plethora of proposed and promoted treatments have been based on any number of untested theories that purport to explain the core symptoms and comorbidities of autism spectrum disorders. On the other hand, Volkmar (2001) has also pointed out that many of these theories have been developed following supposed treatments, suggested by the nature of how the treatments seemed to work. In the following sections, we briefly review some of the biomedical interventions that have been proposed for autistic spectrum disorders and that are currently experiencing a measure of popularity.

Pharmacologic Treatments

Volkmar (2001) has contended that autism medication treatment studies have been complicated by a number of factors associated with the complex nature of the disorder, etiological uncertainties, and methodological problems. For example, population and sampling problems may occur due to diagnostic uncertainty, the range of syndrome expression, and, different associated comorbidities. The short-term nature of studies and the impact of nonspecific effects on longer studies, such as the natural course of developmental change, have also complicated the interpretation of findings. Volkmar has cautioned that the broadband nature of diagnostic instruments and rating scales used to assess outcomes may lead to errors in adequately describing the specificity and magnitude of change, and associational findings may be misinterpreted as causal. The complex nature of the disorder and the differential impact of various symptoms on those who work with these children may also lead to reporting biases. Still, researchers agree that some psychoactive medications seem to be both safe, in terms of toxicity, and effective in beneficially altering some aspects of behavior that parents and teachers feel complicate the lives of people with autism and the people who live and work with them. The relevant research is constantly changing and being updated, both because of improvements in research methods and the advent of new drugs being placed on the market (see Reiss & Aman, 1998, for a broad survey of medication research in developmental disabilities).

Concomitant with the current inadequate understanding of the etiology of autism spectrum disorders, there is a lack of robust animal models. Such models are critical to serve as a foundation in the development of efficacious and safe medications. Current autism animal models express one or more characteristics of autistic behavior but do not come close to modeling the complex repertoire of behaviors displayed by children with pervasive developmental disorders, and, thus, are of limited use in generalizing findings. No animal model can address the failure of autistic children to acquire language normally in typical family environments because no animal other than humans typically learns to talk!

Rapin (2002) has noted that medications cannot cure autism because, in most cases, etiology is probably due to early embryonic atypical cellular development. Medications have been most effective in alleviating symptoms such as aggression, self-injury, attention problems, and stereotypy (Volkmar, 2001). They have not been effective in remediating the core social-communicative deficits in autism, although some children may be more amenable to effective behavioral intervention as a result of reduction in comorbid symptoms (McDougle, 1997). In this capacity, medications may serve an important adjunctive role as part of a comprehensive autism treatment plan, although behavioral and psychosocial approaches remain the gold standard in autism intervention (Phelps, Brown, & Power, 2002). Given the uncertain etiology of autism spectrum disorders, the methodological problems in autism drug studies, and the potentially harmful side effects that can accompany many of these medications, Kerbeshian, Burd, and Avery (2001) have cautioned that it is important to take a cautious clinical approach in prescription practice. When they advise this, moreover, they are referring to the use of drugs that have already been deemed safe and effective enough to be available for prescription, rather than compounds consisting of botanical extracts, nutrients, or hormones of unknown toxicity or efficacy.

Dopamine, norepinephrine, serotonin, and other neuropeptides have been among the wide range of neurochemical systems most implicated in autism spectrum disorders (Volkmar, 2001). It is beyond the scope of this chapter to review the body of literature associated with medication intervention, and the reader is directed to several applied and methodological reviews of pharmacologic interventions for autism spectrum disorders (Phelps et al., 2002; Sikich, 2001; Towbin, 2003; Volkmar, 2001).

Nutritional Fad Interventions

Historically, the diet has had a central place in the armamentarium of medicine. Hippocrates recognized the importance of diet in promoting good health. Specific foods or food groups were often deemed to have curative or illness-causing powers. For example, Chrysippus of Cnidus in the 4th century BC wrote a treatise promoting the curative and health properties of cabbage. In the 17th century Franz de le Boe, founder of the Sylvius approach to medicine, emphasized disturbances in the fermentation process in the stomach as the etiology of many diseases (Williams, 1904). In 17th-century England, lettuce was thought to weaken eyesight and cure insomnia and gonorrhea (Emerson, 1996). As early as the 1920s, excessive sugar ingestion was thought to cause hyperactivity in children. This eventually evolved into the popularity of restrictive diets, such as the Feingold diet, in the 1960s and beyond, despite the fact that there is no clear evidence indicating that dietary exposure to sugar or preservatives plays any causal role in hyperactivity (Wolraich, 1996).

Of course experimentation with herbs and substances led to the development of important modern medicines. Dietary interventions are also used as part of the treatment package in a number of neurological diseases, such as the use of the ketogenic diet to reduce seizures in children with certain seizure disorders (Lefevre & Aronson, 2000; Nordli, 2002), or in other conditions with neurological sequelae, such as the prevention of mental retardation via the elimination of phenylalanine from the diets of individuals with phenylketonuria (NIH Consensus Statement, 2000; Sullivan & Chang, 1999), or the restriction of phytanic acid from the diets of those with Refsum disease (Wierzbicki, Lloyd, Schofeld, Feher, & Gibberd, 2002). Thus, it is understandable that there is some tendency among physicians and parents to consider and try nutritional interventions.

By far the current most popular dietary manipulation is the gluten-free/ cassien-free (GFCF) diet. The "leaky gut" hypothesis, originally proposed by Panksepp (1979), underlies this intervention. In short, it is hypothesized that incomplete breakdown of foods with gluten and casein cross a leaky-gut membrane forming peptides. These cross the blood–brain barrier forming ligands with peptidase enzymes which interferes with neurotransmitter breakdown. This results in increased opioid activity, causing the aberrations in cognition, behavior, and affect characteristic of autism (Cornish, 2002). A number of potential causes have been proposed, including yeast overgrowth, immunological abnormalities, and gastrointestinal disease secondary to immunization (Hyman & Levy, 2000).

Some investigators have found increased urinary peptides in children with autism (Reichelt, Knivsberg, Lind, & Nodland, 1991). Knivsberg, Wiig, Lind, Nodland, and Reichelt (1990) found decreased peptides increased social interaction, environmental interest, and language in a group of autistic children who initially displayed high urinary peptide levels and were on the diet for one year, compared to autistic children with high levels of urinary peptide who could not maintain the diet (Knivsberg et al., 1990). Other investigators have found no such difference in urinary peptides in children with autism (Williams & Marshall, 1992). Some studies have suggested evidence for increased permeability in a minority of autistic children with no previous history of intestinal disorders (D'Eufemia et al., 1996). Page (2000), however, points out that it is important to note that no studies have reported any association between unusual levels of peptides and increased intestinal permeability. Horvath and Perman (2002) have argued that there is increasing evidence to suggest that children with autism suffer from more intestinal problems and dysfunction than typically developing children. This evidence, however, remains correlational. Although the "brain–gut connection" may warrant more study, our opinion is that theories and interventions based on a possible relationship remain unsubstantiated.

Reports of the effectiveness of the GFCF diet have been primarily anecdotal. There are a few studies that have purported to examine the diet's effectiveness (Knivsberg, Reichelt, Hoein, & Nodland, 1998; Knivsberg, Reichelt, Nodland, & Hoein, 1995; Whiteley, Rodgers, Savery, & Shattock, 1999); however, these have been plagued by serious methodological problems. For example, the Knivsberg et al. (1990) study, which reported benefits, suffers from numerous possible methodological difficulties including maturation effects associated with the year-long process, poorly defined and heterogeneous samples, and concurrent educational and medication interventions (Hyman & Levy, 2000). Although the University of Rochester is reportedly planning a large-scale study of the effectiveness of GFCF diet, as of this writing we have found no such completed studies and, consistent with the New York State Department of Health (1999) guidelines, must deem this intervention unproven. Given the restrictions that the diet entails, and the tendency of children with autism to self-restrict their diets, adherence to this diet may place the affected child at risk for malnutrition.

Supplements

The use of megavitamins to treat mental health problems gained popularity in the 1960s, receiving a particular push with Linus Pauling's orthomolecular theory, which hypothesized a link between mental illness and inborn biochemical errors. While numerous vitamin therapies, including vitamins A and C have been advocated, the B6-magnesium combination has been among the most studied and heavily promoted of these therapies. Rimland (1987) reported positive benefits in the 18 studies known to him at that time, benefits including decreased behavior excesses and increased appropriate behaviors.

Pfeiffer, Norton, Nelson, and Shott (1995) reviewed the 12 published studies that they were able to locate through an exhaustive computer search. Most studies reviewed reported positive outcomes in response to B6-magnesium treatment, with about half of the subjects displaying improvements on behavioral indices in a matter of weeks. Specific studies also reported relapse within one to several weeks on discontinuation of the interventions. However, Pfeiffer et al. also noted that most of these studies contained severe methodological flaws, including lack of control groups, small sample sizes, possible repeated use of the same subjects in multiple studies, imprecise outcome measures, lack of long-term follow-up data, and failure to adjust for regression effects in measuring improvements.

Similarly, Nye and Brice (2002) conducted an extensive computer search in several of the major medical and psychological databases for any studies in which subjects were randomly allocated to a group prior to intervention, and in which the treatment group was compared to a placebo or nontreatment group. Of the two double blind crossover studies identified, one (Tolbert, Haigler, Waits, & Dennis, 1993), according to the reviewers, did not provide sufficient data for an analysis. The other (Findling et al., 1997) failed to find significant differences on measures of social interaction, communication, compulsivity, impulsivity, or hyperactivity, when high doses of B6-magnesium were administered. The reviewers concluded that the small number of studies, small sample sizes, and methodological problems did not support the efficacy of B6-magnesium intervention for autism. Even Rimland (1987) has acknowledged that he advocates B6-magnesium as an adjunctive treatment and not as a cure. Although B6-magnesium has been promoted as a "safe" treatment, Hyman and Levy (2001) have pointed out that no long-term studies have been carried out with children, that high dose pyroxidine interventions have resulted in neuromotor side effects in adults, and that magnesium is a potentially toxic metal in high doses.

In recent years several supplements (e.g., dimethylglycine) have been touted as effective interventions for autism. Of these, few have received more public attention and use than secretin, a pancreatic hormone that assists digestion. Secretin suddenly became popular as a possible cure for autism following a case study report about three children by Horvath and his colleagues (1998) reporting improvements in core social-communicative deficits in children who each received a single injection of porcine secretin. The study was publicized and many parents of children with autism spectrum disorders found physicians willing to prescribe secretin in different forms, injected intravenously or administered transdermally. Other recent studies have consistently concluded that secretin was no more effective than placebo in reducing aberrant behaviors or increasing social-communication skills (Carey et al., 2002; Chez et al., 2000; Owley et al., 1999; Sandler et al., 1999).

A recent double-blind, placebo-controlled, crossover study comparing 19 children with and without gastrointestinal difficulties found a reduction in aberrant behaviors in children with chronic active diarrhea when treated with secretin but not with the placebo (Kern, Miller, Evans, & Trivedi, 2002). Kern et al. suggested the possibility of a subtype of children with autism who respond beneficially to secretin. Small sample sizes notwithstanding, we would hypothesize that children without active, chronic diarrhea feel better, are less irritable, and behave better than those with diarrhea. We would also hypothesize that parents of children without diarrhea are more favorably disposed to their children than parents of children with diarrhea! Drug effects and other treatment effects can change behavior by very indirect routes, and a correlated change in behavior simply does not validate, by itself, the theory that led the investigator to try the treatment in the first place.

Despite the absence of studies supporting the efficacy of secretin, or assessing the possibility of side effects, many community physicians regularly prescribe this hormone at the behest of parents. Our own recent attempts to conduct a double-blind, placebo-controlled, crossover study of the effects of transdermal secretin illustrates, in part, some of the difficulties and dangers inherent in prescription practices of this type that are not supported by scientific evidence. In conjunction with our institutional review board, we opted not to carry out this study when it was discovered that the transport agent was DMSO and when the pharmacy that produced topical secretin, whose only purported medical use is autism treatment, refused to release the formulary!

Other Biomedical Interventions

In concluding this section on fad biomedical interventions for autism, we briefly discuss two recent fads: (a) the purported causal link between the MMR (mumps, measles, and rubella) vaccine and autism, and (b) chelation therapy. Both illustrate the misuse of science and the potential danger of fads.

Public concern about the MMR vaccine exploded following a study by Wakefield et al. (1998) of 12 children in Great Britain suggesting the possibility of a causal link between administration of the mumps, measles, and rubella (MMR) vaccine and increased rates of autism. The process underlying this explosion is illustrative. The article by Wakefield and his colleagues reported a series of case studies of 12 children with intestinal symptoms and loss of previously acquired developmental skills who presented to a London gastroenterologist. In two thirds of the cases, parents retrospectively recalled that the skills loss was close in time to the administration of the MMR vaccine. The article was the basis of a story on the television program, *60 Minutes*, resulting in the birth of a fad. The potency of the fad can best be described by the concerns of the American Academy of Pediatrics (AAP) about an upcoming multicity tour in the United States by Wakefield promoting the autism–MMR vaccine link theory and the broad media coverage that is expected. Anticipation of a deluge of concerned parents broaching the topic with their pediatricians and family physicians has prompted the AAP to place a posting on their Web site providing information to pediatricians about the absence of any evidence of an autism–MMR vaccine link (American Academy of Pediatrics, 2003). The AAP also posted a paper written by Offit (2003), chief of infectious diseases and director of the vaccine education center at Children's Hospital of Philadelphia, which summarizes the studies used to support the hypothesis that MMR causes autism, reviews the studies that refute this hypothesis, and provides an overview of other investigations into the causes of autism.

Parental and physician concern may be a legitimate response to questions raised about a vaccine, especially in light of past validated concerns raised about medications such as thalidomide. However, the pronunciations about the MMR vaccine as a cause of autism—which has extended into Congressional subcommittee hearings in the United States—are a dangerous example of what can happen when a fad erupts *sans* scientific substantiation. In fact, the preponderance of evidence to date, epidemiological and scientific, suggests that there is no relationship whatsoever between the MMR vaccine and autism (DeStefano & Chen, 1999; Fombonne & Chakrabarti, 2001; Halsey, Hyman, & the Conference Writing Panel, 2001; Stratton, Gable, Shetty, & McCormick, & the Immunization Safety Review Committee, Institute of Medicine, 2001; Taylor et al., 1999). The Institute of Medicine does recommend ongoing study of the issue. However, should a sufficient mass of parents and physicians decline to administer the MMR vaccine, or cause delay via separate administrations, incidence of these preventable diseases may increase (Halsey et al., 2001). It is ironic that an unsupported concern about a possible cause of autism may actually lead to an increase in maternal rubella, one of the known causes of autism.

Wakefield et al.'s hypothesis about an MMR vaccine–autism link involves a cascade of events initiated by the vaccine. These include intestinal inflammation, intestinal permeability or loss of barrier function, and release of encephalopathic proteins into the blood, and development of autism (Wakefield et al., 1998). In contrast, many parents and doctors have pointed to mercury poisoning as a possible cause of autism. A paper by Bernard et al. (2000) is frequently cited as support for this hypothesis. In this paper, Bernard et al. highlight similarities in the symptoms of autism and mercury poisoning and provide a neurochemical rationale for their hypotheses. They also posited that children varied in their sensitivity to mercury, explaining why only a small subset of children developed autism despite multiple potential environmental sources for mercury poisoning. Mercury is highly toxic and has been implicated in a number of disease processes with neurological sequelae.

After the concerns about the MMR vaccine were raised by Wakefield and his colleagues (1998), parents and some physicians pointed to Thimerisol, an ethylmercury-based preservative once used in many vaccines in the United States including the MMR vaccine, as a possible source of mercury poisoning leading to autism. According to the Autism-Mercury Internet mail-list (2003) FAQ, proponents claim that the amount of Thimerisol in each vaccine exceeded the safety limit of 0.1 mcg/kg/day established by the federal Environmental Protection Agency. Other possible sources of mercury include mercury amalgams in tooth fillings, some types of fish, coal-burning power plants, paint, fluorescent lights, and thermometers, among others. Biochemical assays, such as blood tests and urinalysis, do not reveal excessive levels of mercury as the substance quickly leaves the bloodstream and accumulates in internal organs. Therefore, proponents variously recommend tests such as hair trace analysis to assess for mercury toxicity.

Many parents, and some doctors, have embraced chelation therapy as a means of detoxification (DAN! Subcommittee on Mercury and Autism, 2000). Chelating agents are molecules that form bonds to specific metals in the body. These have long been used for known cases of recent lead or mercury poisoning, with great care and under close medical supervision.

This is an example of a fad based solely on hypothesized connections, in the absence of supportive evidence. A search of the Medline and National Library of Medicine databases revealed only two articles that directly addressed chelation therapy as an autism intervention. Neither of the two articles was a study. In fact, proponents (Holmes, 2002) acknowledge that no child has been cured, but anecdotally report dramatic improvements in behavior. At this writing, however, we have found no empirical studies in professional peer-reviewed journals addressing the efficacy of chelation therapy as an autism treatment.

We have several concerns about this fad. A variety of protocols are promoted, but we have been unable to find empirical evidence supporting either the efficacy or safety of these specific protocols. Parents often try a number of different chelating agents in different amounts and with a variety of administration schedules. Some chelation agents cannot remove heavy metals that are bound in some tissues, and some agents remove beneficial minerals needed by cells for healthy function, which requires that the prescribing physician must use several of them and provide supplements to replace needed minerals. Interactions among chelation agents have not been studied in humans. To us, this fad appears to be a random process of human experimentation without accompanying safeguards, thus posing ethical and safety concerns. Also of concern is the expense inherent in these testing and treatment procedures for mercury toxicity and for other hypothesized autism causing heavy metals and substances. The diagnostic testing process alone can cost many thousands of dollars.

In reviewing the evidence suggesting the absence of scientific support for the major biomedical fad treatments, it is clear to us why the American Academy of Neurology and Filipek et al. (2000) established a guideline, also endorsed by the American Academy of Pediatrics and the American Psychological Association, stating that there is inadequate supporting evidence for hair analysis, celiac antibodies, allergy testing (particularly food allergies for gluten, casein, candida, and other molds), immunologic or neurochemical abnormalities, micronutrients such as vitamin levels, intestinal permeability studies, stool analysis, urinary peptides, mitochondrial disorders (including lactate and pyruvate), thyroid function tests, or erythrocyte glutathione peroxidase studies. Some proponents (Autisminfo.com, 2003) acknowledge that most mainstream physicians find these biomedical hypotheses and treatments questionable, but point to the absence or inadequacy of other available biochemical treatments as a factor motivating parents to pursue these fad interventions.

MECHANICAL FAD INTERVENTIONS

As with other forms of developmental disability, a number of mechanical treatments, based on questionable premises and with little or no empirical support for efficacy, have been embraced as treatments for autism. We classify these treatments as mechanical insofar as they involve physical manipulation of one sort or another.

In this section, we briefly review several of the many such treatments that are currently being promoted and practiced, specifically, those with the most, albeit insufficient, empirical support.

Facilitated Communication

The technique of facilitated communication was first proposed by Crossley and popularized by Biklen (Biklen, 1990; Biklen, Morton, Gold, Berrigan, & Swaminathan, 1992; Crossley, 1994). Underlying facilitated communication, a form of assisted typing, is the notion that autism constitutes a deficit in ability to use or express language, a disorder of output rather than necessarily of cognitive deficit. It was hypothesized that the technique allowed for the revelation of previously untapped cognitive abilities and enabled quicker rates and more sophisticated types of learning, despite deficits in formal education. These more advanced cognitive abilities were purportedly the result of extensive exposure to written and spoken language in the individual's natural environment.

Several comprehensive reviews of the available literature definitively concluded that the claims of supporters of facilitated communication were unsubstantiated. Jacobson, Mulick, and Schwartz (1995) reported a set of controlled studies, noting only four possible positive outcomes out of 126 subjects. The significant methodological difficulties, which could have led to false positives in those studies reporting positive outcomes, were discussed. Reviews by Green (1994) and Simpson and Myles (1995), among others, reached similar conclusions.

It is illustrative that the studies incorporating control procedures find minimal or no support for facilitated communication, that studies using fewer controls result in mixed findings, and that studies using no controls result in findings of efficacy (Mostert, 2001). The American Academy of Pediatrics (1998) concluded that the research did not support the claims of proponents of facilitated communication and recommended against its use except in research. The academy also pointed out that this technique could have potentially harmful side effects, including unsubstantiated allegations of abuse, expense, and the time better spent on effective behavioral and educational interventions.

Despite the preponderance of evidence suggesting that facilitated communication is an unproven treatment for autism, the practice continues (Jacobson, Foxx, & Mulick, chap. 22, this volume). We would argue that the continuation of this fad can be attributed to those practitioners who have a professional stake in this procedure. We would also make the case that the continued propagation of this technique is a direct product of a cruel and harmful side effect of the practice: the hope and false belief of caregivers that they are developing a previously unavailable affective and communicative relationship with their child.

Auditory Integration Training

Like facilitated communication, auditory integration training is an unproven fad treatment for autism. Originally developed by Berard, a French otolaryngologist who based this technique on the work of Tomatis, the technique involves the use of audiograms to identify auditory hypersensitivities in autistic children and exposure to attenuated sounds at high, low, and sensitive frequencies. This is done through the use of narrow band filters and modulation during playing of processed music to a child in approximately 20 half-hour listening sessions conducted over the course of 10 days (i.e., the Berard Method). The goal is to normalize hearing and the manner in which the brain processes auditory information (American Academy of Pediatrics, 1998). There are different methods of auditory integration training, including the Berard and Tomatis Methods. Tomatis Method proponents make claims of reduced hypersensitivity to sound, tactile defensiveness, aggressiveness, and picky eating, as well as increased language, self-image, social skills, and eye contact (Tomatis Method, 2001). Auditory integration training has been touted for numerous disorders, including attention deficit-hyperactivity disorder, learning disabilities, and depression.

Edelson and Rimland (2001) reviewed and critiqued 28 studies reporting on the efficacy of auditory integration training. They concluded that 13 of 16 of the studies resulted in positive outcomes with individuals with autism. They felt that the three studies with mixed or negative findings had serious methodological flaws, attributed to researcher negative bias. Nonetheless, their summaries of the positive outcome studies revealed that the studies uniformly lacked sufficient statistical power, failed to use control groups, used inappropriate control groups, did not use random assignment of subjects to groups, or had other significant methodological faults.

One of the cited studies was by Mudford et al. (2000), who conducted a blind to order of treatment, controlled, crossover design to assess the affects of auditory integration training and a control treatment in a group of 16 autistic children. Significant results were found in favor of the control condition on parent measures of hyperactivity and direct measures of ear occlusion. At some points during the experiment, the control group demonstrated significantly reduced hyperactivity and ear occlusion compared to the auditory integration group. No changes were found in teacher rating measures, IQ, or on measures of language comprehension. Both groups displayed decreases on adaptive behavior, social behavior, and expressive language measures. No individual educational or behavior benefits were noted, and most parents could not correctly identify the order of treatment. Zollweg, Palm, and Vance (1997) conducted a double blind evaluation of auditory integration training efficacy and also found a reduction in behavior problems in the control group in one point in time, no other differences between control and treatment groups, and overall improvements in both groups that could be attributed to nonspecific affects.

Gravel (1994) examined the hypotheses on which auditory integration training is premised, noting a failure of electrophysiological measuring instruments (e.g., auditory evoked brainstem measurements) to detect the differences hypothesized between autistic and nonautistic children. Given the inconsistency of their responses, autistic children are also difficult to reliably test using methods of behavioral audiometry. Concerns have also been raised about the safety of the sound output devices used (Rankovic & Rabinowitz, 1996). In a study of 80 children randomly assigned to an auditory integration training group or a regular music control group, Bettison (1996) found significant improvements in both groups in behavior, as well as verbal IQ and performance IQ, but no differences between the two groups. It is unclear to us if these improvements were due to maturation effects or the effects of other interventions, for example, educational.

As with most fad treatments, reports of efficacy are primarily anecdotal. The American Academy of Pediatrics (1998) concluded that the clinical use of auditory integration training is unsupported and that use of the technique should be limited to research protocols. The continued appeal of this fad appears to us to be in the use of technical equipment and in the relatively short period of treatment.

Sensory Integration Training

Sensory integration training is based on the work of Jean Ayres (1994/1979). According to proponents, sensory integration is a neurological process, that is, the way in which the brain organizes and interprets touch, movement, body awareness, sight, sound, and gravity. It is premised that sensory integration problems, a malfunctioning of this process, can lead to specific behavior and emotional problems. Fisher and Murray (1991) have listed five major assumptions underlying sensory integration:

1. There is plasticity in the central nervous system.
2. The sensory integration process follows a developmental sequence.
3. The brain is made up of hierarchically organized systems but functions as an integrated whole.
4. The relationship between adaptive behavior and sensory integration is circular (i.e., adaptive behavior reflects appropriate sensory integration and learning an adaptive behavior promotes sensory integration).
5. There is an innate drive to develop sensory integration via sensorimotor activities.

Sensory integration therapy is usually performed by occupational or physical therapists who provide a "diet" of sensory stimulation to the child, in an attempt to improve the way in which the child's brain processes and organizes sensory information. This can include vestibular and tactile stimulation, purposeful movements, use of weighted vests, and brushing, among other techniques. Programs are supposed to be individually designed using a scaffolding approach.

While it is accepted that the brain changes as a result of sensory experiences, Arendt, Maclean, and Baumeister (1988) have critiqued some of the neurological assumptions underlying sensory integration theory, specifically those aspects dealing with purported mechanisms of brain functioning and changes. As with many of the other fad treatments described in this chapter, available studies are sparse and tend to be methodologically flawed. In a review, Hoehn and Baumeister (1994) concluded that sensory integration is not only unproven but also ineffective. Similarly, Smith (1996) did not find evidence of decreases in self-injury or ritualistic behaviors. A recent review of sensory and motor interventions for children with autism (Baranek, 2002) concluded that studies that resulted in modest improvements from sensory integration therapy were few and characterized by severe methodological flaws that precluded any conclusive findings about efficacy. A specific limitation was the failure of many studies to link changes in hypothesized dysfunctional mechanisms to functional changes in behavior.

Even though the efficacy of sensory integration therapy and the validity of its underlying assumptions remain unproven, this should not be interpreted to mean that occupational and physical therapies should be discounted. To the contrary, we feel that the valuable time of these therapists is better spent using their knowledge and skills in the teaching, modeling, and shaping of skills in their domains of expertise and in which autistic children are deficient. The contributions of physical and occupational therapists are important as part of a comprehensive treatment plan in the psychoeducational remediation and habilitation of skill deficits.

PSYCHOSOCIAL FAD INTERVENTIONS

As we have previously argued, the preponderance of empirical evidence supports the effectiveness of psychosocial interventions for autism above and beyond most other proposed biomedical and mechanical treatments. Generally, more effective psychosocial interventions aim to teach skill deficits.

It is important to note that there is a plethora of unproven psychosocial treatments premised on other hypotheses. Some psychosocial interventions, such as holding therapy (Welsch, 1989), are rooted in dubious applications of psychodynamic and attachment theory. One study (Myeroff, Mertlich, & Gross, 1999) using this intervention with a heterogenous group of 23 children ages 5 to 14 who displayed destructive behavior and poor attachment to parents reported finding that holding therapy was effective. A review of this study revealed that the treatment group consisted of children who met inclusion criteria and attended the treatment center in question and that the control group included children who did not attend the center due to time or financial constraints or whose parents were information-seeking. There was no evidence for control of nonspecific effects in the treatment group, thus severely limiting the significance of the study findings. At the other extreme are suggestions that holding therapy and its variants, or their misapplications, may be dangerous to children. Sarner (2001) describes the suffocation of 10-year-old Candace Newmaker in Colorado on April 18, 2000. Four therapists and assistants wrapped the 70-pound body of this 10-year-old, who had a history of abuse and multiple foster placements, in a flannel sheet. On top they placed eight pillows and over 650 pounds of adults. The aim of this intervention was "rebirthing therapy." Her adoptive mother, a pediatric nurse practitioner watched the intervention, which was also captured on videotape. As part of the intervention, the girl was impeded and frustrated in her efforts to get out of the sheet as part of the "rebirthing" process, eventually leading to her death. While many potentially efficacious interventions can also be dangerous if misapplied, we believe that this case illustrates the importance of the safeguards that are typically a priority in evidence-based approaches.

In this section, we briefly review three types of psychosocial intervention that have become popular. Generally, the psychosocial interventions that we review aim to remediate the skills that autistic children have difficulty learning in typical ways.

Floortime: A Developmental, Individual Differences, Relationship-Based Approach (DIR)

Greenspan (2000) has attempted to understand the impacts of autism from a developmental perspective rooted in elements of ego and object relations psychology.

His approach to intervention, DIR, is more commonly known as Floortime. Greenspan and Weider (1998; Greenspan, 2001) view autism as an inability to relate to others affectively in a reciprocal fashion in a variety of contexts. The DIR model asserts that each child's unique strengths, developmental capacities, and challenges must be identified. Each child must master, in developmental sequence, six important foundational milestones in order to have the basic capacity for communication, thinking, and emotional coping. Children who have progressed through these milestones develop a positive sense of self, can engage in positive affective relationships, can use language to express a variety of emotions, can tolerate strong emotions without loss of control, can use imagination to create new ideas, can tolerate change, and are flexible in dealing with people and situations. These milestones include (a) self-regulation and interest in the world; (b) the formation relationships, attachment, and engagement; (c) reciprocal communication; (d) complex communication (including development of organized problem-solving interactions and internalization of a competent sense of self); (e) representational capacity (including the ability to create and share symbols, develop pretend play, label feelings, and take others' perspectives); and, (f) representational differentiation (including connecting actions and feelings, understanding what is real and not real, understanding relationships between self and others, and developing logical connections between emotions and ideas).

In autism, biological challenges impede the ability of the child to progress through these milestones. Specific challenges can include sensory reactivity, processing problems, and difficulty planning or sequencing responses. Floortime can be thought of as a means of attempting to compensate for these challenges in an attempt to help autistic children progress through the hypothesized six essential developmental milestones. Therapists provide direct intervention and help parents—through translation, modeling, and coaching—become more effective teachers for their children and establish a better fit between parent interaction styles and the child. An important aim is to help the parent to become a central organizer of their child's world en route to helping the child develop greater functional and emotional independence and capacity. Basic principles of Floortime intervention include creating a play environment with appropriate materials, following the child's lead, joining in at the child's developmental level and building on his or her interests, naturally increasing the child's interest in communication and communication patterns, creating opportunities for interaction, increasing the child's range of interactive experience, broadening the range of processing and motor capacities used in interactions, tailoring interactions to the child's individual sensory motor styles, and attempting to mobilize the six developmental milestones (Greenspan & Weider, 1999).

Unfortunately, we could only locate one study supporting the efficacy of Floortime. This is a retrospective, 200-casechart review of outcomes of children with autism spectrum disorders (Greenspan & Wieder, 1997). The lack of empirical support is unfortunate because, although this form of intervention remains unsupported, we find elements of the Floortime intervention model of interest. Floortime appears to be an intensive and directed extension of traditional play therapy. At its core, the model seems to incorporate an intensive form of incidental teaching, creating and capitalizing on interaction and instructional opportunities and teaching new skills using shaping and reinforcement. These are aspects of intervention important to teaching and generalization of skills that should be an integral part of any intensive intervention program. The emphasis on increasing parent sensitivity to, and skill in, capitalizing on incidental opportunities for instructional intervention and in practice and generalization of skills in natural settings is one, in our experience, that is occasionally missing from many home intensive intervention programs based on principles of applied behavior analysis.

TEACCH

Project TEACCH (Treatment and Education of Autistic and Communication Handicapped Children) was founded by Eric Schopler in the early 1970s at the University of North Carolina, Chapel Hill. It warrants special recognition as one of the first statewide, comprehensive, community programs aimed at improving services for autistic children. According to the TEACCH Web site (Mesibov, 2003), TEACCH is based on the idea of focusing on the person with autism and developing an appropriate program capitalizing on his or her existing skills and interests. The person with autism is understood "where they are" and in the context in which he or she is functioning, and is assisted to progress as much as possible. An important priority is structured teaching, which entails organizing the physical environment, developing work skills and schedules, explicitly clarifying expectations, and using visual materials so that the person can function as independently as possible within a given environment without adult prompts. A second emphasis is placed on cultivating strengths and interests versus a sole focus on remediation of deficits. The TEACCH approach is broad-based and lifelong, focusing on teaching communication, social, and leisure skills that can improve well-being. Briefly, TEACCH attempts to understand autism and the autistic individual, develops appropriate structures, promotes independent work skills, emphasizes strengths and interests, and fosters communication, as well as social and leisure interests and opportunities. TEACCH also attempts to work at a systems level, aiming to integrate services and provider networks over the lifespan of the individual with autism (Mesibov, 2003). A number of studies have found positive outcomes when comparing TEACCH to standard special education programs for children with autism and assessing the effectiveness of elements of TEACCH (e.g., Ozonoff & Cathcart, 1998; Panerei, Ferrante, & Zingale, 2002).

The TEACCH program has been embraced in many school districts looking to provide services for children with autism. Therein lies our concern. The TEACCH program as implemented in North Carolina is a lifelong, integrated, and comprehensive program supported by a legislative mandate by the state of North Carolina. To the best of our knowledge, no other state in the United States has a similar mandate. Thus, in our experience in Ohio, the programs implemented by school districts as TEACCH programs are not in any way comparable to the TEACCH program as implemented via the University of North Carolina at Chapel Hill in North Carolina. School programs do not provide multiagency integrated services, often do not integrate parents, often do not provide for implementation in the home and the community outside of school, and do not provide for follow-up past the specific school program. Rather, school programs tend to incorporate facets of the methods used in TEACCH classrooms in isolation and then claim that they are providing a TEACCH program. They are not.

Applied Behavior Analysis—Is It a Fad?

In 1987, Lovaas published an important paper (Lovaas, 1987) reporting outcome results of a controlled comparison of an intensive intervention program for young children with autism based on principles of applied behavior analysis (ABA), with less intensive and contemporary community-standard educational interventions. Children who participated in the intensive behavioral program displayed dramatic improvements, averaging an IQ boost of approximately 20 points, and significant improvements on other measures of language, adaptive skills, and behavior. About 47% of the children in this program were successfully mainstreamed in a regular education program without further need for support or services. This is arguably the most impressive claim ever made for a psychological intervention.

Although the study was not without methodological flaws (see Gresham & MacMillan, 1998), its most important contribution was in establishing the efficacy and effective dose of behavioral intervention. It had already been known that behavioral techniques were effective in reducing behavior problems in children with autism and in remediating specific skills deficits (Matson, Benavidez, Compton, Paclawskyj, & Baglio, 1996; Matson & Coe, 1992). Results of the Lovaas study, albeit of smaller magnitude, have been replicated in more tightly controlled studies (e.g., Matson et al., 1996; McEachin, Smith, & Lovaas, 1993; Smith, Eikeseth, Klevstrand, & Lovaas, 1997). Thus, it is not surprising that the New York State Department of Health (1999) concluded that ABA programs were the only form of intervention that met the burden of demonstrating significantly positive outcomes under rigorous scientifically controlled circumstances, and constituted the treatment of choice for young children with autism. We agree.

The parental push for ABA increased dramatically following the publication of the Lovaas study and the mass trade book publication of *Let Me Hear Your Voice* by Catherine Maurice (1993), the parent of two children with autism. The Maurice children were described as achieving the same degree of success via participation in ABA programs that was reported by Lovaas (1987). This push has become a highly organized and widespread consumer movement driven by parents (Jacobson, 2000). FEAT (Families for Effective Autism Treatment) groups have been formed in many cities in the United States, Canada, and other countries. These parent-led groups offer parent support, parent education, identification of autism resources and providers, and initiation of advocacy efforts. The push for early intensive behavioral intervention (EIBI) has met considerable resistance from a number of sources. The main resistance has come from educational and governmental agencies not wishing to foot the bill for these very expensive individualized home-based programs. Other opposition has come from professionals unfamiliar with autism, with philosophical perspectives antithetical to behavioral approaches, or with agendas that involve promotion of competing approaches.

Programs based on principles of ABA have not been immune to problems with fads and internal controversies. A recent book edited by Lovaas (2002) contains the warning that program "consultants must have supervisory experience at UCLA or an affiliated site ... in order to consult effectively with families on the UCLA treatment model" (Smith & Wynn, 2002, p. 331). The appropriate and effective design and implementation of these programs is very difficult and requires high levels of training and experience. The fidelity of implementation of properly designed programs is critical. Unfortunately, the implementation of home programs of these types is often inconsistent. Generalization efforts sometimes seems to become secondary to formal direct instruction, or promoting generalization seems to become more important than assuring acquisition (and we have seen well-known professionals in this area make either or both claims at different times). Consultants to these programs have a wide range of knowledge, skills, ability, and experience. Supervision of these consultants can often be inadequate and the quality and quantity of consultation can often be insufficient. Nevertheless, to even suggest that the EIBI treatment effect can only be achieved by someone trained specifically through UCLA and following the "UCLA model" strains the credibility of anyone who understands the progressive nature of all scientific processes. Once the outcome cat is out of the bag, whether the project involves ABA or advanced electronics or making nuclear weapons, if it is an outcome that has scientific validity, it will (and should) be reverse-engineered, replicated, and improved by the scientists and technologists who follow along after the initial discovery. Every significant scientific advance is the result of reported observations and techniques of other scientists who laid the necessary groundwork, and the strong effect of EIBI on the long-term outcome of children with autism is no different, if it is real. We think it is real and that it can, and has been, replicated independently.

Of greatest concern to us is the deplorable "branding" of ABA programs. Implementation of these programs often focuses on specific techniques rather than on the appropriate application of the principles underlying ABA and the proper use of accurate data to make correct and timely program changes. There may be monetary, agenda-driven, or philosophical reasons for this branding. Branding may also occur in the absence of appropriate knowledge. We often hear statements such as, "We do Lovaas [or] discrete trial [or] verbal behavior (pick any one of these terms or any of the many others) therapy." To us, this serves as a red flag that suggests that a child may not be as well served as possible by his or her program, and that elements essential to more favorable outcomes may be missing. The field of behavior analysis benefits from new ideas, understanding, and techniques; and science will only confirm controversial treatment claims if, and only if, independent replication is not only achievable but achieved. Specialized advances and effective demonstrations should become the bases of general principles and new tools and included in the armamentarium of all practitioners. In our opinion, the translation of these new findings and techniques into mere branding causes great harm to the field and to those parents, professionals, and concerned persons attempting to secure effective intervention.

CONCLUSIONS

We close with one last note of caution. Our understanding of autism and the development of effective treatments will not be advanced by the unequivocal dismissal of novel theories and innovative approaches to this complex and refractory disorder. Exploration of new ideas should be encouraged. Science will not advance without new ideas. However, new treatment options should be conceptualized as experimental hypotheses and fully scrutinized through research. Interventions should emanate from a theoretical basis already rooted in what is known about the etiology and course of autism. Further, the intellectual tools of science, namely experimental reasoning, logic, and the absence of contradiction of well-established knowledge, should be shared with enthusiasm with parents. If autism interventions could be approached with a critical and skeptical eye, then ineffective, harmful, or unproven fad treatments could be more often avoided. We have made many advances in pharmacology and behavioral treatment, and although the golden age of successful autism treatment is not yet on us, we can begin to sense it just over the horizon. We believe we will get there through the use of science and because of citizen support of both new research and their insistence on the use of empirically validated treatments for their children.

REFERENCES

Aguirre, B. E., Quarantelli, E. L., & Mendoza, J. L. (1988). The collective behavior of fads: The characteristics, effects and career of streaking. *American Sociological Review, 53*(4), 569–584.

American Academy of Child and Adolescent Psychiatry Working Group on Quality Issues. (1999). Practice parameters for the assessment and treatment of children, adolescents, and adults with autism and other pervasive developmental disorders. *Journal of the American Academy of Child and Adolescent Psychiatry, 38*(12 Supp.), 55S–76S.

American Academy of Pediatrics. (1998). Auditory integration training and facilitated communication for autism. *Pediatrics, 102*, 431–433.

American Academy of Pediatrics. (2003). *MMR and autism background*. Retrieved June 3, 2003, from http:// http://www.cispimmunize.org/fam/mmr/a_back.html

Arendt, R. E., Maclean, W. E., & Baumeister, A. A. (1988). Critique of sensory integration therapy and its applications in mental retardation. *American Journal on Mental Retardation, 92*, 401–411.

Autisminfo.com. (2003). *Medical overview*. Retrieved June 5, 2003, from http://autisminfo.com

Ayres, A. J. (1994/1979). *Sensory integration and the child*. Los Angeles, CA: Western Psychological Services.

Baranek, G. T. (2002). Efficacy of sensory and motor interventions for children with autism. *Journal of Autism and Developmental Disabilities, 32*(5), 397–422.

Benelli, E. (2003). The role of the media in steering public opinion on healthcare issues. *Health Policy, 63*, 179–186.

Bernard, S., Enayati, A., Binstock, T., Roger, H., Redwood, L., & McGinnis, W. (2000). *Autism: A unique type of mercury poisoning*. Retrieved June 3, 2003, from http://www.cureautismnow.org/sciwatch/invest.cfm

Bettison, S. (1996). Long-term effects of auditory training on children with autism. *Journal of Autism and Developmental Disorders, 26*, 361–367.

Bikhchandani, S., Hirschleifer, D., & Welch, I. (1998). Learning from the behavior of others: Conformity, fads, and informational cascades. *Journal of Economic Perspectives, 12*(3), 151–170.

Biklen, D. (1990). Communication unbound: Autism and praxis. *Harvard Educational Review, 60*, 291–314.

Biklen, D., Morton, M. W., Gold, D., Berrigan, C., & Swaminathan, S. (1992). Facilitated communication: Implications for individuals with autism. *Topics in Language Disorders, 12*, 1–28.

California Department of Developmental Services. (2003). *Autistic spectrum disorders changes in the California caseload an update: 1999 Through 2002*. Sacramento, CA: California Health and Human Services Agency, State of California.

Carey, T., Ratliff-Schaub, K., Funk, J., Weinle, C., Myers, M., & Jenks, J. (2002). Double-blind placebo-controlled trial of secretin: Effects on aberrant behavior in children with autism. *Journal of Autism and Developmental Disorders, 32*, 161–167.

Chez, M. G., Buchanan, C. P., Bagan, B. T., Hammer, M. S., McCarthy, K. S., Ovrutskaya, I., et al. (2000). Secretin and autism: A two part clinical investigation. *Journal of Autism and Developmental Disorders, 30,* 87–94.

Cornish, E. (2002). Gluten and casein free diets in autism: A study of the effects on food choice and nutrition. *Human Nutrition and Dietetics, 15,* 261–269.

Crossley, R. (1994). *Facilitated communication training.* New York: Teachers College Press.

DAN! Subcommittee on Mercury and Autism: Bradstreet, J., El-Dahr, J., Homes, A., Cave, S., & Haley, B. (2000). *Position paper on diagnosis and treatment of heavy metal toxicity in autism spectrum disorders (ASD). Version 1.2.* Retrieved June 5, 2003, from http://www.geo-mark.com/docs/chelprot.pdf

DeStefano, F., & Chen, R. T. (1999). Negative association between MMR and autism. *Lancet, 353,* 1987–1988.

D'Eufemia, P., Celli, M., Finocchiaro, R., Pacifico, L., Viazzi, L., Zaccagnini, M., et al. (1996). Abnormal intestinal permeability in children with autism. *Acta Pediatrica, 85,* 1076–1079.

Donnan, G. A., & Davis, S. M. (2003). Controversy: The essence of medical debate. *Stroke, 34,* 372–373.

Edelson, S. M., & Rimland, B. (2001). *The efficacy of auditory integration training: Summaries and critiques of 28 reports (January 1993–May 2001).* Retrieved June 5, 2003, from http://www.up-to-date.com/saitwebsite/aitsummary.html

Eikeseth, S. (2001). Recent critiques of the UCLA young autism project. *Behavioral Interventions, 16,* 249–264.

Emerson, K. L. (1996). *The writer's guide to everyday life in renaissance England.* Cincinnati, OH: Writer's Digest Books.

Filipek, P. A., Accardo, P. J., Ashwal, S., Baranek, G. T., Cook, E. H., Dawson, G., et al. (2000). Practice parameter: Screening and diagnosis of autism. Report of the Quality Standards Subcommittee of the American Academy of Neurology and the Child Neurology Society. *Neurology, 55,* 268–479.

Findling, R. L., Maxwell, K., Scotese-Wojtila, L., Huang, J., Yamashita, T., & Wiznitzer, M. (1997). High dose pyridoxine and magnesium administration in children with autistic disorder: An absence of salutary effects in a double-blind, placebo-controlled study. *Journal of Autism and Developmental Disorders, 27,* 467–478.

Fisher, A. G., & Murray, E. A. (1991). Introduction to sensory integration theory. In A. G. Fisher, E. A. Murray, & A. C. Bundy (Eds.), *Sensory integration: Theory and practice.* Philadelphia: Davis.

Fombonne, E., & Chakrabarti, S. (2001). No evidence for a new variant of measles-mumps-rubella-induced autism. *Pediatrics, 108,* e58.

Gore, A. (2003). The politics of scientific illiteracy. *Global Change (Electronic Edition).* Retrieved May 5, 2003, from http://www.globalchange.org/editall/98dec1.htm

Gravel, J. S. (1994). Auditory integrative training: Placing the burden of proof. *American Journal of Speech and Language Pathology, 3,* 25–29.

Green, G. (1994). The quality of the evidence. In H. C. Shane (Ed.), *Facilitated communication: The clinical and social phenomenon.* San Diego, CA: Singular.

Green, G., Brennan, L. C., & Fein, D. (2002). Intensive behavioral treatment for a toddler at high risk for autism. *Behavior Modification, 26,* 69–102.

Greenspan, S. I. (2000). Children with autistic spectrum disorders: Individual differences, affect, interaction, and outcomes. *Psychoanalytic Inquiry, 20,* 675–703.

Greenspan, S. I. (2001). The affect diathesis hypothesis: The role of emotions in the core deficit of autism and in the development of intelligence and social skills. *Journal of Developmental and Learning Disorders, 5,* 1–45.

Greenspan, S. I., & Wieder, S. (1997). Developmental patterns and outcomes in infants and children with disorders in relating and communicating: A chart review of 200 cases of children with autistic spectrum diagnoses. *The Journal of Developmental and Learning Disorders, 1,* 87–141.

Greenspan, S. I., & Wieder, S. (1998). *The child with special needs: Encouraging intellectual and emotional growth.* Reading, MA: Addison-Wesley.

Greenspan, S. I., & Wieder, S. (1999). A functional developmental approach to autism spectrum disorders. *Journal of the Association for Persons with Severe Handicaps, 24*, 147–161.

Gresham, F. M., & MacMillan, D. L. (1998). Early intervention project: Can its claims be substantiated and its effects replicated? *Journal of Autism and Developmental Disorders, 28*, 5–13.

Halsey, N. A., Hyman, S. L., & the Conference Writing Panel. (2001). Measles-mumps-rubella vaccine and autistic spectrum disorder: Report from the new challenges in childhood immunizations conference convened in Oak Brook, Illinois, June 12–13, 2000. *Pediatrics, 107*, e84–e107.

Hoehn, T. P., & Baumeister, A. A. (1994). A critique of the application of sensory integration therapy to children with learning disabilities. *Journal of Learning Disabilities, 27*, 338–350.

Holmes, A. S. (2002). *Autism treatments: Chelation of Mercury.* Retrieved June 3, 2003, from http://www.healing-arts.org/children/holmes.htm

Horvath, K., & Perman, J. A. (2002). Autism and gastrointestinal symptoms. *Current Gastroenterology Reports, 4*, 251–258.

Horvath, K., Stefanatos, G., Sokolski, K. N., Wachtel, R., Nabors, L., & Tildon, J. T. (1998). Improved social and language skills after secretin administration in patients with autistic spectrum disorders. *Journal of the Association of the Academy of Minority Physicians, 9*, 9.

Hyman, S. L., & Levy, S. E. (2000). Autistic spectrum disorders: When traditional medicine is not enough. *Contemporary Pediatrics, 17*, 101–116.

Jacobson, J. W. (2000). Early intensive behavioral intervention: Emergence of a consumer-driven service model. *The Behavior Analyst, 23*, 149–171.

Jacobson, J. W., Mulick, J. A., & Schwartz, A. A. (1995). A history of facilitated communication: Science, pseudoscience, and antiscience. *American Psychologist, 50*, 750–765.

Johnson, P. (1988). *Intellectuals.* New York: Harper & Row.

Kabot, S., Masi, W., & Segal, M. (2003). Advances in the diagnosis and treatment of autistic spectrum disorders. *Professional Psychology: Research and Practice, 34*, 26–33.

Kasari, C. (2002). Assessing change in early intervention programs for children with autism. *Journal of Autism and Developmental Disorders, 32*, 447–461.

Kerbeshian, J., Burd, L., & Avery, K. (2001). Pharmacotherapy of autism: A review and clinical approach. *Journal of Developmental & Physical Disabilities, 13*, 199–228.

Kern, J. K., Miller, V. S., Evans, P. A., & Trivedi, M. H. (2002). Efficacy of porcine secretin in children with autism and pervasive developmental disorder. *Journal of Autism and Developmental Disorders, 32*, 153–160.

Knivsberg, A., Reichelt, K., Hoein, T., & Nodland, M. (1998, April). Parent's observations after one year of dietary intervention for children with autistic syndromes. In *Psychobiology of autism, current research and practice.* Conference Proceedings, University of Durham.

Knivsberg, A. M., Reichelt, K., Nodland, M., & Hoein, T. (1995). Autistic syndromes and diet. A follow up study. *Scandinavian Journal of Educational Research, 39*, 223–236.

Knivsberg, A. M., Wiig, K., Lind, G., Nogland, M., & Reichelt, K. L. (1990). Dietary intervention in autistic syndromes. *Developmental Brain Dysfunction, 3*, 315–327.

Lefevre, F., & Aronson, N. (2000). Ketogenic diet for the treatment of refractory epilepsy in children: A systematic review of efficacy. *Pediatrics, 105*, e46–e53.

Lovaas, O. I. (1987). Behavioral treatment and normal educational and intellectual functioning in young autistic children. *Journal of Consulting and Clinical Psychology, 55*, 3–9.

Lovaas, O. I. (Ed.). (2002). *Teaching individuals with developmental delays: Basic intervention techniques.* Austin, TX: Pro-Ed.

Marsden, P. (2003). *Untitled.* Retrieved May 15, 2003, from http://www.viralculture.com

Matson, J. L., Benavidez, D. A., Compton, L. S., Paclawskyj, T., & Baglio, C. (1996). Behavioral treatment of autistic persons: A review of research from 1980 to the present. *Research in Developmental Disabilities, 17*, 433–465.

Matson, J. L., & Coe, D. A. (1992). Applied behavior analysis: Its impact on the treatment of mentally retarded emotionally disturbed people. *Research in Developmental Disabilities, 13*, 171–189.

Maurice, C. (1993). *Let me hear your voice: A family's triumph over autism.* New York: Ballantine Books.

McDougle, C. J. (1997). Psychopharmacology. In D. J. Cohen & F. R. Volkmar (Eds.), *Handbook of autism and pervasive developmental disorders* (2nd ed., pp. 169–194). New York: Wiley.

McEachin, J. J., Smith, T., & Lovaas, O. I. (1993). Long-term outcome for children with autism who received early intensive behavioral treatment. *American Journal on Mental Retardation, 97,* 359–372.

McWilliam, R. A. (1999). Controversial practices: The need for reacculturation of early intervention fields. *Topics in Early Childhood Special Education, 19,* 177–188.

Merriam-Webster, Inc. (1998). *Merriam-Webster's collegiate dictionary* (10th ed.). Springfield, MA: Author.

Mesibov, G. B. (2003). *What is TEACCH?* Retrieved June 5, 2003, from http://www.teacch.com/teacch.htm

Mostert, M. (2001). Facilitated communication since 1995: A review of published studies. *Journal of Autism and Developmental Disorders, 31,* 287–313.

Mudford, O. C., Cross, B. A., Breen, S., Cullen, C., Reeves, D., Gould, J., et al. (2000). Auditory integration training for children with autism: No behavioral benefits detected. *American Journal on Mental Retardation, 105,* 118–129.

Myeroff, R., Mertlich, G., & Gross, J. (1999). Comparative effectiveness of holding therapy with aggressive children. *Child Psychiatry and Human Development, 29*(4), 303–313.

National Research Council. (2001). *Educating children with autism.* Committee on Educational Interventions for Children with Autism, C. Lord & J. P. McGee (Eds.), Division of Behavioral and Social Sciences and Education. Washington, DC: National Academy Press.

New York State Department of Health. (1999). *Clinical practice guideline: The guideline technical report, autism/pervasive developmental disorders, assessment and intervention for young children (age 0–3 years).* Albany, NY: Author.

National Institutes of Health Consensus Statement. (2000). Phenylketonuria (PKU): Screening and management. *NIH consensus statement, 17*(3), 1–33.

Nordli, D. (2002). The ketogenic diet: Uses and abuses. *Neurology, 58,* S21–S24.

Nye, C., & Brice, A. (2002). Combined vitamin B6-magnesium treatment in autism spectrum disorder (Cochrane Review). In *The Cochrane Library,* Issue 2. Oxford, UK: Update Software. Retrieved from www.cochranelibrary.com/abs/ab003497.htm

Offit, P. (2003). *The "Wakefield" studies: Studies hypothesizing that MMR causes autism.* Retrieved June 3, 2003, from http://www.cispimmunize.org/fam/mmr/a_wake.html

Owley, T., Steele, E., Corsello, C., Risi, S., McKaig, K., Lord, C., et al. (1999). A double-blind, placebo-controlled trial of secretin for the treatment of autistic disorder. *Medscape General Medicine.* Available from http://www.medscape.com/medscape/GeneralMedicine/journal/1999/v01.n10/mgm1006.owle/mgm1006.owle-01.html

Ozonoff, S., & Cathcart, K. (1998). Effectiveness of a home program intervention for young children with autism. *Journal of Autism and Developmental Disorders, 28,* 25–32.

Page, T. (2000). Metabolic approaches to the treatment of autism spectrum disorders. *Journal of Autism and Developmental Disorders, 30,* 463–469.

Panerai, S., Ferrante, L., & Zingale, M. (2002). Benefits of the treatment and education of autistic and communication handicapped children (TEACCH) programme as compared with a non-specific approach. *Journal of Intellectual Disability Research, 46,* 318–327.

Panksepp, J. (1979). A neurochemical theory of autism. *Trends in Neuroscience, 2,* 174–177.

Pfeiffer, S. I., Norton, J., Nelson, L., & Shott, S. L. (1995). Efficacy of vitamin B6 and magnesium in the treatment of autism: A methodology review and summary of outcomes. *Journal of Autism and Developmental Disorders, 25,* 481–493.

Phelps, L., Brown, R. T., & Power, T. J. (2002). *Pediatric pharmacology: Combining medical and psychosocial interventions.* Washington, DC: American Psychological Association.

Rankovic, C. M., & Rabinowitz, W. M. (1996). Maximum output intensity of the Audiokinetron. *American Journal of Speech and Language Pathology, 5,* 68–72.

Rapin, I. (2002). The autistic spectrum disorders. *New England Journal of Medicine, 347,* 302–303.

Reichelt, K. L., Knivsberg, A. M., Lind, G., & Nodland, M. (1991). Probable etiology and possible treatment of childhood autism. *Brain Dysfunction, 4,* 308.

Reiss, S., & Aman, M. G. (Eds.). (1998). *Psychotropic medications and developmental disabilities: The international consensus handbook.* Columbus, OH: The Ohio State University Nisonger Center.

Rimland, B. (1987). Vitamin B6 (and magnesium) in the treatment of autism. *Autism Research Review International, 1,* 3.

Sandler, A. D., Sutton, K. A., DeWeese, J., Girardi, M. A., Sheppard, V., & Bodfish, J. W. (1999). Lack of benefit of a single dose of synthetic human secretin in the treatment of autism and pervasive developmental disorder. *New England Journal of Medicine, 341,* 1801–1806.

Sarner, L. (2001). *Rebirthers who killed child receive 16 year prison terms.* Retrieved June 22, 2003, from http://quackwatch.org/04ConsumerEducationNews/rebirthing.html

Schreibman, L. (2000). Intensive behavioral/psychosocial interventions for autism: Research needs and future directions. *Journal of Autism and Developmental Disorders, 30,* 373–378.

Schwartz, I. S. (1999). Controversy or lack of consensus? Another way to examine treatment alternatives. *Topics in Early Childhood Special Education, 19,* 189–193.

Schwartz, I. S., & Baer, D. M. (1991). Social-validity assessments: Is current practice state-of-the-art? *Journal of Applied Behavior Analysis, 24,* 189–204.

Sikich, L. (2001). Psychopharmacologic treatment studies in autism. In E. Schopler & N. Yirmiya (Eds.), *The research basis for autism intervention* (pp. 199–218). New York: Plenum.

Silver, L. B. (1995). Controversial therapies. *Journal of Child Neurology, 10*(1), S96–S100.

Simpson, R. L., & Myles, B. S. (1995). Effectiveness of facilitated communication and children with disabilities: An enigma in search of a perspective. *Focus on Exceptional Children, 27,* 1–16.

Smith, T. (1996). Are other treatments effective? In C. Maurice, G. Green, & S. Luce (Eds.), *Behavioral interventions for young children with autism: A manual for parents and professionals* (pp. 45–59). Austin: Pro-Ed.

Smith, T., Eikeseth, S., Klevstrand, M., & Lovaas, O. I. (1997). Intensive behavioral treatment for preschoolers with severe mental retardation and pervasive developmental disorder. *American Journal of Mental Retardation, 102,* 238–249.

Smith, T., & Wynn, J. (2002). Considerations in selecting consultants for home-based programs. In O. I. Lovaas (Ed.), *Teaching individuals with developmental delays: Basic intervention techniques* (pp. 327–331). Austin, TX: Pro-Ed.

Stone, J. E. (1996). Developmentalism: An obscure but pervasive restriction on educational improvement. *Education Policy Analysis Archives 4*(8), [Electronic journal].

Stratton, K., Gable, A., Shetty, P., & McCormick, M. (Eds.), Immunization Safety Review Committee, Institute of Medicine. (2001). *Measles, mumps, rubella and autism.* Washington, DC: National Academy Press.

Sullivan, J. E., & Chang, P. N. (1999). Review: Emotional and behavioral functioning in phenylketonuria. *Journal of Pediatric Psychology, 24,* 281–299.

Taylor, B., Miller, E., Farrington, C. P., Petropoulos, M.-C., Favot-Mayaud, I., & Waight, P. A. (1999). Autism and measles, mumps, and rubella vaccine: No epidemiological evidence for a causal association. *Lancet, 353,* 2026–2029.

Tolbert, L., Haigler, T., Waits, M. M., & Dennis, T. (1993). Brief report: Lack of response in an autistic population to a low dose clinical trial of pyridoxine plus magnesium. *Journal of Autism and Developmental Disorders, 23,* 193–199.

Tomatis Method. (2001). *Autism.* Retrieved June 5, 2001, from http://www.tomatis.com/English/Articles/autism.htm

Towbin, K. E. (2003). Strategies for pharmacologic treatment of high functioning autism and Asperger syndrome. *Child & Adolescent Psychiatric Clinics of North America, 12,* 23–45.

University of Oxford. (2003). *M.Sc. in evidence based social work.* Retrieved May 30, 2003, from http://www.apsoc.ox.ac.uk/Courses_New.html

Volkmar, F. R. (2001). Pharmacological interventions in autism: Theoretical and practical issues. *Journal of Clinical Child Psychology, 30,* 80–87.

Wakefield, A. J., Murch, S. H., Anthony, A., Linnell, J., Casson, D. M., Malik, M., et al. (1998). Ileal-lymphoid-nodular hyperplasia, non-specific colitis, and pervasive developmental disorder in children. *Lancet, 351,* 637–641.

Welsch, M. G. (1989). Toward prevention of developmental disorders. *Journal of Prenatal and Perinatal Psychology and Health, 3*(4), 319–328.

Whiteley, P., Rodgers, J., Savery, D., & Shattock, P. (1999). A gluten free diet as an intervention for autism and associated spectrum disorders. *Autism, 3*, 45–65.

Wierzbicki, A. S., Lloyd, M. D., Schofeld, C. J., Feher, M. D., & Gibberd, F. B. (2002). Refsum's disease: A peroxisomal disorder affecting phytanic acid a-oxidation. *Journal of Neurochemistry, 80*, 727–735.

Williams, H. W., & Williams, E. H. (1904/1910). *A history of science.* New York: Harper.

Williams, K. M., & Marshall, T. (1992). Urinary proteins in autism as revealed by high resolution two dimensional electrophoresis. *Biochemical Society Transactions, 20*, 189S.

Wing, L., & Potter, D. (2002). The epidemiology of autistic spectrum disorders: Is the prevalence rising? *Mental Retardation and Developmental Disabilities Research Reviews, 8*,151–161.

Wolf, M. M. (1978). Social validity: The case for subjective measurement, or how behavior analysis is finding its heart. *Journal of Applied Behavior Analysis, 11*, 203–214.

Wolraich, M. L. (1996). Diet and behavior: What does the research show? *Contemporary Pediatrics, 13*, 29.

Zollweg, W., Palm, D., & Vance, V. (1997). The efficacy of auditory integration training: A double blind study. *American Journal of Audiology, 6*, 39–47.

16

Helping Parents Separate the Wheat From the Chaff: Putting Autism Treatments to the Test

Shannon Kay
The May Institute

Stuart Vyse
Connecticut College

An applied behavior analyst assigned to a new case of a child with developmental disabilities will often find the child's parents have already adopted a treatment strategy that is not supported by scientific evidence. Having heard about facilitated communication or sensory integration therapy from another parent, from a health professional, or in the news media, the parents may have seized on an idea and either have begun to implement the treatment themselves or recruited a professional to do it for them. Often the child is not improving, and much time and money are being wasted; yet, the parents have become committed to their chosen course of action.

Part of this phenomenon stems from the nature of developmental disabilities. Childrearing is typically thought to be the responsibility of parents, and its goal is the instillation of necessary skills and social behavior in the child. Usually, if a child's behavior falls outside the bounds of normal expectations, it is up to her parents to respond accordingly. Psychologists, social workers, or educational specialists may be enlisted to the cause when necessary, but parents rarely relinquish control over their child's educational and social development. As a result, even when working with qualified professionals, parents of children with developmental disabilities often exercise their considerable power to alter the course of treatment.

The role of the parent in behavioral development is further clarified by contrasting it with parental involvement in medical problems. If a child becomes ill or suffers from an identifiable physical condition, in all but the mildest circumstances, the parent is not expected to treat the child directly. The parent's responsibility is simply to recognize when the child is in need of medical attention and to consult with a doctor when necessary. The choice of treatment is typically left up to the physician.

In comparison to behavior specialists, physicians enjoy other benefits that keep them from having to convince parents to abandon unsubstantiated treatments for their children's health problems. First, for many of the most common ailments, a single highly effective approach has become the dominant treatment. Antibiotics are prescribed for infections, and standard surgical techniques have been established to repair a variety of injuries and structural problems. Furthermore, to gain access to these dominant procedures, parents must go through a licensed physician who has completed a standardized training program grounded in evidence-based clinical decision making. In cases where an effective treatment is still lacking or the standard treatment is very unpleasant (e.g., in the later stages of cancer), physicians may find their patients drawn to pseudoscientific or nonscientific treatments (see Vyse, chap. 1, this volume). However, as long as modern medical practice retains its dominance in the western world, most serious physical health problems will be addressed by scientifically validated procedures.

Unfortunately for behavior therapists, scientifically based treatment has not yet captured the high ground in developmental disabilities services. Parents of children with developmental disorders are not automatically presented with a standard treatment approach consistently endorsed by all, or nearly all, practitioners. As a result, the treatments chosen often reflect the random nature of the information parents encounter and the programs that are available locally. In some cases, parents' treatment decisions are influenced by their personal philosophies about human behavior and health, but often these decisions lead to ineffective therapies. Furthermore, even when parents see little evidence that an alternative therapy is working for their child, they may be reluctant to halt its use.

Despite these obstacles, practitioners' efforts to help parents cast off ineffective treatments are substantially aided by two factors. First, the overwhelming majority of parents are highly motivated to see their children improve, and if presented with clear evidence that a program is working, they will often quickly abandon an ineffective approach in favor of an effective one. This kind of motivation can even overcome the initial distaste some parents have for a therapy they perceive as "manipulative and cold" (Maurice, 1993, p. 63). Second, the same empirical tools that have built the knowledge base of applied behavior analysis—in particular, single-case experimental designs—can be employed to help parents discover which treatments will help their children and which will not. In the following pages, we present a simple strategy for using an alternating treatments design to help parents compare the effectiveness of two therapies on the behavior of their children. In addition, we present three illustrative cases.

SEARCHING FOR THE BEST TREATMENT

Parent Education

Sometimes talking to parents and providing them with information is enough to turn them away from fad therapies. Giving parents reading material (e.g., Green, 1996; Herbert, Sharp, & Guadiano, 2002) about the effectiveness of various treatments can be helpful, but parents without a firm understanding of what constitutes reliable evidence of success will have trouble evaluating the available therapies. Often it is necessary to inform parents about the relative value of information found in peer-reviewed articles, chapters from edited books, self-published materials, testimonials, and information from the World Wide Web (Green & Perry, 1999), as well as how to identify the characteristics of sound empirical research.

Even when parents have not yet expressed interest in an alternative therapy, it is better to address the topic directly. The lack of consensus about treatment options makes the parent's job very difficult. Rather than merely hoping that parents will not hear about dolphin therapy (Specter, 1997), gyrogym therapy (Young, 2002), or gluten-free or casein-free diets (Whiteley, Rodgers, Savery, & Shattock, 1999), practitioners should discuss treatment choices when they begin to work with the child and inform parents about the prevalence of unsubstantiated remedies for autism and other developmental disabilities. Finally, practitioners will be more likely to have a positive influence on future decision making if they establish an atmosphere in which parents feel comfortable talking about the alternative therapies they hear about in the news media or elsewhere.

But what if talking and education are not enough? Behavior analysts who, despite their best efforts, are unable to dissuade parents from using unsupported treatment methods are left with several choices. The therapist might (a) ignore the parent's use of an alternative therapy and continue to provide services in the same manner, (b) continue to advise the parent and hope to wear her or him down, or (c) refuse to provide services to children whose parents use unproven treatments. Alternatively, (d) the practitioner may suggest that the parents collect data to help determine the value of the alternative treatment for their child. If presented properly, the option of an empirical test can diffuse conflict and provide a shared goal for both parent and practitioner. Of course, this approach should only be attempted if the unsubstantiated treatment is not likely to cause serious harm to the child or others.

Presenting the Idea of a Data-Based Decision

When the time comes to propose a simple experiment to test the effectiveness of an alternative treatment, practitioners should enumerate some of the advantages of collecting data to help make the decision to continue the treatment or not. First, collecting data will help the parents objectively determine whether the treatment is helping to solve the targeted problem. Second, collecting data will help the parent determine whether the treatment has iatrogenic effects. Without an adequate test, parents often fail to recognize that a treatment is actually causing deterioration rather than improvement in behavior or development. Third, if the intervention lacks empirical evidence but proves to be effective for their child, the parents' efforts may contribute to the literature and help other families. Rather than rejecting the possibility that an unproven therapy will work, the therapist should project an attitude of scientific curiosity and propose that, together with the parents, they will "see what happens." In addition, the practitioner can explain that single-case studies are often the first step in proving that an intervention is effective for some children. If the alternative therapy works, the experiment will have contributed needed objective evidence. If it does not work, the parents may learn to put their efforts elsewhere.

Finally, this kind of test has one tremendous advantage over any other kind of decision-making information: It is based on the parent's own child. Parents may dismiss the results of published empirical studies because they are done on faceless children they have never met. The parent may acknowledge that the evidence for a new therapy is weak while clinging to the belief that it will work for their child. The only way to test whether this belief is justified is to conduct a simple experiment with the child in question.

Designing and Implementing the Test

Identifying the Target Behavior.   The first step in designing a study is to identify which behaviors the parent would like to change with the proposed therapy. Because parents have been educated in a culture that emphasizes the medical model of recovery and cure, they may initially hope that the treatment will simply make their child "less autistic" or more typical. It may be difficult for many parents to develop an operational definition of the behavior that they want to change; as a result, the practitioner may need to give examples of appropriate operational definitions. Frequently, the claims about unproven treatments do not lend themselves to the creation of operational definitions of behaviors, but parents can usually identify a target with assistance. Once the target behavior has been identified, the parent and practitioner can determine how to measure the behavior and how to establish data reliability (Foxx, 1982).

Designing the Test.   The second step is to develop a research design. Several different time-series designs may be used to evaluate whether a particular treatment is effective for an individual child. Reversal designs (e.g., ABA, ABAB) and multiple baseline designs may be useful in some circumstances, but the focus of this chapter is the use of alternating treatments designs to compare the relative efficacy of two treatments or to compare treatment versus no-treatment conditions.

In an alternating treatments design, two treatments are quickly alternated in a single participant (Barlow & Hayes, 1979). The first step in an alternating treatments design is to collect baseline data (although if persistence of a behavior presents ethical concerns, a baseline is not absolutely necessary; Cooper, Heron, & Heward, 1987). After baseline data are collected, the quick alternation of treatments can begin in the intervention phase. During this time, the order of treatments should be randomly selected. For example, one might use a coin flip to determine if the child was going to receive treatment A or treatment B each morning. A follow-up or return to baseline condition may also be used. During this third phase, one might choose to return to the baseline condition or continue to present only the most effective treatment (Barlow & Hayes, 1979).

There are several advantages to using alternating treatments designs. First, it allows for the direct comparison of two interventions and allows for comparisons across baseline, intervention, and follow-up phases. Second, the design is quite flexible. Two to three very different interventions or two similar versions of the same intervention can be compared. Alternatively, a treatment condition can be compared to a no-treatment condition. In addition, because a withdrawal phase is not required, an alternating treatments design may be more socially valid (Bloom, Fischer, & Orme, 1999) and more acceptable to parents or teachers. When using alternating treatments designs, carryover effects can represent a confounding variable when one treatment influences an adjacent treatment (Barlow & Hayes, 1979). However, counterbalancing the order of treatments (i.e., making sure that each type of treatment follows each other type an equal number of times; Ulman & Sulzer-Azaroff, 1975) and carefully selecting the frequency of alternation should minimize the problem of carryover effects. The order of the treatments should be randomized, and when treatments applied within a short time frame are likely to influence each other, the practitioner should make efforts to establish an appropriate pace of alternation (McGonigle, Rojahn, Dixon, & Strain, 1987). Reversal or multiple baseline designs may be most appropriate when the proposed treatment is expected to have a cumulative effect because it will be difficult to avoid carryover effects in this instance.

Next, the practitioner and parents should determine how the data will be collected and by whom. If possible, the observers should be blind to the condition and the hypothesis of the study. The practitioner should give a brief explanation of expectancy effects and emphasize that if a strong research design is used, the parents will be better able to trust that they are getting accurate data for their decision making. If it is not possible to use blind raters, the use of multiple raters and reliability checks may help ensure the integrity of the data.

Developing Decision Rules. Before beginning the experiment, it is recommended that the therapist and parent determine, a priori, the level of behavior change that would indicate the alternative treatment is working. This step is not an essential component of the process, but it can be very helpful when it is time to make a decision about whether to continue or halt use of a treatment. It may be a good idea to for the practitioner and parent to sketch hypothetical graphs that portray their depictions of a positive, negative, and neutral response to the therapy. In addition, parents may want to establish a goal; for example, a percentage reduction of a problem behavior or increase of an appropriate behavior that would constitute an effective outcome.

Collecting the Data. The fourth step is actually collecting the data. If possible, arrangements should be made to establish data reliability for the dependent variable and treatment integrity data for the independent variables (Gresham, 1989). Measuring treatment integrity may require the construction of checklists based on information from the alternative therapy provider. Although these data may be cumbersome to collect, doing so will help to ensure that the alternative treatment was implemented as intended, and the target variable is measured accurately. The parent and practitioner will be more comfortable with the eventual decision if they have confidence that the treatment has been administered correctly and the data are sound.

Evaluating the Results and Making a Decision. After the data are collected and a graph of the results has been constructed, the therapist should meet with the parents to discuss the findings. Because some parents are not experienced in the interpretation graphs, it may be necessary to explain how the figure works and how the data are evaluated. This is also the time when the actual data set should be compared to the hypothetical data that were generated before beginning the study. If the data are highly variable or sloped (Gibson & Ottenbacher, 1988), statistical techniques may help to clarify the results (Gorman & Allison, 1996).

The final step is to support the parents in making a data-based decision. If the data are definitive, the parents may readily make an appropriate decision. If there is no difference between treatment conditions, many parents may want to continue the alternative treatment. At this point, it may be important to discuss the opportunity costs, if any, involved in continuing the treatment. For example, the treatment may take time away from empirically validated methods or it may have other detrimental effects. For example, the elimination of dairy or gluten may not be consistent with good childhood nutrition.

CASE EXAMPLES

In each of the following cases, the child's parents were committed to using empirically validated treatments; however, for various reasons they either became interested in an alternative, unsubstantiated treatment or were encouraged to adopt such a treatment by school officials. Each study was designed collaboratively with the parents and the child's behavior therapy team.

Case 1: Brushing and Joint Compression

This case involved a non-verbal 8-year-old boy with autism who had received limited discrete trial training and one month of intensive applied behavior analytic therapy at his current placement. His problem behaviors included self-induced vomiting, other self-injurious behaviors, feces smearing, aggressive behaviors (hitting), and food selectivity issues.

The occupational therapist at the child's school strongly recommended to his parents that he would benefit from sensory integration therapy (Ayres, 1979; see Dawson & Watling, 2000, for a review). She argued that sensory integration deficits and "sensory overload" probably caused the child's aggressive behavior and recommended brushing and joint compression therapy. After talking to the occupational therapist, the child's parents were interested in giving sensory integration therapy a try. They believed the therapy could only help and "couldn't hurt," but they were willing to undertake a data-based evaluation.

The agreed-on target was episodes of hitting behavior per hour. As defined for this study, hitting included blows directed at himself, staff members, or his table. Ninety-five percent of the boy's hitting episodes consisted of three hits in a quick sequence lasting less than 2 seconds. At other times, he hit once or twice. Each burst of one-to-three hits was counted as a single episode, and a new episode could only be recorded if the child went 2 seconds without hitting. Hitting episodes were recorded in 2-hour blocks during discrete trial training. The 2-hour time period was chosen because the occupational therapist stated that the effects of brushing and joint compression would be most noticeable in the 2 hours after the treatment. Four behavior therapists were trained to count the number of hitting episodes. Interrater reliability averaged 96% during training. The child was always staffed by two behavior therapists, and during 30% of intervals, both therapists collected data so that interrater reliability could be monitored. During the remaining 70% of intervals, the therapist who was not engaging in discrete trial training collected the data. During the study, interrater reliability averaged 94%.

Brushing and joint compression were delivered by the occupational therapist and a trained assistant. During brushing, the child's skin was firmly stroked by a specialized flexible plastic brush. After the child's limbs and torso were brushed, the occupational therapist firmly pushed specific body parts so that the joints were compressed. The occupational therapist developed a treatment integrity checklist that included 10 components of brushing and joint compression, and she recorded whether she had delivered these components correctly each day. Her treatment integrity was 95% during the experiment. On two occasions, the therapy had to be discontinued 2 to 3 minutes early because the child induced vomiting. The joint compression and brushing sessions typically took 10 minutes.

Instruction in completing a shape sorter was chosen as a neutral treatment to be compared with sensory integration. The therapist used a backwards-chaining procedure to teach the child to do the shape sorter, and the boy received rewards for appropriate behavior and completion of the shape sorting task. The therapists completed a five-component treatment integrity checklist. Treatment integrity for the shape sorter teaching procedure was 100%. Between discrete trial training sessions during the intervention phase, the child was taken into another room out of sight of the tutors who collected the data. A coin flip was used to determine whether the boy received the brushing and joint compression therapy or shape sorter instruction, and observers were blind to what treatment had been given. The child received two interventions a day.

The results of the experiment are shown in Fig. 16.1. In every instance except one, the child's rate of hitting episodes was higher after receiving brushing and joint compression therapy, and in that case hitting occurred at the same rate for both treatments. The study showed clear evidence that an unproven treatment—even one that appears benign—can have significant detrimental effects. If they had not conducted this test, the parents would have had considerable difficulty recognizing the negative affects of sensory integration therapy and may have continued it much longer than they did. However, after seeing the data, the parents asked for the brushing and joint compression therapy to be discontinued. The occupational therapist was surprised by the results, but she agreed that the treatment was not beneficial for this child.

Case 2: Prism Glasses

This case involved an 8-year-old boy with autism who had significant problems walking appropriately. He rarely alternated feet and tended to toe walk and gallop clumsily. The child's optometrist told his parents that wearing prism glasses would improve the boy's visual processing. There have been some published studies reporting behavioral changes in children with autism while using prism glasses (Kaplan, Carmody, & Gaydos, 1996; Kaplan, Edelson, & Seip, 1998). The parents reported that their optometrist believed that autism was a result of visual processing problems and that he claimed to have seen children "recover" from autism by wearing the glasses. He said that the first sign the glasses were working would be an increase in appropriate gait and a decrease in toe walking. The par-

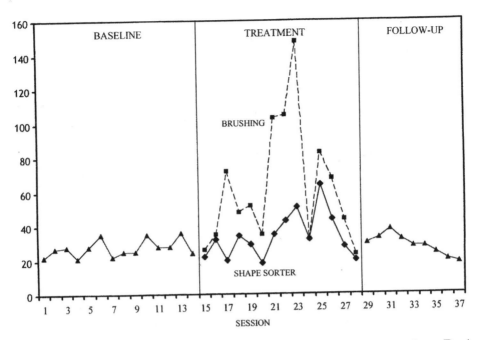

FIG. 16.1. Hitting episodes per hour during discrete trial training sessions. During the intervention phase, the child received sensory integration therapy (brushing and joint compression; broken line) or instruction in using a shape sorter (solid line) just prior to his discrete trial session. The follow-up phase was a return to the baseline condition in which neither sensory integration therapy nor shape shorter instruction was given prior to the daily session.

ents were sufficiently concerned about their child that they wanted to see whether the glasses would help.

Appropriate walking was defined as two steps with alternating feet. For the behavior to be counted as correct, the child had to use a heel–toe motion during each step. Interrater reliability for the dependent variable was 98%. During the baseline phase, the boy was asked to walk nicely and given edible reinforcers for appropriate walking. He did not wear glasses during this condition.

During the intervention phase of this alternating treatments design, the prism glasses were compared to a pair of glasses frames that contained no lenses. Before beginning the "walking nicely" drill, the therapist flipped a coin to determine whether the child would wear prism glasses or the empty frames. Then the therapist said, "Walk nicely." If the child walked appropriately, he was given a preferred edible reinforcer. He was given the same preferred reinforcer, a small piece of candy, in both the play glasses and prism glasses conditions. The therapist completed 10 trials each day. Four therapists participated in the data collection, recording the percentage of trials completed correctly each day. During 35% of the sessions, two raters collected data producing an interrater reliability of 97%. A treatment integrity check was also done during 35% of sessions. The second rater recorded whether the coin was flipped, whether the correct pair of classes was administered, and whether the correct command and consequence were given on each trial. Treatment integrity was 98%.

Figure 16.2 shows the results of the study. After an initial period of appropriate walking, performance while wearing the prism glasses quickly decreased. In the empty glasses condition, the child's appropriate walking steadily increased. The initial positive result with the prism glasses is notable, but the therapists reported that the boy walked extremely slowly during his first experiences with the prism classes, taking very small steps. Even though appropriate walking was reinforced during the prism glasses condition, the boy's walking became quite erratic and he engaged in disruptive behaviors. The therapists reported that he showed high levels of resistance to physical prompts to walk appropriately during the prism glasses condition and that he attempted to turn around in circles when wearing the prism glasses. After viewing the data, the parents chose to discontinue the use of prism glasses.

Case 3: Sensory Integration Therapy to Reduce an Inappropriate Sitting Behavior

This case involved a 5-year-old boy with autism who had received 2.5 years of intensive applied behavior analysis therapy. He had acquired a vocabulary of approximately 500 words and had learned to read simple words, add, and respond to appropriate requests for information. The boy engaged in a variety of behaviors that allowed him to avoid task demands for short periods of time. One of the most problematic of these was throwing himself on the floor when asked to complete tasks. The child had engaged in this behavior when he first started his therapy program, and it had been eliminated in the past with the use of a differential reinforce-

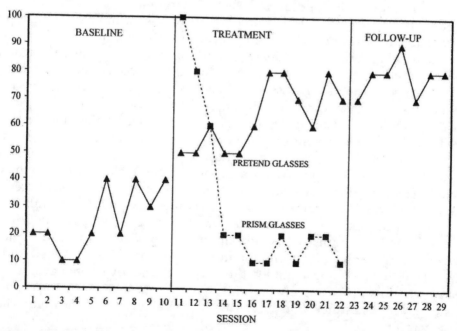

FIG. 16.2. Percentage of correct trials during training in appropriate walking. In the intervention phase, the child alternated wearing prism glasses (broken line) and a pair of empty glasses frames (solid line). The child wore no glasses during either the baseline or follow-up phases.

ment of other behavior (DRO) procedure. However, it had recently reappeared when he moved from a home-based to a school-based program and switched therapists. The boy's occupational therapist believed that this behavior was a result of an "inadequate sensory diet" and that if his vestibular system were balanced through sensory integration therapy, he would not fall out of the chair as much. In this case, the child's parents did not want him to receive sensory integration therapy because of the lack of empirical evidence to support its use; however, the occupational therapist was able to convince the boy's educational team that it was an essential component of the child's therapy program. The occupational therapist also indicated that it could be detrimental to the child if he was denied access to rewarding things when he engaged in the behavior, because she believed it was not truly under his control. Therefore, the parents asked that at a data-based decision be made. As in the previous examples, an alternating treatments design was used, but in this case, sitting behavior following sensory integration therapy was compared to sitting behavior under a differential reinforcement of lower rates (DRL) treatment procedure.

The target behavior for the study was falling out of his chair, which was defined as buttocks or stomach in contact with the floor. Four therapists obtained interrater reliability of 98% before the beginning of the study. The therapists were blind to the hypothesis of the study, but did know that on some days they were asked not to implement the behavioral intervention. The number of times the child fell out of the chair in the hour from 1:00 to 2:00 p.m. was counted during discrete trial training. The tasks that the child was given to complete during this time were the same each day. This time of day was chosen because previous observations revealed that the behavior was most likely to occur in the early afternoon.

On random preselected days, the child received sensory integration therapy before the data collection period. First, the occupational therapist would place the child on a large ball and bounce him for about 5 minutes. Then, the child would be placed in a spinning swing and moved in various directions. The occupational therapist wrote down whether she was able to complete both exercises each day. She completed both exercises on 90% of the days and one exercise on 10% of the days.

On days not selected for occupational therapy, a DRL schedule was implemented. During this intervention, the boy was reminded that the rule for work time was to stay in his seat, and then he chose a reinforcer to earn from an array of choices; often he chose use of a swing as his reinforcer. A clipboard with the written rule "nice sitting during work," a timer, and two pictures of the preferred reinforcer attached was placed in front of him. The timer was set for 15 minutes, and if he fell out of the chair, one of the pictures was removed from the board. When the timer went off, the therapist would prompt him to look at his rule board and say, "Did you follow the rule?" If one picture was left on the board, he would be prompted to say "yes" and would get to play with the toy or engage in the preferred activity for approximately 1 minute. If both pictures were still on the board, he could play for 2 minutes. If he lost both pictures at any point, the timer was immediately reset.

The results of the experiment are presented in Fig. 16.3. The boy's rate of falling out of his chair decreased during the DRL condition and increased during the sensory integration condition. The parents were not surprised to discover that the treatment had a detrimental effect, but they were pleased that they did not have to

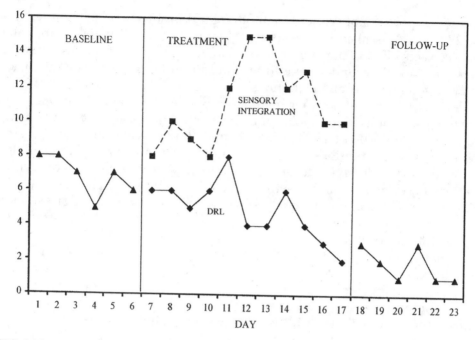

FIG. 16.3.   Frequency of inappropriate sitting behavior (falling out of chair). During the intervention phase, sensory integration therapy (broken line) prior to the daily session was alternated with a differential reinforcement of low rate (DRL) program (solid line) during the session. In the follow-up condition, only the DRL program was in effect.

continue to fight a philosophical battle with the school. After seeing the results, the school quickly agreed to discontinue sensory integration therapy with this child.

CONCLUSIONS

Autism is a serious disorder for which there is no easy, guaranteed cure. Parents of children with autism cannot be blamed for wanting to leave no leaf unturned. But when parents are unable to evaluate the evidence for an unsubstantiated treatment, or are unwilling to dismiss a treatment based on the absence of evidence to support its use, applied behavior analysts are well equipped to help them make sound treatment decisions. As a first step, the practitioner can teach parents the basics of behavioral science problem solving in an effort to turn them into better consumers of the information they encounter and the treatments offered for their children. If parents choose to implement an unproven treatment, practitioners can help them make a data-based decision about whether the treatment is helping their child or not. Simple single-participant designs like the ones used in the cases discussed in this chapter can produce clear results that are readily accepted by both skeptics and believers.

These studies are not without methodological problems. For example, in both Case 2 (prism glasses) and Case 3 (sensory integration/DRL) it was impossible to keep observers blind to the interventions. However, the results of these cases were clear enough to allow for decisions to be made on evidence and not on rumor, ideology, or blind faith in recommendations by professionals.

These cases show that, rather than argue with parents and the proponents of these therapies, practitioners can collaborate with them in the design and implementation of controlled tests. Far from being a theoretical exercise, these simple experiments are evaluations conducted on the most important person of all, the child who everyone is trying to help. And there are potential benefits of such a test for all parties. Parents learn whether they are making wise choices. They have their child's welfare in mind, and most will not want to waste time on false leads. The practitioner's scientifically validated techniques can be demonstrated to be effective for the specific child in question, which may lead to greater parent support. Finally, the proponents of the alternative treatments, such as the occupational therapists and optometrist from the previous examples, enter such an evaluation with the hope of uncovering empirical support for the therapy. If they are disappointed, as they were in each of the present cases, supporters may still maintain their belief in the validity of the treatment, but at the very least, they are forced to accept that it does not work "for this child." As a result, simple single-participant experiments, such as the alternating treatment designs used in these cases, are useful tools that can help all parties reach agreement in their effort to separate the wheat from the chaff of autism therapies.

REFERENCES

Ayres, A. J. (1979). *Sensory integration and the child*. Los Angeles, CA: Western Psychological Services.

Barlow, D. H., & Hayes, S. C. (1979). Alternating treatments design: One strategy for comparing the effects of two treatments in a single subject. *Journal of Applied Behavior Analysis, 12*, 199–210.

Bloom, M., Fischer, J., & Orme, J. G. (1999). *Evaluating practice: Guidelines for the accountable professional*. Boston: Allyn & Bacon.

Cooper, J. O., Heron, T. E., & Heward, W. L. (1987). *Applied behavior analysis*. Englewood Cliffs, NJ: Prentice-Hall.

Dawson, G., & Watling, R. (2000). Interventions to facilitate auditory, visual ad motor integration in autism: A review of the evidence. *Journal of Autism and Developmental Disorders, 30*, 415–421.

Foxx, R. M. (1982). *Increasing behaviors of persons with severe retardation and autism*. Champaign, IL: Research Press.

Gibson, G., & Ottenbacher, R. (1988). Characteristics influencing the visual analysis of single-subject data: An empirical analysis. *The Journal of Applied Behavior Science, 24*, 298–314.

Gorman, B. S., & Allison, D. B. (1996). Statistical alternatives for single-case designs. In R. D. Franklin, D. B. Allison, & B. S. Gorman (Eds.), *Design and analysis of single-case research* (pp. 159–214). Mahwah, NJ: Lawrence Erlbaum Associates.

Green, G. (1996). Evaluating claims about treatments for autism. In C. Maurice, G. Green, & S. C. Luce (Eds.), *Behavioral intervention for young children with autism: A manual for parents and professionals* (pp. 15–28). Austin, TX: Pro-Ed.

Green, G., & Perry, L. (1999, Spring). Science, pseudoscience, and antiscience: What's this got to do with my child? *Science in Autism Treatment*, 5–7.

Gresham, F. M. (1989). Assessment of treatment integrity in school consultation and prereferral intervention. *School Psychology Review, 18*, 37–50.

Herbert, J. D., Sharp, I. R., & Gaudiano, B. A. (2002). Separating fact from fiction in the etiology and treatment of autism. *The Scientific Review of Mental Health Practices, 1*, 25–45.

Kaplan, M., Carmody, D., & Gaydos, A. (1996). Postural orientation modifications in autism in response to ambient lenses. *Child Psychiatry and Human Development, 27*, 81–91.

Kaplan, M., Edelson, S., & Seip, J. L. (1998). Behavioral changes in autistic individuals as a result of wearing ambient transitional prism lenses. *Child Psychiatry and Human Development, 29*, 65–76.

Maurice, C. (1993). *Let me hear your voice: A family's triumph over autism.* New York: Knopf.

McGonigle, J. J., Rojahn, J., Dixon, J., & Strain, P. S. (1987). Multiple treatment interference in the alternating treatments design as a function of the intercomponent interval length. *Journal of Applied Behavior Analysis, 20*, 171–178.

Specter, M. (1997, August 4). Dolphins study war no more (They mend nerves). *The New York Times*, p. A4.

Ulman, J. D., & Sulzer-Azaroff, B. (1975). Multielement baseline design in educational research. In K. A. Ramp & G. Semb (Eds.), *Behavior analysis: Areas of research and application* (pp. 377–391). Engelwood Cliffs, NJ: Prentice-Hall.

Whiteley, P., Rodgers, J., Savery, D., & Shattock, P. (1999). A gluten-free diet as an intervention for autism and associated spectrum disorders: Preliminary findings. *Autism, 3*, 45–65.

Young, D. (2002, March 31). New treatments to improve people with ADD/ADHD. *Pioneer Valley Gazette.* Retrieved June 13, 2002, from http://www.gazettenet.com

Severe Aggressive and Self-Destructive Behavior: Mentalistic Attribution

Steve Holburn
New York State Institute for Basic Research in Developmental Disabilities, Staten Island, NY

In the past 20 years, the field of developmental disabilities has witnessed a surge of interest in identifying the sources of difficult-to-manage behavior, including aggression and severe self-injury. Today's practitioner can take advantage of various assessment strategies that suggest environmental causes of the behavior and assist in the formulation of treatment. For years, practitioners have attempted to generate hypotheses about controlling variables by gathering information about what was happening before and after the occurrence of a given behavioral episode, but when these variables began to be systematically evaluated (Carr, 1977; Iwata, Dorsey, Slifer, Bauman, & Richman, 1982; Schroeder et al., 1982), more accurate methods for assessing the occasioning circumstances and maintaining reinforcement became available to the practitioner.

Forms of such assessment include naturalistic observation (Repp, Felce, & Barton, 1988), behavioral interviews (Sturmey, 1991), pretreatment variable manipulation (Iwata et al., 1982), questionnaires (Durand & Crimmins, 1992; Van Houten & Rolider, 1991), ecobehavioral analysis (Schroeder, 1990), and combinations of these forms (O'Neill, Horner, Albin, Storey, & Sprague, 1990). Other behavioral assessment approaches include the scatterplot procedure (Touchette, MacDonald, & Langer, 1985), free-operant analysis (Holburn & Dougher, 1986), and even Japanese cause–effect diagrams (Kume, 1985; Pfadt & Wheeler, 1995). Most of these assessment procedures can be classified as *functional assessment*.

Despite the availability and reported successes of these recent operant applications, many people who are in the business of helping people with severely challenging behavior believe the sources of the behavior are not as attributable to an

Note: This chapter is dedicated to Donald M. Baer for his work in encouraging people to bring about important social change through the principles of science. This work was supported in part by the New York State Office of Mental Retardation and Developmental Disabilities, but it does not necessarily reflect the views of that organization.

individual's interaction with the environment as the operant approaches hold paramount. Instead, such problems are thought to originate inside of the individual. Accordingly, solutions are aimed toward eliminating or adjusting the inner source, rather than developing new behavior–environment relationships. In this chapter, I argue that mentalistic formulations abound in the field of developmental disabilities, and they foster unhelpful approaches to addressing serious aggression and self-injury. Moreover, mentalistic practices perpetuate resistance to more effective analysis and treatment of such problems.

BEHAVIORISTIC AND MENTALISTIC EXPLANATIONS

The belief that behavior originates from something that happens inside of us, such as a thought, feeling, or impulse, with the resulting behavior being an expression of the mind, from which that thought, feeling, or impulse emanated, is called mentalism (Day, 1983, Skinner, 1953, 1974). The antithesis of mentalism is the philosophy of radical behaviorism (Skinner, 1953, 1974); it is radical because it includes all behavioral phenomena (Branch, 1987) and because there is nothing in its formulation that is mental (Skinner, 1964), including notions that neural, psychic, or conceptual inner states cause behavior (Skinner, 1953). Contrary to popular but inaccurate representations of behaviorism, private feelings, thoughts, and internal states often have an important role in the analysis of behavior (Anderson, Hawkins, Freeman, & Scotti, 2000; Friman, Hayes, & Wilson, 1998).

A typical causal sequence was depicted by Skinner (1986), who wrote, "In a given episode the environment acts upon the organism, something happens inside, the organism then acts upon the environment, and certain consequences follow" (p. 716). The second event in the sequence is not the province of behavioral science, but even if we did understand what takes place inside the person, we are no less affected by the environment. (This does not mean we are uninterested in what happens inside, as demonstrated by how an illness affects us, but what we do about it requires interaction with the environment.) As the previous depiction indicates, a person is not a passive recipient of environmental influences (the learner as a passive participant is another common misconception about behaviorism). Instead, the process is reciprocal and interactive; the person's action changes the environment, which subsequently has a slightly different effect on how the person feels and what the person does. Both behavior and environment continually act on each other and change each other. Accordingly, we can penetrate and influence this reciprocal process by systematically engineering aspects of our environment that are associated with relevant behavior. In fact, it is the identification of such aspects and their consequences that underlies the functional assessment strategies listed earlier.

On the contrary, in a mentalistic formulation, behavior is governed by the intricacies of the mind and its cognitive processes, and the individual is the center of the behavioral universe. This pre-Copernican-like view is well represented by the phrase, "Everything we think, do, and feel is generated by what happens inside of us" (Glasser, 1984, p. 1). Because behavior is believed to originate inside, something inside the individual must be changed before behavior can change. In this framework, people are capable of changing their own behavior by altering the defective inner parts or processes or by acquiring a missing internal element. Alternatively, a behavioristic account holds that one must alter the environmental variables of which the behavior is a function. The mentalistic account holds that a person is autonomous and responsible for his or her actions. Consequently, a person is admired and given credit for achievement, and admonished and blamed for misbehavior (Skinner, 1972, p. 21). In a behavioral account, the credit and the culpability are assigned to the person's interaction with the environment.

In Skinner's reckoning, the concept of mind has stood in the way of the advancement of psychology as a science and of behavior analysis as its method. Its appeal and the accompanying disregard of the environment in accounting for behavior has changed little from its antique roots 25 centuries ago. Although most of our cultural practices and scientific formulations have evolved significantly since then, the concept of mind has remained tenaciously with us and holds a dominant position in our lay community and social sciences alike. Moore (1981) reminds us that mentalistic reasoning derives from the powerful prevailing traditions and preconceptions of the lay community in which the practitioner is embedded. Its influence on the practitioner and scientist is diminished to the extent that the practitioner is influenced by observations and contacts with data and less by the social reinforcement for following the cultural rules of causal explanation.

MENTALISTIC ACCOUNTS OF PROBLEM BEHAVIOR

To illustrate a blatant mentalistic account of self-injurious behavior, I recount a success story about Raphael, a man who gradually reached a precarious state of health while living in an institution in New Mexico. Poor vital signs and emaciation resulted from ruminating food, much of which ended up on the floor. A simple food-satiation procedure (Jackson, Johnson, Ackron, Crowley, 1975; Rast, Johnston, Drum, & Conrin, 1981) rapidly restored his health and prior robust appearance; none of the staff, including me, expected such a speedy and thorough recovery. Later, I learned that some of the mostly Hispanic direct-support staff who cared for Raphael attributed his improvement to my ridding him of *empacho*, a condition in which a bolus of food is thought to be lodged in the intestine. *Empacho* is discussed by Torrey (1972), who explains how the Mexican-American culture commonly ascribes severe psychiatric illness and chronic deviance to *mal puesto*, or witchcraft, in which one person places a hex on another, ostensibly because of some wrongdoing. The staff reasoned that Raphael's hex was the *empacho*, and I had removed it, permitting normal digestion. Although this example probably does not represent how the majority of Mexican Americans conceptualize causation of mental illness today, it does illustrate how unusual behavior is thought to be eliminated by removing some undesirable entity dwelling inside the individual.

Powers (1992) provides a more contemporary example of autonomous action in which person–environment interactions hold no causal role in behavior. What we do is determined solely by the brain: "Violence, aggression, hostility, war, murder—these phenomena do not arise from specialized inborn traits or learned habits, but simply from the normal operation of living systems that are unaware of how they, or more particularly the other systems, work" (p. 292). In this account, our brains are busy sensing and processing various signals on different levels as they strive to control perceptions and regulate experience.

Perhaps the most strident anti-environment sentiment is conveyed in the popular writings of William Glasser (1984), who scolds those with opposing viewpoints: "Nothing we do is caused by what happens outside of us. If we believe that what we do is caused by forces outside of us, we are acting like dead machines, not living people" (p. 1). However, Glasser appears to reverse his thinking in a recent explanation of the World Trade Center attacks, in which the terrorist behavior is seen as satisfying a need for power, and power is said to be equivalent to external forces (Glasser, 2001). Here, external forces are pejoratively linked to human misery: "Throughout recorded history, power has been synonymous with external control. Whether it is a husband attacking a wife or terrorists attacking a city, external control leads to human misery" (p. 1). On this point, there is confusion as to whether the source of the attack is truly external or if the terrorists fell victim to their own harmful inner need for power.

In addition to misattributing an emotion, thought, or other private event as a cause of unacceptable behavior, many people (especially psychologists) use hypothetical constructions to explain the causes of behavior. Examples are "low self-esteem," "poor motivation," and "negative attitude." These latter terms are so commonly used that it is hard to remember that they are inventions; they do not exist as entities, and as such, cannot cause anything. The constructions refer more to patterns of behavior than anything else, and they hint at what a person is likely to do under certain conditions, but they are ultimately traceable to a person's interaction with the environment. As such, they reflect what has happened *to* the person, not what is *inside* the person. If we attempt to find a solution by finding and correcting an inner cause instead of identifying and altering the culpable behavior–environment relationships, we are delaying effective assistance. As popular and appealing as mentalistic accounts may be, they stand in contrast to the more useful behavior-analytic accounts of challenging behavior.

STAFF ATTRIBUTIONS OF PROBLEM BEHAVIOR

A number of researchers have suggested that staff attributions are associated with how staff respond to challenging behavior (Hastings, 1997; Hastings, Remington, & Hopper, 1995). To determine the degree to which staff held mentalistic views about the causes of problem behavior, a modest questionnaire was administered to staff who had direct contact with people who have developmental disabilities and also exhibit aggressive, destructive, or self-injurious behavior. The staff were employed at a multiple-disabilities unit on the grounds of a psychiatric hospital in Staten Island, New York.

The survey was distributed to all direct-care employees at the unit (N = 63). Forty-nine surveys were returned. Respondents were asked to check three of six possible causes of aggressive, destructive, and self-injurious behavior of the people for whom they provided care. Questions were counterbalanced to control for possible position effect. As can be seen in the following list, the second, fourth, and sixth items are representative of mentalistic causes (M); the first, third, and fifth items are representative of behavioristic causes (B). Survey items were constructed arbitrarily, and no psychometric data were available. Each item and number of times it was selected are presented here in the order of greatest to least frequency:

33   The person is reacting to something that has happened. (B)
30   The person needs to release frustration pent up inside. (M)
21   The person behaves this way because of how other people react. (B)
19   Unpleasant memories, thoughts, or feelings go through the person's mind. (M)
12   The problem behavior is a way for the person to control the environment. (B)
11   The person has low self-worth and poor self-esteem. (M)

Overall, 60 mentalistic causes and 66 behavioristic causes were attributed. Nearly all respondents (40 of 42) checked one or more mentalistic attributions. Two respondents checked all behavioristic causes. Thus, it appears that staff who provided treatment in the multiple-disabilities unit believed that a good deal of the source of the aggressive, destructive, and self-injurious behavior of its residents resulted from events occurring inside the person.

These findings are somewhat consistent with the work of McDonnell (1997), who interviewed 81 direct-support staff about their most recent experiences with problematic behavioral incidents and concluded that "a large proportion of staff also classified the causes of incidents in terms of dispositional characteristics of the residents rather than situational factors" (p. 162). Hastings and colleagues (Hastings 1997; Hastings et al., 1995) assessed staff attributions of challenging behavior by using a scenario-based format combined with a checklist. Many of the causes offered by respondents could be classified as mentalistic, although comparative data were not presented as to the relative frequencies of internal and external sources of challenging behavior.

WHY MENTALISM IS COMMON IN THE FIELD OF DEVELOPMENTAL DISABILITIES

Explanations of behavior problems of people with developmental disabilities seem especially vulnerable to mentalistic interpretations because antecedents are often hard to detect, and the topography of the behavior can be unusual (see Foxx, 1996). A person with a developmental disability may not be able to generate a clear verbal account of the circumstances that occasioned the behavior, leaving the first part of the traditional antecedent–behavior–consequence formulation vulnerable to speculative accounts. Because we tend to look toward events that immediately precede behavior as causing it, when antecedents are not obvious, we are likely to attribute the source to an internal event or process. Such attribution is suspected if the problem behavior occurs suddenly and "out of the blue," and it is usually reported as occurring "for no apparent reason." As Hineline (1995) points out, the proclivity to attribute organismic causes under these conditions is associated with the abstract nature of rate, the primary measure of operant responding. "You can look right through a rate; that is, it can be going on right now, even though none of the events that comprise the rate is occurring at this moment. And thus, interpreters of human action commonly ignore diffuse but directly observable events, and instead appeal to impalpable entities, such as mental or presumed physiological processes, as causing overt behavior" (p. 86).

Unfortunately, there is a dearth of applied research examining temporally distant events. A rare demonstration was provided by Gardner, Karan, and Cole (1984), who found that remote antecedents, such as a bad night's sleep, increased the likelihood that certain immediate stimuli would give rise to aggression in the workplace.

Another reason for the apparent vulnerability to mentalistic attribution pertains to the unusual topography of extreme problem behavior by people with developmental disabilities. Behaviors such as pica, air-swallowing, and self-mutilation are atypical response patterns that one might readily assume result from a mind disturbance or brain dysfunction. It is easier to imagine the existence of a structural brain abnormality or dysfunction if the person acts in an atypical manner and also has an atypical physical appearance. Such ascription has technical appeal, as well as convenience, as Skinner's (1974) still-relevant example suggests, "[I]t is simpler to say that 'mental retardates show reactive inhibition' than to examine the defective relation between their behavior and the environments to which they have been exposed" (p. 231).

Still another factor that may tilt explanation of problem behavior of people with developmental disabilities toward an inner source is the notion that aggression results from deficits in processing information or forming cognitive representations (Guerra, Nucci, & Huesmann, 1994). For example, Dodge (1986) proposed that aggression results from deficits in processing social information at any or all of these steps: (a) encoding of social cues, (b) representation and interpretation of cues, (c) response search, (d) response decision, and (e) enactment. These functions are ostensibly mental activities, making it easier to infer that a person with mental retardation would get tripped up at one of these cognitive stages and behave aggressively, particularly if nothing obvious is happening outside of the person to account for the aggression.

AUTHENTIC PHYSICAL STATES RELATED TO BEHAVIOR PROBLEMS

Of course, not all inner states are fictional. For example, we are all familiar with the internal states of fatigue and pain and how they can affect our own behavior, and of course, these body states and conditions also influence the behavior of people with mental retardation. It would be difficult to argue with Russo and Budd's (1987) assertion that various biological factors and syndromes can play a key role in the etiology of severe behavior disorders. Some conditions associated with mental retardation appear to either potentiate or blunt the effects of certain environmental consequences (Gardner & Sovner, 1994). The Lesch-Nyhan syndrome (Lesch & Nyhan, 1964) and Cornelia de Lang syndrome (Berg, 1970; de Lang, 1933) are frequently cited examples of such conditions. More recently, a number of syndromes have been shown to correlate with distinct patterns of aberrant behavior, including fragile X syndrome (Haggerman, 1996), Angelman syndrome (Summers, Allison, Lynch, & Sandler, 1995), Prader-Willi syndrome (Dimitropolis, Feurer, Butler, & Thompson, 2001), and Smith–Magenis syndrome (Finucane, Dirrigl, & Simon, 2001). Through the combined efforts of medical and behavioral researchers, we have reached the point in our assessment and treatment technology that syndrome-based behavioral treatments are accumulating (Dykens, Hodapp, & Finucane, 2000).

In addition to phenotyping or identifying irregular behavior patterns associated with specific syndromes, investigators have linked behavior problems to irregular levels of neurotransmitters such as opiate peptides (Sandman & Hetrick, 1995) and serotonin (Coccaro et al., 1989). These conditions have been treated with medications that affect those neurotransmitter systems, including respective administrations of naltrexone (Sandman et al., 2000) and paroxetine (Davanzo, Belin, Widawski, & King, 1998). Both syndrome-based and neurotransmitter-based treatments are biobehavioral interventions, but the neurotransmitter research provides a clear demonstration of authentic internal events related to problem behavior when the endogenous chemical processes are detected and altered, with corresponding changes in behavior and neurotransmission.

However, despite the technical sophistication of the biobehavioral research, it is difficult to evaluate syndrome-based or neurochemical explanations of severe problem behavior, because even if the existence of a dysfunctional internal state can be reliably demonstrated, it almost always interacts with environmental variables. As concluded by Cataldo and Harris (1982) in their review of biological explanations of self-injury, "No clear evidence has emerged on the biological cause of self-injury in these cases" (p. 34).

Less technical biobehavioral interventions also appear to affect behavior by altering an inner state to which the behavior is related. For example, some investigators have observed changes in aggressive behavior of people with developmental disabilities when temporary physical states were altered with dietary changes. Podboy and Mallery (1977) observed reductions in aggression when caffeine was lowered, and Talkington and Riley (1971) noted increases in aggression after reduction diets were imposed. Although the inner states were not directly measured in these cases, the inference of their existence is likely correct because (a) we know from basic biology that reductions in caffeine and food intake produce physiological changes, and (b) most of us have felt distinct bodily states ourselves under such conditions. (We are calmer after we cut back on coffee and are edgy during a diet.)

It is certain that biological and environmental variables interact and affect behavior, but in rare instances, problem behavior appears to be maintained by an inner state alone. Here, the consequences are not visible, and, as in the case where inconspicuous antecedents give rise to mentalistic explanations of causality, inconspicuous consequences also tend to produce speculation about fictitious mental structures to explain the behavior (Vaughan & Michael, 1982). For example, self-injury might generate an internal effect that automatically reinforces the self-injury, although the veracity of this explanation depends on the extent to which the hypothesized inner cause can be confirmed. Lab reports of unusually high endorphin levels in the blood suggests that a self-generated opiate "high" is maintaining the self-injury, but this hypothesis is confirmed only when both self-injury and endorphin levels decrease following administration of an opiate-blocking drug such as naltrexone. Another example of a likely self-generated reinforcement is a state of dizziness, which was inferred through physiological measures of autonomic functioning during self-injurious air-swallowing (Barrett, McGonigle, Ackles, & Burkhart, 1987). These are interesting but rare examples of severe problem behavior that might be sufficiently explained as a self-sustaining cycle.

INNER-CAUSAL TRAPS

Next I address a few common ways by which practitioners are induced to mis-attribute internal sources as causes of behavior problems, and I discuss harmful effects of the resulting practices. Examples were derived from research literature as well as personal observations while working as an interdisciplinary treatment team member in the role of behavior specialist.

Circular Reasoning

The main point of the preceding section is that if a practitioner believes the source of problem behavior is inside an individual and applies an intervention to alter that source, conclusions about the effect of the intervention on behavior will be weak unless the suspected inner phenomenon is confirmed. However, practitioners and educators sometimes employ techniques that presumably affect complex internal processes believed to be the source of problem behavior, but what is actually measured as the inner source is not appreciably different from what is measured as its perceived result. The practitioner infers the presence or degree of the internal source from the behavior that it is thought to produce when the suspected internal source is difficult or impossible to access. If a treatment that presumably corrects the inner source leads to an improvement in behavior, the improvement is held as evidence that the inner source was corrected.

The story of Raphael described earlier is an example of circular reasoning. A hex was thought to cause rumination, but the existence of the hex was inferred from the rumination. Improvement with food satiation was taken as evidence that the food satiation chased away the hex. Voodoo logic uses circular reasoning that is easily spotted because of the supernatural language used, but circular reasoning can also be detected in cavalier promotions of a technique: "Most people with autism have some sort of noise in their heads," Marilyn stated, "The auditory training program seems to alleviate this problem in varying degrees" (Blatchley, 1994, p. 27). The main problem with such approaches is that any internal mechanism can be posited as causal, and the hypothesis can appear valid with the pseudoconfirmation. Employing techniques based on such rationales might seem harmless, but it diverts time and resources from more fruitful methods of inquiry and delays access to effective treatment.

A more popular intervention typifying circular reasoning is sensory integration therapy (Ayres, 1969, 1979), which is conducted with children and adults with developmental disabilities (see Smith, Mruzek, & Mozingo, chap. 20, this volume). Here, the cause of self-injurious and other difficult-to-manage behavior is assumed to result from either poor nervous system integration or malfunctioning neural pathways in the brain (McGee, 1987). The therapy entails stimulating multiple senses through techniques such as deep physical pressure, brushing and rubbing with objects of different texture, and vestibular stimulation through various movements. Presumably, these techniques repair defective nervous system integration and neural pathways, but what is measured before and after treatment is only behavior. Sensory integration remains in wide use today, despite a literature review that found no evidence that sensory integration produces morphological changes in the nervous system (Arendt, MacLean, & Baumeister, 1988), and a more recent review by Sturmey (2001), who found only one investigation that appeared to demonstrate a reduction in problem behavior from using this method (see also Smith et al., chap. 20, this volume).

The flaw of unverified neurological causation is also apparent in the notion of behavior state conditions, which are said to affect alertness and responsiveness of people with profound physical and cognitive impairments (Guess et al., 1988, 1993). This model further proposes that self-injury and stereotypy are determined by various internally regulated states (Guess & Carr, 1991). However, the internal states are inferred from various observed levels of alertness they are said to cause. For example, self-injury can originate from the "crying/agitated" state, but the definition of this internal state includes the observation "self-injurious behavior possible" (Guess et al., 1993, p. 637). Thus, any correlation between the two would be a comparison of self-injury to self-injury, not self-injury to an internal state. In the case of behavior states, what appears to be the linking of aberrant behavior to biology may be redundant description (Baumeister, 1991).

Subsequent investigations have challenged the procedures and implications of the behavior state model. For example, Mudford, Hogg, and Roberts (1997, 1999) have repeatedly failed to achieve sufficiently reliable interobserver agreement on the definitions of 13 behavior states. Green, Gardner, Canipe, and Reid (1994), using the Guess et. al. (1993) definitions, showed that alertness increased when training programs were instituted, suggesting that alertness was a function of the environment, rather than a manifestation of an internal condition.

The Need to Release

Problem behavior is often misattributed to the release metaphor. It seems reasonable that if behavior originates inside the person, it must somehow exit. Problem behavior is said to *build up inside*, and as if under physical pressure, it can *burst*. Destructive and dangerous actions are called *acting out* behavior. A person exhibiting less intense behavior is *ventilating*, usually through an *outlet*, but a person on the verge of a very intense episode is about to *blow up* or *go off*. Anger is often thought to be the culprit, and like a sneeze that rids the body of an allergen, behaving aggressively or destructively is a way of *getting it out of our system*.

The hazard in the release metaphor is its treatment implications. For example, if aggression is interpreted as a way of expressing anger or releasing tension, a therapist might assume the person should learn anger control, perhaps by rechanneling negative emotions or by practicing tension-reduction techniques. Such strategies are not ineffective per se, but when used alone, they divert attention from establishing operations and environmental variables that occasion and maintain the aggression and destruction. If the conditions responsible for the behavior are not modified, it is likely that the person will continue to act in the same manner, or at best, continue to practice tension-reduction techniques.

An ancient inner causal explanation attributes unusual behavior to demonic possession or evil spirits. It was once popular to practice exorcism on people with mental retardation (Budrikis, 1998). It appears that exorcism is still sometimes practiced for people with developmental disabilities and severe problem behavior after other treatment approaches have failed (D. Clemente, personal communication, June 19,

1998), and if true, it would seem that the practice would be carried out surreptitiously. Occasionally, the dangers of exorcism are exposed in a newspaper or magazine article based on testimony resulting from a lawsuit. For example, a Long Island woman tried to drive a demon from her 17-year-old daughter, Charity, who appeared to be depressed because "a demon would go in and out of her" (McQuiston, 1998, p. B5). Charity died after her mother tried to kill the demon by smothering Charity with a plastic bag. In another account, Krysta, a 3-year-old said to have attachment disorder, died while a nurse was forcing his fist into her abdomen to release her pent-up rage, which was part of her holding therapy to remove the devil (Horn, 1997).

The release metaphor translates to literal release when the source of aggression is thought to be pent-up sexual tension needing discharge. It is not unusual to attribute problem behavior of people with developmental disabilities to an inability to have an orgasm and to consider masturbation as a remedy. Here, the release metaphor seems to pertain more to men than women because ejaculation is eruptive. The question of whether or not the man ejaculates is sometimes addressed in interdisciplinary team meetings in discussion of what to do about his aggression, property destruction, or anxiety. The answer could shed light on a physical problem, but it is not possible for a behavior problem to leave the body.

A graphic and dramatic example of the release metaphor is the notion that some people are prisoners trapped in their own body. This is a very old notion that resurfaced in the facilitated communication (FC) movement (Biklen, 1993; Crossley & McDonald, 1980). In the book *Communication Unbound* (note the metaphor), Biklen (1993) described how people with autism can learn to type messages if the facilitator provides proper physical and emotional support and also perceives the person as a capable learner. The FC movement spread rapidly, aided by dramatic metaphors of release. Following a breakthrough, the person is said to have been freed from a prison of silence or from being trapped in a body the person could not control. Lehr (1992) hints that this trapped person can be detected by the title of her report, *If You Look in Their Eyes You Know: Parents' Perspectives on Facilitated Communication*. The title implies the existence of a visual pathway, perhaps to a location where the entrapped person resides.

Reification

When treatment teams are unable to get behavior under control, it is common to speculate about inner causes and to refer the person to a clinical specialist outside of the team who might confirm their suspicions. I recall an occasion when a treatment team, of which I was a member, could not predict or suppress a person's aggression, so a referral was made to a consulting psychiatrist who detected intermittent explosive disorder (IED). Most members were relieved to hear the diagnosis. They were delighted to know the ostensible cause of the behavior problem and acted as if there was nothing more they could do. In this case, the team fell victim to reification, the practice of regarding something abstract as a real thing. Perhaps an abstraction that materializes into a thing seems more credible as a cause. A closer look at IED reveals a definition that refers to episodes of failing to resist the impulse toward serious assault or property destruction (American Psychiatric Association, 1994). However, this definition is little more than a description of the behavior (with an impulse added) and adds little to what the treatment team already knew. Thus, we reified because we used a description of the behavior to explain its source. Interestingly, McElroy (1999) studied 27 people with IED, some of whom reported internal explanations such as "letting the beast out" and feeling "an adrenaline rush," and a number of subjects reportedly gained control over their impulses by channeling aggression into harmless screaming or punching objects.

Reification is often subtly operating when severe problem behavior is linked to a syndrome. For example, the spoiled child syndrome is said to cause persistent misbehavior (McIntosh, 1989). More dramatically, in the legal defense of Colin Ferguson, the Long Island Railroad killer, William Kunstler argued that black rage was the cause ('Rage' defense, 1994). Similarly, urban survival syndrome was advanced as the source of a teenager's killing in Fort Worth, Texas ('Urban survival,' 1994). These reifications can actually be useful starting points for speculating about the sources of serious problem behavior (e.g., Grier & Cobbs, 1968), but they will misguide treatment efforts if they are viewed as entities that reside inside the person. Most people would agree that these "syndromes" are a result of the person's experiences, but the experiences were not transformed into an entity that menacingly entered the body and now needs attention. The attention should focus on correcting behavior–environment interactions.

CONCLUSION

Environmental accounts of problem behavior do not deny the existence or importance of inner states, such as anxiety and rage, in affecting behavior, but they maintain that the internal state ultimately originates in the environment (except in the rare cases addressed earlier). The practitioner who understands the proper role of the inner state in the causal chain will be in a better position to offer an effective treatment. However, such a practitioner will have to resist persuasions to join the search for more dynamic and colorful reasons for problem behavior, especially severe problem behavior for which the responsible contingencies are nearly imperceptible.

Neurological causation is probably the most prevalent misattribution of severe problem behavior. Perhaps the prestige of neuroscience and brain processes overrides an interest in verification. Nonetheless, verification of an inner state is necessary to confirm the involvement of the suspected internal source. For example, zinc might be administered to treat pica, resulting in cessation of pica (e.g., Lofts, Schroeder, & Maier, 1990), but unless blood tests for trace elements are conducted, one cannot deduce with certainty that low zinc levels are related to the pica.

Mentalism seems to have found a comfortable home in the field of developmental disabilities, but there are inner causal traps to which practitioners of all disciplines are susceptible because they are pervasive in the lay and professional verbal communities alike. The traps described in this chapter include circular reasoning, the need to release, and the propensity to assign a characteristic of a problem behavior to explain its origin. Two or three of these assumptions can blend smoothly together to form a compelling hypothesis, but pseudoexplanations discourage a functional analysis of behavior, and they render the person vulnerable to fruitless therapies, unnecessary medication, and even surgery.

A special problem arises with the mentalistic notion that people are autonomous and responsible for their own actions. If the people who care for those with severe problem behavior believe in the doctrine that one controls one's world with an inner self, they might not support changing environmental contingencies to alter behavior. Instead, a person with problem behavior may undergo numerous internally oriented remedies, and eventually, the person, rather than the contingencies, is likely to be blamed for the behavior. Repeated treatment failures can signify that the person is choosing to be stubborn, lazy, or mean, and team members might conclude that they have done all they can do to change the person's mind. A more compassionate and productive position will guide the search toward the person's interaction with the environment, where the solution can be found.

REFERENCES

American Psychiatric Association. (1994). *Diagnostic and statistical manual of mental disorders* (4th ed.). Washington, DC: American Psychiatric Association.

Anderson, C. M., Hawkins, R. P., Freeman, K. A., & Scotti, J. R. (2000). Private events: Do they belong in a science of human behavior? *The Behavior Analyst, 23*, 1–10.

Arendt, R. E., MacLean, W. E., & Baumeister, A. A. (1988). Critique of sensory integration therapy and its applications in mental retardation. *American Journal on Mental Retardation, 92*, 401–429.

Ayres, A. J. (1969). Deficits in sensory integration in educationally handicapped children. *Journal of Learning Disabilities, 2*, 160–168.

Ayres, A. J. (1979). *Sensory integration and the child*. Los Angeles: Western Psychological services.

Barrett, R. P., McGonigle, J. J., Ackles, P. K., & Burkhart, J. E. (1987). Behavioral treatment of chronic aerophagia. *American Journal on Mental Deficiency, 91*, 620–625.

Baumeister, A. A. (1991). Expanded theories of stereotypy and self-injurious responding: Commentary on "Emergence and maintenance of stereotypy and self-injury." *American Journal on Mental Retardation, 96*, 321–323.

Berg, S. (1970). *The de Lange syndrome*. New York: Pergamon.

Biklen, D. (1993). *Communication unbound: How facilitated communication is challenging traditional views of autism and ability/disability*. New York: Teachers College Press.

Blatchley, D. (1994, January/February). Family care providers who make a difference. *The Journal* (Newsletter), *8*(1), 27.

Branch, N. M. (1987). Behavior analysis: A conceptual and empirical base for behavior therapy. *The Behavior Therapist, 10*, 79–84.

Budrikis, S. (1998). Christians and the mind. [26 paragraphs] *Thinking it through* [On-line serial]. St. Alban's School of Ministry. Available from http://members.iinet.net.au/~stalbans/

Carr, E. G. (1977). The motivation of self-injurious behavior: A review of some hypotheses. *Psychological Bulletin, 84*, 800–816.

Cataldo, F. C., & Harris, J. (1982). The biological basis of self-injury in the mentally retarded. *Analysis and Intervention in Developmental Disabilities, 2*, 21–39.

Coccaro, E. F., Seiver, L. J., Howard, M. K., Maurer, G., Cochrane, K., Cooper, T. B., et al. (1989). Serotonergic studies in patients with affective disorders. *Archives of General Psychiatry, 46*, 587–599.

Crossley, R., & McDonald, A. (1980). *Annie's coming out*. New York: Penguin.

Davanzo, P. A., Belin, T. R., Widawski, M. H., & King, B. (1998). Paroxetine treatment of aggression and self-injury in persons with mental retardation. *American Journal of Mental Retardation, 102*, 427–437.

Day, W. (1983). On the difference between radical and methodological behaviorism. *Behaviorism, 11*, 89–102.

de Lang, C. (1933). Sur un type nouveau de degeneration (Typus Amstelodamensis). *Archives de Medicine des Enfants, 36*, 713–719.

Dimitropolis, A., Feurer, I. D., Butler, ?., & Thompson, T. (2001). Emergence of compulsive behavior and tantrums in children with Prader-Willi syndrome. *American Journal on Mental Retardation, 106,* 39–51.

Dodge, K. A. (1986). A social information processing model of social competence in children. In M. Perlmutter (Ed.), *Minnesota symposium on child psychology* (Vol. 18, pp. 77–125). Hillsdale, NJ: Lawrence Erlbaum Associates.

Durand, V. M., & Crimmins, D. B. (1992). *The Motivational Assessment Scale (MAS) administration guide.* Topeka, KS: Monaco & Associates.

Dykens, E. M., Hodapp, R. M., & Finucane, B. (2000). *Genetics and mental retardation syndromes: A new look at behavior and treatment.* Baltimore: Brookes.

Finucane, B., Dirrigl, K. H., & Simon, E. W. (2001). Characterization of self-injurious behaviors in children and adults with Smith-Magenis syndrome. *American Journal of Mental Retardation, 106,* 52–58.

Foxx, R. M. (1996). Twenty years of applied behavior analysis in treating the most severe problem behavior: Lessons learned. *The Behavior Analyst, 19,* 225–235.

Friman, P. C., Hayes, S. C., & Wilson, K. G. (1998). Why behavior analysts should study emotion: The example of anxiety. *Journal of Applied Behavior Analysis, 31,* 137–156.

Gardner, W. I., Karan, O. C., & Cole, C. L. (1984). Assessment of setting events influencing functional capacities of mentally retarded adults with behavioral difficulties. In A. S. Halpern & M. J. Fuhrer (Eds.), *Functional assessment in rehabilitation* (pp. 171–185). Baltimore: Brookes.

Gardner, W. I., & Sovner, R. (1994). *Self-injurious behaviors: A multimodal approach.* Willow Street, PA: Vida.

Glasser, W. (1984). *Control theory: A new explanation of how we control our lives.* New York: Harper & Row.

Glasser, W. (2001). *A message from Dr. Glasser, September 14, 2001.* Chatsworth, CA: The William Glasser Institute, 22024 Lassen Street, Suite 118, 91311. Accessed on-line at http://www.wglasserinst.com/dr.htm

Green, C. W., Gardner, S. M., Canipe, V. S., & Reid, D. H. (1994). Analyzing alertness among people with profound multiple disabilities: Implications for provision of training. *Journal of Applied Behavior Analysis, 27,* 519–531.

Grier, W. H., & Cobbs, P. M. (1968). *Black rage.* New York: Basic Books.

Guerra, N. G., Nucci, L., & Huesmann, ?. (1994). Moral cognition and childhood aggression. In R. Huesmann (Ed.), *Aggressive Behavior: Current Perspectives* (pp. 13–33). New York: Plenum.

Guess, D., & Carr, E. (1991). Emergence and maintenance of stereotopy and self-injury. *American Journal of Mental Retardation, 96,* 299–319.

Guess, D., Mulligan-Ault, M., Roberts, S., Struth, J., Seigel-Causey, E., Thompson, B., Bronicki, G. B., et al. (1988). Implications of biobehavioral states for the education and treatment of students with the most profoundly handicapping conditions. *Journal of the Association for Persons with Severe Handicaps, 13,* 163–174.

Guess, D., Roberts, S., Seigel-Causey, E., Ault, M., Guy, B., Thompson, B., et al. (1993). Analysis of behavior state conditions and associated environmental variables among students with profound handicaps. *American Journal on Mental Retardation, 97,* 634–653.

Haggerman, R. J. (1996). Physical and behavioral phenotype. In R. J. Haggerman & A. Cronister (Eds.), *Fragile X syndrome: Diagnosis, treatment, and research* (2nd ed.), (pp. 3–87). Baltimore: Johns Hopkins University Press.

Hastings, R. P. (1997). Measuring staff perceptions of challenging behavior: The challenging behavior attributions scale (CHABA). *Journal of Intellectual Disability Research, 41,* 495–501.

Hastings, R. P., Remington, B., & Hopper, G. M. (1995). Experienced and inexperienced health care workers beliefs about challenging behaviors. *Journal of Intellectual Disability Research, 39,* 474–483.

Hineline, P. N. (1995). The origins of environmental-based psychological theory. In J. T. Todd & E. K. Morris (Eds.), *Perspectives on B. F. Skinner and contemporary behaviorism* (pp. 85–106). Westport, CT: Greenwood Press.

Holburn, C. S., & Dougher, M. (1986). The application of response satiation procedures in the treatment of air-swallowing. *American Journal of Mental Deficiency, 91*, 72–77.

Horn, M. (1997, July). A dead child, a troubling defense. *U.S. News & World Report*, 26–28.

Iwata, B. A., Dorsey, M. F., Slifer, K. J., Bauman, K. E., & Richman, G. S. (1982). Toward a functional analysis of self-injury. *Analysis and Intervention in Developmental Disabilities, 2*, 3–20.

Jackson, G. M., Johnson, C. R., Ackron, G. S., & Crowley, R. (1975). Food satiation as a procedure to decelerate vomiting. *American Journal of Mental Deficiency, 80*, 223–227.

Kume, H. (1989). *Statistical methods for quality improvement.* Tokyo: 3A Corporation.

Lehr, S. (1992). *If you look in their eyes you know: Parents' perspectives on facilitated communication* [Report]. Syracuse, NY: Facilitated Communication Institute.

Lesch, M., & Nyhan, W. (1964). A familial disorder of uric acid metabolism and central nervous system function. *American Journal of Medicine, 36*, 561–570.

Lofts, R. H., Schroeder, S. R., & Maier, R. H. (1990). Effects of serum zinc supplementation on pica behavior of persons with mental retardation. *American Journal of Mental Retardation, 95*, 103–109.

Lorenz, K. (1966). *On aggression.* New York: Harcourt, Brace, & World.

McDonnell, A. (1997). Training care staff to manage challenging behaviour: An evaluation of a three day training course. *British Journal of Developmental Disabilities, 43*, 156–162.

McElroy, S. (1999). Recognition and treatment of DSM-IV intermittent explosive disorder. *Journal of Clinical Psychiatry, 60*, 12–16.

McGee, M. (1987). The motor aspects of behavior disorders in mentally retarded individuals: A neuro-developmental approach. In J. A. Mulick & R. Antonak (Eds.), *Transitions in mental retardation: Vol. 2. Issues in therapeutic intervention* (pp. 179–188). Norwood NJ: Ablex.

McIntosh, B. J. (1989). Spoiled child syndrome. *Pediatrics, 83*(1), 108–115.

McQuiston, J. T. (1998). Sister of dead Long Island teen-ager offers account of killing in exorcism. *New York Times*, p. B5.

Moore, J. (1981). On mentalism, methodological behaviorism, and radical behaviorism. *Behaviorism, 9*, 55–78.

Mudford, O. C., Hogg, J., & Roberts, J. (1997). Interobserver agreement and disagreement in continuous recording exemplified by measurement of behavior state. *American Journal of Mental Retardation, 102*, 54–66.

Mudford, O. C., Hogg, J., & Roberts, J. (1999). Behavior states: Now you see them, now you don't. *American Journal on Mental Retardation, 104*, 385–391.

O'Neill, R. E., Horner, R. H., Albin, R. W., Storey, K., & Sprague, J. R. (1990). *Functional analysis of problem behavior. A practical assessment guide.* Sycamore, IL: Sycamore.

Pfadt, A., & Wheeler, D. J. (1995). Using statistical process control to make data-based clinical decisions. *Journal of Applied Behavior Analysis, 28*, 349–370.

Podboy, J. W., & Mallery, W. A. (1977). Caffeine reduction and behavior change in the severely retarded. *Mental Retardation, 15*(6), 40.

Powers, W. T. (1992). *Living control systems II.* New Canaan, CT: Benchpress.

'Rage' defense for LIRR killer. (1994, April 11). *The Staten Island Advance*, p. 11.

Rast, J., Johnston, J. M., Drum, C., & Conrin, J. (1981). The relation of food quantity to rumination behavior. *Journal of Applied Behavior Analysis, 14*, 121–130.

Repp, A. C., Felce, D., & Barton, L. E. (1988). Basing treatment of stereotypic and self-injurious behaviors on hypotheses of their causes. *Journal of Applied Behavior Analysis, 21*, 281–289.

Russo, D. C., & Budd, K. S. (1987). Limitations of operant practice in the study of disease. *Behavior Modification, 11*, 264–285.

Sandman, C. A., & Hetrick, W. P. (1995). Opiate mechanisms in self-injury. *Mental Retardation and Developmental Disabilities Research Review, 1*, 130–136.

Sandman, C. A., Hetrick, W., Taylor, D. V., Touchette, P., Baron, J. L., Martinezzi, V., et al. (2000). Long term effects of naltrexone on self-injurious behavior. *American Journal of Mental Retardation, 105*, 103–117.

Schroeder, S. R. (Ed.). (1990). *Ecobehavioral analysis and developmental disabilities: The twenty-first century.* New York: Springer-Verlag.

Schroeder, S. R., Kanoy, J. R., Mulick, J. A., Rojahn, J., Thios, S. J., Stephens, M., et al. (1982). Environmental antecedents which affect management and maintenance of programs for self–injurious behavior. In J. C. Hollis & C. E. Myers (Eds.), *Life-threatening behavior* (Monograph No. 5, pp. 105–159). Washington, DC: American Association on Mental Deficiency.

Skinner, B. F. (1953). *Science and human behavior.* New York: Macmillan.

Skinner, B. F. (1964). Behaviorism at fifty. In T. W. Wann (Ed.), *Behaviorism and Phenomenology* (pp. 79–108). Chicago: University of Chicago Press.

Skinner, B. F. (1972). *Beyond freedom and dignity.* New York: Knopf.

Skinner, B. F. (1974). *About behaviorism.* New York: Knopf.

Skinner, B. F. (1986). Is it behaviorism? *The Behavioral and Brain Sciences, 9,* 716.

Storr, A. (1968). *The territorial imperative.* New York: Antheneum.

Sturmey, P. (1991). Assessing challenging behavior using semi-structured behavioral interviews: A case transcript. *Mental Handicap, 19,* 56–90.

Sturmey, P. (2001, March). *Chronic aberrant behavior: Research-based intervention.* Invited address at the 34th Annual Gatlinberg Conference on Research in Mental Retardation and Developmental Disabilities, Charleston, SC.

Summers, J. A., Allison, D. B., Lynch, P. S., & Sandler, L. (1995). Behavior problems in Angelman Syndrome. *Journal of Intellectual Disability Research, 32,* 97–106.

Talkington, L., & Riley, J. (1971). Reduction diets and aggression in institutionalized mentally retarded patients. *American Journal of Mental Deficiency, 76,* 370–372.

Torrey, E. F. (1972). *The mind game: Witch doctors and psychiatrists.* New York: Emerson Hall.

Touchette, P. E., MacDonald, R. F., & Langer, S. N. (1985). A scatter plot for identifying stimulus control of problem behavior. *Journal of Applied Behavior Analysis, 18,* 343–351.

'Urban Survival' drove teens to kill, attorneys claim. (1994, April 15). *Syracuse Herald Journal,* pp. A9–A10.

Van Houten, R., & Rolider, A. (1991). Applied behavior analysis. In J. L. Matson & J. A. Mulick (Eds.), *Handbook of mental retardation* (2nd ed., pp. 569–585). New York: Pergamon.

Vaughan, M. E., & Michael, J. L. (1982). Automatic reinforcement: An important but ignored concept. *Behaviorism, 10,* 217–227.

Severe Aggressive and Self-Destructive Behavior: The Myth of the Nonaversive Treatment of Severe Behavior

Richard M. Foxx
Penn State Harrisburg

> *Severe*—Causing distress, especially physical discomfort or pain
> —Merriam-Webster Dictionary (1974)

In the spring of 1991, the Mental Retardation and Developmental Disabilities Branch of the National Institute of Child Health and Development (NICHD) sponsored a conference hosted by the Institute for Disabilities Studies of the University of Minnesota. The conference brought experts together to discuss the diagnosis and treatment of destructive behavior in developmental disabilities. The conference was an extension of the 1989 National Institutes of Health (NIH) Consensus Development Conference (see Foxx, chap. 28, this volume).

My presentation featured a videotape and 18 months follow-up data documenting the successful multifaceted 24-hour treatment of an extremely dangerous 36-year-old man. His most common and dangerous form of aggression was biting others, which had left his victims with permanent scarring and physical damage (e.g., someone lost the end of a finger). The treatment program was comprehensive and included all of the factors recommended in the NIH Consensus Statement (1991), namely, functional analysis, a hypothesis-driven treatment model, choice making, an evaluation of skill deficits and environmental situations, methods for enhancing desired behaviors including social ones, and community integration. It also included contingent shock and the procedure had received the appropriate informed consent and professional and legal review for its use.

Shortly before the conference, I was contacted by one of the organizers and told that there was concern that if I spoke on the topic of shock that the conference would be picketed by the Minnesota Chapter of The Association for the Severely Handicapped (TASH). I replied that I would not attend if my topic was restricted. My invitation was not rescinded, I spoke, there was no picket, and my talk was published in the proceedings book (Foxx, Zukotynski, & Williams, 1994).

I began my talk by expressing a frustration with this conference and previous ones (National Institute of Disability and Rehabilitation Research, 1987; NIH, 1989) regarding the use of the term *severe* or *destructive*. I stressed that the definition of *severe* behavior problems used by me and others who had used aversive or punishment procedures (e.g., Carr & Lovaas, 1983; Foxx, 1991, 2003; Linscheid, Iwata, Ricketts, Williams, & Griffin, 1990; Lovaas & Favell, 1987; Mulick, 1990a, 1990b) was quite different from the one used by the nonaversive movement practitioners (e.g., LaVigna & Donnellan, 1986). Hence, we actually differed not only on what possibly may be needed for successful treatment but also on what constituted severe behavior problems. I pointed out that while the treatment controversy was championed by the nonaversive movement devotees (Foxx, chap. 28, this volume; Newsom & Kroeger, chap. 24, this volume), they had not raised or addressed the definitional division (Mulick, 1990a). The reason was obvious: To do so would expose the fact that whereas nonaversive movement proponents might agree that severe behavior problems could be characterized by repeated hospitalizations, high dosages of neuroleptics, and severe tissue damage to oneself or others, when criticizing the use of aversives/punishment, they were not treating such *severe* behavior problems (LaVigna & Donnellan, 1986). I also pointed out that as in previous conferences, much of the discussion concerned children and milder forms of self-injurious behavior as opposed to adults and dangerous aggression and self-injury. I noted that adults who display dangerous aggression toward others are perhaps the most undertreated of all populations because persons providing treatment are at risk (Foxx et al., 1994). With each conference, it was becoming clearer to me that a myth was being promulgated, reinforced, and utilized, both coercively (Foxx, chap. 28, this volume) and with ever increasing sophistication (Foxx; 1998b; Jacobson & Mulick, 2000; Mulick & Butter, chap. 23, this volume).

This chapter concentrates on the coercive perpetuation of the myth and concludes by briefly addressing its sophisticated promulgation.

THE MYTH

The most virulent of the antipunishment, nonaversive, positive approaches professional proponents (e.g., LaVigna & Donnellan, 1986; Meyer & Evans, 1989) have coercively and actively promoted a myth, namely, that all severe behavior problems can be treated without aversive consequences (Axelrod, 1990). Consider, for example, this sweeping generalization: "[T]here is a great deal of evidence that nonaversive approaches have equal or greater empirical validity than the alternatives. They are more likely to result in significant and lasting behavior changes that are reflective of worthwhile outcomes" (Meyer & Evans, 1989, p. 4).

Several factors work to support this myth. One, nonaversive proponents are opposed to "segregated/restrictive" settings and therefore would not deign to provide treatment in these settings even though most of the individuals with truly severe behavior problems reside there, even today. That is not to say that they won't consult in restricted settings for a substantial fee and recommend a very expensive elaborate intervention that in all likelihood will be not be implemented because of its prohibitive expense and logistical barriers. This, of course, provides the perfect out: My plan would have worked, but the agency wouldn't fund it. (This same open checkbook rational is utilized by positive behavior support adherents. If the program fails, we simply need more supports.) Yet, even when such a program is implemented for a single individual at a cost nearing a million dollars per year, the severe behavior problems may not be treated successfully (Paisey, Whitney, Hislop, & Wainczak, 1991).

Two, because a myth is a belief "given uncritical acceptance by a group" (Donnellan & LaVigna, 1990, p. 50), the myth has a narcotic-like effect on all of the major advocacy groups and reinforces their militancy regarding "aversives" and those who use them (Foxx, chap. 28, this volume; Guess, Helmsteller, Turnbull, & Knowlton, 1987). As Hoffer (1951) stated in discussing mass movements, "Contrary to what one would expect, propaganda becomes more fervent and importunate when it operates in conjunction with coercion than when it has to rely solely on its own effectiveness" (p. 106). Hence, as long as one uses the terms *severe* and *nonaversive*, no one is asking for a definition. This, of course, is why the nonaversive movement has been more effective with governments and politicians than courts. Courts rely on data and definitions (Royko, 1986; Sherman, 1991) whereas agencies such as National Institute on Disability and Rehabilitation Research (NIDRR) in the U.S. Department of Education have demonstrated repeatedly that they put their money where the myth is. All one need do is look at who and what they fund and don't fund.

Another way the myth is perpetuated is by a susceptible audience in the new generation of community providers and funding agencies, who have very little appreciation for empirical validation because of their support of deprofessionalization (another advocacy group goal), which means that there is no one in most agencies with enough expertise to evaluate treatment claims. Furthermore, a philosophical orientation, characterized as political correctness embedded in a social values ideology that borders on fanaticism (Foxx, 1994), dictates that the major community regulatory and funding sources mandate nonaversive approaches.

All of these events, as well as the very legitimate concerns associated with the use of aversive procedures (Foxx, 1982, 1996a , 1996b, 2001; Foxx & Bechtel, 1983; Foxx, Bittle, & Faw, 1989; Foxx & Livesay, 1984; Foxx, Plaska, & Bittle, 1986; Lovaas & Favell, 1987; Mulick, 1990b; Newsom & Kroeger, chap. 24, this volume), have created fertile ground for the belief that truly severe behavior problems can always be treated nonaversively. This ground has been widely planted with books and workshops attacking the use of punishment and tying its use to dehumanization and segregated settings (LaVigna & Donnellan, 1986; Meyer & Evans, 1989).

A BIT OF HISTORY

The most vociferous myth perpetuators have been Donnellan, LaVigna, and Meyer. Evidence of their success can be seen in the NIH consensus conference since one of Carr, Taylor, Carlson, and Robinson's (1991) five recommendations was that "it may be useful to combine several positive approaches in order to produce a compressive treatment intervention. To date, only a few studies have employed this strategy (Berkman & Meyer, 1988; Donnellan, LaVigna, Zambito, & Thvedt, 1985; Heidorn & Jensen, 1984). In every case, outcome data were encouraging" (p. 228). Indeed, Donnellan et al. (1985) and Berkman and Meyer (1988) have long been touted as providing clear evidence for the effectiveness of nonaversive intervention for severe behavior. Heidorn and Jensen (1984) have not, possibly because their research was institution based or because they are not affiliated with any nonaversive research or advocacy group. Because Linscheid and Landau (1993) have already discussed in detail that Berkman and Meyer (1988) failed to acknowledge the relation between the use of large amounts of Thorazine and their "going all out nonaversively" treatment success with severe behavior, I focus primarily on Donnellan and LaVigna's role in the myth. This is followed by a brief discussion of Meyer's role. I conclude with a discussion of the current and more scientifically sophisticated extensions of the myth.

DONNELLAN, LaVIGNA, AND THE TREATMENT OF "SEVERE" BEHAVIOR

The application of the principles of behavior analysis to populations with developmental disabilities, which began in the early 1960s, created the conditions and outcomes that led to the right to education laws, right to treatment laws, and deinstitutionalization. The Association for Behavior Analysis (ABA) is the world's leading behavior analytical organization. In 1988, ABA published a task force report on the right to effective behavioral treatment (Van Houten et al., 1988). Donnellan and LaVigna (1990) described the task force report as "not so different from *Malleus maleficarum* (Kramer & Spranger, 1486/1971), outlining for the inquisition the procedural safeguards to assure that each accused heretic had an opportunity to respond to less intrusive means" (pp. 51–52). The report also was criticized as defending "segregation and institutional placements and the use of aversives within those placements"(p. 51).

The task force was chided for writing more of an encyclical than a scientific paper as ABA "is a good example of how a scientific group, challenged on its basic and dearly held beliefs, begins to operate in ways more similar to religious hierarchies than a group dedicated to open scientific inquiry" (p. 51). Much was made of how behavior analysts value mythology over science in their assertion that what is effective in the treatment of severe behavior problems, such as aggression, self-injury, and pica, may include punishment. For Donnellan and LaVigna (1990), "nonaversive, multielement treatment packages are showing promise in solving even the most difficult problems (Donnellan, LaVigna, Zambito, & Thevedt, 1985) and are rendering the use of punishment unnecessary and in many ways counterproductive (Berkman & Meyer, 1988; LaVigna, 1988)" (p. 44).

Indeed, Donnellan et al. (1985) and the book *Alternatives to Punishment: Solving Behavior Problems With Non-Aversive Strategies* (LaVigna & Donnellan, 1986) were considered by many advocacy groups, advocacy attorneys, and some organizations (e.g., TASH) as the gold standard in the advancement and support of the ideological agenda against aversives, punishment, and in more recent times, behavior analysis. Furthermore, these authors continue to cite these writings as evidence of their expertise with severe behavior in their written reports and testimony in court cases (Donnellan & LaVigna, 1990; LaVigna, 1998).

I now examine Donnellan and LaVigna's challenge and assertions about the treatment of severe behavior problems. Several conclusions are reached. One, people who live in a glass house and have transparent agendas should not throw stones. Two, when it comes to religious fervor, ignoble efforts, and encyclicals, Donnellan and LaVigna provide convincing support for the Freudian defensive mechanism of projection. Three, the real myth is that these individuals have ever convincingly demonstrated in any reliable, peer-reviewed work that they have ever successfully treated *severe* behavior problems as defined by anyone not belonging to a nonaversive advocacy group.

One of the problems in attempting to examine Donnellan and LaVigna's research in support of their model is that very little exists. Most of their citations are to their own books, chapters, unpublished works, and conference presentations (e.g., LaVigna, 1988). Consider that LaVigna's vitae in 1998 (available to me because we were opposing expert witnesses) revealed that in a 25-year career, he published three articles, two coauthored with Donnellan, in what might be described as "peer-reviewed" journals. Perhaps this absence of exposure to peer review may help explain Donnellan and LaVigna's willingness to adopt some of the extreme positions (or beliefs) that individuals who believe in the peer review system find so, to put it delicately, puzzling.

Consider for example, Spitz's critical comments on Donnellan's other writings in support of facilitated communication. Spitz (1994) stated:

> Apparently, Donnellan's science allows her to believe almost anything. Haskew and Donnellan (1993) wrote: "Shortly after facilitation begins ... facilitators often report that their communicators have an uncanny ability to know thoughts in their facilitators' minds" (p. 13). They attributed this up to a "sixth sense" that allows the person being facilitated to "understand what others think, feel, or know, and to transmit their own thoughts to other nonverbal acquaintances and sometimes to their facilitators" (p. 13). This sixth sense is ubiquitous. Haskew and Donnellan noted that "Reports that facilitated communicators seem to be able to read their facilitators' and other people's minds surface wherever facilitation is attempted. We have reports from dozens of sources in several countries, and the numbers continued to grow" (p. 13). (p. 99)

Perhaps, if one does not seek peer review, one does not value it. For example, LaVigna offered his opinion of peer review in regard to the recommendations of the NIH Consensus Development Conference on the treatment of destructive behaviors (Foxx, chap. 28, this volume). Although the preliminary statement issued in the name of the scientists on the consensus panel was by no means an overwhelming endorsement of the use of aversives or contingent shock, LaVigna was quoted in *Science* (Holden, 1990) as stating that there was no research demonstrating its effectiveness. Donnellan (1989) expressed similar sentiments, for example, that the report "misrepresents the present state of the art and science" (p. 2).

My examination of their writings begins with a critical analysis of Donnellan et al. (1985), followed by other reviews of LaVigna and Donnellan (1986) and a brief review of LaVigna, Willis, and Donnellan (1989), and concludes with a look at how they consult "on truly severe behaviors."

Donnellan et al. (1985)

No one knowledgeable about the aversives controversy (e.g., Newsom & Kroeger, chap. 24, this volume) was surprised that the editorial process of *The Journal of the*

Association for Persons with Severe Handicaps (JASH) looked beyond this article's methodological shortcomings and treatment of nonsevere behavior because it supported TASH's philosophical position (Foxx, 1998a; Mulick, 1990b). Indeed, JASH also published Berkman and Meyer (1988). Both were published on the basis of ideological rather than clinical or scientific merit.

Regarding meeting TASH's ideological litmus test, consider that intervention specialists described in Donnellan et al. (1985) were selected on the basis of their commitment to community integration and willingness to be trained in accordance with the philosophy of positive programming and nonpunitive interventions. Indeed, the word *punitive* was used to describe intensive behavior management for severe problems in highly restrictive, institutional settings.

Who were the subjects? Thirteen of the 16 lived at home, 2 in group homes, and 1 in a 60-bed facility. They were selected on the basis of the severity of their behavior "as measured by the potential for damage or injury" and their "level of basic communication and self-care skills" (p. 124). Of the 16, one was 3½, three were 10 years old or under, ten were adolescents, one was 34, and one was 56. Nine were labeled autistic, one with moderate mental retardation (MR), one brain damaged, one mild to moderate MR, one mild to borderline MR, one unknown MR, and one hyperactive.

How severe was their behavior? Although the title stated that the intervention was for severe behavior problems, the manifest behaviors obviously were not (Foxx, 1996b, 1998a, chap. 28, this volume). The baseline frequencies of 11 subjects were fewer than 10 behavior occurrences per week. Two had frequencies of 12 and 14 behaviors per week and the three whose target behaviors exceeded 14 per week had target behaviors that included opening a door and going outside without permission, moving furniture, sticking a tongue out at people, and getting into cupboards. Yet, these and the other subjects were described as being in crisis and likely to be institutionalized "without a dramatic behavior change" (p. 124). Other target behaviors included leaving a bedroom, turning over objects, seeking attention, spitting (two subjects), hyperventilating, putting hands in pants, mouthing objects, hitting and kicking (at a baseline frequency of 0.7 times per week), displaying aggression (once per week), displaying aggression toward others (slightly over once a day), and self-injurious behavior (SIB), that is, hitting, biting, and pinching (less than once per day).

The quasi-experimental design was A-B-C with a single target behavior where A was baseline, B was intervention, and C was follow-up. This design provides no information about what the natural course of the behavior would have been had no intervention occurred (Wolf & Risley, 1971), does not answer whether some unidentified variable coincided with the intervention and actually accounted for the observed changes, can be influenced of a host of confounding variables, and results in rather weak conclusions (Hersen & Barlow, 1978).

The outcomes for two subjects were especially revealing. Subject 3, who was not "successfully treated" for his low frequency SIB, was taken from his natural home and placed in a group home. Not only was he a treatment failure, but he showed an increase in his target behaviors! The parents of Subject 2, who had the highest rate of behavior, over 140 times of opening the door and going outside without permission each week, were described in the section on Consumer Satisfaction as discontinuing the intervention program in the follow-up.

The study had a number of additional shortcomings. Despite having a clinical psychologist and three full-time graduate-level staff (or one professional for every four clients), follow-ups were conducted by telephone, interrater reliability assessments could not be conducted on everyone, and follow-ups were very short. Despite the emphasis on positive approaches, no in-depth reinforcer analysis was conducted. Rather, the mediators were interviewed to determine possible reinforcers to use. There was no information about generalization.

LaVigna and Donnellan (1986)

Naturally, there was great interest in the claims made in LaVigna and Donnellan's *Alternatives to Punishment: Solving Behavior Problems With Non-Aversive Strategies* (1986) in regard to severe behavior problems, and the book was reviewed by a number of professionals specializing in behavior analysis and developmental disabilities. There was clear consensus on a number of points.

Severity of Behavior Addressed.   Bailey (1987): "[I]t takes a discriminating and experienced reader to realize that the positive programming options being presented almost never relate to *severe* [italics original] behavior problems at all" (p. 572). Mulick and Linscheid (1988): "Given the book's intended emphasis on the severely handicapped, we were surprised that so many of the examples were about verbal youngsters in fairly integrated community environments having more or less minor behavior problems. Examples in the book pertained to non-injurious stereotypy (numerous examples), inappropriate verbalizations including 'knock-knock' jokes (pp. 99–101), or off-task behavior in school and mild classroom disruptions which are not sequentially related to more dangerous behavior (numerous examples) (p. 318).

Wieseler (1988), a psychologist at the Faribault Regional Center in Minnesota, a facility discussed by Donnellan and LaVigna (1990), stated: "[T]he cases presented constitute neither the severe problem behaviors that practitioners frequently encounter nor do they contain elements of the scientific rigor essential to demonstrating the effectiveness of procedures" (p. 323).

Axelrod (1987) asked these questions: (a) "[C]ould they [LaVigna and Donnellan] repeatedly provide examples of how the extreme self-injurious or aggressive behavior of severely retarded or autistic individuals could be reduced" and (b) "[C]ould they provide a level of technology that can reasonably be expected to exist at the majority of facilities?" (p. 244). His answer to both of these questions was "No." He found a number of crucial shortcomings. "First a large portion of the book deals with either mild management problems or minimally impaired individuals. Second, the authors frequently used a high technology approach whose cost and technical skill requirements are not always realistic" (p. 244). At various points, "they indicate that their technology can be applied to serious problems exhibited by severely and profoundly impaired learners. I am unconvinced that the latter could be done" (p. 250).

What is perhaps the greatest irony is that those of us who have and do use punishment procedures responsibly would never consider their use with the behaviors that Donnellan and LaVigna treat.

Empirical Support.   Mulick and Linscheid (1988): "The authors had no compunc-
tion about giving the impression of empirical support for their positions by creative
and liberal use of citations. For example, some of our own research was used, without explanation to the reader about how it might apply by extension or logic to support points the study did not really address. In other instances, assertions are
supported with citations to unpublished papers and conference reports which the
reader cannot obtain for independent verification" (pp. 319–320). "Playing fast and
loose with citations, in this manner gives the impression of empirical support where
there is in fact little or none. Unfortunately, the naive reader, such as a beginning
student, parent or non-professional advocate, lack familiarity with the literature
and the easy access to primary citations required to catch them at this game" (p.
320). They concluded "the book has weakness in terms of its scholarship, interpretation of scientific phenomena, and accuracy" (p. 320).

Axelrod (1987) stated that "the book is not one of high scientific merit. It was common to see several consecutive pages of recommendations without relevant citations or with no citations at all. Graphs of data were seldom presented; instead, the
reader had to rely on the conclusions of the authors" (p. 244). They did not "provide
sufficient evidence of offering an effective and feasible technology that resulted in
long-term gains for learners who exhibit serious behavior problems" (p. 244).

LaVigna, Willis, and Donnellan (1989)

This chapter was written for a book on treatment of severe behavior disorders by behavior analysis (sic) approaches. It contains several cases as examples but no published citations to the cases. Regarding severity, one case is a 14-year-old teenager
who hit his teacher an average of once an hour during a 6-hour day. Another is a
young boy who smeared his saliva over shiny surfaces. Yet another is an 18-year-old
who displayed 1.71 episodes of aggression per week! No conclusions can be drawn
regarding what may have been a severe behavior, the high rate of pica of a
6-year-old boy, because the behavior was undefined and no numbers were presented. Nevertheless, the authors concluded, "The researcher's role is clear: to further develop and validate treatment procedures" (p. 81).

Donnellan and LaVigna, 1990

In Donnellan and LaVigna (1990), there is a discussion of the review of patient MU
and the use of contingent shock for the Minnesota Court Monitor (Donnellan &
Negri-Shoultz, 1986). MU was extremely self-injurious and restraint dependent. In
1979, his thumb was amputated due to an infection as a result of his picking at his
thumb with his forefinger while in four-point restraint. His emesis (vomiting) was
so severe in the early 1970s that he had severe weight loss and dehydration. Contingent shock was used successfully in 1975–1976 and 1978–1979 to treat life-threatening emesis (Bruel, Fielding, Joyce, Peters, & Weisler, 1982). I recommended
contingent shock in 1983 to treat multiple forms of severe self-injury and consulted
on the case for several years. Prior to recommending a treatment program that included contingent shock, I evaluated MU on several days on several occasions.

The Minnesota facility's response to the Court Monitor and Donnellan & Negri-Shoultz report (Sauferer, 1986) stated that Dr. Donnellan and her assistant conducted an on-site visit that consisted of observing MU for a total of 30 minutes and subsequently produced a voluminous report of over 274 pages exclusive of references and appendices.

LaVigna assessed and developed an intervention plan for MU in the spring of 1987. His review was based on brief observations of MU, interviews of staff, and a review of historical documents including Donnellan & Negri-Shoultz (1986). He offered the following services from his Institute for Applied Behavior Analysis (LaVigna, 1987; all figures are in 1987 dollars): General training staff training $25,000; on-site training $5,000; monthly on-site consulting $3,000 per month. Also recommended was immediate purchase of an apartment for MU. He included a copy of Donnellan et al., 1985, because "Based on work carried out in California, (see attached reprint), Intensive Intervention has proven to be a viable way to solve the most serious problems in the least restrictive settings" (p. 37). Apparently, his offer was not accepted (Donnellan & LaVigna, 1990).

Berkman and Meyer (1988)

I now examine some of Meyer's efforts in coercively perpetuating the myth. As noted earlier, Berkman and Meyer's (1988) article was frequently cited as demonstrating the effectiveness of positive approaches and in attacks on the use of aversive procedures. It appears that truly severe behavior was being treated, given the description of the individual's SIB and a 1200-mg. daily dosage of Thorazine. However, Linscheid and Landau (1993) reexamined the article and the validity of its conclusions.

Berkman and Meyer (1988) attributed reductions in their client's SIB to their intervention of "going all out nonaversively," and appeared to rule out medication as being responsible as they reported that medication was held constant. However, Linscheid and Landau (1993) obtained the medication records via a court case which indicated "that a) Berkman and Meyer incorrectly reported their client's medication status during their intervention and b) there appears to be a relation between the introduction of Thorazine (with subsequent increases in dosage) and reduction in the client's SIB" (p. 1).

In their response to Lincheid and Landau (1993) regarding their inaccurate reporting, Meyer and Berkman (1993) were evasive and did not deal directly with the issue of medication effects and the changes in dosage. Furthermore, they inferred that my article on Harry, a self-abusive man (Foxx, 1990; Foxx & Dufrense, 1984) was a case study and did not use a single-subject experimental design. This inference followed their section titled, "So who says a single-subject experiment is better than a case study?" (p. 9). In the interest of accuracy, I wrote to the journal and pointed out that Foxx & Dufrense (1984) included an ABA reversal experimental design prior to extending treatment to 24 hours a day (Foxx, 1993).

Meyer and Evans (1989)

This book contains misleading and often inaccurate portrayals of the clinical use of aversive procedures based on selective literature interpretation and unsupported data (Boyle, 1991). Furthermore, as noted earlier, nonaversive approaches are described as (a) offering a great deal of evidence of equal or greater empirical validity than aversive approaches and (b) being more likely to result in significant and lasting behavior changes that reflect worthwhile outcomes.

Meyer and Evans (1989) characterized use of punishment or aversives as being associated with homogenous groupings of people, highly restrictive settings, very undesirable side effects, inadequate or inept functional analysis, ignoring human dignity and quality of life, poorly designed interventions, lack of individualization, rigidity of application, and increased risk for chemical and physical restraint (which is actually truer of positive approaches, Foxx, 2003).

SOPHISTICATED UTILIZATION AND PROMULGATION OF THE MYTH

In discussing mass movements, Hoffer (1951) noted that "a movement is pioneered by men of words, materialized by fanatics and consolidated by men of action (p. 147). The man of action is eclectic in the methods he uses to endow the new order with stability and permanence. He borrows from near and far and from friend and foe. He even goes back to the old order which preceded the movement and appropriates from it many techniques of stability" (p. 151).

There has been a sophisticated promulgation and utilization of the myth and its fundamental role within the nonaversive movement by "men of action" via model building (e.g., positive behavior support, communication-based intervention, educative approaches, multielement interventions) and the ubiquitous marketing of functional assessment. Whether ideology or science is promoted appears to be dependent on the intended audience. Crucial to the maintenance of the myth is blurring of the distinction between problem behavior and severe behavior.

Problem—A source of perplexity or vexation   —(Merriam-Webster, 1974)

The Treatment of Problem Behavior Versus Severe Behavior Problems

Consider the term *problem behavior*. Although Carr et al. (1994), Evans and Meyer (1985), and Repp and Horner (1999) have all written books with "problem behavior" in their titles, little information has been provided in these works on the successful treatment of severe behavior problems and the focus was primarily on children with mild and moderate problem behavior (Newsom & Kroeger, chap. 24, this volume). Indeed, while "there is little current literature that provides empirically valid demonstrations of multi-element interventions in applied settings" for severe behavior problems (Sprague & Horner, 1999, p. 100), there appears to be no shortage of literature on functional analysis, functional assessment, and models for intervention and support (e.g., Durand, 1991; Horner et al., 1990; Repp & Horner, 1999). Perhaps this is why most descriptions of intervention with severe behavior problems continue to be promissory (e.g., Sprague & Horner, 1999) rather than prescriptive and validated.

The use of the descriptor *severe* appears to have evolved with the positive behavior support movement. Consider, for example, that Val, a child with "problem behavior" discussed at length in Carr et al. (1994), is also discussed 5 years later in a chapter on hypothesis-based intervention for severe problem behavior (Carr et al., 1999). In both instances, the behaviors of concern—screaming, spitting at the teacher, grabbing another child's hair or throwing her school work off the desk—would most likely be considered by many classroom teachers and practitioners to be fairly commonplace rather than severe.

AN EXAMPLE OF MYTH UTILIZATION

An example of the sophisticated and creative utilization and extension of the myth (i.e., that nonaversives work with severe behavior problems and that functional assessment can always provide answers to the problem, whereas the use of aversives is not creative, not designed to teach new behaviors, and does not seek to understand a behavior's function) can be found in Repp and Horner (1999). In their introductory chapter, Repp and Horner first contrast differential reinforcement of other behavior (DRO; Repp & Deitz, 1974, mis-cited as 1975 in their chapter) and overcorrection (Foxx & Azrin, 1973), and then provide two paragraphs on the use of functional assessment that conclude that "intervention would not involve a punishment procedure like overcorrection" (p. 3).

> Using overcorrection with clients who frequently had their hands in their mouths (Foxx & Azrin, 1973) or bit their hands (Barnard et al., 1974), we might require clients to brush their teeth for an extended period with a toothbrush that had been immersed in an oral antiseptic, and then to wipe their lips several times with a washcloth dampened with antiseptic. The rationale behind this procedure could be that 'mouthing of objects or parts of one's body results in exposure to potentially harmful microorganisms through unhygienic oral contact' (Foxx & Azrin, 1973, p. 4). Using DRO with *the same clients* [italics added] we might determine the mean interval between episodes of biting, select an interval 25 percent or so smaller, provide each client a token for each of the smaller intervals in which he or she does not engage in biting, and allow the clients to exchange the tokens for favored activities (Repp & Dietz, 1975). (p. 3)

The implication is clear. Why use aversive extended tooth brushing when you can simply provide DRO for favored activities via tokens?

The first creative myth was suggesting that Repp and Dietz (1974) only used DRO (a positive reinforcement procedure), whereas Foxx & Azrin (1973) used punishment. Unmentioned was that Repp and Dietz (1974) used punishment with all four of their clients including physical restraint, timeout, and response cost, and that Foxx and Azrin had demonstrated that DRO was ineffective with their clients.

The second myth was suggesting that the clients in both studies were similar. The two clients in Foxx and Azrin (1973) had equivalent developmental age characterizations of 1.4 and 1.9 years, high rates of mouthing, and behavior that was self-stimulatory or automatically reinforced. The two clients in Repp and Dietz (1974), for whom tokens were exchangeable for items such as camera film and cassette tapes, had IQs of 47 and 54 and low rates of aggressive behavior that was reinforced by attention. Not surprisingly, Repp and Dietz (1974) used bits of candy rather than tokens in their DRO program for their two clients who functioned at 8 and 12 months, as did Foxx and Azrin (1973) with their clients.

The third myth was when Repp and Horner (1999) switched the discussion of the target behavior to self-biting, which Repp and Dietz (1974) did not treat, and implied that Barnard et al. (1974) only treated their clients by brushing their teeth. Given that Barnard et al. (1974) was a convention talk, an examination of Barnard et al. (1976) reveals that their use of overcorrection for hand biting included a 2-minute oral hygiene procedure followed by 2 minutes of hand washing, 1 minute of hand drying, and finally 2 minutes of applying hand cream. In effect, this overcorrection procedure included 5 minutes of positive, educational activities via positive practice and only 2 minutes of oral hygiene (Foxx & Bechtel, 1983).

In the following two paragraphs on functional assessment, the behavior of concern, self-biting, conveniently became escape motivated (i.e., simply treat by changing stimulus conditions) and then attention seeking (i.e., simply intervene by changing reinforcement contingencies). A self-stimulatory hypothesis was not advanced. Oft trod ground was covered, that is, identify conditions under which biting may have occurred, examine the role of tasks, analyze the behavior of other students, and change stimulus conditions. The chapter (Repp & Horner, 1999) contained no citation to any literature on the use of functional assessment to successfully design a program to treat self-biting.

Apparently one roadblock to the treatment of severe behavior problems, especially low-frequency, high-intensity problems, is that their successful treatment "will require the development of expanded alternatives to existing single-subject research methodologies whose limitation is that they require relatively high-frequency behaviors for observation and diagnosis" (Sprague & Horner, 1999, p. 101). By way of example, Sprague and Horner stress that a reversal design would be ethically unacceptable to use with head banging and in fact, might even result in a strengthening of the behavior. The profundity of this observation leaves one eagerly awaiting the proliferation of expanded alternative research methodologies that no doubt will be available in the *Journal of Positive Behavior Support* (see Mulick & Butter, chap. 23, this volume).

CLOSING REMARKS

Over 40 years ago, behavior analysis entered the institutional world and began to use science to bring freedom and dignity to individuals who displayed severe behavior by freeing them from drugs and restraint and providing them with treatment and functional and adaptive skills. These individuals often were considered untestable because the main function of many professionals at that time was to assign an IQ score and a repugnant label such as "trainable" or "imbecile." Although great advances have been made in education, quality of life, choice making, and self-determination for individuals with developmental disabilities (e.g. Foxx et al., 1993), we practitioners have, in many ways, come full circle with those who display severe behavior problems due, in large part, to the myths regarding treatment that continue to be perpetuated.

Consider that even though these individuals no longer reside in segregated settings, they now may receive high doses of sometimes toxic drugs and restraint (but noncontingently!) in the community. While they may not receive effective treatment for their severe behavior problems (Van Houten et al., 1988), there is no question that these behaviors have been or will be fully assessed. Full circle, indeed, because whereas in the past, someone in a helmet who was self-abusive and on high dosages of Thorazine was labeled *untrainable*, that same helmeted, self-abusive, drugged person now is labeled *escape motivated*.

In their chapter on myths about punishment, Donnellan and LaVigna (1990) begin with a quote attributed to John F. Kennedy: "The great enemy of the truth is very often not the lie—deliberate, contrived and dishonest—but the myth—persistent, persuasive and unrealistic." I shall leave it to the reader to judge where the material and events discussed in this chapter fall on the continuum set forth by Kennedy.

REFERENCES

Axelrod, S. (1987). [Review of *Alternatives to punishment: Solving behavior problems with non-aversive strategies* by G. W. LaVigna & A. M. Donnellan]. *The Behavior Analyst, 10,* 243–251.

Axelrod, S. (1990). Myths that (mis)guide our profession. In A. C. Repp & N. N. Singh (Eds.), *Perspectives on the use of nonaversive and aversive interventions for persons with developmental disabilities* (pp. 59–72). Pacific Grove, CA: Brooks/Cole.

Bailey, J. S. (1987). [Review of *Alternatives to punishment: Solving behavior problems with non-aversive strategies* by G. W. LaVigna & A. M. Donnellan]. *Contemporary Psychology, 32,* 571–572.

Barnard, J. D., Christophersen, E. R., Altman, K. & Wolf, M. M. (1974). *Parent-mediated treatment of self-injurious behavior using overcorrection.* Paper presented at the meeting of the American Psychological Association, New Orleans, LA.

Barnard, J. D., Christophersen, E. R., & Wolf, M. M. (1976). Parent-mediated treatment of self-injurious behavior using overcorrection. *Journal of Pediatric Psychology, 1,* 56–61.

Berkman, K. A., & Meyer, L. H. (1988). Alternative strategies and multiple outcomes in the remediation of severe self-injury: Going "all out" nonaversively. *Journal of the Association for Persons with Severe Handicaps, 13,* 76–86.

Boyle, T. D. (1991). [Review of *Nonaversive intervention for behavior problems: A manual for home and community* by L. H. Meyer & I. M. Evans]. *Child & Family Behavior Therapy, 13*(2), 96–100.

Bruel, H. H., Fielding, L., Joyce, M., Peters, W., & Weisler, N. (1982). Thirty-month demonstration project for treatment of self-injurious behavior in severely retarded individuals. In J. H. Hollis & C. E. Meyers (Eds.), *Life-threatening behavior: Analysis and intervention* (pp. 191–275). Washington, DC: American Association on Mental Deficiency.

Carr, E. G., Langdon, N. A., & Yarbrough, S. C. (1999). Hypothesis-based intervention for severe problem behavior. In A. C. Repp & R. H. Horner (Eds.), *Functional analysis of problem behavior* (pp. 9–31). Pacific Grove, CA: Wadsworth.

Carr, E. G., Levin, L., McConnachie, G., Carlson, J. I., Kemp, D. C., & Smith, C. E. (1994). *Communication-based intervention for problem behavior.* Baltimore: Brookes.

Carr, E. G., & Lovaas, O. I. (1983). Contingent electric shock as a treatment for severe behavior problems. In S. Axelrod & J. Apsche (Eds.), *The effects of punishment on human behavior* (pp. 221–245). New York: Academic Press.

Carr, E. G., Taylor, J. C., Carlson, J. I., & Robinson, S. (1991). Reinforcement and stimulus-based treatments for severe behavior problems in developmental disabilities. In *Treatment of Destructive Behaviors in Persons with Developmental Disabilities* (pp. 173–229). Bethesda, MD: NIH Consensus Development Conference.

Donnellan, A. (1989, September 6). *Preliminary response to draft report: Treatment of destructive behaviors in persons with developmental disabilities.* Madison, WI: University of Wisconsin.

Donnellan, A. M., & LaVigna, G. W. (1990). Myths about punishment. In A. C. Repp & N. N. Singh (Eds.), *Perspectives on the use of nonaversive and aversive interventions for persons with developmental disabilities* (pp. 33–57). Sycamore IL: Sycamore.

Donnellan, A. M., LaVigna, G. W., Zambito, J., & Thvedt, J. (1985). A time-limited intensive intervention program model to support community placement for persons with severe behavior problems. *Journal of Association for Persons with Severe Handicaps, 10*(3), 123–131.

Donnellan, A. M., & Negri-Shoultz, N. (1986). *A review and evaluation of interventions implemented by Fairbault State Hospital for selected class members in Welsch v. Levine.* Minneapolis: Office of the Court Master, Welsch v. Levine.

Durand, V. M. (1991). *Functional communication training: An intervention program for severe behavior problems.* New York: Guilford.

Evans, I. M., & Meyer, L. H. (1985). *An educative approach to behavior problems: A practical decision model for interventions with severely handicapped learners.* Baltimore: Brookes.

Foxx, R. M. (1982). *Decreasing the behaviors of persons with severe retardation and autism.* Champaign, IL: Research Press.

Foxx, R. M. (1990). Harry: A ten year follow-up of the successful treatment of a self-injurious man. *Research in Developmental Disabilities, 11,* 67–76.

Foxx, R. M. (1991). Decreasing severe behavior with punishment procedures: Discontinuing their use while maintaining long-term treatment effects. *Treatment of Destructive Behaviors in Persons with Developmental Disabilities* (pp. 48–51). Bethesda, MD: NIH Consensus Development Conference, U.S. Department of Health and Human Services.

Foxx, R. M. (1993). A clarification regarding Foxx and Dufrense. *Mental Retardation, 31,* 34.

Foxx, R. M. (1994, Fall). Facilitated communication in Pennsylvania: Scientifically invalid but politically correct. *Dimensions,* 3–9.

Foxx, R. M. (1996a). Translating the covenant: The behavior analyst as ambassador and translator. *The Behavior Analyst, 19*(2), 147–161.

Foxx, R. M. (1996b). Twenty years of applied behavior analysis in treating the most severe problem behavior: Lessons learned. *The Behavior Analyst, 19*(2), 225–235.

Foxx, R. M. (1998a). *Rebuttal report in Messier v. Southbury Training School.* Available by request to the author.

Foxx, R. M. (1998b). *Self-injurious behavior: Perspectives on the past, prospects for the future.* Panel discussion presented at the annual convention of the Association for Behavior Analysis, Orlando, FL.

Foxx, R. M. (2001). Thirty years of applied behavior analysis in treating problem behavior. In C. Maurice, G. Green, & R. M. Foxx (Eds.), *Making a Difference: Behavioral Intervention for Autism* (pp. 183–194). Austin, TX: Pro-Ed.

Foxx, R. M. (2003). Treating dangerous behaviors. *Behavioral Interventions, 18,* 1–21.

Foxx, R. M., & Azrin, N. H. (1973). The elimination of autistic self-stimulatory behavior by overcorrection. *Journal of Applied Behavior Analysis, 6,* 1–14.

Foxx, R. M., & Bechtel, D. R. (1983). Overcorrection: A review and analysis. In S. Axelrod & J. Apsche (Eds.), *The effects of punishment on human behavior* (pp. 133–220). New York: Academic Press.

Foxx, R. M., Bittle, R. G., & Faw, G. D. (1989). A maintenance strategy for discontinuing aversive procedures: A 52-month follow-up of the treatment of aggression. *American Journal on Mental Retardation, 94,* 27–36.

Foxx, R. M., & Dufrense, D. (1984). "Harry": The use of physical restraint as a reinforcer, timeout from restraint, and fading restraint in treating a self-injurious man. *Analysis and Intervention in Developmental Disabilities, 4,* 1–13.

Foxx, R. M., Faw, G. D., Taylor, S., Davis, P. K., & Fulia, R. (1993). "Would I be able to …" ? Teaching clients to assess the availability of their community living life style preferences. *American Journal on Mental Retardation, 92,* 235–248.

Foxx, R. M., & Livesay, J. (1984). Maintenance of response suppression following overcorrection: A ten year retrospective examination of eight cases. *Analysis and Intervention in Developmental Disabilities, 4,* 65–79.

Foxx, R. M., Plaska, T. G., & Bittle, R. G. (1986). Guidelines for the use of contingent electric shock to treat aberrant behavior. In M. Hersen, A. Belleck, & P. Miller (Eds.), *Progress in Behavior Modification* (Vol. 20, pp. 1–34). New York: Academic Press.

Foxx, R. M., Zukotynski, G., & Williams, D. E. (1994). Measurement and evaluation of treatment outcomes with extremely dangerous behavior. In T. Thompson & D. Gray (Eds.), *Treatment of Destructive Behavior in Developmental Disabilities* (Vol. 2, pp. 261–273). Newbury Park, CA: Sage.

Guess, D., Helmstetter, E., Turnbull, H. R., III, & Knowlton, S. (1987). *Use of aversive procedures with persons who are disabled: An historical review and critical analysis* (Monograph). Seattle, WA: The Association for Persons with Severe Handicaps.

Haskew, P., & Donnellan, A. M. (1993). *Emotional maturity and well-being: Psychological lessons of facilitated communication.* Madison, WI: DRI Press.

Heidorn, S. D., & Jensen, C. C. (1984). Generalization and maintenance of the reduction of self-injurious behavior maintained by two types of reinforcement. *Behaviour Research and Therapy, 22,* 581–586.

Hersen, M., & Barlow, D. H. (1978). *Single case experimental designs.* New York: Pergamon.

Hoffer, E. (1951). *The true believer: Thoughts on the nature of mass movements.* New York: Harper & Row.

Holden, C. (1990, August). What's holding up "aversives" report? *Science, 249,* 980–981.

Horner, R. H., Dunlap, G., Koegel, R. L., Carr, E. G., Sailor, W., Anderson, J. A., et al. (1990). Toward a technology of "nonaversive" behavioral support. *Journal for Persons with Severe Handicaps, 15*(3), 125–132.

Jacobson, J. W., & Mulick, J. A. (2000, Fall). MR/DD consulting for dummies. *Psychology in Mental Retardation and Developmental Disabilities, 26*(2), 3–11.

Kramer, H., & Spranger, J. (1971). *Malleus maleficarum* (M. Summers, Trans.). New York: Dover. (Original work published 1486)

LaVigna, G. W. (1987, April 13). *Behavioral assessment report and intervention plan.* Los Angeles: Institute for Applied Behavior Analysis.

LaVigna, G. W. (1988, May). *Analysis and treatment after removal from a "last resort" punishment program.* A symposium presented at the Annual Convention of the Association for Behavior Analysis, Philadelphia, PA.

LaVigna, G. W. (1998, January 15). *An evaluation of behavioral services at Southbury Training School, Messier v. Southbury Training School.*

LaVigna, G. W., & Donnellan, A. M. (1986). *Alternatives to punishment: Solving behavior problems with non-aversive strategies.* New York: Irvington.

LaVigna, G. W., Willis, T. J., & Donnellan, A. M. (1989). The role of positive programming in behavioral treatment. In E. Cipani (Ed.), *The treatment of severe behavior disorders* (pp. 59–84). Washington, DC: American Association on Mental Retardation.

Linscheid, T. R., Iwata, B. A., Ricketts, R. W., Williams, D. E., & Griffin, J. C. (1990). Clinical evaluation of the Self-Injurious Behavior Inhibiting System (SIBIS). *Journal of Applied Behavior Analysis, 23,* 53–78.

Linscheid, T. R., & Landau, R. J. (1993). Going "all out" pharmacologically? A re-examination of Berkman and Meyer's "Alternative strategies and multiple outcomes in remediation of severe self-injury: Going "all out" nonaversively." *Mental Retardation, 31*(1), 1–6.

Lovaas, O. I., & Favell, J. E. (1987). Protection for clients undergoing aversive/restrictive interventions. *Education and Treatment of Children, 10,* 311–325.

Merriam-Webster Dictionary. (1974). New York: Pocket Books.

Meyer, L. H., & Berkman, K. A. (1993). What's straw and what's real: A reply to Linscheid and Landau. *Mental Retardation, 31,* 7–14.

Meyer, L. H., & Evans, I. M. (1989). *Nonaversive intervention for behavior problems: A manual for home and community.* Baltimore: Brookes.

Mulick, J. A. (1990a). Ideology and punishment reconsidered. *American Journal on Mental Retardation, 95,* 173–181.

Mulick, J. A. (1990b). The ideology and science of punishment in mental retardation. *American Journal of Mental Retardation, 95,* 142–156.

Mulick, J. A., & Linscheid, T. R. (1988). [Review of *Alternatives to Punishment: Solving Behavior Problems with Non-Aversive Strategies* by G. W. LaVigna & A. M. Donnellan]. *Research in Developmental Disabilities, 9,* 317–320.

National Institutes of Health. (1989). *Treatment of destructive behaviors in persons with developmental disabilities.* NIH Consensus Development Conference, Washington, DC: U.S. Department of Health and Human Services.

National Institutes of Health. (1991). *Treatment of destructive behaviors in persons with developmental disabilities.* NIH Consensus Development Conference, Washington, DC: U.S. Department of Health and Human Services.

National Institute of Disability and Rehabilitation Research. (1987). *State of the art conference on the treatment of severe behavior disorders.* Lawrence, KS: Author.

Paisey, T. J. H., Whitney, R. B., Hislop, M., & Wainczak, S. (1991). Case study 5: George. In R. Romanczyk (Ed.), *Self-injurious behavior: Etiology and treatment* (Tech. Rep.). Binghamton, NY: State University of New York at Binghamton, Department of Psychology.

Repp, A. C., & Dietz, S. M. (1974). Reducing aggressive and self-injurious behavior of institution-alized retarded children through reinforcement of other behaviors. *Journal of Applied Behavior Analysis, 7,* 313–325.

Repp, A. C., & Horner, R. H. (1999). *Functional analysis of problem behavior.* Pacific Grove, CA: Wadsworth.

Royko, M. (1986, May 29). A brain disorder in bureaucracy. *Chicago Tribune,* p. 3.

Sauferer, W. G. (1986, December 10). *Response to court monitor report, Welsh v. Levine.* Fairbault Regional Center, State of Minnesota.

Sherman, R. A. (1991). Aversives, fundamental rights and the courts. *The Behavior Analyst, 14,* 197–206.

Spitz, H. H. (1994). Comment on Donnellan's Review of Shane's (1994) Facilitated Communication: The Clinical and Social Phenomenon. *American Journal on Mental Retardation, 10,* 96–100.

Sprague, J. R., & Horner, R. H. (1999). Low-frequency high-intensity problem behavior: Toward an applied technology of functional assessment and intervention. In A. C. Repp & R. H. Horner (Eds.), *Functional analysis of problem behavior* (pp. 98–116). Pacific Grove, CA: Wadsworth.

Van Houten, R., Axelrod, A., Bailey, J. S., Favell, J. E., Foxx, R. M., Iwata, B. A., et al. (1988). The right to effective treatment. *Journal of Applied Behavior Analysis, 21,* 381–384.

Wieseler, N. A. (1988). [Review of *Alternatives to Punishment: Solving Behavior Problems With Non-Aversive Strategies* by G. W. LaVigna & A. M. Donnellan]. *Research in Developmental Disabilities, 9,* 321–323.

Wolf, M. M., & Risley, T. R. (1971). Reinforcement: Applied research. In R. Glaser (Ed.), *The nature of reinforcement* (pp. 310–325). New York: Academic Press.

Part V

Intervention-Specific Issues

Person-Centered Planning:
A Faux Fixe in the Service of Humanism?

J. Grayson Osborne
Utah State University

In this chapter, I examine skeptically person-centered planning approaches (PCAs) for people who have developmental disabilities and I relate them to behavior analysis, which is my orientation. In so doing, I determine whether PCAs constitute *faux fixes* (Osborne, 1999) in their approaches to those who have developmental disabilities.

WHAT IS APPLIED BEHAVIOR ANALYSIS?

Principles of behavior, initially researched and developed in the laboratory, have been applied to persons who have mental illness, developmental disabilities, or both with some success (for an early compendium, see Ulrich, Stachnik, & Mabry, 1966, 1970, 1974). Individuals who work in this area approach their work as behavior scientists (Baer, Wolf, & Risley, 1968, 1987). Called applied behavior analysts, in the beginning, they faced considerable opposition and were given cases of last resort, many of which were dealt with successfully (e.g., Wolf, Risley, & Mees, 1964). As a result of this success, application of behavior principles to people with developmental disabilities became commonplace in institutional and many other settings (see, e.g., all of the volumes of the *Journal of Applied Behavior Analysis*).

A basic premise of behavior analysis is that all, including human, behavior is lawful. As such, it is related functionally to an individual's genetic makeup, to an individual's history of conditioning, and to an individual's present context. Given that behavior analysts cannot alter genetic makeup or an individual's history of conditioning, they confine themselves to treatments in the present that relate an individual's behavior to its current and future contexts (Baer et al., 1968). Context is broadly construed to connote not only the immediate antecedent and consequent conditions that relate to an individual's behavior, but also the broader environment in which these antecedents and consequences are embedded.

WHAT IS A PERSON CENTERED APPROACH (PCA)?[1]

A person-centered approach is a conglomeration of philosophy, values, ideas, and methods that attempt to improve the lives of individuals who have developmental disabilities and are typically located in state-run intermediate care facilities for persons with developmental disabilities (ICF-MR), or state-sponsored, but privately run, institutions such as community homes (e.g., O'Brien & O'Brien, 2002). It has been noted that "the assortment of terms used to refer to person-centered approaches both exemplifies their comprehensive impact and obscures their common essence and shared features" (Schwartz, Jacobson, & Holburn, 2000, p. 236).

Where Did PCAs Come From?

PCAs appear to have arisen from shifts in developmental disability policy of the late 1980s toward total inclusion, family supports, and personal empowerment (Davidson & Adams, 1989). In turn, these policy shifts appeared to result from the civil rights movement, concurrently with a counterreaction to the precise application of scientific principles and technology to human behavior (Wagner, 2002). Initially, PCA implementers desired to form communities of practice (O'Brien & O'Brien, 2002).

Some PCAs may be antiquantification as an aspect of the rejection of the values of science. In the sense in which it is said that PCA procedures cannot be accurately specified and replicated (Holburn & Vietze, 2002b), scientific analysis of their would-be effects appears to be precluded. It is further claimed that PCAs are philosophically postmodern and deconstructive, two phrases that are often construed as antiscientific (e.g., contrast Jacobson, Mulick, & Schwartz, 1995; and Sailor, 1996).

An Example of the Context of a PCA: Personal Futures Planning (Mount, 1994)

Mount (1994) contrasts what she calls "traditional forms of planning" and personal futures planning. How do applied behavior analysis and PCAs relate in general? Presented here are four statements from Mount (1994) that provide a values context for PCAs and my reactions, as behavior analyst, to them.

1. "*PCAs envisage a new, positive, inclusive future for the focus person.*" This focus is antithetical to what Mount calls the traditional developmental model, which is thought to emphasize "the deficits and needs of people, overwhelming people with endless program goals and objectives, and assigning responsibility for decision-making to professionals" (p. 98). Apparently, the developmental model has erroneously emphasized the positive development of the focus person, has wrongly established meaningful program goals and objectives for that person, and—analogous to a cultural revolution—has wrongly entrusted experts to oversee the job. There are serious implications here: goals and objectives—the stuff of accountability and assessment are out; professionals are out.

---

[1] I use PCA in the generic sense to cover many similar approaches, for example, person-centered planning (Holburn, 2001; O'Brien & Lovett, 1992) and personal futures planning (Mount, 1994; Mount & Zwernick, 1988).

Moreover, "the underlying values of traditional [developmental] planning [are said to] communicate subtle messages, for example: The [focus] person is the problem and should be fixed but never will be. Learning to adapt to impossible situations is expected; the more a [focus] person protests, the more of a problem he or she is. Professionals know best, and the [focus] person must stay in segregated programs until he or she is ready for [the] community. These messages undermine [focus?] people's confidence and growth" (p. 98).

These are serious charges. Let me stipulate that applied behavior analysis participates in the traditional developmental model. First, applied behavior analysts have primarily focused on positive change.[2] The idea that persons who are the focus of applied behavior analysis "will never be fixed" is anathema in applied behavior analysis, which has always taught that the behavior of the person of interest is always correct. If a person behaves in a particular context in a way we are unable to understand, as behavior analysts, we do not throw out behavior analysis. If a procedure doesn't work, it is considered to be the fault of the procedure, not the focus person, and new procedures are sought. Historically, such new procedures have been found, successfully. Indeed, an entirely new area of applied behavior analysis—functional analysis/assessment—has arisen to determine precisely what behavior relates to in situations where the applied behavior analyst may not be able to easily ascertain the controlling variables (e.g., Derby et al., 1992; Iwata et al., 1994). Those promoting PCAs apparently have decided that the system needs to be thrown out. They have done so because "developing skills in small steps—were insufficient to carry people into as full a life as developing technologies of assistance and instruction could support" (O'Brien, O'Brien, & Mount, 1997, p. 480). Insofar as applied behavior analysis is a part of the traditional model, these assertions appear to throw it out along with the rest of that model. These assertions are made in the face of the gains by applied behavior analysis in understanding the behavior of people with developmental disabilities over the last half century.

On the other hand, that PCAs envision a better future for persons with developmental disabilities is extremely positive. On this, the two approaches can agree.

2. *"People with disabilities have important gifts and capacities that seek expression."* Applied behavior analysts have no objection to this statement. Applied behavior analysts have never been comfortable with the way in which ICF-MRs are run, which is why over the years applied behavior analysts have suggested systems that focus on changes in staff behavior in them (e.g., see Rea, Martin, & Wright, 2002, on the history of Parsons State Hospital and Training Center).

There are two points of discussion here: What do personal futures planners envisage the important gifts and capacities of people with developmental disabilities to be? Behavior analysis has conceptually considered that the capacities of people with disabilities (or without) are infinite. It has done so from a framework that has shown the validity of (the above-denigrated) step-wise progress, with proofs (also

---

[2]I agree with Holburn & Vietze (2002) that applied behavior analysis has a "tendency toward decelerating behavior" (p. 61). Behaviors to be decelerated are usually the problems the system wants dealt with first, and, for the most part, applied behavior analysts have complied. However, philosophically, applied behavior analysis has always wanted to do the right thing, and acceleration of positive behavior remains that right thing.

denigrated) that the progress toward fulfilling capacity is real and not ephemeral. This progress, which may have taught a focus person to dress appropriately (Azrin, Schaeffer, & Wesolowski, 1976) or to use the telephone (Test, Spooner, Keul, & Grossi, 1990) certainly involves real world goals and objectives, but these goals and objectives are not "endless lists" and they do not "lead nowhere." Instead they lead directly to new competencies, broadened behavioral repertoires, and the increased freedoms that accompany them.

Dealing with the phrase "capacities that seek expression" is more difficult because the wording is vague. On the one hand, the phrase may imply that a person will be a fine trumpet player, if only someone would give him a trumpet. But, with rare exception, few people evidence high levels of skill without incremental change in those skills, which clearly reflects the behavior analytic model. Perhaps the reference to capacity is more to emotional capacity? If the reference is to emotional well-being, behavior analysts have no objection, understanding something about how the presence of reinforcers, the absence of punishers, and the presence of choices relate to happiness. In fact, applied behavior analysts have been instrumental in conducting research into indices of happiness for persons with developmental disabilities (e.g., Green, Gardner, & Reid, 1997).

3. "*Professionals need to learn to listen to, and take direction from, individuals and families.*" This statement, too, is replete with overtones of cultural revolution. The word *professionals* includes a large assortment of fields and individuals, all apparently being tarred with the same broad brush. As a behavior analyst, the frame of reference is simple: Every person is a locus of stimuli and responses. As such, a person acts on the environment and, in turn, the environment acts on her or him. In so doing, probabilistically, the person's behavior changes, and, in turn, the environment may change as well. This is a continuous process. It is this framework that is brought to discussions of next steps in aiding a focus person. This framework neither entails nor rejects taking direction from individuals and families, who may have good ideas. And it is not incompatible with working with anyone "so that people have many ways to be part of community life" (p. 98). It also does not mean *not* listening. It only means retaining a behavior-analytic frame of reference because that reference is still the most valid one with which to understand human behavior.

4. "*When situations frustrate people it means that the setting, environment, activity, or people in the situation need to change.*" Yes and no. Yes, behavior in every situation is relevant to the positive and negative aspects of the situation, and so forth, and may reflect a person's intent not to be where they are, doing what they are doing, and their desires to be somewhere else, doing something else. No, in the sense that it is impossible not to occasionally be somewhere, having to do something, not wanting to be doing it, and wanting to be somewhere else. Most of us cannot cease what we are doing, unless we don't care about being employed. Although behavior change is a goal of behavior analysis, behavior analysts understand that it is not always possible to effect such change under wholly positive conditions. For, it is a fact, that in order to establish a positive reinforcer that may then be used to increase the probability of behavior, an establishing operation is necessary (Michael, 1982, 1993, 2000). One may not go out to play until one has practiced one's trumpet. That is a trade most of us are willing to make. Apparently, some personal future planners are unwilling to make this kind of trade on behalf of, or with the agreement of, their charges. Where challenging behavior occurs to produce escape from an undesired

environment, applied behavior analysts have led the way to determine the function of these contingencies and have combined this knowledge with the teaching of new communicative skills that help to decrease the challenging behavior and that permit one to escape situations that are aversive by emitting socially acceptable behavior (Carr & Durand, 1985; Durand & Carr, 1991).

The foregoing suggests some contextual underpinnings of PCAs. But what actually occurs when a PCA is applied to the circumstances of a person with developmental disabilities?

Personal Planning Methods

In the personal planning process, a planning committee is formed. It develops a plan for a focus person, and then sees that the plan is carried out, modifying it as needed.

The Planning Committee as Ouija Board.   As an integral part of personal futures planning, a planning committee is formed to plan the focus person's future. Committee composition is vital. Experts are not wanted. Family, friends, and the focus person are. Staff who have good knowledge of the focus person are. Committee members speak of what they know of the focus person's wishes, capacities, vision of the future, and, if necessary, challenging behavior. Consensus is the objective via cooperative interaction (Kincaid, 1996). This is noble.

Members of the committee see the focus person through their own unique lenses, so the committee functions as ouija board. In fact, it is recommended that they do (Kincaid, 1996; O'Brien, 1987). Unfortunately, the opinions of others may not validly map the preferences of individuals with profound disabilities (Green et al., 1988; Reid, Everson, & Green, 1999). Notwithstanding the nobility of this exercise, the committee functions *in loco parentis*.

The Personal Futures Plan.   As a part of personal futures planning, the planning committee develops a plan for the focus person (see, e.g., Kincaid, 1996). Interestingly, it is expected that this planning process will change not the individual for whom the plan is developed, but the group assisting in the formation of the plan (Kincaid, 1996; Mount, 1994). "They [the committee] begin to see that the [focus] person has been traumatized by being a recipient of human services along with many other frustrations and failures" (Kincaid, 1996, p. 457). It is from this conversion of the planning group that the plan takes shape. The plan is to be reflective of the essential goals of the planning process and will include the domains of home, work, community, competencies, and relationships (Kincaid, 1996). Does this mean that change in a focus person is less important than the conversion of the committee planning the focus person's future?

Carrying out the Plan.   Having developed a plan, the committee determines how the plan can be accomplished. This necessitates having persons on the committee who are capable of modifying the system to accommodate the focus person in different environments. A number of authors note that without the ability to change the system, operationally, one will be unable to accomplish the goals of personal futures planning (Holburn, 1997; Kincaid, 1996; Mount, 1994). It is clear that committee members who would be change agents must be dedicated and creative because without such dedication the planning process will fail and become just another "service fad" (O'Brien et al., 1997).

Faux Fixes

Elsewhere (Osborne, 1999), I have argued that PCAs, such as personal futures planning, are the latest in a long line of *faux fixes*, all purportedly techniques to deal with persons who have developmental disabilities. A *faux fixe* is literally a false fix of a problem. Usually it is a politically correct (for the moment at least) procedure or movement in the social sciences, of which there is uncritical adoption (see Schwartz et al., 2000), in the face of difficult-to-solve problems.

Characteristics of Faux Fixes

Dramatic Breakthroughs. *Faux fixes* are often marked by claims of dramatic breakthroughs. Facilitated communication is a good example (Jacobson, Foxx & Mulick, chap. 22, this volume). Dramatic change is claimed in PCAs, typically in the form of anecdotes (e.g., Amado & McBride, 2002). Moreover, it has been stated that "it is the most powerful and dynamic approach ... in the field of developmental disabilities (Holburn & Vietze, 1998, p. 485). Yet, anecdotes notwithstanding, this type of assertion seems largely empty.

A New Term/Phrase Is Coined. There are many reasons to coin new terms: new findings, new laws, new relations, and new procedures among them. Typically, a new term/phrase is a clue to a *faux fixe* if it refers to procedures that are unsupported with respect to their effectiveness. The procedures designated by the following new terms/phrases are not supported currently by summative data of their effectiveness—person-centered planning; personal futures planning (Mount, 1994); Planning Alternative Tomorrows with Hope (PATH; Pearpoint, O'Brien, & Forest, 1993); life arrangement and life coaching (Risley, 1996); whole life planning (Butterworth et al., 1993); and essential lifestyle planning (Smull & Harrison, 1992)—but their effectiveness is, for the most part, uncritically assumed. If the new term/phrase refers to procedures, the procedures are often poorly specified (Reid et al., 1999).

With the New Term/Phrase Comes New Jargon. Another clue to a *faux fixe* is the presence of new nontechnical jargon, for example, wraparound services (Risley, 1996; Sailor, 1996); respect (O'Brien, 1987); alternative tomorrows (Pearpoint et al., 1993); focus person (Holburn, 1997); and preference mapping (Everson, 1996). By nontechnical, I mean that there is usually no tie of the term to operations that define the procedures and to relations that describe their functions. In fact, with respect to person-centered planning, it has been stated that technical language is to be avoided because it is thought to exclude ordinary citizens (Holburn, 2001; Holburn & Vietze, 2000b). Ironic, then, is it not, that PCAs have developed their own jargon? Even the founders of the PCA movement consider the adoption of acronyms such as PCP, for person-centered planning, a sign that the movement has become unmoored from its origins (O'Brien et al., 1997).

The Absence of Scientifically Proven Procedures. *Faux fixes* are characterized also by the absence of scientifically proven procedures. In fact, the promulgators of *faux fixes* appear to denigrate and avoid science (Jacobson et al., 1995). In the realm of human behavior, *faux fixes* often appear first in workshops (for staff and teachers) and in the workbooks that accompany them. Notably, such sources are not peer reviewed, another possible clue to the presence of a *faux fixe*.

The Absence of Research on the Topic. Hand-in-glove with the foregoing, *faux fixes* are also characterized by the absence of research into them, at least in the initial stages, and later by their rejection of well-conducted research into their alleged effectiveness (e.g., Mostert, 2001). Given the ambiguity in their procedures, *faux fixes* may be also difficult to research. Person-centered approaches appear not to have sprung initially from research (see, e.g., O'Brien et al., 1997). Rather, they originated from the desire to help others (O'Brien & O'Brien, 2002). Nothing wrong with that, if the help is successful. There is considerable wrong, however, if the wholesale adoption of the *faux fixe* steals valuable time away from more effective procedures (Osborne, 1999). Indeed, it has been argued that *faux fixes* "are not benign [because] they supplant use of proven and reliable methods when these methods do not also appear to produce dramatic breakthroughs" (Jacobson et al., 1995). The wholesale acceptance of PCAs by states and institutions (as cited in Schwartz et al., 2000) suggests that such supplanting reflects the current developmental disabilities environment.

The Absence of Overall Evaluation. *Faux fixes* are often marked by the absence of either plans for, or actual, overall evaluation. PCAs have now been around for more than 20 years (O'Brien & O'Brien, 2002, mark 1979–1992 as the formative period). One might ask, where are the evaluations? There are few. From those who appear to be antiobjective and antigoal, perhaps, one should expect neither measurement nor assessment. Two studies have approximated overall evaluation (i.e., Holburn & Vietze, 2002b; Magito-McLaughlin, Spinosa, & Marsalis, 2002),[3] whereas others are analyzing components specific to the process (e.g., Green, Middleton, & Reid, 2000; Reid et al., 1999; Reid & Green, 2002).

Absence of a Technical Vocabulary. Again, though not critical, a clue to the presence of a *faux fixe* lies in the absence of any technical vocabulary. By technical vocabulary, I mean words that refer to scientific procedures and laws. PCAs appear to be free of technical vocabulary. Indeed, their founders rule such vocabulary out.

Presence of Fuzzy (or No) Goals. *Faux fixes* may also contain fuzzily stated goals, if they contain statements of goals at all. Given that goals and objectives are anathema to PCAs, it may not be surprising that the goals they do contain are vague and not easily measured. Indeed, there is no currently accepted definition of person cen-

---

[3]Magito-McLaughlin et al.'s study appears to be only 5 weeks long with the reported data a 1-week sample from that time period. Obviously, this is not much time in which to obtain more than a brief snapshot of the outcomes. Their study, therefore, cannot be used to infer longitudinal outcomes. Although Holburn and Vietze's measures are also snapshots, the snapshots occur across 4 years.

teredness and only recently have there been attempts to fabricate one (Schwartz et al., 2000). In the absence of an accepted definition, goal specification is impossible.

Feeling Good.   In lieu of objective and measurable goals, *faux fixes* attempt to help everyone feel good. Indeed, this may be critical to their acceptance. Feeling good appears to characterize much of what transpires in PCAs. The planning committee is to do its job without rancor. The vision for the focus person is positive. The planning committee is to reach consensus. Naysayers (professionals?) are *personna non grata*.

What Is a PCA Supposed to Accomplish? Fuzzy Goals and Fuzzy Outcomes

For this analysis, I have used O'Brien's (1987) goals as presented by Holburn (2001) as they seem common to the genre.

Community Presence.   As a result of a well-planned and well-implemented PCA, the focus person should have community presence. As Holburn (2001) points out, it is difficult to know what this means, probably because the phrase is an example of the use of new jargon. How does one measure this? Two ways are to measure the number of hours focus persons spend in inclusive environments and the numbers of such environments they encounter (e.g., Holburn & Vietze, 2002a; Magito-McLaughlin et al., 2002). These examples are but two of many that applied behavior analysts might use to begin to measure community presence. For others, community presence is likely to be a feeling that the focus person's presence is felt in the community. When community presence is defined as an abstraction such as this, a typical measurement attempt leads to an opinion survey. For behavior analysts, such a survey, where inference levels are kept low, would constitute a decent set of secondary data after the primary sense data were gathered. With the two exceptions cited previously, at this writing, there do not seem to be any evaluative studies of community presence as an outcome variable of a PCA.

Community Participation.   As a result of a well-planned and carried out PCA, the focus person should participate in the community. Does this mean that the residents of the group home use public transport? Does it mean that a person in supported living shops for his own groceries? These are ways that applied behavior analysts might begin to define community participation (e.g., Holburn & Vietze, 2002a; Magito-McLaughlin et al., 2002). Such measures are overt and observable, and low level inferences are all that are required to judge whether or not the behaviors they refer to exist. Secondarily, a survey of the neighbors could determine whether they have noted that the focus person exhibits specific behaviors (e.g., uses public transportation). Again, with the exception of the same two studies (i.e., Holburn & Vietze, 2002a; Magito-McLaughlin et al., 2002), at this writing, there do not seem to be any evaluative studies of community participation as an outcome variable of a PCA.

Choice.   In a well-planned and well-implemented PCA, the focus person should have choices, both big choices ("I don't like my job, so I think I'll quit") and little choices ("No thanks on the green beans. Could I have some ice cream instead?"), and the availability of choices is to be maximized. Will a well-planned and well-implemented PCA measure these choices, and will the number of these choices relate to a better quality of life? It is difficult to know because many authors of PCAs don't appear to think in these terms. On the other hand, behavior analysts do (e.g., Foxx, Faw, Taylor, Davis, & Fulia, 1993; Harding, Wacker, Berg, Barretto, & Rankin, 2002). Choice is well studied in behavior analysis in situations where there are known numbers of possibilities that result in differential reinforcement at various delays (Fisher & Mazur, 1997). Of course, one must see choice as a behavior, subject to its consequences, in order to deal with it objectively (see also Wagner, 2002).

Choice acquires additional philosophical complexities in relation to individuals who have developmental disabilities and who are under state control. This is because their caretakers operate under rules that restrict what they are permitted to allow the focus person to do. Typically, the focus person may be counseled as to which choice is the most acceptable. Is this, then, really a choice? Or is it just a subtle, nonquantified, nonmeasured source of control over the individual's behavior (Baer, 1998)? The focus person may really not want to work at a particular job anymore, notwithstanding that in the regular world this may not be adaptive. The individual who has developmental disabilities may not have many real choices when the choices are big, but the same is true for many without developmental disabilities. In fact, it is the job of the planning committee to ensure that the large choices are realistic ones. In other words, on the big choices, the committee will select and counsel out the unreasonable ones during planning, confirming the committee's status *in loco parentis*. PCAs have the greatest difficulty with the big choices because these choices necessitate substantial systems change—what systems least tolerate. The purveyors of PCAs reluctantly acknowledge this, noting that making these big choices destabilizes and upsets the system (Holburn & Vietze, 1999). Where substantial-sized choices are possible, they may only be possible when dealing with very small numbers of focus persons.

There may be more possibilities on the little choices. Individuals with developmental disabilities can certainly be informed as to these choices. As Holburn (2001) points out, applied behavior analysts have developed programs to do so (e.g., Cooper & Browder, 1998; Faw, Davis, & Peck, 1996; Foxx et al., 1993). Moreover, the system may tolerate these little choices because they are not disruptive of the system as a whole. Granted, if the choice is to stay and watch television or go to a baseball game, some staff person may have to be delegated to remain with the focus person who decides that tonight he'd rather watch television. Most often in these circumstances, staff wheedle the reluctant participant until that person agrees to go, because none of them wants to stay and watch television either when a ball game paid for by the state or the contractor is the alternative. Where's the choice here? And, whose choice is it? And who is concealing what from whom (Baer, 1998)? At this writing, there do not seem to be any evaluative studies that measure directly changes in choice as an outcome variable of a PCA. Notably, the two studies mentioned previously as exceptions rely on survey data with respect to choice (i.e., Holburn & Vietze, 2002a; Magito-McLaughlin et al., 2002).

Being free to make more choices, it is assumed, will lead to an improved quality of life. But defining quality of life and then determining whose quality of life it is are tasks not yet well accomplished in the PCA movement and are fraught with their own difficulties (Hatton, 1998).

Competence.   Competence means being able to satisfactorily interact with one's environment. Specifically, perhaps, it means knowing how to operate a vending machine (Browder, Snell, & Wildonger, 1988; Sprague & Horner, 1984) or count money (Bellamy & Buttars, 1975). The development of specific competencies has substantial behavior analytic research behind it. In one PCA evaluation, goal-based, formal ("system-driven") instructional activities were more frequent in the traditional group, whereas in the person-centered group, formal instructional activities tended to be more self-determinative (Magito-McLaughlin et al., 2002). In Holburn & Vietze's (2002a) study of Hal, raters rated Hal's capabilities. Other than these two attempts, at this writing, there do not seem to be any evaluative studies of changes in competence as an outcome variable of a PCA.

Respect.   PCAs understandably have trouble with respect, because it is difficult to define (Holburn, 2001). Kincaid (1996) suggests that these are behaviors and attributes that are viewed as positive or negative by the community (e.g., very cute = positive; tantrums = negative). As such, respect is an abstraction to be inferred by community members. Measurement of this variable will probably require a high level of inference on the part of the raters, not the low levels of inference necessary to decide the outcomes of most applied behavior analysis. Interestingly, Magito-McLaughlin et al. (2002) refer to changes in this variable by counting episodes of challenging behavior (the exhibition of which it is assumed is contra respect) and the numbers of contexts in which challenging behavior occurred. Lower numbers occurred in fewer contexts in their PCA group, but notably they failed to match their focus persons on this variable. Moreover, who said that absence of challenging behavior equates with respect? Holburn & Vietze infer this variable's outcome via survey. Again, with these two exceptions, at this writing, there do not seem to be any evaluative studies of changes in respect as an outcome variable of a PCA.

Evaluation, Evaluation, Evaluation

Holburn and Pfadt (1998) suggest that process measures might be best used to evaluate the effectiveness of PCAs. Using a process measure, the operations of the approach are themselves evaluated (Schwartz et al., 2000). For example, did the team function well? Did it develop vision-based goals? A plan? Did the team use person-centered principles? Is the system now more sensitive to personal issues? Are there changes in staff performance, attitudes, time spent with the focus person? Note that all of the foregoing measures relate to changes in the system, not the focus person. They are measures of internal validity rather than outcome. However, at this writing, there do not seem to be any evaluative studies of process measures, such as the foregoing, as they relate to outcome variables of a PCA.

Almost totally lost in all of this is the focus person's behavior. Granted, it is said that "perhaps the most obvious measure of the effectiveness of person-centered planning for a person with challenging behavior is a change in that behavior itself" (Holburn & Pfadt, 1998, p. 85). The foregoing statement specifies "a person with challenging behavior." Apparently, where there is not some challenging behavior, measures of behavior are less obviously needed. Indeed, it is next revealed that "more central to person-centered planning are considerations about quality of life, which generally can be described in terms of goodness of fit between the person and the social ecology, and more specifically refer to the quality of one's home life, relationships, community participation, health, and so forth" (p. 85). Improvements in these domains are designated as "valued outcomes" (Horner et al., 1996). It is important to determine how well defined these valued outcomes really are, and how they are measured and validated. In these measures the individual again appears to be lost. Rather than a direct measure of that individual's behavior, one instead measures an abstract "fit" between the individual and the "social ecology." Are these outcomes the result of direct observation? For instance, have temper tantrums decreased? Has smiling increased? Or are the measures derived from high level inferences based on the perceptions of others? (e.g., "On a scale of 1 to 10, how much more happy do you think John is?") At this writing, there do not seem to be any evaluative studies of the attainment of valued outcomes as a result of a PCA. (Both of the studies cited repeatedly in this section, because they alone have attempted evaluation, seemed not to attempt global evaluation, perhaps reflecting the difficulty of doing so validly.)

The Issue of Social Validation

This skepticism does not imply that social validation is not necessary. Applied behavior analysts recognized the importance of social validation of their outcomes well before PCAs were formulated, but only as data secondary to the primary outcomes of well-controlled studies (Wolf, 1978). Moreover, there are ways to make social validation via survey reliable and less subjective. These have been alluded to earlier in this chapter. They involve keeping the level of inference of the respondent as low as possible. Responses to low-level inference items tend to be more reliable and more valid than responses to high inference items. Low inference items tend, therefore, to be less subjective than higher inference items.

Where a construct, such as quality of life, is highly abstract, social validation is fraught with problems, particularly where one aspect of the process involves trying to measure subjective well-being (Hatton, 1998).

Positive Behavioral Support

The PCA known as Positive Behavioral Support (PBS; e.g., Carr et al., 1999; Koegel, Koegel, & Dunlap, 1996) has the weight of some of applied behavior analysis behind it (see Risley, 1999). Therefore, of all PCAs, we should expect PBS to show the most and best evaluations. "Positive behavior support (PBS) is an approach for dealing with problem behavior that focuses on the remediation of deficient contexts (i.e., environmental conditions and/or behavioral repertoires) that by functional analyses are documented to be the source of the problem" (Carr et al., 1999, p. 16). Without going into specifics, it can be noted that this approach is research based in terms of seeking and finding functional relations between problem behavior and context manipulations (Carr et al., 1999). Carr et al. have undertaken a meta-analysis of the available studies in the area of positive behavioral support. Of interest here is that as one of the outcome variables in their review they specifically evaluated lifestyle change. They defined positive lifestyle change as "increased engagement in normative social, vocational, family, recreational, and academic activities" (p. 33), and they measured these changes as a percentage increase from baseline. This definition of lifestyle change maps the primary focus of most PCAs.

It is worth quoting Carr et al.'s (1999) summary in its entirety:

> As the ultimate purpose of PBS is to enable individuals to live more normalized lives, lifestyle change is an important index of effectiveness. Surprisingly, the database for this outcome measure was extremely small. Lifestyle change was a stated intervention goal for only 24 out of 230 participants in the sample (i.e., 10.4% of the sample). A formal intervention directed specifically at improving lifestyle was recorded for 8 out of the 230 participants (i.e., 3.5% of the sample). Finally, success in improving lifestyle was measured for only 6 participants (i.e., 2.6% of the sample). Of these, anecdotal (nonquantified) improvement was noted for 4 participants. Data (percentage improvement from baseline) were taken on only 2 participants, and showed a 100% improvement with respect to increased engagement in community activities. (p. 62)

Given that the studies reviewed by Carr et al. (1999) were those focused on the PBS program, it may not be totally appropriate to use these outcomes to characterize all PCAs. However, in so doing note that this is the PCA that should be the most research oriented of all.[4] And it is. The others pale in comparison. Yet, clearly, only a small fraction of the PBS studies reviewed attempted to measure change in lifestyle. However small the numbers are, they are still higher than those for other PCAs for whom such numbers do not appear to exist. The fact that those involved in PBS programs have such numbers all-be-they small is, nevertheless, encouraging. However, such approximations do not characterize this field in general at this time.

What If PCAs Are Not Faux Fixes?

At this point in their development, PCAs certainly seem to be *faux fixes*. But what if they are not? Recall that it is currently difficult to ascertain this because their goals are often fuzzy, data collection is absent, procedures are poorly described, and evaluation is nonexistent. That is, without substantial refinements, how will we know? Nevertheless, it is claimed via anecdote that good results have been observed (e.g., Amado & McBride, 2002; Turnbull & Turnbull, 1996). These results aside, there are a number of reasons why PCAs may not be worth implementing. First, their implementation necessarily upsets and destabilizes institutional procedures and, in so doing, may upset staff and administration (Holburn & Vietze, 1999). Because the procedures are demanding of committee time and effort, the originators only planned on applying the procedures to a single person at a time, much in the same vein as applied behavior

---

[4]Not the direct focus of this chapter, in their review, Carr et al. show that PBS approaches are largely successful in the reduction of problem behavior. The reader is reminded again that PBS appears to be the sole PCA that has problem behavior reduction as a central focus, and, is, therefore, different from the many other PCAs that have neither any specific behavior as their focus nor any summative analysis of any aspects of their programs.

analysis.[5] Institutions have been quick to recognize that this results in unequal treatment of their populations. Furthermore, there are ethical problems: Practitioners who usually attempt an objective stance, must substantially engage another's life (O'Brien, 2002). Indeed, paradoxically, PCAs may actually extend the control over another's life, rather than reduce it (Hatton, 1998). Moreover, the system changes required by PCAs will more than likely have to occur as unfunded mandates with the usual resentments of those who have to carry out the mandates. Indeed, it is even suggested that massive implementation of PCAs will surely be the demise of the movement because PCA procedures will not be appropriately carried out (O'Brien et al., 1997). There are even worries that standardizing the training of future practitioners will cause loss of sight of the values base on which PCAs depend (Kincaid & Fox, 2002). In sum, it looks as though—its *faux fixe* status notwithstanding—the PCA movement will have difficulty being true to itself.

The Role of Applied Behavior Analysis

Unfortunately, some of those who see the necessity that applied behavior analysis comport with PCAs to improve the status of the latter (Holburn & Vietze, 2002b) don't seem to get it. How can applied behavior analysis and PCAs get fully together when it is stated that "[a person-centered team] cannot administer a uniform and fully replicable intervention, as is typical in controlled research" (p. 58)? From the beginning, applied behavior analysis has understood its limitations. As an applied science, it has been willing to forego the comforts of the laboratory and has done so successfully (Baer et al., 1968). Notably, internal validity has been a high priority (Carr, 1997). However, understanding and, indeed, accepting the inevitability of the absence of treatment integrity (i.e., internal validity) of any set of procedures appears to open an unbridgeable chasm between those who are applied scientists and those who are not (see also Risley, 1999). Rather, it is suggested that positive behavior support become a "companion approach" to behavior analysis (Horner, 1997) and with that I can agree, but not, of course, at the expense of good applied science (Singer, 1997).

SUMMARY

PCAs, for the most part, appear to be a new *faux fixe* with respect to the treatment of people who have developmental disabilities. There are few data to support their widespread adoption; their goals, if they have them, are fuzzy; there is little consensus as to what constitute the necessary and sufficient conditions that make them work—if they work at all; there is little research that supports them; and there is little evidence of their success. Moreover, with the exception of PBS programs, among those who support PCAs, there seems little interest in their evaluation. Yet PCAs have been widely adopted. The Pied Piper appears to have successfully played his pipe again.

---

[5]This comparison ignores the fact that applied behavior analysis of single cases occurs in ways that permit generalization of the outcomes to similar subjects, responses, and environments.

REFERENCES

Amado, A. N., & McBride, M. W. (2002). Realizing individual, organizational, and systems change: Lessons learned in 15 years of training about person-centered planning and principles. In S. Holburn & P. Vietze (Eds.), *Person-centered planning: Research, practice, and future directions* (pp. 361–377). Baltimore: Brookes.

Azrin, N. H., Schaeffer, R. M., & Wesolowski, M. D. (1976). A rapid method of teaching profoundly retarded persons to dress by a reinforcement-guidance method. *Mental Retardation, 14,* 29–33.

Baer, D. M. (1998). Commentary: Problems in imposing self-determination. *Journal of the Association for Persons with Severe Handicaps, 23,* 50–52.

Baer, D. M., Wolf, M. M., & Risley, T. R. (1968). Some current dimensions of applied behavior analysis. *Journal of Applied Behavior Analysis, 1,* 91–97.

Baer, D. M., Wolf, M. M., & Risley, T. R. (1987). Some still current dimensions of applied behavior analysis. *Journal of Applied Behavior Analysis, 20,* 313–327.

Bellamy, T., & Buttars, K. L. (1975). Teaching trainable level retarded students to count money: Toward personal independence through academic instruction. *Education and Training in Mental Retardation, 10,* 18–26.

Browder, D. M., Snell, M. E., & Willdonger, B. A. (1988). Simulation and community-based instruction of vending machines with time delay. *Education and Training in Mental Retardation, 23,* 175–185.

Butterworth, J., Hagner, D., Heikkinen, B., Faris, S., DeMello, S., & McDonough, K. (1993). *Whole life planning: A guide for organizers and facilitators.* Boston, MA: Institute for Community Integration, University of Massachusetts.

Carr, E. G. (1997). The evolution of applied behavior analysis into positive behavior support. *Journal of the Association for Persons with Severe Handicaps, 22,* 208–209.

Carr, E. G., & Durand, M. V. (1985). Reducing behavior problems through functional communication training. *Journal of Applied Behavior Analysis, 18,* 111–126.

Carr, E. G., Horner, R. H., Turnbull, A. P., Marquis, J. G., McLaughlin, D. M., McAtee, M. L., et al. (1999). *Positive behavioral support for people with developmental disabilities: A research synthesis.* Washington, DC: American Association on Mental Retardation.

Cooper, K. J., & Browder, D. M. (1998). Enhancing choice and participation for adults with severe disabilities in community-based instruction. *Journal of the Association for Persons with Severe Handicaps, 23,* 252–260.

Davidson, P. W., & Adams, E. (1989). Indicators of impact of services on persons with developmental disabilities: Issues concerning data collection mandates in P. L. 100–146. *Mental Retardation, 27,* 297–304.

Derby, K. M., Wacker, D., Sasso, G., Steege, M., Northrup, J., Cigrand, K., et al. (1992). Brief functional assessment techniques to evaluate aberrant behavior in an outpatient setting. *Journal of Applied Behavior Analysis, 25,* 713–721.

Durand, M. V., & Carr, E. G. (1991). Functional communication training to reduce challenging behavior: Maintenance and application in new settings. *Journal of Applied Behavior Analysis, 24,* 251–264.

Everson, J. (1996). Using person-centered planning concepts to enhance school-to-adult life transition planning. *Journal of Vocational Rehabilitation, 6,* 7–13.

Faw, G., Davis, P. K., & Peck, C. (1996). Increasing self-determination: Teaching people with mental retardation to evaluate residential options. *Journal of Applied Behavior Analysis, 29,* 173–188.

Fisher, W. W., & Mazur, J. E. (1997). Basic and applied research on choice responding. *Journal of Applied Behavior Analysis, 30,* 387–410.

Foxx, R. M., Faw, G. D., Taylor, S., Davis, P. K., & Fulia, R. (1993). "Would I be able to …?" Teaching clients to assess the availability of their community living life style preferences. *American Journal on Mental Retardation, 98,* 235–248.

Green, C. W., Gardner, S. M., & Reid, D. H. (1997). Increasing indices of happiness among people with profound multiple disabilities: A program replication and component analysis. *Journal of Applied Behavior Analysis, 30,* 217–228.

Green, C. W., Middleton, S. G., & Reid, D. H. (2000). Embedded evaluation of preferences sampled from person-centered plans for people with profound multiple disabilities. *Journal of Applied Behavior Analysis, 33,* 639–642.

Green, C. W., Reid, D. H., White, L. K., Halford, R. C., Brittain, D. P., & Gardner, S. M. (1988). Identifying reinforcers for persons with profound handicaps: Staff opinion versus systematic assessment of preferences. *Journal of Applied Behavior Analysis, 21,* 31–43.

Harding, J. W., Wacker, D. P., Berg, W. K., Barretto, A., & Rankin, B. (2002). Assessment and treatment of severe behavior problems using choice-making procedures. *Education and Treatment of Children, 25,* 26–46.

Hatton, C. (1998). Whose quality of life is it anyway? Some problems with the emerging quality of life consensus. *Mental Retardation, 36,* 104–115.

Holburn, S. (1997). A renaissance in residential behavior analysis? A historical perspective and a better way to help people with challenging behavior. *The Behavior Analyst, 20,* 61–85.

Holburn, S. (2001). Compatibility of person-centered planning and applied behavior analysis. *The Behavior Analyst, 24,* 271–281.

Holburn, S., & Pfadt, A. (1998). Clinicians on person-centered planning teams: New roles, fidelity of planning and outcome treatment. *Mental Health Aspects of Developmental Disabilities, 1,* 82–86.

Holburn, S., & Vietze, P. (1998). Has person-centered planning become the alchemy of developmental disabilities? A response to O'Brien, O'Brien and Mount. *Mental Retardation, 36,* 485–488.

Holburn, S., & Vietze, P. (1999). Acknowledging barriers in adopting person-centered planning. *Mental Retardation, 37,* 117–124.

Holburn, S., & Vietze, P. (2002a). A better life for Hal: Five years of person-centered planning and applied behavior analysis. In S. Holburn & P. Vietze (Eds.), *Person-centered planning: Research, practice, and future directions* (pp. 291–314). Baltimore: Brookes.

Holburn, S., & Vietze, P. (2002b). Person-centered planning and cultural inertia in applied behavior analysis. *Behavior and Social Issues, 10,* 39–70.

Horner, R. H. (1997). Encouraging a new applied science: A commentary on two papers addressing parent-professional partnerships in behavioral support. *Journal of the Association for Persons with Severe Handicaps, 22,* 210–212.

Horner, R. H., Close, D. W., Frederick, H. D., O'Neill, R. E., Albin, R. W., Sprague, J. R., et al. (1996). Supported living for people with severe problem behaviors: A demonstration. In D. H. Lehr & F. Brown, (Eds.), *People with disabilities who challenge the system* (pp. 209–240). Baltimore: Brookes.

Iwata, B. A., Pace, G. M., Dorsey, M. F., Zarcone, J. R., Volmer, T. R., Smith, R. G., et al. (1994). The functions of self-injurious behavior: An experimental epidemiological analysis. *Journal of Applied Behavior Analysis, 27,* 215–240.

Jacobson, J. W., Mulick, J. A., & Schwartz, A. A. (1995). A history of facilitated communication: Science, pseudoscience, and antiscience. *American Psychologist, 50,* 750–765.

Kincaid, D. (1996). Person-centered planning. In L. K. Koegel, R. L. Koegel, & G. Dunlap (Eds.), *Positive behavioral support: Including people with difficult behavior in the community* (pp. 439–465). Baltimore: Brookes.

Kincaid, D., & Fox, L. (2002). Person-centered planning and positive behavior support. In S. Holburn & P. M. Vietze (Eds.), *Person-centered planning: Research, practice, and future directions* (pp. 29–49). Baltimore: Brookes.

Koegel, L. K., Koegel, R. L., & Dunlap, G. (1996). *Positive behavioral support: Including people with difficult behavior in the community.* Baltimore: Brookes.

Magito-McLaughlin, D., Spinosa, T. R., & Marsalis, M. D. (2002). Overcoming the barriers: Moving toward a service model that is conducive to person-centered planning. In S. Holburn & P. M. Vietze (Eds.), *Person-centered planning: Research, practice, and future directions* (pp. 127–150). Baltimore: Brookes.

Michael, J. (1982). Distinguishing between discriminative and motivational functions of stimuli. *Journal of the Experimental Analysis of Behavior, 37,* 149–155.

Michael, J. (1993). Establishing operations. *The Behavior Analyst, 16,* 191–206.

Michael, J. (2000). Implications and refinements of the establishing operation concept. *Journal of Applied Behavior Analysis, 33*, 401–410.

Mostert, M. P. (2001). *Facilitated communication* since 1995: A review of published studies. *Journal of Autism and Developmental Disorders, 13*, 287–313.

Mount, B. (1994). Benefits and limitations of personal futures planning. In V. J. Bradley, J. W. Ashbaugh, & B. C. Blaney (Eds.), *Creating individual supports for people with developmental disabilities: A mandate for change at many levels* (pp. 97–108). Baltimore: Brookes.

Mount, B., & Zwernick, K. (1988). *It's never too early, it's never too late: A booklet about personal futures planning* (Publication No. 421-88-109). St. Paul, MN: Metropolitan Council.

O'Brien, J. (1987). A guide to life-style planning: Using The Activities Catalog to integrate services and natural support systems. In B. Wilcox & G. Bellamy (Eds.), *A comprehensive guide to The Activities Catalog: An alternative curriculum for youth and adults with severe disabilities* (pp. 175–189). Baltimore: Brookes.

O'Brien, J. (2002). Numbers and faces: The ethics of person-centered planning. In S. Holburn & P. M. Vietze (Eds.), *Person-centered planning: Research, practice, and future directions* (pp. 399–414). Baltimore: Brookes.

O'Brien, J., & Lovett, H. (1992). *Finding a way toward everyday lives: The contribution of person centered planning*. Harrisburg, PA: Pennsylvania Office of Mental Retardation.

O'Brien, C. L., & O'Brien, J. (2002). The origins of person-centered planning: A community of practice perspective. In S. Holburn & P. M. Vietze (Eds.), *Person-centered planning: Research, practice, and future directions* (pp. 3–27). Baltimore: Brookes.

O'Brien, C. L., O'Brien, J., & Mount, B. (1997). Person-centered planning has arrived … or has it? *Mental Retardation, 35*, 480–484.

Osborne, J. G. (1999). Renaissance or killer mutation? A response to Holburn. *The Behavior Analyst, 22*, 47–52.

Pearpoint, J., O'Brien, J., & Forest, M. (1993). *PATH: A workbook for planning positive possible futures and planning alternative tomorrows with hope for schools, organizations, businesses, and families* (2nd ed.). Toronto: Inclusion Press.

Rea, J. A., Martin, C., & Wright, K. (2002). Using person-centered supports to change the culture of large intermediate care facilities. In S. Holburn & P. M. Vietze (Eds.), *Person-centered planning: Research, practice, and future directions* (pp. 73–96). Baltimore: Brookes.

Reid, D. H., Everson, J. M., & Green, C. W. (1999). A systematic evaluation of preferences identified through person-centered planning for people with profound multiple disabilities. *Journal of Applied Behavior Analysis, 32*, 467–477.

Reid, D. H., & Green, C. W. (2002). Person-centered planning with people who have severe multiple disabilities: Validated practices and misapplications. In S. Holburn & P. M. Vietze (Eds.), *Person-centered planning: Research, practice, and future directions* (pp. 183–202). Baltimore: Brookes.

Risley, T. R. (1996). Get a life! Positive behavioral intervention for challenging behavior through life arrangement and life coaching. In L. K. Koegel, R. L. Koegel, & G. Dunlap (Eds.), *Positive behavioral support: Including people with difficult behavior in the community* (pp. 425–437). Baltimore: Brookes.

Risley, T. R. (1999). Forward: Positive behavioral support and applied behavior analysis. In E. G. Carr et al. (Eds.), *Positive behavior support for people with developmental disabilities: A research synthesis* (pp. 11–13). Washington, DC: American Association on Mental Retardation.

Sailor, W. (1996). New structures and systems change for comprehensive positive behavioral support. In L. K. Koegel, R. L. Koegel, & G. Dunlap (Eds.), *Positive behavioral support: Including people with difficult behavior in the community* (pp. 163–206). Baltimore: Brookes.

Schwartz, A. A., Jacobson, J. W., & Holburn, S. C. (2000). Defining person centeredness: Results of two consensus methods. *Education and Training in Mental Retardation and Developmental Disabilities, 35*, 235–249.

Singer, G. H. S. (1997). Participatory action research meets the emic, the etic, and program evaluation: A response to Vaughan et al. and Fox et al. *Journal of the Association for Persons with Severe Handicaps, 22*, 215–217.

Smull, M. W., & Harrison, S. B. (1992). *Supporting people with severe retardation in the community.* Alexandria, VA: National Association of State Mental Retardation Program Directors.

Sprague, J. R., & Horner, R. H. (1984). The effects of single instance, multiple instance, and general case training on generalized vending machine use by moderately and severely handicapped students. *Journal of Applied Behavior Analysis, 17,* 273–278.

Test, D. W., Spooner, F., Keul, P. K., & Grossi, T. (1990). Teaching adolescents with severe disabilities to use the public telephone. *Behavior Modification, 14,* 157–171.

Turnbull, A. P., & Turnbull, H. R. (1996). Group action planning as a strategy for providing comprehensive family support. In L. K. Koegel, R. L. Koegel, & G. Dunlap (Eds.), *Positive behavioral support: Including people with difficult behavior in the community* (pp. 99–114). Baltimore: Brookes.

Ulrich, R., Stachnik, T., & Mabry, J. (1966). *Control of human behavior* (Vol. 1). Glenview, IL: Scott Foresman.

Ulrich, R., Stachnik, T., & Mabry, J. (1970). *Control of human behavior* (Vol. 2). Glenview, IL: Scott Foresman.

Ulrich, R., Stachnik, T., & Mabry, J. (1974). *Control of human behavior* (Vol. 3). Glenview, IL: Scott Foresman.

Wagner, G. A. (2002). Person-centered planning from a behavioral perspective. In S. Holburn & P. Vietze (Eds.), *Person-centered planning: Research, practice, and future directions* (pp. 273–289). Baltimore: Brookes.

Wolf, M. M. (1978). Social validity: The case for subjective measurement or how applied behavior analysis is finding its heart. *Journal of Applied Behavior Analysis, 11,* 203–214.

Wolf, M. M., Risley, T. R., & Mees, H. I. (1964). Application of operant conditioning procedures to the behavior problems of an autistic child. *Behaviour Research & Therapy, 1,* 305–312.

Sensory Integrative Therapy

Tristram Smith
Daniel W. Mruzek
Dennis Mozingo
University of Rochester Medical Center

In 1972, Ayres introduced the construct of sensory integration (SI). She defined SI as "the neurological process that organizes sensation from one's own body and from the environment and makes it possible to use the body effectively within the environment" (p. 11). According to Ayres (1972), SI occurs in the brain cortex, and it requires balance between the central and peripheral nervous systems, as well as between excitatory and inhibitory neurological systems (Bundy & Murray, 2002; Galvin Cook & Dunn, 1998). SI is viewed as necessary to maintain a personal "map" of one's body (i.e., being aware of the body and what it is doing) and to perform sophisticated cognitive activities (e.g., planning, attending to the environment, and using language).

Ayres (1972) and subsequent writers have implicated problems with SI in a variety of disorders, including physical disabilities such as cerebral palsy (Anzalone & Murray, 2002), learning disabilities, ADHD (Shellenberger & Williams, 2002), and developmental disabilities such as autism (Linderman & Stewart, 1998). These writers refer to problems with SI as "sensory integration dysfunction," which is "the inefficient neurological processing of information received through the senses, causing problems with learning, development, and behavior" (Stock Kranowitz, 1998, p. 292). Sensory integration dysfunction is thought to impair the vestibular, proprioceptive, and tactile systems. The vestibular system provides sensory input to the brain about the body's movement through space. Ostensible signs of vestibular impairment include poor posture and dyspraxia (difficulty planning or sequencing motor activities). The proprioceptive system provides sensory input from muscles and joints. Proprioceptive impairment is said to be manifested by stereotyped body movements such as flapping one's hands or rocking one's body back and forth. Finally, in SI theory, impairments in the tactile system, or one's sense of touch, are evidenced by over- or undersensitivity to sensory stimuli.

Sensory integrative therapy (SIT) is designed to restore effective neurological processing by enhancing each of these systems. For example, SIT often incorporates activities intended to stimulate the vestibular system such as swinging, rolling, jumping on a trampoline, or riding on scooter boards. Activities to stimulate the proprioceptive or tactile systems include "smooshing" the individual between gymnasium pads or pillows to provide "deep pressure," brushing a client's body, providing "joint compression" by repeatedly tightening the individual's joints such as at the wrist or elbow, and playing with textured toys (Bundy & Murray, 2002).

The application of a "sensory diet" is a related clinical practice in which practitioners implement individualized activity plans to meet the presumed sensory needs of the individual. Such a plan might include engaging an individual in gross motor games, having her wear weighted vests, putting a body sock over her, conducting oral motor exercises, and modifying her environment (e.g., adjusting the lighting) in order to improve or alter arousal states and affect (Alhage-Kientz, 1996; Wilbarger, 1995; Wilbarger & Wilbarger, 1991).

SIT practitioners are usually occupational therapists (OTs). These practitioners typically conduct 30- to 60-minute sessions one to three times per week and often direct parents and paraprofessionals, such as classroom aides, to carry out the intervention at other times throughout the day (Bundy & Murray, 2002). SIT may take place in a variety of settings, including classrooms, homes, swimming pools, and even on horseback (Case-Smith & Miller, 1999; Lawton-Shirley, 2002).

SIT practitioners report three types of benefits: (a) enhanced ability to focus on relevant materials in educational, therapeutic, and social environments (Wilbarger & Wilbarger, 1991); (b) reduction in the rate of aberrant behaviors such as self-injury (Bright, Bittick, & Fleeman, 1981; Reisman, 1993); and (c) generalized improvements in nervous system functioning, reflected in gains in high-level cognitive activity such as language and reading (Ayres, 1974, 1979; Brody, Thomas, Brody, & Kucherawy, 1977; Magrun, McCue, Ottenbacher, & Keefe, 1981). Because practitioners attribute these improvements to increased organization and functional efficiency in an impaired central nervous system (CNS), they often describe SIT as a "process" therapy (Cermak & Henderson, 1999). Ayres (1979) asserted that, although consumers may be skeptical of SIT, it should take precedence over other interventions:

> It may be difficult for a parent to believe that riding a scooter board could really help his child with speech, reading, or behavior. On the surface, it seems obvious that he needs speech therapy, reading lessons, or more discipline. However, the brain is so complex that its operations are never obvious on the surface of things. If speech and reading and behavior are poor because the brain is not working well, it makes good sense to build a foundation upon which the brain can work better. After therapy has accomplished as much as it can, and if the child still has difficulty, it may be appropriate to provide him with tutoring. (p. 145)

EVALUATION OF SIT

Theory

Ayres (1972) and subsequent writers such as Lane (2002) have portrayed SI concepts as rooted in well-established scientific models of neurological structure and function. For example, they correctly note that research supports the role of the cortex in integrating sensory input and the need for balance (homeostasis) in the brain. A major limitation in SI theory, however, is the dearth of reliable evidence for its main tenet, which is that integration of sensory input is necessary for high level cognitive functioning. As Arendt, MacLean, and Baumeister (1988) noted, this tenet is based on the outmoded position that the development of the individual human mirrors the evolutionary development of the species (i.e., "ontogeny recapitulates phylogeny"). Specifically, a key rationale for SIT is that sensory systems arose relatively early in the evolutionary history of humans and were prerequisite for the emergence of more complex cognitive skills: "The manner in which the sensory systems evolved influences the way in which they develop and function in man today" (Ayres, 1979, p. 39). For this reason, according to SI theory, individuals must optimize their sensory systems before they can acquire cognitive skills. SIT proponents also assert that the vestibular, proprioceptive, and tactile systems are ancestors of other senses such as hearing or seeing (Ayres, 1979, pp. 39–43). Therefore, these systems, rather than other senses, are the main focus of SIT. The systems are said to reside in "primitive," subcortical pathways that must develop before the formation of advanced cortical systems that are unique to humans (Ayres, 1972).

In actuality, there is no sound scientific basis for any of these assertions (Arendt et al., 1988). For instance, the sequence of development for an individual often differs from the evolutionary history of the individual's species (Gould, 1977). Many individuals who have sensory impairments excel at cognitive tasks (Spitz, 1986). It is doubtful that vestibular and tactile systems were forerunners of other senses, that they must develop before cortical systems or, more generally, that they are a prerequisite for cognitive functioning (Arendt et al., 1988). Thus, SI theory is inextricably linked to unsubstantiated and even refuted models.

Other tenets of SI theory also conflict with research. Despite repeated and elaborate attempts, investigators have been unable to link learning disabilities to vestibular dysfunction (Hoehn & Baumeister, 1994). Proprioceptive, tactile, and other sensory dysfunctions identified by SI theorists have received less research attention but are also unconfirmed. The view that individuals with disabilities have an imbalance or lack of homeostasis in nervous system functioning is similarly uncorroborated by research (Arendt et al., 1988).

In the SI literature, biological theories are complemented by hypothetical personality constructs such as spiraling "inner drives" for a sense of mastery and self-actualization (Bundy & Murray, 2002), "decreased self-regulation," "diminished optimal arousal," "sensory deprivation and/or overload," and "sensory and/or tactile defensiveness" (Wilbarger & Wilbarger, 1991). These constructs do not have clear definitions that would permit their valid and reliable measurement, or any demonstrated scientific basis.

Assessment

The three main methods for diagnosing sensory integrative dysfunction are direct assessments such as the Sensory Integration and Praxis Tests (SIPT; Ayres, 1989), rating scales such as the Sensory Profile (Dunn, 1999), and clinical observations. The SIPT was derived from factor-analytic studies, beginning with Ayres (1965), and is a standardized instrument designed to assess vestibular, proprioceptive, tactile, and visual processing in children aged 4 through 8 years. It has been described as "the most comprehensive and statistically sound means for assessing some important aspects of sensory integration, most notably praxis and tactile discrimination" (Bundy, 2002, p. 170). However, research indicates that 5 of the 17 subtests are unstable, meaning that results are likely to vary each time they are given to the same individual (Mailloux, 1990). Although Ayres (1989) reported that SIPT scores differed between children with and without learning disabilities, subsequent analyses of her studies showed that there were actually no reliable differences (Hoehn & Baumeister, 1994). As well, Ayres (1989) did little testing of the utility of this test for children with other disabilities. A more fundamental concern is that a key index of SI dysfunction in the SIPT is hyponystagmus, which is an especially long duration of involuntary eye rolling following a rapid rotation of the individual. Studies indicate that hyponystagmus is unrelated to learning disabilities (Hoehn & Baumeister, 1994).

Another SI measure is the Sensory Profile (Dunn, 1999), which is a 125-item questionnaire completed by parents to characterize their child's unique sensory preferences and aversions. Although studies indicate that the Sensory Profile discriminates among different clinical populations (Dunn & Westman, 1997), its utility for identifying sensory integration dysfunction remains empirically untested.

Another diagnostic practice involves observing behaviors and making inferences about sensory difficulties associated with those behaviors. Galvin Cook and Dunn (1998) describe this practice as a functional analysis, although it differs markedly from standard functional analytic procedures. Specifically, a functional analysis consists of systematically presenting or removing different environmental events (e.g., attention from others or demands to perform tasks) and objectively measuring how these events influence operationally defined behaviors (Iwata, Dorsey, Slifer, Bauman, & Richman, 1982). In contrast, the practice described by Galvin Cook and Dunn (1998) does not involve making environmental changes or operationally defining the sensory difficulties said to be affected by these changes. The practice is also unsupported by research. Thus, there are currently no objective, validated methods for identifying sensory integrative dysfunction.

Treatment Outcome

Arendt et al. (1988) identified only eight studies on SIT with individuals with developmental disabilities. Three were descriptive case studies that "contain no empirical support" (p. 403) of SIT effectiveness. The remaining five each had significant methodological limitations, including failure to use dependent measures with established reliability, apply appropriate statistical techniques, and incorporate control groups. Arendt et al. (1988) concluded, "Until the therapeutic effectiveness of sensory integration therapy with mentally retarded persons is demonstrated, there exists no convincing empirical or theoretical support for the continued use of this therapy with that population outside of a research context" (p. 409).

In a meta-analysis of 32 SIT treatment effectiveness studies across several diagnostic categories (e.g., learning disability or motor delay), Vargas and Camilli (1999) reported that, although studies before 1982 indicated moderate improvement with SIT, subsequent studies revealed essentially no benefit. Studies with rigorous procedures such as the use of multiple, objective measures of outcome were particularly likely to show SIT to be ineffective. This meta-analysis incorporated five studies of individuals with mental retardation, including two studies

(Brody et al., 1977; Montgomery & Richter, 1977) that Arendt et al. (1988) previously reviewed. Table 20.1 summarizes the studies and methodological safeguards employed to ensure that the results are valid (random assignment to treatment groups, manuals to describe the interventions in enough detail that others can replicate it, checks on whether the intervention is implemented properly, and validated outcome measures given by examiners who are "blind" to the study hypothoses). As shown, two studies (Close, Carpenter, & Cibiri, 1986; Morrison & Pothier, 1972) identified benefits from SIT but contained many significant methodological weaknesses that cast doubt on the validity of the results. Another study (Montgomery & Richter, 1977) revealed that individuals who received SIT did not differ on most outcome measures from individuals who attended physical education, although they did improve more than individuals who participated in arts and crafts. Limitations of the study included nonrandom assignment to intervention groups and unclear descriptions of treatment procedures. In addition, Huff and Harris (1987) reported no significant differences on pre- and post-measures between a group of adults with mental retardation who participated in a SIT group and a control group. Lastly, Brody et al. (1977) incorporated adequate experimental control and did not find a difference between SIT and operant conditioning in the promotion of vocalizations by individuals with profound mental retardation. Vocalizations occurred at a higher rate in the operant conditioning group than the SIT group, but this difference was not statistically significant.

In a review of treatment methods, Dawson and Watling (2000) identified a total of four studies containing objective measures to evaluate SIT for individuals with autism. This group consisted of one case study (Ray, King, & Grandin, 1988), two uncontrolled studies with small samples and inadequate experimental controls (Case-Smith & Bryan, 1999; Linderman & Stewart, 1999), and one study with a larger sample that failed to demonstrate gains in speech following participation in sensory activities (Reilly, Nelson, and Bundy, 1984). With regard to contrasting SIT and traditional occupational therapy in the treatment of autism, Dawson and Watling wrote, "There exist so few studies that conclusions cannot be drawn" (p. 419). These findings prompted Goldstein (2000) to ask, "Can we allow treatments that are too good to be true? Can we allow anecdotal reports, case studies, and uncontrolled experiments to continue to guide the field and families of children with autism?" (p. 424).

THE ENDURING APPEAL OF SIT

Despite the limited and mostly negative research findings on SIT, a survey of OTs revealed that 82% of respondents reported that they "always" use a sensory integrative approach when working with children with autism (Watling, Dietz, Kanny, & McLaughlin, 1999). The popularity of SIT extends to other professionals and clinical populations. Shore (1994) cited a survey in which 24% of residential program directors endorsed SIT for individuals with developmental disabilities. Smith and Antolovich (2000) found that most families reported enrolling their child in SIT on the recommendation of individuals identifying themselves as speech therapists, behavior analysts, or other professionals. A few families even reported having been compelled to accept SIT in order to receive other services.

TABLE 20.1

Controlled studies of SIT effectiveness in persons with developmental disabilities cited by Vargas and Camilli (1998)

Study	Sample	Treatment Groups	Random Assignment	Manuals	Integrity Checks	Validated Outcome Measures	"Blind" Assessment	Findings
Brody et al. (1977)	27 Adults with Profound MR	SIT, Operant Conditioning, and SIT/Operant Combined	Yes	Yes	Yes	Yes	Yes	No significant difference between groups
Close et al. (1986)	12 Adults with Profound MR	SIT and Control (no treatment)	No	No	No	No	No	SIT group improved more than Control group
Huff & Harris (1987)	34 Adults with MR	SIT and Control (no treatment)	No	No	No	Yes	No	No significant differences between groups
Montgomery & Richter (1977)	75 Children with Trainable MR	SIT, Physical Education (PE), and Arts and Crafts	No	No	Yes	Yes	Yes	SIT group improved more than Arts and Crafts group; no difference between SIT group and PE group on 16 of 18 outcome measures[a]
Morrison & Pothier (1972)	27 Children with MR	SIT[b], Gross Motor Treatment, and Attention Control	No	No	No	Yes	Yes	SIT group improved more than two other groups[a]

[a]Pairwise comparisons between groups were not reported by the investigators; hence, the data were re-analyzed for presentation in this table.
[b]SIT intervention included systematic use of behavior-analytic methods such as shaping, chaining, and contingency management (p. 257).

How do SIT proponents justify this practice in the absence of scientific validation? Some emphasize subjective reports supporting SIT and view research as a
"potential threat" because it may cast doubt on subjective reports (Dubouloz, Egan,
Vallerand, & von Zweck, 1999). Other practitioners believe that SIT should become
"evidence-based" (Tickle-Degnen, 1999). These individuals acknowledge the lack
of scientific validitation for SIT. Still, they expect that the research will "catch up"
with their professional beliefs and practices over time. For example, Bundy and
Murray (2002) noted, "In recent years, the evidence in support of intervention based
on the principles of sensory integration theory is mixed at best and downright negative at worst" (p. 22). They added that perceived gains might not be due to any particular SIT exercise, but, rather, due to "reframing" of the child's behavior by
parents and others or the result of experimenter bias. They anticipate, however, that
a body of methodologically sound studies to validate SIT will emerge.

Smith (chap. 4, this volume), identified two factors that contribute to continued
belief in the therapeutic value of SIT: First, its practitioners promise vague benefits
that are difficult to test. Second, they contend that these benefits occur because the
treatment corrects a central, underlying deficit. Some representative comments of
Ayres (1979) illustrate the presence of these factors:

> After a course of therapy, clients say things like, "It helped me pull my life together,"
> and "I used to plan a lot of things and nothing happened; now I can pull it off." (p. 143)

> Sensations [from riding a scooter board] and the resulting movements leave memories
> stored in his brain, and so the child gradually makes his body percept more accurate.
> The internal sensory "maps" that develop on the scooter board help the child to motor
> plan at home or at school. His improved sensory integration helps the parts of the ner-
> vous system that organize his thoughts and also his emotions. In addition, success in
> these tasks makes him feel more confident about himself. (p. 145)

> Riding the bolster [swing] as though it were a horse helps develop postural and equi-
> librium responses. (p. 147)

Although pulling one's life together, making body percepts more accurate, enhancing sensory integration, organizing thoughts and emotions, feeling more confident, and improving posture all may be important worthwhile outcomes, they are
extremely nebulous. There is no clear way to determine whether or not SIT can help
children pull their lives together, develop more accurate body percepts, and so on,
unless one develops and uses reasonably objective measures and definitions of
these outcomes. Still, Ayres (1979) contended that SIT is the most important intervention to implement: "Therapy involving sensory stimulation and responses to
stimulation is often more effective than drugs, mental analysis, or rewards and punishments in helping the dysfunctional brain to correct itself" (p. 135). Ayres added
that the treatment is "completely natural" (p. 135) and based on "a holistic approach" (p. 142). As Smith (chap. 4, this volume) discussed, these terms are meaningless in evaluating whether a treatment is helpful but are alluring to many
consumers and service providers.

In addition to a focus on vague benefits and a hypothesized central deficit, a reason for the popularity of SIT may be that it has real (though unintended) effects on
behaviors. For example, Mason and Iwata (1990) indicated that SIT activities may

provide positive reinforcement (e.g., attention) or negative reinforcement (e.g., escape from undesired settings or activities). This reinforcement, instead of the prescribed SIT activities, may bring about behavior change, and represents a more straightforward, simple, and testable explanation for the change than does improved mental "balance." SIT may have other unintended effects such as promoting relaxation (Siegel, 1996), though this possibility has not been tested empirically. Because SIT may influence behaviors in some ways and may be pleasurable, practitioners and consumers may be encouraged to believe that it also has therapeutic benefit.

EVALUATING SENSORY INTEGRATION AND SENSORY DIETS IN APPLIED SETTINGS

Given that widespread use of SIT continues in the absence of research support, we believe that professionals and consumers cannot simply wait and hope that this problem resolves itself. Rather, they are obliged to find constructive ways to respond when SIT is recommended or implemented. In our experience, the most useful response is to advocate for evaluating SIT objectively while minimizing threats to the integrity and intended outcome of other interventions. Next, we present specific ways to address SIT at different stages of implementation. For the purposes of this discussion, we assume that treatment teams include one or more professionals familiar with the research on the effectiveness of SIT and other interventions under consideration. Figure 20.1 summarizes the most common scenarios, possible responses to them, and options associated with each scenario.

Responding to Recommendations for SIT

In the best case scenario, before starting SIT, families and treatment teams have an opportunity to review research findings on this intervention. To enable teams to make informed decisions, professionals need to state directly that studies fail to show any therapeutic effectiveness. For example, they might say that, although many families and service providers consider SIT to be a standard, beneficial intervention for individuals with developmental disabilities, research indicates that the intervention does not help individuals function better. In addition, it is important to point out that the time and resources devoted to administering SIT take away opportunities to implement scientifically validated procedures.

To make these statements acceptable, professionals in disciplines that incorporate research findings as a matter of course in applied practice (e.g., behavior analysts) should recognize that they may antagonize SIT practitioners and consumers by citing data-based studies. In particular, they may come across as close-minded or even unaware of current practices. Professionals can often avoid this impression by emphasizing an empiricist perspective wherein SIT is seen as an approach that can be evaluated like any other intervention and may show therapeutic value. Thus, SIT practices are presented as amenable to and worthy of the kind of empirical evaluation that other interventions routinely undergo.

Second, SIT practices should be conceptualized analytically, within a framework of scientifically validated principles such as learning theory and educa-

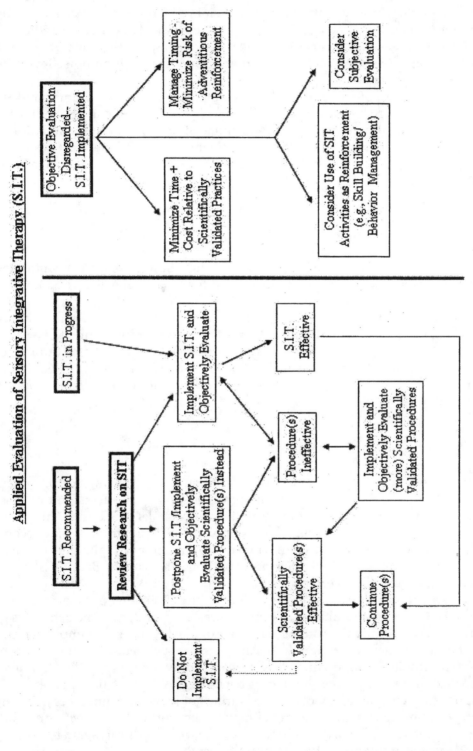

Applied Evaluation of Sensory Integrative Therapy (S.I.T.)

FIG. 20.1. Courses of action in the applied evaluation of sensory integrative therapy (SIT) when recommended prior to treatment, when in progress, or when objective evaluation is disregarded.

tional or treatment methods such as applied behavior analysis (Cooper, Heron, & Heward, 1987). For example, using principles of learning, service providers can identify specific behaviors to be changed in SIT, and they can conduct functional analyses to identify antecedents to these behaviors or consequences that may reinforce them. In their functional analyses, they can objectively evaluate whether SIT procedures are antecedents or consequences, just as they would study other environmental events (e.g., instructional staff attention, curriculum, noise levels, or termination of demands).

Following a review of research on SIT, a treatment team, including family and SIT practitioners, may proceed in one of three ways: (a) decide not to use SIT as part of the individual's treatment package, (b) postpone SIT until after the completion of an evaluation of a scientifically validated treatment, or (c) implement SIT systematically, with a plan for objectively evaluating its benefit, as described later in this section. Any of these outcomes should lead to informed, data-based decisions about SIT in the individual case.

Responding to SIT in Progress

Because SIT is often implemented without question about its empirical validation and without procedures to evaluate its benefit for a particular individual, many professionals and even families discover that SIT is being employed only after it has been initiated. In this scenario, an objective evaluation should be attempted (see "Methods of Objective Evaluation" later in this section). Emphasizing the empiricist perspective previously described may increase the likelihood that SIT practitioners and parents will support the evaluation. Once a team arrives at a decision to evaluate, further decisions about intervention can be made empirically, as shown in Figure 20.1.

Responding to a Decision Against an Objective Evaluation

Despite a recommendation for objective evaluation, practitioners and consumers may opt to continue SIT without systematically assessing its effects. In this case, other practitioners are obligated to reduce the clinical risks of SIT and limit its encroachment on other interventions. For example, an SIT practitioner may recommend brushing or bouncing on a ball when a person becomes "agitated," or, more specifically, when an individual attempts to hit himself or others. Because SIT may provide adventitious (inadvertent) reinforcement (Mason & Iwata, 1990), this procedure poses a risk of worsening the agitation. Figure 20.1 shows options for reducing this risk. One way is to employ SIT procedures independent of the behaviors of concern (e.g., scheduling them at regular times of the day instead of implementing them when a person becomes agitated). Another approach is to evaluate the procedures to confirm their reinforcing properties and apply them as positive reinforcement for acquiring skills or self-managing behavior problems. A final possibility is to propose subjective assessment, such as ratings of perceived outcomes of SIT. If this kind of assessment suggests that SIT may not be working, an objective evaluation or replacement of SIT with validated treatment methods can again be considered and may be of interest to the SIT practitioner.

Methods of Empirical Evaluation

Service providers have developed rigorous methods for "determining the effects of interventions ... and the reasons for these effects" in applied settings (Hayes, Barlow, & Nelson-Gray, 1999). These methods may be used to evaluate treatments derived from many theoretical perspectives, including SIT (Dura, Mulick, & Hammer, 1988). The methods involve the use of single-case designs. The designs are applicable to a wide range of clinical situations, but require that a member of the treatment or educational team have some expertise in implementing them (see Bailey & Burch, 2002; Cooper et al., 1987; Hayes et al., 1999).

In a single-case design, the first step is to select the behaviors to be changed. An SIT practitioner may propose that these be behaviors that are difficult to measure such as improving an individual's "organization" or helping them "modulate." Other team members can help clarify these behaviors by asking what they will see if the individual improves. They can also suggest possible outcomes, such as decreases in motor movements (e.g., buttocks remaining on a chair) or increases in accurate responding to instructor requests. Once team members agree on readily observable target behaviors, they then write definitions and procedures for scoring the behaviors (e.g., recording how often, or how long, or what percent of time intervals that the behaviors occur). Next, they identify the interventions that the SIT practitioner and other team members will implement to change the target behaviors (e.g., particular SIT procedures such as brushing or swinging), describe these procedures carefully, and develop a plan for implementing them consistently throughout the evaluation.

After specifying target behaviors and interventions, team members pick a design for testing whether the interventions produce changes in the target behaviors. Table 20.2 shows designs and their applicability for evaluating SIT methods. Typically, each design involves comparing a baseline phase in which individuals receive no SIT intervention to one or more treatment phases in which interventions are provided. Data are collected continuously on the target behavior throughout both conditions. If the behavior improves in a SIT treatment phase, relative to the baseline phase, one may conclude that the treatment may have produced this improvement.

The first method listed in Table 20.2, the multielement design (also called alternating treatment design), may be especially useful because it yields quick results. The design consists of implementing a treatment on alternate days or in alternate sessions. During the other days or sessions, a baseline is in effect (i.e., no intervention is provided), or another treatment is provided. Dura et al. (1988) used this design to evaluate the effects of SIT on self-injurious behavior in an individual with mental retardation. They alternated 10 sessions of vestibular stimulation with 10 baseline sessions in which the individual engaged in social interaction but did not receive vestibular stimulation. Self-injury was less frequent during the sessions with vestibular stimulation than during the baseline sessions. However, the sessions with vestibular stimulation had no apparent effect on the rate of self-injury outside of treatment sessions. For this reason, the intervention was stopped.

Figure 20.2 illustrates the alternating treatments design with one of our students. Clara, a 5-year-old girl with autism who attended an applied behavior analytic classroom, flapped her hands beside her head and covered her ears with her wrists. Her OT asserted that these behaviors occurred because Clara craved deep pressure

TABLE 20.2

Single-case designs for objectively Evaluating Sensory Integration Therapy (SIT)

Type of Design	Procedure	Target Behaviors (Dependent Measures)	Intended Treatment Effects (Independent Variables)	Comments
Multiple Element/ Alternating Treatments	Administer treatment on alternate days or sessions. During other days or sessions, implement a different treatment or no treatment (baseline).	One behavior already in the individual's repertoire.	Treatment produces immediate behavior change, observable in a single day or session.	Fastest evaluation of treatment, high acceptability to service providers and families, but appropriate only when treatment effects are expected to be immediate.
Reversal (ABAB)	Administer a baseline phase (A), then a treatment phase (B). Remove the treatment and begin another baseline phase (A); then introduce a second treatment phase (B).	One or more behaviors displayed by a single individual.	Treatment produces immediate or gradual behavior change.	Most stringent evaluation of treatment effects, but ethics must be considered (e.g., removing an apparently beneficial treatment and returning to the baseline phase may be inappropriate).
Multiple Baseline	Implement two or more baseline phases that are of varying lengths. Then apply treatment to one baseline at a time.	One behavior displayed by different individuals, several behaviors displayed by one individual, or one behavior displayed by an individual in different settings.	Behavior change occurs when treatment begins, regardless of the length of baseline. Change may occur immediately or gradually during the treatment phase.	Broadest applicability of all single-case designs.
AB (pre–post)	Administer baseline phase (A), then a treatment phase (B).	One or more behaviors displayed by a single individual.	Treatment produces immediate behavior change.	Often the easiest design to use in applied settings, but least rigorous test of whether treatment produces behavior change, requires lengthy, stable baseline and treatment phases.

on her wrists and recommended a sensory diet that consisted of wearing weighted wristbands. Frequency of hand-flapping and ear-covering was evaluated in an alternating treatments design with Clara wearing the weighted wristbands every other day.

In Fig. 20.2, the days when assessment took place are on the horizontal axis, and the frequency of hand-flapping is on the vertical axis. The figure shows virtually no difference between "wristbands-on" and "wristbands-off" conditions, though the target responses gradually decreased in both conditions during the 2-week period of the assessment. The decrease occurred at least partly because the use of wristbands was reduced to a partial day after Day 4, when the team discovered that Clara was attempting to remove them during activities that required her to raise her hands (lunch, physical education, art, and other activities requiring extensive hand movements). Subsequently, during these activities, the wristbands were withheld and data were not collected. Following the 2-week evaluation, team members decided to end Clara's use of wristbands.

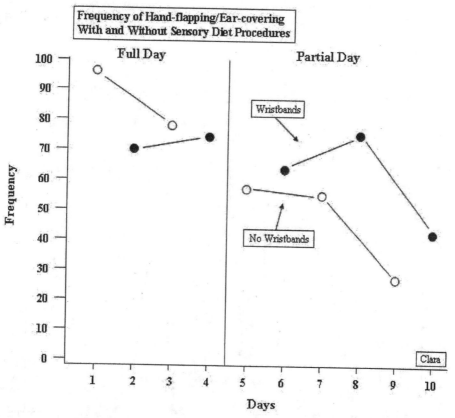

FIG. 20.2. The frequency of Clara's hand-flapping and ear-covering with and without weighted wristbands is depicted in an alternating treatments/multiple-element design. During the full-day condition, procedures and frequency measures occurred throughout the school day. During the partial-day condition, procedures and frequency measures occurred in all activities except those requiring use of hands (e.g., lunch, physical education).

A limitation of the alternating treatment design is that it is appropriate only when treatment effects are observable within a single day or session. Thus, if an SIT intervention is said to require multiple days or weeks to change the target behavior, other designs must be considered. A useful one is the reversal design, in which a baseline phase is followed by a treatment phase, followed by a return to the baseline phase, and so on. Each phase lasts several sessions, days, or weeks.

Figure 20.3 illustrates the use of a reversal design. Robert was a 4-year-old boy with autism who was receiving home-based early intensive behavioral intervention and who engaged in tantrums (screaming, crying, throwing objects, falling to the floor). Functional assessment data pointed to escape and avoidance of task demands as variables associated with the tantrums. Nevertheless, Robert's OT recommended an SIT procedure that consisted of brushing his body with a surgical brush, with the goal of reducing tantrums. We used a reversal design to evaluate the effects of brushing on the frequency of tantrums. During the baseline phases, Robert played with favored toys or briefly watched videos when he had breaks in teaching activities. During treatment phases, Robert's mother performed the brushing at break times, with training and guidance by the OT. Instructors, who were unaware of whether Robert was in the baseline or treatment condition, collected frequency data on tantrums during teaching sessions. Figure 20.3 shows that SIT failed to reduce this behavior, and may

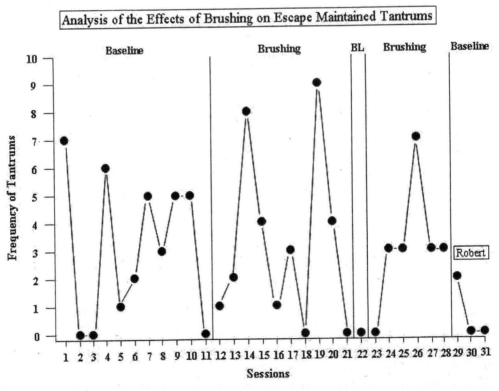

FIG. 20.3.   Robert's frequency of tantrums (screaming, crying, throwing objects, falling to the floor) during sensory brushing and baseline (no brushing) conditions is illustrated in an ABABA reversal design.

have been related to an increase in the behavior. When the findings were discussed with the family, a decision was made to discontinue SIT.

A potential problem with the reversal design is that it may be unethical to return to a baseline phase if the treatment was effective, or to introduce a treatment again if it was ineffective the first time. Table 20.2 shows another option, the multiple base-line design. This approach involves having two or more baseline phases that are of varying lengths and then applying treatment to one baseline at a time (Bailey & Burch, 2002). For example, three individuals could be in a baseline phase and then begin treatment at different times (a procedure called multiple baseline across participants). Alternatively, three different behaviors displayed by the same individual could be in a baseline phase and targeted for intervention beginning at different times (multiple baseline across behaviors). If the rate (or other measurement) of the target behavior remains about the same during baseline, regardless of the length of the baseline, but changes when treatment starts, one can infer that the treatment produced the change. Because the baseline and treatment phases are each implemented only once, the multiple baseline design avoids the ethical concerns that may arise in a reversal design.

Mason and Iwata (1990) used a multiple baseline design in their study of SIT. At the beginning of the study, three children with developmental disabilities were in a baseline phase. Then, one child began SIT while the other two children remained in baseline. Next, a second child began SIT while baseline continued for the third child. In addition, within the treatment phase for one child, SIT was implemented either without attending to the child or by providing continuous attention to evaluate whether attention received during SIT was responsible for behavior change. Mason and Iwata found that SIT increased the rate of self-injury in one child and decreased this behavior for the other two children only when it involved attending to the children. Thus, the investigators concluded that SIT by itself did not reduce self-injury.

As a last resort, a simple AB design can be employed. In this design, "A" refers to the baseline phase, which is followed by a treatment phase (B). This design is often the only available method in applied settings, where opportunities to modify educational or treatment programming may be limited. Because the shift from baseline to treatment occurs only once, the target behavior must change rapidly and dramatically when treatment begins in order for team members to have confidence that the treatment was effective. To allow detection of this kind of change, the AB design must include a lengthy baseline phase, and the target behavior must be stable in both the baseline and the treatment phases (Bailey & Burch, 2002), as illustrated by the hypothetical data in Figure 20.4. The AB design can yield valuable information about the benefit of treatments, but the results obtained with this design are usually not as clear as those obtained with the other designs in Table 20.2.

CONCLUSIONS AND FUTURE DIRECTIONS

Studies indicate that SIT is ineffective and that its theoretical underpinnings and assessment practices are unvalidated. Although the lack of research support for SIT has been apparent for many years (Arendt et al., 1988), it remains as popular as ever (Watling et al., 1999). As a result, professionals and consumers must ensure

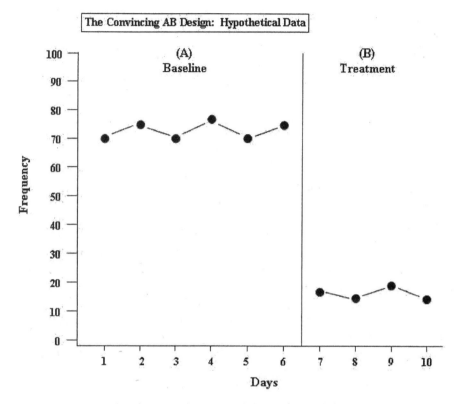

FIG. 20.4.   An example of an AB design with hypothetical data.

that educational and treatment teams carefully and objectively evaluate the intervention when they implement it in schools, homes, residential facilities, and other applied settings.

In addition to supporting informed decisions about whether to begin or continue SIT for a particular individual with a developmental disability, objective evaluations may have a broad impact on service delivery. The examples of evaluations in the preceding section all led to the conclusion that SIT was not beneficial for the recipient and should be discontinued. If other evaluations by educational or treatment teams consistently lead to the same conclusion, the popularity of SIT may finally wane. However, if carefully designed evaluations yield favorable results, appropriate uses of SIT may emerge.

To facilitate evaluations, SIT practitioners and other professionals would benefit from formal training on how to conduct single-case assessments in applied settings. Also, because many SIT practitioners believe that this intervention yields gains that studies have failed to detect, it would be advantageous for them to develop expertise in treatment outcome research involving large numbers of participants or to collaborate with investigators who have this knowledge. Such steps would enable them to improve the design of studies on SIT. Although single-case experiments and treatment outcome studies have the potential to support SIT, history shows that this result is unlikely. Research indicates that not only SIT but also many other sensorimotor therapies are unsuccessful (Kavale & Forness, 1999). Because of this history, investigators must go beyond evaluating SIT and examine how to break the cycle in which sensorimotor therapies are continually proposed and then refuted.

One possible strategy is to study the adventitious effects of SIT and other sensorimotor therapies. For example, although these therapies do not appear to work as intended, there is some evidence that they serve as reinforcement (Mason & Iwata, 1990), and they may have other benefits, such as promoting healthy physical exercise. Thus, if research confirms that SIT activities are reinforcing and healthy, they could be offered as leisure options. Alternatively, investigators may discover that other activities such as climbing on playground equipment are equally beneficial without requiring the involvement of a professional. In either case, a more sophisticated understanding of the effects of sensory activities would emerge, and the appeal of sensorimotor therapies that are "too good to be true" (Goldstein, 2000) may diminish.

Another promising strategy is to focus on the genuine sensorimotor issues present in many disabilities. For example, some individuals with language delays may respond slowly to auditory information such as speech sounds (Merzenich et al., 1996). Many individuals with autism are hypo- or hypersensitive to auditory stimuli and other sensations (American Psychiatric Association, 2000). Individuals with Down syndrome tend to be more proficient at processing visual than auditory information, whereas the reverse is true of individuals with Williams syndrome (Dykens, Hodapp, & Finucane, 2000).

The downfall of interventions such as SIT may be that they are based not on known sensorimotor issues but on speculative constructs, such as impaired vestibular systems. A strategy of starting with known sensorimotor issues and developing interventions that address these issues, based on scientifically sound principles of learning or biology, may have a much higher probability of success. Because different disabilities are associated with different sensorimotor issues, a multiplicity of interventions may be needed, rather than a single set of approaches as is used in SIT. Because changes in any one area of functioning usually do not lead to widespread changes in other areas of functioning (Smith, chap. 4, this volume), research-based sensorimotor interventions are likely to yield limited benefits rather than cures. Nevertheless, even complex interventions with limited benefits would be a significant advance.

REFERENCES

Alhage-Kientz, M. (1996). Sensory-based need in children with autism: Motivation for behavior and suggestions for intervention. *AOTA Developmental Disabilities Special Interest Section Newsletter, 19*(3), 1–3.

American Psychiatric Association. (2000). *Diagnostic and statistical manual of mental disorders* (4th ed., text revision). Washington, DC: Author.

Anzalone, M. E., & Murray, E. A. (2002). Integrating sensory integration with other approaches to intervention. In A. C. Bundy, S. J. Lane, & E. A. Murray (Eds.), *Sensory integration: Theory and practice* (2nd ed., pp. 371–396). Philadelphia: Davis.

Arendt, R. E., MacLean, W. E., & Baumeister, A. A. (1988). Critique of sensory integration therapy and its application in mental retardation. *American Journal on Mental Retardation, 92*, 401–411.

Ayres, A. J. (1965). Patterns of perceptual-motor dysfunction in children: A factor analytic study. *Perceptual and Motor Skills, 20*, 335–336.

Ayres, A. J. (1972). *Sensory integration and learning disorders.* Los Angeles: Western Psychological Services.

Ayres, A. J. (1974). *The development of sensory integrative theory and practice.* Dubuque, IA: Kendall/Hunt.

Ayres, A. J. (1979). *Sensory integration and the child.* Los Angeles: Western Psychological Services.

Ayres, A. J. (1989). *Sensory Integration and Praxis Tests manual.* Los Angeles: Western Psychological Services.

Bailey, J. B., & Burch, M. R. (2002). *Research methods in applied behavior analysis.* Thousand Oaks, CA: Sage.

Bright, T., Bittick, K., & Fleeman, B. (1981). Reduction of self-injurious behavior using sensory integrative techniques. *American Journal of Occupational Therapy, 35,* 167–172.

Brody, J. F., Thomas, J. A., Brody, D. M., & Kucherawy, D. A. (1977). Comparison of sensory integration and operant methods for production of vocalization in profoundly retarded adults. *Perceptual and Motor Skills, 44,* 1283–1296.

Bundy, A. C. (2002). Assessing sensory integrative dysfunction. In A. C. Bundy, S. J. Lane, & E. A. Murray (Eds.), *Sensory integration: Theory and practice* (2nd ed., pp. 169–198). Philadelphia: Davis.

Bundy, A. C., & Murray, E. A. (2002). Sensory integration: A. Jean Ayres' theory revisited. In A. C. Bundy, S. J. Lane, & E. A. Murray (Eds.), *Sensory integration: theory and practice* (2nd ed., pp. 3–34). Philadelphia: Davis.

Case-Smith, J., & Bryan, T. (1999). The effects of occupational therapy with sensory integration emphasis on preschool-age children with autism. *American Journal of Occupational Therapy, 53,* 489–497.

Case-Smith, J., & Miller, H. (1999). Occupational therapy with children with pervasive developmental disorders. *American Journal of Occupational Therapy, 53,* 506–513.

Cermak, S. A., & Henderson, A. (1999). *The efficacy of sensory integration procedures.* Available from www.Sinetwork.org

Close, W., Carpenter, M., & Cibiri, S. (1986). An evaluation study of sensory motor therapy for profoundly retarded adults. *Canadian Journal of Occupational Therapy, 53,* 259–264.

Cooper, J. O., Heron, T. E., & Heward, W. L. (1987). *Applied behavior analysis.* Columbus, OH: Merrill.

Dawson, G., & Watling, R. (2000). Interventions to facilitate auditory, visual, and motor integration in autism: A review of the evidence. *Journal of Autism and Developmental Disorders, 30,* 415–421.

Dubouloz, C. J., Egan, M., Vallerand, J., & von Zweck, C. (1999). Occupational therapist's perceptions of evidence-based practice. *American Journal of Occupational Therapy, 53,* 445–453.

Dunn, W. (1999). *Sensory Profile user's manual.* San Antonio, TX: Psychological Corporation.

Dunn, W., & Westman, K. (1997). The sensory profile: the performance of a national sample of children without disabilities. *American Journal of Occupational Therapy, 51,* 25–34.

Dura, J. R., Mulick, J. A., & Hammer, D. (1988). Rapid clinical evaluation of sensory integrative therapy for self-injurious behavior. *Mental Retardation, 26,* 83–87.

Dykens, E., Hodapp, R. M., & Finucane, B. (2000). *Genetics and mental retardation syndromes: A new look at behavior and interventions.* Baltimore: Brookes.

Edelson, S., & Rimland, B. (2001, May). *Summaries and critiques of research on auditory integration training: January, 1993 - May, 2001: 28 reports* (information packet). San Diego, CA: Autism Research Institute.

Galvin Cook, D., & Dunn, W. (1998). Sensory integration for students with autism. In R. L. Simpson & B. Smith Myles (Eds.), *Educating children and youth with autism: Strategies for effective practice* (pp. 191–239). Austin, TX: Pro-Ed.

Goldstein, H. (2000). Commentary: Interventions to facilitate auditory, visual, and motor integration: "Show me the data." *Journal of Autism and Developmental Disorders, 30,* 423–425.

Gould, S. J. (1977). *Ontogeny and phylogeny.* Cambridge, MA: Harvard University Press.

Hayes, S. C., Barlow, D. H., & Nelson-Gray, R. O. (1999). *The scientist practitioner* (2nd ed.). Boston: Allyn & Bacon.

Hoehn, T. P., & Baumeister, A. A. (1994). A critique of the application of sensory integration therapy to children with learning disabilities. *Journal of Learning Disabilities, 27*, 338–351.

Huff, D. M., & Harris, S. C. (1987). Using sensorimotor integrative treatments with mentally retarded adults. *American Journal of Occupational Therapy, 41*, 227–231.

Iwata, B. A., Dorsey, M. F., Slifer, K. J., Bauman, K. E., & Richman, G. S. (1982). Toward a functional analysis of self-injury. *Analysis and Intervention in Developmental Disabilities, 2*, 3–20.

Kavale, K. A., & Forness, S. R. (1999). *Efficacy of special education and related services.* Washington, DC: American Association on Mental Retardation.

Lane, S. J. (2002). Structure and function of the sensory systems. In A. C. Bundy, S. J. Lane, & E. A. Murray (Eds.), *Sensory integration: theory and practice* (2nd ed., pp. 35–70). Philadelphia: Davis.

Lawton-Shirley, N. (2002). Hippotherapy. In A. C. Bundy, S. J. Lane, & E. A. Murray (Eds.), *Sensory integration: theory and practice* (2nd ed., pp. 350–353). Philadelphia: Davis.

Linderman, T. M., & Stewart, K. B. (1998). Sensory-integrative based occupational therapy and functional outcomes in young children with pervasive developmental disorders: A single-subject design. *American Journal of Occupational Therapy, 53*, 207–213.

Linderman, T. M., & Stewart, K. B. (1999). Sensory integrative-based occupational therapy and functional outcomes in young children with pervasive developmental disorders: A single-subject study. *American Journal of Occupational Therapy, 53*, 207–213.

Magrun, W. M., Ottenbacher, K., McCue, S., & Keefe, R. (1981). Effects of vestibular stimulation on spontaneous use of verbal language in developmentally delayed children. *American Journal of Occupational Therapy, 35*, 101–104.

Mailloux, Z. (1990). An overview of the sensory integration and praxis tests. *American Journal of Occupational Therapy, 44*, 589–594.

Mason, S. A., & Iwata, B. A. (1990). Artifactual effects of sensory-integrative therapy on self-injurious behavior. *Journal of Applied Behavior Analysis, 23*, 361–370.

Merzenich, M. M., Jenkins, W. M., Johnston, P., Schreiner, C., Miller, S. L., & Tallal, P. (1996). Temporal processing deficits of language-learning impaired children ameliorated by training. *Science, 271*, 77–81.

Montgomery, P., & Richter, E. (1977). Effect of sensory integrative therapy on the neuromotor development of retarded children. *Physical Therapy, 57*, 799–806.

Morrison, D., & Pothier, P. (1972). Two different remedial motor training programs and the development of mentally retarded pre-schoolers. *American Journal of Mental Deficiency, 77*, 251–258.

Ray, T. C., King, L. K., & Grandin, T. (1988). The effectiveness of self-initiated vestibular stimulation in producing speech sounds in an autistic child. *Occupational Therapy Journal of Research, 8*, 186–190.

Reilly, C., Nelson, D. L., & Bundy, A. C. (1984). Sensorimotor versus fine motor activities in eliciting vocalization in autistic children. *Occupational Therapy Journal of Research, 3*, 199–212.

Reisman, J. (1993). Using a sensory integrative approach to treat self-injurious behavior in an adult with profound mental retardation. *American Journal of Occupational Therapy, 47*, 403–411.

Shellenberger, S., & Williams, M. S. (2002). "How does your engine run?" The Alert Program for self-regulation. In A. C. Bundy, S. J. Lane, & E. A. Murray (Eds.), *Sensory Integration: Theory and Practice* (2nd ed., pp. 342–345). Philadelphia: Davis.

Shore, B. A. (1994). Sensory-integrative therapy. *Self-Injury Abstracts & Reviews, 3*(1), 1–7.

Siegal, B. (1996). *The world of the autistic child: Understanding and treating autistic spectrum disorders.* New York: Oxford Press.

Smith, T., & Antolovich, M. (2000). Parental perceptions of supplemental interventions received by young children with autism in intensive behavior analytic treatment. *Behavioral Interventions, 15*, 83–97.

Spitz, H. (1986). *The raising of intelligence.* Mahwah, NJ: Lawrence Erlbaum Associates.

Stock Kranowitz, C. (1998). *The out-of-synch child: Recognizing and coping with sensory integration dysfunction.* New York: Perigree.

Tickle-Degnen, L. (1999). Organizing, evaluating and using evidence in occupational therapy practice. *The American Journal of Occupational Therapy, 53*, 537–539.

Vargas, S., & Camilli, G. (1999). A meta-analysis of research on sensory integration treatment. *American Journal of Occupational Therapy, 53,* 189–198.

Watling, R., Deitz, J., Kanny, E. M., & McLaughlin, J. F. (1999). Current practice of occupational therapy for children with autism. *American Journal of Occupational Therapy, 53,* 489–497.

Wilbarger, P. (1995). The sensory diet: Activity programs based on sensory processing theory. *Sensory Integration: Special Interest Section Newsletter, 18*(2), 1–4.

Wilbarger, P., & Wilbarger, J. (1991). *Sensory defensiveness in children aged 2–12: An intervention guide for parents and caregivers.* Denver, CO: Avanti Educational Programs.

Auditory Integration Training: A Critical Review

Oliver C. Mudford
TreeHouse Trust, London, UK

Chris Cullen
Keele University, Staffordshire, UK

WHAT IS AUDITORY INTEGRATION TRAINING?

Auditory integration training (AIT) is a procedure in which acoustically modified music is played to a person for 10 hours. Two 30-minute sessions per day, several hours apart, are conducted for 10 days in a fortnight. Commercial popular music with wide frequency range is used. Output from a compact disk player is connected to a box (AIT device, i.e., Audiokinetron, Audio Tone Enhancer/Trainer, or Ears Education and Retraining System) containing electronic circuitry that can modify the signal in two ways, modulation and narrow-band filtering. Modulation entails random clipping of frequencies above or below 1000 Hz for random durations between .25s and 2.0s. Filtering is reduction of volume for frequencies at which the individual recipient has hyperacute (unusually sharp) hearing as determined from prior audiological testing. The client wears headphones connected to the output from the AIT device. There are alterations made during the course of treatment in some dimensions of the musical stimuli, for example, changing volume levels for individual ears and in narrow-band filtering (Berkell, Malgeri, & Streit, 1996). These variables in AIT procedure have not been studied and are not mentioned further in this chapter.

EARLY HISTORY OF AIT

AIT was invented in the 1960s by French otolaryngologist (medical ear, nose, and throat specialist) Guy Berard (1993). He described his method as retraining the auditory system, and specifically dissociated AIT from auditory therapies (e.g., the Tomatis Method) that share some similar features:

> In the last number of years a number of sound processing centers have opened in Europe and the United States. These establishments attempt to cure hearing problems with a variety of techniques, ranging from simply listening to tapes of music, selected

according to the operator's subjective assessment of the patient, to much more sophisticated methods using filtered sounds supposedly reproducing the intrauterine hearing of the fetus. These approaches, whatever their worth, bear only a distant
resemblance to the auditory retraining concept, based upon the most precise
audiographic testing of the patient. (Berard, 1993, pp. 78–79)

Audiological testing to determine narrow-band hyperacuity (Berard's "trauma-
tizing frequencies") for individual AIT recipients was clearly prescribed as a key
component of AIT. Frequencies at which an audiogram shows relative peaks[1] of sensitivity are filtered, a "peak" when defined by AIT practitioners being greater than
or equal to a 10 dB (Bettison, 1996; Veale, 1994a) or 5 dB (Rimland & Edelson, 1994)
lower threshold than adjacent frequencies. Berard compared the effects of AIT on
the structures of the ear implicated in hyperacuity with physical therapy for stiff
joints: graded and increasing exercise. Audiographically, the aim is to bring hearing
to similar sensitivity across the range of frequencies, that is, flatten the peaks.
     Berard had used AIT with other populations before he started treating persons
with autism. He reported 76.2% "very positive results" from 1,850 cases with dyslexia, and 93% of 233 cases of "depression, suicidal tendencies" which were "cured
after first course of treatment" (Berard, 1993, p. 97). It should be emphasized that no
peer-reviewed scientific studies of the effects of AIT on persons with these disorders were located through database searches (Medline, PsycInfo, Web of Science)
nor in reference citations in articles published by AIT providers or advocates.
     Berard (1993) wrote that he was influenced to try AIT with persons with autism
after reading Condon (1975). Berard interpreted Condon's article as showing similarities in audiological anomalies between children with autism and those with dyslexia. Condon had analyzed film, frame-by-frame, of movements of children and
adolescents with a variety of diagnoses. What Condon concluded was that children
with autism seemed to respond to discrete sounds more than once, with intraindi-
vidually consistent delays of .5 to nearly 1.0 seconds. As an aside, these findings
may best be considered quirky as they have not been replicated, nor were they rediscovered in auditory event-related brain potential studies of persons with autism
(e.g., Courchesne, Lincoln, Yeung-Courchesne, Elmaison, & Grillon, 1989). Nevertheless, Condon's study did not address hyperacuity, and he reported on audiometric testing on only 1 of 25 participants. Berard's (1993) original stated
justification for using AIT with autism was scientifically tenuous at best.
     The first client with autism who received AIT was 12-year-old Georgiana Stehli in
late 1976 or early 1977 (Berard, 1993; Stehli, 1991). Berard stated that "1 case [i.e.,
Georgiana] experienced complete cure" (p. 97). Her mother, Annabel Stehli, wrote
that she believed that AIT was a contributory factor (Stehli, 1991), and her father
was reported to have averred that AIT was the sole factor in Georgiana's improvements (Rimland, 1991). Berard reported that, of 48 clients with autism who received
AIT, "47 experienced disappearance of fear of noise, 47 had pronounced modification in behavior [and] 31 experienced progressive restoration or improvement of

---

[1]Audiograms display hearing thresholds as minimum sound pressure level to which the individual
responded in dB on the vertical axis with lower dB values (i.e., more acute hearing) uppermost. Frequencies (Hz) at which thresholds are determined are shown on the horizontal axis, increasing from
left to right.

speech [and] 16 developed speech where it had not existed ..." (p. 97). Despite Berard's emphasis on accurate audiological pre-AIT assessment, audiograms were obtained from only 12 of these 48 clients (p. 80).

PUBLICITY, POPULARITY, PROFESSIONAL CONTROVERSY AND SUPPORT

Annabel Stehli's (1991) book *The Sound of a Miracle*, accompanied by magazine articles and television interviews, provided wide publicity for AIT to parents in the English-speaking world (Walker, 1991). AIT was adopted as a treatment by some professionals, particularly speech–language pathologists (e.g., Veale, 1994a, 1994b; Tharpe, 1996). By 1994, over 10,000 American children and adults had received AIT (Gravel, 1994). The cost then to parents was in the region of $1,000 (Rimland & Edelson, 1994) to $1,300 (Berkell et al., 1996) for the 10-hour treatment, so AIT provision had quickly become a multimillion dollar industry. More recently, the highest quoted cost of AIT known to us has approached $2,000 (Mudford et al., 2000).

AIT aroused heated controversy within the communication sciences' professional community. Critics (e.g., Berkell et al., 1996; Gravel, 1994; Tharpe, 1996, 1999) pointed out that (a) there was no scientific evidence for the type of peripheral hearing abnormalities in autism that Berard reported (Gravel, 1994); (b) AIT is theoretically inconsistent with knowledge about structures and mechanisms of the ear (Tharpe, 1996); (c) there is no audiometric measurement sufficiently valid and reliable to discriminate 5 or 10 dB peaks of hypersensitivity, especially in children with autism (Gravel, 1994; Tharpe, 1996); (d) there was only weak, irrelevant or insignificant "evidence" for AIT's claimed positive effects; and (e) sound pressure levels produced by some AIT devices were potentially unsafe (Gravel, 1994; Lucker, 1998; Rankovic, Rabinowitz, & Lof, 1996; Tharpe, 1996). Rankovic et al. (1996) reported average sound pressure level of 110dB from an Audiokinetron in use by an AIT provider. Average level from the device at maximum setting was 118 dB. These levels "exceed the maximum allowable exposure for 1 hour per day specified by OSHA [U.S. Occupational Safety and Health Administration], which is 105 dB" (Rankovic et al., 1996, p. 72). Rankovic et al. concluded that damage to hearing, particularly in children, could be caused by the device. The U.S. Food and Drug Administration (FDA) had disallowed import of Audiokinetrons in 1993 (Rankovic et al., 1996) "because the safety and efficacy of the treatment [AIT] have not been established" (Tharpe, 1996, p. 355). Audiokinetrons (manufactured by SAPP in France) and some other auditory integration devices (manufactured by Tomatis Electronics, also in France) are still (June 2002) listed as subject to U.S. import ban (see http://www.fda.gov/ora/fiars/ora_import_ia8908.html).

AIT was reviewed by several professional organizations. They recommended that AIT be used within experimental research protocols only (American Academy of Pediatrics, 1998; American Academy of Audiology, cited in Gravel, 1994; American Speech-Language and Hearing Association, cited in Tharpe, 1996).

Meanwhile, the Society for Auditory Integration Training (SAIT), now known as Society for Auditory Intervention Techniques, was formed in 1992 and included AIT researchers Bernard Rimland and Stephen M. Edelson among its organizational leading lights. Publicity for the claimed positive benefits of AIT continued through the SAIT newsletter and website (www.sait.com) and Rimland's Autism Research Institute publications. Being asked to give an expert informed opinion about any proposed intervention in the absence of high quality information (i.e., research data) induces a dilemma faced by most professionals in developmental disorders. A mixture of caution and optimism about AIT gave an ambiguous message to parents. Examples from a circular to parents and professionals that included advertisements for the sale of AIT treatment, AIT devices, AIT practitioner training, and pre-publication copies of Rimland and Edelson (1995) illustrate that ambiguity: "Please note that while we are optimistic, we are *not* stating that auditory training is a proven method .... We feel that parents have a right to try AIT on their children if they wish, even before final research results are known .... Now we believe that it may be possible that children with normal hearing might also benefit" (Rimland, 1992). It was a relatively small step for AIT merchants with Edelson and Rimland listed on their promotional material as on their Board of Advisors to be less ambiguous, for example, "GIVE YOUR CHILD A REAL CHANCE AT LAST ... a combined two week Sensory Integration Programme of Auditory Integration Training combined with Light Therapy" (Light & Sound Therapy Centre advertising material to parents, undated, received by authors February 1997, emphasis in original). As a matter of interest, this center (see Howlin, 1996) also sold the thoroughly discredited facilitated communication as part of their treatment package with AIT (Light & Sound Newsletter, Summer '93).

RESEARCH REVIEWS

Berard's claim that AIT improved behaviors of people with autism is the most important aspect for families with autistic children and the majority of professionals who advise them about treatment options. Therefore, our review of the relatively small body of published research on AIT focuses mainly on behavior change rather than on possible underlying peripheral or central mechanisms that may be responsible for claimed changes in behaviors. This is not to denigrate research on these mechanisms, but the first question is: Does AIT improve behaviors of persons with autism as claimed? If the research evidence points to the affirmative, the second question is: How does AIT work?

Reports Claiming Beneficial Effects of AIT

With one exception (Rimland & Edelson, 1994), we consider only research reports that were subject to peer review before publication and employed an experimental design that provided some comparison of the effects of AIT with a control or placebo group or condition. The results of three studies were viewed by their authors as favoring AIT treatment over control treatments (Edelson et al., 1999; Rimland & Edelson, 1994, 1995).

The first study (Rimland & Edelson, 1995) was conducted in 1991 (Rimland & Edelson, 1994). Eight children and young people with autism aged 4–21 years received AIT. An equal number of participants for a placebo treatment were matched with experimental subjects on age, sex, and history of ear infections. Placebo treatment was identical to the AIT condition except that the music was not modulated or filtered by the AIT device. Intergroup effects were assessed by analyzing changes in individual's scores on three assessment instruments completed by parents who were blind to group assignment, that is, they did not know until the study was complete whether their child had received AIT or not. Two of these assessment instruments were questionnaires of unknown reliability or validity: Fisher's Auditory Problems Checklist (FAPC) and Hearing Sensitivity Questionnaire (HSQ). The other was the 58-item Aberrant Behavior Checklist (ABC; Aman, Singh, Stewart, & Field, 1985). The ABC provides scores on five subscales: irritability, lethargy, hyperactivity, stereotypy, and inappropriate speech (formerly, excessive speech), and evidence on their psychometric properties has been published (Aman et al., 1985; Aman & Singh, 1986).

Rimland and Edelson (1995) analyzed treatment effects by calculating difference scores for individuals, the difference being between pretreatment and 3-month posttreatment measures. They reported significant improvements ($p < .05$) for the AIT group compared with the placebo group on FAPC, ABC mean score per item, and ABC subscales irritability, stereotypy, hyperactivity, and inappropriate speech. Rimland and Edelson interpreted their reported findings as supporting their hypothesis that AIT was a potentially beneficial treatment for people with autism.

Critical review of this first study highlights omissions, errors, and possible alternative explanations that diminish enthusiasm for the findings. First, groups differed on ABC and FAPC pretreatment scores. Rimland and Edelson (1995) did not report what those differences were, thus preventing independent review of the effects of those preexisting differences. If individuals in the AIT group had more extreme (higher) scores before treatment, the findings could be due to *regression to the mean*, which is the tendency of individual's initial extreme scores to be closer to the group average score on further measurement independent of any treatment effects (or lack thereof). Defending their conclusions, Edelson and Rimland (2001, review of study 10) wrote, "Regression analysis suggested the effects observed were not artefacts of the initial differences." However, this claim was not supported in the Rimland and Edelson (1995) publication.

Second, the use of a single score from average ABC ratings is not psychometrically legitimate due to the independence of the subscales. This was stated explicitly by the developers of the rating scales (Aman & Singh, 1986). Therefore, use of changes in mean total ABC scores, a common index of AIT-supportive effects, is invalid. To explain, the five subscales represent qualitatively different types of aberrant behavior, either too much (e.g., hyperactivity) or too little (i.e., lethargy). Scores are obtained on each subscale. Combining five valid (i.e., meaningful) subscale scores or averaging them across the whole ABC produces an invalid score (i.e., a meaningless number).

Third, Rimland and Edelson (1995) did not report how many statistical tests they performed with just eight pairs of subjects, but there were at least 32: six on ABC scores, 26 on FAPC score and items, with an unreported number on four HSQ scores and two further sets of ABC and FAPC scores. Selecting a statistical significance level of $p < .05$ under these conditions and failing to warn readers of the increasing likelihood of detecting positive but chance findings with additional tests misleads unsophisticated consumers of this research, that is, nonscientist parents of children with autism and advocates (including retailers) of AIT who do not have skills in scientific review.

To explain: When researchers write that an analysis produced a significant result at $p < .05$, this means that they are accepting the likelihood that 5% of significant results will be chance findings (i.e., not real experimental effects). This risk of misleading positive results is called the *alpha-level*. If 20 tests are conducted in the same study, the odds are that at least one statistically significant result will be an error; that is, a false conclusion will be accepted by the researchers. Especially when assessing an intervention that has never been researched before, as was the case with AIT in 1991, the potential for such errors must be highlighted. Alternatively, they can be avoided. One way is to use what is called the Bonferroni correction procedure to adjust the alpha-level depending on the number of statistical tests conducted. The adjusted alpha-level is determined by dividing the alpha-level selected for one test (e.g., accepting $p < .05$ as significant) by the number of tests conducted. It can be noted here that Edelson and Rimland (2001) criticized a study unsupportive of AIT by Gillberg and colleagues (1997) for applying the Bonferroni correction procedure to guard against chance findings with $p < .005$ as minimally significant. Rimland and Edelson (1995) had chosen to accept a ten-fold risk of finding benefits of AIT that were, in fact, chance findings.

The Bonferroni procedure is widely recommended and used by researchers in psychology and medicine to provide some protection for consumers and patients from the nefarious or naïve practice of data-snooping (i.e., excessive use of significance testing that was not directed by theory-based hypotheses and was not part of the originally planned data analysis). Edelson and Rimland (2001) wrote that an AIT study reviewed later (Mudford et al., 2000) was "deeply flawed" and "demonstrated an alarming bias favoring negative results" only on the grounds that the researchers would not engage in data-snooping.[2]

Yet another controversial statistical practice that increases (actually, further doubles) the chance of finding false-positive significant findings is to choose to conduct one-tailed significance testing. Rimland and Edelson (1995) reported one-tailed significance, which means that they were looking for confirmation of their hypothesis that AIT was beneficial rather than assuming, as researchers are generally trained, that AIT and the placebo condition will produce the same effects. In the latter case, a two-tailed statistical test should be used. Again, that is usually considered essential when researching a novel intervention, that is, one for which there is no existing strong empirical research concerning the direction of effects.

The second study of AIT started in 1991 (Rimland & Edelson, 1994). Subjects were 445 children and adults with autism whose families paid $1,000 for AIT and took them at their own expense from all over the United States to Oregon for the 10-day treatment. There was no control for placebo effects, so the results were compared with the placebo group from the earlier study (i.e., Rimland & Edelson, 1995). As previously described, that set of results may have been biased. So the Rimland and Edelson (1994) study cannot be interpreted to determine whether AIT had a beneficial effect or not. Indeed, Rimland and Edelson (1994) did write cautiously "the results nevertheless are *felt* [italics added] to provide some, albeit limited, insight into [post-AIT] behavior changes" (p. 21). Because this study was not subject to prepublication peer-review procedures (Gravel, 1994), there is no suggestion that any other

---

[2]Specifically, Edelson and Rimland (2001) noted that they had requested further analyses of published statistically significant results that were likely to have been purely due to chance.

researchers have agreed with Rimland and Edelson's feelings. Later interpretations of the results of this study by the authors were less guarded: "A growing body of experimental evidence supports the initial clinical reports that … AIT confers significant improvement to many children and adults with autism (Berard, 1993; Rimland & Edelson, 1994, 1995)" (Edelson et al., 1999).

Comparison of variations of AIT methods within the 1994 study was not hindered by the same problem. Rimland and Edelson (1994) reported that (a) the type of AIT device did not affect outcomes, (b) using filtering by the device made no difference, (c) persons with or without preexisting sensitivity to sounds had similar outcomes, and (d) subjects who scored lower on a prior test of intelligence improved (lowered) their scores on the total ABC and the 93-item Conners' Rating Scales child behavior checklist. As an aside: Conners' test results, like the ABC, do *not* provide a meaningful single overall score (Conners, 1989), so Rimland and Edelson (1994) erred again by deriving "a summary score … by summing the responses to each question" (p. 19).

In the third study, Edelson et al. (1999) compared changes in ABC, Conners', and FAPC total scores from pretreatment to 3-month posttreatment for nine subjects who received AIT and nine who received a placebo treatment. This is the only existing AIT study that was interpreted by its authors as showing behavioral benefits from AIT exceeding possible placebo effects and had an unbiased allocation of subjects to groups with respect to behavioral measures. As in their previous studies (Rimland & Edelson, 1994, 1995), ABC total mean score showed reduction at three months after AIT: "This reduction was statistically significant, $t(8) = 1.89$, $p < .05$" (Edelson et al., 1999, p. 77). The critical value for $t(8)$ with alpha at 5% is 2.31, so this result is only significant from a one-tailed test for which critical $t(8)$ is 1.86. Again, multiple testing without the protection of the Bonferroni correction means that this single indicator of AIT benefit could well be a chance finding. Many reviewers would reject such a weak result.

The profile of ABC change over 3 months in Edelson et al. (1999) was different from that shown in the previous studies, in which graphs had shown increasing reduction in this measure over time, a factor that Rimland and Edelson (1994) had noted as "reassuring" (p. 21). Edelson et al. (1999) failed to replicate that pattern of change. Data from the Conners' Scales and FAPC did not show posttreatment differences. So, the Edelson et al. (1999) study fails to replicate Rimland and Edelson (1994) with regard to the Conners' score and Rimland and Edelson (1995) with regard to FAPC. These failures may result from the research group's preparedness to accept statistically weak findings that could be false-positive results. Despite our criticisms of the misuse of the Conners' and ABC average scores, the failure to replicate results on these scores across studies, which Edelson et al. (1999) acknowledged, seems not to concern that research group.

The scientific approach to evaluating new treatments is to repeat studies to determine the reliability of original findings: That is what "replication" is (Sidman, 1960). Potential consumers of new treatments (e.g., children and adults with autism and their parents) should prefer to select a treatment that has been shown empirically to produce known benefits reliably. A research group should express a large measure of caution concerning the reliability of its findings about a treatment when it cannot repeat those findings from one study to the next. Examination of Rimland, Edelson, and colleagues' studies of AIT finds no reliable and valid results across their studies, although they have de-emphasized that. This represents a failure at direct replication (Sidman, 1960) and a failure to highlight that as a warning to consumers. Edelson et al., 1999) wrote in their discussion that "the efficacy of AIT is well documented ..." (p. 80). Other reviewers may share with us the view that the ephemeral unreplicable findings from Rimland, Edelson, and their colleagues' published work do not support this claim.

Further Failures to Replicate

In this section, we review all other peer-reviewed publications reporting AIT research that included at least some persons with autism and that included some control condition. Thus, Yencer's (1998) study with children with central auditory processing disorders (not autism) was excluded as was the open, uncontrolled trial of children with autism by Gillberg et al. (1997). All studies reviewed in this section included procedures to keep raters or observers of behaviors blind to treatment.

Bettison (1996) compared the effects of AIT with those of a control condition, 40 children in each group. Questionnaire measures about behaviors were completed by parents and teachers before treatment and at 1, 3, 6, and 12 months posttreatment. In general, results showed improvement for both groups at the 1-month follow-up. The gains were maintained for both groups at 12 months. Although Bettison (1996) argued that both "treatments" had brought these changes about, she acknowledged that ratings of behaviors could have been influenced by practice effects; for example, parents' and teachers' ratings could have changed as a result of repeated use of the questionnaires rather than by real change in children's behavior. Bettison also suggested that parents' (and, to a lesser extent, teachers') posttreatment ratings could have been influenced by their expectations that their children's behavior had been improved by AIT, even though there was a 50% chance that the child had not received that treatment. Despite not finding that AIT was any more beneficial than a control condition in her own study, Bettison is currently (as of June 2002) listed as an AIT practitioner at the Autism Research Institute website (www.autism.com).

Zollweg, Palm, and Vance (1997) provided AIT or a control treatment to groups of 15 subjects aged 7 to 24 years with diagnoses of autism or "cognitive impairment." The ABC was completed by residential facility staff before treatment and at intervals of 1, 3, 6, and 9 months after treatment. Although there was no significant difference between groups on ABC subscale scores before or after treatment, the scores of both groups declined over time, similar to Bettison's (1996) result. Zollweg et al. (1997) discussed this finding in detail, positing a variety of placebo effects as responsible. Although Edelson et al. (1999) and Edelson and Rimland (2001) reject the Zollweg et al. (1997) negative findings because of the mixed diagnoses of subjects, the study was important in showing trends towards reductions in ABC subscale ratings across time regardless of AIT. Data from 24-hour direct observational measures of aberrant behavior described in the Method section of Zollweg et al. (1997) were not provided in their results. Therefore, it was not clear whether reduced ABC scores were subject to placebo effects or were corroborated by reduced occurrences of aberrant behavior recorded by staff as those behaviors occurred.

Our Study of AIT (Mudford et al., 2000)

By 1996, there were six businesses selling AIT to the parents of children with autism in the UK for up to £1250 (about US$1,880, at the June 2002 exchange rate). We were alerted to AIT by colleagues Lorna Wing and Richard Mills working for the National Autistic Society (NAS), an organization that (among other functions) advises UK parents about the scientific evidence concerning treatments. The NAS was receiving many enquiries about AIT but, in the absence of research findings of sufficient quality, were unable to recommend for or against AIT. We and NAS professionals Wing and Mills obtained research funding to study the effects of AIT (Mudford et al., 2000).

All 16 children aged 5–13 years who completed the study had a confirmed diagnosis of autism and, with Vineland Adaptive Behavior Scale Composite scores > 3 SD below the mean of 100, consistent with moderate or severe mental retardation. All had significant levels of problem behavior. These were children we believed would be most likely to show benefit following Rimland and Edelson's (1994) report. We interviewed all UK AIT providers who had expressed interest in collaborating in the study. AIT was provided by practitioners trained by a SAIT-approved trainer. Not only were they acceptable to SAIT, they were prepared to provide AIT or placebo alone. That is, they did not insist on providing other "treatments" concurrently. Also, they did not have an excessive financial interest in the outcome as AIT provided a small proportion of the income of their employers.

Among other monthly measures (32 in all) in the 14-month study, we employed direct observational recording of children's individually defined idiosyncratic, stereotypical, and disruptive problem behaviors throughout a school day. Ear occlusion (covering or blocking ears) was measured too, as that was viewed as a behavioral indicator of hypersensitivity to noises. Instead of relying solely on rating scales completed by parents or staff for assessing effects on behaviors as in all other AIT research to date, we collected reliable observational data as a criterion measure of behavior change. This enhanced interpretation of the questionnaire data.

All children received the prescribed 10-hour AIT treatment. They also had a 10-hour control/placebo treatment (same environments with same music, not modulated). Seven children received AIT at least 4 months before control treatment. The other nine children had AIT at least 4 months after control.

Results were obtained from analyzing changes in behaviors across the whole study and following treatments (AIT and control). In summary, many questionnaire-based measures showed that children's behavior improved somewhat across the study as judged by parents' responses. In other words, the more often parents rated the behavior of their children, the better were the ratings of their children's behavior. However, none of these changes followed AIT. Direct observational measures showed no changes across the 14 months, except that ear occlusion worsened following AIT, a statistically weak effect that could have been due to chance. We wondered whether parents had noticed changes in their children that were not detected by any of the measures we employed. A minority (7 of 16) were able to guess correctly the order in which their child had received AIT or control treatment. Four said that negative side effects influenced their guess.

Our conclusion was that AIT did not benefit any of the children in the study. The decreasing trends in behavioral ratings were consistent with findings by others

(Bettison, 1996; Zollweg et al., 1997). However, direct observational measurement of aberrant behaviors did not corroborate those ratings. This suggests that repeated questionnaire measures in AIT studies, whether completed by parents (Bettison, 1996; Mudford et al., 2000) or staff (Bettison, 1996; Zollweg et al., 1997), may be prone to "instrumentation" effects; that is, ratings of behavior drift across times of measurement to become increasingly independent of the rate of occurrence of behavior (Campbell & Stanley, 1966).

Summary of Reviews

SAIT-associated researchers (Edelson et al., 1999; Rimland & Edelson, 1994, 1995) have reported some helpful findings that make the AIT treatment easier to provide in research studies; for example, filtering is no longer a necessary component of the therapy. Berard's theoretical basis for AIT has been discarded by SAIT on empirical grounds (Edelson et al., 1999), so supporters of AIT are in functional agreement with communication sciences' critics that Berard erred in explaining the audiological rationale for AIT. These findings have made AIT an experimentally testable treatment, which was not necessarily the case when impractically fine-grained audiometry was stipulated by proponents to be an essential precondition.

SAIT researchers have interpreted their studies as showing AIT to be beneficial for people with autism. Rimland had predicted this well in advance of the first peer-reviewed research publication (Rimland & Edelson, 1995). "Based on what I know thus far, I have little doubt that the experimental studies of auditory training now under way, and soon to get under way, will indeed show that auditory training is a valid method for improving the status of many (certainly not all) autistic children" (Rimland, 1992, p. 229). Critical examination showed that their findings were not always replicated across their own studies, their measures were often psychometrically invalid, and they employed unconventional statistical methods that, by chance or design, maximized the likelihood of positive but chance findings supportive of AIT (see Goldstein, 2000, for further examples).

None of the other studies reviewed showed that AIT produced beneficial changes in behavior, although one study (Bettison, 1996) was interpreted by its author as showing that either 10 hours of AIT or 10 hours of listening to unmodified music reduced questionnaire ratings of problem behavior. Nevertheless, the results of that study do not suggest that AIT itself was useful.

CONCLUSIONS

There does not appear to be any evidence from published research that AIT is helpful for changing behaviors of people with autism to their benefit. SAIT associates and, presumably, AIT-provision businesses seem to be the only surviving advocates for the treatment. Berard's method of using electronic filters to remove hyperacute frequencies, which was the original core component of the treatment, appears to have no remaining advocates.

Reviews of treatment research typically conclude with recommendations for further research. Future research efforts might better be put to studying potential treatments other than AIT. However, if more AIT studies are conducted, reliable direct observational measurement of behaviors should be included to provide data independent of carers' opinions about behaviors. The skill and resources required to collect these data over prolonged times, for example, 14 months in the Mudford et al. (2000) study, may be difficult to justify when there seems little a priori empirical or theoretical justification for doing so.

Finally, our unambiguous recommendation for families considering purchasing AIT: There is no good evidence that AIT will change behavior beneficially. No independent studies have shown that AIT has positive effects on behavior of children or adults with autism.

REFERENCES

Aman, M. G., & Singh, N. N. (1986). *Aberrant Behavior Checklist: Manual*. E. Aurora, NY: Slosson Educational Publications.

Aman, M. G., Singh, N. N., Stewart, A. W., & Field, C. J. (1985). The Aberrant Behavior Checklist: A behavior rating scale for the assessment of treatment effects. *American Journal of Mental Deficiency, 89*, 485–491.

American Academy of Pediatrics. (1998). Auditory integration training and facilitated communication for autism. *Pediatrics, 102*, 431–433.

Berard, G. (1993). *Hearing equals behavior*. New Canaan, CT: Keats.

Berkell, D. E., Malgeri, S. E., & Streit, M. K. (1996). Auditory integration training for individuals with autism. *Education and Training in Mental Retardation and Developmental Disabilities, 31*, 66–70.

Bettison, S. (1996). The long-term effects of auditory training on children with autism. *Journal of Autism and Developmental Disorders, 26*, 361–374.

Campbell, D. T., & Stanley, J. C. (1966). *Experimental and quasi-experimental designs for research*. Chicago: Rand McNally.

Condon, W. S. (1975). Multiple response to sound in dysfunctional children. *Journal of Autism and Childhood Schizophrenia, 5*, 37–56.

Conners, C. K. (1989). *Manual for Conners' Rating Scales*. North Tonawanda, NY: Multi-Health Systems.

Courchesne, E., Lincoln, A. J., Yeung-Courchesne, R., Elmaison, R., & Grillon, C. (1989). Pathophysiologic findings in nonretarded autism and receptive developmental language disorder. *Journal of Autism and Developmental Disorders, 19*, 1–17.

Edelson, S. M., Arin, D., Bauman, M., Lukas, S. E., Rudy, J. H., Sholar, M., et al. (1999). Auditory integration training: A double-blind study of behavioral and electrophysiological effects in people with autism. *Focus on Autism and Other Developmental Disabilities, 14*(2), 73–81.

Edelson, S. M., & Rimland, B. (2001). *The efficacy of auditory integration training: Summaries and critiques of 28 reports (January, 1993 – May, 2001)*. Available from www.sait.com and www.autism.com

Gillberg, C., Johansson, M., Steffenburg, S., & Berlin, O. (1997). Auditory integration training in children with autism: Brief report of an open pilot study. *Autism, 1*, 97–100.

Goldstein, H. (2000). Commentary: Interventions to facilitate auditory, visual, and motor integration: "Show me the data." *Journal of Autism and Developmental Disorders, 30*, 423–425.

Gravel, J. S. (1994). Auditory integration training: Placing the burden of proof. *American Journal of Speech-Language Pathology, 3*(2), 25–29.

Howlin, P. (1996, May). *A visit to the Light & Sound Therapy Centre*. London: National Autistic Society.

Light & Sound Newsletter '93. (1993). London: The Light & Sound Therapy Centre.

Lucker, J. R. (1998). Is auditory integration training safe? *Journal of Autism and Developmental Disorders, 28*, 267.

Mudford, O. C., Cross, B. A., Breen, S., Cullen, C., Reeves, D., Gould, J., et al. (2000). Auditory integration training: No behavioral benefits detected. *American Journal on Mental Retardation, 105*, 118–129.

Rankovic, C. M., Rabinowitz, W. M., & Lof, G. L. (1996). Maximum output intensity of the audio-kinetron. *American Journal of Speech-Language Pathology, 5,* 68–72.

Rimland, B. (1991). Afterword and postscript. In A. Stelhi (Ed.), *The sound of a miracle: A child's triumph over autism* (pp. 221–230). London: Fourth Estate.

Rimland, B. (1992, June). *To: Parents and/or professionals who have written or phoned for information on auditory integration training* (Letter). San Diego, CA: Autism Research Institute.

Rimland, B., & Edelson, S. M. (1994). The effects of auditory integration training. *American Journal of Speech-Language Pathology, 3*(2), 16–24.

Rimland, B., & Edelson, S. M. (1995). Brief report: A pilot study of auditory integration training in autism. *Journal of Autism and Developmental Disorders, 25,* 61–70.

Sidman, M. (1960). *Tactics of scientific research.* Boston: Authors' Co-operative.

Stelhi, A. (1991). *The sound of a miracle: A child's triumph over autism.* London: Fourth Estate.

Tharpe, A. M. (1996). Concerns regarding auditory integration training. *Current Opinion in Otolayngology & Head and Neck Surgery, 4,* 353–355.

Tharpe, A. M. (1999). Auditory integration training: The magical mystery cure. *Language, Speech, and Hearing Services in Schools, 30,* 378–382.

Veale, T. K. (1994a). Auditory integration training: The use of a new listening treatment within our profession. *American Journal of Speech-Language Pathology, 3*(2), 13–15.

Veale, T. K. (1994b). Weighing the promises and the problems: AIT may be a risk worth taking. *American Journal of Speech-Language Pathology, 3*(2), 35–37.

Walker, N. (1991). Can hearing problems be corrected ... and "cure"autism? *Autism Society Canada, 10*(3), 1–4.

Yencer, K. A. (1998). The effects of auditory integration training for children with central auditory processing disorders. *American Journal of Audiology, 7*(2), 32–44.

Zollweg, W., Palm, D., & Vance, V. (1997). The efficacy of auditory integration training: A double blind study. *American Journal of Audiology, 6*(3), 39–47.

Facilitated Communication: The Ultimate Fad Treatment

John W. Jacobson
Sage Colleges Center for Applied Behavior Analysis

Richard M. Foxx
Penn State Harrisburg

James A. Mulick
The Ohio State University and Columbus Children's Hospital

Facilitated communication (FC) is a fad treatment that began in the late 1980s in Australia and spread with astonishing rapidity in the early 1990s to the United States and other westernized nations, primarily Canada and Western Europe. Although FC was initially targeted to individuals with cerebral palsy in Australia (Crossley, 1992), encouragement of its use was rapidly generalized to people with autism spectrum disorders in the United States (Biklen, 1990, 1992a; Biklen, Morton, Gold, Berrigan, & Swaminathan, 1992; Biklen, Saha, & Kliewer, 1995), and the Facilitated Communication Institute at Syracuse University was established. The use of FC has been demonstrated, disseminated, supported, and promoted through training and workshops in other nations, and linkages to providers of FC services (see Biklen, 2001a). In the United States at this writing, FC is still promoted and disseminated under the auspices of the state developmental disability service agency in Vermont and by many private and university-based service agencies that receive public funding support throughout North America.

Facilitated communication (FC) has been described as:

> a means by which many people with major speech difficulties type or point at letters on an alphabet board or use a typing device to convey their thoughts. It involves a facilitator who provides physical support to help stabilize the arm, to isolate the index finger if necessary, to pull pack the arm after each selection, to remind the individual to maintain focus and to offer emotional support and encouragement; the facilitator progressively phases out the physical support. (Biklen, 1992a, p. 243)

A fundamental premise of FC is that some people with autism and mental retardation have "undisclosed literacy" or linguistic competence akin to average or above average intellectual functioning. Indeed, while receiving facilitation, people with severe or profound retardation or autism who had never conveyed even the simplest message or idea via standard methods of augmented communication, nevertheless, appeared to be displaying linguistic competence by writing poetry replete with literary devices such as similes and metaphors, self-advocating by expressing sophisticated lifestyle decisions and preferences, and writing sentences with perfect syntax and grammar. Yet, the individuals doing the communicating often appeared disinterested in the FC activity and paid virtually no attention to the keyboard (Foxx, 1994). To the facilitators, FC output was always reported to seem to be the expression of the person being assisted. But to the skeptic, it appeared that the facilitated messages were those of the facilitator and not the person with the disability.

A FANTASTIC AND INCREDIBLE FAD

Research on FC has confirmed these skeptical suspicions. The process has not been verified in numerous peer-reviewed scientific studies (Green, 1994; Jacobson, Mulick, & Schwartz, 1995) because virtually all researchers found that the facilitators were literally speaking on behalf of the person, albeit unknowingly, because they were responsible for whatever meaningful statements were produced.

The FC movement not only created false hopes for families and professionals, but it had additional negative consequences. These included violation of an individual's right to self-expression and self-determination, improper control over important life decisions, denial of disability and hence appropriate treatment and education, and misdirection and misappropriation of financial and human resources (e.g., Maul, 1994). One particularly sinister outcome was that FC was used to make allegations of sexual misconduct against parents and caregivers. How could this happen?

The immediate and widespread acceptance of FC by large numbers of individuals in the developmental disabilities community may be explained, in part, because it fit perfectly with the self-advocacy movement. With FC, universal self-advocacy was possible because facilitated persons could allegedly communicate their desires for the socially defined roles that the movement had created for them. No longer would lack of language skills be an impediment to discovering what an individual thought, wanted or feared. In effect, FC provided the means to achieve the goals of those in the social values advocacy movements who felt that all people with developmental disabilities must be involved in every aspect of their own life planning. Thus, conditions were right for a fad such a FC to take root and flourish, because with FC there was no longer any communication barrier to full participation. As much as any fad discussed in this book, FC serves both as an example of fad but false treatments and of the phenomenon that appearances, if not further investigated, can be extremely and sometimes tragically, misleading.

The influence of FC continues today on the Internet. On numerous Internet sites FC is averred to be a useful and valid instructional or treatment method for use with people who have an ever-expanding variety of disabling conditions: "Children, teenagers, and autistic adults (with or without speech impairment), the ESN (the educationally subnormal), trisomic, the mentally defective, the multiply-disabled, patients suffering from concussion, dysphasics, persons suffering from Rett's or Angelman's syndrome, and so on" (The Association, 2003).

Furthermore, through one of several academic centers, particularly the Facilitated Communication Institute at Syracuse University, the use of FC continues to be demonstrated, disseminated, supported, and promoted through training and workshops in other nations, and linkages to providers of FC services. These linkages include those in Austria (operated by VHN), Finland (by Saloviita), France and Belgium (by EPICEA and The Association), Italy (by Centro Studi Sulla Communicazione Facilittata), Germany (by FC Forum), Switzerland (by EPICEA), and the United Kingdom (see Biklen, 2001a).

Other chapters in this book discuss FC, among other fad interventions. In this chapter, we focus on the characteristics of FC as a "bogus" or fad therapy, and review more recent research on FC completed primarily since the mid-1990s. For research prior to the mid-1990s, a number of excellent earlier reviews are available (e.g., Green, 1994; Jacobson et al., 1995). In addition, we will respond to the continuing depiction of FC by its disseminators.

FC AND CRITERIA FOR BOGUS OR FAD TREATMENTS

The research published by proponents of FC is characterized by features of what Park (2003) has described as "bogus" science (i.e., invalid and unsupported claims based on an illusory patina of research support). Bogus science is, of course, not science but something more along the lines of marketing. Park identified seven warning signs of bogus science:

1. *The discoverer pitches the claim directly to the media.* In the United States, the initial dissemination of claims for the validity of FC was via a lengthy article published in a student-run journal (Biklen, 1990), a trade book (Biklen, 1993), and numerous newspaper articles and interviews, as well as television news segments (see Jacobson et al, 1995).

2. *The discoverer says that a powerful establishment is trying to suppress his or her work.* This theme is self-evident both in the initial U.S. articles (Biklen, 1990, 1992a) and follow-up publications (e.g., Biklen & Cardinal, 1997a; Cardinal, 1994) and responses to critics of FC by its founder (Borthwick & Crossley, 1999; Crossley, 1993).

3. *The scientific effect involved is always at the very limit of detection.* Even prior to previous major reviews of FC (Green, 1994; Jacobson et al., 1995), it was clear that evidence for the authenticity of communications by people with severe disabilities through FC was minimal. Indeed, even research studies that are cited by proponents of FC have tended to find a preponderance of inaccurate, inadequate, and nonfunctional responses. Accurate responses under conditions where facilitators were unaware of content had been and continue to be vanishingly rare (Green, 1994).

4. *Evidence for a discovery is anecdotal.* Proponents of FC have relied on qualitative anecdotal studies characterized as observational or nonexperimental case studies, neither of which meets conventional standards for demonstrating cause and effect (i.e., see Biklen, n.d., Olney, 2001). As Simpson and Myles

(1995) noted, "Much of the purported qualitative research on facilitated communication fails to follow accepted qualitative protocol .... What often is presented as qualitative research actually is anecdotal or case study methodology. These reports nonetheless are presented as qualitative research ... " (para. 27). This reliance on qualitative methods as evidence of the authenticity of FC content has continued to the present, and remains unable to unambiguously and factually demonstrate authenticity, because of its nature (see Wolfensberger, 1992).

5. *The discoverer says a belief is credible because it has endured for centuries.* Original claims of the value of FC in the United States focused on children and youth with autism spectrum disorders (ASD; Biklen, 1900, 1992b). These sources referred to earlier work on touch facilitation of response (e.g., Oppenheim, 1974), and alluded to hidden competencies (e.g., "hidden knowledge" among individuals with ASD, later expanded to include others with almost any disability who have few verbal communication skills, as we have noted; see also Hill & Leary, 1993). "After the rise and fall of 'hidden knowledge,' one teacher seemed to have revised it. It is also mainly the same, relatively small number of people who seem to promote the technique in the professional journals (Biklen, Crossley, Donnellan, Duchan, Remington-Gurney and Sabin) .... [D]ue to the impact of North American views on the professional world at large, having for the first time become a major media event in North America, it may spread wider than before" (von Tetzchner, 1994).

6. *The discoverer has worked in isolation.* More than a decade after the introduction of FC to the United States, the network of academics and their departments participating in active advocacy and dissemination of FC techniques comprises largely the same professionals and institutions that aligned themselves with FC in the early 1990s, although the network of individuals and organizations offering FC services or training has expanded and contracted as the 6 years have passed (Facilitated Communication Institute [FCI], 1999). Since the inception of FC's promulgation, a number of national organizations have issued cautionary statements regarding the use of FC, including the American Psychological Association, American Academy of Child and Adolescent Psychiatry, American Speech-Language and Hearing Association, and American Association on Mental Retardation in 1994, and the Association for Behavior Analysis in 1995 (Association for Science in Autism Treatment [ASAT], n.d.), indicating the marginal status of the procedure from the perspective of accepted professional practice. FC has been the subject of several highly negative reports in the U.S. mass media and was described as the "cold fusion of developmental disabilities" (Foxx, 1994).

7. *The discoverer must propose new laws of nature to explain an observation.* From its inception in the United States, the underpinning rationale for FC has consisted of facilitative effects of human touch, assumption of hidden competence, and the attribution of disabilities to motor disturbances, referred to at some times as apraxia and at others as dyspraxia. None of these assumptions has been independently sustained in research, although specious arguments have been offered to support them. Consider, for example, Biklen's (2001a) summary of a study by Brighenti, Teatin, and Malaffo (available only in that summary) that purports to present findings demonstrating apraxia in individ-

uals with ASD, but which can be explained more parsimoniously by concurrent intellectual disabilities and limited receptive language skills. A second example is found in a study by Bara, Bucciarelli, and Colle (2001), reviewed by Biklen (2001b), of people with autism who were assessed on theory of mind tasks using FC and found to have hidden language competence. However, in this study, because facilitators were entirely aware of the content of the test items, but not the "aim of the research," a more parsimonious explanation of the findings is that facilitators influenced the results that were interpreted as suggesting hidden language competence. Very little of the research that FC proponents identify as supporting the validity or authenticity of FC is sensible unless one first assumes that FC is valid based on the unwarranted assumptions previously listed.

RESEARCH ON FC FROM THE MID-1990S TO THE PRESENT

Since the mid-1990s, little evidence supporting FC has emerged, although proponents claim otherwise (see Biklen & Cardinal, 1997b). Representative studies that addressed the impact of FC on communication and other aspects of functioning and found FC wanting in either specific or collateral effects include Myles, Simpson, and Smith (1996a), regarding collateral effects on social behavior; Myles, Simpson, and Smith (1996b), regarding instructional benefits of using FC as an assistive method; Montee, Miltenberger, and Wittrock (1995), with respect to authenticity of communications and facilitator control; and Kerrin, Murdock, Sharpton, and Jones (1998), who also demonstrated unwitting facilitator control over responses (as did Burgess et al., 1998, and Kezuka, 1997, who provided even more extensive analyses of facilitator control). Other studies reporting negative findings include Bebko, Perry, and Bryson (1996); Beck and Pirovano (1996); Bomba, O'Donnell, Markowitz, and Holmes (1996); Braman, Brady, Linehan, and Williams (1995); Edelson, Rimland, Berger, and Billings (1998); Hirshorn and Gregory (1995); and Simon, Whitehair, and Toll (1996). During this period, another book critical of FC was published. Spitz (1997) elucidated the correspondence of FC messages to automatic writing, among other nonconscious perceptual biases common to humans.

There were also a number of publications on FC or related issues that were sympathetic to its use, including Borthwick and Crossley (1999); Duchan (1999); Duchan, Calculator, Sonnenmeier, Diehl, and Cumley (2001); and Danforth (1997, 1999). Two qualitative studies portraying FC in a positive light were published: Broderick and Kasa-Hendrickson (2001) and Schubert (1997; with a participant who could independently both speak and sign), but neither used a plausibly causal methodology to ascertain the authenticity of communications or verify that observed changes were attributable to FC. A very recent study, Niemi and Kärnä-Lin (2002), analyzed the correspondence of the developmental course of facilitated messages for one individual to the developmental course of acquisition typical of his native language, but failed to note correspondence of a number of these elements to typical, almost stereotypic features of automatic writing.

During the late 1990s, there were also signs of growing acrimony between supporters and critics of FC:

During the past year, the Center [on Human Policy] decided to step into the fray ....
Critics of FC have had the opportunity to present their position in JASH, AAMR(s *Mental Retardation* (MR), and other forums. That's fair game. But misleading and one-sided
resolutions and policy statements against FC such as those adopted by the American
Psychological Association (APA) and New York State Office of Mental Retardation and
Developmental Disabilities (OMRDD) cross the line .... Most recently, FC opponents
have attempted to undermine a consensus conference on FC underwritten by federal
agencies concerned with people with disabilities. The conference represented an attempt to bring together persons with different positions on FC, including independent
researchers and disability leaders. Not only have opponents refused to participate in a
discussion of FC on neutral grounds, they have attempted to have political pressure
exerted to prevent any conference from being held. (Taylor, 1998, February, paras. 1–2)

STUDIES SAID TO SUPPORT THE USE AND EFFECTIVENESS OF FC

An Internet document, Biklen (undated, but probably current to 1994), posted at the
Facilitated Communication Institute Web site cites observational studies and autobiographical studies that "provide evidence that ... [FC] works." Because neither
observational studies nor autobiographical accounts *can* provide convincing demonstrations of cause and effect (e.g., Park, 2003; Shavelson et al., 2002; Stanovitch,
2001) this claim is not very convincing. Biklen (n.d.) also cites findings from "controlled studies" as indications that FC works. He cites the Intellectual Disabilities
Review Panel (IDRP, 1989); Calculator & Singer (1992); Vazquez (1994); and Weiss,
Wagner, & Bauman (in press, at that time; published in 1996). To this list of "controlled studies" we can add Cardinal, Hanson, and Wakeman (1996); Ogletree,
Hamtil, Solberg, and Scoby-Schmelzle (1993); Olney (1997, 2001); and Sheehan and
Matuozzi (1996; see Olney, 2001). Australian researchers who are not responsible
for the IDRP report, however, have reported elsewhere that the evidence presented
in that source is flawed and unconvincing (Cummins & Prior, 1992; Hudson, 1995,
also Jacobson et al., 1995) and thus, here we focus on the remaining studies as candidates for evidence that FC "works."

What Studies Actually Show

Calculator and Singer (1992). This "article" was a letter to the editor of the journal *Topics in Language Disorders*, which reported enhanced performance on a receptive language measure under conditions that included FC. However, this letter was
not peer reviewed, which means that the credibility of the conclusions drawn from
the procedures used was not assessed by conventional standards for professional
publications. The effectiveness of FC was not experimentally demonstrated in any
case. Perry, Bebko, and Bryson (1994), reporting in another letter to the editor in the
same journal, failed to replicate the findings of Calculator and Singer. They concluded that FC was inefficacious generally and resulted in lower receptive language
scores for some subjects based on their intimate knowledge of all aspects of their
study, and suggested that Calculator and Singer's findings may have been contaminated by facilitator knowledge of the stimulus words spoken to the subjects. In response, Calculator (1995) suggested that Perry et al. did not constitute a replication
per se, because their use of white noise and earphones by facilitators (which prevented them from *hearing the words* spoken to subjects in the study, a "single blind"

procedure) "may have caused facilitators to have difficulty facilitating" (Calculator, 1995, abstract). Obviously, it did cause facilitators difficulty hearing the words, but that was the point of the masking sound. Calculator and others have not replicated their initial findings, and Calculator (1999) subsequently questioned whether FC can "overcome" the purported dyspraxic difficulties that are a component of the rationale for use of FC.

Cardinal, Hanson, and Wakeham (1996). This study is widely cited as the most scientific demonstration of the utility of FC, perhaps because it uses a message-passing procedure that has been used with other specific procedures in several previous studies that had not validated FC. It also should be noted that this study was published in *Mental Retardation* under the editorship of Steven Taylor, who is not only in the same academic department at Syracuse University as Biklen, but also characterized the resolutions critical of FC by several national professional organizations that were based in good part on research findings as "misleading and one-sided" (Taylor, 1998). Cardinal et al. hypothesized that the failure to validate FC in previous studies had been associated with inadequate prior exposure of subjects to the experimental conditions (i.e., habituation to situational demands). To overcome this "problem," Cardinal et al. incorporated extensive practice in a word set selected for their study, containing some words previously familiar to subjects, and possibly some facilitators, and used a baseline of 10 trials with 5 words each without facilitation, followed by facilitation over 90 trials with 5 words each, followed by a baseline similar to the first one. Readers are referred to the article for a complete description of the procedures used.

Statistically, in terms of effect size (an index of degree of difference between before and after accuracy scores), the benefits found were massive, both in comparison of the highest first baseline session to the highest FC session score for each subject, and of the first baseline to the second baseline. Strikingly, however, relative to the group standard deviations, and although the average level of performance with FC seemed most superior, the effect size for the comparison of the average total scores for the two baselines is greater than that for the comparison of best baseline to best facilitation scores, a finding not explored or noted by Cardinal et al. (1996). Other considerations that affect interpretation of the findings include the fact that the number of words that began with specific letters of the alphabet varied substantially—only one word each began with G, J, K, or O, two each began with A, and three with N or R, and four with E, H, or M; in contrast, 16 began with B, 11 with P, and 12 with S. This means that the likelihood that a word could be inadvertently or unknowingly cued accurately by a facilitator based on correct delayed typing by a subject of the first letter of the word varied from about 6% (for B) to 100% (for G, J, K, or O), depending on possible facilitator exposure to the word previously. Cardinal et al. do conduct an analysis of accuracy for words used more than once, but do not analyze the possible impact of the nonrandom distribution of first letters of words.

In addition, a true blind condition was not used, in the sense that each session included continued presence of the facilitator (who was blind to the presentation of the word) and the recorder, who had randomly selected and shown, spoken, and defined the word to the subject. Although procedures included prohibition of verbal comments by the recorder, the recorder was in the field of view of the facilitator during the trial typing, and no controls were employed to prohibit unknowing nonverbal cuing of the facilitators. Readers who doubt the effects of subtle nonverbal cues on subject behavior, in this case, that of the facilitator, should consult Milgram (1963) and Wilder and Shapiro (1984) as exemplars of such concerns.

There are limitations of this study that relate to the meaningfulness of findings: On one level it seems that the findings reflect benefits of FC, but at another, more fundamental and less abstract level, the findings can also be attributed to differential social reinforcement of accurate delayed typing of simple words, without comprehension or "communicative intent," and it is possible that variability across subjects in their scores, if indeed uncontaminated by the factors listed previously, reflect differences in individual memory for something as simple as short sequences of letters. Because no standardized assessments of prelinguistic or functional communication skills were reported by Cardinal et al. (1996), although many such measures exist, differences in such skills and their relationship to tested performance are unknown for these subjects and may account for differences in subject performance. Moreover, although 14 of the 43 subjects correctly reproduced stimulus words on four or five of five exposures with FC at least once, 20 subjects correctly reproduced no more words or only one more word in their best session under the same conditions. This is a poor level of accuracy and is hardly accurate enough for intentional communication. As well, the average for best FC sessions was reported as 2.23 out of 5 words, indicating that in a majority of responses, on average, more errors occurred than accurate reproduction (and for trials 81–90, accuracy was at an average of only 32% of words). As noted by Cardinal et al. (1996, Table 3), most errors (73%) consisted of misspellings or no detectable patterns of letters forming a word. Thus, although the findings of Cardinal et al. suggest a practice effect, it is unclear whether this is a practice effect reflecting changes in comprehension or simply delayed reproduction: The responses of subjects were more characterized by errors or complete *non-communication* rather than successful demonstration of the effectiveness of FC methods. It is important, finally, to note that the findings from this study have not been replicated, in principle as well as in substance, and hence cannot be considered definitive on any grounds with respect to standards in behavioral science or quantitative educational research (e.g., Shavelson et al., 2002; Stanovitch, 2001). For an extensive critique of the Cardinal et al. study, see Mostert (2001).

Ogletree, Hamtil, Solberg, and Scoby-Schmelzle (1993).   This study is cited in support of the validity of facilitated communication even though it did not claim to do so. Ogletree et al. (1993) assessed the accuracy of FC utterances involving play activities not witnessed by the facilitator. They reported

'It could be argued that L.B.'s performance during free-play provides clear evidence of independent communication .... In contrast, L.B.'s performance during both evaluation/play contexts could be interpreted as evidence of facilitator participation. The agreement between L.B.'s typed messages and free-play events could be dismissed as predictable, given that many of the events could have been part of routines familiar to L.B.'s mother ....' and 'Although both of the above-mentioned arguments are plausible, it is these authors' opinion that there is not sufficient evidence to suggest that L. B. used FC independently in either play context.' (p. 6)

Nor did the authors either attempt to resolve the issue or to provide sufficient evidence.

Olney (1997, 2001).   These are two separate accounts of what is apparently the same study, in which nine subjects were exposed to a variety of learning games (e.g., *Word Attack*) displayed on a computer screen. Performance was compared without facilitation and with facilitation and blinding of the facilitator. There were 83 sessions of facilitating or responding without facilitation, in which sufficient data to perform statistical testing were obtained for five subjects in either two games for two subjects or one game for the other three. Data collection proceeded for a period of months, in hour-long sessions, but in the data analysis, some subjects' comparisons were based on their first responses to items whereas comparisons for others were based on second responses (i.e., corrected responses given when asked to respond again). For these reasons, the results cannot be interpreted comparably in terms of the demonstration of skill, and they cannot be legitimately combined as scores, although Olney does so, comparing the percent of responses correct with blind facilitation to percent correct, overall, under the unfacilitated post-baseline condition. There was also an open facilitation condition, when the facilitator could see stimulus materials. In every case, subject performance was superior when the facilitator could see or was aware of the materials, than when she could not. Hence, a clear pattern of potential facilitator influence was evident.

Because months of real time passed during data collection, with an average of only nine sessions per subject, these data should be considered quite limited and the extent to which they reflect the responding of the subjects over time, and the adequacy of these samples of responses in general terms, can reasonably be questioned. Then, there is the question, what happened to the other four subjects? One made sufficient responses to be tested, but the "Scores did not meet validation criterion"; this finding is unexplained. For the others, data were not collected sufficiently to include them in the study. Thus, potential findings for four of nine (or 44%) of the original subjects were either dropped or discarded in the 1997 report, but they seem to show up in the 2001 report.

It is possible that the subjects for which there were insufficient data in 1997 may have provided, over time, sufficient data for the 2001 analysis. Yet, it appears that generally, fewer comparisons are made in the later report between facilitator-blind and posttest unfacilitated scores than in the 1997 report. Although both studies reported that facilitator blind scores were numerically higher than unfacilitated scores, there was evidence for facilitator influence in both articles. Consider that there were repeated interactions involving a variety of materials to which the facilitator had been possibly exposed during facilitator-aware trials. There also was some degree of prompting by the researcher, not completely described, during blind trials as well. Furthermore, in neither study was it stated that the facilitators were naive regarding the content of the learning games prior to the study. All of these considerations call into question whether the facilitators *were* actually blind in the "blind condition."

Sheehan and Matuozzi (1996).   In this study, also published in *Mental Retardation* under Taylor's editorship, message passing was used to ascertain whether information unknown to the facilitator was provided by the subject under facilitation.

Three people with autism had their individualized preferences assessed through FC via message passing that had been procedurally adapted in various ways. Each subject had engaged in FC for at least 18 months. Varied types of stimuli were used and facilitators were blind to the materials presented; however, the original facilitator who was present when the stimuli were presented remained inexplicably present when the second blinded facilitator entered the setting. Sheehan and Matuozzi report:

> The presence of the original facilitator at the information disclosure sessions raises a question about the possibility of cuing. With this awareness, we made significant efforts to disallow both obvious and subtle cuing, such as voice intonation, head nodding, bodily cues, visual gaze, and facial expression that would inadvertently shape or prompt a desired response from the participant. To date, the only research suggesting that what is typed may not be the product of the facilitated speaker is the research on facilitator influence. There is nothing to support visual cuing based solely on the presence of a person who knows the correct response. (para. 31)

As noted earlier, extensive psychological research has revealed that human beings frequently engage in nonverbal and unknowing but influential cuing, a phenomenon well known in perception science and cinematography (Castelhano & Henderson, 2002). Thus, it seems likely that naive facilitators can be as readily influenced by subtle and inadvertent nonverbal cues as the person on the street or college students who have been often studied. The conclusion, "There is nothing to support visual cuing based solely on the presence of a person who knows the correct response," ignores this robust body of research, is groundless, and poses a major threat to the validity of this study.

The subjects in this study were reported to communicate "unknown" information in 49 of 289 interactions (27%) over four sessions, in 25 of 292 interactions (9%) over six sessions, and in 3 of 139 interactions (2%) over three sessions. Between 19% and 37% of these communications occurred in the context of interactions that were not open-ended (e.g., closed responses or yes or no questions), which Sheehan and Matuozzi (1996) suggest might be discounted by some readers because the structure or content of the response formats might diminish the blinding of the second facilitator. They noted:

> The significance of some instances of the participant's disclosure of unknown information may be diminished because we designed the study to allow the naive facilitator to offer feedback, redirection, or, at times, yes/no questions or choices in order to elicit a response. Certainly, in those instances when participants responded to yes/no questions or were provided with multi-choice formats, a significant level of shared information with the naive facilitator was involved, even before the disclosure …. However, that leaves unexplained those instances when the participants required nothing but an inquiry and some encouragement preceding their correct responses. (p. 104)

Sheehan and Matuozzi (1996) do not state that implicit feedback through "feedback, redirection, or, at times, yes/no questions or choices in order to elicit a response" always *followed* rather than preceded instances of communication of unknown information for each subject. If this did not occur, then subsequent disclosures that are depicted as structured without cues may indeed be contaminated, because this information was also provided to the facilitators, and may have altered the likelihood of later responses if the individual understood the information given (i.e., results were no longer based on the spontaneous response of the individual). This is a particular concern because the rates at which unknown information was reported to occur, with adjustment for those that could directly provide cues (see Table 3, p. 102) ranged from only 17% at best to about 2%, among the three subjects. In the context of message passing, it appears that the performance of these subjects was characterized by inaccurate and nonfunctional or irrelevant typing. In any case, would 17% accuracy be sufficient for any practical purpose?

Given that each subject had been regularly facilitating for 18 months, and that facilitated communication interactions by motivated facilitators might total 1 hour (and probably more) daily, one could conclude that the subjects had the equivalent of 500 to 600 hours of facilitated communication practice. Yet, this resulted in accurate, useful, functional communication in very few interactions. Far from supporting the utility or validity of FC, this study's findings seem to portray it as remarkably ineffective and of negligible benefit. Furthermore, the three people who were assessed had been chosen for the study because they were considered by those around them to be communicating with a reasonable degree of effectiveness. So much for first impressions!

Vazquez (1994). This study involved three subjects in message passing related to picture identification, video viewing, and object identification. Rather than providing clear evidence of the accurate responding of individuals, as proponents of FC might hope, Vazquez reported her findings to be mixed; among one of the key issues was that one subject could speak and would "blurt out" some responses. Vazquez (1994) noted, "While there is no doubt that Eva spoke these names, it was not so clear that she, and not the facilitator who could hear the names, did the typing" (p. 375). Eva was also reported to be able to type without facilitation, and so the question must be posed of why a verbal person, who could also type, was participating in FC at all. Vazquez also noted "evidence for cuing in the picture identification task was quite strong" (p. 375) and "these subjects who are believed to be doing grade-level work with [FC] were quite erratic in their ability to perform simple tasks without cuing from the facilitator" (p. 376). One of the subjects got all of the blind items incorrect and all of the items known to the facilitator correct. Vazquez concludes in part "if facilitated communication is characterized as ... a training procedure for developing linguistic and cognitive skills over a period of years ... then cuing may be seen as part of this process" (p. 376). This is not how FC was pitched originally, but it has been increasingly characterized in this manner, as a means of adapting to scientific criticism.

The difficulty with this interpretation of Vazquez (1994) is the denial of cuing by facilitators and the attribution that the content of the typing is a genuine expression of the person with a disability when facilitator control of utterances in FC has been found to be ubiquitous. When the information produced is found so consistently to be biased in this manner, how can the information be used to judge that a child is making progress in linguistic development, as it can when there is independently produced content? In summary, it appears that the "evidence" for the authenticity of facilitated communications from this study was the product of a child who could accurately verbalize responses and type at least some responses without FC. This is rather thin support.

Weiss, Wagner, and Bauman (1996).   This study, published in *Mental Retardation*, was a partially controlled message-passing study with a single 13-year-old boy with autism, using brief one-paragraph moral stories as stimuli. Each story was told to the child, facilitation was provided in response to a series of questions, and then a naive facilitator was introduced, using the same person as facilitator in each session. Weiss et al. provide a verbatim transcription of three sessions of FC message passing and report that "13 of Kenny's responses were factually correct, 4 responses were factually incorrect, and one question was partially correct across all three of the sessions" (p. 226). In fact, the pattern of responses differs from the one suggested by this statement, in that during facilitation by the naive facilitator, in the second session, *none* of four questions posed by the researcher was answered accurately by the child, a point noted by Weiss et al.

Weiss et al. (1996) noted further that "Clearly, it is possible that these words came from the uninformed facilitator and not Kenny" (p. 225), but did not evaluate the implications of this pattern and did not introduce distractor information to the facilitator because "it would be dissimilar from the common use of facilitated communication" (p. 228). This rationale is irrelevant, because if the child is validly and functionally communicating through FC, the child would never find out that different information had been given to the facilitator, so the only disruption, if any, would be due to facilitator control of typing. Weiss et al. also did not assure that during the first session, when Kenny made 5 of 13 "correct" responses, the facilitator was factually uninformed about the story presented to the child, and although the facilitator was escorted to and from the third session, the distance of the location where she waited and the actual inaudibility of the story presented to the child for the facilitator was never verified (i.e., "the ... referee ... supervised the facilitator's *departure* and *return* to Kenny," p. 222). Kenny had been receiving one-to-one assistance from the facilitator for 30 hours weekly for 15 months.

At best, the structure of this evaluation study reflects a weak design, and one in which it is apparent that reasonable precautions (which should have been reported in the article if taken) to prevent contamination of communications were never used. Although this is an article that is widely cited as evidence that some people can effectively use FC, the evidence from it is weak. Thus, while Weiss et al. (1996) suggest that "it is reasonable to conclude from the data already available that the phenomenon of facilitated communication does exist in some fashion with as yet unspecified incidence, validity, or reliability" (p. 229), and that their data contribute to this perspective, experimental design requirements dictate that this is not the case. Readers should also see Mostert (2001) for a critique.

BIKLEN AND CARDINAL (1997A)

Claims About FC Make Sense Only if One First Assumes FC Is Usually Real, First and Foremost

Biklen and Cardinal (1997) edited a book on FC in an attempt to stop the hemorrhaging of the status of FC caused by quality research demonstrating that FC was invalid and to respond to statements from every major professional organization questioning its efficacy and cautioning against its use. Indeed, perhaps at no time in the history of the field of developmental disabilities had agreement been reached on the identification and condemnation of a fad. Part of this, no doubt, was the result of the size and extent of the claims, including Donnellan's assertion that mental telepathy was involved in FC (see Spitz, 1994).

What Is Said That Should Not Be Said About FC (Cardinal & Biklen, 1997b)

One chapter in the book (Cardinal & Biklen, 1997b) dealt with what should not be said about FC by posing statements made by critics of FC and then refuting them.

"Facilitated communication has been proven to be a hoax or a fraud." Taylor (1998) in defending FC asserted that the accusation has been made that FC is a "fraud," "hoax," "sham" ... (para. 3). Cardinal and Biklen (1997b, p. 203) cite several legal cases in support of the position that FC is not regarded as a hoax or fraud. Yet, none of the decisions they cited considered (in the legal sense) whether FC was a hoax or a fraud. However, the appeal decision in Storch v. Syracuse University (1995) asserts that as a "matter of fact," the facilitator knowingly influenced the responses of the child. At the very least, this raises the question of how proponents of FC define "sham."

"Facilitated communication has been proven to not be real." Cardinal and Biklen (1997b) assert that FC "has been authenticated under both natural and controlled conditions" (p. 203) in articles published in peer-reviewed journals. In contrast to this position, the more appropriate question to raise becomes "Is FC real, and if so, under what circumstances?" The answer is no, based on the limitations of the articles reviewed in this chapter and the findings of other reviews of articles supporting and refuting FC (Green, 1994, 1996; Green & Shane, 1994; Mostert, 2001; Jacobson et al., 1995).

"Facilitated communication originates with the facilitator rather than with the FC user." Cardinal and Biklen (1997b, p. 203) cite "controlled studies" noted elsewhere in this chapter. Yet recall that none provide convincing and adequate procedural controls to rule out facilitator influence, control, or determination of the content of typing. Whereas one cannot, by scientific or other methods, conclude that all typing at all times by all people using FC is controlled by the facilitator, advocates of FC have yet to convincingly demonstrate, by ruling out influence adequately, that claimed instances of validated typing are bonafide. Of course, exceptions need to be made for people who now type independently, without the presence of a facilitator (or past facilitator), but the number of people who have approached or attained this status is minuscule (numbering no more than 23 people; see FCI, 1999) despite a decade of FC provision in the United States.

"Facilitated communication is magic or a trick." Cardinal and Biklen (1997b) argue that "No reputable studies have concluded that facilitated communication show that FC is a trick or illusion" (p. 204). Since 1997, however, research by Kirsch et al. (1998) has demonstrated that the FC process entails ideomotor responses and perceptual illusions that affect the facilitator. These considerations have been discussed elsewhere by Dillon (1993), Dillon, Fenlason, and Vogel (1994), Kezuka (1997), Mostert (2002), and Spitz (1997).

"Facilitated communication works for everyone." Although Cardinal and Biklen (1997b, p. 204) noted that the claim that FC "works for everyone" is not reasonable, Biklen (1992b) stated that virtually everyone with autism should be able to benefit from FC. To the best of our knowledge, Biklen is the only person who has made a statement of this nature in print, and thus the significance of his assertion is not clear, other than to deny his own earlier statement.

"No one has ever 'validated' their communication through facilitation." Cardinal and Biklen (1997b, p. 204), state that "Many people using FC have 'validated' their authorship" (and cite, among other studies, Simon, Toll, & Whitehair, 1994, in support of this position). However, in their original article, Simon et al. (1994) expressed reservations regarding the surety of their validation findings. They subsequently reiterated their reservations (Simon, Whitehair, & Toll, 1995, 1996), but apparently failed to telegraph them to proponents.

"Everyone using facilitated communication will demonstrate excellent literacy skills, write poetry, have perfect spelling, perform at super accelerated levels." Although Cardinal and Biklen (1997b, p. 204) cite several studies where variability in performance among facilitated individuals was evident, none of these studies (i.e., Biklen, 1993, Biklen et al., 1995; Biklen, Morten, Gold, Berrigan, & Swaminathan, 1992) employed credible means to validate communications, and hence cannot stand as indications of whether or not the actual communication changes that could be engendered by FC are heterogenous.

"Everyone using facilitation will facilitate best (or conversely, not at all) with their mothers and fathers, facilitate best (or conversely, not at all) with only one person, learn to use facilitated communication immediately." The point that Cardinal and Biklen (1997b, p. 205) seem to be making here is that responses to FC are idiosyncratic; however, as evidence they refer to studies that contain insufficient controls to verify that typing style or apparent typing progress of the people being facilitated were not being controlled or influenced by their facilitators, and hence, the property of variability of responses is uninterpretable.

What Is Said That Should Be Said About FC (Cardinal & Biklen, 1997b)

Cardinal and Biklen (1997b) also addressed what they believed should be said about FC. Once again, their logic, rationale, and use of scholarly citation of sources were flawed.

"Facilitated communication appears to work for some people." Cardinal and Biklen (1997b) stated that "peer-reviewed controlled studies report that some people can use facilitated communication to communicate to a degree that is significantly greater than they can without facilitation" (p. 205). As we have noted and reviewed, either the procedures of these studies or the very statements of the authors of these studies belie this conclusion.

"Authorship studies in facilitated communication achieve mixed results, but when studies possess certain procedures, some level of facilitated communication can be measured." With respect to this conclusion, Cardinal and Biklen conveniently refer to studies in Cardinal and Biklen (1997a). In that chapter, in addition to citing studies that present logical problems for this conclusion, they also cite the Department of Family Services (1993) *Queensland Report*. This report, which we have reviewed, is aptly summarized by Green (1994), paraphrasing or quoting as follows:

A coding system was applied to transcripts for elements that it was presumed, but not verified, that certain information was unknown to facilitators .... Independent, non-participating judges were not involved .... A single person apparently served as advisor, trainer, sometime facilitator, and data analyst .... No objective evidence from controlled observations was provided in the report .... For no observations were there any controls for possible facilitator influence .... Validity was assumed or inferred from circumstantial evidence ... from facilitators that FC users displayed spelling and word usage patterns that were supposedly unique to the FC user. (pp. 179–180)

As readers will note, these provisions fail to provide sufficient control of facilitator control to allow the conclusion that the statements made through FC were valid.

"*Authorship studies have reported that the facilitator can influence the user's communicative output or that participants may seek/derive cues from the facilitator.*" Cardinal and Biklen (1997b, p. 206) note that "some controlled studies have indicated that the facilitator can control," influence, or cue FC users' responses. In fact, the degree of influence in most studies approaches perfect control of FC user responses; studies published in 1995, 1996, and later confirm these findings and support the conclusion that influence is far from subtle, but is instead clearly evident and pragmatically significant. Even more critically, there is no evidence that well-meaning facilitators who are unintentionally controlling responses have any control, by intent or agreement, over the influence they exert on responses (i.e., there is no evidence that warning or admonishing a facilitator about cuing, influencing, or control has any impact on the degree of control of the FC users' responses that occur).

"*Testing for authorship of facilitated communication is still very complex and there are many unanswered questions, but our understanding of it is greater now than even a few years ago.*" Again, Cardinal and Biklen (1997b) refer to conclusions drawn from analysis of studies in Cardinal and Biklen (1997a), but limitations on their interpretations in that chapter—related to the extent to which three studies demonstrate effective communication via FC and which they ignore—undermine the logical conclusion that "our understanding is greater now." Our understanding, however, of their position as unsupportable, in contrast, is substantially greater. Contrary to the obfuscation inherent in all writing published in support of FC, testing for authorship is not a complex enterprise, but does require strict procedures to guarantee and verify that facilitators are actually blind to message content on at least some trials of message passing. There are also numerous other methodologies that differ from message passing that could be used to verify the authenticity of authorship, and which have not been used by proponents of FC during the past decade of advocacy for the method (e.g., see Jacobson & Mulick, 1994).

"*Not all people with autism, Down syndrome, pervasive developmental disorder, or other developmental disabilities benefit from facilitation.*" We find little to disagree with in this statement as a generalization except that it is an understatement. The extent to which facilitator control is detected when adequate methods are incorporated in studies clearly indicates that FC effects, in the sense of growing communicative competency as a typical pattern, if they do occur, are very much the exception rather than the rule (see Green, 1994, 1996; Mostert, 2001).

"*Not all professionals make good facilitators, regardless of experience in the field.*" Existing research has not sufficiently documented and validated useful, functional communication across a range of facilitator–FC user dyads. When attempts are made in the course of clinical or educational services to validate authorship, it is typically done in a manner that does not permit clear conclusions to be drawn. Thus, there are no grounds for drawing conclusions about who is or is not a "good facilitator."

"Many facilitated communication users have difficulty passing validation tests under controlled conditions." We agree with the tenor of this generalization, although our reasons center on the findings from controlled studies indicating that facilitators are controlling the authorship otherwise attributed to the FC user. In contrast, Cardinal and Biklen (1997b) would attribute this problem to the imposition of controls in studies that they purport reduce confidence, undermine the relationship between the facilitator and FC user, or affect the confidence of the facilitator. They also purport that the FC user might find the implementation, of what could only be considered to be benign methodological controls, to be confrontational and demeaning. The research shows that under validation testing, the overwhelming majority of people fail validation, so this generalization is another understatement. In addition, virtually all of the evidence offered to support the perspective that confrontational factors inhibit authorship comes from people who "uttered" confirming statements in the course of FC. Findings indicating that the authorship of these utterances may well be under control of the facilitator mean that conclusions that these factors impair the quality of validation are based on circular reasoning. The only diminution we perceive in this argument is with regard to analytical competence.

"Some facilitated communication users show remarkable increases in communicative performance, others show less than remarkable performance, and others show no increase at all." Again, we concur on this issue with Cardinal and Biklen, but are compelled to note that the results of controlled studies clearly show that independent authorship is vanishingly less common than suggested in Biklen and Cardinal (1997a, 1997b) or by others' earlier and later qualitative research. The implications of the controlled studies are clear in that reasoned caution would suggest that without systematic and procedurally adequate validation, authorship may only be assumed in those instances where independent typing or *de novo* verbal conversational skills are achieved in the physical absence of current or past facilitators. It is important to recognize that minor gestural prompts that an FC user can see, with no physical contact, or physical facilitation at the arm, back, or shoulder have significant potential to compromise authenticity of FC user responses (Castelhano & Henderson, 2002). To argue otherwise would suggest, for example, that people with autism cannot learn from prompting to display particular multistep behaviors using the same types of prompts to which apes, horses, dogs, and canines respond effectively (Burch & Bailey, 1999; Sebeok & Umiker-Sebeok, 1980). These considerations greatly reduce the number of people for whom proponents of FC can validly claim they have demonstrated remarkable increases. Moreover, there is little evidence that people who demonstrate remarkable, less than remarkable, or very small increases in communicative performance differ in the degree to which their communications are controlled by their facilitators; that is, "remarkable increases" in and of themselves do not indicate greater "independence" from facilitator control.

"Findings from qualitative and quantitative studies have produced convergent findings about validation." Cardinal and Biklen (1997b) note that "controlled studies

in which individuals have demonstrated authorship incorporate factors that have been discussed in qualitative studies" (p. 207). A more accurate interpretation of findings from controlled studies is that those with adequate controls have continued to demonstrate that authorship lies substantially with the facilitator, whereas controlled studies conducted in a less adequate or conclusive manner, or which have not fully disclosed findings, are more likely to indicate FC user authorship.

CONCLUSION

"Facilitated communication is important." According to Cardinal and Biklen (1997b), "To the extent that facilitated communication can provide a voice to some people with disabilities, it is crucially important" (p. 208). Giving a voice to these persons was part of the initial strategy for promoting FC. Consider for example, that a Pennsylvania State Office of Mental Retardation Bulletin (Number 00-94-11, March 1, 1994) was devoted solely to FC. The bulletin supported FC, described Department of Public Welfare (DPW) sponsored training in FC, and established a *Right to Communicate* as DPW policy. Displaying what could only be described as a colossal leap of faith, the Office of Mental Retardation (PA OMR) stated policy was "Facilitated communication is based upon a *belief* [italics added] in the competence of the individual regardless of his or her label" (p. 4). A month later, PA OMR promoted the FC notion of "undisclosed literacy consistent with normal functioning" by supporting a FC workshop that stated as its goal, "This service is funded by the Office of Mental Retardation to promote and enhance the values that guide services to people who are *perceived to be* cognitively impaired" [italics added].

In summary, the voices provided by FC to persons with disabilities have been shown in virtually every appropriately designed study to be not theirs but rather those of the facilitators. Controlled research that is capable of identifying actual authorship continues to show that when these concerns are responsibly, professionally, adequately, and ethically addressed, the extent to which FC has actually represented the communicative intent of individuals with severe disabilities is very small, bordering on negligible, relative to the large number of people with whom it has been attempted for sustained periods over a decade or more. This finding has emerged repeatedly in research conducted internationally with children and adults, with a range of specific disabilities, using a variety of research designs including variations on message passing, and completely different quasi-experimental designs. By the standard set forth by Cardinal and Biklen (1997a, 1997b), facilitated communication can be understood as essentially a very ineffective treatment or intervention, and of very little importance, because it does *not* give a voice to a person with a disability. Rather, research shows that FC substitutes the thoughts of the facilitator and thus, there is no true self-determination displayed by the individual receiving facilitation. On the other hand, FC could be viewed as an important phenomenon because of how the movement to support FC resists disconfirmation of any nature, from any source, at any time, and exemplifies the enormous waste of time, money, and human resources that such fad and bogus treatments and interventions represent.

REFERENCES

Association for Science in Autism Treatment. (n.d.). *Description of facilitated communication.* Retrieved March 24, 2003, from http://www.asatonline.org/autism_info09.html

The Association. (2003). *Ta main pour parler.* Retrieved March 21, 2003, from www2.tmpp.net

Bara, B. G., Bucciarelli, M., & Colle, L. (2001). Communicative abilities in autism: Evidence for attentional deficits. *Brain and Language, 77,* 216–240.

Bebko, J. M., Perry, A., & Bryson, S. (1996). Multiple method validation study of facilitated communication: II. Individual differences and subgroups results. *Journal of Autism and Developmental Disorders, 26,* 19–42.

Beck, A. R., & Pirovano, C. M. (1996). Facilitated communicators' performance on a task of receptive language. *Journal of Autism and Developmental Disorders, 26,* 497–512.

Biklen, D. (1990). Communication unbound: Autism and praxis. *Harvard Educational Review, 60,* 291–314.

Biklen, D. (1992a). Autism orthodoxy versus free speech: A reply to Cummins and Prior. *Harvard Educational Review, 62,* 242–256.

Biklen, D. (1992b, Summer). Questions and answers on facilitated communication. *The Advocate,* 16–18.

Biklen, D. (1993). *Communication unbound: How facilitated communication is challenging traditional views of autism and ability/disability.* New York: Teachers College Press.

Biklen, D. (2001a, March). Expanding horizons for new research into facilitated communication. *Facilitated Communication Digest* (The newsletter of the Facilitated Communication Institute Syracuse University), *9*(2). Retrieved March 14, 2003, from http://soeweb.syr.edu/thefci/9-2bik.htm

Biklen, D. (2001b, September). Review of "Communicative abilities in autism: Evidence for attentional deficits" by Bara, Bucciarelli, & Colle. *Facilitated Communication Digest* (The newsletter of the Facilitated Communication Institute Syracuse University), *9*(4). Retrieved March 16, 2003, from http://soeweb.syr.edu/thefci/9-4bik.htm

Biklen, D. (n.d.). *Facts about facilitated communication.* Retrieved March 19, 2003, from http://soeweb.syr.edu/thefci/fcfacts.htm

Biklen, D., & Cardinal, D. N. (Eds.). (1997a). *Contested words, contested science: Unraveling the facilitated communication controversy.* New York: Teachers College Press.

Biklen, D., & Cardinal, D. N. (1997b). Reframing the issue: Presuming competence. In D. Biklen & D. Cardinal (Eds.), *Contested words, contested science* (pp. 187–198). New York: Teachers College Press.

Biklen, D., Morton, M., Gold, D., Berrigan, C., & Swaminathan, S. (1992). Facilitated communication: Implications for individuals with autism. *Topics in Language Disorders, 12*(4), 1–28.

Biklen, D., Saha, N., & Kliewer, C. (1995). How teachers confirm authorship of facilitated communication. *Journal of the Association for Persons with Severe Handicaps, 13,* 155–162.

Bomba, C., O'Donnell, L., Markowitz, C., & Holmes, D. L. (1996). Evaluating the impact of facilitated communication on the communicative competence of fourteen students with autism. *Journal of Autism and Developmental Disorders, 26,* 43–58.

Borthwick, C., & Crossley, R. (1999). Language and retardation. *Psycoloquy: 10,* #38. Retrieved March 23, 2003, from http://psycprints.ecs.soton.ac.uk/archive/00000673/

Braman, B. J., Brady, M. P., Linehan, S. L., & Williams, R. E. (1995). Facilitated communication for children with autism: An examination of face validity. *Behavioral Disorders, 21,* 110–119.

Broderick, A. A., & Kasa-Hendrickson, C. (2001). "SAY JUST ONE WORD AT FIRST": The emergence of reliable speech in a student labeled with autism. *Journal of the Association for Persons with Severe Handicaps, 26*(3), 13–14.

Burch, M. R., & Bailey, J. S. (1999). *How dogs learn.* New York: Wiley.

Burgess, C. A., Kirsch, I., Shane, H., Niederauer, K. L., Graham, S. M., & Bacon, A. (1998). Facilitated communication as an ideomotor response. *Psychological Science, 9,* 71–74.

Calculator, S. N. (1995). "Validity of facilitated communication: Failure to replicate Calculator & Singer (1992)": Response to Perry, Bebko, and Bryson. *Topics in Language Disorders, 15*(2), 87–89.

Calculator, S. N. (1999). Look who's pointing now: Cautions related to the clinical use of facilitated communication. *Language, Speech, and Hearing Services in the Schools, 30*(4), 408–414.

Calculator, S. N., & Singer, K. M. (1992). Letter to the editor: Preliminary validation of facilitated communication. *Topics in Language Disorders, 12*(4), ix–xvi.

Cardinal, D. N. (1994). Researchers and the press: A cautionary tale. *The Chronicle of Higher Education, XLI*(7), b-3.

Cardinal, D. N., & Biklen, D. (1997a). Suggested procedures for confirming authorship through research: An initial investigation. In D. Biklen & D. N. Cardinal (Eds.), *Contested words, contested science* (pp. 173–186). New York: Teachers College Press.

Cardinal, D. N., & Biklen, D. (1997b). Summing up: What should not and what can be said about facilitated communication. In D. Biklen & D. Cardinal (Eds.), *Contested words, contested science* (pp. 199–208). New York: Teachers College Press.

Cardinal, D. N., Hanson, D., & Wakeham, J. (1996). Investigation of authorship in facilitated communication. *Mental Retardation, 34*(4), 231–242.

Castelhano, M. S., & Henderson, J. M. (2002). Detailed visual memory for objects in scenes following intentional and incidental learning tasks. *Michigan State University Eyelab Technical Report, 3*, 1–15. (http://eyelab.msu.edu/documents/niki/tech2002_3.pdf)

Crossley, R. (1992). Getting the words out: Case studies in facilitated communication training. *Topics in Language Disorders, 12*, 46–59.

Crossley, R. (1993, April). *Flying high on paper wings - Facilitated communication training In North America: An Australian Perspective.* Retrieved March 21, 2003, from http://home.vicnet.net.au/~dealccinc/Flying.htm

Cummins, R. A., & Prior, M. P. (1992). Autism and assisted communication: A response to Biklen. *Harvard Educational Review, 62*(2), 228–240.

Danforth, S. (1997). On what basis hope? Modern progress and postmodern alternatives. *Mental Retardation, 35*(2), 93–106.

Danforth, S. (1999). Pragmatism and the scientific validation of professional practices in American special education. *Disability & Society, 14*, 733–751.

Department of Family Services and Aboriginal and Islander Services, Division of Intellectual Disability Services. (1993). *The Queensland report on facilitated communication.* Brisbane, Queensland, Australia: Author.

Dillon, K. M. (1993). Facilitated communication, autism, and ouija. *Skeptical Inquirer, 17*(3), 281–287.

Dillon, K. M., Fenlason, J. E., & Vogel, D. J. (1994). Belief in and use of a questionable technique, facilitated communication, for children with autism. *Psychological Reports, 75*(1, Pt. 2), 459–464.

Duchan, J. F. (1999). Views of facilitated communication; What's the point? *Language, Speech, and Hearing Services in Schools, 30*, 401–407.

Duchan, J. F., Calculator, S., Sonnenmeier, R., Diehl, S., & Cumley, G. D. (2001). A framework for managing controversial practices. *Language, Speech, and Hearing Services in the Schools, 32*, 133–141.

Edelson, S. M., Rimland, B., Berger, C. L., & Billings, D. (1998). Evaluation of a mechanical hand-support for facilitated communication. *Journal of Autism and Developmental Disorders, 28*, 153–157.

Effeta. (2003). *Formations et stages en Suisse Romande.* Retrieved March 21, 2003, from http://site.voila.fr/effeta

Facilitated Communication Institute, Syracuse University. (1999a). *Articles by facilitated communication users.* Retrieved March 26, 2003, from http://soeweb.syr.edu/thefci/fcauths.htm

Facilitated Communication Institute, Syracuse University. (1999b). *Facilitated communication resource directory – 1999.* Retrieved March 26, 2003, from http://soeweb.syr.edu/thefci/7-4ric.htm

Foxx, R. M. (1994). Facilitated communication in Pennsylvania: Scientifically invalid but politically correct. *Dimensions*, 1–9.

Green, G. (1994). The quality of the evidence. In H. C. Shane (Ed.), *Facilitated communication: The clinical and social phenomenon* (pp. 157–226). San Diego, CA: Singular.

Green, G. (1996). Evaluating claims about treatments for autism. In C. Maurice, G. Green, & S. C. Luce (Eds.), *Behavioral intervention for young children with autism* (pp. 15–28). Austin, TX: Pro-Ed.

Green, G., & Shane, H. C. (1994). Science, reason, and facilitated communication. *Journal of the Association for Persons with Severe Handicaps, 19*, 151–172.

Hill, D. A., & Leary, M. R. (1993). *Movement disturbance: A clue to hidden competencies in persons diagnosed with autism and other developmental disabilities.* Madison, WI: DRI Press.

Hirshorn, A., & Gregory, J. (1995). Further negative findings on facilitated communications. *Psychology in the Schools, 32*, 109–113.

Hudson, A. (1995). Disability and facilitated communication: A critique. *Advances in Clinical Child Psychology, 17*, 197–232.

Intellectual Disability Review Panel. (1989). *Investigation into the reliability and validity of the assisted communication technique.* Melbourne, AU: Department of Community Services, Victoria.

Jacobson, J. W., & Mulick, J. A. (1994). Facilitated communication: Better education through applied ideology. *Journal of Behavioral Education, 4*, 93–105.

Jacobson, J. W., Mulick, J. A., & Schwartz, A. A. (1995). A history of facilitated communication: Science, pseudoscience, and antiscience. *American Psychologist, 50*, 750–765.

Kerrin, R. G., Murdock, J. Y., Sharpton, W. R., & Jones, N. (1998). Who's doing the pointing? Investigation facilitated communication in a classroom setting with students with autism. *Focus on Autism and Other Developmental Disabilities, 13*(2), 73–79.

Kezuka, E. (1997). The role of touch in facilitated communication. *Journal of Autism and Developmental Disorders, 27*, 571–593.

Kirsch, I., Shane, H. C., Burgess, C. A., Niederauer, K. L., Graham, S. M., & Bacon, A. (1998). Facilitated communication as an ideomotor response. *Psychological Science, 9*, 71–74.

Maul, T. A. (1994, February 8). *Advisory to the field and model guideline on facilitated communication.* Albany, NY: Office of Mental Retardation and Developmental Disabilities.

Milgram, S. (1963). Behavioral study of obedience. *Journal of Abnormal and Social Psychology, 67*(4), 371–378.

Montee, B. B., Miltenberger, R. G., & Wittrock, D. (1995). An experimental analysis of facilitated communication. *Journal of Applied Behavior Analysis, 28*, 189–200.

Mostert, M. P. (2001). Facilitated communication since 1995: A review of published studies. *Journal of Autism and Developmental Disorders, 31*, 287–313.

Mostert, M. P. (2002). Letter to the editor: Teaching the illusion of facilitated communication. *Journal of Autism and Developmental Disorders, 32*, 239–240.

Myles, B., Simpson, R. L., & Smith, S. M. (1996a). Collateral behavior and social effects of using facilitated communications with individuals with autism. *Focus on Autism and Other Developmental Disabilities, 11*, 163–169, 190.

Myles, B. S, Simpson, R. L., & Smith, S. M. (1996b). Impact of facilitated communication combined with direct instruction on academic performance of individuals with autism. *Focus on Autism and Other Developmental Disabilities, 11*, 37–44.

Niemi, J., & Kärnä-Lin, E. (2002). Grammar and lexicon in facilitated communication: A linguistic authorship analysis of a Finnish case. *Mental Retardation, 40*, 347–357.

Ogletree, B., Hamtil, A., Solberg, L., & Scoby-Schmelzle, S. (1993). Facilitated communication: A naturalistic validation method. *Focus on Autistic Behavior, 8*(4), 1–10.

Olney, M. (1997). A controlled study of facilitated communication using computer games. In D. Biklen & D. N. Cardinal (Eds.), *Contested words, contested science: Unraveling the facilitated communication controversy* (pp. 96–114). New York: Teachers College Press.

Olney, M. F. (2001). Evidence of literacy in individuals labeled with mental retardation, *Disability Studies Quarterly, 21*(2). Retrieved March 22, 2003, from www.cds.hawaii.edu

Oppenheim, R. (1974). *Effective teaching methods for autistic children.* Springfield, IL: Charles C. Thomas.

Park, R. L. (2003). The seven warning signs of bogus science. *The Chronicle Review, 49*(21), B20. Available on-line at http://chronicle.com/free/v49/i21/21b02001.htm

Perry, A., Bebko, J., & Bryson, S. E. (1994). Validity of facilitated communication: Failure to replicate Calculator & Singer (1992) [Letter to the Editor]. *Topics in Language Disorders, 14*(4), 79–82.

Saolovita, T. (1996). *Tukiviesti 6/1996.* Retrieved March 21, 2003, from http://www.sci.fi/~biopteri/e-ref3.html

Schubert, A. (1997). "I want to talk like everyone": On the use of multiple means of communication. *Mental Retardation, 35,* 347–354.

Sebeok, T., & Umiker-Sebeok, J. (Eds.). (1980). *Speaking of apes.* New York: Plenum.

Shavelson, R. J., & Town, L. (Eds.). (2002). *Scientific research in education.* Washington, DC: National Academy Press.

Sheehan, C., & Matuozzi, R. (1996). Validation of facilitated communication. *Mental Retardation, 34*(2), 94–107.

Simon, E. W., Toll, D. M., & Whitehair, P. M. (1994). A naturalistic approach to the validation of facilitated communication. *Journal of Autism and Developmental Disorders, 24,* 647–657.

Simon, E. W., Whitehair, P. M., & Toll, D. M. (1995). Keeping facilitated communication in perspective. *Mental Retardation, 33,* 338–339.

Simon, E. W., Whitehair, P. M., & Toll, D. M. (1996). A case study: Follow-up assessment of facilitated communication. *Journal of Autism and Developmental Disorders, 26,* 9–18.

Simpson, R. L., & Myles, B. S. (1995). Facilitated communication and children with disabilities: An enigma in search of a perspective. *Focus on Exceptional Children, 27*(9), 1–16.

Spitz, H. H. (1994). Comment on Donnellan's Review of Shane's (1994) Facilitated Communication: The Clinical and Social Phenomenon. *American Journal on Mental Retardation, 101,* 96–100.

Spitz, H. H. (1997). *Nonconscious movements: From mystical messages to facilitated communication.* Mahwah, NJ: Lawrence Erlbaum Associates.

Stanovich, K. E. (2001). *How to think straight about psychology* (6th ed.). Upper Saddle River, NJ: Allyn & Bacon.

Storch v. Syracuse University, 165 Misc.2d 621 (1995). 629 N.Y.S.2d 958.

Taylor, S. J. (1998, February). *A time to speak out on the FC controversy.* Retrieved March 24, 2003, from http://web.syr.edu/~thechp/tash-fc.htm

Vazquez, C. A. (1994). Brief report: A multitask controlled evaluation of facilitated communication. *Journal of Autism and Developmental Disorders, 24*(3), 369–379.

von Tetzchner, S. (1994). Research issues in facilitated communication. In J. Brodin & E. Björck-Åkesson (Eds.), *Methodological issues in research in augmentative and alternative communication.* Jönköping, Sweden: Jönköping University Press (English language manuscript version, courtesy S. von Tetzchner).

Weiss, M. J. S., Wagner, S. H., & Bauman, M. (1996). A validated case study of facilitated communication. *Mental Retardation, 34*(4), 220–230.

Wilder, D. A., & Shapiro, P. N. (1984). Role of out-group cues in determining social identity. *Journal of Personality & Social Psychology, 47*(2), 342–348.

Wolfensberger, W. (1992). The facilitated communication craze: The cold fusion of human services. *Training Institute Publication Series 12*(2/3), 39–46.

Positive Behavior Support:
A Paternalistic Utopian Delusion

James A. Mulick
Eric M. Butter
The Ohio State University and
Columbus Children's Hospital

> The credo of liberal science imposes upon us two moral obligations: to allow everybody to err and criticize, even obnoxiously, and to submit everybody's beliefs—including our own—to public checking before claiming that they deserve to be accepted as knowledge. Today, activists and moralists are assailing both halves of the creed. They are assailing the right to err and criticize, when the error seems outrageous or the criticism seems hurtful; they are assailing the requirements for public checking, when the result is to reject someone's belief. They have a right to pursue their attack (nonviolently), but they, and we, should understand that they are enemies of science itself, and even ultimately, of freedom of thought. And those of us who hold sacred the right to err and the duty to check need to understand that our defense of liberal science must preach not only toleration but discipline: the hard self-discipline which requires us to live with offense.
>
> —Rauch (1993, p. 154)

Positive behavior support (PBS) has been presented to the education and disability services sectors as a new science of behavior. It is sold as a science that has special relevance to solving behavior problems encountered in school and community settings. This is not a trivial claim. In this chapter, we take a critical look at this claim, examine its emergence in developmental disability and education circles, and assess what PBS may mean for people with disabilities, the people who care for and about them, and for serious students of psychology and education.

Our general thesis has two parts. The first part is that whatever else it may be, PBS is not science, but rather a form of illusion that leads to dangerously biased decision making. This leads us to examine the basis of what a science of behavior, or of education or of anything else, must be in order to be called a science. The second part of our analysis shows that PBS is not new, if by new, it refers to either the synthesis of values with a technology or the content adherents claim it encompasses. In establishing these points we are led, and hope to lead the reader along with us, to an inescapable conclusion about PBS; namely, that it represents little more than propaganda designed to promote the professional interests of a group of social and educational reformers. Further, what little benefit in education or community service settings PBS practitioners might be able to provide is more than offset by the cost to them and their students of distorting the reality of the very behavioral processes they seek to alter and use to benefit people with disabilities.

For our purposes, we must take some statement of what PBS is supposed to be as a starting point. A recent paper by Carr et al. (2002) serves nicely; it is titled, "Positive Behavior Support: Evolution of an Applied Science." Surely, the content and description of any field evolves over time, and most of these authors have been involved in what may be considered the social movement behind PBS since its earliest beginnings. The paper asserts that PBS is a *new applied science* that is based on three important sources: applied behavior analysis, the normalization movement in human services, and person-centered values. The first of these is arguably an applied science, whereas the other two are ideologies or value systems. The concept of ideology traces its roots to Marxist political philosophy, and refers to the social influences that both generate and sustain the ways in which people come to understand their world and to shape their social agenda (Belkin, 1998). Values refer to the things people actively pursue, both for themselves and for others whom they wish to influence. Thus, the novelty of PBS is in the combination of science and value systems. In other words, it is a value-based applied science. This gives us a starting point.

SCIENCE AND VALUES

Like oil and water, science and values are impossible to mix completely. You get a layered combination that may swirl around feverishly when agitated, or entwine and flow with convection when heated, but which ultimately separates as soon as removed from forced association. A lava lamp works on the latter of these two models, but lava lamps rightly are regarded as cheap curiosities that give poor illumination at best. Likewise, science is a system with rules which make it work and work well, but which conflict with some ideologies and cultural systems that serve other ends than those for which science evolved to achieve; that is, of finding the truth.

Jonathan Rauch (1993), who was quoted at the opening of this chapter, looks on science as a great and recent cultural invention. The morality he refers to is centered on the material and civil progress he thinks science has made possible since it was more or less invented and adopted as an important cultural practice a few short centuries ago. He sees the preservation of the practice of science as a moral obligation in modern society. He does not seek to derive morality from science, a mistake that others have made in the 20th century to the detriment of millions.

Social Darwinism was such a mistake. In its incarnation as the eugenics movement, which sought to improve the human race through the elimination of *people* who displayed undesirable characteristics, it was briefly influential in American political and legal thought (Mulick & Antonak, 1992). The mentally and physically disabled, the dishonest, and even the immoral were to be discouraged from having children (Weiss, 1987). The horror of this negative eugenic thinking was finally and widely perceived in the revelations that followed the defeat of Fascism in Europe in World War II. In the name of race hygiene, "people worthless to live" had been killed in the Nazi-dominated countries, beginning with people with mental and physical disabilities, moving on to homosexuals, and finally focusing on those from specific ethnic backgrounds, including Gypsies and Jews (Friedlander, 1995).

The idea of the struggle for existence and the survival of the fittest had been offered as a *scientific value system*. It was based on the belief that superiority was its own justification, and that social good was achieved by the triumph of superiority over inferiority by any means. Of course, this was a deep misunderstanding of both natural selection and its relevance to social ideology. The real lesson of natural selection is that the variability within populations provides the opportunity for successful reproduction, and for the unbroken continuity of life via natural selection, under ever-changing environmental conditions. Thus, if anything, a moral system derived from Darwinian thought would encourage diversity as preparation for possible unanticipated environmental change!

But any proposal for a scientific value system, or for a value-based science, is bound to lead at the very least to scientific error and likely to political failure too. This is the lesson of the fall of the Soviet system, which based its instrumentality on the presumed scientific Marxist–Leninist "truth" that the progressive power of the state should (and could) shape the individual into the "New Soviet Man." The resulting chimera, after a 70-year gestation (and untold human suffering and economic failure), died without issue in the vast Russian cultural and ethnic landscape. It could hardly have been otherwise.

Science is the systematic search for true relations in nature, in the material universe. One knows that one is closer to scientific truth when people who perform roughly the same actions get roughly the same results. It is method, neither good nor bad; neither positive nor negative. While the scientific method's rules are neither good nor bad in themselves, and they do represent a cultural system of sorts among those who practice science, they are first and foremost completely pragmatic, emphasizing simplicity, generality, honesty, completeness, and openness. Finally, they demand a willingness, as Rauch (1993) pointed out, to check everything and to be checked by others. This emphasis on letting no assertion of fact go unchecked is the essence of the *success* of this approach in achieving progress in understanding and controlling the material processes we find in nature. It permits no dogma to persist for long that contravenes physical reality, no authority to completely quiet criticism. Absolutely no appeal to faith or authority or custom has a place in scientific checking. In fact, proclaiming one's authority concerning the revelation of truth about some issue is the surest way of all to get other scientists to try to disprove the same thing. Science only thrives in a broader culture of openness (hence, Rauch's "liberal science"). This is because unless propositions are put before the relevant audience for critical evaluation, for disproof, error can accumulate as undisclosed, and self-serving distortions lead to further distortions and cause accepted ideas to depart more and more from reality.

Unavoidable Bias

There are even two major subdivisions in science and in the kinds of truth for which scientists seek: (a) the truth about the structure of a thing and (b) the truth about the function of a thing. True structures are mainly, but not exclusively, investigated by ever more sophisticated means of imaging, dissecting, and magnifying. True functions are investigated by ever more sophisticated means of correlating changes among events, and of isolating things in order to systematically vary the isolated parts of complex systems to determine their causal role in those systems. B. F. Skinner (1954, 1963) strongly advocated for an emphasis on the functional analytic method as the most appropriate approach for the study of behavior, emphasizing the lawful way behavior changed as a function of changes in the external environment.

Structural and functional truths about natural phenomena and natural objects are often strongly related, but not always or necessarily directly. For example, there is evidence that the human brain is specialized to perceive the human face (de Haan, Humphreys, & Johnson, 2002). This specialization to orient to the human face provides the assurance of much practice in differentiating among faces, some of whom will be more individually important than others. Preference to look at faces also provides for attention to the expressive vehicle of most human communication (i.e., the eyes and mouth). Further, the structure of the human visual system provides most people with the capacity to respond to, say, the color red. Knowledge of the visual sensory system alone will not, however, inform us in the least about the likelihood of approach or withdrawal with respect to a red object, or whether a red object will be highly valued, or whether it will be recalled later. Nevertheless, a potential functional relation, like consistent selection of a particular preferred fruit (or a color), will not be possible for an individual who cannot physically distinguish among fruits by using some physical characteristic. Physiological structure sets important limits on possible functional relations. Thus, if the way to tell the difference between a poisonous fruit and a similar looking delicious safe fruit without tasting it is *only* on the basis of one fruit's reflectance of infrared light, a physically unequipped but hungry human will be completely out of luck. Humans can't see in this portion of the spectrum. The honeybee, in contrast, can see in the infrared portion of the light spectrum, and could unerringly discriminate these fruits. Evolutionary biologists speculate that many flowering plants evolved pigments that reflect light in the infrared spectrum precisely because bees and other appropriately equipped animals assist them with pollination, an interesting and common interspecies complex of functional relations. Organisms evolve to be able to work with aspects of nature that contribute to their survival and reproduction, remaining quite blind to other aspects of nature.

Humans are blind not only with respect to what they are unable to detect, but also as a result of what they are particularly equipped to detect. Human detection of some aspects of the physical environment is so keen that it can mask reality. Psychologists have studied these *perceptual biases* extensively. Visual illusions are an easily demonstrated type of perceptual bias that leads to perceiving something that isn't there. The Muller–Lyer illusion can be demonstrated with a pencil and paper (or put *Muller–Lyer illusion* into an Internet search engine to see many versions of this visual illusion). Draw two exactly equal 4-inch parallel lines, one about 1.5 inches exactly above the other. Add to the top line inward pointing arrows, like this: > and this <. To the bottom line, add outward pointing arrows, like this: < and this >. The lines will appear to be of different lengths, the one with outward pointing arrowheads seemingly shorter. The next time you open your

Internet browser, perform a search on these words: Poggendorf illusion, Titchner illusion, Herring illusion, and the Zollner illusion. All are illusions of size or orientation that trick the eye into seeing falsely. There are many other sorts of visual illusion, some evoking motion where there is none, some color shifts or afterimages, some solidity or transparency or depth (just type *illusion* into your search engine and explore the fantastic variety available on the Internet, but one of our favorites is http://www.grand-illusions.com/), and others even inducing failure to notice real changes that happen right before the observer's eyes (see Simons, 2003) Movies, which are really frequently substituted still frames, fuse into an illusion of motion because of the high speed with which each frame is flashed on the screen, a rate higher than the so-called critical flicker fusion frequency.

Perceptual biases can shift with a person's state of health. For example, people with cirrhosis of the liver due to alcoholism or hepatitis eventually show brain damage because the toxins that accumulate in the blood are not efficiently removed by the liver. Damage to the brain may alter its function, independent of age, time of day, and training experience. Ordinarily, extensive neuropsychological tests are required to detect the onset of cognitive impairment. Kircheis, Wettstein, Timmermann, Schnitzler, and Haussinger (2002) showed that the early stages of this brain damage can be detected reliably before they are otherwise apparent in a person's everyday function by changes in the critical flicker fusion threshold, or the flash rate required to achieve apparent constant illumination (i.e., a solid image). Healthy subjects required a higher flicker rate to perceive a constant light that was really turning on and off rapidly than did cirrotic patients. The flicker rate required for apparent fusion tended to decrease with increasing cognitive impairment.

We are structured by inheritance, health, and also by our experiences to *see* important aspects of the environment, and to ignore other aspects, even if under other conditions we might have the capacity to see and respond to the same stimuli. One example of this can be seen in studies of the effects of work load on perception. Researchers have shown that as the amount of effort to perform a task increases a person's sense of time passing becomes more inaccurate and variable (Brown & Boltz, 2002). Workload affects the details of what is both seen and what is later remembered. Another particularly interesting phenomenon is that of recalling things that never actually happened; false memories. False memory can be induced by suggestion and leading questions, which makes the style of interrogation so very important in questioning eyewitnesses. But a person's own prior experience can concoct very false recollections of even recent events. A simple experiment by Roediger and McDermott (1995) demonstrated this phenomenon. First, they had subjects memorize a list of common words (e.g., *bed, rest, awake*). The list was made up of words commonly associated with a single word that was not actually in the list (e.g., *sleep*). Subjects later reported about 40% of the time with high confidence that the list had included the absent but often associated word. People remembered not only the words they had studied, but also the words they associated with these words but never actually saw. Their memories were fooled by their own prior but unrelated learning of relations among words.

Finally, the phenomenon of experimenter bias or *expectancy effects* must be emphasized. Experimenter beliefs, expectations, and the resulting subtle differences in behavior with respect to the objects (or people) studied can distort findings and make things turn out the way the experimenter expects them to turn out (Rosenthal,

1976). Some of these effects can be minimized by strict adherence to procedural guidelines and even scripts for experimenter behavior, and by making sure when possible that experimenters are not informed about whether subjects or observations are from a treatment or a control condition when they work with them. Nevertheless, in nonlaboratory settings, such as classrooms and clinics, or in private homes and during advocacy meetings, expectancy effects can warp reality sharply.

Sugar Coatings Make You Feel Nice

The foregoing is similar to the placebo effect, in which the subject or patient in a therapy experiment is led to believe that a similar appearing but inert treatment is actually the *active* treatment. To the extent that patients report improvement or are observed to improve when they are given a placebo treatment instead of the active treatment, they exhibit a placebo effect. Placebo effects are real and often large. The impact or size of the "real" treatment's effects are usually understood as the extent to which they exceed the placebo effect; and the placebo effect is judged on the basis of how greatly its effect exceeds a no-treatment control condition (Bowers & Clum, 1988).

In one well-designed study of a treatment for autism known as auditory integration training (AIT), Mudford et al. (2000) evaluated AIT in a crossover design procedure in which all children experienced AIT and a sham or placebo condition. Children with autism were assigned at random to one of two groups to which AIT was administered either before the sham procedure or afterward, and parent and teacher raters and research assistants collecting the data were uninformed (i.e., double blind conditions) about which treatment the children were receiving at any particular time as a control for expectancy effects. AIT was administered using procedures taught to the researchers by one of the Directors of the Society of Auditory Intervention Techniques and the special AIT machine used met the Society's standards for such devices. In AIT, the person with autism listens to specially filtered sounds through headphones. In this experiment, this was done during the AIT condition, but during the placebo condition the identical music, now unfiltered, was piped in through speakers in the room and nothing was played through the headphones the children wore. Mudford et al. (2000) found that the children did better on parent-report and teacher rating measures of behavior following the placebo condition! In school, behavior observation detected only a trend for children to put their hands over their ears more during the AIT treatment condition. Interestingly, promoters of AIT, Rimland and Edelson (1995) reported exactly opposite results, but their study was on children whose parents had paid $1,000 plus hotel and travel expenses for the 10 days the treatment required, and no one had been blind to the treatment condition. The degree of commitment alone by parents who bore such expenses would tend to bias them to see improvement in their children, to say nothing of their hopes and desires and their trust in Rimland and Edelson.

There are a variety of nonspecific effects of "doing something good for others" on the outcomes of medical and behavioral treatments. These can be recognized operating in the Rimland and Edelson report, important factors including social pressure, such as others knowing and asserting the treatment is supposed to work; overt suggestion with instructions as forceful as those used in hypnotic induction; and respected social characteristics of the person administering the treatment (Zane, 1989). The size of nonspecific effects of medical interventions on real illnesses can be substantial. Roberts, Kewman, Mercier, and Hovell (1993) reported a study that yielded findings nothing short of sobering. Five medical and surgical treatments were examined, each of which had been performed on many people and written up in medical journals. Clinicians had concluded that all five treatments were efficacious, but the studies demonstrating this had lacked controls for nonspecific effects of merely doing something. All five treatments were later shown not to work in controlled experiments, using such control procedures as random assignment of eligible patients to treatment and sham treatment groups, and keeping the subjects and the people who assessed them unaware of which treatment condition had been administered (double blind control procedures). Nevertheless, despite the demonstrated uselessness of these medical and surgical treatments, when both the patient and physician believed they would work, they did seem to work. The uncontrolled studies had reported glowing outcomes in about 40% of patients, good outcomes in about 30%, and poor outcomes in about 30%. Not bad for just faith and trust.

Beliefs can affect the perceptions of both experimenters and subjects, professionals, and patients, to the extent that they falsely attribute cause and effect. People see the things they look for and miss what they are not looking for. Stage magicians and psychics rely on our susceptibility to be led astray in order to entertain us. Bogus faith healers and quacks similarly rely on props, misdirection, and our own commitments and beliefs to make people feel better long enough to generate gratitude, loyalty and contributions, or payment. More importantly, sincere healers and their followers can be led astray in the same way unless they take effective steps to control perceptual biases. In the end, humans are prepared by their physical structure and their experience to perceive patterns in the world that are consistent with their own needs and desires. The scientific method has evolved procedures to mitigate the perceptual biases to which all of us are otherwise susceptible.

A sort of obverse effect may be operating among people who are attracted to PBS. PBS is about being *positive*. Positive is by connotation pleasing, especially when juxtaposed against fear-inspiring aversive behavioral intervention, which is a strategy PBS advocates have been following for many years (Brown, 1990; Guess, Helmstetter, Turnbull, & Knowlton, 1987). We have already seen how common word associations can create false memories; here is a straightforward example of false impressions created by common word associations. What ever could be bad about doing something *positive*? What good could ever come from something felt as bad?

Finding the Source

PBS authorities are very clear about the origin of their "science" in applied behavior analysis. Citing the early statement by Baer, Wolf, and Risley (1968), PBS leaders Carr et al. (2002) say PBS owes the basic concepts of how to understand, measure, and change behavior to the many researchers who have conducted applied behavior analysis research in past decades. We all owe those things to the database amassed by applied behavior analysts over the years. But there is more to it. Applied behavior analysts in turn owe those methods and concepts to earlier (as well as contemporary) researchers who labored under the rubric of the Experimental Analysis of Behavior (Skinner, 1963) and those who worked over the past century or more in the broader tradition of the experimental psychology of learning and conditioning (Kimble, 1967). It is customary—no, obligatory as an aid to *checking*—to cite the original source of a scientific finding or procedure in subsequent scientific writing so that the reader can follow the evolution of a finding or theory.

This raises the issue of the consistent style of self-citation characteristic of PBS authors who publish extended replications of earlier work that has a long tradition in research done in the applied behavior analysis tradition. Sometimes they fail to point out how well trod their research paths have been before they found them. Scientific writing is supposed to avoid pointless replication of well-established findings, but extended replication in which methods are applied to new problems or in new settings or represent systematic variation of procedural elements is legitimate. Extended replication with some new element or twist supports the generality of a proposed relation between behavior and environment. PBS, however, has tended to enhance the appearance of its own originality by neglecting to recognize earlier work along the same lines. PBS authors attempt to erect the illusion that their writings are original even when they are as old as the field of applied behavior analysis itself.

Nonmembers of this in-group might generously regard this as mere cliquishness and self-promotion. The group has a history, however, which seems to involve rewriting history. Isn't this just a form of telling lies? PBSers have developed a unique jargon by which initiates can easily recognize work by those with allied philosophical and ideological commitments. Thus, PBS authors do not tend to write about behavior patterns that have scientific or practical interest, such as self-injurious behavior or phobic reactions or aggression; instead, they write about "challenging behavior." They do not write about "behavioral suppression" through "extinction and alternative response training" (even when they use it) or admit that a complex series of actions taken by teachers or therapists contains elements that produce aversive motivation in the students whose behavior changes—when in fact it does (Mulick & Linscheid, 1988). Nothing endorsed or done by PBSers is allowed to involve any aversive motivation. They write instead about "student support" and euphemistically refer to "a continuum of procedures for discouraging displays of rule-violating behavior." For at least 15 years, some of us have pointed out at every opportunity that this word-substitution game can only be meant to mislead students and consumers.

Students who use library or Internet search tools use key words and author names to find research studies related to their topic of interest. When they use PBS euphemisms as key words or PBS authors' names as search terms, they get neatly isolated writings that omit pre-PBS articles or relevant articles written by people who remain committed to scientific writing conventions and refuse to use euphemism to describe what they do. Thus, students and consumers are deprived by this insidious strategy from ever contacting literature that is not consistent with the PBS party line. Vladimir Illich Lenin could not have devised a better strategy for "active propaganda of the idea" in order to keep the decadent alternate views of the vacillating *bourgeoisie* from confusing the *proletariat* in the information age.

Is this really a problem? Yes. Scientific writing has to rely on the voluntary commitment of scientists to acknowledging the contributions of previous researchers to solutions to a given problem, because all scientific writing relies on evidence of consistency with other evidence to establish the truth of a proposed relation between events in the subject under consideration. Consumers also need to know the range of available solutions to a problem so that they can evaluate the relative risks, costs, and benefits of a treatment procedure according to their own values (Meinhold & Mulick, 1992; Mulick & Meinhold, 1992), and not someone else's set of values (Meinhold, Mulick, & Teodoro, 1994).

So What's New in PBS?

It remains difficult to ascertain what is new, unique, or additive from the research base presented by PBS investigators. Carr et al. (1999), for example, identified two categories of PBS intervention strategies: stimulus-based interventions and reinforcement-based interventions. Stimulus-based interventions were described as those actions that would change the environment to promote positive behavior change. Examples included interspersal training, expanding choice, curricular modification, and manipulation of setting events. Reinforcement-based interventions were described as strategies designed to increase positive behavior directly. These included functional communication training, differential reinforcement of alternative behavior, and self-management.

These intervention strategies identified by Carr and colleagues do not represent discoveries or inventions of PBS, nor are any of them unique to PBS. The use of interspersal training, which involves the presentation of a stimulus that elicits problem behavior with stimuli that elicit positive behavior, has not been limited to practitioners of PBS (Neef, Iwata, & Page, 1980). Harking further back in history, it can be said that interspersal training is related to the Premack Principle in that high frequency behaviors serve as reinforcement for low frequency behaviors (Premack, 1959). Choice opportunity in behavior analysis is as old as Skinner's box equipped with not one but two levers. Similarly, the use of curricular modifications to remove negative aspects of a task has been an established intervention for many years, with good examples preceding the PBS movement (Ayllon, Layman, & Burke, 1972). Errorless learning procedures, which involve the gradual transfer of stimulus control, were identified decades before PBS came into existence (Martin & Pear, 1983; Terrace, 1963). The manipulation of setting events was discussed much earlier than the advent of positive behavior support (Bijou & Baer, 1961; Kantor, 1970; Rojahn, Mulick, McCoy, & Schroeder, 1978) and relies on Skinner's identification of the motivational functions of stimuli (Skinner, 1957). Further, the related concept of establishing operations (Michael, 1982) has been discussed extensively outside of PBS circles (Agnew, 1998; Leigland, 1984; Michael, 2000; Northup, Fusilier, Swanson, Roane, & Borrero, 1997; Worsdell, Iwata, Conners, Kahng, & Thompson, 2000).

Similarly, there is nothing new about the reinforcement-based strategies advocated by PBS proponents. Functional communication training, though an effective technology, is merely one way to utilize knowledge about functional relationships, which is the very foundation of applied behavior analysis (Baer et al., 1968). Self-management procedures had been identified as a positive treatment option prior to the PBS movement (Kazdin, 1975; Mahoney, 1972) and had first been considered by B. F. Skinner (1953). PBS does not claim to have invented reinforcement schedules, which would be too laughable even for them. However, Carr et al. (1999) do contend that differential reinforcement of other behaviors (DRO) is not a *positive* procedure and should be avoided. The reinforcement of any behavior other than targeted problem behavior could lead, PBSers contend, to no reinforcement during long periods of time. Instead, positive behavior support interventionists should use *differential reinforcement of alternative behaviors (DRA)*. Making this point, the PBS movement argues for the teaching of functional alternative behaviors, but it is unclear with whom they are arguing. We do not disagree; neither do other behavior analysts who pre-date the PBS movement (Deitz & Repp, 1983; Deitz, Repp, & Deitz, 1976; Mulick, Hoyt, Rojahn, & Schroeder, 1978; Mulick, Schroeder, & Rojahn, 1980). The "DRA/DRO controversy" is based on the misleading premise that DRA procedures had never been used and that DRO procedures were used unethically prior to the advent of PBS. But, really, logic dictates that at the very least reinforcement of response withholding *does* reinforce a positive act of using competing muscle groups that must be used to result in behavior other than the previous response. We have always advised that it is preferable to teach functional replacement skills, and not the mere absence of observable undesired behavior, but such values do not make a new applied science, and in this case seem to have distorted perception of underlying behavioral processes.

The true folly, and indeed real danger, of the PBS movement is this drive to find something new. For instance, antecedent control, through the manipulation of setting events and establishing operations, has become a hallmark of PBS interventions (Luiselli & Cameron, 1998). The use of establishing operations to create motivation has a long tradition in behavior analysis (Michael, 1982) and is not unique to PBS. What is peculiar to PBS is the selection of setting events or establishing operations that are "person-centered," "individualized," and directed toward achieving "meaningful outcomes" (Anderson & Freeman, 2000), as if there could be an establishing operation that was not individualized.

This foolishness was manifested in a recent study by a group of PBS researchers who sought a new application of setting events to improve the lifestyle of people with developmental disabilities. Carr, McLaughlin, Giacobbe-Grieco, and Smith (2003) studied the role of "mood" as an establishing operation or setting factor for problem behaviors. After defining mood, not as an internal emotional state but as a "confluence of a number of setting events" (p. 33), such as yelling, pouting, and appearing to be irritable, angry, and frustrated, Carr et al. (2003) demonstrated that "bad mood" ratings by staff members predicted more severe problem behaviors (e.g., aggression, self-injury, and property destruction) than "neutral" or "good mood" ratings in demand situations. They used these data to develop an intervention to reduce problem behaviors. The intervention involved the induction of positive mood when a bad mood was identified. Positive mood was induced by the implementation of a preferred activity or access to a preferred tangible reinforcer. Positive mood induction took as little as 15 minutes of positive interaction or as much as 45 minutes. Compliance with task demands increased and severe behavior problems were eliminated over baseline after positive mood induction for each subject.

The study was presented as a powerful example of how a complex, contextual, and highly individualized variable (i.e., bad mood) could be manipulated to prevent the occurrence of severe problem behaviors. Yet, it could just as easily have been interpreted as positive reinforcement for "yelling, pouting, and appearing to be irritable, anger, and frustrated." Merely calling it a mood intervention is disingenuous when the actual criteria have been made explicit.

Further, as we read the study, the implementation of positive mood induction contingent on the presence of bad mood suggests that bad mood might have been powerfully reinforced. In this way, it could be reasoned that the positive mood induction intervention served to maintain or perhaps even increase bad moods. Carr et al. (2003) commented that bad moods were infrequent, but they did not provide any data about the stability or possible increase of bad mood over time, and without this kind of follow-up data it is difficult to interpret the efficacy of this antecedent control intervention. In an effort to individualize treatment and obtain meaningful outcomes, this group of researchers appears to have overlooked the possibility that their intervention may be related to an unfortunate outcome—the proliferation of a bad mood.

The long-term follow-up of these patients could reveal overall increases in irritability and an eventual return of severe destructive behavior when staff tired of implementing mood induction procedures. A scientific approach to this study could have considered the role of the three-term-contingency and could avoid this plausible longitudinal outcome. These researchers were blinded by their quest to discover something new and to make lifestyle changes in their subjects, neither of which may be durable or operating in this instance.

PBS Promises

In PBS, then, it is not what they do that is so very different in theory from practices of mainstream behavioral psychologists and other practitioners of behavior analysis; rather, it is how they *see* what they do, how they want *others* to see what they do, and *why* they do what they do that constitute the difference. Carr et al. (2002) could not have made it more explicit. They tell us that their new science is to be consistent with normalization ideology (Wolfensberger, 1972, 1983), inclusion goals in school and in society, and person-centered values. To this they add an additional aim, that of changing the focal person's lifestyle, sometimes together with the lifestyles of those who regularly deal with the focal person. Moreover, some advocates of PBS, including leading PBSers, even disagree about whether the procedures they use are those of applied behavior analysis or of something quite different (Carr & Sidener, 2002).

Mulick and Kedesdy (1988) warned that normalization was an ideology, a sociopolitical program, and that when treatment decisions were based on it first and on empirical findings second, disquieting things happened. They showed that effective behavioral treatment for self-injurious behavior in people with mental retardation—treatments that worked—could not be derived from normalization philosophy. They also showed that interventions consistent with normalization could not be supported by the findings of research demonstrating effective applications of behavioral intervention with these problems. This disconnect suggested that ideology and science as applied to effective treatment of destructive behavior were not compatible *at the same level of analysis*; that of treatment verification (Foxx, chap. 18, this volume).

Normalization emphasizes trying to achieve the most normal modes of living and behaving for people with mental retardation, and to help this along by helping others to perceive them as normal. These are feasible goals, to an extent, by using principles and methods of behavioral science. The problem comes when there are inconsistencies with reality; with the realities of producing reliable behavior change in people with mental retardation, and with the effectiveness of cosmetic enhancement of their appearance in producing normal reactions to them by people in the general population.

Abnormal behavior can be caused and maintained by very normal reactions of people to the abnormal behavior of those with mental retardation. For example, typical sorts of attending to and sympathizing with a person whose destructive behavior is maintained by social attention, a common enough relation in clinical practice, often serves to worsen it. At the very least in such a case, the normal and immediate expression of sympathy should be withheld and a somewhat atypical set of maneuvers carried out to either discourage or displace the destructive behavior. In addition, the conscious arrangement of behavioral contingencies, prompts, and systematic environmental rearrangements characteristic of applied behavior analysis interventions are themselves far from typical of routine human interaction. To put it bluntly, it is abnormal to be as systematic and consistent as is often required for effective behavioral treatment, or, for that matter, effective counseling or psychotherapeutic, services. Effective interventions have to be consistent with the laws of nature, not merely with how ordinary folks react in every day situations. After all, it is most often the case that ordinary living in the ordinary world (inevitable warts and all) is what has caused the person (who may have a defect or disability that creates vulnerability) to acquire the "challenging" undesired behavior.

Inclusion is another insufficient therapeutic concept. In our work, we have seen children placed with age-peers in music and art and gym classes in schools where neither normalization of their behavior nor of their peers' behavior toward them was achieved. Instead, children without prerequisite skills of understanding language or knowing what to do practiced the behavior they did know how to do, that of rocking, or gazing at lights, or touching themselves and others. They literally were given practice opportunities in ignoring group instruction, ignoring the teacher and the ongoing activity, and ignoring their otherwise engaged peers, at which they could be expected to get better and better with the additional practice. People learn all the time. They learn the actions they actually perform, utterly independently of our hopes and intentions for them.

A scientific approach would suggest that beneficial inclusion has to follow after there has been sufficient learning of prerequisite skills to be able to respond appropriately to the inclusive setting, or at least that extensive prerequisite skill training is provided in and continues after entry to the setting. People who find themselves in a setting look normal only when they can respond to the demands on their behavior in that setting, otherwise they behave abnormally. When people look abnormal, they are less often treated normally or given equal opportunities. In the early stages of inclusion, there will often be the need for systematic help, prompts, and extra reinforcement. This permits strengthening of participation skills in the setting in which they are called for. Further, it can easily be seen that inclusion is a fraud in the absence of participation, and participation is sometimes impossible without prerequisite learning. When inclusion simply in the form of physical presence has greater or equal weight than assuring that the behavioral relations needed to support participation are in place, little normalization will occur. There is a good possibility that *ab*normalization of everyone and the inclusive setting will follow instead. When a student is ready for inclusion, however, it can be shown that they learn how to behave more normally in classes with typical peers than with peers who behave atypically (Smith, Lovaas, & Lovaas, 2002). Readiness is all, but readiness is no accident, no mere moral choice.

Person-centered values are another set of considerations in PBS. As applied to planning the therapeutic or educational or habilitative programs for people with disabilities, person-centered values are supposed to emphasize the autonomy and community in which the focal person lives. But Carr et al. (2002) actually suggested that "humanistic" (sic; they seem to mean "humanitarian" as opposed to "humanistic," because the latter term involves adopting solutions to problems based on what is possible for people to accomplish without supernatural help from a deity) values should "inform empiricism." This is exactly the wrong order, because when values inform science, the outcome is predetermined by the values. When values inform us about what must be done, by whom, and by what means, before we find out what is actually feasible or possible, then ineffective, even absurd choices may be inevitable. The right order is for humanitarian values to be employed first in formulating our questions and then only after the data have been collected, after what is feasible has been determined, and after what is possible is ascertained. Humanitarian choices must follow what science determines is feasible, given the social context, or the full range of options may never even be discovered, and the people whom we seek to help may be made helpless rather than helped.

Experience in many aspects of life informs us that bad seeming options seem much better after they are discovered to be the only ones that might actually work. In this regard, while constantly trying to improve the underlying science and specific technological applications, we will still accept risks of serious reactions by accepting, say, vaccination for dangerous diseases, of accidental injury and death from high speed travel in modern vehicles, of unemployment and obsolescence from embracing ever more automation in our lives, and from readily accepting a host of other risks from modern tools and technologies. Indeed, when given the freedom to do so, we reject paternalistic interference with these choices by government (and do-gooders who intrude on our freedoms "for our own good") if we believe the benefit justifies the risk. What if person-centered plans, then, reflect our own values more than those of the person for whom we plan?

Lest the reader think these admonitions are self-evident and not at all characteristic of PBSers, a few examples will help to establish that from the earliest days of PBS, in its first incarnation as the "non-aversive behavior modification movement," leaders of the movement have acted in ways previously suggested. These actions have been consistent in the past, serve the interests of their advocates, embrace convenient falsehoods, and continue to the present time. We address them one at a time.

PBS Reality

Using the Freedom of Information Act, colleagues at Ohio State University had a chance to examine a copy of the first grant application that established the "non-aversive behavior modification consortium." Examination of the proposal, submitted to the U.S. Department of Education in the early 1980s, revealed that already standard behavior modification procedures were described as innovative and as generally effective as any other sort of procedure that might involve aversive motivation in changing behavior. Neither assertion had been demonstrated to be true (and still has not been), but that did not stop members of the consortium or the U.S. Department of Education from setting up a national network of training programs designed to disseminate these "innovations." The consortium eventually morphed into the national network of Rehabilitation Research and Training Centers on Positive Behavioral Support, and funding and publications continue to flow. PBS leaders even managed to use their inside status with the U.S. Department of Education to insert a vague and somewhat ungrammatical reference to the following in the student discipline section of the 1997 reauthorization of IDEA (Public Law 105-17):

(B) CONSIDERATION OF SPECIAL FACTORS- The IEP Team shall—

(i) in the case of a child whose behavior impedes his or her learning or that of others, consider, when appropriate, strategies, including *positive behavioral interventions, strategies, and supports* [italics added] to address that behavior. (Public Law 105–17, p. 57)

and later:

(C) REQUIREMENT WITH RESPECT TO REGULAR EDUCATION TEACHER—

The regular education teacher of the child, as a member of the IEP Team, shall, to the extent appropriate, participate in the development of the IEP of the child, including the determination of appropriate *positive behavioral interventions and strategies* [italics added] and the determination of supplementary aids and services, program modifications, and support for school personnel consistent with paragraph (1)(A)(iii). (Public Law 105–17, p. 57)

Although the specific words in the law are vague, PBS insiders have lost no time in numerous writings claiming federal authority for PBS, and that this authority is whatever they happen to feel like saying it is. There is no other reference even vaguely related to PBS in the law. However, if PBSers state that the methods they use are the methods of applied behavior analysis (ABA)—as has been found to be the case by Carr and Sidener, 2002, in their review—then the inclusion of PBS in federal legislation, factually, also includes ABA.

Professor Rob Horner of the University of Oregon, a leader of the original nonaversive consortium, sent letters in the early 1980s to professionals in developmental disabilities asking them to become members of a referral network consisting of those who would be willing to treat destructive behavior disorders in people with developmental disabilities. To be a network member, the professional had to sign a statement saying that aversive procedures would not be used in treatment. In that this amounted to deciding on treatment before the client had been assessed, or even identified, it violated the most basic tenets of professional psychology's ethics code requiring that such decisions are only made in the context of a professional relationship (American Psychological Association, 1981, 1992). The senior author of this chapter and many of his colleagues were unable to sign this agreement. It also, of course, made no scientific sense.

More recently, we tried to refer a child and his concerned parents to an agency in a nearby state where we had had contact with professionals specializing in behavioral interventions of a kind we knew the child needed immediately. Based on this contact, we knew the agency staff would know how to meet the child's treatment needs if the family moved to that state. The situation was then complicated by a custody conflict between the now separated father and mother. A court appointed *guardian ad leitem* became involved, and tried to verify the availability of behavioral treatment services like the ones we recommended for the child in both the nearby state and the other parent's location. The *guardian ad leitem* was a lawyer, unfamiliar with services of this type, and phoned the agency we had indicated in the other state to verify that they offered behavioral services. We were astonished that the person responding to the lawyer said that the agency did not offer applied behavior analysis services, but *rather positive behavioral support*; something different! The custody decision was delayed several months as a result, and the child remains at this writing denied appropriate services as the parents continue their legal enmeshment.

Peer review is the hallmark of scientific publication. This involves the review of research papers by experts in a given field prior to publication to assure that they meet standards of originality, validity, and value to the field. These reviews are supposed to be based on scientific standards, not ideological ones. As early as the 1980s, however, The Association for Persons With Severe Handicaps (TASH), after passing a resolution banning the use of aversive procedures, began using an ideological standard for publishing articles in their journal and for papers presented at their national conference. This was confirmed by telephone calls placed at the time by the senior author to Professors Rob Horner, then editor of the TASH journal (*JASH*, now *Research to Practice*), and Lou Brown, a founder of TASH, who were asked about the kinds of papers that could be presented at conferences. Brown indicated that papers, say, about a comparison between timeout and overcorrection in the treatment of dangerous behavior (both validated treatment procedures) would have been unacceptable for the conference because parents attend the conference and should not hear such things. So much for peer review, unless by peers only certain paternalistic ideologues qualify.

TASH, as would be expected, endorses PBS (TASH, 2000b). Then again, Lou Brown (1990) described TASH as unique among disability organizations in, among other things, "addressing the ideological." True enough, and fair enough because TASH describes itself on its Web site as a "civil rights organization" (TASH, n.d.). It does not follow, then, that publications in its journal are peer reviewed in the same sense as articles in behavioral science journals, or as a result that articles in their journal can be cited in support of scientific assertions of truth. Yet, such is implied by PBS advocates in many of their writings. Alas, the newly established *Journal of Positive Behavior Interventions* published by Pro-Ed (2002) may not be much more scientifically defensible, but at least the title represents truth in advertising. The same players, however, publish in both places, may have difficulty differentiating their beliefs from reality consistent with PBS ideas, and will probably continue to wrap up reinforcement in fancy new clothes. It has to be hoped that the research this new journal will publish will not misrepresent aversive processes in behavior analysis, other behavior analysts, and sincere efforts to help others when some element of aversive motivation is openly employed, as has characterized some TASH articles (Mulick, 1990).

Inclusion is the setting in which to hone prosocial skills; to learn how to participate in normative ways in the typical activities of the community. We have already indicated that prerequisite learning may be necessary to enable a person with a disability to truly participate. Some TASH activists, now associated with PBS, realized this as well, but saw that some people seemed not even to understand language, much less the subjects being taught in school. The answer for their inclusion was facilitated communication (FC). FC, now generally recognized as unequivocally bogus (except by TASH; see TASH, 2000a), was an apparent solution to the problem of achieving universal inclusion. Gullible people who were introduced to FC were admonished to assume that all people could communicate, even if they never had communicated before (Mulick, Jacobson, & Kobe, 1993). This was a direct attempt to induce an illusion of communication, and it often worked unless control procedures were used to disprove it (Jacobson, Mulick, & Schwartz, 1995). One of the authors of the Carr et al. (2002) paper, said of FC: "It is constructivism in communication. It is understood as a product of sender and receiver processes rather than standing back and interpreting what a sender is trying to send. Facilitated communication is a product of an interactive process" (Sailor, 1994, p. 10).

But it was never that. It was a false representation constructed by the facilitator out of his or her nonconscious behavior (Spitz, 1997), beliefs, possibly even hopes, but it was not true. Not being true, it failed the person with the handicap because it misrepresented his or her real desires and needs. Without anyone realizing it in many cases, FC subjected the person with the handicap to another person's possibly antithetical desires and needs. Once again, it can be seen how powerful a distortion basing one belief on another can be when one of them is just not true. Why must we repeat this shameful history with yet another admonition to place our hopes and beliefs ahead of verifiable evidence from some of the same individuals and agencies; to join their chorus in praise of the superiority of their "new science" based on overriding and antecedent beliefs?

CONCLUSION

We can, and should have a science of values, a way of understanding how values come to be held. We agree that it is scientifically vital to measure the effects that values exert on choices people make for themselves and others. Skinner (1971) began such a study when he wrote his classic *Beyond Freedom and Dignity*. Ironically, he made the point that aversive contingencies in society contribute to the *illusion* of human autonomy and dignity. In contrast, a scientific analysis of values suggested to him that values are, as are other choices, the direct biological result of past individual (and species) interactions with the real world and the present availability of relevant opportunities for action; are *completely determined* by these types of selection, controlling relations and reinforcers. We cannot, however, have a value-based science, because science requires the goal of discovering the truth, whether we like it or not, whether we say so or not, and whether we can do what we want with it or not. What we want for ourselves and for others has to take a secondary place to what is real, or we will run a much heightened risk of frustration and failure.

PBS fails as a science because it does not indicate how to differentiate reality from desire. It fails because it subordinates method and measurement. It is an example of an effort by people driven to seek leadership to achieve their political goals through convincing others to surrender their critical faculties. We insist that it matters greatly how leadership and position are achieved. Konrad Lorenz, known today as the Nobel Laureate in Medicine whose fatherly image as the white bearded scientist followed by ducklings to illustrate his discovery of the early critically timed learning phenomenon of species imprinting, was also the former young man who could write in 1940:

> The only resistance which mankind of healthy stock can offer ... against being penetrated by symptoms of degeneracy is based on the existence of innate schemata ... Our species-specific sensitivity to the beauty and ugliness of members of our species is intimately connected with the symptoms of degeneration, caused by domestication, which threaten our race .... We must—and should—rely on the healthy feelings of our Best and charge them with the selection which will determine the prosperity or the decay of our people .... (quoted in Eisenberg, 1972)

It was not necessarily a subsequent coincidence that his pro-eugenic writings so impressed authorities in the Third Reich that he was appointed to a full university chair at an unusually early age; nor was it necessarily an oversight that some of these writings failed to appear on later editions of his curriculum vitae (Eisenberg, personal communication, 1973). We are led to wonder what, really, those who advance PBS hope to achieve by their over-promising, by their use of deceptive language, by their selective scholarship, and very little else.

As we write, we realize that our values, in fact, are not so very different from those described in the PBS literature. We do not believe children or people with disabilities should be humiliated or harmed by professionals, the government, or anybody. We do not hold ourselves out as father figures or arbiters of the lifestyles of others. We think the needs of the patient and his or her family should be the focus of treatment. We agree that treatment should lead to outcomes characterized by more choices, more freedom from external coercion, and more satisfaction. These are our values, and we do not feel a need to have them endorsed by a group of special educators and professional advocates in order to hold them or to work toward them. We recognize them as *our* values, and remind ourselves that working toward these outcomes on a short-term basis is a matter of dealing with three important realities. First is that choices lie with all parties in the therapeutic contract: we practitioners, the focal person or patient, and the people who will live with the focal person and the treatment priorities established. Second is that wishful thinking leads to error. The only way such error can be ameliorated is by second-guessing ourselves; by insisting that we are continuously checked. By checking, we mean that our assertions will be examined using methods designed to verify our beliefs about cause and effect, about efficacy and efficiency, and about whether or not our values are held as widely as we hope and believe. Finally, we realize that the world often needs to be changed, as opposed to the individual nominally said to have a problem. We temper this by recognizing that some forces are not ours to control, and that urgency may require us to make, together with the people with whom we work, hard choices in the short term to achieve the greatest benefit in the long term.

REFERENCES

Agnew, J. (1998). The establishing operation in organizational behavior management I. *Journal of Organizational Behavior Management, 18*(1), 7–19.

Allyon, T., Layman, D., & Burke, S. (1972). Disruptive behavior and reinforcement of academic performance. *Psychological Record, 22*, 315–323.

American Psychological Association. (1981). Ethical principles of psychologists. *American Psychologist, 36*, 633–638.

American Psychological Association. (1992). Ethical principles of psychologists. *American Psychologist, 47*, 1597–1611.

Anderson, C. M., & Freeman, K. A. (2000). Positive behavior support: Expanding the application of applied behavior analysis. *The Behavior Analyst, 23*, 85–94.

Baer, D. M., Wolf, M. M., & Risley, T. (1968). Current dimensions of applied behavior analysis. *Journal of Applied Behavior Analysis, 1*, 91–97.

Belkin, J. M. (1998). *Cultural software: A theory of ideology.* New Haven, CT: Yale University Press.

Bijou, S. W., & Baer, D. M. (1961). *Child development: Vol. 1. A systematic and empirical theory.* New York: Appleton-Century-Crofts.

Bowers, T. G., & Clum, G. A. (1988). Relative contribution of specific and nonspecific treatment effects: Meta-analysis of placebo-controlled behavior therapy research. *Psychological Bulletin, 103*, 315–323.

Brown, L. (1990, September). *Who are they and what do they want? – An essay on TASH.* Retrieved February 21, 2003, from http://www.tash.org/misc/loubrown.htm

Brown, S. W., & Boltz, M. G., (2002). Attentional processes in time perception: Effects of mental workload and event structure. *Journal of Experimental Psychology: Human Perception and Performance, 28*, 600–615.

Carr, E. G., Dunlap, G., Horner, R. H., Koegel, R. L., Turnbull, A. P., Sailor, W., et al. (2002). Positive behavior support: Evolution of an applied science. *Journal of Positive Behavior Intervention, 4*(1), 4–16, 20.

Carr, E. G., Horner, R. H., Turnbull, A. P., Marquis, J. G., McLaughlin, D. M., McAtee, M. L., et al. (1999). *Positive behavior support for people with developmental disabilities: A research synthesis.* Washington, DC: American Association on Mental Retardation.

Carr, E. G., McLaughlin, D. M., Giacobbe-Greico, T., & Smith, C. E. (2003). Using mood ratings and mood induction in assessment and intervention for severe problem behavior. *American Journal on Mental Retardation, 108*, 32–55.

Carr, J. E., & Sidener, T. M. (2002). On the relation between applied behavior analysis and positive behavioral support. *Behavior Analyst, 25*, 245–253.

de Haan, M., Humphreys, K., & Johnson, M. H. (2002). Developing a brain specialized for face perception: A converging methods approach. *Developmental Psychobiology, 40*, 200–212.

Deitz, D. E. D., & Repp, A. C. (1983). Reducing behavior through reinforcement. *Exceptional Education Quarterly, 3*, 34–46.

Deitz, S. M., Repp, A. C., & Deitz, D. E. D. (1976). Reducing inappropriate classroom behavior of retarded students through three procedures of differential reinforcement. *Journal of Mental Deficiency Research, 20*, 155–170.

Eisenberg, L. (1972). The human nature of human nature. *Science, 176*, 123–128.

Friedlander, H. (1995). *The origins of Nazi genocide: From euthanasia to the final solution.* Chapel Hill, NC: The University of North Carolina Press.

Guess, D., Helmstetter, H., Turnbull, H. R., & Knowlton, S. (1987). *Use of aversive procedures with persons who are disabled: An historical review and critical analysis.* Seattle, WA: The Association for Persons With Severe Handicaps.

Jacobson, J. W., Mulick, J. A., & Schwartz, A. A. (1995). A history of facilitated communication: Science, pseudoscience, and antiscience. *American Psychologist, 50*, 750–765.

Kantor, J. R. (1970). An analysis of the experimental analysis of behavior. *Journal of the Experimental Analysis of Behavior, 13*, 101–108.

Kazdin, A. E. (1975). *Behavior modification in applied settings.* Homewood, IL: Dorsey Press.

Kimble, G. A. (Ed.). (1967). *Foundations of conditioning and learning.* New York: Appleton-Century-Crofts.

Kircheis, G., Wettstein, M., Timmermann, L., Schnitzler, A., & Haussinger, D. (2002). Critical flicker frequency for quantification of low-grade hepatic encephalopathy. *Hepatology, 35,* 357–366.

Leigland, S. (1984). On "setting events" and related concepts. *Behavior Analyst, 7,* 41–45.

Luiselli, J. K., & Cameron, M. J. (Eds.). (1998). *Antecedent control: Innovative approaches to behavioral support.* Baltimore: Brookes.

Mahoney, M. J. (1972). Research issues in self-management. *Behavior Therapy, 3,* 45–63.

Martin, G., & Pear, J. (1983). *Behavior modification: What is it and how to do it.* Englewood Cliffs, NJ: Prentice-Hall.

Meinhold, P. M., & Mulick, J. A. (1992). Social policy and science in the treatment of severe behavior disorders: Defining and securing a healthy relationship. *Clinical Psychology Review, 12,* 585–603.

Meinhold, P. M., Mulick, J. A., & Teodoro, J. M. (1994). Risks and costs of SIBIS-treatment litigation: Focus on the family. *Journal of Child and Family Studies, 3,* 403–415.

Michael, J. (1982). Distinguishing between discriminative and motivational functions of stimuli. *Journal of the Experimental Analysis of Behavior, 37,* 149–155.

Michael, J. (2000). Implications and refinements of the establishing operation concept. *Journal of Applied Behavior Analysis, 33,* 401–410.

Mudford, O. C., Cross, B. A., Breen, S., Cullen, C., Reeves, D., Gould, J., et al. (2000). Auditory integration training for children with autism: No behavioral benefits detected. *American Journal on Mental Retardation, 105,* 118–129.

Mulick, J. A. (1990). The ideology and science of punishment in mental retardation. *American Journal on Mental Retardation, 95,* 142–156.

Mulick, J. A., & Antonak, R. F. (1992). The legacy of eugenics. *Psychology in Mental Retardation and Developmental Disabilities, 18*(1), 5–9.

Mulick, J. A., Hoyt, P., Rojahn, J., & Schroeder, S. R. (1978). Reduction of a "nervous habit" in a profoundly retarded youth by increasing independent toy play. *Journal of Behavior Therapy and Experimental Psychiatry, 9,* 25–30.

Mulick, J. A., Jacobson, J. W., & Kobe, F. H. (1993). Anguished silence and helping hands: Autism and facilitated communication. *The Skeptical Inquirer, 17*(3), 270–280.

Mulick, J. A., & Kedesdy, J. H. (1988). Self–injurious behavior, its treatment, and normalization. *Mental Retardation, 26,* 223–229.

Mulick, J. A., & Linscheid, T. R. (1988). A review of LaVigna and Donnellan's *Alternatives to Punishment: Solving Behavior Problems with Non–aversive Strategies. Research in Developmental Disabilities, 9,* 317–327.

Mulick, J. A., & Meinhold, P. M. (1992). Analyzing the impact of regulations on residential ecology. *Mental Retardation, 30,* 151–161.

Mulick, J. A., Schroeder, S. R., & Rojahn, J. (1980). Chronic ruminative vomiting: A comparison of four treatment procedures. *Journal of Autism and Developmental Disorders, 10,* 203–312.

Neef, N. A., Iwata, B. A., & Page, T. (1980). The effects of interspersal training versus high-density reinforcement on spelling acquisition and retention. *Journal of Applied Behavior Analysis, 13,* 153–158.

Northup, J., Fusilier, I., Swanson, V., Roane, H., & Borrero, J. (1997) An evaluation of methylphenidate as a potential establishing operation for some common classroom reinforcers. *Journal of Applied Behavior Analysis, 30,* 615–625.

Premack, D. (1959). Toward empirical behavioral laws: I: Positive reinforcement. *Psychological Review, 66,* 219–233.

Pro-Ed. (2002, March 4). *Journal of Positive Behavior Interventions: Author guidelines.* Retrieved February 21, 2003, from http://www.proedinc.com/submission_jpbi.html

Rauch, J. (1993). *Kindly inquisitors.* Chicago: The University of Chicago Press.

Rimland, B., & Edelson, S. M. (1995). Auditory integration training in autism: Brief report of a pilot study. *Journal of Autism and Developmental Disorders, 25,* 61–70.

Roberts, A. H., Kewman, D. G., Mercier, L., & Hovell, M. (1993). The power of nonspecific effects in healing: Implications for psychological and biological treatments. *Clinical Psychology Review, 13,* 375–391.

Roediger, H. L., III, & McDermott, K. B. (1995). Creating false memories: Remembering words not presented in lists. *Journal of Experimental Psychology: Learning, Memory, and Cognition, 21,* 803–814.

Rojahn, J., Mulick, J. A., McCoy, D., & Schroeder, S. R. (1978). Setting effects, adaptive clothing, and the modification of head–banging and self–restraint in two profoundly retarded adults. *Behavioral Analysis and Modification, 2,* 185–196.

Rosenthal, R. (1976). *Experimenter effects in behavioral research* (enlarged ed.). New York: Irvington.

Sailor, W. (1994, March). *Untitled luncheon presentation.* Remarks presented at the Fourth Annual Integration Institute (conference), Cosa Mesa, CA.

Simons, D. J. (2003). *Surprising studies of visual awareness* [DVD]. Boulder, CO: Viscog Productions. Available from http://www.viscog.com

Skinner, B. F. (1953). *Science and human behavior.* New York: Macmillan.

Skinner, B. F. (1954). Critique of psychoanalytic concepts and theories. *Scientific Monthly, 79,* 300–305.

Skinner, B. F. (1957). *Verbal behavior.* New York: Appleton-Century-Crofts.

Skinner, B. F. (1963). Behaviorism at fifty. *Science, 140,* 951–958.

Skinner, B. F. (1971). *Beyond freedom and dignity.* New York: Knopf.

Smith, T., Lovaas, N. W., & Lovaas, O. I. (2002). Behaviors of children with high-functioning autism when paired with typically developing versus delayed peers: A preliminary study. *Behavioral Interventions, 17,* 129–143.

Spitz, H. H. (1997). *Nonconscious movements: From mystical messages to facilitated communication.* Mahwah, NJ: Lawrence Erlbaum Associates.

Terrace, H. S. (1963). Discrimination learning with and without errors. *Journal of the Experimental Analysis of Behavior, 6,* 1–27.

The Association for Persons With Severe Handicaps. (2000a). *TASH resolution on facilitated communication.* Retrieved February 21, 2003, from http://www.tash.org/resolutions/res02faccom.htm

The Association for Persons With Severe Handicaps. (2000b). *TASH resolution on positive behavioral supports.* Retrieved February 21, 2003, from http://www.tash.org/resolutions/res02behavior.htm

The Association for Persons With Severe Handicaps. (n.d.). *TASH: Equity, opportunity and inclusion for people with disabilities since 1985.* Retrieved February 21, 2003, from http://www.tash.org/misc/index.htm

Weiss, S. F. (1987). *Race hygiene & national efficiency: The eugenics of Wilhelm Schallmayer.* Berkeley, CA: University of California Press.

Wolfensberger, W. (1972). *The principle of normalization in human services.* Toronto, Canada: National Institute on Mental Retardation.

Wolfensberger, W. (1983). Social role valorization: A proposed new term for the principle of normalization. *Mental Retardation, 21,* 234–239.

Worsdell, A. S., Iwata, B. A., Conners, J., Kahng, S. W., & Thompson, R. H. (2000). Relative influences of establishing operations and reinforcement contingencies on self-injurious behavior during functional analyses. *Journal of Applied Behavior Analysis, 33,* 451–461.

Zane, N. W. S. (1989). Change mechanisms in placebo procedures: Effects of suggestion, social demand, and contingent success on improvement in treatment. *Journal of Counseling Psychology, 36,* 234–243.

Nonaversive Treatment

Crighton Newsom
Southwest Ohio Developmental Center

Kimberly A. Kroeger
Xavier University

A number of developments beginning in the 1970s coalesced in the 1980s to elevate concerns about the treatment of serious problem behaviors in people with developmental disabilities to a high level of visibility and, inevitably, controversy. Concern focused on the use of aversive procedures, primarily punishment procedures. This chapter begins with the trends leading to the "nonaversive movement," the attempt to eliminate the use of aversive procedures (also referred to as "aversives") with this population. Then the major events of the movement at its height in the 1980s are described, followed by a discussion of its continuing legacy and some implications of adopting a totally nonaversive approach to treatment.

TRENDS LEADING TO THE NONAVERSIVE MOVEMENT

Increasing Attention to Clients' Rights

The civil rights movement of the 1960s created a climate of increased sensitivity to the rights of all minorities, expanding to include people with developmental disabilities by the 1970s. Judicial remedies for abusive institutional conditions and practices (e.g., *Wyatt v. Stickney*, 1972) established fundamental rights to due process protections whenever intrusive behavior management interventions were proposed (Hannah, Christian, & Clark, 1981; Scheerenberger, 1987). Federal Medicaid regulations, which govern the use of specific procedures such as timeout, restraint, and aversive consequences in institutions, adopted the *Wyatt* standards and became increasingly stringent and more rigorously enforced. State agencies promulgated regulations controlling behavior modification procedures in both residential and educational settings, although this happened later and more slowly in education (Morgan, Striefel, Baer, & Percival, 1991). The increased regulation of treatment procedures produced a sharper, more critical focus on the use of intrusive procedures of all kinds and created the impression that most aversive procedures were dangerous. It was therefore only a small additional step to argue for the abolition of aversive procedures.

Increasing Awareness of the Limits of Aversive Interventions

Applied behavior analysis became increasingly technology oriented during the 1970s, concerned more with demonstrating and evaluating treatments for problem behaviors than discovering their causes (Deitz, 1978; Hayes, Rincover, & Solnick, 1980). One consequence was that the use of aversive procedures resulted in a large body of evidence that increasingly revealed the limits of these procedures (Axelrod & Apsche, 1983; Johnson & Baumeister, 1978; Lennox, Miltenberger, Spengler, & Erfanian, 1988; Matson & Taras, 1989; Schroeder, Schroeder, Rojahn, & Mulick, 1981). Professionals opposed to aversives became increasingly able to buttress their ethical and ideological arguments with arguments based on the research. In turn, this gave the nonaversive movement credibility in some quarters well in advance of any solid achievements.

Abuse of Aversive Procedures

Aversive procedures were sometimes used inappropriately or abusively (Guess, 1990; LaVigna & Donnellan, 1986). Although regulations existed, weak oversight at the administrative level, bad judgment at the professional level, and poor training, implementation, and supervision at the direct-care level still sometimes occurred. Professional associations had limited authority to intervene in specific cases except in an advisory capacity. Formal certification of behavior analysts did not begin in earnest until the 1990s. Muddying the picture were cases of obvious abuse masquerading as "behavior modification." Although hardly mainstream, such cases made easy targets for those advocating the elimination of aversive procedures.

Increasing Availability of Alternative Treatments

Discontent with aversive procedures would have smoldered in some quarters but gone no further were it not for the discovery of nonaversive alternatives. The initial development of such procedures was motivated only partly by the desire to create nonaversive treatments. In most cases, the discovery of the causes of problem behaviors through functional assessment often led to nonaversive treatments as logical outcomes. Functional analyses prior to treatment became increasingly common following early studies by Carr, Newsom, and Binkoff (1976, 1980); Iwata, Dorsey, Slifer, Bauman, and Richman (1982); and others. The success of such procedures in certain cases led some to assume that all problem behaviors could be successfully treated with nonaversive procedures. Indeed, it was argued that the mere fact that most problem behaviors were learned meant that they could be "shaped out" through solely positive reinforcement procedures (LaVigna & Donnellan, 1986).

The Discovery of Severe Problem Behaviors by Special Education

Children with severe problem behaviors were routinely placed in institutional and private school settings prior to 1975. When public school districts were finally forced to serve children with severe disabilities by the Education for All Handicapped Children Act of 1975, academic special educators involved in teacher preparation turned to the existing literature on the treatment of severe problem behaviors for guidance on behavior management. They found its recommended practices to be couched in the unfamiliar terms and concepts of behaviorism, difficult to implement in classrooms for practical or regulatory reasons, and, quite often, personally objectionable. Not surprisingly, most of the early pressure for banning aversives came from educators.

Other trends were present which, while not directly related to developmental disabilities, were parts of the Zeitgeist providing fertile ground for the nonaversive movement. These included the increasing litigiousness of society, the rise of various rights movements (e.g., women, children, crime victims), and the extension of postmodernist philosophical concepts from philosophy and literature into the social sciences.

THE NONAVERSIVE MOVEMENT

The confluence of the foregoing trends was a contentious period from the early 1980s through the mid-1990s in which courteous disagreement was often replaced with heated rhetoric and splintered professional relationships. All who were active in the field during that era can recount tales of harsh arguments at professional conferences, verbal assaults on presenters by hostile members of the audience, and the splitting of professional organizations into "anti-aversive" and "pro-treatment choice" camps. Some examples of the acrimony are provided by Schroeder & Schroeder (1989). In essence, a major episode of the countercontrol that Skinner (1953) had warned can occur when salient behavior control methods are used was being undertaken by advocates who viewed themselves as speaking for the clients involved in aversive treatment programs.

Although controversies about aversive procedures have existed as long as they have been used in formal behavior change programs (e.g., Lucero, Vail, & Scherber, 1968; Miron, 1968), what became the most recent "aversives controversy" began in 1981. The executive board of an organization then known as The Association for Persons with Severe Handicaps (now known simply by its acronym, TASH) approved a resolution calling for the complete cessation of the use of all aversive procedures (*TASH Resolution on Intrusive Interventions*, reprinted in Evans & Meyer, 1985, p. 47). Its definition of aversive procedures focused on the immediate subjective effects of a procedure on the individual and the reaction of the social environment. Banned were not only procedures that produced "obvious signs of physical pain experienced by the individual," but also those that were "normally unacceptable for persons who do not have handicaps," those that produced "extreme ambivalence and discomfort by family, staff, and/or caregivers," and procedures that resulted in "obvious repulsion and/or stress felt by peers and community members." In addition to these criteria was a prohibition on procedures that inflict "tissue damage, physical illness, severe physical or emotional stress, and/or death." Why this item was added is unclear; perhaps it was directed at a particular facility or meant as a general prohibition of client abuse. Its relevance to the practice of behavior analysis was moot, since there was no documentation that the aversive procedures most commonly used at the time (response cost, verbal reprimands, timeout, overcorrection, personal restraint) produced such effects.

The current revision of the TASH resolution (TASH, 2002) continues the conflation of "aversive" with "abusive" and creates additional problems. The first notable change is the omission of a phrase in the original resolution calling for "habilitative procedures free from indiscriminant use of drugs," creating the impression that drugs are now considered benign. The definition of "aversive procedures" is expanded by the addition of two items, "rebellion on the part of the individual" and "permanent or temporary psychological or emotional harm," items that invite arbitrary decisions about whether or not a certain procedure is aversive. There is, finally, the sweeping claim that "… it has now been irrefutably proven that a wide range of methods are available which are not only more effective in managing dangerous or disruptive behaviors, but which do not inflict pain on, humiliate, dehumanize or overly control or manipulate individuals with disabilities" (p. 1).

The original TASH resolution was based in part on the board's belief that evidence for the effectiveness of aversive interventions was "questionable" and "on the observations among board members that these procedures were being both abused and misused in a variety of settings that serve persons with disabilities" (Guess, 1990). However, even Guess' own literature review (Guess, Helmstetter, Turnbull, & Knowlton, 1987), like those of other reviewers, actually showed that punishment procedures were generally effective in reducing behaviors. The evidence was "questionable" only in the sense that punishment was faulted for failing to do more than it was ever intended to do, that is, produce not only response reduction but also long-term maintenance and generalization. (There was, however, no acknowledgment that reinforcement also does not automatically produce maintenance and generalization of treatment gains.) The main issue was actually the second mentioned, the misuse of punishment procedures. But instead of addressing what is a regulatory, credentialing, training, and oversight problem with a proposal for better controls, the TASH board chose to eliminate aversives as an option altogether.

The TASH resolution had little impact at first. Most psychologists in the field regarded it as an issue among a relatively small group of special educators. Although it was true that the field had erred in generalizing the use of punishment from severe cases to all cases (Carr, 1988), now it appeared that the opposite error was being made, that of generalizing from mild cases to all cases.

The situation changed abruptly on the publication of a monograph whose lead author had credentials respected in the developmental disabilities community. Guess et al. (1987) provided retroactive support for the TASH resolution in a monograph reviewing much of the literature on punishment and presenting their legal and philosophical views on the use of aversive procedures. The authors stated their bias against aversive procedures in the Introduction: "It [the monograph] was, in fact, prepared in response to a growing concern of the authors that aversive procedures continue to be used extensively with persons who have severe disabilities and that the perpetuation of this practice must be analyzed, and indeed critiqued, from several new and different perspectives" (p. 1). Why Guess et al. thought that strong aversive procedures were used "extensively" with people with disabilities is never made clear, except as their inference from the fact that research on punishment was generally taught in college classes and described in textbooks. Late in the monograph (p. 35), there is a hint that the authors' main concern was with special education classrooms, which typically lacked the protections then common in institutional and clinic settings for clients with behavior programs. Rather than propose solutions to perceived overutilization of punishment in classrooms, Guess et al. mounted a broadside against all aversive procedures in all settings as well as the professionals who use them. This was a major tactical error that provoked considerable resistance from many who would otherwise have supported the "skill-building," "educative" (Evans & Meyer, 1985) approach to behavior management then emerging.

The Guess et al. (1987) monograph first covered well-trodden ground on the limitations of research on aversive procedures, then went on to present its "new and different perspectives," specifically, demographic, legal, and ethical issues, doing so with the tone and style of the ideological tract it was intended to be. Its conceptual and methodological deficiencies were thoroughly described by Mulick (1990) and need not be repeated here. Instead, we mention some of the main points that alienated many behavior analysts.

Guess et al. (1987) argued that the use of aversives was practiced in a discriminatory manner. The unsurprising finding in their demographic analysis that punishment procedures were most often studied in institutional settings, where most individuals with severe behavior problems lived, led to the surprising conclusion that persons with severe and profound disabilities were singled out for harsh treatment.

Equally objectionable was the authors' portrayal of behavior analysts as "depersonalizing" the people with whom they work. Professionals who used aversive procedures were described as having an "excess of enthusiasm for aversives" because they may view people with disabilities as "so distinguishable from nondisabled people as to be different and therefore able to be treated differently and less favorably" (p. 30). In the absence of any evidence for this assumption, Guess et al. reasoned rather sophomorically that the precise, emotionally restrained writing style required by journals indicated a corresponding coldness toward participants by researchers. Behaviorism itself was incorrectly characterized as "mechanistic" and "reductionistic." One of the more egregious ploys in the monograph was a table highlighting the formal resemblance between some punishment procedures and some torture techniques used with political prisoners in repressive countries. The intended implication about those using aversive procedures was as false as it was obvious.

The monograph concluded with three recommendations. The first was that there should be a determination of the extent to which aversives were being used, apparently to find some substantiation of the authors' claim that their use was "widespread" and "of enormous magnitude." Second, the authors advocated "expanded discourse on the ethical/moral issues involved in using aversive procedures," a hollow call given their foreclosure of the validity of any ethical stance but their own in the monograph and in a contemporaneous philosophical paper (Turnbull & Guess, 1986). Third, there was a recommendation for research into alternatives to aversive procedures, certainly a worthy pursuit, but one that should obviously have come before rather than after both the resolution and the monograph. Given what the authors acknowledged to be "a scant amount of research" on alternative treatments, the overall message of the monograph to many seemed to be that all use of aversive procedures should stop and essentially no treatment be offered to people with disabilities displaying severe problem behaviors.

Far from stimulating "desirable" and "necessary" dialogue, one of the professed purposes of the TASH monograph, it effectively eliminated, at least in the near term, any remaining chance of *rapprochement* between the two sides in this controversy. Nor was the antiaversive position helped when a survey of traditional ethical principles, undertaken by some of the same authors to show that the use of aversive procedures is always morally wrong, actually proved to offer limited support for that position (Turnbull & Guess, 1986). Nevertheless, the authors concluded, "Given the inadequate efficacy of aversive interventions, the potential results of aversive interventions for the person with a disability and for others, and the availability of efficacious positive interventions, it is more wrong than right on moral grounds to use aversive procedures" (Turnbull & Guess, 1986, p. 208). Given the lack of empirical support for any of the three propositions in this syllogism, it seemed to be example of drawing an invalid conclusion from false premises.

Soon the call for a ban on all aversives moderated a bit, but in ways that added confusion instead of clarity. In his presidential address at the annual convention of the American Association on Mental Deficiency (AAMD), Turnbull (1986) stated, "Not every intervention that is unwelcome by the client or that may cause unpleasant consequences should be regarded as presumptively questionable. To take that approach would be to exclude, for example, timeout, seclusion, medications, or modest repetitions of skill-developing tasks" (p. 266). Did this leave other aversives, such as strong verbal reprimands and response cost, on the forbidden list or not? What about manual or mechanical restraint? Saying they were "obviously not opposed to all punishers," Evans and Meyer (1990) stated that "people with disabilities can learn from the same kinds of correction that are culturally acceptable for those who do not have disabilities" (p. 134). Many certainly can learn; some cannot. Were such a statement remotely valid for all individuals with disabilities, self-injury and aggression would never reach serious levels, institutions would have all closed long ago due to a lack of admissions, and aversive procedures would never have been developed. By ignoring consensual, scientific definitions of *aversive* and admitting the need for some aversive consequences yet failing to specify which met the TASH standard of "community acceptability," the stage was set for recurring disputes about specific procedures. Procedures that are unnecessarily painful or stigmatizing, such as water squirts, ammonia capsules, pinching, and hair pulling, have since become unacceptable in virtually all settings, but a number of aversive consequences remain. "Community acceptability," by itself, can be a poor standard for making decisions about treatment procedures. A recent survey found that 94% of parents of normal children used some form of physical punishment (including slaps and spankings) with their 3- and 4-year-old children (Straus & Stewart, 1999). What antiaversive advocates actually preferred was their own instead of the community's definition of community acceptability.

As the controversy intensified, behavior analysts began to split on the aversives issue. To those on the antiaversive side, the message was clear that strong aversive procedures lacked social validity. Some support for this conclusion occurred when the TASH resolution tapped into a vein of discontent with aversive procedures shared by the leaders of other organizations. Within a few years, it was adopted with only minor changes by the AAMD (1987) and the Autism Society of

America (1988), among other advocacy groups. (It is a minor irony of history that the Autism Society's rejection of aversives came within a year of the publication of the first study showing recovery to normal functioning in autistic children in a program in which aversive consequences had been used [Lovaas, 1987].) Reaction by some constituents of AAMD was swift. Keyes, Creekmore, Karst, Crow, and Dayan (1988) conducted a survey of Louisiana AAMR (formerly AAMD) members and found that support for the resolution varied sharply by discipline: 92% of educators agreed with the resolution but only 43% of psychologists did. The authors attributed this split to the fact that psychologists in developmental disabilities generally worked with clients with severe problem behaviors to a greater extent than did educators. Contrary to a cardinal position of those opposed to aversive procedures, 81% of respondents with doctoral degrees did not believe that there was sufficient research evidence to conclude that all complex behavior problems can be effectively managed using only nonaversive procedures. Keyes et al. (1988) suggested that the position statement be withdrawn and replaced with a comprehensive review of empirical research on treatment procedures. Instead, despite the input of a task force involving members in the field, the AAMD (now the American Association on Mental Retardation [AAMR]) statement was revised only slightly, by the addition of two inconsequential paragraphs stating that it was not meant to be regulatory and that community integration should be a goal (American Association on Mental Retardation, 1990).

The controversy received attention beyond the confines of the professional and advocacy groups directly involved. In September 1989, a panel gathered at the National Institutes of Health to report the summary of their months of study of the existing state of knowledge on the treatment of severe destructive behaviors and to present a consensus statement of treatment recommendations (National Institutes of Health, 1989). Considerable effort was expended to get the views of parents, advocacy groups, and professional organizations on both sides of the aversives issue. The statement produced by the panel indicates that the panel took pains to write a balanced set of recommendations. The recommendation regarding punishment procedures, in particular, was a model of caution: "Behavior reduction procedures should be selected for their rapid effectiveness *only* if the exigencies of the clinical situation require such restrictive interventions and *only* after appropriate review. These interventions should *only* be used in the context of a comprehensive and individualized behavior enhancement treatment package" (p. 19; italics in original). This recommendation fell short of the wishes of antiaversive advocates. While the panel held a news conference to announce their findings, a separate news conference was held by a group of opponents of aversive treatment to complain that the consensus statement failed to recommend that aversives should only be used after all positive procedures had been tried, and to suggest that the conference was premature and should have been delayed another 5–10 years (Landers, 1989).

By the late 1980s, the split within the behavior analysis community, which had been simmering for years at professional meetings, became obvious. An eminent behavioral scientist, Murray Sidman, published a book detailing the pervasive extent to which everyday behavior is controlled by aversive contingencies (Sidman, 1989). In addition, Sidman argued forcefully against the use of punishment as a treatment procedure by behavior analysts, both on the grounds that more effective alternatives were available and out of his concern that the positive contributions of behavior analysis were being overshadowed by its public perception as a field completely invested in coercive methods. Repp and Singh (1990) published the definitive anthology on the issue, with chapters contributed by individuals on both sides. The division of the behavior analysis community indicated in Sidman's and Repp and Singh's books, although moderated somewhat by time and perspective, remains to the present day.

Politically active opponents of aversive procedures initiated actions beyond the customary arenas of research and debate. In some states, activists sought changes in state laws to eliminate or severely restrict the use of such procedures in schools (e.g., California Senate Bill 520, 1987; Massachusetts Assembly Bill 1709, 1987). A group of advocacy organizations petitioned the Food and Drug Administration to withdraw approval for a new device (Self-Injurious Behavior Inhibiting System [SIBIS]) that could be programmed to deliver low-intensity electric shocks precisely contingent on head-directed self-injurious behaviors and to remotely activate reinforcement dispensers (Meyer, 1988). The AAMR prevented the company making the device from renting exhibit space at its annual convention in 1988 (Linscheid, 1989). Two prominent behavior analysts' applications for Fellow status in AAMR were tabled by the executive board for 6 months due to their involvement in the initial research and development of SIBIS (American Association on Mental Retardation, 1989).

Partly in response to such developments, behavior analysts in favor of preserving choice in decisions about treatment began a "right to effective treatment" countermovement (Matson, 1987). The Association for Behavior Analysis established a Task Force on the Right to Effective Treatment, which issued a position paper that reflected the views of many of its members (Van Houten et al., 1988). The authors noted that a procedure's overall level of restrictiveness is a combined function of its absolute level of restrictiveness, the amount of time required to produce an acceptable outcome, and the consequences of delayed intervention. Procedures should not be based solely on personal preference and should not be judged simply by whether they manipulate antecedent rather than consequent stimuli or reinforcement rather than punishment. Division 33 (Mental Retardation and Developmental Disabilities) of the American Psychological Association issued comprehensive *Guidelines on Effective Behavioral Treatment for Persons with Mental Retardation and Developmental Disabilities* (American Psychological Association, 1989). It required psychologists' involvement in training efforts and presented guidelines for the selection, implementation, and monitoring of behavioral interventions, with particularly stringent standards for the use of highly restrictive procedures.

ATTEMPTED RESOLUTIONS

The heated rhetoric began to cool somewhat when various investigators proposed approaches that refocused the discussion on the critical issues. An article by Horner et al. (1990) succeeded where the TASH monograph had failed in making the case for a new approach to behavior management. Horner et al. stated that the problem lay not with all aversives, but only with painful or abusive procedures, and that the term *nonaversive behavior management* diverted attention away from what should be an emphasis on building replacement behaviors and judging effectiveness by improvement in quality of life. They argued that the routine use of painful or humiliating consequences was unacceptable in the community, but allowed for the rare use of painful procedures in extremely unusual situations, as had been advocated by Lovaas and Favell (1987).

Meinhold and Mulick (1990, 1992) noted that there are well-established formal decision-analysis models that are used in government and business to aid in deciding whether or not to go forward with new technologies involving significant risks and costs. They argued that the full range of available information on social costs, risks, and benefits needs to be considered in making ethical clinical decisions about the use of aversive procedures. Meinhold and Mulick showed how the model could be applied to a variety of positive and aversive treatment alternatives (1990), including controversial ones like the SIBIS device (1992).

Carr, Robinson, and Palumbo (1990) argued that the debate about aversive interventions had been misdirected all along because it failed to address the more important point of whether or not treatments are influenced by functional assessment. They argued that in the absence of knowledge about the causes of a client's problem behavior, both positive and aversive treatments are nonfunctional, that is, unrelated to the causes of the behavior, reactive instead of proactive, and limited to short-term crisis management instead of long-term preventive solutions. They made a compelling case that treatment efforts must focus on skill building and environmental rearrangements *between* disruptive episodes, not the application of consequences *during* episodes.

By the mid-1990s, a satisfactory resolution of the controversy had not been achieved, but the issue had largely been exhausted. Everything useful that could be said had been said, and most people were simply tired of hearing about it. Other issues moved it off center stage in the journals and at professional conferences. Professionals who used aversive procedures continued to use them, though with greater selectivity and increased understanding of others' views. The nonaversive movement evolved into the "community-referenced behavior management" movement and then the "positive behavior support" movement (described in Mulick & Butter, chap. 23, this volume). The legacy of the controversy includes both significant contributions and lasting harm.

CONTRIBUTIONS OF THE NONAVERSIVE MOVEMENT

To dismiss the nonaversive movement as merely ideological is to fail to appreciate the most important point that it was groping toward, however heavy-handedly, that treatment outcome standards were changing. Behavioral procedures, both positive and aversive, had become victims of their own success. The reduction or elimination of a problem behavior for a short time in a circumscribed setting was expected to occur almost routinely and was no longer sufficient to show the actual value of a procedure in the life of the client. Instead, the bar had been raised and there was growing support for the view expressed by Horner (1990), that "Behavioral support should result in changes in what people do, where they do it, with whom they spend time, the level of support of paid staff, and the extent to which response patterns (activities) reflect personal preference" (p. 167). This does not mean that there is no longer a place for innovative treatments and novel applications of known treatments in classical small-N designs, but that attempts should also be made to measure quality-of-life changes and to consider additional research methodologies (Meyer & Evans, 1993). Although ignored by the nonaversive movement, some behavior analysts had in fact provided comprehensive treatment across all aspects of clients' lives over periods of many years and had documented their enhanced quality of life (Foxx, 1990; Foxx, Bittle, & Faw, 1989; McEachin, Smith, & Lovaas, 1993). Still, the nonaversive movement deserves some credit for accelerating progress toward a systems perspective on problem behaviors, a trend emphasized more directly in the positive behavior support movement. The practical problem remains, however, that in most settings the clinician directly responsible for treatment has limited ability to effect changes in many of the parts of the system that need changing, even at the local level of a group home. Further, large-scale systems change at the state or national level is invariably a complex, multilayered, and slow endeavor (Jacobson & Otis, 1992).

A second contribution of the nonaversive movement was its championing of functional assessment. Studies explicitly mentioning functional assessment began to accelerate in 1989 (Dunlap & Kincaid, 2001), and it became a required practice in schools with the 1997 amendments to the Individuals with Disabilities Education Act. Some journals now require a functional analysis of the problem behavior in all reports on behavior-reduction procedures submitted for publication. In addition to often (though not always) showing the way to more effective treatments, advances in functional assessment methodology have had two further beneficial sequelae: First, there has been a shift in focus from consequences to the stimulus control of behaviors and the subsequent development of antecedent interventions (Carr, Robinson, Taylor, & Carlson, 1990; Luiselli & Cameron, 1998). Second, multicomponent packages of interventions, although present for many years, came to be the preferred alternative to single-procedure interventions (Carr & Carlson, 1993).

A third contribution was one recommended in the TASH monograph: increased research on nonaversive treatment procedures. In the last 15 years, there has been an explosion of research reports, books, Web sites, and conferences on nonaversive treatment. The growth would have occurred without the TASH recommendation, as part of the natural progression of research, but the nonaversive movement undoubtedly provoked increased interest in positive procedures. Most of this information has been helpful, but some has not. In some cases, "nonaversive" simply became a trendy label used to repackage old techniques, a few of which could probably be regarded as actually aversive, as may be the case with some "therapeutic holding" restraints (e.g., Stirling & McHugh, 1997). Overall, studies have tended to focus primarily on relatively mild and moderate problem behaviors in children rather than on severe behaviors in children and adults, and few reports of extensive lifestyle change have been published. The new literature shows little evidence of the paradigm shift of Kuhnian proportions initially proclaimed by postmodernist advocates of nonaversive treatment (Guess, Turnbull, & Helmstetter, 1990; Meyer & Evans, 1993).

HARM DONE BY THE NONAVERSIVE MOVEMENT

Offsetting the positive contributions of the nonaversive movement are its equally enduring harmful effects. The first of these is the overextension of the approach, sometimes at the expense of common sense as well as basic learning principles and responsible practice. Guess et al. (1990) noted what they called the "spread effect," or the tendency of aversive procedures to be used more and more inappropriately over time. But inappropriate applications can occur with any technology, including the nonaversive approach. Procedures deemed aversive by some people in policy-making roles began to include various relatively mild procedures, just as many behavior analysts had originally feared. The TASH resolution expanded from procedures that inflict "physical pain" to those that may cause "temporary psychological or emotional harm." The problem with the latter is not only that detection of such effects is usually quite subjective, but also that they are easily interpreted to mean that it is harmful to do anything that might temporarily irritate or upset a client. The nonaversive movement has led directly to school and provider policies in many communities of excessive "consumer choice" and "hands-off behavior support," policies that over time can and have produced individuals who become increasingly self-injurious, routinely damage their homes or classrooms, or intimidate and injure peers and staff. In the name of treating such individuals with "respect and dignity," such providers are condemning them to certain institutionalization or incarceration. Examples of misguided policies occur frequently at meetings about adult clients' problem behaviors in community settings, usually in the context of discharging the client. At one such meeting recently, the workshop supervisor mentioned that their new behavior support policy classifies "telling a consumer not to do something they want to do" as aversive, because "there's this big push to give people choices and let them do whatever they want to do regardless." The issue under discussion was whether or not the client should be allowed to run out of the workshop into a busy street. The group home manager stated, "We have no consequences. If a person needs hands-on to control his behavior, he's not appropriate for our program."

Distrustful of regulatory approaches and the efforts of professional associations to control the use of aversives, some professionals wondered at the time what would happen if we simply cut the Gordian knot of the controversy by prohibiting painful or stigmatizing procedures altogether? The resulting pressure should produce a dramatically increased effort to develop new positive approaches and to disseminate existing nonaversive methods (Durand, 1990). Such outcomes have, in fact, come about with the ascendance of the nonaversive philosophy and the decline in the use of aversives during the 1990s. But rarely is the nonaversive philosophy, once adopted by a treatment provider, backed up with sufficient staffing and training resources to make it work. As a result, unintended consequences of excessive client choice and hands-off policies are often the increased use of psychotropic drugs and the frequent utilization of hospital emergency rooms or developmental centers to deal with crises. At the present time, in fact, we suspect that one factor indirectly perpetuating the existence of institutions is the half-hearted implementation of nonaversive policies by community providers.

Finally, the nonaversive movement (like behavior modification in its early years) can be faulted for raising false hopes of widespread, indeed universal, effectiveness. To be fair, some proponents pointed out limitations, as, for example, Carr et al. (1994) did with regard to functional communication training (pp. 7–8), discouraging its use with behaviors controlled by sensory, homeostatic, and organic variables instead of social factors. Meyer and Evans (1989), however, attributed any limitations in using nonaversive treatment to "limitations in organizing resources in certain ways," as though this were a simple logistical problem, unencumbered by funding, policy, and administrative issues. Most other proponents simply did not mention limitations. But even under ideal conditions, some individuals fail to show clinically significant behavior changes or the changes fail to endure. Paisey, Whitney, and Hislop (1990) presented the case histories of seven individuals, four of whose problem-behavior reductions failed to generalize in spite of a commitment to nonaversive treatment, expert outside consultation, comprehensive functional analysis, community placement, and generous staffing, in short, all the ingredients purportedly sufficient to solve behavior problems. Successful interventions can be quickly derailed by misguided program philosophies and unresponsive service systems. Moreover, the behavioral expertise, staffing, and other resources needed to "go all out nonaversively" (Berkman & Meyer, 1988) with especially difficult clients are prohibitively expensive for most settings. Although short-term cost obviously should not, ethically, constrain the selection of the procedures used, in real-world educational and residential services it actually plays a major and often decisive role in treatment selection. When limitations in effectiveness and high cost cannot be overcome, one result may be disenchantment with all behavioral interventions and the embrace of fads like those described in this volume.

Granting the logic of the theoretical argument that because most problem behaviors are learned they can be treated by building replacement behaviors, experience still suggests that even some socially motivated behaviors in some clients are resistant to positive-only approaches, at least initially, and sometimes indefinitely. The logic of the replacement behavior approach requires that the replacement behavior and the problem behavior be functionally equivalent, or controlled by the same class of reinforcers (Carr, 1988). Functionally equivalent replacement behaviors may not be identifiable or be acquired in every case. Sometimes a nonequivalent alternative response will serve, but sometimes even this strategy of overriding the controlling variables of a problem behavior with reinforcement will fail. The more knowledgeable proponents of nonaversive treatment have acknowledged at least a limited role for aversive interventions, either to deal with crises or to create a window of opportunity to begin positive procedures (Carr et al., 1994; Sidman, 1989). If progress then occurs, creating and solidifying effective social and environmental arrangements that will maintain and enhance behavioral changes become the real challenges of challenging behaviors.

More important than the need for the frequently requested development of more nonaversive procedures is the need for better ways of effecting systems change at the level of service providers, state agencies, and legislatures. Models of productive collaboration between consumers, providers, and funders in the redesign of social service systems have been developed, yet still await wider implementation (Risley, 1996; Sailor, 1996). Further, intensive behavioral early intervention already has an enviable track record and could eventually obviate the need for strong aversives later in life if pursued on a larger scale (Drash, Raver, & Murrin, 1987; Dunlap, Johnson, & Robbins, 1990; McEachin et al., 1993).

IS TOTALLY NONAVERSIVE TREATMENT DESIRABLE?

A utopian ideal of totally nonaversive intervention seems to be the message that was understood by many educational, vocational, and residential programs in the years since the TASH resolution and monograph were first published, although such a goal was denied by some of those who formulated those documents (Evans & Meyer, 1990; Turnbull, 1986). However, the philosophies and practices of programs seeking to avoid all use of aversive consequences ignore what we know about human development. As Sidman (1989) showed convincingly, many behaviors in the natural environment are controlled by aversive contingencies. A totally non-aversive approach would constitute poor preparation for a client transitioning to an ordinary community residential or work setting (Tennant, Hattersley, & Cullen, 1978). Further, research with children indicates an important role for aversives in learning and development.

To understand why punishment often led to faster learning in children than did praise (Walters & Grusec, 1977), Paris and Cairns (1972) observed the use of naturally occurring consequences in special education classrooms. They found social reinforcement to be a relatively ambiguous, weak event because it occurs frequently, serves various functions, and is less contingent on specific behaviors than is negative feedback. A verbal reprimand or statement of disapproval is usually accompanied by a clear indication of inappropriate behavior, making it easier for the child to learn what not to do. Pfiffner and O'Leary (1987) studied conduct-problem children in a special education classroom while the children worked on typical educational tasks. The researchers found that an enhanced positive approach (praise and individualized token programs with choices from a reward menu) must be combined with or preceded by aversive consequences (reprimands, timeout) for disruptive behavior to create acceptable levels of academic performance and on-task behavior. Similarly, other investigators working with oppositional children have found that imitation, social interaction, and compliance increased only when timeout for noncompliance was added to reinforcement for compliance (Nordquist & McEvoy, 1983; Wahler, 1969; Wahler & Nordquist, 1973). Finally, several studies with autistic children show that learning may be very slow and unstable due to the interference of problem behaviors, even with highly consistent positive reinforcement for appropriate behaviors over a long period of time. Progress does not improve for some children until interfering behaviors are reduced by punishment (Ackerman, 1980; Koegel & Covert, 1972; Koegel, Firestone, Kramme, & Dunlap, 1974; McEachin & Leaf, 1984). A number of other beneficial effects of punishment on learning and social relatedness in individuals with developmental disabilities have long been known (Harris & Ersner-Hershfield, 1978; Newsom, Favell, & Rincover, 1983) but are routinely neglected by antiaversive advocates.

Studies of good childrearing practices in normal children also fail to support a totally nonaversive approach (Baumrind, 1996; Dornbusch, Ritter, Leiderman, Roberts, & Fraleigh, 1987; Larzelere, 2000; Phillips, 1993; Steinberg, Elmen, & Mounts, 1989). In a classic series of studies, Baumrind (1967, 1971; Baumrind & Black, 1967) found that *authoritative* parents, who use a combination of firm discipline, reasoning, and warmth, rear children who are happy, self-reliant, responsible, and competent. *Authoritarian* parents, who are highly controlling but less nurturant, rear children who tend to be dysphoric, anxious, and unaffiliated with peers. *Permissive* parents, who are nurturing but undemanding and lax in discipline, have children who are lacking in self-control, dependent, and immature. Parallels can be drawn to suggest that authoritarian childrearing is similar to strictly aversive behavior management, while permissive childrearing is comparable to totally nonaversive treatment. If so, a reasonable conclusion would be that a consistently nonaversive approach would be likely to foster students or clients who show little self-control and are excessively dependent. A better treatment philosophy would resemble Baumrind's (1983) characterization of authoritative parenting in its "consistent balancing of high control with high responsiveness." Although normal development is not a perfect model for the treatment of people with disabilities, knowledge of effective childrearing does provide a rough template for the design of an intervention philosophy, one that is more likely to promote clients' psychological growth than designs derived solely from ethical abstractions or advocates' personal values.

REFERENCES

Ackerman, A. B. (1980). *The role of punishment in the treatment of preschool-aged autistic children: Effects and side effects.* Unpublished doctoral dissertation, University of California, Los Angeles.

American Association on Mental Deficiency. (1987). The AAMD position statement on aversive therapy. *Mental Retardation, 27,* 119–125.

American Association on Mental Retardation. (1989). Minutes: Board of directors meeting. Standing committee reports. *Mental Retardation, 25,* 120.

American Association on Mental Retardation. (1990). Minutes: Board of directors meeting. Recommendations of aversive task force. *Mental Retardation, 26,* 130.

American Psychological Association, Division 33. (1989). Guidelines on effective behavioral treatment for persons with mental retardation and developmental disabilities. *Psychology in Mental Retardation and Developmental Disabilities, 14,* 3–4.

Autism Society of America. (1988). *Resolution on abusive treatment and neglect.* Washington, DC: Author.

Axelrod, S., & Apsche, J. (Eds.). (1983). *The effects of punishment on human behavior.* New York: Academic Press.

Baumrind, D. (1967). Child care practices anteceding three patterns of preschool behavior. *Genetic Psychology Monographs, 75,* 43–88.

Baumrind, D. (1971). Current patterns of parental authority. *Developmental Psychology Monographs, 4* (1, Pt. 2), 1–103.

Baumrind, D. (1983). Rejoinder to Lewis's reinterpretation of parental firm control effects: Are authoritative families really harmonious? *Psychological Bulletin, 94,* 132–142.

Baumrind, D. (1996). The discipline controversy revisited. *Family Relations: Journal of Applied Family & Child Studies, 45,* 405–414.

Baumrind, D., & Black, A. E. (1967). Socialization practices associated with dimensions of competence in preschool boys and girls. *Child Development, 38,* 291–327.

Berkman, K. A., & Meyer, L. H. (1988). Alternative strategies and multiple outcomes in remediation of severe self-injury: Going "all out" nonaversively. *Journal of the Association for Persons with Severe Handicaps, 13,* 76–88.

California Senate Bill 520, California Legislature, Reg. Sess. (1987).

Carr, E. G. (1988). Functional equivalence as a mechanism of response generalization. In R. H. Horner, G. Dunlap, & R. L. Koegel (Eds.), *Generalization and maintenance: Life-style changes in applied settings* (pp. 221–241). Baltimore: Brookes.

Carr, E. G., & Carlson, J. I. (1993). Reduction of severe behavior problems in the community using a multicomponent treatment approach. *Journal of Applied Behavior Analysis, 26,* 157–172.

Carr, E. G., Levin, L., McConnachie, G., Carlson, J. I., Kemp, D. C., & Smith, C. E. (1994). *Communication-based intervention for problem behavior: A user's guide for producing positive behavior change.* Baltimore: Brookes.

Carr, E. G., Newsom, C., & Binkoff, J. (1976). Stimulus control of self-destructive behavior in a psychotic child. *Journal of Abnormal Child Psychology, 4,* 139–153.

Carr, E. G., Newsom, C., & Binkoff, J. (1980). Escape as a factor in the aggressive behavior of two retarded children. *Journal of Applied Behavior Analysis, 13,* 101–117.

Carr, E. G., Robinson, S., & Palumbo, L. W. (1990). The wrong issue: Aversive vs. nonaversive treatment. The right issue: Functional vs. nonfunctional treatment. In A. C. Repp & N. N. Singh (Eds.), *Perspectives on the use of nonaversive and aversive interventions for persons with developmental disabilities* (pp. 361–379). Sycamore, IL: Sycamore.

Carr, E. G., Robinson, S., Taylor, J. C., & Carlson, J. I. (1990). *Positive approaches to the treatment of severe behavior problems in persons with developmental disabilities: A review and analysis of reinforcement and stimulus-based procedures.* Seattle, WA: The Association for Persons with Severe Handicaps.

Deitz, S. M. (1978). Current status of applied behavior analysis: Science versus technology. *American Psychologist, 33,* 805–814.

Dornbusch, S. M., Ritter, P. L., Leiderman, P. H., Roberts, D. F., & Fraleigh, P. W. (1987). The relation of parenting style to adolescent school performance. *Child Development, 58,* 1244–1257.

Drash, P. W., Raver, D. A., & Murrin, M. R. (1987). Total habilitation as a major goal of intervention in mental retardation. *Mental Retardation, 25,* 67–69.

Dunlap, G., Johnson, L. F., & Robbins, F. R. (1990). Preventing serious behavior problems through skill development and early intervention. In A. C. Repp & N. N. Singh (Eds.), *Perspectives on the use of nonaversive and aversive interventions for persons with developmental disabilities* (pp. 273–286). Sycamore, IL: Sycamore.

Dunlap, G., & Kincaid, D. (2001). The widening world of functional assessments: Comments on four manuals and beyond. *Journal of Applied Behavior Analysis, 34,* 365–377.

Durand, V. M. (1990). The "aversives" debate is over: And now the real work begins. *Journal of the Association of Persons with Severe Handicaps, 15,* 140–141.

Evans, I. M., & Meyer, L. H. (1985). *An educative approach to behavior problems.* Baltimore: Brookes.

Evans, I. M., & Meyer, L. H. (1990). Toward a science in support of meaningful outcomes: A response to Horner et al. *Journal of the Association of Persons with Severe Handicaps, 15,* 133–135.

Foxx, R. M. (1990). "Harry": A ten year follow-up of the successful treatment of a self-injurious man. *Research in Developmental Disabilities, 11,* 67–76.

Foxx, R. M., Bittle, R. G., & Faw, G. D. (1989). A maintenance strategy for discontinuing aversive procedures: A 52-month follow-up of the treatment of aggression. *American Journal on Mental Retardation, 94,* 27–36.

Guess, D. (1990). Transmission of behavior management technologies from researchers to practitioners: A need for professional self-evaluation. In A. C. Repp & N. N. Singh (Eds.), *Perspectives on the use of nonaversive and aversive interventions for persons with developmental disabilities* (pp. 157–172). Sycamore, IL: Sycamore.

Guess, D., Helmstetter, E., Turnbull, H. R., & Knowlton, S. (1987). *Use of aversive procedures with persons who are disabled: An historical review and critical analysis.* Seattle, WA: The Association for Persons with Severe Handicaps.

Guess, D., Turnbull, H. R., & Helmstetter, E. (1990). Science, paradigms, and values: A response to Mulick. *American Journal on Mental Retardation, 95,* 157–163.

Hannah, G. T., Christian, W. P., & Clark, H. B. (1981). *Preservation of client rights.* New York: Free Press.

Harris, S. L., & Ersner-Hershfield, R. (1978). Behavioral supression of seriously disruptive behavior in psychotic and retarded patients: A review of punishment and its alternatives. *Psychological Bulletin, 85,* 1352–1375.

Hayes, S. C., Rincover, A., & Solnick, J. V. (1980). The technical drift of applied behavior analysis. *Journal of Applied Behavior Analysis, 13,* 275–285.

Horner, R. (1990). Ideology, technology, and typical community settings: Use of severe aversive stimuli. *American Journal on Mental Retardation, 95,* 166–168.

Horner, R. H., Dunlap, G., Koegel, R. L., Carr, E. G., Sailor, W., Anderson, J., et al. (1990). Toward a technology of "nonaversive" behavioral support. *Journal of the Association for Persons with Severe Handicaps, 15,* 125–132.

Iwata, B. A., Dorsey, M. F., Slifer, K. J., Bauman, K. E., & Richman, G. S. (1982). Toward a functional analysis of self-injury. *Analysis and Intervention in Developmental Disabilities, 2,* 3–20.

Jacobson, J. W., & Otis, J. P. (1992). Limitations of regulations as a means of social reform in developmental services. *Mental Retardation, 30,* 163–171.

Johnson, W. L., & Baumeister, A. A. (1978). Self-injurious behavior: A review and analysis of methodological details of published studies. *Behavior Modification, 2,* 465–487.

Keyes, J. B., Creekmore, W. N., Karst, R., Crow, R. E., & Dayan, M. (1988). The AAMR position statement on aversive therapy: The controversy. *Mental Retardation, 26,* 314–318.

Koegel, R. L., & Covert, A. (1972). The relationship of self-stimulation to learning in autistic children. *Journal of Applied Behavior Analysis, 5,* 381–388.

Koegel, R. L., Firestone, P. B., Kramme, K. W., & Dunlap, G. (1974). Increasing spontaneous play by suppressing self-stimulation in autistic children. *Journal of Applied Behavior Analysis, 7,* 521–528.

Landers, S. (1989). Self-injury "consensus" stirs strife, not accord. *APA Monitor, 20,* 26–27.

Larzelere, R. E. (2000). Child outcomes of nonabusive and customary physical punishment by parents: An updated literature review. *Clinical Child and Family Psychology Review, 3,* 199–221.

LaVigna, G. W., & Donnellan, A. M. (1986). *Alternatives to punishment.* New York: Irvington.

Lennox, D., Miltenberger, R., Spengler, P., & Erfanian, N. (1988). Decelerative treatment practices with persons who have mental retardation: A review of five years of literature. *American Journal on Mental Retardation, 92,* 492–501.

Linscheid, T. R. (1989). SIBIS article facts disputed [Letter to the editor]. *AAMR News & Notes, 2,* 6.

Lovaas, O. I. (1987). Behavioral treatment and normal educational and intellectual functioning in young autistic children. *Journal of Consulting and Clinical Psychology, 55,* 3–9.

Lovaas, O. I., & Favell, J. E. (1987). Protection for clients undergoing aversive/restrictive interventions. *Education and Treatment of Children, 10,* 311–325.

Lucero, R. J., Vail, D. J., & Scherber, J. (1968). Regulating operant conditioning programs. *Hospital and Community Psychiatry, 19,* 53–54.

Luiselli, J. K., & Cameron, M. J. (1998). *Antecedent control: Innovative approaches to behavior support.* Baltimore: Brookes.

Massachusetts Senate Bill 1709, Reg. Sess. (1987).

Matson, J. (1987). *Open letter on the Committee for the Right to Treatment, May 19, 1987.* Available by request to J. L. Matson, Department of Psychology, Louisiana State University, Baton Rouge, LA.

Matson, J., & Taras, M. E. (1989). A 20 year review of punishment and alternative methods to treat problem behaviors in developmentally delayed persons. *Research in Developmental Disabilities, 10,* 85–104.

McEachin, J. J., & Leaf, R. B. (1984, May). *The role of punishment in the motivation of autistic children.* Paper presented at the annual convention of the Association for Behavior Analysis, Nashville, TN.

McEachin, J. J., Smith, T., & Lovaas, O. I. (1993). Long-term outcome for children with autism who received early intensive behavioral treatment. *American Journal on Mental Retardation, 97,* 359–372.

Meinhold, P. M., & Mulick, J. A. (1990). Risks, choices and behavioral treatment. *Behavioral Residential Treatment, 5,* 29–44.

Meinhold, P. M., & Mulick, J. A. (1992). Social policy and science in the treatment of severe behavior disorders: Defining and securing a healthy relationship. *Clinical Psychology Review, 12,* 585–603.

Meyer, L. (1988). TASH joins with other organizations to protest electric shock device. *TASH Newsletter, 14,* 1–3.

Meyer, L. H., & Evans, I. M. (1989). *Nonaversive intervention for behavior problems.* Baltimore: Brookes.

Meyer, L. H., & Evans, I. M. (1993). Science and practice in behavioral intervention: Meaningful outcomes, research validity, and usable knowledge. *Journal of the Association for Persons with Severe Handicaps, 18,* 224–233.

Miron, N. B. (1968). Issues and implications of operant conditioning: The primary ethical consideration. *Hospital and Community Psychiatry, 19,* 226–228.

Morgan, R. L., Striefel, S., Baer, R., & Percival, G. (1991). Regulating behavioral procedures for individuals with handicaps: Review of state department standards. *Research in Developmental Disabilities, 12*, 63–85.

Mulick, J. A. (1990). The ideology and science of punishment in mental retardation. *American Journal on Mental Retardation, 95*, 142–156.

National Institutes of Health. (1989). *NIH Consensus Statement: Treatment of destructive behaviors in persons with developmental disabilities, 7*(9), 1–26.

Newsom, C., Favell, J. E., & Rincover, A. (1983). Side effects of punishment. In S. Axelrod & J. Apsche (Eds.), *The effects of punishment on human behavior* (pp. 285–316). New York: Academic Press.

Nordquist, V. M., & McEvoy, M. A. (1983). Punishment as a factor in early childhood imitation. *Analysis and Intervention in Developmental Disabilities, 3*, 339–357.

Paisey, T. J. H., Whitney, R. B., & Hislop, P. M. (1990). Client characteristics and treatment selection: Legitimate influences and misleading inferences. In A. C. Repp & N. N. Singh (Eds.), *Perspectives on the use of nonaversive and aversive interventions for persons with developmental disabilities* (pp. 175–197). Sycamore, IL: Sycamore.

Paris, S. G., & Cairns, R. B. (1972). An experimental and ethological analysis of social reinforcement with retarded children. *Child Development, 43*, 717–729.

Pfiffner, L. J., & O'Leary, S. G. (1987). The efficacy of all-positive management as a function of the prior use of negative consequences. *Journal of Applied Behavior Analysis, 20*, 265–271.

Phillips, E. L. (1993). *Permissiveness in child rearing and education—A failed doctrine?* Lanham, MD: University Press of America.

Repp, A. C., & Singh, N. N. (Eds.). (1990). *Perspectives on the use of nonaversive and aversive interventions for persons with developmental disabilities.* Sycamore, IL: Sycamore.

Risley, T. (1996). Get a life! Positive behavioral intervention for challenging behavior through life arrangement and life coaching. In L. K. Koegel, R. L. Koegel, & G. Dunlap (Eds.), *Positive behavioral support* (pp. 425–437). Baltimore: Brookes.

Sailor, W. (1996). New structures and systems change for comprehensive positive behavioral support. In L. K. Koegel, R. L. Koegel, & G. Dunlap (Eds.), *Positive behavioral support* (pp. 163–206). Baltimore: Brookes.

Scheerenberger, R. C. (1987). *A history of mental retardation: A quarter century of promise.* Baltimore: Brookes.

Schroeder, S. R., & Schroeder, C. S. (1989). The role of AAMR in the aversives controversy. *Mental Retardation, 27*, iii–v.

Schroeder, S. R., Schroeder, C. S., Rojahn, J., & Mulick, J. A. (1981). Self-injurious behavior: An analysis of behavior management techniques. In J. L. Matson & J. R. McCartney (Eds.), *Handbook of behavior modification with the mentally retarded* (pp. 61–115). New York: Plenum.

Sidman, M. (1989). *Coercion and its fallout.* Boston: Authors Cooperative.

Skinner, B. F. (1953). *Science and human behavior.* New York: Free Press.

Steinberg, L., Elmen, J. D., & Mounts, N. S. (1989). Authoritative parenting, psychosocial maturity, and academic success among adolescents. *Child Development, 60*, 1424–1436.

Stirling, C. S., & McHugh, A. (1997). Natural therapeutic holding: A non-aversive alternative to the use of control and restraint in the management of violence in people with learning disabilities. *Journal of Advanced Nursing, 2*, 304–311.

Straus, M. A., & Stewart, J. H. (1999). Corporal punishment by American parents: National data on prevalence, chronicity, severity, and duration, in relation to child and family characteristics. *Clinical Child and Family Psychology Review, 2*, 55–70.

TASH. (2002). *TASH resolution opposing the use of aversive and restrictive procedures* [On-line]. Available: http://www.tash.org/resolutions/res02aversive.htm

Tennant, L., Hattersley, J., & Cullen, C. (1978). Some comments on the punishment relationship and its relevance to normalization for developmentally retarded people. *Mental Retardation, 16*, 42–44.

Turnbull, H. R. (1986). Presidential address 1986: Public policy and professional behavior. *Mental Retardation, 24*, 265–275.

Turnbull, H. R., & Guess, D. (1986). A model for analyzing the moral aspects of special education and behavioral interventions: The moral aspects of aversive procedures. In P. R. Dokecki & R. M. Zaner (Eds.), *Ethics of dealing with persons with severe handicaps* (pp. 167–210). Baltimore: Brookes.

Van Houten, R., Axelrod, S., Bailey, J. S., Favell, J. E., Foxx, R. M., Iwata, B. A., et al. (1988). The right to effective behavioral treatment. *Journal of Applied Behavior Analysis, 21,* 381–384.

Wahler, R. G. (1969). Oppositional children: A quest for parental reinforcement control. *Journal of Applied Behavior Analysis, 2,* 159–170.

Wahler, R. G., & Nordquist, V. M. (1973). Adult discipline as a factor in childhood imitation. *Journal of Abnormal Child Psychology, 1,* 40–56.

Walters, G. C., & Grusec, J. E. (1977). *Punishment.* San Francisco: Freeman.

Wyatt v. Stickney, 344 F. Supp. 373, 344 F. Supp. 387 (M.D. Ala. 1972).

Gentle Teaching

Chris Cullen
Keele University

Oliver C. Mudford
The Treehouse Trust

SOME CONTEXTUAL NOTES

In order to understand phenomena such as gentle teaching, it is necessary to set the "movement" in its historical context.

The way we treat people with intellectual impairments (mental retardation) has always caused concern for society. In the UK and in the United States, the late 19th century saw the growth of a movement to build asylums in which people who would otherwise be at serious risk of exploitation and harm would be cared for and "educated." Alaszewski (1986) described how intellectually impaired people were often incarcerated in local work houses and private mad houses, in circumstances which caused considerable concern. In England, Parliament set up a Select Committee on Madhouses, which published its report in 1815. This Select Committee obtained and made public the plans for a model asylum. In the middle of the 19th century, it became clear that intellectually impaired people should not be mixed in with the "insane," and the mental deficiency colonies were born. The aim of many of these institutions was philanthropic, and historical evidence suggests that some people's lives were much improved.

However, the asylums soon became places of cruelty and deprivation, losing sight of their original aims. Beliefs in society at large contributed to this. In the 19th century, there were fears of overpopulation and that the "lower orders" in particular were breeding too fast. Utilitarianism was a significant political force, arguing for the greatest good for the greatest number, with the implication that resources for those least able to contribute to society were wasted. Some interpretations of Christianity suggested that intellectual impairment was explicable only in terms of divine will, and therefore the misfortune of "idiots" and "imbeciles" was probably their own fault and certainly not something that others could—or should—do much about. Populist interpretations of evolutionary theory told society that only the fittest should survive, leading directly to the eugenics movement (Rothman, 1980; Scheerenberger, 1976; Tully, 1986).

In the 1960s, there was an increasing number of public exposés of the inhumane conditions in the institutions. Society at large began to realize that something had to be done, and a program of deinstitutionalization began. Part of the solution, though, was to try to improve the lives of individuals in the institutions, because it was clear that their mere closure would not be a solution on its own.

Educators of all kinds had been working in institutions, but research that was first carried out with pigeons in the unlikely setting of the Harvard University psychology department was to have a significant influence. In the 1940s, the work of B. F. Skinner (Catania & Harnad, 1988) and an increasing number of his collaborators and students led to the founding of a science now known as *behavior analysis*. It became clear that by arranging environmental contingencies, behavior would change. One of the first attempts to use these methods led to an increase in the behavioral repertoire of an 18-year-old man described as a "vegetative human organism" (Fuller, 1949). Using a reinforcer of a warm sugar–milk solution, Fuller was able to increase arm-raising from a baseline of once per minute to three times per minute, thus challenging the notion that the man was incapable of learning.

By the 1960s, there were so many published examples of behavior analysis being able to help people that a new journal, the *Journal of Applied Behavior Analysis*, was launched. In their seminal paper, published in the first issue of the new journal, Baer, Wolf, and Risley (1968) wrote that "[b]etter applications, it is hoped, will lead to a better state of society" (p. 91). Although the large majority of behavior analytic work is constructional—in the sense that nonaversive procedures are used to increase behavioral repertoires (Cullen, Brown, Combes, & Hendy, 1999; Goldiamond, 1974)—there are cases where aversive procedures have been used to decrease socially inappropriate behavior (e.g., Axelrod & Apsche, 1983). Usually these are used in situations where they seem to be the only alternatives to help with very serious or even life-threatening situations (Foxx, chap. 18, this volume; Foxx, in press; Mulick, 1990a, 1990b). However, as with any powerful technology, there are those who have misused punishment procedures. Moreover, even apparently nonaversive procedures have sometimes been used to achieve outcomes that are, in the long term, socially dubious (Holland, 1974). One now classic paper complained that behavioral procedures used in the classroom were teaching children to "be still, be quiet, be docile" (Winett & Winkler, 1972).

What was happening was that, at its worst, a powerful behavioral technology was being used in socially inappropriate ways to achieve socially inappropriate outcomes. This is not something which has gone unchallenged by behavior analysts (Sidman, 1989; Wolf, 1978) and, as B. F. Skinner himself frequently pointed out, this is not a problem intrinsic to behavioral science, but is one inherent in the nature of society (Skinner, 1971). Those who would control others will use the most effective and available procedures to do so. When the control is benign, there appears to be no problem. When there is no countercontrol, as is usually the case with people with intellectual impairments, this can lead to an abuse of power.

THE ADVENT OF GENTLE TEACHING

It is against this background that approaches such as gentle teaching arise. The scenario seems to be like this: Some people with intellectual impairments present behaviors that hurt themselves or others, or which otherwise lead to them being devalued; professionals try to help, using behavioral procedures, sometimes successfully and sometimes not, sometimes in sophisticated and valuing ways and sometimes less so, either because some of the interventions have not worked or because they have low social validity (see Wolf, 1978). Usually the cause of "failure" can be traced to individuals who have an incomplete understanding of the science and technology of behavior. They have often not understood the need for an analysis of what has been involved in bringing about the behavior in the first place, nor have they grasped that, whereas it might be relatively straightforward to stop or prevent a particular behavior, replacing it with a socially appropriate alternative, which would be maintained in the person's environment, requires a sophisticated understanding. There is public and/or professional criticism and opprobrium; the criticism and opprobrium attaches to all behavioral interventions, whether successful or not, whether socially valid or not. A "savior" comes forward with alternative ways of dealing with the behavior, arguing that not only are the previous methods faulty, but the analysis of what brings about the behavior is also wrong. This is particularly appealing to those who have not acquired or understood the science of behavior, especially if they perceive the new approach to be easy to use and understand. In fact, approaches which are apparently easier to understand, which appear to be intuitive, and which clearly have at least face validity, especially when they are propounded by compelling and charismatic individuals, often do not have to present data on their efficacy to become accepted by naïve service administrators, managers, and direct care staff.

GENTLE TEACHING DEFINED

The first use of the term *gentle teaching* appeared in professional journals in 1985, although the approach had its roots in earlier work which asserted the importance of the nature of interactions between people: in this case, care providers and service users (Watzlawick, Beavin, & Jackson, 1967). It is worth mentioning that behaviorists have always recognized the importance of the nature of the relationship between people (cf. Skinner, 1953), although much of the earlier work of behavior analysts, with some notable exceptions, had been with individual participants, concentrating less on their relationship with other people than with the identification of important environmental antecedents and consequences.

It is somewhat difficult to identify the essential characteristics of gentle teaching because it is often described in terms of what it is *not*. For example, Brandon (1990) described it as "a profound reaction against often extreme behaviorist techniques" (p. 62) and "completely opposed to punishment and aversion techniques of any kind" (p. 62). The most common descriptions of gentle teaching used terms such as *non-aversive approach, human presence and participation*, and *bonding* (Cheseldine & Stansfield, 1995). For a period in the 1990s, many authors tried to identify the precise descriptors appropriate to gentle teaching, so that they could assess its effectiveness and efficacy as a therapeutic approach, but in recent years this has ceased to be an issue as the term and approach have waned in popularity with staff and care providers. Whereas 10 years ago there were scores of conferences and workshops featuring gentle teaching as the "latest solution" for behavior problems, today a service wishing to have its staff trained in gentle teaching would have to search far and wide for a workshop. More likely than not they would have to turn to the two gentle teaching Web sites.

Current Descriptions

When gentle teaching first developed, there was a group of proponents. The first book-length treatment was by McGee, Menolascino, Hobbs, and Menousek (1987). The second was by McGee and Menolascino (1991). Menolascino, a psychiatrist, had worked earlier with McGee at the University of Nebraska, writing on the importance of humane and valuing approaches to people with intellectual impairments (see Menolascino & McGee, 1981, 1983). Searching for gentle teaching on the Internet now leads mainly to a site maintained by the Gentle Teaching Institute in the Netherlands, and to Gentle Teaching.com, a site apparently maintained by McGee and those devoted to his current activities.

On March 15, 2002, Gentle Teaching.com had posted the following "Primer on Gentle Teaching" (Gentle Teaching International, 2002).

> Gentle Teaching is many things. Gentleness towards others, in spite of what anyone does or does not do, is the critical factor …. Cursing is met with words of affection and nurturing. Spiteful eyes are met with warmth …. It starts with caregivers and, hopefully, touches those who are most marginalised. Its central focus is to express unconditional love. It is the framework around a psychology of interdependence. The main idea of gentleness is not to get rid of someone else's behaviors, but to deepen our own inner feelings of gentleness in the face of violence or disregard. Gentle Teaching is also a teaching approach. As such it has four initial teaching purposes—*to teach others to feel safe, loved, loving and engaged.*

On the same day, the Gentle Teaching Institute had the following on their Web site:

> *Gentle Teaching* is a non-violent approach for helping people with special needs and sometimes challenging behavior that focuses on four primary goals of care-giving:
>
> • teaching the person *to feel safe* with us
> • teaching the person *to feel engaged* with us
> • teaching the person *to feel unconditionally loved* by us
> • teaching the person *to feel loving* towards us
>
> Gentle Teaching is a strategy based on a Psychology of Interdependence that sees all change as being mutual and bringing about a feeling of companionship and community.

It should be noted that these and earlier descriptions of gentle teaching involve relatively vague and ill-defined statements combining both process and outcome. There is no clear description of independent or dependent variables, which makes it very difficult to address questions of effectiveness and efficacy. In some ways, given the obviously laudable aims and processes outlined in these and myriad other quotes, investigating gentle teaching would be seen in the same category as trying to determine whether democracy works; whether Yogacara Buddhism or Mordyamika Buddhism, or Roman Catholicism as opposed to Anglicanism, are better religions; or whether Leon Trotsky or V. I. Lenin had the more accurate interpretations of Marxism. Nevertheless, some have tried.

EVALUATIONS OF GENTLE TEACHING

The first publications specifically mentioning gentle teaching appeared in New Zealand (McGee, 1985a, 1985b, 1985c). McGee was challenged on claims made in these papers and during public presentations, but asserted that gentle teaching had "never failed" (Mudford, 1985, 1995). Several authors have attempted to examine the veracity of such claims made about gentle teaching. Jones and McCaughey (1992) produced a "critical review," examining issues such as the definitions of, and assumptions underlying, gentle teaching; the specific techniques used by proponents; the misrepresentation of other approaches by proponents; whether gentle teaching is aversive or even dangerous; and so on. They concluded that there might be similarities in the specific procedures used in applied behavior analysis and gentle teaching, and that it is inappropriate to dismiss gentle teaching "out of hand" (p. 864). They did, however, identify the need for research and analyses addressing the data, to determine, for example, whether the procedures of gentle teaching result in the outcomes claimed and whether the procedures are more or less effective than other, alternative procedures.

There have been attempts to do this. For example, Jones, Singh, and Kendall (1991) compared gentle teaching and visual screening with a profoundly mentally retarded 44-year-old man. Therapists were trained in behavioral observation, gentle teaching, and in the use of visual screening. An alternating treatments design, along with a no-treatment control condition, was used. Both procedures were effective in reducing head-slapping, with visual screening being more effective than gentle teaching. Other self-injurious repertoires were not affected by either intervention.

Jordan, Singh, and Repp (1989) compared gentle teaching to visual screening with three profoundly retarded people, using an alternating treatments design. Visual screening was the most effective intervention, although gentle teaching was more effective than task training for two of the three people.

Barrera and Teodoro (1990) described a study with a 33-year-old profoundly retarded man, who had an extensive history of self-injurious behavior. They alternated baseline periods of no gentle teaching with treatment phases entailing four formats of gentle teaching. Video samples of the teaching sessions were reviewed by McGee, and his recommendations were incorporated. Barrera and Teodoro found no positive effects for the gentle teaching intervention, even though they were following McGee's instructions.

Cullen and Mappin (1998) introduced gentle teaching into a day center for 13 people with severe or profound disabilities and challenging behavior. Staff were already highly trained in implementing individual educational programs, so the effectiveness of such programming served as the A condition in a simple A–B design. The B condition was gentle teaching, which was introduced by a systematic staff training program. Video recordings were made of staff interacting with students at a number of different times, and real-time observations of student behaviors were made using a hand-held computer. More than 50 hours of video recording and around 45 hours of direct behavioral observations over several months were analyzed. With respect to students' challenging behaviors, there were no changes after the introduction of gentle teaching, as evidenced by the direct behavioral observations.

Among the defining characteristics of gentle teaching, the nature of the interaction between caregiver and client is considered to be crucial. In earlier expositions, this was referred to as "bonding." Jordan et al. (1989) and Jones et al. (1991) operationally defined this as smiling directed at the therapist, physical approaches to the therapist, and making eye contact with the therapist. Both studies found no evidence of an increase in bonding associated with the introduction of gentle teaching.

Cullen and Mappin (1998) also examined this aspect of gentle teaching in more detail. They used two observational systems described by McGee and Gonzalez (1990): the Caregiver's Interactional Observation System (CIOS) and the Person's Interactional Observation System (PIOS). These were said to reflect the essential elements of gentle teaching, viz:

> The continuous delivery of non-contingent value-centered interactions ...; The deceleration of the use of punishment, restraint, and other dominative interactions ... to remove the barriers that impede bonding, friendship, and interdependence; and ... the concurrent acceleration of the caregiver's value-giving and warm assistance [facilitating and leading] to mutual and reciprocal prosocial relationships. (p. 238)

Following the introduction of the gentle teaching intervention, there were statistically significant increases in value-centered interactions and significantly fewer dominative interactions, as measured on the CIOS. With respect to student behavior, there were significantly more interactions on the participatory dimensions. This effect was made up of more "value reciprocation," more "value initiation" during room management, and more "interdependence centering" during mealtimes. Although gentle teaching appeared to have "added value" to the IEP system already in use, the absolute magnitude of the differences was relatively modest.

McGee and Gonzalez (1990) reported a "preliminary study" in a book chapter involving 30 caregivers and 15 persons with "severe behavioral disorders." In this chapter, there was little ranting against behaviorism other than the occasional comment demonstrating some of the more common misunderstandings of behaviorism. Instead, they prefaced their study with a reasoned discourse on the multiple determination of challenging behavior, arguing that the nature of the dyadic relationships which persons with mental retardation have with caregivers ought to be a matter of concern to researchers.

The observational instruments used—the CIOS and PIOS—were comprehensively described. An A–B design was used. Data were presented graphically and tests for significant differences between baseline and the gentle teaching intervention were presented. They concluded that the results "provide tentative support that Gentle Teaching effectuates substantial change in both care givers and persons with behavioral difficulties" (pp. 249–250). They recognized and identified important methodological limitations in such a study—similar to those in the later Cullen and Mappin (1998) study—and go on to say, "Further studies will concentrate on larger groups, more precise analysis of variables and subvariables, relationships between them, and the qualitative dimensions of this change process" (p. 251). We have not been able to find their further studies.

IS GENTLE TEACHING EFFECTIVE?

With respect to how the data reflect on the efficacy of gentle teaching, there have been no reliable studies which would lead us to accept the more grandiose claims of McGee that the approach is "universally effective." Mudford (1995) provided a detailed examination of some of McGee's published data, raising many doubts about the accuracy of McGee's claims. In particular, details which would allow the replication of McGee's studies, or which would allow the verification of his participant details, are notably absent.

Mudford (1995) also reviewed other studies which had independently evaluated gentle teaching. He concluded, "In summary, these independent studies showed the following: 9 clients received gentle teaching and 2 of them benefited by clinically significant reductions in problem behaviors; for 2 gentle teaching increased self-injurious behaviours; and for the other 5, there were no clinically significant changes in levels of behaviors" (p. 351).

Cullen and Mappin (1998) showed that there may be some positive changes in interactions between staff and clients after the introduction of gentle teaching, but that was not surprising, given a highly competent and motivated staff group, trained in the importance of warm and caring reactions. Mudford (1995) pointed out that regular behavioral procedures are usually more effective than gentle teaching when included in the comparisons. Cullen and Mappin (1998) did not find any effects of gentle teaching on their measures of difficult behavior.

In recent years, interest in empirical evaluations of gentle teaching has diminished, and now it is virtually impossible to find published studies. There has been no major data set, or randomized controlled trial, to suggest that gentle teaching *as a procedure* should be taught to staff and used systematically in services for people with intellectual impairments. There have been some reports of gentle teaching being associated with positive client outcomes, and a few examples, usually anecdotal or apocryphal, of its association with negative outcomes. For example, Mudford (1995) reported McGee being shown on Canadian television poking a fingertip under the eye of a client in response to having his (McGee's) hair pulled. However, it would be inappropriate to dismiss gentle teaching outright as a result of such examples, just as we declaim McGee and his associates dismissing applied behavior analysis when they find examples of cruelty being perpetrated in the name of behaviorism.

GENTLE TEACHING'S USE OF BEHAVIORAL PROCEDURES

With respect to the recorded benefits of gentle teaching, it is perfectly plausible to see these as coming about as the result of the use of well-known behavioral procedures. McGee (1992) refers to errorless teaching, task analysis, environmental management, prompting, identifying precursors to target behaviors, reducing verbal instructions and demands, choice-making, fading assistance, and integrating caregivers and peers into the relationship as all being part of gentle teaching. This paper (McGee, 1992) was written for the *Journal of Applied Behavior Analysis*; however, there are many other occasions where McGee presents gentle teaching as the very antithesis of the behavioral approach. In common with McGee, some of those who have espoused gentle teaching have presented it as a clear alternative to behaviorism (e.g. Brandon, 1989, 1990). Others have tried to identify the behavioral procedures used in gentle teaching (cf. Turnbull, 1990) and some have even described it as "behaviorism at its best" (Jones, 1990).

However, it is certain that those proponents who are still "selling" the approach, notably John McGee himself, would resist attempts to describe gentle teaching in behavioral terms alone. Instead, they resort to notions such as "bonding" and "valuing," combining and confusing techniques and procedures conflated with philosophical and value statements.

It is this confusion which, for some, is the attraction of gentle teaching, (e.g. Cheseldine & Stansfield, 1993), whereas for others it indicates a muddle which cannot be resolved (e.g. Bailey, 1992). Gentle teaching has been an approach built on shifting sands. To some audiences, notably behavioral ones, it has been presented as a set of sophisticated techniques that incorporate a humane value system, addressing the issue of behavior problems as one of communication. To other audiences, it has been presented as the antithesis of torture (which is equated with behavior modification) and the solution to many of society's ills. It is the latter stance which seems to be the most favored now, according to the content of the gentle teaching Web sites.

These web pages present a mixture of folk psychology, rhetoric, and unsubstantiated claims. For example, on 15 March 2002, the following was posted: "A sad example … is a woman who was treated with Electro Aversive Therapy for over 22 years. She received over 1,200,000 electro-shocks and still had self-injuries (sic) behavior."

No other information is presented, so there is no way to verify or refute this claim or indeed to ascertain whether it was made up out of whole cloth. Having set the scene, however, the anonymous author then goes on to imply that gentle teaching is a solution. But what is offered is a "psychology of interdependence," which consists of eight "basic values": bodily integrity, feeling safe, feeling self-worth, having a life structure, a sense of belongingness, social participation, having meaningful daily activities, and inner contentment. It is not made clear how these "basic values" relate to the care of the person with self-injurious behavior.

If one were to challenge gentle teaching on this point, it would seem that one is attacking some or all of the "basic values." But who would possibly object to the importance of these? Ergo, it becomes impossible to challenge gentle teaching.

What has happened is that gentle teaching has moved away from being a set of procedures that could be tested for effectiveness and efficacy. It is now more in the realm of a religion which depends for its success on other, competing religions to be seen as "false." Bailey (1992) described this as "euphemism, metaphor, smoke and mirrors" (p. 879). There is no doubt that the eight basic values are laudable, and would be central to the value system of any of us who have devoted our professional careers to the service of people with intellectual disabilities, but they tell us little about what procedures to implement in our efforts to help people.

REFERENCES

Alaszewski, A. (1986). *Institutional care and the mentally handicapped: The mental handicap hospital.* London: Croom Helm.

Axelrod, S., & Apsche, J. (Eds.). (1983). *The effects of punishment of human behavior.* New York: Academic Press.

Baer, D. M., Wolf, M. M., & Risley, T. R. (1968). Some current dimensions of applied behavior analysis. *Journal of Applied Behavior Analysis, 1,* 91–97.

Bailey, J. S. (1992). Gentle teaching: Trying to win friends and influence people with euphemism, metaphor, smoke, and mirrors. *Journal of Applied Behavior Analysis, 25,* 879–883.

Barrera, F. J., & Teodoro, G. M. (1990). Flash bonding or cold confusion? A case analysis of gentle teaching. In A. C. Repp & N. N. Singh (Eds.), *Perspectives on the use of nonaversive and aversive interventions for persons with developmental disabilities* (pp. 199–214). Sycamore, IL: Sycamore.

Brandon, D. (1989, April). How gentle teaching can liberate us all. *Community Living,* 9–10.

Brandon, D. (1990). Gentle teaching. *Nursing Times, 86,* 62–63.

Catania, A. C., & Harnad, S. (Eds.). (1988). *The selection of behaviour. The operant behaviourism of B. F. Skinner: Comments and consequences.* Cambridge, UK: Cambridge University Press.

Cheseldine, S., & Stansfield, J. (1993). *Gentle teaching: A guide for carers.* Glasgow, UK: University of Strathclyde.

Cheseldine, S. E., & Stansfield, J. (1995). Research to practice: An evaluation of gentle teaching descriptors in the classroom. *European Journal on Mental Disability, 2*(7), 3–12.

Cullen, C., Brown, F., Combes, H., & Hendy, S. (1999). Working with people who have intellectual impairments. In J. Marzillier & J. Hall, (Eds.), *What is clinical psychology?* (3rd ed., pp. 112–133). Oxford, UK: Oxford University Press.

Cullen, C., & Mappin, R. (1998). An examination of the effects of gentle teaching on people with complex learning disabilities and challenging behavior. *British Journal of Clinical Psychology, 37,* 199–211.

Foxx, R. M. (in press). Treating dangerous behaviors. *Behavioral Interventions.*

Fuller, P. R. (1949). Operant conditioning of a vegetative human organism. *American Journal of Psychology, 62,* 587–590.

Gentle Teaching International. (2002). *Primer on gentle teaching.* Retrieved March 15, 2002, from www.gentleteaching.com

Goldiamond, I. (1974). Toward a constructional approach to social problems. *Behaviorism, 2,* 1–84.

Holland, J. G. (1974). Political implications of applying behavioral psychology. In R. Ulrich, T. Stachnik, & J. Mabry (Eds.), *Control of human behavior: Behavior modification in education* (pp. 413–419). Glenview, IL: Scott, Foresman.

Jones, J. L., Singh, N. N., & Kendall, K. A. (1991). Comparative effects of gentle teaching and visual screening on self-injurious behaviour. *Journal of Mental Deficiency Research, 35,* 37–47.

Jones, R. (1990). Gentle teaching: Behaviorism at its best? *Community Living, 3,* 9–10.

Jones, R. S. P., & McCaughey, R. E. (1992). Gentle teaching and applied behavior analysis: A critical review. *Journal of Applied Behavior Analysis, 25,* 853–867.

Jordan, J., Singh, N. N., & Repp, A. C. (1989). An evaluation of gentle teaching and visual screening in the reduction of stereotypy. *Journal of Applied Behavior Analysis, 22,* 9–22.

McGee, J. J. (1992). Gentle teaching's assumptions and paradigm. *Journal of Applied Behavior Analysis, 25,* 869–872.

McGee, J. J. (1985a). Bonding as the goal of teaching. *Mental Handicap in New Zealand, 9*(4), 5–10.

McGee, J. J. (1985b). Examples of the use of gentle teaching. *Mental Handicap in New Zealand, 9*(4), 11–20.

McGee, J. J. (1985c). Gentle teaching. *Mental Handicap in New Zealand, 9*(3), 13–24.

McGee, J. J., & Gonzalez, L. (1990). Gentle teaching and the practice of human inter-dependence: A preliminary group study of 15 persons with severe behavioral disorders and their caregivers. In A. C. Repp & N. N. Singh (Eds.), *Perspectives on the use of non-aversive and aversive interventions for persons with developmental disabilities* (pp. 237–254). Sycamore, IL: Sycamore.

McGee, J. J., & Menolascino, F. J. (1991). *Beyond gentle teaching: A nonaversive approach to helping those in need.* New York: Plenum.

McGee, J. J., Menolascino, F. J., Hobbs, D. C., & Menousek, P. E. (1987). *Gentle teaching: A non-aversive approach to helping persons with retardation.* New York: Human Sciences.

Menolascino, F. J., & McGee, J. J. (1981). Persons with severe mental retardation and behavioral challenges: From disconnectedness to human engagement. *Mental Retardation, 19,* 215–220.

Menolascino, F. J., & McGee, J. J. (1983). The new institutions: Last ditch arguments. *The Journal of Psychiatric Treatment and Evaluation, 5,* 187–193.

Mudford, O. C. (1985). Treatment selection in behavior reduction: Gentle teaching versus the least intrusive treatment model. *Australia and New Zealand Journal of Developmental Disabilities, 11,* 265–270.

Mudford, O. C. (1995). Review of the gentle teaching data. *American Journal on Mental Retardation, 99,* 345–355.

Mulick, J. A. (1990a). The ideology and science of punishment in mental retardation. *American Journal of Mental Retardation, 95,* 142–156.

Mulick, J. A. (1990b). Ideology and punishment reconsidered. *American Journal on Mental Retardation, 95,* 173–181.

Rothman, D. J. (1980). *Conscience and convenience: The asylum and its alternatives in progressive America.* Boston: Little, Brown.

Scheerenburger, R. C. (1976). *Deinstitutionalization and institutional reform.* Springfield, IL: Charles C Thomas.

Sidman, M. (1989). *Coercion and its fallout.* Boston: Authors Cooperative.

Skinner, B. F. (1953). *Science and human behavior.* New York: Macmillan.

Skinner, B. F. (1971). *Beyond freedom and dignity.* New York: Knopf.

Tully, K. (1986). *Improving residential life for disabled people.* London: Churchill Livingstone.

Turnbull, J. (1990). Gentle teaching: The emperor's new clothes? *Nursing Times, 86,* 64–68.

Watzlawick, P., Beavin, J. H., & Jackson, D. D. (1967). *Pragmatics of human communication.* New York: Norton.

Winett, R. A., & Winkler, R. C. (1972). Current behavior modification in the classroom: Be still, be quiet, be docile. *Journal of Applied Behavior Analysis, 5,* 499–504.

Wolf, M. M. (1978). Social validity: The case for subjective measurement or how applied behavior analysis is finding its heart. *Journal of Applied Behavior Analysis, 11,* 203–214.

Part VI

Ethical, Legal, and Political Concerns

Ethical Dilemmas and the Most Effective Therapies

Peter Sturmey
Queens College and The Graduate Center
City University of New York

Ethics is a term that is bandied about with a sense of near abandon in the field of developmental disabilities. Broadly, in this context, the term *ethics* or *ethical* is generally used to refer to a position, or rule, stated in the form of a moral imperative, with the implication that if one's conduct is guided by this rule, one will be acting in an ethical manner. Over the past 150 (or so) years of organized developmental disabilities services, these moral imperatives, and therefore the nature of ethical conduct, have changed dramatically, and at an increasing pace during the past 15 years. In some cases and over the short term, changing moral imperatives have consisted of a subtle re-cloaking of past imperatives; on the other hand, some of the more aspirational imperatives of the 1970s that developed as providers and clinicians sought to develop alternatives to then prevalent institutional care have not been completely realized today. Nonetheless, while there are some aspects of ethical conduct that have changed dramatically over time, for example, the conduct of workers within services as the nature of those services progressively changes, there are some aspects, of professional conduct, as a contrasting example, that endure and have not changed to the same degree. This chapter will focus on the contrast between ethical positions set forth in publications within the field, and more typical perspectives in society and among ethicists with respect to how and on what basis conduct is judged to be ethical or unethical.

A SIMPLE ETHICAL ISSUE

Green (1999) published a chapter, "Science and Ethics in Early Intervention for Autism," which I want to present as a point of departure for this discussion and analysis of ethics. In her chapter, she cites "The Right to Effective Behavioral Treatment" (Van Houten et al., 1988) as a basis for ethical practice in applied behavior analysis (ABA). She notes that this document states that recipients of ABA services "... have the right to: (1) a therapeutic environment, (2) services whose overriding goal is personal welfare, (3) treatment by a competent behavior analyst, (4) programs that teach functional skills, (5) behavioral assessment and ongoing evaluation, and (6)

435

the most effective treatment procedures available" (Van Houten, et al., 1988, abstract; italics added). Green contrasts science with pseudoscience. Science is based on publicly observable phenomena, controlled replicable experiments, and clear distinction between facts, opinions, and conclusions; whereas pseudoscience uses some of the vocabulary of science, but appeals to the new and innovative, and does not conduct science itself to back up its claims. She uses the research on facilitated communication as a good example of pseudoscience that led to ineffective treatment, harm to clients by denying them effective treatment, and harm to family members who were falsely accused of abuse. She appeals to the reader: "I hope most behavior analysts would agree that pseudoscientific practices are unethical" (p. 17). (Who has proposed that pseudoscientific practices and ineffective or harmful therapies *are* ethical? The debate is not whether or not pseudoscientific, unethical, and ineffective therapies are ethical, but rather which therapies are effective and what constitutes evidence for effective therapies. Yet, there may be some who *believe* that the therapies they provide are efficacious, despite scant evidence aside from that stemming from such faith.) She goes on to note that there are many certification programs for many therapies, including ineffective and harmful therapies that give the appearance of an aura of effectiveness. Finally, she notes the variable quality of many programs that claim to be based on ABA.

Green ends her chapter with a call for action. The actions she calls for include urging readers to get more data on different forms of ABA, child characteristics, treatment integrity, and complete cost–benefit analyses of ABA. She also calls for reduction of polarization within the behavior analytic community, basing practice more closely on science and certifying practitioners. Finally, she called for behavior analysts to speak out against pseudoscience and ineffective therapies.

A similar appeal is made in Van Houten's (1999) revisitation of the right to effective treatment issue, but his appeal is based on a claim that clients have specific rights related to behavioral treatment.

Where did these rights come from? They did not come from an ethical treatise or from the Constitution of the United States of America. These "rights" are not "rights" in a legal sense; the Constitution of the United States of America does not explicitly guarantee these rights. Rather, these so-called rights are espoused in the work of a committee, admittedly a committee of some of the most influential and well-published ABA researchers in the world, but nevertheless, still, a committee.

Green and Van Houten appeal to the reader for the adoption of the most effective forms of treatment as an ethical thing to do. Their call for ethical action in ABA is an interesting one, but one which I argue actually contains no analysis of ethical issues. Rather, these sources appeal to authority, specifically Van Houten et al.'s position paper, and the right stated therein to the most effective treatment. In this chapter, I argue that this position does not include a systematic and broader analysis of what ethics are, and how they might apply to treatment of children or adults with autism or other developmental disabilities or other members of society. Such documents are rhetorical devices that serve a variety of purposes, but do not contain an analysis of ethical issues. Can we not do better than an appeal to authority in our analysis of ethics? We should consider the manner in which an ethics code is characteristic of a profession. We should differentiate professional ethics from foundational ethics, with the former perhaps derivative of the latter. Consensus on professional ethics does not necessarily mirror an appeal to authority; rather, it reflects a social contract with society, in which professionals are granted certain prerogatives in exchange for accountability in a variety of forms, including ethics as principles or guidelines for conduct. So, what are ethics?

CONVENTIONAL ETHICS

Ethics

Webster's dictionary defines ethics as a branch of philosophy that is concerned with morals and the science of moral duty. Ethics includes a variety of approaches, including ethics based on the greatest good, the search for perfection, and absolute moral standards. Thus, Webster's definition of ethics identifies at least three different ideas about what ethics are. Society enshrines a version of ethics in professional standards, position papers, laws, and regulations. However, it is easy to point out that many things that are or have been legal are not ethical. It has been legal to sterilize, kill, and starve people with disabilities; it remains legal to abort fetuses because they have developmental disabilities. Not everyone would argue that all of these legal acts are ethical. One might also point out that psychological, medical, and other scientists have engaged in many egregious unethical practices, including infecting people with diseases without their informed consent, committing fraud, lying about data and lying about procedures, participating in the murder of people with developmental disabilities, and coercing their scientific colleagues in various ways. Scientists and professionals have no special status or claim to innocence when it come to ethics, and society attempts to protect its citizens from the unethical behavior of scientists, as it does from the unethical behavior of other groups. Similarly, therapists and therapy, including psychological therapies and therapists, may not merely be ineffective and neutral, but may be dangerous and harmful in their practices or behavior as private citizens. Thus, the FDA attempts to protect the public from harmful drugs, such as thalidomide. Likewise, psychological therapies can cause positive harm: Witness the recent case where a client was killed, apparently by her two therapists, during rebirthing (*Colorado*, 2001). Thus, society moves to protect citizens from unethical and harmful therapies and therapists.

Professional Ethical Standards

One source of ethical behavior is professional standards developed and revised by committees that have been set up for this purpose. The American Psychological Association (APA, 1992) promulgates ethical standards for its members. These ethical standards include competence, integrity, professional and scientific responsibility, concern for others' welfare, and social responsibility. In addition to broad and aspirational ethical standards, the APA also promulgates specific ethical standards that prohibit or require certain specific actions from psychologists. Many professional organizations (including those of counselors, occupational therapists, physicians, and behavior analysts) also have similar kinds of ethical standards (Sturmey & Gaubatz, 2003, chap. 2). Indeed, Van Houten et al.'s position paper is one example of such a cultural practice. For some of these ethical principles and specific standards of conduct, there are no corresponding laws or regulations (although in some cases there are; e.g., National Commission, 1979). In addition, many states have practice acts, or regulatory boards that can take actions, that have the force of law. These practice acts or regulatory boards often refer back to professional codes of conduct or ethical codes in order to identify responsibilities and prerogatives. Federal law may also apply to the provision of therapies to people with developmental disabilities. For example, the Individuals with Disabilities Education Act (IDEA) requires that students must receive a Free and Appropriate Public Education (FAPE). Exactly what each of these four words means and how they apply to individual students continues to evolve. Exactly what constitutes an "appropriate" education is not simple. Debate continues over whether anyone, including students with or without disabilities, is entitled to a good, or the best, education. So far, American courts have ruled that students in regular or special education do not have a right to the best education, or even a good education. Thus, it may be legally sufficient to demonstrate any change in functioning as the minimum progress required by law. Where a child makes absolutely no progress, regresses, or is harmed by education, then school districts may have a harder time demonstrating that a legally sufficient education has taken place. Perhaps a carefully documented program of good faith efforts to teach the child might be a defense, but hearing officers and juries may be influenced a great deal by the outcome for the child, even if extensive good faith efforts were made. Similarly, what constitutes "education" is clear neither to lawyers nor educators, and minimal progress seems to be legally sufficient (Driscoll, 2001), even if parents and professionals want more for the children.

Another set of standards for ethical conduct is practice guidelines. For example, the New York State Department of Health issued a series of practice guidelines for both the assessment and selection of therapies in services for young children with autism spectrum disorders (New York State Department of Health, 1999a, 1999b, 1999c). These practice guidelines are not binding on anyone, as they do not regulate any licensed profession or members of any specific profession or have the force of law. However, they create a precedent for professional ethical conduct that might be applied in a judicial context or considered to be precedent-setting. For example, when a specific type of therapy is described as useless or harmful and a practitioner nevertheless proceeds to use the therapy *and* that action results in some harm to the child or someone else, then a case could be made that the therapist did or should have known not to engage in that form of therapy. Further, applying the principles of tort, one could easily argue that the actions of the therapist caused the harm when they had a relationship to the client and a duty of care, and hence, he or she is liable for the harm caused. Of course, if a therapist knowingly engaged in a contraindicated therapy, but obtained informed consent from the parents and guardian, including an explanation of all the risks and benefits of the treatment, then even if harm ensued, they *might* be on safer ground. After all, many of us choose to engage in experimental treatments with uncertain outcomes and negative side effects under certain circumstances; many of us value the freedom to make that choice if we so wish.

Indeed, although people generally disapprove of restrictive or coercive treatments, they may approve of them if they are effective, at least under some circumstances, especially if they are lifesaving, other treatments have been attempted or ineffective, or if a focal behavior involves social taboos (e.g., Sturmey, Thomsett, Sundaram, & Newton, 2003). Many would argue that the central ethical question is not the use of ineffective or harmful treatment, but rather the lack of informed consent and deceptive practices on the part of charlatans or incompetent therapists.

Consider a case of a therapy that practice guidelines had deemed to be contraindicated, and it was unclear if the child benefited or was actually harmed by the treatment. Perhaps the best defense that a therapist might have would be accurate, reliable, and valid data on that child's response to treatment to demonstrate that there was "benefit", or at least a lack of harm to the child. Clinical impressions, narrative notes, and therapist verbal behavior would probably not suffice for this purpose.

Practitioners and researchers are also subject to common law such as malpractice. Malpractice is a *tort*, or wrongdoing, in which (a) a professional relationship exists between two parties, (b) there is a demonstrable standard of care, (c) harm or injury occurs to the client, and (d) the legal proximate cause of harm or injury was the action of the therapist (Bennett, Bryant, VandenBos, & Greenwood, 1990). Thus, practitioners in the field of autism using any kind of therapy may be sued for malpractice if all four criteria for malpractice are met.

PHILOSOPHICAL APPROACHES TO ETHICS

Not only are ethics a code of professional conduct enshrined in law and codes of conduct, but ethics is also a branch of philosophy. Thiroux (2001) distinguishes two broad approaches to ethics. Consequentialist, or teleological, ethics are approaches in which behavior is judged on the basis of its consequences. An action might be deemed ethical because it leads to the greatest good, happiness, or money for oneself, others, or society. Robin Hood might have been adopting a consequentialist ethic when he robbed a few rich people to make many poor people happy. Nonconsequentialist or deontological ethics are those based on some absolute standard; here it would be unethical to consider the consequences of one's actions: One must do what is right. For example, a physician might truthfully tell their patient they are going to die and that chemotherapy is hopeless. They might do so even though they knew it was going to cause terrible distress to the patient and their family. However, the physician might do this from an ethical standpoint that people should be respected and told the truth, irrespective of the consequences.

BEHAVIOR ANALYTIC VIEWS OF ETHICAL BEHAVIOR

Skinner's (1953) model of behavior identified three sources of behavior: (a) behavior that has evolved with the species, (b) behavior that evolved during the course of the organism's lifetime, and (c) behavior that evolves as part of cultural evolution; he termed this last source "group control" of behavior. Skinner discussed how group control took place through controlling agencies such as the government, law, religion, psychotherapy, economic control, education, and through the deliberate design of cultural practices. Skinner argued that group control of an individual's behavior occurred when the group defines behavior as "good" or "bad," "right" or "wrong," and the group applies reinforcement or punishment—often punishment—accordingly. Such classifications of behavior may not be formally codified and may be consequated imperfectly and only by some members of the group. Such contingencies generate secondary punishers, such as emotional behavior called shame. Thus, Skinner considered ethics to be the controlling practices of the group on the individual.

For example, a government may control the behavior of individuals by specifying contingencies of punishment, by taking away a person's property or restricting a person's access to reinforcers, through house arrest. A government achieves this by codifying laws, and assigning tasks of behavior control to different government agencies and parts of agencies. Governments also periodically use punishment with certain citizen behaviors, such as use of the police or armed forces to suppress rioting or to detain potentially harmful citizens. Thus, the law and ethics are examples of one kind of cultural control of the behavior of therapists.

So how do such cultural practices evolve? Skinner (1953, pp. 430–436) hypothesized that cultural practices evolve by contributing to the survival value of the culture. Hence, cultural practices that avoid famine or extinction of too many members of the culture or other aversive states are likely to be selected and maintained within the culture. Diamond (1991, 1998) provided multiple examples of cultural selection and extinction of a wide variety of cultural practices during human history. Thus, ethical behavior may be seen as the product of cultural evolution that contributes to the survival of the culture.

Hayes, Adams, and Rydeen (1994) took this functional analytic perspective on the cultural evolution of ethical behavior and offered a behavior analytic view of ethics, choice, and value based on Kantor's analysis of cultural behavior (Kantor, 1982; Kantor & Smith, 1975). Although Kantor's view of cultural evolution includes many common elements with Skinner's view, there are some differences between these two (Lahten, 1999). Kantor and Smith (1975) distinguished three kinds of behavior based on their origin. Universal actions are those that are shared across members of a species, such as salivation to lemon juice in the mouth. Idiosyncratic actions are those that individuals acquire over the course of their lifespan. These vary from person to person because their learning histories are different. Finally, there are cultural actions that are conventional, limited to the culture in which the person lives and are relatively stable over time. These three kinds of behavior roughly correspond to reactions to unconditional stimuli, the products of individual histories, and cultural or conventional behaviors (Lahten, 1999).

Cultural behavior is limited in distribution over time, geography, and people. It is conventional in that cultural behavior is not based on any other kind of reason. Laws and ethical standards too are cultural artifacts that are often the product of verbal behavior and the special form of verbal behavior called logic. Further, it is arbitrary in that it there are no fixed or absolute standards of the behavior imposed from outside. Hence, Hayes et al. (1994) argued that ethical behavior is conventional, culturally specific and relatively enduring over time—that it is an example of a cultural action. Using this framework, Hayes et al. argued that values are not absolute, but rather, relative, and fairly specific to each society, time, and place. Skinner took a different position from this, arguing that that which is ethical contributes to the survival of the individual and culture. Survival of the culture may not be immediately evident. Cultures change, and some fade away. Thus, both concur that values are not absolute or idealized, but rather exist in the natural world (Lahten, 1999).

IMPLICATIONS OF CONVENTIONAL ETHICS

One might ask a number of ethical questions relating to choosing data-based, effective treatments or fads. Some of these questions are listed in Table 26.1. What do conventional ethics tell us about such choices? Green (1999) *inter alia* and Van Houten et al. (1988) argued that clients have a right to the *most* effective treatment. This standard is not shared with ethical standards. Professional ethical standards may require the professional to do no harm; the law of tort may require a professional not to harm their client; IDEA may require educators to provide a FAPE; however, none explicitly require that clients receive the most effective treatment or education. Indeed, in contrast to Green and Van Houten et al., some elements of society are completely up front that people are *not* entitled legally or constitutionally to the most effective treatment.

When writing about a class action lawsuit in Texas for a mental patient, the Federal Judge could plainly write that the case was about protection of constitutional rights and nothing more: the constitution did not guarantee a high quality program (Pharis, 1999). Articles during 2001 in the *New York Times* reported that state courts have affirmed that typical students have no right to a good education or one that prepares them for a good job (Dewan, 2002). Rather, the state constitution perhaps guarantees them sufficient education to know how to vote, participate in a jury, and get an unskilled manual job, but no more—this differs from state to state. Society is of course free to do more; it may vote in a government that raises taxes and expands the education budget; so far the behavior of the American electorate has spoken clearly on this issue.

If we apply a Skinnerean-like definition to ethical behavior, there does appear to be a society-wide consensus that people with disabilities, as with the rest of us, should be protected from positive acts of harm. However, there does not appear to

TABLE 26.1

Ethical Dilemmas Created by the Use of Nonvalidated or Fringe Therapies

Should clinicians be held accountable for nonhabilitative impacts of nonempirically validated or fringe therapies and how should they be held accountable?

Should professional organizations be held accountable for the nonhabilitative impacts of nonempirically validated or fringe therapies if these therapies have been promoted at their conferences or endorsed by the organization?

Should an organization develop an ethical code of conduct regarding the promulgation of therapies by it or its members?

How should a member of an organization deal with the organization's promotion of nonempirically validated or fringe therapies?

Should an human services agency or school district be held accountable for the nonhabilitative impacts or effects of nonempirically validated or fringe therapies if these therapies have been delivered by employees or endorsed by the agency?

Do professionals have a duty to warn consumers and parents of the nonhabilitative effects of nonempirically validated or fringe therapies?

Should the assessment of whether or not a therapy has empirical validation become one of the responsibilities of an organization's peer review and human rights committees?

Should universities or colleges be held accountable for the nonhabilitative impacts of nonempirically validated or fringe therapies that were part of the curriculum developed and taught by faculty members?

Do developmental disabilities professionals or human services professionals need a Hippocratic oath?

be such a consensus over lack of effective treatment, even when more effective alternatives exist. Likewise, there appears to be a broad, but incomplete consensus within American society that people, including people with autism or other developmental disabilities, do not have a right to the *most* effective treatment or education available (see Table 26.1 for some examples of common ethical questions raised by ineffective treatments).

Thus, position statements, such as those by Green (1999) and Van Houten et al. (1988), should not be regarded as an analysis of the ethical issues, but rather as an aspirational call by advocates for better services for people with disabilities. On the other hand, there are provisions that are more affirmative; for example, the remaining aspects of the Americans with Disabilities Act, the Olmstead decisions, and Good Samaritan laws that prohibit prosecution of health care professionals who provide aid in emergencies in order to encourage such aid. The FDA has banned the purchase of the audiokinetron for auditory integration therapy due to the absence of scientific evidence for its use. Federal rules of evidence stress that expert testimony in fields where scientific methods are relevant must meet demonstrable standards of science, that is, have a scientific foundation.

There seems to be greater consensus within society over other ethical issues related to fads and data-based therapy as opposed to those relating to effectiveness of treatment per se. Professional ethical standards and laws do agree on ethical principles such as honesty and competency. When a therapist misrepresents treatment cost, effectiveness, and outcome, and some harm occurs to the client or others, then society is more likely to agree that this is unethical and that sanctions should be applied against the therapist. Inasmuch as professional societies and large universities have deep pockets and hefty insurance policies, it is possible that they might be held accountable for their actions as well if there is some link between their behavior and negative impact on the client, although universities cannot be held directly accountable under contemporary law for teaching or encouraging the use of ineffective or damaging therapies by therapists who later use these methods in their practices.

Lawyers have no problem rounding up groups of clients who may have been harmed by corporate pollution or drugs that were harmful. Responding to the contingencies of legal work done on contingency fee basis, they have even been successful in leveraging hefty payments from industry for alleged damage to clients when the scientific community concurs that there is no evidence of a causal relationship between the product and the harm that may have occurred, as in the case of silicon breast implants (see Huber, 1993).

As ABA services entered the realm of routine professional practice, the dangers of program dilution and therapist competency immediately became apparent (Green, 1999). Individual behavior analysts—motivated by profit, gratification from family members, professional reputations for Prospero-like powers, and the notoriety, controversy, adulation and shrimp of the conference circuit—are increasingly vulnerable to making excessive claims, shorting the families out of hours, and engaging in hours of billable but ineffective service. In a marketplace where demand far exceeds supply, they may carefully select only the pliant, intelligent families with values and vocabularies most congruent to their own. For-profit companies are motivated by profit. For them, the largest number of families they can sign up and the number of hours they can bill for with the cheapest available labor will enhance their profits most efficiently. Parents or school districts may still pay for less than optimal or even ineffective behavior analytic services, if there are no alternatives if no positive harm is done, or if no one complains. A fad of ineffective, but billable behavioral services could easily evolve in some local cultures. Even not-for-profit agencies have to pay the bills, including the sometimes generous salaries and benefits of their directors and supervisors.

Conventional ethics already has answers to these problems. Individual therapists can be held personally liable for any fraud or bill padding through the law. If they fail to act in the best interest of their client, then they can be held accountable for the harm that they have done in the court of professional ethics.

Implications of Effective Therapies

Previous appeals for ethical behavior by implementing the most effective treatment available (Green, 1999; Van Houten, 1999; Van Houten et al., 1988) focused on the outcome for the client, that is, the avoidance of client harm from ineffective or harmful therapies. By focusing on the most obvious examples of unethical behavior, these analyses have avoided other, equally important ethical questions raised by the presence of effective therapies. For example, such analyses have focused on the child with developmental disabilities, but have not acknowledged other interested parties, such as family members, therapists, impact on services, and impact on society more generally. What does the right to the most effective treatment mean? Does it mean that the most effective treatment must be implemented at any cost? *Should* parents sell their house and cash in their retirement and their parents' retirement to fund the most effective treatment? *Should* other children with disabilities and typically developing children forego a better education, let alone their own most effective treatment, in order to fund the most effective treatment for children with disabilities? *Should* family members undergo extraordinary distress, depression, divorce, or unemployment to facilitate the most effective treatment for a child with a disability? *Should* the development and education of siblings be held back in order to facilitate the development of a child with developmental disabilities? *Should* members of the general taxpayer community work harder and pay more taxes to fund the most effective treatment for all children with autism, which can not be funded out of current budgets (Jacobson, Mulick, & Green, 1998). *Should* resources be diverted from other programs, such as drug programs for seniors or mainstream education, to fund the most effective treatment? These ethical questions have been greatly underplayed in current discussions of ethical of treatment by behavior analysts. This is because current ethical analyses focus on the client and emphasize the contrast between data-based behavioral interventions and other treatments, many of which typically lack empirical evaluation or have been evaluated and found wanting (New York State Department of Health, 1999a, 1999b, 1999c).

One strand in ethical thinking that does address greater societal considerations is that which analyzes the costs and benefits of an intervention. Jacobson et al. (1998) present a cost–benefit model of early intensive behavioral intervention (EIBI), which appears to show massive savings in terms of avoidance of costs of human services associated with reduced use of special education and reduced consumption of adult services. This model has been contested because of possibly making overly optimistic assumptions about the proportions of children who make substantial benefit, for failing to consider the costs and benefits of alternate programs, and for using cost–benefit analysis methodology, as opposed to other costing methods (Marcus, Rubin, & Rubin, 2000). However, the use of cost–benefits analysis as an ethical justification for effective therapies raises some interesting ethical questions. Clearly, this is a consequentialist argument of some sort. The ethical stance here may be that by saving society the costs of services that are not used, society will benefit in terms of increased happiness that results from investing the saved money in other public programs or through reduced suffering for taxpayers who pay fewer taxes and perhaps have to work less.

If better financial efficiency for tax-funded programs is truly the ethical imperative for EIBI, this places EIBI on a very slippery slope. If there were children who did not contribute to society's cost benefit, would we deny them services on the basic of this ethical principle? If new programs were developed that saved society more money, would we advocate for the wholesale shutting down of EIBI, and transfer of the funds to those programs that saved society more money? Probably not! Why? Because, concerns over cost savings are unlikely to be the ethical imperative behind EIBI. Rather, cost savings are another rhetorical device to advance these services, which we believe to be ethical for *other* reasons; if not a rhetorical device, then at the least cost savings are a secondary consideration, except as it may weigh heavily in governmental policymaking.

The underlying consequentionalist ethical arguments for EIBI are various. They include reducing human suffering and increasing happiness, and autonomy in children with autism, their families, and staff. Even if some of these outcomes are very modest for some of the children—those who learn useful skills, but who will continue to have severe intellectual, social, language, and behavioral disabilities—many behavior analysts, other professionals, and staff value these goals alone as worthy ones. Behavior analysts should also recognize other personal consequences of disseminating effective interventions. We gain paychecks, status, and other personal benefits. Reducing one's own suffering and increasing one's own happiness are worthy, ethical goals in many circumstances; (Thiroux, 2001), and we should at least recognize that these are important consequences for ourselves. Another ethical imperative for the dissemination of EIBI is that behavior analysts believe that behaviorism is not merely the basis for effective therapy, but is a coherent and true worldview. In this sense, EIBI is a vehicle for disseminating behaviorism, a vehicle for disseminating a truth, which is a kind of philosophy, the love of truth.

Equity of Access to Effective Treatments.   A final ethical question concerning the existence of effective treatments is that of equity of access and nondiscrimination on grounds of class, race, gender, ethnicity, skin color, religion, age, sexual orientation, language, immigrant status, or other irrelevant personal qualities. If behavior analysis has the most effective treatments, does behavior analysis have a responsibility to ensure that they are delivered without discriminatory practices? Society (in general) and professional codes of conduct and many American laws (specifically) would indicate that they should. And yet, education and health services are pervasively distributed in an inequitable manner, as any sociology textbook shows (e.g., Bilton et al., 1981).

These issues show up directly in the literature on people with developmental disabilities. For example, the mean lifespan of African Americans with Down syndrome in the 1990s was a mere 25 years, compared to an average of 50 years for whites with Down syndrome (Friedman, 2001). No biological basis for this difference in mortality is known to account for this difference. It is much more likely that this difference in mortality is due to inequitable access to health care in general and cardiac care specifically for African Americans (Editor's note, 2001). A similar issue related to ethnicity and childhood disability comes from Sharma, Nicholson, Briderick, and Poyser (2002), who reported higher rates of severe mental retardation, sensory disability, and slight increases in cerebral palsy and autism in children from Pakistani families compared to Continental Indian and White families. They also observed a 10-fold increased risk of genetic disorders. Sharma et al. speculated that these findings may reflect higher rates of consanguineous marriages within the Pakistani families. To date, we have no data on access to behavior analytic treatments and race. Recent scale immigration into Europe, the United States, and Canada has changed the ethnic and cultural mix of these societies. We can not assume that service models that were developed 10 or 20 years ago are uniformly appropriate for our present culture. Similarly, we can not unquestioningly generalize the results of outcome research done in the past with different populations to current populations.

Social class may also an important variable accounting for access to services for people with autism and other developmental disabilities. For example, there is general convergence of findings from several empirical studies that the prevalence of autism, unlike mild and moderate mental retardation of unknown etiology, is not related to social class (Fombonne, 1999). However, there is both direct and indirect evidence that social class affects the likelihood that families of children with autism will obtain access services. Wing (1980) found that fathers from upper socioeconomic backgrounds were much more likely than fathers of working-class background to self-refer to an outpatient clinic and to the National Society for Autistic Children. Schopler, Andrews, and Strupp (1979) compared families with an autistic child and found that those from a higher socioeconomic background were more likely to report an early age of onset, give a more detailed child history, travel further for services, and have greater access to services. In contrast, DeGiacomo and Fombonne (1998) found that social class was not related to age of recognition of onset of autism.

Although not directly addressing social class, there is considerable evidence that parental stress and related family characteristics might be related to social class and access to the most effective treatment. Johnson and Hastings (2002) surveyed 141 families who were receiving intensive early behavioral intervention services for their children with autism. The parents were asked to name common facilitative factors for, and barriers to, the services they were receiving. Commonly named barriers included recruitment and retention of therapists and lack of time and personal energy. Henderson and Vandenberg (1992) found that maternal social support and perceived efficacy correlated with family adjustment to having a child with autism. Inasmuch as the factors identified in these two studies might be related to social class, the two studies also suggest that social class might be important in determining access to the most effective interventions.

An important ethical question that has not been addressed rigorously by the current literature on the most effective treatment is equity of access to the most effective treatment by all families with a child with autism. There is some limited evidence that social class and ethnicity mediate access to treatment for children with autism. To date, research has not yet directly explored this issue. In order to ensure that the most effective services are delivered in an equitable and nonbiased manner, future research should address this question.

Cultural Design and Promotion of Ethical Behavior

Some aspects of this analysis might give the reader cause for pessimism: The values of society generally do not coincide with those of behavior analysts advocating for a better situation for people with disabilities. However, behaviorism is not passive with regard to cultural evolution. Skinner's *Science and Human Behavior* (1953) devotes an entire chapter to cultural design, and his *Walden Two* (Skinner, 1948) was an attempt to outline how to design an Utopian community as well as a statement about what behaviors we should find prevalent in a Utopian community. Some, such as the Los Horcones community in Mexico, have taken up Skinner's challenge and continue to work on the design and evolution of their own culture.

Skinner (1953) argued that the deliberate design of cultures is an activity in which many cultures engage. We place alarms to deter violence. We fine people for double parking. We tax to minimize consumption or remove taxes to stimulate consumption in our own neighborhood. Skinner suggested that much of this deliberate cultural design is operant behavior. We emit such cultural practices to avoid negative consequences such as famine or inflation; cultures that do not have such a cultural repertoire are generally no longer around. Skinner also noted that these cultural practices are emitted not because of the possibility of future or even distant consequences, but because of the culture's learning history and experience of consequences in the *past*. Thus, we might infer that society's general avoidance of implementing the most effective treatment is a practice that has been reinforced. Why does society continue to engage in such practices, even when there might be long-term benefits (Jacobson et al., 1998)? First, it may be that society has not yet come into contact with the benefits of such practices (e.g., the practices may rely on developing technologies). Second, it seems likely that avoidance of such practices has been negatively reinforced through loss of resources and increased effort. The situation seems analogous to self-control problems in which an individual's behavior that is harmful in the long run is reinforced by immediate consequences. Practices do change; for many years, early intervention was funded as a haphazard and almost exclusively state-initiative service. When IDEA was implemented, it required that early intervention be put in place in each state, in order to receive other education funds. The resistance to this new cultural practice is evident in that nearly a decade later, after the enactment of IDEA, many states had only just begun to implement early intervention. It remains a service seldom funded in the manner and to the degree that either preschool services or primary and secondary educational services are funded. Perhaps aversive contingencies for states are an essential component of maintaining this new cultural practice, at least initially. A model of cultural evolution must account for changes as well as resistance to changes.

Implementation of EIBI nationally might be viewed as a nascent indicator of a growing right to treatment. Perhaps in time this might be transformed to a right to effective treatment. It may be useful to distinguish a right to treatment from a right to effective treatment. Prior to IDEA, hundreds of thousands of American children with disabilities were excluded from any form of education. Similar practices existed in the United Kingdom and elsewhere. The precursor to IDEA guaranteed *some* form of education; it did not guarantee the *most* effective form of education. Over time, some children now have gained what their families and advocates believe to be the most effective form of intervention. Likewise, some children have gained access to preventative forms of intervention, some of which are highly effective, such as PKU (phenylketonuria) diets.

Several authors have noted that the behavior of many parents, therapists, policymakers, and legislators is not greatly under the control of data, or least behavioral outcome data from individual clients or programs (Howard, 1999). Yet, I suggest that their behavior is under the control of other data: data on costs, outcomes of regulatory surveys, budgets, and profits. We may regard such behavior as unethical, but it may be a description of the natural world as it is. If this is the case, the gauntlet is thrown down to advocates for the most effective treatments to establish their data as more reinforcing than these other data. How can we do that? Currently we do so by adding punitive contingencies to these other data through due process hearings and court cases. By demonstrating that all a school district or other service provider cares about is the bottom line, but not client outcomes, we shame, coerce effortful responses, and then take away the callous providers' reinforcers. By taking such action, we set up contingencies of negative reinforcement. Unfortunately, the escape behavior of providers associated teaches them to make the minimum responses required to avoid the contingency—to meet the letter of the law—but does not teach the provider to love the most effective treatments and repeatedly approach them because such approach responses are positively reinforced. Can advocates for the most effective treatments design contingencies for providers under which they approach these effective treatments?

A LAST WORD ON ETHICS

Behavior analysts have been very active in advocating for effective behavioral treatments. We cite endorsements from the New York State Department of Health (1999a, 1999b, 1999c) and the Surgeon General of the United States (Satcher, 2002) and readily point to the shortcomings of many other treatments that generally have little empirical basis to support their use. Some may find these endorsements a little too shrill. We should be aware that the evidence in favor of behavior analysis is strong, but imperfect. Further, we know treatment efficacy is important, but not a sufficient criterion for society to adopt an intervention (Howard, 1999). So, appeal to treatment efficacy may help or hinder the evolution of evidence-based treatments; as yet, we do not have the data to see how our culture will evolve.

Let me give Skinner the last word on ethics. Skinner (1953, p. 434) noted that cultural evolution parallels evolution of organisms and the operant. Some mutation or variation in behavior must occur for selection to occur. Some forms of behavior or cultural practice will be extinguished, and others selected, according to Skinner, if they promote the survival of that culture. We can promote such variation in order to design new cultures. Obviously some forms of cultural practices—slavery, aggression, some forms of fertility control—may promote the survival of cultures, but would today in our culture be considered ethically odious. (Who says we will survive, anyway?)

What can we say about these new cultural mutations, the fads *du jour*? Most fads, by definition, are passing and do not endure: They are weeds on the margins of cultural evolution, which grow too tall only to die away when the host culture no longer selects such practices, through punishment or extinction. But what of these other cultural mutations, the newly developed effective forms of treatment? We know that many effective forms of cultural practice arise and rapidly extinguish (Howard, 1999). Diamond's (1998) book is replete with examples of new cultural practices that arose and rapidly extinguished, for example, the possible development of printing in ancient Greece and the arrival of bows and arrows in New Zealand hundreds of years before the arrival of Europeans. Are data-based effective treatments to follow the way of bows and arrows in New Zealand? Skinner (1953) answers this question as follows:

> We have no reason to suppose that any cultural practice is always right or wrong according to some principle or values regardless of the circumstances or that anyone can at any given time make an absolute evaluation of its survival value. So long as this is recognized, we are less likely to seize upon the hard and fast answer as an escape from indecision, and we are more likely to continue to modify cultural design in order to test the consequences. (p. 436)

REFERENCES

American Psychological Association. (1992). *Ethical principles for psychologists and code of conduct.* Washington, DC: Author.

Bennett, B. E., Bryant, B. K., VandenBos, G. R., & Greenwood, A. (1990). *Professional liability and risk management.* Washington, DC: American Psychological Association.

Bilton, T., Bonnett, K., Jones, P., Stanworth, M., Sheard, K., & Webster, A. (1981). *Introductory sociology.* London: MacMillan.

Colorado Governor signs 'rebirthing' ban. (2001). CNN.com/law center. Downloaded January, 23, 2003, from http://www/cnn.com2001/LAW/04/17/rebirthing.ban/index.html

De Giacomo, A., & Fombonne, E. (1998). Parental recognition of developmental abnormalities in autism. *European Journal of Child and Adolescent Psychiatry, 7,* 131–136.

Dewan, S. K. (2002, September 13). Pataki attacks June ruling that 8th-grade education is enough. *New York Times,* Final, p. B6.

Diamond, J. (1991). *The rise and fall of the third chimpanzee. How our animal heritage affects the way we live.* London: Vintage.

Diamond, J. (1998). *Guns, germs and steel: The fates of human societies.* New York: Norton.

Driscoll, D. P. (2001, November 20). *Administrative advisory SPED 2002-1: Requirement to review refusals to evaluate for special education eligibility—Guidance on the change in the special education standard of service from "maximum possible development" to "free appropriate public education" ("FAPE").* Boston: Department of Education, Commonwealth of Massachusetts.

Editor's Note. (2001). [No title]. *Morbidity and Mortality Weekly Report, 50,* 464–465.

Fombonne, E. (1999). The epidemiology of autism: A review. *Psychological Medicine, 29,* 769–789.

Friedman, J. M. (2001). Racial disparities in median age at death of persons with Down syndrome–United States, 1968–1997. *Morbidity and Mortality Weekly Report, 50,* 463–465.

Green, G. (1999). Science and ethics in early intervention for autism. In P. M. Ghezzi, W. L. Williams, & J. E. Carr (Eds.), *Autism: Behavior analytic perspectives* (pp. 11–28). Reno, NV: Context.

Hayes, L. J., Adams, M. A., & Rydeen, K. L. (1994). Ethics, choice and value. In L. J. Hayes, G. J. Hayes, S. C. Moore, & P. M. Ghezzi (Eds.), *Ethical issues in developmental disabilities* (pp. 1–39). Reno, NV: Context.

Henderson, D., & Vandenberg, B. (1992). Factors influencing adjustment in the families of autistic children. *Psychological Reports, 71,* 167–171.

Howard, J. (1999). Data are not enough. In P. M. Ghezzi, W. L. Williams, & J. E. Carr (Eds.), *Autism: Behavior analytic perspectives* (pp. 29–32). Reno, NV: Context.

Huber, P. (1993). *Galileo's revenge: Junk science in the courtroom.* New York: Basic Books.

Jacobson, J. W., Mulick, J. A., & Green, G. (1998). Cost-benefit estimates for early intensive behavioral intervention for young children with autism: General model and single state case. *Behavioral Interventions, 13,* 202–226.

Johnson, E., & Hastings, R. P. (2002). Facilitating factors and barriers to the implementation of intensive home-based behavioural intervention for young children with autism. *Child: Care, Health & Development, 28,* 123–129.

Kantor, J. R. (1982). *Cultural psychology.* Chicago: Principia.

Kantor, J. R., & Smith, N. M. (1975). *The science of psychology.* Chicago: Principia.

Lahten, B. (1999). Ethical behavior. In L. J. Hayes, G. J. Hayes, S. C. Moore, & P. M. Ghezzi (Eds.), *Ethical issues in developmental disabilities* (pp. 40–43). Reno, NV: Context.

Marcus, L. M., Rubin, J. S., & Rubin, M. A. (2000). Benefit–cost analysis and autism services: A response to Jacobson and Mulick. *Journal of Autism and Developmental Disorders, 30,* 595–598.

National Commission for the Protection of Human Subjects of Biomedical and Behavioral Research. (1979). *The Belmont report: Ethical principles and guidelines for the protection of human subjects of research.* Washington, DC: Department of Health, Education, and Welfare.

New York State Department of Health. (1999a). *Clinical practice guidelines: Report of the recommendations. Autism / Pervasive Developmental Disorders. Assessment and intervention for young children (age 0–3 years)* (Publication No. 4215). Albany, NY: Author.

New York State Department of Health. (1999b). *Clinical practice guidelines: Quick reference guide. Autism / Pervasive Developmental Disorders. Assessment and intervention for young children (age 0–3 years)* (Publication No. 4216). Albany, NY: Author.

New York State Department of Health. (1999c). *Clinical practice guidelines: The guideline technical report. Autism / Pervasive Developmental Disorders. Assessment and intervention for young children (age 0–3 years)* (Publication No. 4217). Albany, NY: Author.

Pharis, D. (1999). *State hospital reform. Why was it so hard to achieve?* Durham, NC: Carolina Academic Press.

Satcher, D. (2002). *Report of the Surgeon General's conference on children's mental health: A national action agenda.* Washington, DC: Office of the Surgeon General of the United States, Public Health Service, Department of Health and Human Services.

Schopler, E., Andrews, E., & Strupp, K. (1979). Do children with autism come from upper-middle-class parents? *Journal of Autism and Developmental Disorders, 9,* 139–152.

Sharma, M. R., Nicholson, J., Briderick, M., & Poyser, J. (2002). Disability in children from different ethnic groups. *Child, Health Care and Development, 28,* 87–93.

Skinner, B. F. (1948). *Walden two.* London: MacMillan.

Skinner, B. F. (1953). *Science and human behavior.* New York: Collier-MacMillan.

Sturmey, P., & Gaubatz, M. D. (2003). *Clinical and counseling practice. A case-guided approach.* Boston: Allyn & Bacon.

Sturmey, P., Thomsett, M., Sundaram, G., & Newton, J. T. (2003). The effects of method of behavior management, client characteristics, and outcome on public perception of intervention in pediatric dentistry. *Behavioural and Cognitive Psychotherapy, 31,* 169–176.

Thiroux, J. (2001). *Ethics: Theory and practice.* Upper Saddle River, NJ: Prentice-Hall.

Van Houten, R. (1999). The right to effective behavioral treatment. In P. M. Ghezzi, W. L. Williams, & J. E. Carr (Eds.), *Autism: Behavior analytic perspectives* (pp. 103–119). Reno, NV: Context.

Van Houten, R., Axelrod, S., Bailey, J. S., Favell, J. E., Foxx, R. M., Iwata, B. A., et al. (1988). The right to effective behavioral treatment. *Journal of Applied Behavior Analysis, 21,* 381–384.

Wing, L. (1980). Childhood autism and social class: A question of selection? *British Journal of Psychiatry, 137,* 410–417.

Judicial Remedies for Fads
and Fraudulent Treatment Practices

Edmond Tiryak
Private Practice, Philadelphia, PA

No reasonable observer of human culture and civilization could come away with anything other than the conclusion that our primary, if not virtually exclusive, manner of enforcing behavior is through punishment. The world is divided into nation states which enforce their borders against each other through death and violence, and even the poorest devote significant percentages of their gross national products to ensuring that they possess sufficient firepower to succeed. Within each nation, there are literally roomfuls of books setting forth criminal and civil rules and behavioral requirements, with specific punishments identified for each violation. Each nation, state, county, and township has additional sets of rules, with concomitant punishments. Numerous prisons are built and maintained with which to incarcerate violators.

Even our workplaces typically have volumes of employee conduct manuals, which again demand certain behavioral conduct, and which list the punishments that flow from a failure to behave appropriately. Millions of additional regulatory requirements enforce rules in virtually every area of our lives. The sheer number and levels of rules and punishments, if reviewed on a national or international scale, is staggering. That there are so many levels of punishments which we accept and which form the basis of our everyday lives gives support to the motto of one of George Bernard Shaw's most famous characters: "Nothing is ever done in this world until men are prepared to kill one another if it is not done" (Undershaft weapon's foundry motto, *Major Barbara*, Act III, Scene 1).

Given this uniform and pervasive belief among all world races and cultures that punishment is the primary mechanism to ensure conduct, it would come as a great surprise to most Americans that many governmental entities, not to mention the majority of advocacy groups, have concluded that there is one subset of individuals who, no matter the problem, situation, or behavior, will *always* engage in proper conduct if they are solely provided with positive encouragement to do so. For this group of exceptional people, punishment is never necessary under any circumstances. If most Americans were asked to identify which subset of people in this country were to possess this superhuman quality, it would be reasonable to assume that those with developmental disabilities might well be last on the list of those selected. Whereas society demands that nuns, scholars, and orphans be subject to punishment, people with developmental disabilities require no such sanction.

In this context, it is worth asking and exploring how such a fanciful notion could have gained any significant acceptance at all, much less developed into a consensus in the field. After reviewing how it can be that such ideas could gain acceptance in our field, I discuss the legal risks in adopting these types of politically driven beliefs, how the courts view these types of ideas, and how fads and other fraudulent treatment practices might be subjected to judicial review.

FADS AND IDEOLOGY

It is now well-documented that ideologically driven treatment methodologies are capable of perpetrating vast frauds on people with developmental disabilities. The rapid and widespread acceptance and utilization of facilitated communication (FC) on people with developmental disabilities (Biklen, 1990) was in all likelihood the most significant fraud perpetrated on such individuals since their massive institutionalization in the early 20th century. In my view, such a widespread and massive acceptance of a blatantly carnival-like treatment mechanism could only have been achieved as a result of several independent but related developments in the field. First, given that FC in this context could so easily be established through minimal scientific testing to be a hoax (Gorman, 1998), its widespread acceptance can only be explained by means of a significant trend in the field: to accept ideology over science. Second, the use of FC and other fraudulent treatment practices evidences serious and pervasive flaws and ethical problems in advocacy mechanisms in the disabilities community.

Advocacy and Fads

Imagine for a moment a crisis-stricken family meeting with a surgeon or a trial lawyer, seeking a remedy for some momentous problem that had enveloped them. Imagine further that, after a legal or medical analysis, the sought-after expert offers several courses of action to the family, with an explanation of the risks and benefits of each approach. Now, in this hypothetical situation, suppose an "advocate" for the family (with no degree or particular expertise in the field) announces at the same meeting that "there are no experts" and proceeds to propose an entirely different approach, a technique that the advocate cannot legally provide, given his or her lack of training, and for which there is no scientific support.

In the normal world of hiring experts, can one imagine any result other than the advocate being escorted from the room? Yet, in the field of developmental disabilities, there is nothing at all unusual about this scenario. Many advocates and advocacy organizations openly disdain science and expertise, and adopt virtually as a motto the notion that "there are no experts." Once the notion is accepted that expertise, science, and data are unnecessary, facilitated communication and acceptance of other fad treatments cannot be far behind.

Fads and Ethics

The proper role of advocacy has been undermined by an equally significant other dynamic, which involves ethics. Even though one may not be able to hold out the legal profession as one evidencing a stellar record with regard to ethics, even the dumbest, most unethical attorney is aware of the fact that he or she is an agent for a client. Every jurisdiction in the United States has disciplinary rules for attorneys which demand that the client's wishes be obeyed. Typical of these kinds of rules is Rule 1.2 (a) of the Rules of Professional Conduct of the Supreme Court of Pennsylvania, which says, "A lawyer shall abide by a client's decisions concerning the objectives of representation, ... and shall consult with the client as to the means by which they are achieved" (Supreme Court of Pennsylvania, 1988, p. 10).

No attorney in the United States could imagine that he or she could seek some relief for a client without that client's express wishes, and if the client cannot, by reason of a disability, express such a belief, the Rules permit the attorney to seek a guardian so that there is always a capable client who can provide him with instructions. (See, e.g., Rule of Professional Conduct, 1.14 (b), Supreme Court of Pennsylvania, 1988, p. 39.)

The reason for these rules are obvious: Attorneys have a duty of loyalty to their client, and that duty is violated if their actions on behalf of a client further either the interest of the attorney, or do not follow the client's wishes.

A significant flaw in the structure of disability advocacy is the complete lack of similar rules concerning loyalty and agency. Advocacy groups generally do not feel obliged to advocate on behalf of clients who seek results that differ from the advocacy group's own philosophy. Consider a developmentally disabled client, for example, who prefers to remain in a sheltered workshop, which an advocacy group would consider to be a "segregated setting" and therefore undesirable. Many advocacy groups would make no attempt whatsoever to follow the client's preferences and would simply conclude that the client "needed education" and would advocate for alternatives that allowed the person to make a "more informed decision."

There is no doubt that in this situation, the client's preference could well be the result of habit or the lack of experience in other, more interesting or beneficial settings. So an education effort here could well be worthwhile. Were I representing that client, I would surely advise the client to review alternative settings and would view it as an important part of my job to do so.

However, after providing assistance in reviewing the problem, if my client still insisted on remaining in this "segregated" environment, I would have no choice but to follow that wish. Attorneys have a duty of loyalty to their clients, and in the final analysis, their wishes control the actions of the attorney. The danger presented by current disability advocacy mechanisms is that there is no duty of loyalty to the client: No rule or ethical standard would prevent an advocacy organization from seeking, against their client's wishes, a change in a preferred placement. Advocacy groups not only believe that "there are no experts," they also believe there are no clients who disagree with them.

These twin pillars of ignorance—the disdain for science coupled with a lack of loyalty to clients—can and have created significant problems for people with disabilities and their families. As we shall see infra, the legal system while operating in a deliberate fashion, can be an effective tool to prevent the imposition of fads and other fraudulent treatment methodologies on people with disabilities.

THE JUDICIAL SYSTEM AND PEOPLE WITH DISABILITIES

At the outset, I should note that there is a natural and historic relationship between the federal courts and people with developmental disabilities. Nearly three decades ago, the federal courts began widescale interventions to provide protection for people warehoused in institutions (See, e.g., *Wyatt v. Aderholt*, 503 F.2d 1305 (5th Cir. 1974); *Welsch v. Likins*, 373 F. Supp. 487 (D.Minn.1974), *aff'd in part and vacated and remanded in part*, 550 F.2d 1122 (8th Cir. 1977), retarded individuals involuntarily committed to state institutions have a constitutional right to treatment). And for 20 years, the Supreme Court has afforded significant constitutional protections to such individuals (*Youngberg v. Romeo*, 457 U.S. 307 (1982). Moreover, Congress, in passing the Americans with Disabilities Act of 1990, 42 U.S.C.A. § 12101 et seq. and the Fair Housing Amendments Act of 1988, 42 U.S.C. § 3601 et seq. has significantly broadened the ability of people with disabilities to utilize the federal judiciary to live and work in the community, obtain needed social services, and live free of discrimination.

Given this historic relationship, it comes as no surprise that individuals with disabilities and their families would turn to the federal courts to remedy injuries or other harms created by the use of fads or other forms of fraudulent treatment practices. I shall now explore the benefits and problems associated with the use of judicial remedies in these areas, and review how such cases could be brought and litigated. But first I shall examine some basic legal principles that will enable the reader to fully appreciate the issues involved in seeking judicial intervention in such cases.

Basic Legal Principles

Strengths and Weaknesses of the Legal System in Dealing With Fads and Other Fraudulent Treatment Practices. To effectively utilize the legal system in dealing with the ongoing problem of fads and other fraudulent treatment practices, it is necessary to have some basic understanding about how the system works. A reasoned view of the effectiveness of legal processes in this area leads to the twin conclusions that while legal processes can be slow—and sometimes maddeningly so—they also can provide a very effective remedy.

How Courts Develop the Law. The courts operate on a system of decision making that has at its core the principle of *Stare decisis*. This principle as a general proposition means that once the courts finally decide on a legal principle, they will not change that interpretation except for extraordinary reasons. It is this principle which allows people to write wills or contracts for interpretation decades later, with the firm confidence that the terms of the document will be interpreted in the manner intended, without settled legal principles changing. As Justice Brandeis put it, "Stare decisis is usually the wise policy, because in most matters it is more important that the applicable rule of law be settled than that it be settled right" *Burnet v. Coronado Oil & Gas Co.*, 285 U.S. 393, 406 (1932) (Brandeis, dissenting).

Because final legal decisions have such a longlasting and binding effect, the courts have developed a deliberate process designed to make such decisions wisely. The federal judicial system, for example, has three levels of courts. The federal district courts are the lowest level and are the courts at which trials are held. If a federal district judge makes a legal decision in an area in which there are no prior precedents (referred to in the legal system as a decision "of first impression"), that decision is binding on no other courts at all, although the logic and reasoning used can clearly be reviewed and applied by other judges.

The next level of judicial review is the Federal Courts of Appeal, which cover geographic regions encompassing several states and numerous district courts. These courts hear appeals from the district courts, and their decisions are considered binding in the geographic region that they cover. Although a Court of Appeals decision is not binding on district courts in other geographic areas, or on other Courts of Appeal, the decision is reviewed and given weight by judges in other regions when considering the same issue.

One of the principal duties of the Supreme Court of the United States is to decide cases on legal issues in situations where two or more Courts of Appeal disagree on a legal principle. In these cases, the Supreme Court can decide to hear such cases and finally resolve them and the legal principles involved. By the time that the Supreme Court sets out to resolve such cases, there are usually a variety of appellate and district court decisions available for it to draw on, with the result that all of the competing arguments on all sides of the issue are there for the Court to review.

The result of this process is that whereas an individual person seeking legal relief is able to obtain decisions generally within a year, final judicial determinations of legal questions can take several years to develop. There was a gap of 8 years between the initial district court decision in *Welsch v. Likins*, for example, and the final Supreme Court decision in *Youngberg v. Romeo*.

How Courts Apply Science.   The federal courts have adopted strict guidelines to limit the use of scientific testimony. Under Rule 701 of the Federal Rules of Evidence, the average person is not permitted to testify concerning matters involving "scientific, technical, or other specialized knowledge"; that testimony is limited to expert witnesses. Whether an opinion concerning science may be offered as evidence is dependent on meeting two significant hurdles. The first is Rule 702 of the Federal Rules of Evidence, which provides that:

> If scientific, technical, or other specialized knowledge will assist the trier of fact to understand the evidence or to determine a fact in issue, a witness qualified as an expert by knowledge, skill, experience, training, or education, may testify thereto in the form of an opinion or otherwise, if (1) the testimony is based upon sufficient facts or data, (2) the testimony is the product of reliable principles and methods, and (3) the witness has applied the principles and methods reliably to the facts of the case. (Rule 702, 28 U.S.C.)

This rule requires that before a person may testify about a scientific procedure, a variety of safeguards are applied to ensure that actual science, as opposed to unfounded opinions or philosophy is being offered. In any case, a party could object to the use of their opponent's expert, asserting that the witness is not "qualified," that the testimony is not data based, or that the data are not being utilized in a scientifically reliable or valid manner. When such objections are made, the court will review the testimony, apply the principles of Rule 702 to the testimony, and decide whether the testimony should be allowed.

The second major hurdle potential expert testimony has to overcome before it may be heard in a case are the precepts set forth by the Supreme Court of the United States in *Daubert v. Merrell Dow Pharmaceuticals, Inc.*, 509 U.S. 579 (1993). That decision significantly affected the manner in which scientific information may be presented through expert witnesses, and the decision has enormous implications for litigation involving fads and other fraudulent treatment practices.

For 70 years prior to the *Daubert* decision, the courts had permitted expert scientific testimony based on representations that the scientific issue to be discussed was " 'generally accepted' as reliable in the relevant scientific community" (see, e.g., *Frye v. United States*, 293 F. 1013, 1014 (1923). Over the years, that standard had broadly been interpreted to permit expert testimony in a whole host of areas.

The Supreme Court, in *Daubert*, substantially changed these standards, and required that "the trial judge must ensure that any and all scientific testimony or evidence admitted is not only relevant, but reliable" (509 U.S. at 589). Moreover, in the event that the scientific validity of an expert's opinion is challenged, the Supreme Court required that the trial court conduct an inquiry or hearing, outside of the hearing of the jury, to determine the validity of the expert's opinions before that expert may testify. "The inquiry envisioned by Rule 702 is, we emphasize, a flexible one. Its overarching subject is the scientific validity and thus the evidentiary relevance and reliability—of the principles that underlie a proposed submission" (509 U.S. at 594–595).

The Supreme Court instructed trial courts to conduct "a preliminary assessment of whether the reasoning or methodology underlying the testimony is scientifically valid" (509 U.S. at 593). "Ordinarily, a key question to be answered in determining whether a theory or technique is scientific knowledge that will assist the trier of fact will be whether it can be (and has been) tested" (509 U.S. at 593).

According to the Supreme Court, "Another pertinent consideration is whether the theory or technique has been subjected to peer review and publication" (509 U.S. at 593). Although the Court stated that publication did not necessarily prove the validity of the science in a work, "submission to the scrutiny of the scientific community is a component of 'good science,' in part because it increases the likelihood that substantive flaws in methodology will be detected" (509 U.S. at 593).

Other factors that the trial court should consider before permitting expert testimony include "the known or potential rate of error" and "the existence and maintenance of standards controlling the technique's operation" (509 U.S. at 594).

In my view, the heightened scrutiny required of experts and expert testimony by the Supreme Court can only aid people with disabilities and their attorneys in using the judicial forum to rid themselves of fads and other fraudulent treatment methods. This heightened scrutiny may, in some instances, turn close cases into clear victories.

I now examine how these principles would likely be applied in a case involving fads. Indeed, in my view, it is likely that the next major civil rights issue that will be decided could be a test of the scientific validity of the concept of Positive Approaches.

THE NEXT MAJOR CIVIL RIGHTS ISSUE EXAMINED

Charlie, a person with developmental disabilities, lives in a group home operated by Positive Approaches Corporation ("PA Corp."), with another resident, "Mark," who has significant and dangerous aggressive behaviors. PA Corp. has adopted Positive Approaches as its sole method of managing behavior and has eschewed other applied behavior analysis (ABA) principles in attempting to reduce or eliminate Mark's aggression. Mark seriously injures Charlie, whose parents hire counsel to sue PA Corp.

Note that there are at least two significant legal theories which could be advanced in this circumstance to establish negligence or worse. The first legal theory was that PA Corp. failed to utilize scientifically proven principles to deal with the challenging behaviors. This legal argument would essentially be that the use of Positive Approaches itself amounts to negligence.

But an equally important second legal theory exists. It would contend that PA Corp. never considered and never advised Mark's family of the existence of other ABA treatment regimens. In essence, this argument says that PC Corp. chose ideology (which ruled out kindred methods) over science, and never advised or obtained consent to do so.

There is no question in this situation that the plaintiff's attorney could obtain an ABA-trained psychologist and qualify him or her as an expert. That expert could review the numerous peer-reviewed and published studies showing a variety of techniques that have been proven effective in reducing or eliminating Mark's type of aggression. That expert could testify that these scientifically tested behavioral techniques were never considered, much less implemented by PA Corp., and that Charlie was seriously injured as a result.

In my view, this would be a strong case for the plaintiff even if the defense were permitted to present a Positive Approaches expert to the jury. But given the recent rulings about scientific validity, there is a very serious question whether such an expert would even be viewed as an expert by a Federal Court. In order to qualify such a witness over the plaintiff's objection, *Daubert* requires a hearing at which time the court would need to decide whether Positive Approaches had "scientifically valid" reasoning or methodology, whether that theory can be and has been tested, whether the theory has been subjected to peer review and publication, and the known or potential rate of error of the technique.

In my view, there is a substantial probability that Positive Approaches cannot meet these standards. While I review the reasons infra, it is worth noting first that if PA Corp.'s expert is disqualified from testifying in the a case, victory is all but assured for the plaintiff. What was a strong case for liability becomes virtually guaranteed. The jury would hear expert testimony that PA Corp.'s methods were improper, with no expert to even dispute the point. Simply put, those individuals or companies who use these principles in providing treatment for dangerous behaviors should take note.

Federal Courts would not, in my opinion, accept Positive Approaches as a scientifically valid basis for expert testimony, for the reason that Positive Approaches is a belief, value, or ideology, not a scientifically based theory. At the core of the concept is the notion that no human on earth with any constellation of problem behaviors would under any circumstances ever require any sort of punishment to change. Indeed, the use of any punishment at all is a certain disqualification for status as a practitioner of Positive Approaches. If you ever believe punishment is necessary, you are not, by definition, an adherent of this approach.[1]

This basic principle that punishment is always unnecessary is not science. Like discussions about the existence of God, it is not susceptible to being proven or disproven. It is either believed or not believed. And under the right circumstances it would be unlikely, in my opinion, that a Federal Judge would conclude that Positive Approaches is scientifically valid, given that it cannot be proven or disproven.

The major point here is not that Positive Approaches can never work. Certainly, the use of positive reinforcement for behavior change is a universally accepted principle. The least restrictive alternative (LRA) model insists that positive reinforcement be attempted to deal with problem behaviors initially, at least in cases where such methods have been proven effective, or when the risks of using positive approaches are warranted. In these cases, the LRA model requires that more restrictive approaches not be attempted until the positive ones are demonstrably futile.[2] The distinction between the two approaches is that whereas the LRA accepts that punishment may be used as a behavior tool when all else fails, proponents of positive approaches assert that this is never necessary.

There are two points here worth considering. The first is that if a LRA model is applied, and all behavior would respond to positive approaches at all times, then the use of the LRA model would always result in the use of positive means in all cases. Indeed, if there were merit to the position that reinforcement always worked, the LRA model would already have established this fact and there would be no need for Positive Approaches in the first place.

Finally, and most importantly, the core principle of Positive Approaches—that all behavior of persons with disabilities can be altered by positive reinforcement—cannot be proven in any scientific manner. But in my view, it can be disproven, and there is evidence that the approach is ideologically and not scientifically driven and ultimately harmful to those persons it was designed to assist.

In my experience, there has been a significant increase in the number of persons with developmental disabilities who are diagnosed with mental illness and who receive psychiatric medications since Positive Approaches arrived on the scene. Individuals residing in group homes, which formerly prided themselves on being able to deal with the most challenging behaviors, now use drugs and psychiatric hospitalizations as a remedy for behavioral problems.

I recently was involved in a case involving the deinstitutionalization of a State Center for people with developmental disabilities, and watched as advocacy groups created more and more obstacles to behavioral management efforts. Even-

---

[1] I am defining Positive Approaches here consistent with the vast majority of groups and practitioners who consider the theory to exclude the use of punishment in all cases. There is a minority of practitioners who consider this theory to be the preferred method of treatment, but who recognize that punishment may be used when positive approaches do not succeed, or when the behaviors are so inherently dangerous that the risk of attempting positive methods is too high. The points I make *infra* have no applicability to this second group.

[2] One point not recognized by many Positive Approaches advocates is that the use of positive approach mechanisms that have not been proven in the literature to be effective would constitute engaging in research without all the safeguards required.

tually, they created so many procedural roadblocks to behavioral treatment that such treatment essentially ceased to be provided. The result was that larger and larger numbers of institutionalized individuals suddenly evidenced psychiatric symptoms, were diagnosed with mental illness, and were treated with medications.

A more cynical observer than I could note, with evidentiary support, that there was proof that the presence of advocacy groups on the campus was clearly linked to substantially increased levels of mental illness in the residents. A cheap shot? Perhaps. But advocacy positions which result in large numbers of persons for whom you advocate being classified as mentally ill and requiring psychotropic medication raises serious issues that cannot be explained away with ideological slogans.

CONCLUSION

The core belief among most Positive Approaches advocates, that all behavior can be addressed through solely positive mechanisms, is an ideology, not a scientifically valid conclusion. The sad part of this extreme position is that it is quite unnecessary to the Positive Approaches position. There is no question that in many respects, Positive Approaches can do much good. It recognizes and reaffirms the integrity of disabled persons, advances the view that the environment has fundamentally powerful effects on behavior, and represents a necessary reaction to some of the poorly conceived and designed behavioral oriented approaches that were used in the 1970s.

Today, virtually any behavioral consultant would most certainly reject the use of punishment prior to taking significant steps towards positive reinforcement, environmental changes, and similar techniques. To that extent, Positive Approaches advocates have won the day and deservedly so. It is the next step taken by Positive Approaches advocates, that is, the concept of banning all punishments no matter the circumstances while vilifying those who disagree in the process, that crosses the line.

A relevant analogy might be to the medical community, where there is a belief that some surgeons adopt a surgical approach too quickly. Other physicians take a more conservative approach and would recommend a variety of less invasive techniques before surgery is used. As long as they counsel their patients on the risks and benefits of such a position, it would seem that this approach was reasonable and proper.

But suppose some physicians, in a outbreak of zealousness, took the position that no surgery was ever needed on any patient for any reason? And that those who perpetrated the outrage of surgery should be driven from the profession? Such an approach would surely be rejected as unscientific and unprofessional, and clearly not in the best interest of patients. But more than that, it would be unnecessary to convey the point that was initially intended.

So too it is with Positive Approaches. Starting with a premise of respecting each individual's innate integrity, the movement has turned to an extreme position that has no scientific basis, restricts professional options, and has perpetrated great injury to professionals who disagree.

I have established that significant numbers of advocates and professionals in the field of developmental disabilities have eschewed science, instead adopting ideology over data, and their own beliefs over their loyalty to the people with disabilities that they seek to represent. As it was with other serious harms inflicted by our society on people with disabilities, the legal system stands ready to once again provide a remedy for injuries inflicted by fads and other fraudulent treatment practices. The courts have had to choose between ideology and science, and the verdict is in: The courts have chosen science.

REFERENCES

Americans with Disabilities Act of 1990, 42 U.S.C.A. § 12101 et seq.

Biklen, D. (1990). Communication unbound: Autism and praxis. *Harvard Educational Review, 60,* 291–314.

Burnet v. Coronado Oil & Gas Co., 285 U.S. 393, 406 (1932) (Brandeis, dissenting).

Daubert v. Merrell Dow Pharmaceuticals, Inc., 509 F. 579 (1993).

Fair Housing Amendments Act of 1988, 42 U.S.C. § 3601 et seq.

Frye v. United States, 293 F. 1013, 1014 (1923).

Gorman, B. J. (1998). Facilitated communication in America: Eight years and counting. *Skeptic, 6*(3), 64–71.

Major Barbara, Act III, Scene 1.

Rule 1.2 (a) of the Rules of Professional Conduct of the Supreme Court of Pennsylvania (Supreme Court of Pennsylvania, 1988, p. 10).

Rule 1.14 (b) of the Rules of Professional Conduct of the Supreme Court of Pennsylvania, (Supreme Court of Pennsylvania, 1988, p. 39).

Rule 702, Federal Rules of Evidence, 28 U.S.C.

Satcher, D. (2002). *Report of the surgeon General's conference on children's mental health: A national action agenda.* Washington, DC: Office of the Surgeon General of the Unites States, Public Health Service, Department of Health and Human Services.

Wyatt v. Aderholt, 503 F.2d 1305 (5th Cir. 1974).

Welsch v. Likins, 373 F. Supp. 487 (D.Minn.1974), aff'd in part and vacated and remanded in part, 550 F.2d 1122 (8th Cir. 1977).

Youngberg v. Romeo, 457 U.S. 307 (1982).

The National Institutes of Health Consensus Development Conference on the Treatment of Destructive Behaviors: A Study in Professional Politics

Richard M. Foxx
Penn State Harrisburg

Newsom and Kroeger (chap. 24, this volume) provide an excellent overview of the genesis, principal players, organizations, and tactics of the nonaversive treatment movement. Perhaps no other event more clearly illustrates the movement's willingness to dismiss science and reasonableness and play hard ball than its actions surrounding the National Institutes of Health (NIH) Consensus Development Conference (CDC) on the Treatment of Destructive Behaviors in Persons with Developmental Disabilities in 1989.

NIH CDCs are intended to help clinicians by creating an authoritative, credible consensus statement that sums up the scientific evidence on treatments for a specific condition. A broad-based panel chosen by a planning committee issues the consensus statement after evaluating both scientific evidence from topic experts and statements from interested parties, and responding to a series of previously posed questions. The Consensus Statement is an independent report and not a policy statement of the NIH or Federal Government (NIH, 1989).

The CDC program was begun in 1977 and, on average, seven conferences are held each year. CDCs are jointly sponsored and administered by one or more NIH agencies and sometimes cosponsored by other Federal agencies or private professional organizations (NIH, 1989). The typical CDC lasts 2½ days. The first day and a half is a plenary session in which invited experts present scientific evidence on the consensus topic. Panelists, speakers, and the audience have ample opportunity for open discussions. During the afternoon and evening of the second day, the panel meets in executive session and drafts the consensus statement. The following morning, the statement is presented publicly to the audience, modified at the discretion of the panel on the basis of any comments, and adopted. The consensus statement that emerges is widely circulated through both the lay and scientific/professional media. NIH considers public participation, in a town meeting tradition, to be crucial to the development of the consensus position.

The CDC on treatment of destructive behaviors was held September 11–13, 1989. It was sponsored by the National Institute of Child Health and Human Development (NICHHD) and by the Office of Medical Applications of Research (OMAR). Cosponsors were the National Institute of Neurological Disorders and Stroke, the National Institute of Mental Health, and the Bureau of Maternal and Child Health and Resources Development of the Health Resources and Services Administration. The impetus for the conference was the need to scientifically clarify a raging public controversy on the use of various treatment modalities, for example, punishment/aversives for the treatment of the destructive behaviors. This controversy/topic clearly fit within the CDC's scope and purpose of publicly evaluating a body of scientific information and arriving at a Consensus Statement that would be useful to practitioners, the public, and scientists.

The topic also met the three CDC selection criteria:

1. It was medically important and had a potential for impact. Destructive behavior, either aggression toward others or self-injurious behavior (SIB), clearly qualified given the numbers of developmentally disabled persons who suffer from chronic, violent SIB, including constant head-banging, eye-gouging, or biting off their own fingers or severely injuring others (Foxx, 2003). For the CDC to be useful, there had to be either a gap between knowledge and practice and/or a scientific controversy that the CDC would clarify.
2. It could be adequately defined and had an available science base that could be examined.
3. It was thought be resolvable on technical grounds and the outcome should not depend mainly on the value judgments of the CDC panelists (NIH, 1989).

THE PLANNING COMMITTEE

Once the topic was selected and defined, a formal planning committee met. The committee consisted of a parent of an individual with a developmental disability, expert consultants and representatives from all of the sponsoring agencies as well as the U.S. Department of Education, the Administration on Developmental Disabilities, the Health Resources and Services Administration, the Department of Health and Human Services, and the President's Committee on Mental Retardation. Some members of the committee included Duane Alexander, Director of NICHD; Thomas Bellamy; Michael Cataldo; Eleanor Dibble; Carolyn Doppeit Gray; David Gray; James Hill, Chief of the Office of Planning and Evaluation of NICHD; Sharon Landesman; Stephen Schroeder; and Robert Sprague. R. Rodney Howell, Professor and Chairman of the Department of Pediatrics at the University of Miami School of Medicine, served on the planning committee and was selected by it to serve as chair of the CDC Panel.

The planning committee had several tasks. One, it identified the disciplines to be represented on the panel and individuals from them who would serve as panel members. Given the controversy, it was critical that the composition of the panel be constructed to insure that there was a balanced mixture of expertise and disciplines that would permit the panel to understand the range of issues being addressed (NIH, 1989). Two, it formulated the consensus questions that would be addressed because they would determine the scope and substance of the conference. Three, it identified the topics of background papers to be prepared prior to the CDC and the scientists qualified to develop them. Four, it selected the conference's invited experts.

THE PANEL

A panel generally includes active researchers in the topic, professionals who employ the technology, methodologists or evaluators, and public representatives such as lawyers, ethicists, consumers, parents, or patients. Such a broad range of panelists bolsters the credibility of the Consensus Statement because the conclusions come from more than proponents or practitioners of a technology/topic (NIH, 1989). Indeed, the NIH guidelines are very clear that during their deliberations, panel members are expected to express intellectual differences of opinion and views, be thoughtful, able to weigh data, capable of compromise, and ultimately seek consensus. Overall, the responsibilities of the panel are "to be objective in reaching consensus without prejudgment or promotional position with respect to the consensus topic" after listening to the speakers and experts, reading background reports and speakers' papers, and addressing the previously posed questions (NIH, 1989). Howell, the panel chair, participated in all steps of the conference planning and chaired the CDC plenary session and panel deliberations. His charge was to "maintain a balanced interest in, and sensitivity to, the range of data and opinions brought to bear on the consensus topic" (NIH, 1989).

The panel members were David Braddock, Director of the UAF Program, University of Illinois at Chicago; Joseph Brady, Professor of Behavioral Biology and Neuroscience, Johns Hopkins School of Medicine; Robert Cooke, Parent and Professor Emeritus of Pediatrics from SUNY Buffalo; Jo Ann Derr, Parent, Department of Mental Retardation, Commonwealth of Massachusetts; Joseph French, Clinical Professor of Neurology and Pediatrics, SUNY Health Center; Leonard Krasner, Clinical Professor, Department of Psychiatry and Behavioral Science, Stanford University School of Medicine; Marty Wyngaarden Krauss, Director of Social Research, Eunice Kennedy Shriver Center; Victor Laties, Professor of Toxicology, Pharmacology, and Psychology, University of Rochester School of Medicine and Dentistry; Gerald Nord, Department of Human Services, State of Minnesota; Joseph Noshpitz, Clinical Professor of Psychiatry and Behavioral Science, George Washington University; Gene Sackett, Associate Director, Child Development and Mental Retardation Center, University of Washington; Sara Sparrow, Professor and Chief Psychologist, The Child Study Center of Yale University School of Medicine; and Naomi Zigmond, Special Education Program, University of Pittsburgh School of Education.

CONSENSUS STATEMENT QUESTIONS

Six questions served as the basis for the CDC:

1. What are the nature, extent, and consequences of destructive behaviors in persons with developmental disabilities?
2. What are the approaches to prevent, treat, and manage these behaviors?
3. What is the evidence that these approaches, alone or in combination, eliminate or reduce destructive behaviors?
4. What are the risks and benefits associated with the use of these approaches for the individual, family, and community?
5. Based on the answers to the questions 1–4 and taking into account (a) the behavior; (b) the diagnosis and functional level of the individual; (c) possible effects on the individual, family, and community; (d) the treatment setting; and (e) other factors, what recommendations can be made at present regarding the use of the different approaches?
6. What research is needed on approaches for preventing, treating, and managing destructive behaviors in persons with developmental disabilities?

BACKGROUND PAPERS AND BIBLIOGRAPHY

The panel first met in December 1988 and received an extensive bibliographic search on the treatment of destructive behaviors that examined six databases. Detailed plans for the background papers were also presented. The bibliography was updated 2 months prior to the conference and contained 751 references (Patrias & Gray, 1989).

The planning committee chose five background papers to be written for the panel and conference:

1. "Treatment of Destructive Behaviors Among People With Mental Retardation and Developmental Disabilities: Overview of the Problem" (Schroeder, Rojahn, & Oldenquist, 1991).
2. "Reinforcement and Stimulus-Based Treatments for Severe Behavior Problems in Developmental Disabilities" (Carr, Taylor, Carlson, & Robinson, 1991).
3. "The Effects of Punishment and Other Behavior Reducing Procedures on the Destructive Behaviors of Persons With Developmental Disabilities" (Cataldo, 1991).
4. "Pharmacological Treatments for Behavior Problems in Developmental Disabilities" (Thompson, Hackenberg, & Schaal, 1991).
5. "Overview of the Neurobiology of Pain and Its Relationship to SIB" (French, 1991).

TREATMENT APPROACHES REVIEWED

Four approaches were identified as being used in the prevention, treatment, and management of destructive behaviors: behavioral, educational, ecological, and pharmacological (NIH, 1991).

The behavioral approaches were further divided into reduction and enhancement approaches. Behavior reduction approaches were functionally defined as punishment (e.g., faradic shock, overcorrection, time-out, response cost, etc.) although extinction was included. Thus, examples of "aversive techniques" ranged from withdrawing attention to SIBIS, a new electric shock device (Holden, 1990). Enhancement approaches consisted of two broad classes: differential reinforcement of other behavior (DRO) and differential reinforcement of incompatible behavior (DRI).

Educational/skills acquisition approaches were defined as reinforcing responses that are believed to enhance the individual's ability to perform competently in the daily environment. The emphasis was on teaching new behaviors likely to increase the person's social competence. Four approaches were listed: compliance training, self-management training (self-monitoring, evaluation, and reinforcement), communication skills training (replacement of destructive behavior by new requesting forms that enhance the individual's social interactions), and functional independence training (training socially useful behaviors to correct deficits presumed to trigger destructive behavior). Functional analysis was considered to be an essential step.

Ecological approaches and stimulus-based treatments were defined as identifying the triggers for destructive behavior as well as the situations and settings that are correlated with low rates of destructive behavior. After this identification, stimuli that evoke destructive behaviors are modified to reduce their triggering function, and situations correlated with low rates of destructive behavior are scheduled more frequently throughout the day. The literature for this approach was noted to be relatively new.

Pharmacological methods used to reduce destructive behavior either directly or indirectly included neuroleptics, sedative-hypnotics, stimulants, antianxiety drugs, antidepressants and mood stabilizers, anticonvulsants, and antihypertensives.

PANEL MEETINGS PRIOR TO THE CONFERENCE

Four subsequent panel meetings were held in which the background papers were presented by their authors and extensively discussed and reviewed by the panel. The papers' authors made substantial revisions based on the panel's questions and feedback (NIH, 1991).

INVITED EXPERTS

The speakers selected by the planning committee were Alfred Baumeister, Magda Campbell, Judith Favell, Richard Foxx, Barbara Herman, Robert Horner, Brian Iwata, Thomas Linschied, William Nyhan, Raymond Romanczyk, Murray Sidman, Robert Sprague, Paul Touchette, and David Wacker. Gary LaVigna was added the day of the conference to apparently appease nonaversive adherents. Prior to the conference, the speakers provided abstracts of their presentations for the panel and participants.

CONFERENCE PLANNING AND PUBLICITY

In January 1989, NIH made a broad and concerted effort to involve the greatest possible number of interested participants, organizations, and agencies in order to give them sufficient time to indicate whether they wished to participate in the public conference presentations. In July 1989, more than 13,000 announcements inviting participation were mailed to groups and individuals with an interest in the topic. There was a *Federal Register* announcement.

PUBLIC SPEAKERS

Based on their spoken and written comments, the public speakers represented two clearly distinct groups (NIH, 1991). One group consisted of individuals supporting the use of science, options, and rationality in treatment decisions. It included scientists and professionals, John Jacobson, representing American Psychological Association, Division 33, the Division of Mental Retardation and Developmental Disabilities; Saul Axelrod, representing the Association for Behavior Analysis; James Harris, representing the American Academy of Child and Adolescent Psychology; David Holmes, Executive Director of the Eden Institute; Michael Hazel, the developer of the Self-Injurious Behavior Inhibiting System (SIBIS); and two parents and one grandparent. The other group consisted of individuals representing advocacy groups/organizations that were antiaversive/punishment in their resolutions, political efforts, publications, and rhetoric. This group included Jim Ellis, American Association on Mental Retardation (AAMR); Martha Snell, The Association for Persons with Severe Handicaps (TASH); Colleen Wieck, Association for Retarded Citizens (ARC); Tom Nerney, Autism Society of American (ASA); Ralph Maurer, Advocacy Center for Persons with Disabilities (ACPD); Jane Salzano, Community Services for Autistic Adults and Children (CSAAC); and Joni Fritz, National Association of Private Residential Resources (NAPRF).

THE CONFERENCE

The conference began with opening remarks, a charge to the Panel, and Howell's discussion of the Panel's activities to date. The expert presentations followed with each speaker and discussion session having 15 minutes. The morning session featured the Origins of Destructive Behavior (Baumeister, Favell, & Nyhan), discussion, the Definition of the Problem (Sackett), discussion, Description of Interventions (Brady), Criteria for Selection of Interventions (Cooke), discussion, Evidence of Effectiveness (Zigmond), discussion, and Presentation of Critical Issues (Howell). The afternoon session included Deceleration and Elimination Treatments (Linscheid, Foxx, & Romanczyk), Behavioral Treatments (Sidman), discussion, Pharmacological Treatments (Sprague, Campbell, & Herman), discussion, Positive Reinforcement Therapies (Horner, Wacker, & Touchette), the addition of LaVigna, discussion, and adjournment.

The second day began with a one and a half hour general discussion of question 5, the recommendations for interventions. This was followed by an hour of public comment from individuals and organizations. Speakers had 5 to 10 minutes to present their position. Their extended remarks had been submitted in advance. Some of these comments concerned a panel draft report that was circulated prior to the conference and which was presented in summary form at the conference. No individual or organization requesting to speak was denied the opportunity. All material received from respondents was distributed promptly to panel members (NIH, 1991).

After the public meeting, the panel met in executive session for several hours to review and incorporate information from the meeting into the consensus statement.

On the third day, the Consensus Statement was presented for public comment. The actual sequence was statement presentation, public discussion, a return to executive session to amend the statement as appropriate, and then final adoption. A public press conference was held, followed by the conference adjournment. The consensus statement then was disseminated widely to the disabilities world and the public.

THE CONTROVERSY CREATED BY THE CONSENSUS STATEMENT

The Consensus Statement draft and final answers to questions 3, 4, and 5 were balanced, yet not well received by the nonaversive movement. Question 3 dealt with the evidence of effectiveness of various approaches, 4 with risks and benefits, and 5 with the recommendations regarding the different approaches. However, it was summary recommendation 6, a cautious statement that specifically dealt with the conditions under which behavior reduction approaches should be used, which caused great consternation among nonaversive proponents. Let us now examine these answers.

Question 3: What Is the Evidence That These Approaches, Alone or in Combination, Eliminate or Reduce Destructive Behaviors?

Efficacy of Treatment.   Treatment efficacy was determined by examining peer-reviewed, published research that reported empirical data from controlled experimental designs. To establish a firm scientific basis, the panel focused on those studies where a direct treatment effect attributable to a single treatment modality was discernable although the entire treatment research literature was carefully examined (NIH, 1991).

Using a criterion of 90% target behavior reduction from baseline, the behavior reduction interventions appeared to be effective with some individuals, particularly those displaying SIB. Noting the paucity of research on behavior enhancement approaches, the report stated that DRO and DRI appeared to be effective with some individuals. The literature on educational/skills acquisitions and stimulus-based approaches were described as being in infancy with few published studies. The available data were described as showing promising results.

Rapidity of Effects.   The majority of the behavior reduction intervention studies showed 90% or greater suppression of the target behaviors within 1 to 10 days. Rapidity of effect was described as not being a primary goal of either behavior enhancement procedures or educational or ecological treatments. Rather, they were described as emphasizing increasing the probability that socially desirable behaviors would occur and eventually replace the problem behaviors.

Durability of Effects.   Follow-up studies of behavior reduction approaches were described, for the most part, as demonstrating suppressive effects for months and for up to 2 years after the intervention was discontinued. Follow-up studies of behavior enhancement, educational/skills acquisition, and ecological approaches were rare, but demonstrated maintenance of effects for 9 months or more, providing evidence of long-term gains.

The prevalence of drug treatment was described as being disturbingly high and lifetime prevalence (the percentage of individuals who have ever received a drug) as being even higher. The overall conclusions for pharmacological approaches regarding treatment efficacy and rapidity and durability of effects were not encouraging.

Question 4: What Are the Risks and Benefits Associated With the Use of These Approaches for the Individual, Family, and Community?

When discussing the positive and negative side effects of the four approaches, the panel used the term *suppression* when discussing the research findings regarding the intervention's effectiveness and durability of the response. This was of importance, given that suppression is a term typically associated with punishment effects (see Foxx, 1982). Furthermore, the panel noted that positive collateral effects were reported significantly more often than negative ones following the suppression of destructive behavior. This point, plus the answer to the earlier question on effectiveness, revealed that even though the panel may have lumped the three non-pharmacological approaches together, it was clear to the objective and knowledgeable reader that positive side effects and outcomes were associated with the use of behavior reduction approaches.

The only discussion of negative side effects for nonpharmacological approaches was with respect to the enhancement and reductive interventions. The panel did note that some "less visible side effects noted for behavior reduction approaches include potential procedural abuse, psychological effects on staff, and most important, the negative and demeaning social image that the use of some of these procedures conveys to the general public about persons with developmental disabilities" (NIH, 1991, p. 18).

The panel also addressed the controversy:

A major controversy has erupted in the last decade regarding the use of behavior reduction approaches (also called aversive treatments). The controversy includes both the credibility of the scientific evidence regarding the effectiveness of such techniques and the ethical, legal issues, and social acceptability of these procedures. A bitter and acrimonious debate has developed among families, advocates, professionals, organizations, and governmental agencies. Additional research is urgently needed on the risks and benefits of the use of various behavioral as well as psychopharmacologic interventions .... (NIH, 1991, p. 18)

This research has not been forthcoming. In the ensuing 13 years, research on behavior reduction approaches or comparisons across the various approaches has been virtually nonexistent. Indeed, rather than being the subject of research, the study of the most effective approach in 1989, behavior reduction procedures, has been effectively stopped by the various political forces aligned against aversives, whereas there remains a dearth of evidence on the true effectiveness of educational and ecological approaches despite widespread claims to the contrary by the non-aversive (Foxx, chap. 18, this volume; Newsome & Kroeger, chap. 24, this volume), positive approaches (Foxx, 2003) and positive behavior support camps (Mulick & Butter, chap. 23, this volume).

Question 5: Based on the Answers to the Above Questions and Taking Into Account (a) The Behavior; (b) The Diagnosis and Functional Level of the Individual; (c) Possible Effects on the Individual, Family, and Community; (d) The Treatment Setting; and (e) Other Factors, What Recommendations Can Be Made at Present Regarding the Use of the Different Approaches?

The panel answered this question by stating that although single treatment modalities are demonstrably effective, the most successful approaches are likely to involve multiple elements of therapy environment and education. It added that treatment should be based on an analysis of biological and environmental conditions that may maintain the destructive behavior. The panel's conclusion stated that the goal of all treatment approaches should be to maximize an individual's potential and adaptive abilities so that they can live in as culturally normal an environment as possible, and that the primary treatment objective must be to develop and implement an individualized comprehensive behavior enhancement strategy that protects the individual's health safety and promotes appropriate social and cognitive skills. It recommended careful consideration when using psychopharmacologic agents and that they only be selected and continued when there is objective evidence of beneficial change and acceptable levels of undesirable side effects (NIH, 1991).

The final recommendation 6, regarding behavior reduction approaches, was cautious and carefully written. They "should be selected for their rapid effectiveness *only* if the exigencies of the clinical situation require short-term use of such restrictive interventions and *only* after appropriate review and informed consent are obtained …. [T]he interventions should *only* be used in the context of a comprehensive and individualized behavior enhancement treatment package" (p. 22).

These consensus answers and recommendations in the draft and final statements produced a number of major outcomes. As discussed next, the nonaversive/anti-behavior-reduction groups severely criticized the draft prior to and during the conference. Immediately following the conference, they launched a concerted effort to disparage the panel's findings in the media. They applied a great deal of political pressure (Holden, 1990). Their political effectiveness is indisputable given how easily they had earlier infiltrated the U. S. Office of Special Education and Rehabilitative Services and affected its policies (Will, 1987) and were able to delay the publication of the report for almost 2 years (Holden, 1990).

CRITICISMS AT THE CONFERENCE

Criticism on the second day was swift (Scott, 1989). Maurer (1991) said the report advocates "harm in the name of health" (p. 512). He criticized the report for its "lack of attention to ethical considerations" and maintained that the panel members did not understand that scientific and clinical methods are different. He was upset that the panel's report, favorable to punishment, would be used to lobby the Florida legislature to permit the use of the SIBIS shock device.

Ellis (1991), representing AAMR said he was worried about divorcing the report from the legal and ethical concerns and questioned the scientific accuracy of the draft. "NIH," he said, "should take the lead in putting an end to painful, degrading, or punitive treatment methods, yet there is not evidence of this in the report" (p.

512). He asserted that this century we have punished, degraded, and even killed persons with developmental disabilities and have failed to recognize their worth. The report, he said, was "inconsistent with modern understanding of disabilities" (p. 513). He concluded that the draft report was scientifically inaccurate and did not address real research needs.

Snell (1991), speaking for TASH, had concerns about the composition of the panel. TASH wanted to go on record as objecting to the bias of the panel in that no one on the panel was noted for their advocacy of positive approaches. She charged that professions represented on the panel did not represent a broad enough range, specifically education and rehabilitation and especially the individuals focusing on new adaptive skills. "The panel was not composed of the best people in the fields that were represented" (p. 515). She was concerned that state-of-the-art research on treatment approaches was not reflected and "that the individuals presenting on the first conference day are not cited in the research literature and that none are associated with positive reinforcement approaches while some are clearly pro aversive techniques" (p. 515).

ARC weighed in as well. Wieck (1991), saying she spoke for 160,000 members, distributed a formal position statement. She advocated the elimination of aversive techniques that induce "pain, humiliation or which involve withholding food and water" (p. 515). (The latter three were not advocated by anyone at the conference or in the scientific literature.)

Nerney, ASA, said the consensus conference was not fair, that the draft document was skewed and devoid of objectivity and could not be used to arrive at a fair, unbiased consensus statement. He questioned the panel's promotion of SIBIS. Interestingly, Michael Hazel, the developer of SIBIS, noted that the same groups testifying against its use and claiming that there is a lack of SIBIS research were the same groups that have blocked its use in research ("Representatives of U.S.," 1988).

Salzano, CSAAC, protested the bias of the conference toward the use of aversive techniques and questioned the absence of persons who were pro positive reinforcement. She compared the use of aversives to Nazi experiments. Fritz, NAPRF, stated that the scientific literature was misleading in that many remedial success stories using positive reinforcement do not appear in the literature because the people involved are too busy to write up success stories.

A "COUNTER PRESS" CONFERENCE

A "counter press" conference was held immediately following the CDC by a coalition of disability groups (e.g., AAMR, ARC, ASA, Mental Health Law Project, TASH, National Association of Protection and Advocacy Systems). The draft report was described as biased and unscientific. The groups wanted a new process that would be accurate and include a more scientific and objective approach ("Parents," 1989b).

This coalition was essentially the same consortium that conducted a press conference in Washington, D.C. at the U.S. House of Representatives to petition the U.S. Food and Drug Administration (FDA) to halt the registration of SIBIS, which was being marketed to treat self-injurious behavior ("Representatives of U.S.," 1988). (A few years earlier, I was asked to participate in a clinical evaluation of SIBIS but declined to do so. My reasoning was simple. I strongly felt that any attempt to develop and market a standardized shock device would justifiably cause great concern for individuals and groups seeking to ban the use of punishment and would galvanize their resistance. I was concerned because I thought it sent the wrong message. Rather than standardizing shock devices, I felt that we needed to always restrict considering of the use of shock to only the most severe and intractable cases [Foxx, 2003].) The promotion of SIBIS did provide the antiaversives camp with strong political and ethical fodder because SIBIS, "with its high tech overtones, has become a rallying symbol among those opposed to aversives" (Holden, 1990). While the coalition's concerns regarding SIBIS were very apparent at the CDC, their overall agenda was much larger. They had gone beyond simply seeking to outlaw SIBIS and now their quest became to eliminate all "aversives."

PRE-CONFERENCE CRITICISMS

A large document titled "Parents and Researchers Charge Draft NIH Report "Biased and Unscientific" ("Parents," 1989a) was circulated at the press conference. It contained a statement from the coalition that "neither the conference nor authors of the draft are representative of the clear emerging consensus regarding behavior interventions" ("Parents," 1989b). It challenged the legality of NIH closing the conference to the public when the panel went to executive session, which of course all consensus panels do. It was concerned that the conference report could allow greater use of outmoded, punitive devices and treatments that are painful and harmful. It contained letters written from several nonaversive movement proponents, that is, Guess, Donnellan, Evans, Durand, Turnbull, Smith, and Meyer, to the governmental organizers of the conference Hill (NICHD) and Ferguson (OMAR) and others.

Guess (1989) wrote that the draft report was an "inaccurate summary of the efficacy of aversive procedures." He added that there was no discussion of "the potential self-serving use of these procedures to maintain a professional identity."

Donnellan (1989) described the report as poorly conceived and slanted in two ways. One, it was "limited to a rigidly defined behavioral analytic approach to scientific inquiry" and two, it was "biased toward the continued study and use of aversive procedures .... " The report "supports the right of certain scientists to continue and even expand their study and use of punishment using dependent populations as their subjects .... The bias of the report is self-evident." She suggested that "those best served by the report are those who controlled the process of developing it" and suggested the possibility that this was worthy of further inquiry.

Evans (1989) was concerned that the report and five background papers did "not adequately reflect contemporary scientific scholarship in this important area." Indeed, he stated that Carr et al. (1991) misrepresented the nature of reinforcement-based procedures by "suggesting that skill acquisition approaches were limited to four areas ... which is a major distortion of widely accepted educational practices." He also was critical of Carr et. al. (1991) for using an outdated concept "that appropriate positive reinforcement typically consisted of highly preferred foods ...."

In a letter to Tom Nerney of ASA, Durand (1989) expressed concerns that the conference "will not reflect the massive changes observed in the field in recent years." Turnbull (1989) found that the report contained "a magnificent paucity" of the enlightened discussion of moral, ethical, and legal issues and no expert on the panel in these issues.

Smith (1989), perhaps the least well-known, wrote the longest critique. She noted that "The failure of the panel to grasp the important clinical issues is apparent in the section on behavior enhancement approaches" (p. 12). She concluded that the presentations were one-sided and inadequate that the panel made recommendations with no objective basis, and lacked preparedness on the subject.

Meyer (1989) wrote a nine-page critique. She noted that the "Draft Report reflects such obvious prejudice and lack of scientific objectivity along with major inaccuracies and omissions of relevant data" that she needed to reply. She stated that not "even one prominent researcher-clinician in this area who has advocated for the validation of positive and educative approaches" was invited to testify. She noted the absence of well-known and widely published researcher–clinicians whose non-averisve treatment alternatives are widely cited, including Donnellan, Durand, Evans, LaVigna, and Meyer. She contrasted this with "the inclusion of advocates for the use of aversives who have questionable credentials … " (p. 2).

She was quite critical of the individuals providing overviews and testimony. She stated that "generalist behavioral psychologists and methodologists who have never published treatment research in this area are providing overviews" and as examples she listed Sackett, Brady, and Sidman. She was bothered that "a summary on 'Positive Reinforcement Therapies' is being provided by individuals whose credentials as experts in the treatment of destructive behavior are minimal (Horner & Wacker) or whose work relates instead to stimulus control (Touchette)." She noted that the report contained unacceptable stereotypes and misperceptions.

Meyer also had problems with the background papers. For example, regarding Carr et al. (1991), she stated " The narrow behavioral psychology framework of the authors occasionally leads to non-authoritative citations for 'ideas,' as illustrated by citing the 1988 Horner, Dunlap, and Koegel book as an authoritative reference for the concept of 'life-style change,' which it is not" (p. 8). She was concerned that Carr et al. (1991) suggested that positive treatment approaches were somehow "too slow" to use in crisis situations. The pharmarcological review (Thompson et al., 1991) was also problematic because Thompson "is an experimental psychologist, not a psychiatrist or physician," which supports her "earlier concerns regarding the apparent tendency throughout the conference for participants to take on responsibilities that are technically outside of their disciplinary training and expertise" (p. 9).

POST-CONFERENCE CRITICISMS

Others criticized in print although what they said differed depending on the publication. In the November 1989 *APA Monitor* (Landers, 1989), LaVigna stated that the report should have stated that "aversives should be used only after all other more positive methods of treatment have been tried" (p. 26). Later in a *Science* interview, he described the report as "what they've done is sanction shock … there is no research demonstrating its effectiveness" (p. 980). Horner (same APA Monitor article) said the consensus conference was premature. Regarding the controversy, he said,

"It's such a shame ... "We don't need to be drawing black and white hats" (p. 26). However, in a New York times article that was critical of aversives ("Panel backs punishment," 1989), Horner stated, "Most people being treated by aversives alone are kept in institutions, because people in the community won't put up with seeing someone being slapped, pinched, or shocked."

Contrast the previous statements with Favell's comments in the same APA Monitor issue. The consensus "statement accurately reflects the state of our science as well as calling for future research ... it was "very thoughtful" (p. 26). Similarly, Bijou (1990) stated, "The recommendation for treating destructive behavior by means of behavior reduction and enhancement methods seemed reasonable in light of the literature and in consideration of all other facets that must be taken into account in initiating a treatment program" (p. 43).

NEWSPAPER HEADLINES

Many newspaper headlines after the conference helped in the coalition's efforts to devalue the draft report. Consider these titles: "Pain Therapy Method Questioned" (Coeur d'Alene, ID), "Experts Back Use of Pain in Treatment of Retarded" (Milwaukee, WI), "Pain Endorsed as Means to Stop Self-Destructive Behavior" (Tulsa, OK), "Pain Called Good Therapy" (Hackensack, NJ), "Punishing the Retarded" (*U.S. News and World Report*), "Pain Backed as Control Method" (Syracuse, NY), "A Panel Back Punishment Therapy" (*New York Times*), "Pain Treatments for Head-Bangers" (*San Francisco Chronicle*). Some of the pain methods listed included foul-tasting chemicals or smells, forcing the patient to smell strong ammonia salts, pinches, slapping, and mild electric shock.

Some of the most influential periodicals fed the controversy. *U.S. News and World Report* reported that "Parents and guardians of severely retarded children and adults who injure themselves will soon be asked to let doctors and caretakers 'punish' patients to alter their behavior" ("Punishing the retarded," 1989). A *New York Times* article ("Panel backs punishment," 1989) contained these descriptions: "Punishments, sometimes called aversives .... Far more common punishments are slaps and hard pinches that pierce the skin .... Critics argue that such punishment methods sharply limit a person's access to social situations."

What's Holding Up "Aversives" Report? Sometimes Factors Other Than Science Intrude (Holden, 1990).

Preliminary consensus statements are usually released immediately following the conference. Noting that this was not the case for the Treatment of Destructive Behaviors Statement, Holden (1990), writing in *Science*, titled her article "What's holding up 'Aversives' Report"? What she reported was a disturbing view of politics and advocacy. Holden noted that many observers attributed the hold-up to the "long-running, highly emotional debate over one subject dealt with in the report— aversive treatments" ... because "even qualified acceptance of any aversive techniques is vehemently opposed by some advocacy groups ..." (p. 980). For example, she reported that "No sooner had the conference closed when several advocacy groups, including the Autism Society of America (ASA) and the Association for Retarded Citizens (ARC) tried to discredit the verdict" by claiming that "the scientific panel ... was biased and the conference process flawed."

Holden stated that while the preliminary statement was cautious and hardly a ringing endorsement of aversives, it resulted in protests and rather unusual actions on the part of the Department of Health and Human Services (HHS). She reported the following series of events. Immediately after the conference, NICHD director Duane Alexander and John Ferguson of the NIH were "summoned downtown to HHS headquarters to defend the conference proceedings." The ARC wrote several times to Department of Health and Human Services Secretary Louis Sullivan "urging him to block the final report." Senator Sam Nunn of Georgia asked the HHS Inspector General to investigate whether the conference was properly conducted. On July 20, 1990 Secretary Sullivan told the ARC that he had asked Martin Gerry, HHS Assistant Secretary for planning and evaluation to " 'review our current policy in light of the assessment of current knowledge provided by the consensus statement as well as the concerns of your organization ... ' " (p. 981). Regarding this action, James Hill, chief of the office of science policy and analysis at NICHD, said "it is 'most unusual' for the assistant secretary for planning and evaluation to be given the job of "assuring someone that the result of any DHHS effort is above board." Hill described the CDC report as a "thorough, scholarly monograph."

Holden further reported that "Some observers believe it is Gerry who has been responsible for stalling the publication of the conference proceedings. Gerry is a lawyer who was formerly a consultant to Sullivan. For the past decade he has been a member of TASH and he has done legal work for groups that oppose aversives." Gerry denied having anything to do with delaying the statement or final report, but did say he was concerned that the CDC panel's conclusions "not be seen as the department's policy."

Addressing the question of whether the issue was methods or politics, Holden quoted Eric Schopler, who called the critics "self-serving ideologues" who drastically oversimplify the issue with emotional arguments and "are making a fortune going around doing workshops on how to never use aversives" (p. 981).

THE REPORT IS PUBLISHED

The final report was published in July 1991, almost 2 years after the conference. It included the panel's Consensus Statement and Report as well as all of the materials used to develop them. The final report stated that "No panel member was committed to a specific form of treatment for destructive behavior" (NIH, 1991). Of the 75 consensus panels through 1989, the only other NIH consensus conference as contentious was on electroconvulsive therapy to treat depression (NASMRPD, 1989).

The actions of the nonaversive movement in regard to the destructive behaviors conference is perhaps best summed up by a few quotes from Eric Hoffer's classic 1951 book, *The True Believer: Thoughts on the Nature of Mass Movements*:

Where a mass movement can either persuade or coerce, it usually chooses the latter. Persuasion is clumsy and its results uncertain. (p. 109)

Mass movements can rise and spread without belief in a God, but never without belief in a devil. (p. 91)

Those movements with the greatest inner contradiction between profession and practice-that is to say with a strong feeling of guilt-are likely to be the most fervent in imposing their faith on others. (p. 111)

REFERENCES

Bijou, S. W. (1990). Treatment of destructive behaviors in persons with developmental disabilities: National Institutes of Health Consensus Development Conference. *Journal of Autism and Developmental Disorders, 20,* 43.

Carr, E. G., Taylor, J. C., Carlson, J. I., & Robinson, S. (1991). Reinforcement and stimulus-based treatments for severe behavior problems in developmental disabilities. In *Treatment of destructive behaviors in persons with developmental disabilities* (pp. 173–229). Bethesda, MD: NIH Consensus Development Conference.

Cataldo, M. F. (1991). The effects of punishment and other behavior reducing procedures on the destructive behaviors of persons with developmental disabilities. In *Treatment of destructive behaviors in persons with developmental disabilities* (pp. 231–341). Bethesda, MD: NIH Consensus Development Conference.

Donnellan, A. (1989, September 6). *Preliminary response to draft report: Treatment of destructive behaviors in persons with developmental disabilities.* Madison, WI: University of Wisconsin.

Durand, V. M. (1989, September 7). *Letter to Tom Nerney.* Available by request from R. M. Foxx, Behavioral Sciences, Penn State Harrisburg, Middletown, PA.

Ellis, J. (1991). Comments from organizations and individuals. In *Treatment of destructive behaviors in persons with developmental disabilities* (pp. 512–513). Bethesda, MD: NIH Consensus Development Conference.

Evans, I. M. (1989, September 7). *Letter to John H. Ferguson.* Available by request from R. M. Foxx, Behavioral Sciences, Penn State Harrisburg, Middletown, PA.

Experts back use of pain in treatment of retarded. (1989, September 14). *Sentinel,* Milwaukee, WI. Available from news clipping service at www.nytimes.com

Foxx, R. M. (1982). *Decreasing behaviors of persons with severe retardation and autism.* Champaign, IL: Research Press.

Foxx, R. M. (2003). Treating dangerous behavior. *Behavioral Interventions, 18,* 1–21.

French, J. H. (1991). Overview of the neurobiology of pain and its relationship to SIB. In *Treatment of destructive behaviors in persons with developmental disabilities* (pp. 441–445). Bethesda, MD: NIH Consensus Development Conference.

Fritz, J. (1991). Comments from organizations and individuals. In *Treatment of destructive behaviors in persons with developmental disabilities* (pp. 516–517). Bethesda, MD: NIH Consensus Development Conference.

Guess, D. (1989, September 7). *Letter to James G. Hill.* Available by request from R. M. Foxx, Behavioral Sciences, Penn State Harrisburg, Middletown, PA.

Hoffer, E. (1951). *The true believer: Thoughts on the nature of mass movements.* New York: Harper & Row.

Holden, C. (1990, August). What's holding up "aversives" report? *Science, 249,* 980–981.

Landers, S. (1989, November). Self-injury 'consensus' stirs strife, not accord. *APA Monitor,* pp. 26–27.

Maurer, R. (1991). Comments from organizations and individuals. In *Treatment of destructive behaviors in persons with developmental disabilities* (p. 512). Bethesda, MD: NIH Consensus Development Conference.

Meyer, L. H. (1989, September 11). *Letter to John H. Ferguson.* Available by request from R. M. Foxx, Behavioral Sciences, Penn State Harrisburg, Middletown, PA.

National Association of State Mental Retardation Program Directors. (1989, September 28). *Federal panel examines management of destructive behaviors.* Bulletin No. 89–86.

National Institutes of Health. (1989). *Participants' guide to consensus development conferences.* Bethesda, MD: Author.

National Institutes of Health. (1991). *Treatment of destructive behaviors in persons with developmental disabilities.* Washington, DC: NIH Consensus Development Conference, U.S. Department of Health and Human Services.

Nerney, T. (1991). Comments from organizations and individuals. In *Treatment of destructive behaviors in persons with developmental disabilities* (p. 515). Bethesda, MD: NIH Consensus Development Conference.

Pain backed as control method. (1989, September 14). *Post-Standard*, Syracuse, NY. Available from news clipping service at www.nytimes.com

Pain called good therapy. (1989, September 14). *The Record*, Hackensack, NJ. Available from news clipping service at www.nytimes.com

Pain endorsed as means to stop self-destructive behavior. (1989, September 17). *World*, Tulsa, OK. Available from news clipping service at www.nytimes.com

Pain therapy method questioned. (1989, September 14). *Press*, Coeur d'Alene, ID. Available from news clipping service at www.nytimes.com

Pain treatments for head-bangers. (1989, September 14). *San Francisco Chronicle*. Available from news clipping service at www.nytimes.com

Panel backs punishment therapy. (1989, September 14). *New York Times*. Available from news clipping service at www.nytimes.com

Parents and researchers charge draft NIH report "biased and unscientific." (1989a, Fall). *The Advocate, 21*(3), 21.

Parents and researchers charge NIH report "biased and unscientific." (1989b, September 13). *Press Advisory.* Available by request from R. M. Foxx, Behavioral Sciences, Penn State Harrisburg, Middletown, PA.

Patrias, K., & Gray, D. B. (1991). Treatment of destructive behaviors in persons with developmental disabilities. In *Treatment of destructive behaviors in persons with developmental disabilities* (pp. 550–559). Bethesda, MD: NIH Consensus Development Conference.

Punishing the retarded. (1989, October 2). *U.S. News & World Report.* Available from news clipping service at www.nytimes.com

Representatives of U.S. and international professional and disability rights association. (1988, April 13). *Press conference on self-activating shock device: Call for halt to FDA registration of SIBIS.* Washington, DC. Available by request from R. M. Foxx, Behavioral Sciences, Penn State Harrisburg, Middletown, PA.

Salzano, J. (1991). Comments by organizations and individuals. In *Treatment of destructive behaviors in persons with developmental disabilities* (pp. 515–516). Bethesda, MD: NIH Consensus Development Conference.

Schroeder, S. R., Rojahn, J., & Oldenquist, A. (1991). Treatment of destructive behaviors among people with mental retardation and developmental disabilities: Overview of the problem. In *Treatment of destructive behaviors in persons with developmental disabilities* (pp. 125–171). Bethesda, MD: NIH Consensus Development Conference.

Scott, K. M. (Ed.). (1989, September 14). NIH report on destructive behaviors inaccurate, disability group says. *Mental Health Report, 13*(19), 145–147.

Smith, M. D. (1989). *Community services for autistic adults and children.* National Institutes of Health Consensus Panel: Call for Balance, Bethesda, MD.

Snell, M. (1991). Comments by organizations and individuals. In *Treatment of destructive behaviors in persons with developmental disabilities* (pp. 514–515). Bethesda, MD: NIH Consensus Development Conference.

Thompson, T., Hackenberg, T. D., & Schaal, D. W. (1991). Pharmacological treatments for behavior problems in developmental disabilities. In *Treatment of destructive behaviors in persons with developmental disabilities* (pp. 343–439). Bethesda, MD: NIH Consensus Development Conference.

Turnbull, H. R. (1989, September 6). *Letter to James G. Hill.* Available by request from R. M. Foxx, Behavioral Sciences, Penn State Harrisburg, Middletown, PA.

Wieck, C. (1991). Comments from organizations and individuals. In *Treatment of destructive behaviors in persons with developmental disabilities* (p. 515). Bethesda, MD: NIH Consensus Development Conference.

Will, M. (1987). Address to the Second Annual Symposium on the advancement of non-aversive technology. *The Advocate, 19*(4), 12–13.

Afterword

James M. Johnston
Auburn University

On reaching this last chapter, readers may find they have experienced a range of emotional reactions to the contributors' reviews and arguments in this volume. Certainly many will find the collective revelations in these chapters depressing. How could one not be depressed by being confronted with the breadth of challenge posed by the attraction of so many otherwise well-meaning individuals to problematic approaches to providing services to persons with developmental disabilities?

Many contributors to this volume make clear that the problem is not merely a few misguided theories or even the unfortunate effects of economic contingencies. If the needed agenda required only confronting some errant theories or procedures (as chronicled by the editors' chapter on facilitated communication, chap. 22), it might seem a more manageable task. The editors and authors, however, wisely chose to look behind the "fads, frauds, and follies" at the darker explanation of their origins and supports. Here, chapters by Smith, Greenspan, Vyse, Favell, Zane, Holburn, and Kozloff, among others, describe the more difficult challenges of overcoming the insidious effects of culturally supported ignorance and superstition. There is so far to go.

Some readers might find themselves not just depressed but angry. Ignorance or misguided theory somehow seem more excusable motivations for adherence to ineffective approaches than mere personal benefit, though the net effect on consumers might be indistinguishable. It is not too difficult to read between the lines of some chapters and conclude that some individuals who promote approaches of dubious value likely do so out of personal economic interest, even though they are sufficiently well-informed to know the limitations of what they are offering. Although we must all make a living, those who allow what seems to be selling well at the moment to guide their professional focus might be described as "having cash registers for frontal lobes," a characterization offered by Richard Foxx some years ago. How much does this motivation explain the interests of some professionals in offering a values-based approach that minimizes technical clarity and plays on cultural ignorance?

Finally, one is at some point likely to confront sadness at the opportunities and lives lost by the failure to offer consumers and their families the best capabilities science has developed. Perhaps this is the untold story behind these carefully argued and referenced chapters. The continuing appeal of sensory integration training, for example, continues to lead parents away from science-based alternatives that are likely to offer meaningful improvement in their child's behavior. A person-centered planning process that offers passive supports in place of active treatment continues an individual's lifestyle of dependency and limitations. Any behavior analyst working in developmental disabilities settings has seen countless individuals whose reality is tragically far short of their potential. Were we just selling cereal, the diversity of prescientific approaches represented in these chapters might be tolerable, but we are dealing with peoples' lives. In medicine, physicians who stray too far from established, science-based technology can lose their licenses, face lawsuits, and even go to jail. Where is the limit on professionals who offer behavioral, educational, or therapeutic flimflam, even if well-intended?

A FAILURE TO EDUCATE

One of the implicit themes integrating these chapters is the failure of our education system to confront and work toward overcoming cultural ignorance. A number of chapters raise this issue, if only indirectly, but Kozloff (chap. 11) meets it head-on. His explanation of the ineffectiveness of our education system identifies too many colleges and schools of education as "the primordial soup of fad, folly, and fraud." The criticism here is not merely that they fail to teach teachers to teach effectively but the more damaging complaint that their pervasive influence on educational values and curricula is ineffective in producing an educated populace that has learned how to think critically.

There is no more seminal an influence on parents, families, providers, and professionals alike than our shared educational history. It is this history that prepares us to evaluate our experiences and make decisions that will yield important consequences, whether as parents or professionals. It is this history that allows many to be seduced by the approaches cataloged in this book. It might seem a stretch to argue that kindly old education professors are the root of all evil, but it is undeniably true that the power structure of the educational industry, as well as its troops, share undergraduate and graduate degrees from colleges of education. It is this power structure that both generally and specifically influences the K–12 curriculum that spawns citizens who are uncritically susceptible to adoption of and implicit or explicit support for others' use of poorly founded instructional practices.

The effects of our resulting educational history are on display when a parent is attracted to holding therapy for their autistic child. It is an outcome of our educational system when a social worker on a habilitation team insists that there is no reason to set up measurement procedures to evaluate whether placing a consumer in a new day program reduces her self-injurious behavior. When a regional director of community services finds it appealing to hear from a workshop presenter that the most important aspect of how we provide services is that staff exhibit positive values in their actions, it is a consequence of how she has learned to think about what she hears and reads.

It is our educational system that has allowed—indeed, encouraged—the enemies of modern science. The prevalence of postmodernism and its ilk is one of the more discouraging subthemes of some of these chapters. The recitation of reasons fads arise, offered in chapters by Vyse, Smith, Greenspan, Zane, Kozloff, and others, is in part a story of how, in a society that in so many ways depends on the fruits of science, its citizens have learned from their educational experiences to view human nature from fundamentally antiscientific perspectives. Behavior analysts, of course, have long since grown fatigued with the seemingly endless struggle to confront prescientific views of behavior. It might be too much to expect that our educational system would be able to challenge the subtleties of mentalism in a society that has yet to even acknowledge the problem. However, it is surely not unreasonable to hope that the educational enterprise should at least aid in the effort to further acceptance of the nature and consequences of scientific ways of understanding the world.

CAREERS IN DEVELOPMENTAL DISABILITIES

If our system of K–12 education fails to adequately prepare citizens for life in a society that is, in so many ways, driven by science, at least our system of higher education presents some fundamental differences. Faculty in many disciplines are prepared to teach relatively narrow and technical curricula, often as demanded by the workplace. This agenda allows the possibility of explicitly preparing individuals for careers in developmental disabilities. Unfortunately, there is no such established and widely available career track, and this may be a background factor conducive to the deprofessionalization of developmental services.

Ask any roomful of professionals who work in the field of developmental disabilities if they knew when they were in school that they would build a career in developmental disabilities. Few will answer in the affirmative, and most will never have even taken a course in developmental disabilities. Only some will even be working in the area of their college major (e.g., clinicians working as managers). Although those in fields offering well-established professional credentials (e.g., physical therapy, occupational therapy, speech–language pathology and communication, audiology, social work, and nursing) are likely to be employed in their specialty, a number of these individuals will not be in positions that use their professional skills. They may be serving as a QMRP (Qualified Mental Retardation Professional), directing a service program of some sort, or serving in some general administrative capacity. Many individuals will hold degrees in fields that are unrelated to developmental disabilities (e.g., English, history) or that do not provide meaningful specialization and specific skills at the baccalaureate level (e.g., psychology, human development).

What this lack of career specification, planning, and direction means is that the opportunity for professional specialization in developmental disabilities, particularly at the baccalaureate level, is generally not available. Instead of preparing a cadre of professionals sharing a common educational history and set of market-driven skills, the field of developmental disabilities, as large and stable an employment market as it is, typically attracts the leftovers, or at least an excess, of social science and liberal arts majors who are not absorbed by the employment markets most consistent with their majors. It might be argued that the most relevant field of study for a general career track in developmental disabilities is psychology and human development. Unfortunately, such a focus is unusual in departments of psychology, which tend to produce graduates with only a scattered and superficial background in the highly diverse field of psychology at the bachelor's level. Most departments lack even a single faculty member with primary training or experience in developmental disabilities and who would therefore be prepared to teach specialty courses in this area.

Realties aside, the chapters in this volume provide some guidance for a specialization in developmental disabilities. (This book should be required reading, of course.) Surely a course in the basic principles of conditioning would be mandatory. How could anyone who is in any way responsible for services to individuals who share a difficulty in learning not need to understand how learning works? Such a course would be insufficient for most students, however. As behavior analysts have learned, the necessary skill is being able to look at behavior in context, see the embedded contingencies, and then relate these contingencies to the nature of conditioning processes and environmental options. In other words, students should learn how behavior works and be skilled at applying that understanding in their everyday work.

This book makes clear that a developmental disabilities curriculum would also need to teach students not only how science works but also a respect for the importance of quantitative empirical, if not experimental, methods as a basis for decision making. A traditional course in research methods, even one focusing on direct behavioral measurement and within-subject designs, would often not accomplish this objective. The required course would need to focus not on training would-be researchers but on teaching students how to think about theories, arguments, statements, and hypotheses in a way that is implicit in scientific methods.

Finally, these chapters make all too clear the importance of teaching students a way of talking about behavior that recognizes the insidious dangers of mentalism. Naturally, this is asking a great deal of any course of study housed in a psychology department, but so many of the chapters cry out for professionals in developmental disabilities who appreciate this problem. Holburn (chap. 17) clarifies the need for this understanding. It is not that individuals working in this field need to be radical behaviorists, although it is entertaining to consider the sequelae of such a circumstance. It may be sufficient instead to insure that students learn to identify and avoid the pitfalls of egregious mentalism in discussions of the behavior of consumers. The objective would be to produce professionals who would offer not "frustration" as an explanation of a consumer's behavior but a search for causal events in the environment.

"The Truth Will Out"

This phrase has long been a mantra for behavior analysts. Over a time scale measured in decades, we have seen some truths emerge into the light of general acceptance. It is now widely recognized, for example, that applied behavior analysis methods *can* be broadly effective in addressing the needs of individuals with developmental disabilities. In appreciating this basis for cautious optimism, it is useful to accept that our culture, and the particular culture of developmental disabilities, is somewhere in the midst of a gradual and necessarily slow transition from a pre-scientific view of behavior to a scientifically bound perspective. The same transition is in progress in other areas of the culture, of course, but as behavior analysts we are in a unique position to understand the special challenges of abandoning centuries of cultural conditioning about invented causes of behavior. (If Joe and Jane Public read in the morning paper that a new element has been discovered, they are likely to accept this revelation without hesitation. If, however, the headline announces that science has shown that our choices are always determined by the external environment, it will certainly spark distress and disagreement.)

The chapters in this book would not have been written 100 years ago, but they now constitute evidence that a cultural transition from prescientific to scientific ways of thinking about behavior is in progress, though far from complete. Although this book may suggest that we are moving backward rather than forward, a sufficiently long view of the transition should reassure us that progress is being made. It helps quite a lot that behavior analysis offers a science-based technology, that is, a body of procedures that, when properly applied, is pretty consistently effective for reasons that are reasonably well-understood in terms of scientifically established, basic processes of conditioning.

The recent credibility of behavioral interventions for children with autism provides an example of why this scientific foundation is so important. Although the book by Maurice (1993) brought behavior analysis to the attention of this community, the rapid growth of this interest might have had some of the characteristics of a fad were it not for the field's scientific underpinnings. Objective reviews of this literature (e.g., New York State, 1999) have reassured parents and professionals that behavior analysis is not merely another theory or promotional agenda but a scientifically sound technology that may, to an extent not yet fully established, justify some of their hopes.

Tiryak (chap. 27) offers further encouragement that the scientific foundation of behavior analysis will further the transition from prescientific to scientific views of behavior. He describes how the judicial system approaches decisions about services and how courts consider evidence. As experience has already shown, he reports that behavior analysis is likely to fare relatively well, compared to other approaches, when the legal issues turn on objective or scientific evidence.

Maurice's (1993) book suggests another approach that is likely to facilitate this transition. As described by Jacobson (2000), the autism community is especially driven by the involvement of parents. Although their role as parents of an autistic child hardly prepares them to make decisions about treatment models, their ability to learn about their options and to share their experiences via the Internet have made them a potent force in determining the direction of treatment services. These capabilities, together with their relentless desire for effective services for their children, have revealed the power of an informed consumer of behavioral services. As one would expect in a market economy, their interests now seem to be driving the focus and availability of treatment services, and behavior analysis is justifiably the beneficiary of their demand.

It would be a more difficult challenge to create a similar demand from families of individuals with mental retardation. For a variety of reasons, this community has typically played a less directive role in decisions about services than have parents of autistic children. One of these reasons may be that they are generally unaware of what can be accomplished by the timely availability of intensive behavior analysis services. Although such evidence is certainly available, it is not marketed in a way that is accessible and appealing. Parental demand on behalf of children with mental retardation for early and intensive behavior analysis services would do much to blunt the promotion of fads and frauds.

Finally, books such as this are an important part of the transition. Observing the emperor's state of undress puts pretenders on notice and provides a detailed caution to both consumers and providers of services. The chapters of this volume provide damning arguments that call for a defense while setting the standards for any justification. Nevertheless, the persistence of facilitated communication, as surely staked through the heart as any fad could be, shows that this struggle will take a while.

REFERENCES

Jacobson, J. W. (2000). Early intensive behavioral intervention: Emergence of a consumer-driven service model. *The Behavior Analyst, 23*, 149–171.

Maurice, C. (1993). *Let me hear your voice.* New York: Ballantine.

New York State Department of Health. (1999). *Clinical practice guideline: The guideline technical report—Autism/pervasive developmental disorders, assessment, and intervention.* Albany, NY: Early Intervention Program, Author.

Author Index

Subject Index